DEMOCRACIES AND AUTHORITARIAN REGIMES

Democracies and Authoritarian Regimes

First Edition

ANDREA KENDALL-TAYLOR
NATASHA LINDSTAEDT
ERICA FRANTZ

OXFORD
UNIVERSITY PRESS

OXFORD
UNIVERSITY PRESS

Great Clarendon Street, Oxford, OX2 6DP,
United Kingdom

Oxford University Press is a department of the University of Oxford.
It furthers the University's objective of excellence in research, scholarship,
and education by publishing worldwide. Oxford is a registered trade mark of
Oxford University Press in the UK and in certain other countries

Public sector information reproduced under Open Government Licence v3.0
(http://www.nationalarchives.gov.uk/doc/open-government-licence/open-government-licence.htm)

Published in the United States of America by Oxford University Press
198 Madison Avenue, New York, NY 10016, United States of America

British Library Cataloguing in Publication Data
Data available

Library of Congress Control Number: 2019940328

ISBN 978–0–19–882081–9

Printed in Great Britain by
Bell & Bain Ltd., Glasgow

Acknowledgements

I first want to thank Andrea and Erica for all of the hard work they put into writing the book and for their invaluable expertise. Additionally, I would like to thank the team at Oxford University Press for their help and support throughout this process. Finally, I would like to thank René for his constant love and support and Annika and Karolina for being such wonderful girls.

Professor Natasha Lindstaedt

Thanks to Natasha and Erica for their collaboration and partnership. Thanks to my family for their support and inspiration. And thanks to students former and future for their interest in this important topic.

Dr Andrea Kendall-Taylor

I would like to thank Natasha and Andrea for bringing me on board to contribute to this important and timely project. Many thanks, as well, to Oxford University Press for excellent assistance throughout all stages of this process. Lastly, thank you to my family for their support and encouragement.

Dr Erica Frantz

Outline Contents

Detailed Contents

List of Abbreviations

AD	Acción Democrática (Venezuela)
AI	Artificial intelligence
AKP	Adalet ve Kalkınma Partisi (Turkey)
ASEAN	Association of Southeast Asian Nations
AU	African Union
Brexit	British exit (from the EU)
CCP	Chinese Communist Party
CIS	Commonwealth of Independent States
COPEI	Comité de Organización Política Electoral Independiente (Venezuela)
DPP	Democratic Progressive Party (Taiwan)
EPRDF	Ethiopian People's Revolutionary Democratic Front
EU	European Union
FSB	Federal Security Service (Russia)
FSLN	Frente Sandinista de Liberación Nacional (Nicaragua)
GDP	Gross domestic product
ICT	Information communication technology
ILO	International Labour Organization
IMF	International Monetary Fund
IPA-CIS	Inter-parliamentary Assembly of the Commonwealth of Independent States
KANU	Kenya African National Union
KMT	Koumintang of China (Taiwan)
LDP	Liberal Democratic Party (Japan)
MB	Muslim Brotherhood
NCA	National Constituent Assembly (Tunisia)
NGO	Non-governmental Organization
NPC	National People's Congress (China)
OAS	Organization of American States
OECD	Organisation for Economic Co-operation and Development
OSCE	Organization for Security and Cooperation in Europe
PAN	Partido Acción Nacional (Mexico)
PAP	People's Action Party (Singapore)
PARM	Partido Auténtico de la Revolución Mexicana
PCC	Partido Comunista de Cuba (Cuba)
PDP	People's Democratic Party (Nigeria)

PFCRN	Partido del Frente Cardenista de Reconstrucción Nacional (Mexico)
PML-N	Pakistan Muslim League-Nawaz
PoR	Party of Regions (Ukraine)
PPP	Pakistan People's Party
PR	Proportional representation
PRD	Partido de la Revolución Democrática (Mexico)
PRI	Partido Revolucionario Institucional (Mexico)
ROC	Republic of China (Taiwan)
SCO	Shanghai Cooperation Organization
UAE	United Arab Emirates
UCDP	Uppsala Conflict Data Program
UMNO	United Malays National Organisation (Malaysia)
UN	United Nations
UNHCR	UN High Commissioner for Refugees
UR	United Russia
USAID	United States Agency for International Development
USSR	Union of Soviet Socialist Republics
ZANU-PF	Zimbabwe African National Union – Patriotic Front

List of Figures, Tables, and Boxes

How to use this book

Democracies and Authoritarian Regimes is the only introduction to cover the full spectrum of political systems, from democracy to dictatorship and the growing number of systems that fall between, equipping readers to think critically about democracy's future trajectory.

This book features a number of engaging learning features to help you navigate the text and contextualize and reinforce your understanding:

 Box 6.2: **Authoritarian tactics**

The absence of a viable alternative to the incumbent regime is a key source of authoritarian durability. If elites and citizens cannot envision a future under different leadership, they have little choice but to acquiesce to the current regime. Autocrats frequently use the following tactics to pre-emptively weaken challengers from the elite, opposition, and public to prevent the emergence of an alternative and maintain their control:

Divide and rule

Authoritarian regimes seek to use fissures within society—including inter-ethnic or geographic divisions—to create opposing factions they play off one another. Such '**divide and rule**' strategies make it difficult for opponents to coordinate, which prevents the emergence of a unified

Boxes

In-chapter boxes feature a diverse range of case studies, helping you to apply key concepts in the context of contemporary cases, including hybrid regimes such as Malaysia, the impact of corruption in Nigeria, and the personalization of power in the Chinese Communist Party. They also highlight key terms to ensure relevant terminology and research is translated in a clear, engaging format.

Key Questions

1. Why is the difference between 'authoritarian breakdown' and 'democratization' significant?
2. How does economic crisis affect an authoritarian regime's risk of breakdown?
3. What are the primary external factors that affect authoritarian regime stability? In your opinion, *should* outside actors ever seek to destabilize authoritarian regimes? What factors consider in developing your response?
4. What were the most significant causes of the Arab Spring? Which other regimes are most vulnerable to a wave of protests? Why?

Key Questions

Each chapter features a set of carefully devised questions to help you assess your comprehension of core concepts and facilitate critical reflection on key arguments.

Further Reading

DIAMOND, L. 2008. *The Spirit of Democracy: The Struggle to Build Free Societies th World*. Macmillan.

The Spirit of Democracy explains why democracy advances and how this process tak book argues that many authoritarian regimes like Iran or China could democratize ev the book also highlights some of the challenges to building democracy in the worl why there has been a democratic recession in some previously democratic states lik

KNACK, S., 2004. 'Does Foreign Aid Promote Democracy?' *International Studies Qua* pp. 251–66.

As the article indicates, the question of whether or not foreign aid promotes d

Further Reading

Reading lists support you to broaden your understanding of key academic literature and pursue areas of further research interest.

How to use the Online Resources

www.oup.com/he/kendall-taylor

This text is supported by a range of online resources to encourage deeper engagement with the most current developments in the subject matter. These resources are free of charge and provide opportunities to consolidate understanding and further develop skills of critical analysis.

For students

Updates to supplement the text ensuring you are fully informed of the latest developments in the field.

For lecturers

Assignments to use in class help to reinforce key concepts and facilitate the development of key skills of critical analysis and argumentation.

1

Introduction

Democracy is in crisis. By most accounts, this is the most trying period democracy has faced since the 1930s when **fascism** spread over much of Europe. Even the most optimistic observers posit that democracy will decline unless rich countries address vexing challenges such as inequality, cultural and demographic shifts, and technological change. Pessimists fear we have already crossed a critical threshold and that the democratic dominance we have grown accustomed to has ended (Rose, 2018). A 2019 report by Freedom House underscored the gravity of the crisis. The democracy watchdog documented that global political rights and civil liberties have declined for thirteen consecutive years—the longest downward slide since the organization began measuring these trends over forty years ago.

Some of the decline in political and civil liberties has occurred in the usual authoritarian suspects such as China and Russia. Both Chinese President Xi Jinping and Russian President Vladimir Putin have increased repression to retain control. Their efforts to export their authoritarian tactics and models to sympathetic leaders have also contributed to a broader 'authoritarian hardening' as several autocrats have tightened control. But perhaps more importantly, the observed erosion in political and civil liberties has increasingly taken place outside of the usual suspects, including in many long-established democracies. In the last five years there has been a remarkable decline in respect for democratic norms and practices in Hungary, Poland, and the Philippines. The **backsliding** has been so severe in Turkey—a long-time model of a successful secular democracy in the Middle East—that we can no longer call it a democracy. In short, there is a real risk that the democratic gains that have occurred since the end of the Cold War will be rolled back, paving the way for a widespread resurgence of autocracy across the globe.

How did we get here? After all, for the last twenty-five years, momentum had been squarely on democracy's side. In 1991, there were sixty-five democracies in power (Geddes, Wright, and Frantz, 2018). By 2014, this number climbed to ninety-four, such that democracies governed a majority of the world's countries. The end of the Cold War and the triumph of democracy set in motion a number of changes to the international environment that allowed democracy to spread and put authoritarian governments on the defensive. **Authoritarian regimes** were caught off-guard and their numbers rapidly declined. With **communism** discredited, a broad swath of countries scrambled to adopt—at least cosmetically—the trappings of democratic rule. Democracy, it seemed, had secured its status as the world's preferred form of governance.

Threats to democracy

Today, we face a different reality. Although the number of democracies in the world remains at or near historic highs, there are a number of important trends accelerating beneath the surface that threaten to reverse democracy's progress. In particular, democracies are facing mounting challenges from within; autocracies are evolving and adapting their survival strategies in ways that make them a more formidable challenge to democracy; and international developments, including the growing assertiveness of influential countries such as China and Russia, are creating conditions conducive to the spread of autocracy.

These dynamics provide the backdrop, or the broader context in which this book is situated. We will delve more deeply into many of these issues throughout this textbook, including through discussions of the contemporary challenges facing democracy (Part IV) and changes in the survival strategies of today's authoritarian regimes (Part III). More generally, however, we intend our discussion of the challenges facing democracy in the next section to set the stage for the chapters that follow. Each of the following chapters will go on to provide a different lens through which to examine these challenges. The goal of this book is to provide readers with the foundational research and cutting-edge insights that deepen their understanding of the challenges facing democracy and what we can do to respond.

Democracy's internal challenges

The first of these trends—the growing threat to democracy from within—significantly raises the risk of a global democratic retreat. Until recently, we could safely assume that Western societies would be governed by moderate political parties and remain committed to liberal democratic values, open economies, and multilateral cooperation (Norris, 2017). We also assumed that respect for the core principles of free and fair elections, rule of law, human rights, and civil liberties were secure in a large and growing number of countries. And yet events such as **Brexit**, the election of Donald Trump, and the rise of right-wing populist parties across Europe signal that these assumptions are no longer valid. Instead, factors such globalization, migration, rising inequality, and stagnating living standards for broad swaths of citizens in Western democracies have led many to believe that the political establishment no longer works. These factors have also contributed to a loss in citizens' perceived security (Hacker, 2006; Beck, 1999; Giddens, 1990). Research suggests that when individuals feel threatened or insecure, they are more likely to support strong, decisive leaders they perceive as able to hold back the forces of change and protect them from what they see as dangerous outsiders that jeopardize their jobs and benefits (Inglehart and Norris, 2016).

The rise in the number of citizens that are discontent with inequality, stagnating living standards, and changing values is fuelling the political polarization so apparent in Western democracies today. Information technologies and social media amplify these divisions. While many authoritarian regimes are harnessing social media to tighten their control, these same technologies are fraying the social bonds of democratic societies. The digital technologies that promise to connect people and enable a free exchange of ideas are increasingly being used by populists and other extreme voices to amplify their messages. These dynamics have contributed to a decline in popular support for the political centre and fragmented politics across Europe. Such political polarization and fragmentation is contributing to gridlock that threatens to undermine people's support for democratic rule. The dysfunction that polarization and fragmentation breed also invigorate Russian and Chinese narratives that democracy does not deliver.

These trends in Western democracies are creating fertile ground for the rise of **populism**. Once in power, many populist parties pursue policies that slowly erode democracy from within. Today's populist leaders have learned from earlier strongmen such as Venezuela's Hugo Chávez, Russia's Vladimir Putin, and Turkey's Recep Tayyip Erdoğan, who incrementally undermined democracy. Such leaders assume power through relatively free and fair elections and subsequently leverage societal dissatisfaction to gradually undercut institutional constraints on their rule, sideline opponents, and weaken **civil society**. Despite coming to power in different historical and cultural contexts, their approach is the same: they stack key political institutions with loyalists and allies (particularly in the judicial and security sectors) and muzzle the media through legislation and censorship. Their slow and piecemeal approach makes it difficult to pinpoint when the collapse of democracy actually happens (Bermeo, 2016; Kendall-Taylor and Frantz, 2016).

The gradual erosion of democratic rules and norms at the hands of democratically-elected incumbents, what scholars refer to as 'authoritarianization' (Geddes, Wright, and Frantz, 2018), constitutes a major change in the ways that democratic governments have traditionally collapsed. Until recently, coups have been the biggest threat to democracy (Kendall-Taylor and Frantz, 2016). From 1946 to 1999, 64 per cent of democracies collapsed via coups. In the last decade, however, authoritarianizations have been on the rise. They now comprise 40 per cent of all democratic failures and equal coups in frequency. If current trends persist, authoritarianizations will soon become the most common route to autocracy.

The evolution of autocracy

The change in the way that today's aspiring autocrats are dismantling democracy is a poignant example of the way that authoritarianism is evolving. Instead of seizing power overtly and via force, which risks inciting domestic and international condemnation, today's aspiring autocrats have learned that incremental power grabs are far more difficult to oppose. Because they are slow and subtle, there is no single action that generates a massive backlash. And in those instances where opponents do sound the alarm bell that democracy is under threat, populist leaders can easily frame them as unpatriotic provocateurs who solely seek to stir trouble.

But it is not just the tactics that autocrats use to seize power that have evolved. Autocracies are also adapting their survival strategies in ways that make them a more formidable challenge to democracy. In the face of what seemed to be an inevitable extinction in the 1990s and early 2000s, dictators changed their strategies and grew more resilient. As an indicator of this, research shows that today's authoritarian regimes are more long-lasting than their predecessors. From 1946 to 1989, the typical autocracy lasted fourteen years in power. This number has nearly doubled since the end of the Cold War to an average of twenty years. As authoritarian regimes become more durable and savvier, global democracy is likely to suffer (Kendall-Taylor and Frantz, 2015).

One of the most notable changes in contemporary authoritarian regimes is the extent to which they have learned to mimic democracy. Since the end of the Cold War, there has been a substantial rise in the number of countries that combine democratic characteristics with authoritarian tendencies. These 'hybrid' regimes—the broad label used to describe countries that mix democratic and authoritarian elements—have proliferated to such an extent that scholars contend they are now 'the modal type of political regime in the developing world' (Schedler, 2006, p. 3; Brownlee, 2007). Hybrid systems adjust their survival tactics and pursue a softer, subtler form of authoritarian rule. Whereas autocracies of the past relied heavily on overtly repressive methods of control and were more likely to ban political activities, censor opponents, and limit public demonstrations of dissent to maintain power, today's autocrats often embrace seemingly democratic institutions and rule of law, but manipulate these institutions to serve their own self-interests.

Authoritarian regimes have similarly adapted to manage the threats initially posed by social media. In the early 2000s, there was widespread optimism that social media would serve as a great democratizing force. Such optimism was most pronounced in the early days of the Arab Spring, as political activists harnessed social media in their efforts to topple four long-lasting dictators in Tunisia, Egypt, Libya, and Yemen. Over time, however, authoritarian regimes have co-opted these technologies to deepen their grip internally, curb basic human rights, spread illiberal practices beyond their borders, and undermine public trust in open societies. New advances in facial recognition and artificial intelligence will only intensify and accelerate these practices. China, for example, is developing new methods of political control, including mass surveillance and a data-driven 'social credit' system. These dystopian approaches raise serious concerns, including their potential to spread to other parts of the developing world. In sum, since the end of the Cold War, dictators have evolved to withstand and even flourish amid a changing global landscape.

International developments

In addition to changes taking place within democracies and authoritarian regimes, there have also been changes in the international environment that are conducive to the spread of autocracy. As Western democracies are increasingly distracted with their own domestic challenges, authoritarian regimes—especially Russia and China—have grown more assertive on the global stage. Russia and China are convinced of the threat of Western-backed revolutions and have responded by adapting their survival tactics and exporting their best practices for guarding against the 'threat' of engagement with the democratic West. Russian and Chinese efforts to counter democracy promotion are not new. But they have changed in scope and intensity. Since 2014, Russia in particular has gone on the offensive with its efforts to undermine Western democracies. Because Moscow and Beijing gauge their power in relation to the United States, they view weakening Western democracy as a means of enhancing their own standing (Kendall-Taylor and Shullman, 2018).

Shifts in geopolitical power are increasing the potency of Russian and Chinese actions. China's rise and Russia's assertiveness provide other leaders with examples of viable alternatives to the West and alter perceptions about what constitutes a legitimate regime. For the past few decades, China in particular has sought to portray itself as a compelling alternative to democracy. According to the **World Bank**, China's GDP growth has averaged nearly 10 per cent a year—the fastest sustained expansion by a major economy in history—and has lifted more than 800 million people out of poverty. Many now view China as demonstrating that the road to prosperity no longer needs to run through liberal democracy. Even without a deliberate strategy to export his model of governance, Putin has also offered one that others seek to emulate. Hungarian Prime Minister Viktor Orbán and Turkish President Recep Tayyip Erdoğan, for example, seem to admire Putin's strongman tactics and have adopted elements of his repertoire to enhance their control.

Beyond demonstration effects, a shift in the balance of economic and military power away from the democratic West is increasing the potency of the threat that countries such as Russia and China pose to democracy. For decades, established democracies such as the United Kingdom and the United States made up the bulk of global GDP. But now, for the first time in over a hundred years, democracies' share of global GDP has fallen below half (Mounk and Foa, 2018). According to forecasts by the **International Monetary Fund (IMF)**, it will slump to a third within the next decade. Moreover, U.S. President Trump is scaling back U.S. global leadership and disrupting the cohesion of the democratic alliance system.

These geopolitical changes amplify the effects of long-standing Russian and Chinese actions by enabling these countries to engage with a broader spectrum of states. China's rising power and Russia's assertiveness allow them to increase political, economic, and military ties with many states at once—as the United States did in the aftermath of the Cold War—creating greater opportunities to encourage authoritarian tendencies. But even beyond buttressing like-minded autocrats, Russia's and China's international activism may also work to weaken democracies. Research shows that extensive linkages with the West (through aid, trade, and social networks) encouraged democracy and its consolidation after the Cold War (Levitsky and Way, 2005). Although neither Russia nor China seek to export their authoritarian models, their growing ties now raise the risk of a growing global tide of authoritarianism.

These trends highlight some of the critical challenges we face today in preserving the democratic gains that have accrued since the fall of the Berlin Wall. Today, democracies are facing internal threats that are shaking the very foundations of these systems. Autocracies are adapting and evolving their tactics in ways that make them a more formidable threat to democracy. And international developments, including the growing assertiveness of influential countries like China and Russia, are trending in ways that are increasingly conducive to the spread of autocracy.

The bright spots

Although these developments make it easy to grow pessimistic about democracy's future, it is important not to lose sight of the relative bright spots.[1] In Southeast Asia, for example, Timor Leste held free and fair elections in 2017 that saw a clean transfer of power, helping strengthen democracy in one of the world's newest countries. Likewise, the election of Lenín Moreno in Ecuador in 2017 moved that country away from the brink of authoritarianism following the democratic backsliding that occurred during Rafael Correa's decade in power. In Africa, as well, we have seen democratic openings in a number of places, such as Burkina Faso following the ouster of long-time leader Blaise Compaoré in 2014 and the Gambia, where strongman Yahya Jammeh was forced to resign in 2016 after more than two decades in power.

Just as important, we cannot lose sight of the fact that democratic decline is not inevitable. Western democracies have proved remarkably resilient over time. They have faced challenges before, and they have found ways to renew themselves to surmount them. That is the task before us. We are living in time of rapid change and change can be uncomfortable. We are learning that the ideologies, policies, and even the institutions that fit Western democratic societies a generation ago are steadily becoming less applicable to the problems they face today. History suggests that it will be the democracies—and not the far more rigid authoritarian structures—that will be able to harness change into advancement and achievement. Yes, authoritarian regimes are evolving and adapting. But it is unlikely in the long term that these political systems will have the flexibility to change to the extent that today's challenges will require. Because they are flexible and more capable of learning, democracies will always have the upper hand in the long term. Walter Russell Mead (2018) wrote that, 'there is resiliency and flexibility in the creative disorder of a free society'.[2] Democracies now need to develop new ideas, new paradigms, new approaches—and the leadership to execute them—to maintain their competitive edge.

With these points and backdrop in mind, we know provide an overview of the book and how it will unfold.

---

[1] For more information on these cases, see 'Freedom in the World 2018: Democracy in Crisis', *Freedom House*, 2018, https://freedomhouse.org/report/freedom-world/freedom-world-2018 (accessed 13 February 2019).

[2] https://www.foreignaffairs.com/articles/united-states/2018-04-16/big-shift (accessed 29 May 2019).

Overview of the book

This book analyses the political dynamics of democracy and authoritarianism and the ideological struggle between them. The goal of this book is to provide insight into current challenges facing democracy and to inform the solutions needed to safeguard it. We do this by providing in-depth discussion and analysis of democracy and autocracy based on foundational research and cutting-edge scholarship in these fields. Critically, we discuss trends and developments unfolding across the political spectrum—in democracies, authoritarian regimes, and the growing number of countries that fall in between. Only by understanding the dynamics taking place across the full spectrum of countries will scholars and practitioners be able to develop the comprehensive set of solutions needed to preserve democracy. Enhancing the strength and resilience of democracies will likely be the most effective way to protect democracy's future. But the growing confidence and assertiveness of autocracies today mean that doing so will also require innovative approaches to managing and countering autocracies.

In many ways this book returns to the basics and addresses a number of fundamental questions about democracy and authoritarianism. What are the key ingredients of democracy and how can we strengthen its component parts? Are there factors that can encourage the deepening of democracy or that raise a country's vulnerability to democratic decline? How should we conceptualize contemporary authoritarian regimes? How do they maintain their hold on power, how have they evolved, and what factors are most likely to precipitate their collapse? By addressing these questions, this book aims to provide insight that will enhance readers' understanding of current trends and better enable citizens to strengthen and/or preserve democracy's foundations. Likewise, by articulating the political dynamics of contemporary autocracies, we help observers to navigate the murkiness of these closed systems. Without an appreciation of the changes taking place within dictatorships, actors will continue to operate from an outdated understanding of politics in such contexts. Staying abreast of what motivates contemporary autocrats—both in power and aspiring—to do what they do is fundamental to developing strategies to engage, interact, and enhance outcomes in these settings.

We tell this story in four parts.

Part I: Defining Democracy and Dictatorship

Part I of the book provides readers with an in-depth discussion of the full spectrum of political regimes, including democracies, autocracies, and the growing number of countries that fall in the middle. In **Chapter 2**, we discuss democracy. We provide a brief survey of the various approaches to conceptualizing and defining democracy and an overview of its key components. In **Chapter 3**, we examine authoritarian regimes. We emphasize that authoritarian regimes are not one and the same. There are important differences in the way autocracies are structured that dramatically affect their behaviour. We also discuss the most recent wave of democratization and the subsequent proliferation of countries that cannot be classified as fully democratic or authoritarian. In **Chapter 4**, we highlight the wide variation in political systems today and define a number of different types of 'hybrid systems', or those political systems that mix democratic attributes with authoritarian tendencies. We conclude Part I with a discussion of why regime type matters. **Chapter 5** reviews the latest research showing how regime type affects a host of outcomes of interest, including economic growth, quality of life, conflict propensity, terrorism, and corruption.

Part II: Political Dynamics of Autocracies

In Part II of this book, we examine the political dynamics of autocracies, including what explains their durability, the factors that destabilize them, and the pathways of their demise. **Chapter 6** focuses on the authoritarian pillars of stability. We identify the reasons why some authoritarian regimes are long-lasting, such as the monarchic dictatorship in Oman that has been in power for nearly three hundred years, while others are short-lived, such as the military dictatorship in Haiti that governed for only three years from 1991 to 1994. After highlighting sources of their durability, **Chapter 7** identifies triggers of instability. We review the role that elite splits, popular resistance, economic crisis, diffusion, and linkages with the West can have on the breakdown of authoritarian regimes. Finally, in **Chapter 8**, we cover pathways of change, including the top-down and bottom-up forces that can drive incumbent autocrats from power. Here, we emphasize that how autocrats exit office has important consequences for the future trajectory of the regime. More specifically, we show that whether an authoritarian leader is ousted by a coup, protest, or insurgency affects the odds that the entire regime will fall with the leader or that democratization will occur.

Part III: Drivers of Democracy

In Part III of this book, we discuss the drivers of democracy. We address a number of important questions, such as: why do some democracies survive—and even thrive—while others revert to dictatorship after only a brief democratic period? What structural factors are relevant for stable democracy? Does a country have to develop a 'democratic culture' for democracy to emerge and endure? Why do some democracies deteriorate over time? We divide the drivers of democracy into four major thematic groups: cultural (**Chapter 9**); economic (**Chapter 10**); institutional (**Chapter 11**); and international (**Chapter 12**).

Interestingly, many of the same variables that encourage democracy, when working in the negative or opposite direction, can cause it to break down. In other words, the academic literature has largely treated democratic consolidation and democratic backsliding as opposite sides of the same coin. For this reason, the factors we discuss in this section should be understood as *drivers of democracy*. They encourage democratic consolidation when they are discussed in the positive. The absence (or opposite) of the same factor, however, should also be viewed as raising the risk of democratic backsliding. For example, high levels of economic development support democracy's development. Low levels of development, by contrast, raise the risk that democracy will fail.

Part IV: Contemporary Challenges to Democracy

The fourth and final part of the book unpacks contemporary trends in democracy, the factors driving these trends, and the implications for the future trajectory of democracy. Though democracy is currently under threat in a broad swath of countries, understanding this new reality is the first step in determining how to effectively push back against the growing autocratic tide. In **Chapter 13**, we discuss the rise of populism. Across Europe, in the United States, and most recently in Brazil, support for populist parties and leaders has grown. We define populism, explain how right-wing and left-wing populism differ, and discuss the factors that have fuelled populism's rise. In **Chapter 14** we focus on changes in the way that democracies are breaking down. As we noted earlier in this introduction, the way that democracies fall apart has changed. There has been a rise in the proportion of democracies that are collapsing at the hands of leaders who come to power through free and fair elections and that subsequently dismantle democratic norms and practices. We document this change and articulate the playbook that today's aspiring autocrats use to undermine democracy. In **Chapter 15**, the concluding chapter of the book, we lay out those factors that are likely to be most pivotal in shaping the future trajectory of democracy. In particular, we focus on global economic conditions, levels of instability and conflict, technological change, and China's development.

Key definitions and caveats

Before we jump into the substance of the book, it is important to lay a few ground rules for engagement.

First, this book is predominately based on key findings from large-scale cross-national statistical analyses. While we go to great lengths to weave in historical examples, case studies, and other qualitative evidence of the theories and ideas we discuss, the insights are derived mainly from quantitative political science research. This means that the factors and dynamics we discuss help readers understand how political dynamics in democracies and dictatorships *tend* to unfold. Empirical analysis provides an estimate of the baseline odds that something will (or will not happen). For example, a robust body of research shows that economic crises make regimes more likely to collapse. But this does not mean that all regimes that experience an economic crisis will fail. Instead, it tells us that when the economy in a particular country declines, that country is at greater risk of regime failure than if the economy was strong.

The flip side of understanding that certain variables raise the likelihood of future events is that the analysis helps us to put deviant cases into proper perspective. You will always be able to find an example of a regime that experienced an economic crisis but did not fall (as recent experiences in Venezuela and Iran illustrate). Likewise, there is a preponderance of statistical support for the idea that greater education facilitates democratization. Germany, however, succumbed to dictatorship many decades ago despite the country's advanced educational system. Germany's experience, however, is not sufficient for rejecting the hypothesis. Instead, we must take it for the outlier that it is, and understand that generally speaking, greater education will lead to more democratic politics.

Second, there are several definitional issues we seek to clarify from the outset. Most important, is our definition of **democracy** and **authoritarianism**. Scholars have intensely debated democracy's definition. For the most part of this book we adopt a binary view of democracy and autocracy and distinguish between them by using a minimalist definition of democracy. As we discuss at greater length in Chapter 2, a minimalist conception of democracy views a country as democratic if it holds regular, competitive elections (meaning the outcome of an election is not a foregone conclusion) in which citizens can participate equally and where elections direct government actions. A country is authoritarian if it fails to meet these minimalist, procedural criteria. We recognize that a growing number of political systems blend authoritarian and democratic characteristics and therefore focus on these hybrid systems at length in Chapter 4. Throughout the book, we also address the implications of these mixed regime types explicitly. That said, our underlying perspective is that political systems are either democratic or not (and vice versa).

We also highlight that we view the terms **autocracy**, **authoritarian regime**, and **dictatorship** as interchangeable. Although there are some observers who see dictatorship as a distinct category of authoritarianism, this view contrasts with most contemporary research in comparative authoritarian politics. We therefore follow with the conventions of comparative political science research and use these terms interchangeably.

Finally, it is also important to clarify the difference between a political system and a regime. A **political system** refers to the broad type of government in power in a given year (typically a democracy or autocracy). Once a country fails to meet the minimal criteria of democracy, we must further differentiate an authoritarian spell from an authoritarian regime. An authoritarian **regime** refers to the 'rules that identify the group from which leaders can come and determine who influences leadership choice and policy' (Geddes, Wright, and Frantz, 2014, p. 314). It is possible, for example, that a country could be continuously authoritarian (as in, part of a continuous authoritarian spell) but be governed by distinct authoritarian regimes that are organized and behave quite differently. Iran illustrates this dynamic. Iran's authoritarian spell began in 1925. However, the **monarchy** that lasted until 1965 looked and operated very differently than the theocracy that came to power after the Shah's ouster. In other words, despite the continuity of authoritarian rule, the two regimes in Iran bear little resemblance to each other and demand different policy responses (Geddes, Wright, and Frantz, 2014).

In the not-so-distant past, there was widespread enthusiasm about democracy and its future around the globe. Yet as we discussed in this introductory chapter, recent years have seen the emergence of a number of trends that spell trouble for democracy's future. Illiberalism and authoritarianism have experienced a revival in many corners of the world and the prevailing mood about democracy's future course has grown substantially gloomier in many circles. Only time will tell if these pessimistic conclusions will come to pass or whether democracies will similarly be able to adapt their institutions and practices to meet contemporary challenges. This book is designed to give readers the tools to understand the logic of these political systems, the factors that drive them, and the opportunities that exist to safeguard the future of democracy.

PART I

Defining Democracy and Dictatorship

There is tremendous variation in governments across the globe. Democracies like Australia and Sweden share little in common with autocracies such as Belarus or Egypt. Likewise, there are often just as many differences between autocracies as there are between a democracy and an autocracy. Russian President Vladimir Putin's strongman system, for example, is organized and operates very differently from Iran's theocracy or Vietnam's one-party state, which has been dominated by the ruling Communist Party of Vietnam (CPV) for decades. The objective of Part I of this book is to help readers to organize and understand this extraordinary diversity across political systems.

Before we begin, it is important to outline the approaches that political scientists have used to organize and measure political systems. Broadly speaking, there are two approaches that scholars use to disaggregate political systems: categorical and continuous measures of regime type. These two approaches to organizing political systems provide the framework for Part I of this book.

Categorical measures start from the premise that all political systems can be classified as either democracy or dictatorship. To distinguish between a democracy and a dictatorship, scholars apply a minimalist definition of democracy that is based on the quality of elections (see Chapter 2). Once systems are separated into democracies and dictatorships, these categories are further subdivided based on a country's institutional and organizational structure. Categorical measures do not take into account how authoritarian or democratic a given country is. Instead, they focus on how the system is organized and the groups that governments draw on for support.

In contrast, **continuous measures** disaggregate political systems based on how 'authoritarian' or 'democratic' they are. In essence, these typologies line up political systems on a spectrum with fully democratic systems at one end and fully authoritarian systems on the other. Researchers make decisions about where a system falls along this continuum based on the extent of electoral competition, including the freedom, fairness, inclusiveness, and meaningfulness of elections (Schedler, 2002).

Scholars have criticized continuous typologies on several grounds. The most common critique is that the continuous approach lacks conceptual clarity. The boundaries between categories of countries—especially those that sit in the middle of this autocracy–democracy spectrum—are blurry and often require difficult and disputable judgements (Diamond, 2002).

There has also been such a proliferation of categories based on the continuous approach that it is difficult to compare across studies using different categories. Furthermore, some scholars argue that continuous measures oversimplify differences in regime type. Political systems are not necessarily distributed in a linear fashion along a single continuum (Wigell, 2008). Reducing all differences between governments into a matter of the degree of 'democraticness' hinders our understanding of important political dynamics at play. For example, some continuous measures of democracy assign the same score to Argentina's populist regime under President Juan Perón as they do to the military regime that took power in the country in 1976. Because continuous measures emphasize the degree of democracy or authoritarianism, they do not convey how systems may be differently democratic, or differently authoritarian.

Similarly, continuous typologies prohibit researchers from accurately understanding or forecasting authoritarian regime change (Frantz, 2018). Continuous measures do not allow scholars to identify cases in which one authoritarian regime succeeds another, but where both are equally authoritarian (e.g. the change from the Mobutu regime to the Kabila regime in 1997 in the Democratic Republic of Congo). This is problematic because scholars and policy-makers alike have an interest in understanding the transition from one autocracy to another. These transitions have real policy implications, and in some cases can be accompanied by violence and/or instability that Western policymakers must navigate. By using continuous measures, scholars are unable to test and understand the factors that increase the risk of these types of events.

Nonetheless, the continuous approach to disaggregating regimes plays an important role in comparative politics. The recognition that many regimes have in fact become stuck in between the extremes of full dictatorship and full democracy has greatly enhanced our understanding of post-Cold War politics. Importantly, the continuous perspective allows researchers to recognize that regimes can move away from authoritarianism (i.e. liberalize) without actually becoming a full democracy (Conroy-Krutz and Frantz, 2017). Moreover, all major democracy indices such as POLITY, Freedom House, the Economic Intelligence Unit, and Bertelsmann, use the continuous approach to disaggregating regimes. These measures are widely used and have enabled scholars to study a number of political dynamics, including the causes of liberalization and the effect of regime type on a host of outcomes, including prospects for instability.

We emphasize that there is no right or wrong approach to disaggregating political systems. Instead, the decision about which approach to use should be based on the question at hand. If researchers seek to understand the factors that make political liberalization more likely, for example, then continuous measures are the most appropriate tool. Categorical measures, in contrast, are better suited for answering questions about authoritarian durability and collapse, the focus of Part II of this book. Because the tool you use depends on the question you seek to answer, it is important to understand the theoretical ideas and arguments behind each approach, including their limitations and advantages.

To this end, Part I of this book delves into both the categorical and continuous approaches to disaggregating regimes. Chapter 2 and Chapter 3 are based on a categorical conception of regime type. In these two chapters our discussion of democracy and dictatorship is binary—we discuss the criteria and definitions that scholars use to separate political systems into two discrete categories. In Chapter 3 we open up the black box of autocracy and examine the differences in these regimes, based on a categorical conception of regime type.

We discuss the most widely accepted types of authoritarian regimes—namely personalist dictatorships, military regimes, single-party regimes, and monarchies—to emphasize that authoritarian regimes are not one and the same.

We also recognize that political systems have evolved in the post-Cold War era. There are now a large number of countries that do not fit neatly into the democracy or autocracy camp. Instead, a growing number of countries today mix democratic characteristics with authoritarian tendencies. In Chapter 4 we discuss these **hybrid regimes**, and based on the continuous approach, map the messy middle between democracy and authoritarianism.

Finally, Chapter 5 focuses on the implications of these different types of political systems. We show how regime type affects a number of outcomes of interest, such as inter-state war, civil war, economic growth and development, and terrorism. This chapter lays out both foundational and cutting-edge research that helps us understand why we should care if a country is democratic, authoritarian, or somewhere in between.

2

Defining Democracy

'Democracy' and 'dictatorship' are familiar concepts. We generally think we know one when we see one. Sweden, Germany, and the United States, for example, are quite clearly democratic. And North Korea and Turkmenistan are unequivocally authoritarian. But how should we think about Hungary, Poland, or Venezuela? Should they be considered democracies? Do the political dynamics in these countries meet the minimum requirements of democracy? What are the minimum requirements of democracy?

Answers to these questions are not simple. Despite democracy's more than 2,000-year history—dating back to its advent in Athens around the fifth century BC—there is still little consensus about what in fact it means. The word 'democracy' is derived from the Greek words 'demos' (people) and 'kratia' (rule). In simplest terms, democracy is a system of rule by the people. It gives citizens a central role in governance—a view that stands in stark contrast to monarchy, military rule, or other forms of dictatorship where government serves the interests of a narrow and often parasitic elite. But beyond assigning a fundamental role to citizens, definitions of democracy are varied and have evolved over time.

Many early political philosophers, including Plato and Aristotle, were sceptical of democracy. According to political philosopher C.B. MacPherson (1992), 'Everybody who was anybody knew that democracy, in its original sense of rule by the people or government in accordance with the will of the bulk of the people would be a bad thing—fatal to individual freedom and to all the graces of civilized living' (p. 2). By the time of World War I, however, democracy assumed a more positive meaning. People came to define democracy as more than majority rule. In particular, people began to incorporate liberal ideals into their expectations of democratic government, particularly protection for individuals and minorities. After World War II, the concept of 'liberal democracy' was widespread and became a defining feature of the post-' international order.

The end of the Cold War and **communism**'s defeat dramatically accelerat' racy's acceptance across the globe. In the battle for ideas, democracy ha' scientist Francis Fukuyama famously captured the optimism of the time in an article published in 1989, 'The End of History?' Fukuyama posited that the absence of any serious ideological competitors to democracy signalled the end of humankind's ideological evolution, with democracy standing as the final form of government. Indeed, after the fall of the Berlin Wall and the collapse of the Soviet Union, political regimes of all stripes began to describe themselves as democratic, including the Democratic Republic of Congo and the People's Democratic Republic of Algeria. If these countries are 'democratic', then what does democracy really mean?

Today, the most common definitions of democracy focus on institutions and procedures. If citizens can participate equally in competitive elections and if elections direct government actions, then democracy's standards are met. Other conceptions of democracy place more emphasis on outcomes. According to these views, democracy is defined in terms of the freedoms and liberties that citizens enjoy. Democratic institutions such as elections are a necessary component in any democracy, but adherents of this perspective view them more as a means to achieve outcomes like freedom and liberty rather than an end in themselves. Finally, some people view democracy as having an economic element, including the provision of social services and economic welfare. Proponents of this view argue that democratic principles like participation are meaningless if individuals do not have sufficient resources to meet their basic needs. Particularly in developing nations, people's views of democracy are often conflated with economic development (Dalton et al., 2007). In sum, contemporary conceptions of democracy start from the premise of contested elections, but they subsequently diverge in the range and extent of political and economic attributes considered in the definition.

In this chapter we review two broad approaches to defining democracy: a minimalist or procedural approach and a more maximalist account. It is important to note that our discussion of regime type in this chapter is binary—we identify the attributes that scholars use to determine whether a state is democratic or not. In Chapter 4 we use a continuous conception of democracy and address the growing number of countries that now seemingly fall somewhere in between.

After examining the most fundamental components of democracy, we conclude this chapter with a brief overview of four models of democracy. These models—namely protective, pluralist, participative, and deliberative—are useful because they go beyond defining what democracy is and provide contrasting visions of how democracy *should work* in practice.

Why define democracy

Developing clear definitions and conceptions of democracy is important for a number of reasons. For scholars, having clear definitions is essential for examining democracy's causes and consequences. There is a large body of literature, for example, that seeks to identify the factors that make democracy more likely to emerge and endure (see Part III). Likewise, scholars are interested in understanding democracy's effects, including whether regime type influences a state's likelihood of going to war, economic performance, and human development (see Chapter 5). The way that researchers define democracy influences the results they get.

Beyond the academic realm, a clear and consistent understanding of democracy's attributes is essential for tracking its development, including changes in democracy within a country over time. Especially for those countries transitioning away from dictatorship, having a shared understanding of democracy is critical for building the programmes, institutions, and norms that enable democratic governance to endure. Moreover, just as democracy can develop and deepen, so too can it deteriorate. History shows that a substantial share of democratic transitions fail. Having consistent definitions of democracy enables policymakers and practitioners to monitor and interpret events, helping them to differentiate the developments they should respond to from the normal push and pull of politics. Finally, consistent definitions allow us to recognize similar processes occurring in different countries, despite different historical or cultural conditions. Clear and consistent frameworks for democracy, including for how it breaks down, can provide objective warning signs and early indicators of **democratic backsliding**. Because democratic backsliding tends to play out in patterned ways, having a clear conception of democracy is a useful tool for protecting democracy's institutions, norms, and practices.

Conceptualizing democracy

Scholars define democracy in a number of ways. We can generally separate these definitions into two camps. The first is a 'thin' or '**minimalist**' approach, which emphasizes the procedural side of democratic politics and generates a minimal list of requirements that countries must satisfy to be deemed democratic (Boix, 2003; Dahl, 1971; Munck, 2009; Przeworski, 1991; Przeworski et al., 2000; Schumpeter, 1942). Most multi-national empirical studies use minimalist definitions of democracy. The second 'thick' or more maximalist approach adopts a larger number of substantive attributes, creating more demanding standards for countries to qualify as democratic. **Thicker** conceptualizations of democracy are used for in-depth case studies and qualitative comparative research. Thicker conceptions are also used for assessing the *quality* of democracy. The proliferation of democracy in the aftermath of the Cold War led scholars to shift their analytic focus from regime transitions to evaluating the character and progress of these new states (Diamond and Morlino, 2005). The following section describes the criteria used to define minimal and thick conceptions of democracy and highlights the strengths and criticisms of both approaches.

Minimalist definition of democracy

Minimalist conceptions of democracy focus on elections (Przeworski et al., 2000; Schumpeter, 1947). Political economist Joseph Schumpeter was one of the most influential voices advocating for a minimalist definition. Schumpeter defined democracy as a system 'for arriving at political decisions in which individuals acquire the power to decide by means of a competitive struggle for the people's vote' (p. 269). For proponents of this perspective, the essence of democracy lies in people's ability to regularly replace one government with another. This process empowers citizens by enabling them to select and subsequently discipline leaders. As long as governments can be changed, and the electorate has a free choice between (at least two) broadly different policy platforms, the threat of tyranny can be checked (Held, 1999).

Today minimalist definitions of democracy most closely resemble Robert Dahl's definition of **polyarchy**, a term he developed to distinguish between democracy as he viewed it in practice and democracy as an ideal (see Box 2.1). The two most central components of polyarchy are *inclusion* and political *contestation* (Dahl, 1971). In addition to these two attributes, most minimalist definitions also include some consideration of political and civil liberties, without which the first two cannot be meaningful.

 Box 2.1: **Dahl's polyarchies**

In the 1950s, political theorist Robert Dahl developed the idea of 'polyarchy' to differentiate between democracy as an ideal and the type of government that was achievable in practice. No government, Dahl believed, could achieve the conditions that full democracy requires. Instead, Dahl (1971) sought to 'maintain the distinction between democracy as an ideal system and the institutional arrangements that have come to be regarded as a kind of imperfect approximation of an ideal' (p. 9n). Dahl defined polyarchy as the set of institutional arrangements that permits public opposition and establishes citizens' rights to participate in politics. He viewed polyarchy as a spectrum—all political systems fall somewhere between full polyarchy and the absence of polyarchy, or hegemony. To differentiate between political systems, Dahl established a set of criteria that include the following procedural conditions:

- Control over government decisions vested in elected officials
- Frequent and fairly conducted elections
- Practically all adults have the right to vote in the election of officials
- Practically all adults have the right to run for office
- Freedom of expression
- Freedom of information
- Freedom of association

Inclusion, or the widespread right of citizens to participate in elections and run for office, is a distinct attribute of democracy. For a state to be considered democratic, most of its adult citizens must be afforded an equal right to vote and compete for office. Those countries in which large portions of the population are restricted from voting or contesting power are considered authoritarian. Elections that entail widespread reports of disenfranchisement on the basis of class, gender, ethnicity, religion, or education, for example, indicate a country is authoritarian. For this reason, some observers question whether the United States should be considered fully democratic prior to the Voting Rights Act in 1965 that fully enfranchised African Americans. Similar questions are raised about whether Switzerland should be considered democratic prior to the 1971 referendum that granted women the right to vote (Bertocchi, 2011).

Minimalist definitions of democracy also typically exclude countries with reserved domains of power that prevent the elected government from having effective power to rule. To be a democracy, elected officials 'must be able to exercise their constitutional powers without being subjected to overriding (albeit informal) opposition from unelected officials' (Schmitter and Karl, 1991, p. 81). In Myanmar, for example, Aung San Suu Kyi's National League for Democracy won a supermajority in both houses of the Assembly in 2015 in what were regarded as relatively free and fair elections. Nonetheless, most scholars classify Myanmar as authoritarian because the military reserves 25 per cent of legislative seats, enabling it to retain influence over politics. Likewise, in Iran, the president and parliament are popularly elected, but the Supreme Leader—who is not popularly elected—retains significant veto power over major aspects of national policy. Iran is therefore classified as a dictatorship.

The second key criteria of minimalist definitions, *contestation*, requires that voters have at least two alternatives to choose from and that elections are free and fair. Those countries that hold elections in which a single party competes, or in which voters are presented with a single list, for example, are authoritarian. However, just because multiple parties compete in elections does not necessarily mean that a country should be viewed as democratic. It is notable that as of 2008 over 80 per cent of all dictatorships allowed multiple political parties to run in regularly held elections (Kendall-Taylor and Frantz, 2015). As Adam Przeworski et al. note, to be democratic, not only do voters need to have more than one choice, but the opposition must have some chance of winning office as a result of the election (Przeworski et al., 2000). In authoritarian Russia, for example, multiple candidates were allowed to compete in the 2018 presidential election, but Vladimir Putin's victory was never in question. Likewise, Mexico's dictatorship under the Partido Revolucionario Institucional (PRI) held regular elections every six years for the seventy years it was in power, though it was always certain that the PRI would win. In other words, to be a democracy, the outcome of an election cannot be a foregone conclusion before the vote occurs.

Minimalist definitions of democracy have a number of benefits, particularly in terms of hypothesis testing. Because minimalist definitions enable researchers to separate claims about whether a system *is* democratic from democracy's *consequences*, they are well suited for empirical research. Democracy may serve a variety of ends, including freedom and equality, but advocates of minimalist approaches argue that we should not confuse these ends with democracy itself. In other words, the question of whether citizens' ability to periodically choose their government actually produces superior outcomes is an empirical one that we would like to be able to test objectively (Munck and Verkuilen, 2002).

Minimalist definitions of democracy are also well suited for quantitative analysis because they are easier to operationalize, or measure. Although determining the quality of an election can be challenging, it is decidedly less subjective than establishing how much participation, freedom, or equality is required for a state to be considered democratic. To this end, proponents of minimalist definitions argue that including additional attributes beyond competitive elections adds more confusion than utility. Political philosopher Karl Popper (1945), for example, recognized and valued the role of democratic attributes such as freedom, but argued that those dimensions are abstract, prone to be misused, and add little value to any definition. The comparative benefits of a minimalist, procedural-based definition, therefore, include analytical stringency, precision, and clarity (Przeworski et al., 2000).

Despite their frequent use, however, minimalist definitions of democracy have been criticized. Critics of the minimalist approach argue that elections occur only intermittently and are not sufficient for securing democracy in between elections (Diamond, 1999; Schmitter and Karl, 1991). Without consideration of citizen participation, for example, politics becomes removed from the everyday concern of citizens. One needs additional institutional guarantees, requiring that the definition of democracy be broadened. Critiques of minimalist views of democracy have gained validity in the last twenty years as many countries that adopted free and fair elections remained deficient in their actual practice of civil and political liberties (Inglehart and Welzel, 2005). Proponents of thicker definitions of democracy assert that elections are no longer (if they ever were) a sufficient proxy for substantive democracy and that the limitations of minimalist definitions are increasingly apparent (Munck, 2016).

When applied in the policy sphere, in particular, minimalist conceptions of democracy have the potential to lower the threshold of what constitutes a democracy by labelling countries as democracies too easily. In 2015, for example, United States President Barack Obama travelled to Ethiopia and twice described the country's government as 'democratically elected'. Ethiopia's ruling party—the Ethiopian People's Revolutionary Democratic Front—however, won almost 100 per cent of the seats in elections earlier that year, and the government was widely criticized for its harassment and jailing of journalists and bloggers and its intimidation of the opposition. Democracy and human rights groups criticized Obama for lowering the standard of democracy and damaging U.S. credibility on human rights.

Critics of minimalist definitions, therefore, argue that when undemocratic leaders get positive recognition for holding flawed elections, it creates a 'curse of low expectations' and generates incentives for leaders to continue doing the bare minimum (Klaas, 2018, 81). Moreover, once these leaders make it over the minimalist democracy bar, the policy community often reallocates its limited resources for democracy support. These new democracies, therefore, face an elevated risk of backsliding because other institutions and norms often have not developed in conjunction with the electoral process. Likewise, when a country's citizens live in a 'democracy' that holds elections but doesn't really give them a voice, the result is governance that does not deliver and disillusionment with 'democracy'. Proponents of this view assert that a minimalist definition runs the risk of degrading public support for democracy.

Box 2.2: **Liberalism and its relationship to democracy**

Over twenty years ago Fareed Zakaria (1997) wrote that the threads holding together democracy and liberalism were fraying. Since that time, the trends underlying Zakaria's analysis have only accelerated, and in recent years the discussion about the retreat of Western liberalism and the rise of '**illiberal democracy**' has grown (Luce, 2017). In various chapters of this book, we examine why this is the case. But what exactly is liberalism and what is its relationship with democracy? Like many of the concepts we discuss in this book, liberalism is a contested concept—philosophers and scholars have different definitions of the term, and these definitions have evolved with time.

At its core, liberalism is about individual rights. It is a set of ideas that emphasizes, 'faith in individuals and their capacity for growth (individual growth) . . . a belief in open debate and the possibility of persuasion, an insistence on secularism in the public realm, [and] an orientation towards civil rights and civil liberties' (Traub, 2018).[1] **Liberalism**, in other words, holds that people are endowed with natural rights that provide each individual with the space to live according to his or her own propulsion and according to his or her own values. Such freedom, in turn, provides people with the opportunity to live life to its full potential and spurs self-improvement.

Liberalism gained prominence through the work of John Locke. Subsequent thinkers, including Montesquieu, James Madison, and John Stuart Mill, built on his commitment to rights, reason, and equality. For Locke, every person is born in a natural state of freedom and every citizen has an innate and equal right to life, liberty, and property. Locke argued that the best way to protect these rights is through a system of government that is based on the consent of the governed. Liberalism sees the state as existing to protect individuals from coercion by other individuals or groups and to widen the range within which individuals can exercise their freedom. Accordingly, liberalism holds that government must be restricted in scope and contested in practice to ensure the maximum possible freedom of every citizen (Held, 2006). Establishing such restraint also requires limits on the state's ability to impose religious beliefs on individuals, explaining liberalism's adherence to the separation between church and state.

Although liberalism and democracy are frequently intertwined, they do not necessarily go hand in hand. Historically, there have been many societies that were democratic, but not liberal. In ancient democracies, for example, democracy was direct and based on majority rule. But these societies held extremely narrow conceptions of who could participate in politics and did not allow for freedom of speech or religion or the protection of private property. Likewise, liberalism has existed without democracy, as in the nineteenth-century European monarchies, although this has become an uncommon combination in contemporary times (Plattner, 1998). Though one does not guarantee or imply the other, since the end of World War II we tend to see liberalism and democracy go together.

Today, the threats to **liberal democracy** are mounting. Many scholars have sounded the alarm bells and raised the spectre that liberalism, in particular, may have run its course. One of the biggest challenges to liberalism today is populism (see Chapter 13). **Populism** and its emphasis on majority rules, illuminates the tensions that exist between democracy and liberalism. Populism is not inherently anti-democratic, but it is illiberal. Populist governments profess to speak for 'the people' but in many cases their definition of 'the people' excludes minority groups. Moreover, populists tend to view 'the people' as speaking with a singular, homogenous voice, disregarding the inherent plurality that exists within society. These views elevate some social groups over

---

[1] https://www.theatlantic.com/politics/archive/2018/02/liberalism-trump-era/553553/ (accessed 29 May 2019).

others and do little to protect the rights of individuals or minorities—principles that run counter to liberal ideals.

Although the challenges to liberalism today are significant, liberalism has demonstrated its ability to adapt and reform itself and address its internal problems. Maintaining liberalism, however, will require overcoming any complacency about its future and identifying workable solutions to protect it.

Maximalist definitions of democracy

Maximalist (or thick) definitions of democracy start from the premise that a democracy must hold contested elections, but do not consider the presence of elections as sufficient to call a state democratic. Put differently, **maximalist definitions** assert that no democracy can exist in the absence of contested elections, but not all systems that are based on contested elections may be called democratic. In addition to repeated, competitive elections, supporters of a maximalist approach include a variety of other attributes in their definitions of democracy. Some of the criteria are procedural (the rule of law, participation, and accountability), while others are substantive (equality and political and civil liberties) (Diamond, 2015). The dimensions are closely related, frequently overlap, and largely depend on the presence of the others.

We identify the key attributes of maximalist definitions of democracy. Maximalist definitions, by many accounts, conform to contemporary conceptions of liberal democracy (Diamond, 2015). Strengthening each of these aspects in newly created democracies and preserving them in already consolidated systems is key to maintaining the health of liberal democracy worldwide.

Representation

In modern society, direct participation—the basis of the original notion of democracy in ancient Greece—is no longer feasible. Countries are geographically vast and the number of citizens too large to make direct democracy realistic. Since 'the room will not hold all', modern-day democracy requires that the people must rule themselves vicariously, through their representatives (Arendt, 1972, p. 238). Political representation, therefore, involves the permanent transfer of government to a 'small number of citizens elected by the rest' (Madison (1787) *The Federalist Papers*, no. 10). Thick conceptions of democracy view government as representative when elections are freely contested, participation is widespread, and citizens enjoy political liberties. These conditions help ensure that representatives who disregard their constituents' views and positions will be pushed out of office.

In addition to addressing problems of coordination, representation also enables societies to avoid the 'tyranny of the majority'—a threat that several political philosophers, including John Stuart Mill and James Madison worried would undermine democracy. When the majority forms a faction, there is danger that such a group will 'sacrifice to its ruling passions or interests both the public good and the rights of other citizens' (Madison). Representative democracy, therefore, requires that representatives act as trustees of the electors, making up their own minds and exercising their own judge-ment about their constituents' interests (Held, 1999, p. 73). In *The Federalist Papers,* Madison argued that such representation is important because it allows elected leaders to 'refine and enlarge' the views of ordinary citizens by filtering them through a wise, responsible elite better able to 'discern the true interests of their country' (Hamilton et al., 2003: pp. 43–5).

Representative government, however, must walk a fine line between protecting people from the threat of a tyrannous majority and becoming disconnected—in prac-tice or perception—from the citizens it represents. Democracy is likely to become less effective if citizens feel alienated, powerless, and resentful of an elite they view as insu-lated, out of touch with ordinary citizens, or hostage to special interests. Hannah Arendt (1963) suggested that '**representative government** has in fact become **oligarchic gov-ernment**' where 'once more, the people are not admitted to the public realm ... the business of government has become the privilege of a few' (Arendt, 1963, pp. 273, 240). If representation is not effective, it opens the door to populist movements that reject liberal, representative democracy in favour of direct and vertical linkages between the leader and the people.

Beyond contested national elections, proponents of thick conceptions of democ-racy also emphasize the importance of representation at local levels (Arendt, 1963; Pitkin, 1967). Effective democracy requires that citizens have access to strong political parties that can aggregate and advocate the views of their supporters (Sartori, 2005). Representation also encompasses extensive provisions for political and civic plural-ism and individual and group freedoms. Cultural, ethnic, religious, and other minority groups should be afforded equal opportunities to express their interests in the political process. In these ways, thick conceptions of democracy define representation as more than just the presence of leaders that are authorized by voters (Pitkin, 1967).

Accountability

Key to democratic governance is the ability of its founders to devise a political system capable of keeping power in check. James Madison famously wrote in the *Federalist Papers No. 51,* 'If men were angels no government would be necessary ... In framing a government ... the great difficulty lies in this: you must first enable the government to control the governed; and in the next place oblige it to control itself.' Thick conceptions of democracy, therefore, are not just concerned with '**vertical accountability**' of the ruler to the ruled, but also '**horizontal' accountability** of officeholders to one another. To this end, scholars view accountability as having two distinct components: answer-ability and enforcement (Schedler, 1999). Answerability requires that public officials provide information about their actions and decisions and justify those choices to the public and organizations with the authority to monitor their conduct. Enforcement requires that citizens and government agencies have the capacity to punish leaders in cases of misconduct.

Though regular elections ensure 'vertical accountability' (i.e. that elected officials are held accountable by the electorate), thick conceptions of democracy also empha-size 'horizontal' accountability (meaning that other institutions serve as a check on the executive). Horizontal accountability is important because citizens alone are often unable to discern if governments are acting in their best interest. A number of barriers, such as lack of information and insight into the actions of leaders, constrain citizens' ability to ensure that elected leaders are acting in good faith. The task of holding leaders accountable, therefore, falls in practice to a relatively small number of individuals, such as senior judges, auditor-generals, and members of the legislative public accounts committees. Thick conceptions of democracy recognize that effective democracy requires a network of autonomous powers that can call into question and ultimately punish officials for improperly executing their responsibilities. These networks of horizontal accountability constrain executive power and so help protect constitutionalism, the rule of law, and the deliberative process (Diamond, 1999; Merkel, 2004). Where actors are unwilling or unable to exercise their prescribed authority over state institutions, accountability is compromised and democracy is put at risk.

In addition to the perennial challenge of holding delegated power to account, scholars have identified a number of contemporary dynamics that are making it more difficult for governments to create accountability. First, some suggest that globalization is contributing to democratic deficits within established democracies (Goetz and Jenkins, 2004). In particular, there has been a proliferation of powerful non-state actors capable of influencing the lives of ordinary people—multi-national corporations, wealthy individuals, and Non-governmental Organizations (**NGO**s)—that are not directly accountable to the communities they serve. NGOs, for example, have important functions for the populations they serve, but citizens do not delegate this task to them. Likewise, communities are unable to sanction NGOs if they are not satisfied with the way they perform those roles (Papadopoulos, 2014).

In addition to the proliferation of political actors, the growing clout of supranational governments and regional organizations such as the **European Union** (EU) make it difficult to hold national leaders to account. In the case of the EU, concerns are growing that the shift from national, state-based policymaking to multi-level European governance is not being matched by an equally forceful creation of accountability mechanisms (Bovens et al., 2010; Fisher, 2004; Schmitter, 2000). An erosion of political accountability raises the risk of democratic decline. Leaders and parties (like Hungarian Prime Minister Viktor Orbán and Poland's Law and Justice Party, for example) are tapping into citizen concerns about the lack of EU accountability and other anti-EU sentiment to fuel support for their efforts to undermine respect for democratic norms and practices.

Rule of law

The **rule of law** is a system in which laws are publicly known, clear in meaning, and apply equally to everyone. The rule of law is one of the most fundamental attributes of democracy because it serves as the basis for individual rights and provides the foundation upon which all other dimensions of democracy rest. As Guillermo O'Donnell explains:

> Without a vigorous rule of law, defended by an independent judiciary, rights are not safe and the equality and dignity of all citizens are at risk. Only under a democratic rule of law

will the various agencies of electoral, societal, and horizontal accountability function effectively, without obstruction and intimidation from powerful state actors. And only when the rule of law bolsters these democratic dimensions of rights, equality, and accountability will the responsiveness of government to the interests and needs of the greatest number of citizens be achieved. (O'Donnell, 2004, p. 32)

Governments with a strong rule of law are embedded in a comprehensive legal framework. Officials accept that the law will be applied to their own conduct, and the government seeks to be law-abiding. Western conceptions of the rule of law can include attributes such as trial by jury, a constitution that is rarely changed, an expansive view of defendant rights, and a sharp separation of powers (Carothers, 1998). However, like concepts such as 'liberty' and 'equality', the rule of law is a 'contestable concept' and has come to mean different things to various legal traditions (Rosenfeld, 2000).

While the rule of law is fundamental to thick conceptions of democracy, it is difficult to establish and entrench. Legacies of patronage-based politics, corruption, and abuse of power are hard to overcome. Moreover, because laws and political limits can be disobeyed or ignored, the rule of law requires much more than laws to prevent violations (Weingast, 1997). In strong democracies, citizens have arrived at a consensus about the appropriate limits on state action and citizens' rights. This consensus facilitates their collective ability to oppose state violations and makes the rule of law self-reinforcing as politicians know they will be punished for their transgressions. Over time, the rule of law becomes a norm that citizens uphold. In new democracies, in contrast, there is an absence of such consensus. Without such a societal consensus the collective action required to punish abuses is harder to muster. The state and its backers, therefore, face fewer costs for using the law as a political weapon against their adversaries.

Proponents of thick definitions contend that incorporating the rule of law into our frameworks is critical for safeguarding democracy's development. They point to an uptick in the number of countries that hold free and fair elections, but where considerable lawlessness and corruption remains. The persistence of lawlessness and corruption undermines the legitimacy of these regimes, raising the risk of backsliding. Disrespect for the rule of law, or its inconsistent application, undermines the legitimacy of new democracies. Max Weber, for example, argued that in contemporary states, government legitimacy is predominately based on 'legal authority' as opposed to habit, tradition, or the charisma and personal appeal of individual leaders. More specifically, governments are likely to be perceived as legitimate when they follow a set of reasonable procedures in a predictable and trustworthy fashion (Levi et al., 2009). When citizens judge authorities to have violated these principles—such as in cases of corruption or the selective application of laws—political authorities lose legitimacy (Clawson et al., 2001; Farnsworth, 2003; Gangl, 2003; Murphy, 2004). Implementing and adhering to the rule of law, therefore, is critical to sustaining the legitimacy of democratic governments.

As we will discuss at greater length in Chapter 13, judicial independence has come under attack from a number of leaders seeking to expand their power. With greater influence over the judiciary, leaders can use the courts and the semblance of the rule of law to remove barriers to their power and opportunistically target their opponents.

In other words, these leaders can transform judicial authorities into instruments of prosecution, targeting opposition politicians, businesspeople, and independent media (Levitsky and Loxton, 2013). Viktor Orbán and his Fidesz party and the Law and Justice Party in Poland have, to varying degrees, taken steps to undermine judicial independence in their countries.

Participation and engagement

Minimalist definitions of democracy view participation as important in as much as citizens must mobilize in and around elections. Thick conceptions of democracy, in contrast, have a more expansive view of the necessity of participation. To be healthy, participation must occur in between elections and be based on the active participation of an informed citizenry in a wide range of activities. Alexis de Tocqueville was one of the earliest scholars to underscore the importance of participation for the functioning of democracy. When Tocqueville visited the United States in the 1830s, he was most impressed with Americans' propensity for civic association and viewed participation as the key to America's unprecedented ability to sustain democracy. Likewise, in his highly influential *Making Democracy Work*, Robert Putnam (1993) argued that high citizen participation—including voter turnout, newspaper readership, membership in choral societies and football clubs—was the primary factor explaining the superior performance of Italy's northern regional governments compared to those of the south. Since Putnam's study, a body of research has shown that civic engagement affects democracy's ability to deliver public goods, hold officials accountable, and provide effective government.

Participation requires that citizens make use of their formal rights to influence the political decision-making process, including through voting, organizing, assembling, protesting, and lobbying (Allan, 2003; Verba and Nie, 1987). Participation in political life is important in the democratic process because it creates direct interest in government and serves as a basis for an informed citizenry. An informed and engaged population, in turn, shapes society's goals, priorities, and approach to allocating benefits. Citizen engagement is also crucial for upholding and safeguarding rights. The best safeguard of an individual's rights consists of his or her routine participation in the articulation of those rights (Held, 1999, summarizing Mill). Finally, participation is important for upholding accountability. If voters seek to hold their elected officials to account, they must be engaged, knowledgeable about the performance of those officials, and turn out at the polls in large numbers.

Participation in many established democracies is declining. For example, by almost every measure, Americans' direct engagement in politics and government has fallen steadily since the 1960s. This decline has occurred despite the fact that average levels of education—the best individual-level predictor of political participation—have risen throughout this period (Putnam, 1995). Citizen apathy, disenchantment with democratic performance, and alienation from the political process represent particular risks to the functioning of democracy. This is cause for concern because participatory citizens are the last line of defence against executive efforts to undermine democratic norms and practices.

Liberty

Proponents of thick conceptions of democracy go beyond the liberties required for meaningful electoral competition and contend that to be democratic, governments must fully protect the political and civil liberties required to maintain transparency, accountability, and responsiveness. Proponents of this view assert that democracy requires that people have access to free and impartial information; have multiple channels for expression and representation, including the ability to join parties, trade unions, associations, and movements; and are unconstrained in their ability to select candidates, express political and religious beliefs and opinions, assemble and petition, and enjoy personal liberty, security, and privacy.

Liberty is intricately linked with many of the attributes of democracy we have discussed. To protect liberty, there must also be accountability, participation, and rule of law. The presence of a constitutionally protected bill of rights and an autonomous, capable, and constitutionally authoritative judiciary are especially important for protecting basic liberties and freedom. Moreover, separation of powers is crucial to the protection of liberty. Writing in the seventeenth and eighteenth centuries, Montesquieu argued that liberty would not be possible 'were the same man or the same body, whether the nobles or of the people, to exercise those three powers, that of enacting laws, that of executing public resolutions, and of trying the causes of individuals' (De Montesquieu, 1989, p. 70).

Just as liberty depends crucially on the health of other democratic attributes, so too is liberty required to uphold democracy's procedural mechanisms (Bobbio et al., 2005). Take political participation, for example. Without basic liberties such as the freedom to communicate or associate, citizens will be less likely to become politically active, or even participate in the associational life of **civil society**. As David Beetham (2004) noted, 'draw out any strand of the complex web of democracy, and you will find it leads to some specific civil or political right, without whose security the fabric will start to unravel' (p. 65).

Equality

Participation, representation, and liberty are intimately related to political equality. Even if everyone's formal rights of participation are upheld, economic inequality can make it harder for lower-status individuals to exercise those rights, influence political decisions, and protect their interests from arbitrary acts of the state or fellow citizens. The greater the inequality within society, the more disproportionate will be the influence of the privileged. Thus, the broad diffusion of basic education and literacy is a fundamental condition for effective participation (Diamond and Morlino, 2004).

Although most thick definitions of democracy no longer include economic factors, some scholars continue to advocate that economic equality should also affect how we think about the quality of democracy (Bermeo, 2009). Dahl, for example, did not include economic factors in his list of attributes of polyarchy, but equality remained an important thread throughout his analysis (Munck, 2016). He viewed democracy as embedded in a socio-economic system that granted a privileged position to business interests. In his view, 'inequalities in economic and social resources' are a problem for democracy 'because those with greater resources naturally [tend] to use them to influence the political system to their advantage' and because 'the existence of such inequalities [constitute] a persistent obstacle to the achievement of a satisfactory level of political equality' (Cited in Munck, 2016, p. 20). Inequality, in other words, violates political liberty and therefore democratic politics. Likewise, Beetham (2004) similarly argued that government should provide some minimum basic welfare and education in order for people to have a chance to be politically active and reduce the advantages of the wealthy.

High and growing levels of inequality in the developed West pose critical challenges for democracy in these countries. We address inequality and its relationship with democratic backsliding at greater length in Chapters 10 and 13. Here we note, however, that scholars have shown that economic inequality lowers levels of political interest and voter turnout and raises support for authoritarian rule (Przeworski, 2008). High levels of inequality, for example, lead many citizens to calculate that the political establishment no longer serves their interests, making them more willing to support anti-establishment or extreme parties and leaders that disavow liberalism. Economic inequality can also lead to high levels of political polarization (Karl, 2000) that can generate dissatisfaction with the functioning of democracy, weakening its quality over time.

 Box 2.3: **Authoritarian regimes seek to mimic democratic attributes**

Since the end of the Cold War, authoritarian regimes have adapted and evolved. Faced with what looked like slow but certain extinction in the 1990s and early 2000s, dictatorships have altered their tactics, including through their adoption of many of the democratic attributes we discuss in this chapter. Dictatorships' incorporation of these seemingly democratic practices is not necessarily a sign that their governments are becoming more democratic. Instead, authoritarian regimes have learned to incorporate these tactics in ways that enhance perceptions of their governments, and ultimately prolong their duration. We discuss **hybrid systems**—or those regimes that mix democratic characteristics with authoritarian tendencies—at great length in Chapter 4. Here, however, we wish to note some of the ways that non-democratic governments encourage democratic practices like deliberation and participation.

China provides an important example of a regime that has successfully learned to co-opt democratic institutions to prolong itself in power (Truex, 2014). Because authoritarian regimes don't hold free and fair elections, they often suffer from a lack of accurate information about the extent of public support for and effectiveness of public policies. In order to help inform and legitimate public policies, the Chinese Communist Party has introduced a series of consultative channels through which Chinese citizens can offer feedback on specific policy issues (He and Thogersen, 2010). Though Chinese citizens cannot vote in national elections, they can comment on draft legislation that would be debated at the National People's Congress (NPC) and attend hearings and policy debates to voice their opinions. For example, in 2006, China's NPC announced that the draft version of the Labor Contract Law was open for public comment. Within thirty days the NPC had received almost 200,000 online comments (Gueorguiev, 2014). China has also held local political consultative conferences to enable the public to play a bigger role in politics (Xiaojun, 2011). Consultation and collaboration in cities such as Beijing ensure that service delivery is taking place efficiently (Teets, 2013). The result of all the regime's ability to mimic democracy's consultative mechanisms is that Chinese citizens feel as though they are taking part in the political system and that they have some political efficacy. Surveys from 2014 indicate that citizens, particularly those that are less educated, that use the online participation portals feel more satisfied with the regime compared to those citizens who do not use the portals (Truex, 2014).

Some authoritarian regimes also encourage participation to sustain regime support. The **fascist** and **totalitarian** regimes of the inter-war period mobilized widespread citizen participation—including mass membership in the party and party-controlled organizations—as part of their efforts to exercise complete control over the public. Latin America's populist-fuelled autocrats, particularly Hugo Chávez (1999–2013), also encouraged participation to consolidate and sustain their hold on power. Chávez sought to mobilize the poor, women, and others who had been excluded from Venezuelan politics (Self, 2008). He created, for example, 'Bolivarian circles'—a network of voluntary associations that at their peak had 2.2 million members. Each circle was comprised of up to eleven members who sought to uphold the ideals of Simón Bolívar and serve the interests of the community (Ellner and Salas, 2006). The circles proved instrumental in enabling Chávez to maintain power (Canache, 2002). When street protests against him turned violent in 2002 and Chávez was briefly removed in a military coup, a furious counter-mobilization organized through his Bolivarian Circles restored him to the presidency (Roberts, 2006). Similarly, in 2006 Chávez's government created a vast network of Communal Councils—neighbourhood-based elected councils tasked with overseeing local policies and community development. These councils were dependent on government funding. Chávez's oversight was often intrusive, and he leveraged the councils to help him win elections (Mainwaring, 2012). In addition to community organizations, Chávez also integrated a number of other participatory activities including referendums, constitutional and constituent initiatives, and citizen assemblies (Hawkins, 2010).

It is important to emphasize the limits of these seemingly democratic dynamics in the authoritarian context. Citizen input and participation rarely alters the substance of government policies. Instead, these channels largely serve as tools to enhance perceived legitimacy and to provide the regime with information about citizen dissatisfaction, which enables authoritarian officials to address such discontent before it spirals into something more threatening to the regime. In other words, many authoritarian regimes have learned to mimic aspects of democracy in ways that enhance positive public perceptions and the durability of the regime.

Models of democracy

As we have discussed, democracy constitutes a unique way of organizing relations between the ruler and the ruled. We identified a number of components, procedures, and norms that—from a maximalist perspective—are needed for democracy to thrive and endure. Although these lists help us define what democracy is, they do not tell us how it is supposed to function in practice (Schmitter and Karl, 1991). To what ends should government serve? What are the appropriate limits of state action? What role should citizens play in society? To address these questions, political theorists have developed several models of democracy that articulate various perspectives on what democracy should mean and how it should function in practice. The following section provides an overview of four prominent models of democracy: protective, pluralist, participatory, and deliberative.

Protective democracy

For protective democrats, the goal of democracy is to defend the rights of citizens from an intrusive state and other citizens (MacPherson, 1977). The major theorists contributing to conceptions of **protective democracy**, including John Locke, Jeremy Bentham, and John Stuart Mill, viewed individuals as self-interested, and ultimately determined to maximize their own utility and satisfaction. Individuals' pursuit of their own self-interest ultimately puts people in conflict with one another. Elected officials, also guided by the same self-interest, are motivated to use corruption and other abuses of office to maximize their own power. This view of democracy sees government, and especially separation of powers and accountable institutions, as serving to protect citizens' rights and liberty from leaders' despotic use of power. A government's role is to create the conditions that allow individuals to pursue their own interests (Held, 2006).

Although elections, separation of powers, and institutions of accountability are necessary for reducing the dangers citizens face when left to their own devices, protective democrats envision a limited role for government. Politics is regarded as distinct and separate from the economy, culture, and family life (Held, 2006). For protective democrats, limiting the government's scope and power in these spheres enhances social cohesion by reducing the number of issues subject to political conflict (Friedman, 2009). Protective democrats especially emphasize the need to limit government intervention in the economy and viewe the right to private property as being among individuals' natural rights. The role of government, therefore, is to secure life, liberty, and property from the tyranny of local majorities. The right to own property, compete in competitive exchanges, and pursue individual interests with minimal state interference is the key to maximizing the public good (Held, 2006).

More recently, economist and political philosopher Friedrich Hayek (1899–1992) developed one of the strongest contemporary statements of protective democracy (Terchek and Conte, 2001). For Hayek, modern democracy had become too intrusive, constituting a threat to liberty. Hayek believed that democracy had grown intertwined with the modern welfare state, such that the scope of government services (including education, transportation, health and safety regulations) extended far beyond earlier government intentions to protect the poorest and most vulnerable segments of society. Both the political left and right had become overly intent on pleasing special interest groups (working groups and the poor, on the left, and trade associations and professional groups, on the right). For Hayek, the endless cycle of government promises to interest groups at every election caused the scope of government to grow, undermining liberty and ultimately democracy (Terchek and Conte, 2001). Hayek's explication of protective democracy was influential with dissidents during the Cold War, and with conservative politicians including U.S. President Ronald Reagan and British Prime Minister Margaret Thatcher.

Pluralist democracy

Like all theories of democracy, **pluralist democracy** starts from the premise that meaningful elections are the primary distinguishing factor between democracy and dictatorship. Pluralists, however, view this minimalist definition as partial and incomplete (Held, 2006). Instead, this model of democracy focuses on the role played by the myriad groups that mediate between voters and elected leaders and sustain a continued political presence between elections. Pluralists hold that society is composed of individuals with assorted concerns. Liberty can be upheld only if people are given the right to pursue these interests. Governments, therefore, must allow like-minded citizens to join together to pursue their shared interests. Such groups often emerge out of particular economic or cultural **cleavages,** such as class, race, ethnicity, and religion, and include organizations such as political parties, trade unions, and business associations. According to this view, the role of democracy is to protect the freedom of interest groups to advance their goals and reach political decisions by mediating and adjudicating between competing demands. Democracy is seen as an endless process of bargaining between a range of diverse and overlapping interest groups.

In contrast to participatory and deliberative democracy, pluralist democracy does not require active and widespread citizen engagement or participation in politics. Pluralists accept the claim that the electorate is generally disinterested and less well informed than many democratic theories assume. Instead, this model views most citizens as having little if any, direct influence on the political process. Not only do pluralists accept disengagement, but they also view a degree of inaction as beneficial to the stability of the political system. According to some pluralists, extensive participation can readily lead to increased social conflict (Parsons, 1970).

Pluralist democracy views power as being dispersed throughout society. Although inequalities exist within society that advantage certain groups, the sheer plurality of interests ensures competition between multiple groups. Because no one faction can monopolize power, the threat of the 'tyranny of the majority' can be checked. Moreover, the presence of multiple decision-making centres also protects citizens from the risk of power accumulating in the hands of a narrow elite. Pluralist thinkers viewed competition between groups as a more secure check on democracy than even legal or constitutional arrangements. If competitive electoral systems are characterized by a plethora of groups or minorities that feel intensely enough about diverse issues, then democratic rights will be protected and severe inequalities avoided (Dahl, 1973).

Subsequent scholars have highlighted several difficulties with the pluralist view of democracy. Perhaps the most significant criticism stems from the model's faith in the power of competition between groups—a view that many see as suffering from an inadequate grasp of the nature and distribution of power (Held, 2006). In particular, many groups simply do not have the resources to compete at the national level against powerful lobby organizations or corporations. Political pluralism, therefore, has been criticized because it reinforces conventional arrangements as powerful groups work to freeze inequality. Unorganized and vulnerable groups simply do not have the resources or capacity to challenge more entrenched groups. Likewise, the existence of multiple power centres does not guarantee that government will listen to them equally, as governments are most likely to respond to the most powerful among them.

Participatory democracy

Participatory democracy provides a bottom-up model of democracy that views democratic governance as most likely to thrive when citizens engage in public life, participate in a broad range of community activities, and learn how to cooperate to achieve collective goals. Through engagement and participation, people can construct a community ethos, or 'an evolving framework of shared values, which all subcultures will be expected to endorse and support, without losing their distinct identities and subculture' (Etzioni, 1995, p. 167). When people come together in common projects, in other words, they construct a strong civic sense that they can use in their local settings and bring to national debates. Constructing this community ethos requires a large reservoir of social capital built through an active and robust civil society (Putnam, 2000). The primary site of democracy, therefore, is not in government, but in towns and neighbourhoods, and conventionally non-political areas of social life like the workplace, schools, and families. Although representative government is important, citizens must seek to participate in and shape decision-making. In the words of political scientist Robert Putnam (2000), 'citizenship is not a spectator sport' (p. 341).

Proponents of the participatory model of democracy view community development as key to safeguarding and strengthening democracy, including through building strong civil societies, educating citizens, and equipping people with the kind of knowledge and information that facilitates collective action, participation, and engagement. U.S. President Bill Clinton, for example, was a strong proponent of participatory democracy, and these views largely shaped his domestic policy agenda. Policies and programmes such as the Family Leave Act and the AmeriCorps national service programme were inspired by a participatory view of democracy (Galston, 1992). In South Africa, as well, the Community Development Worker initiative, launched in 2003, was a project to enhance greater participation, debate, and engagement with the government at all levels (Modise, 2017). Another example is the case of Porto Alegro in Brazil, where citizens actively participated in putting together the city's budget (Aragones and Sánchez-Pagés, 2009).

Participatory democrats push back on the fear of some that the general public (who lack specialized training or even sufficient knowledge) should not be empowered to shape political decisions. From this perspective, while voters should not decide on the specifics of politics, they should determine its general direction. As American philosopher John Dewey (1859–1952) observed, expert opinion had usurped the prerogative of citizen influence in key processes of decision-making. For this reason, Dewey advocated for creating opportunities for citizens to educate themselves on the findings of experts and then employ common sense and act responsibly. Like other participatory democrats, Dewey viewed education as critical for allowing citizens to fulfil their roles as democratic actors.

Deliberative democracy

Deliberative democracy is a form of democracy in which decisions are made by discussion among free and equal citizens (Elster, 1998). Leaders are expected to publicly justify their decisions and participate in a deliberative process with citizens (Gutmann and Thompson, 2004). **Deliberative democracy**, therefore, rejects conceptions of democracy that base politics on power, interest group bargaining, or the notion that decisions should simply emerge from an aggregation of preferences (such as voting). Instead, decisions should evolve through an argumentative process in which individuals advance their points and maintain a willingness to change their minds based on the arguments of others. Deliberative democracy holds that the government should embody the will of the people formed through the public reasoning of citizens (Habermas, 1979).

In many ways deliberative and participatory democracy are similar, given their strong emphasis on the role of citizens in driving democracy. They differ, however, in that deliberative democracy assumes that citizens invest their time and energy in *deliberating* social issues and legislation. The deliberative process aims to reach a reasoned consensus, achieved through rational persuasion by strong argument, among those affected by a decision. Decisions are legitimate when they are ideas that everyone can accept, or at least not reasonably reject. Participatory democracy, by contrast, has a less intellectual emphasis and instead emphasizes the participatory element—citizens are involved in community projects and drive the general direction of policies and decision-making, but they do not necessarily have to engage with the specifics of political decisions.

Proponents of deliberative democracy recognize that the fissures and persistent moral disagreements in modern societies could obstruct the social consensus that deliberation seeks to achieve. They view deliberation, however, as the best way to address and resolve such societal disputes and cleavages. Deliberative democracy, therefore, can encourage spirited perspectives on public issues and promote mutually respectful processes of decision-making (Gutmann and Thompson, 2004). In southern India, for example, village level deliberations, known as *gram sabhas*, had a positive effect in mobilizing civic agency among the poor (Rao and Sanyal, 2010).

Theories of deliberative democracy became mainstream in the 1980s. Since that time, hundreds of books and articles have been devoted to refining the ideal, identifying the institutional design and feasibility of deliberation, and empirically testing scholars' central claims about its effects. Deliberative democracy has been criticized on several grounds, including its procedural practicality and the value of political participation. For example, how can societies move beyond the ideal and apply deliberative democracy in practice? And is there any evidence that deliberation improves political outcomes? Some researchers have sought to empirically test the theory's claims (for a review see Thompson, 2008). Using focus groups and other settings they consider deliberative, John Hibbing and Elizabeth Theiss-Morse (2002) argue, 'real-life deliberation can fan emotions unproductively, can exacerbate rather than diminish power differentials among those deliberating, can make people feel frustrated with the system that made them deliberate, is ill-suited to many issues, and can lead to worse decisions than would have occurred if no deliberation had taken place' (p. 191).

Conclusion

Although the concept of democracy appears straightforward, this chapter underscored that this is not necessarily the case. Definitions of democracy have evolved over time and there are a number of different ways and criteria used to measure and evaluate it.

The first approach to defining democracy we identified in this chapter was the minimalist approach, or those definitions of democracy that focus primarily on the competitiveness of elections. Minimalist definitions are useful for large, cross-national quantitative analysis. Such empirical research has allowed us to better understand the causes and consequences of democracy. Studies that use minimalist definitions have produced rigorous analysis that guides practitioners in focusing their efforts on the policies and actions most likely to encourage the onset and consolidation of democracy (which we discuss in Part III of this book). Likewise, empirical studies based on minimalist definitions of democracy have also enhanced our understanding of why democracy matters. We will revisit the consequences of regime type in Chapter 5. Here, however, we note that much of the research that forms the basis of our understanding of why democracy matters is based on studies using minimalist definitions of democracy.

The second approach to defining democracy we discussed in this chapter was the maximalist approach, which holds that democracy must be viewed as more than the presence of regularly held, competitive elections. Thicker conceptions of democracy are especially useful for assessing the quality of democracy and for developing frameworks to both deepen democratic quality and identify early warning signs of democratic decline. Frameworks based on maximalist definitions of democracy have gained particular relevance in the current era in which there has been a rise in the number of countries that hold competitive elections but that continue to have severe deficiencies in their actual practice of civil and political liberties. Just as importantly, we have begun to see declining respect for democratic norms and practices in countries considered fully consolidated democracies, like Hungary and Poland. Thick conceptions of democracy add clarity to analytic efforts to gauge political dynamics in these countries. They enable researchers to develop objective indicators that can provide early warning signs of declining respect for democratic practices. The definitions and models of democracy we lay out in this chapter also provide an important foundation for thinking through the policies and actions that will be needed to sustain democracy worldwide.

In the next chapter, we turn our focus to authoritarian regimes. Just as there are different ways to define and conceptualize democracy, so too are there different ways to conceptualize and define authoritarian regimes. Chapter 3 will open up the black box of autocracy. The primary takeaway from the next chapter is that authoritarian regimes are not one and the same. There are important differences in the way they are structured and the segments of society they draw on for support. These differences provide insight into the decisions that these governments make and the overall political and economic dynamics at play in these countries.

Key Questions

1. What are the strengths and weakness of using a thin (minimalist) versus thick (maximalist) definition of democracy? Imagine you work for an international organization aiming to measure democracy around the world, what type of definition of democracy would you use and why?

2. Can a country be democratic without being liberal? Why or why not?

3. Of the attributes of democracy that we discussed in this chapter, which do you think are the most robust in your country and why? Which attributes do you think are the weakest and why?

4. Of the attributes of democracy that we discussed in this chapter, which do you think are most at risk globally?

5. What role do citizens play in different models of democracy? Which of the models we discussed in this chapter fits most closely with your view of how democracy should function and why?

6. What function do democratic attributes such as deliberation and participation play in authoritarian settings? Can you identify other ways in which autocracies are mimicking democratic characteristics?

Further Reading

BEETHAM, D. ed., 1994. *Defining and Measuring Democracy* (Vol. 36). Sage.
Defining and Measuring Democracy is an edited volume that goes over the key debates about how to measure democracy. In doing so it explores what measurements are appropriate for assessing democracy and how democracy may be defined differently in different contexts.

DAHL, R.A., 1973. *Polyarchy: Participation and Opposition.* Yale University Press.
Polyarchy provides a useful framework for examining democracy, looking at competition and participation. Dahl outlines the benefits of the democracy and the conditions that need to be met for democracy to be realized.

DIAMOND, L., 1999. *Developing Democracy: Toward Consolidation.* JHU Press.
Developing Democracy focuses on how to define democratic consolidation and what conditions are necessary for democratic consolidation to take place. Diamond focuses on political institutions, civil society, freedom, transparency, and the rule of law—which he sees as critical to democratic consolidation.

HELD, D., 2006. *Models of Democracy.* Stanford University Press.
Models of Democracy provides a through overview of different classical models of democracy, the variants of democracy from the twentieth century, and how democratic governance should be defined today.

3

Defining Autocracy

In Chapter 2, we defined democracy and identified the key characteristics of democratic regimes. In this chapter, we turn our attention to the other side of the political ledger and delve into the world of authoritarianism. Even a casual scan of international news headlines—filled with stories on Russian President Vladimir Putin's latest feats, China's rise, and Turkish President Erdoğan's consolidation of power—reinforces the notion that today's autocrats are resurgent. After a turbulent decade following the end of the Cold War, many authoritarian regimes have regained their footing and grown bolder and more capable of dealing with dissent.

The resurgence of authoritarian regimes raises the imperative to better understand the political dynamics at play in these countries. Consider for a moment those countries that constitute the greatest challenges to the United States and Western democracies. These countries include North Korea, Iran, Russia, Syria, and China—all authoritarian regimes. Not only do dictatorships present today's most pressing national security challenges, but their number and influence are likely to grow. This is problematic from a U.S. and Western national security perspective, because (as we talk about in greater depth in Chapter 5) autocracies are the countries most likely to fight inter-state wars, spawn major refugee crises, pursue the most volatile—and disastrous—economic policies, and disregard basic freedoms and liberties. Add to this troubling mix the fact that dictatorships are the hardest countries to study and analyse. Media outlets are censored, government propaganda is widespread, and their leadership deliberately conceals information from the public view. In other words, authoritarian regimes present the most significant foreign policy challenges and at the same time are the most difficult political systems to study and analyse.

In this chapter, we provide a framework for understanding authoritarian regimes. Historically, political science research focused predominately on democracy. Authoritarian rule was largely considered a residual category defined in the first place by what democracy is not. The result was an exceptionally diverse set of countries that were unified perhaps only by their failure to meet one or more criteria for democracy (Svolik, 2012). In the last twenty years, however, there has been an explosion of academic work on these regimes. Rather than viewing authoritarianism as a black box, scholars are producing insightful research that helps us make sense of the political dynamics at play in these countries, including how the structure of the regime shapes incentives, behaviour, and outcomes. Through improved understanding of how these regimes function and the logic that motivates their decision-making, we are better positioned to anticipate how events unfold in these contexts.

As you will see in this chapter, authoritarian regimes are not one and the same. Although all autocracies share a disregard for competitive elections and pluralism, the structural differences between them are vast. In the first section we discuss totalitarian regimes. Scholars developed theories of totalitarianism to take account of the new type of dictatorship that emerged in Germany under Hitler and the Soviet Union under Stalin. This research represents some of the earliest efforts to disaggregate autocracy. Political science research subsequently built on these early efforts, and scholars developed a number of ways to distinguish between different types of authoritarian systems. In the remainder of the chapter, we present a categorical framework for understanding differences across autocracies based on whether political power and decision-making reside with a single individual (**personalist rule**), a party (**single party rule**), the military (**military rule**), or a royal family (**monarchy**) (Geddes,1999). As you will see throughout this book, the way that autocracies are structured affects the decisions they make and the outcomes they produce.

Totalitarian regimes

Early work seeking to understand differences across autocracies focused on distinguishing between authoritarian and **totalitarian regimes** (Linz, 2000; Friedrich and Brzezinski, 1956; Brzezinski, 1962). This work began in the late 1930s and 1940s as scholars sought to explain the emergence of a new political phenomenon—the rise of a previously unseen type of dictatorship in Hitler's Germany, Stalin's Soviet Union, and Mussolini's Italy. Scholars viewed totalitarianism as falling into the general classification of authoritarian rule, but as distinct from other forms of autocracy. Juan Linz, for example, in his influential work *Totalitarian and Authoritarian Regimes*, characterizes a system as totalitarian if it has an ideology, a mass party and other mobilizing organizations, and concentrated power in an individual or small group that is not accountable to any large constituency and cannot be dislodged from power through institutionalized and peaceful means. As Linz highlights, each of these elements can be found separately in other autocracies; their simultaneous presence, however, makes a system totalitarian.

Totalitarian regimes seek to maximize their power over the population. Other authoritarian regimes, in contrast, often seek only the extent of power required to keep them in office (Wintrobe, 1998). In her highly influential *The Origins of Totalitarianism* (1958, pp. 323–4), Hannah Arendt describes totalitarian systems as striving for total domination in every domain and of every individual. 'Compared with other parties and movements', she writes, 'their most conspicuous external characteristic is their demand for total, unrestricted, unconditional, and unalterable loyalty of the individual member'. In part, this goal is achieved through the 'atomization' of human relationships—the destruction of classes, interest groups, and other relationships between people.

To achieve such total control, totalitarian regimes rely heavily on ideology and propaganda. In their *Totalitarian Dictatorship and Autocracy* (1956), Carl Friedrich and Zbigniew Brzezinski identified a 'totalist ideology' as the first of their six characteristics of totalitarian government (1956). This ideology tends to be intellectually elaborate and geared toward providing the leader with a source of legitimacy, as well as opportunities to manipulate, adapt, and selectively interpret the ideology to reinforce control. Totalitarian ideologies go beyond the particular programme or definition of the appropriate boundaries of the state and offer some ultimate meaning, sense of historical purpose, and interpretation of social reality (Linz, 2000).

Not only do totalitarian systems seek to advance a particular ideology, but they also seek to mobilize society around these ideas on a significant scale (Linz, 2000). In this sense, totalitarianism suggests a destruction of the line between state and society. These regimes are in essence revolutionary movements, whose aim is to reconstruct society, mobilize their citizens, politicize the public, and ultimately transform human nature. The participatory nature of these regimes—including mass membership in the party and party-controlled organizations—is a key factor that distinguishes totalitarian systems from other authoritarian systems. In autocracies, the regime often relies on a narrow set of backers to maintain control and citizens have limited opportunities to actively participate in the society and state. In totalitarian regimes, the party and other mobilizing organizations give people a share in power. Such voluntary (or manipulated) mobilization allows these regimes to carry out change using fewer resources than those governments that solely rely on coercion to force participation (Linz, 2000).

Nonetheless, totalitarian regimes do employ high levels of **repression**. In addition to their creation of a legitimizing narrative, totalitarian regimes have also relied on the massive and/or arbitrary use of terror, such as concentration camps, purges, and show trials, to force compliance. In Cambodia, for example, Pol Pot and the Khmer Rouge (1975–79) killed over a third of the country's eight million people as the regime sought to revolutionize society through collectivization. Likewise, forced collectivization in the Soviet Union precipitated a famine (1930–33) that killed more than five million people, and the Soviet purges (known as the Great Terror) killed almost a million people (Snyder, 2010). The political party and its related components, including the secret police, play an important role in the execution of terror. These institutions reach down into society and serve as the eyes and the ears of the state. An active party also provides opportunities for latent coercion, allowing the regime to exclude citizens from the benefits of the party, thereby raising the costs of their opposition. Several scholars have argued, however, that repression is neither a necessary nor sufficient characteristic of totalitarian systems. Nonetheless, there appears to be a greater probability that repression will be higher in totalitarian compared to authoritarian regimes (Linz, 2000).

Today, North Korea is the one regime that most closely resembles a totalitarian system. The government has sought to maintain an activated citizenry that is fully committed to the regime. North Koreans are indoctrinated to believe the ideological tenets of the regime, known as *juche*, or self-reliance (Armstrong, 2016). The ideology provides guidelines for 'all fields of human endeavour from poetry to potato farming' (Oh and Hassig, 2004, p. 13). The regime inculcates its ideas into the North Korean people through every possible medium, including education, arts and entertainment, monuments, and memorialization. Another important aspect of North Korean ideology is the Supreme Leader (*suryong*) system which established Kim Il-sung as the 'sun of the nation' and the 'eternal President of the Republic' (Byman and Lind, 2010; Kim, 2001). The *suryong* system is propagated through a ubiquitous cult of personality (See Box 3.1). Even after his death, Kim Il-sung remains the Supreme Leader and head of the North Korean family.

In addition to ideology, the North Korean regime is the most repressive government in power today. Kong Dan Oh and Ralph Hassig write that, 'to the extent that ideological indoctrination fails to bind the people to the party and the leader, social control measures must be employed' (2004, p. 127). The North Korean regime completely controls the media and goes to great lengths to deny its people the ability to access foreign information. It relies on an elaborate system of informants. Andrew Scobell writes that 'the climate of terror is instilled not just by the visible elements of the coercive apparatus ... but also by a fear of being informed on by a colleague, friend or even a loved one' (Scobell, 2006, p. 34). The state exercises such total control over society that no one is exempt from investigation and being watched (Oh and Hassig, 2004). Moreover, punishment for suspected disloyalty is severe. People accused of relatively minor offenses are assigned a short period of 're-education'. Those accused of more serious transgressions are sent to political prison camps—some 200,000 North Koreans are potentially in such camps—or executed. In many cases, the regime punishes not just the accused individual, but (according to the 'three generations' policy) his or her entire family (Byman and Lind, 2010).

The conditions required to sustain a totalitarian system of governance—especially the complete control of the information space that is required to sustain such a pervasive ideology—make it unlikely that new totalitarian systems will emerge in the years to come. Aside from the few holdouts that approach this pervasive and devastating system of governance—such as perhaps Turkmenistan and Eritrea (Tronvoll and Mekonnen, 2014)—totalitarianism will hopefully be confined to the pages of history.

  Box 3.1: **Personality cults**

Early studies of totalitarianism emphasized the role of the leader (Neumann, 1942; Tucker, 1968). Numerous studies placed the personality cults established by Joseph Stalin (USSR), Adolf Hitler (Germany), and Benito Mussolini (Italy) at the centre of their conceptualization of totalitarianism. Though totalitarianism has waned, **personalist cults** continue to exist outside the totalitarian context, including the cults created by Mustafa Kemal Atatürk (Turkey), and more recently Gnassingbé Eyadéma (Togo) and Saparmurat Niyazov (Turkmenistan).

Cults of personality are synonymous with what sociologist Max Weber termed 'charismatic authority' (Weber, 1947). A charismatic leader, according to Weber, owes his or her position not to legal or traditional authority, but to the 'virtue of which he is set apart from other men and treated as endowed with supernatural, superhuman, or at least specifically exceptional powers or qualities' (Weber, 1947, p. 358). Supporters perceive these leaders as superhuman, they blindly believe them, follow them unconditionally, and give them unqualified emotional support (Post, 1986).

A number of factors facilitate a leader's creation of a personality cult. According to Weber, charismatic leaders tend to emerge in times of 'psychic, physical, economic, ethical, religious, and political distress'. A confluence of multiple stressors, in particular, generates conditions conducive to the emergence of a personality cult (Tucker, 1968). Hitler, for example, acquired a mass following when Germany was confronting many issues, including high unemployment and poverty after the great depression, economic troubles and status anxiety among the lower middle class, and injured national feelings following defeat in World War I and the terms of the Versailles treaty. To build a personality cult, leaders must exploit these moments and convince followers that they are uniquely qualified to lead them out of their predicament (Tucker, 1968).

Personality cults are also more likely to emerge when there is relative weakness within the regime's political party structure (Gill, 1984). The cults of Stalin (1929) and Mao (early 1940s), for example, both arose at a time of relative weakness in the Russian and Chinese communist parties (Gill, 1984). Although these parties emphasized collective leadership, neither had effective rules or norms that could constrain ambitious individuals and ensure that collectivism was realized in practice. Other factors, such as acute elite conflict and massive party membership expansion further eroded party strength and created an opening for Stalin and Mao's charismatic leadership to take root.

Finally, the media can play an important role in fostering personality cults. Writing in the 1960s—long before the advent of social media and other information communications technologies—Robert Tucker (1968) asserted that 'modern communications media make possible the projection of a charismatic leader . . . to a far greater number of people than ever before' (p. 733). The media facilitate personality cults via the repeated dissemination of images and information portraying the leader as a god-like figure incapable of wrongdoings (Tucker, 1968). In Turkmenistan, for example, Niyazov's picture appeared in the upper right-hand corner of every TV screen and monuments, including a golden statue of him that rotated to face the sun, were pervasive throughout the country.

Personality cults are, unsurprisingly, most pervasive in personalist dictatorships. Given the global rise in personalist dictatorship we are witnessing globally (which we discuss elsewhere), personality cults have the potential to become more common.

Contemporary approaches to disaggregating autocracy

Totalitarianism is largely a relic of the past. That said, scholarship on totalitarianism gave rise to a large body of research seeking to better understand the political dynamics of authoritarian regimes. In particular, scholars have developed numerous approaches to disaggregating dictatorship based on the structure and strategies of these regimes. In the remainder of this chapter, we present a framework for disaggregating autocracy based on the work of political scientist Barbara Geddes. Geddes (1999) pioneered an approach to disaggregating autocracy based on who makes decisions, controls access to the security apparatus, and the identity of the group the leadership draws on for support. Based on these criteria, Geddes argues that autocracies can be designated as personalist, single party, or military regimes. Although Geddes did not initially analyse monarchies, we add this regime category to our discussion. Throughout the chapter we seek to incorporate key insights from other scholars who have pursued different approaches to disaggregating autocracy.

It is important to note that some observers see dictatorship as a distinct category of authoritarianism, whereas others use the term interchangeably with authoritarianism. Following Geddes and other contemporary scholars, we take the latter approach. This means that in what follows we use the terms dictatorship, authoritarian regime, and autocracy interchangeably.

Personalist dictatorship

Personalist dictatorships are perhaps the most colourful form of authoritarianism. Because power is concentrated in the hands of an individual, policies often reflect personal whims and impulses. Muammar al-Qaddafi of Libya, for example, replaced the Gregorian calendar with a solar calendar, changing all of the months with names that he invented himself (Black, 2000). Hastings Banda of Malawi decreed that women were forbidden from wearing trousers. And in Turkmenistan, President Gurbanguly Berdymukhammedov allegedly prohibited black cars in the country because he preferred white. Not only do policies tend to be variable within these countries, but personalist dictatorships also differ from one another given the outsized influence of the leader. Some personalist dictatorships feature hollowed-out political parties, legislatures, and elections, while others do not. Some have a single military force, while others operate multiple military and paramilitary units.

Although the proclivities of individual leaders (and the institutions they inherit) make these systems appear quite different from one another, the underlying logic of personalist dictatorships is the same. In personalist dictatorships, a leader exercises power with little restraint, at his own discretion, and unencumbered by rules or commitment to an ideology. The expansive nature of a leader's power often makes it difficult to distinguish between the regime and the state (Chehabi and Linz, 1998). Although discretion in these regimes largely resides with a single person, it is important to recognize that, in practice, such discretion is maintained by balancing the interests of multiple competing groups within the dictator's support coalition. No leader rules alone. In personalist dictatorships, however, the size of this support group is small.

Personalist dictators may be current or former members of the military or head a political party. However, neither the military nor the party wields real influence over decisions. In addition to be being largely unconstrained by their ruling circles, personalist dictators also dismantle those institutions with the potential to limit their power. The legislature acts as a rubber stamp on executive decisions; the judiciary is politicized and typically used as a tool for thwarting regime opposition; and the regime controls the media. The lack of institutional constraints on personalist dictators means they have the latitude to impose their preferred domestic and foreign policies. The way that personalist dictators hollow out political institutions, sideline competent individuals, and disregard norms also creates conditions that are inhospitable for democracy after the personalist regime falls from power. Of all the types of autocracies we discuss, personalist dictatorships are the least likely to democratize upon their collapse.

The elite in personal dictatorships typically owe their positions to personal connections with the leader. In contrast, elite in other types of dictatorships tend to advance through established career lines, such as the military ranks or a civil service. Personalist dictators hand-pick their advisors and senior government officials serve entirely at the discretion of the leader. Most often the leader's inner circle and key positions of power are occupied by family, friends, business associates, or individuals directly involved in using violence to sustain the regime. To consolidate his control over the political system, for example, Russian President Vladimir Putin installed members of the *siloviki*, or the security services, in key positions of power. Moreover, the loyalty of the political elite to the leader is typically not ideologically motivated, but determined by a mixture of fear and rewards. Of all the regime types, personalist dictators are the most reliant on the distribution of patronage to sustain their hold on power.

Geddes's definition of personalist dictatorship is consistent with what other scholars have termed 'patrimonialism' or 'sultanism', an extreme form of patrimonialism (Weber, 1978; Bratton and van de Walle, 1994). In Max Weber's conception of patrimonialism, a leader derives his legitimacy from traditional forms of authority. According to Weber, 'patrimonialism, and in the extreme case sultanism, tends to arise whenever traditional domination develops an administration and military force which are purely personal instruments of the master . . . Where domination is primarily traditional, even though it is exercised by virtue of the ruler's personal autonomy, it will be called patrimonial authority; where indeed it operates primarily on the basis of discretion, it will be called sultanism' (1978, pp. 231–2). Scholars such as Michael Bratton and Nicolas van de Walle (1994) used the term 'neo-patrimonial' to characterize many postcolonial African regimes that are consistent with what we are calling personalist dictatorships. **Neo-patrimonial regimes** are political systems where the right to rule is ascribed to a person rather than an office, relationships of loyalty and dependence are pervasive, and leaders occupy office less to perform public service than to acquire personal wealth.

Very often, personalist dictators come to power with the support of clearly recognizable groups—sometimes even through reasonably fair elections, as in the case of Russian President Vladimir Putin, Venezuelan President Hugo Chávez, and Philippine President Ferdinand Marcos. Other personalist leaders, although less often, seize power with the backing of the military, as in the case of Ugandan President Idi Amin. How then do these leaders dismantle the constraints posed by the people and institutions that launched them into power? As soon as a new leader seizes power, the dictator and the backers that brought him to power engage in a dynamic interaction. All of them seek to preserve the regime's hold on power, yet each faction (the leader and various groups within the elite) seeks to enhance its own power and resources at the expense of the others (Geddes, Wright, and Frantz, 2018).

Within this context, the only way that the elite can prevent the leaders from expanding his personal power is by credibly threatening to remove the leader from power if he oversteps agreed-to limits (Svolik, 2012 and Magaloni, 2008). Such threats will be less credible when the elite are factionalized, undisciplined, or lack experience in governing (Geddes, Wright, and Frantz, 2018). Militaries riven by ethnic, ideological, or personal factions, for example, face greater challenges in collectively working to constrain a new leader making personalization more likely. Likewise, newly formed political parties, particularly those parties that the leader himself creates, are also likely to struggle to constrain a leader's efforts to expand personal control. For these reasons the beginning of personalist dictatorships can usually only be dated in hindsight (Chehabi and Linz, 1998) as a leader's moves to personalize power typically happen gradually. In Box 3.2 we identify the indicators of personalism.

Since the end of the Cold War, personalist dictatorships have becoming an increasingly prevalent form of authoritarianism. In 1988, personalist regimes comprised 23 per cent of all dictatorships. Today, 40 per cent of all autocracies are ruled by strongmen (Kendall-Taylor et al., 2017). Examples of personalist dictatorships in power today include Russia (where Vladimir Putin has ruled since 1999), Belarus (where Alexander Lukashenko has ruled since 1994), Rwanda (where Paul Kagame has been in power since 2000), and more recently, Turkcy (where Recep Tayyip Erdoğan has been in power since 2003). As we discuss in Chapter 5, whether leaders rule largely at their own discretion or face institutional constraints from a powerful party or influential military dramatically affects how policy decisions are made. The rise of personalist dictatorship is problematic because these systems produce the worst outcomes of any regime type— a theme we return to in Chapter 5.

 Box 3.2: **Indicators of personalist dictatorship**

The personalization of authoritarian regimes is likely to pose a significant foreign policy challenge. Given the continued movement toward personalization and the dangers inherent in this trend, one study reviewed all dictatorships since 1946 to identified indicators that signal an effort to personalize (Kendall-Taylor et al., 2017). These five indicators can be used as 'alarm bells' to gauge when leaders are seeking to concentrate power.

Install loyalists. Leaders looking to consolidate their personal control over the political system install loyalists in key positions of power including in the courts, the security apparatus, the military, the ruling political party, and the bureaucracy. Individuals with viewpoints that run counter to those of the leader are replaced with individuals the leader can trust, even if they lack competence. In Venezuela, for example, President Hugo Chávez placed his Chavistas 'in key positions of power across the judiciary, army, central bank, and the state-owned oil industry . . . Technical ability [was] a secondary consideration to fealty' (Mander, 2012, Financial Times).

Promote family. Leaders set on amassing power seek to place close family members in influential positions, regardless of government experience. Like other loyalists, family members help insulate a leader from opposing views and are reliable implementers of a leader's agenda. Iraq under Saddam Hussein provides an extreme example: Hussein's son Qusay controlled the Revolutionary Guard, his son Uday ran the Fedayeens, and his cousin Barzan Abd al-Ghafur led the Special Republic Guard. None of these family members had the experience or qualifications necessary to run an elite military force; all were considered lacking in aptitude (Woods et al., 2006).

Create a new party or movement. Leaders intent on personalizing the system try to create new political organizations or movements. They use these movements to signal their break with the political establishment, enabling them to build a new base of support and sideline the traditional establishment. In Peru, for example, Alberto Fujimori ran as a self-professed anti-establishment candidate in the 1990 presidential election and formed the Cambio 90 movement to support his candidacy. Fujimori stacked Cambio 90 with his own personal acquaintances, enabling him to develop a base of power independent of pre-existing political parties. Fujimori's marginalization of the traditional powers that be paved the way for one-man rule following his assumption to power.

Use of direct rule or referendum. Leaders pursuing a power grab seek to appeal directly to the public through referendum or plebiscites to legitimate their rule or extend their time in office. In Nazi Germany, for example, the German government used the referendum of 1934 to gain public approval for Adolf Hitler's illegal combination of the powers of the President of the Reich with the office of the Chancellor following President Paul von Hindenburg's death (Douglas, 2005). Just under 90 per cent of voters voted 'yes', and the media reported that the referendum gave Hitler 'dictatorial powers unequalled in any other country, and probably unequalled in history' (Birchall, 1934).

Create of new security services. Leaders looking to concentrate power create new security services outside of the domain of the traditional military command. This gives them direct access to an armed organization that is personally loyal and has the capacity to counterbalance the formal military. In Haiti, for example, Francois (Papa Doc) Duvalier created the Tonton Macoute in 1959, a militia comprised of a consortium of young illiterate men from the countryside who were fiercely loyal to him. The group functioned as a security police in Haiti, eventually becoming more powerful than the military. Such a tactic increases the leader's grip on power by lessening the credibility of the threat of military ouster.

Single party dictatorship

Single party dictatorships are regimes in which policymaking control and political offices are in the hands of a single party (Geddes, 1999). Other parties may be allowed to operate, compete in elections, and hold political posts, but their influence is minimal. In single party regimes, the party remains influential because it is well organized and autonomous, which prevents the leader from taking personal control over policy decisions and the selection of regime personnel (Geddes, 2003). The leader of the regime is typically the head of the party and is selected to this post by the party's central committee or politburo or via some sort of electoral process controlled by the party. Examples of single party dictatorships in power today include China, Laos, Vietnam, Angola, and Cuba.

In single party regimes, the party controls nearly all of the state's institutions and dominates most aspects of the political sphere, such as local government, civil society, and the media. Even the military is subordinate to the party. There are two broad types of single party regimes. The first type prohibits opposition parties' participation in elections, such as China or Vietnam today. The second type is those that scholars have called dominant party regimes. These regimes permit the opposition to compete in multiparty elections, but the elections are so unfair that the incumbent party is assured victory, as in Malaysia until 2018, Tanzania, and Mexico until 2000 (Magaloni and Kricheli, 2010).

Some single party regimes can appear similar to democracies, as most have elections and legislatures and most emphasize the importance of public participation in the political process. Some even impose term limits on leaders and elites and have rules that dictate how key political posts are filled. Single party dictatorships differ from democracies, however, in that legislatures are nearly always stacked (or entirely filled) with party supporters, enabling them to change the rules of the game continuously in the party's favour. Likewise, opposition parties (if they are not banned) face institutional disadvantages and/or constant threats and harassment. In his study of Mexico's Partido Revolucionario Institucional (PRI), for example, Simpser (2013) shows how the party used its near-hegemonic status to weaken and discourage the opposition. The ability of these parties to orchestrate massive electoral victories shapes peoples' perceptions of the prospects of defeating the regime. This signal of party invincibility reinforces elite loyalty to the party and dissuades other actors such as businesses or security forces from supporting the opposition.

Single party regimes have also historically been associated with totalitarianism. Many of the single party regimes during the Cold War were often referred to as totalitarian, such as the Soviet Union, Albania, and Romania. These regimes were led by parties with clear ideologies that were responsible for implementing policy. The difference is that while totalitarian regimes are led by a single party, there are many single party regimes that are *not* totalitarian. In fact, given the virtual elimination of totalitarianism as a contemporary form of authoritarianism, it is safe to say that the vast majority of single party regimes today are not totalitarian.

Of all the regime types, single party regimes tend to be the longest lasting (Huntington, 1968; Geddes, 2003; Magaloni, 2008), experience the fewest coups (Cox, 2009; Geddes, 2008), and enjoy higher economic growth (Keefer, 2007; Gandhi, 2008; Gehlbach and Keefer, 2011; Wright, 2008) than other authoritarian regime types. What explains the superior performance of single party regimes?

In their review of single party regimes, Beatriz Magaloni and Ruth Kricheli (2010) posit that the ruling party plays two related functions that account for one-party rule's effectiveness: a bargaining function, whereby dictators use the party to bargain with the elites and minimize potential threats to their stability; and a mobilizing function, whereby dictators use the party machine to mobilize mass support. When they are well institutionalized, ruling parties should thus be understood as giant patronage systems that give citizens a vested interest in the perpetuation of the regime (Magaloni, 2006; Geddes, 2006; Pepinsky, 2007). In this sense, strong political parties function as a 'punishment regime' wherein the party distributes rents to citizens who remain loyal and withdraws rents from those who are not. This requires that the ruling party also has the capacity to penetrate society to monitor citizen loyalties. This system is particularly effective at trapping poor voters into supporting the dictatorship because their livelihood depends on state transfers (Blaydes, 2006; Magaloni, 2006).

Those single party regimes in which the ruling party is powerful and cohesive tend to be the most durable. Powerful and cohesive ruling parties, in turn, are most likely to emerge through violent power struggles. Samuel Huntington and Clement Moore, for example, argued that those parties that experienced the fiercest struggle for power tend to be the strongest (Huntington and Moore, 1970). Several of the highly durable Communist parties took power through full-blown class warfare that often coincided with civil war, as in Russia, China, and Vietnam. These regimes built what Selznick refers to as 'organizational weapons' to survive their early years. Violent social revolution creates cohesive ruling parties, a fusion of the ruling party and military actors, vast coercive capacity, and a generation of leaders with extraordinary legitimacy and authority within the regime (Levitsky and Way, 2012). Moreover, single party regimes are also especially durable because they have agreed-upon rules for guiding succession (Geddes, 1999). The Communist Party in China, for example, has had eleven leaders during its almost seventy years in power (although President Xi Jinping removed term limits in 2018, raising new questions about succession). Because rules for succession are typically in place in single party regimes, there is less uncertainty over who is going to take power, making destabilizing struggles over the leadership less likely to arise (Smith, 2005).

Military regimes

Since World War II, military officers have overthrown numerous civilian governments. In many cases, these military officers claim to be defending democracy and promise to hold elections to return to civilian rule. But history has shown that the military frequently clings to power longer than it initially indicates. Military rule was most prevalent in the 1960s, 1970s, and 1980s. During these three decades, military regimes made up about a fifth of the world's autocracies. Military regimes were especially prevalent in Latin America, but also existed in a number of places elsewhere, such as Turkey (1980–83) and Nigeria (1966–79 and 1983–93). Since the end of the Cold War, however, military regimes have become far less common. In 2018, Myanmar and Thailand were the only military regimes in power.

We adopt Geddes's conception of military dictatorship, which defines it as rule by a somewhat collegial body representing the officer corps, in which multiple officers influence decision making (Geddes, 2003). According to the definition, members of the executive branch are members of the military who have been installed as a result of a military coup, and the military (as an institution) controls policy and the security forces. Military regimes, therefore, represent a more collegial form of autocracy than personalist regimes because members of the ruling junta make decisions jointly. During the Brazilian military dictatorship (1964–85), for example, consultation among military officers remained important throughout the regime's time in power, most visibly during negotiations over planned presidential successions every few years (Stepan, 1971).

Other scholars have defined military rule differently. In particular, some researchers define military regimes as those led by a military officer, regardless of the makeup and influence of the rest of the leadership group. In many cases, this boils down to what is known as 'military strongman rule', which refers to the subset of dictatorships in which power is concentrated in the hands of a single military officer. Examples of military strongmen include Uganda's Idi Amin or the Dominican Republic's Rafael Trujillo. Amin and Trujillo were military officers, but the military did not rule 'as an institution' because each leader had concentrated so much power in his own hands that he did not usually need to bargain with other officers (Geddes et al., 2014).[1] The emergence of military strongman rule follows the process of personalization we discussed in the section on personalist dictatorships. Immediately after seizures of power, most military governments are unstructured and somewhat chaotic. How decisions will be made and enforced is unclear even to participants. Hierarchies and routines for making and implementing decisions are not yet established and personnel within the junta may change rapidly (Geddes, 2006). Strongmen are the dictators who prove especially adept at the manipulation of factions within the ruling alliance, leading to the gradual marginalization of other officers from decision-making (Geddes et al., 2014). Military regimes, in contrast, continue to rely on and bargain with the military to govern.

Monarchic dictatorship

Monarchies are defined as those systems in which a person of royal descent inherits the position of head of state in accordance with accepted practice or the constitution (Hadenius and Teorell, 2007). To be a monarchic dictatorship, the monarchy is more than ceremonial. The ruling family occupies key positions of power; exercises control over the military, security services, and access to political office; and dictates domestic and foreign policies. All of today's monarchic dictatorships are located in the Middle East and North Africa, with the exception of Brunei (1959–present) and Swaziland (1968–present). Within comparative politics, monarchies have been the least studied 'type' of authoritarian regime. Political science research long held that monarchy is an outdated form of rule with limited capacity to accommodate modern demands. Huntington (1968), for example, argued that a 'king's dilemma', or the challenge inherent in modernizing without losing control, would render monarchies untenable. The **Arab Spring**, however, led to a surge in research seeking to understand why the monarchies proved to be so resilient relative to the more personalized forms of autocracy that were toppled by protest in Tunisia, Egypt, Libya, and Yemen.

Like single party regimes, monarchies tend to be particularly durable. Some scholars have suggested that the traditional religious and tribal legitimacy that these regimes enjoy induces strong citizen support. Historical-religious claims to legitimacy have been especially important in Morocco and Jordan where the Alaouite Crown of Morocco and the Hashemite House of Jordan claim descent from Muhammad himself. The dynastic families ruling Bahrain, Kuwait, Oman, Qatar, Saudi Arabia, and the UAE also command respect among the tribal confederations in their societies. Sean Yom and F. Gregory Gause (2012) cite Saudi sociologist Khalid al-Dakhil who contends monarchies' historical-religious claims to legitimacy make monarchies 'closer to the society

---

[1] Geddes classifies both Trujillo and Amin as personalist dictators.

they govern' than republics, because their traditions produce reverence and support from Arab subjects wooed by such powerful cultural appeals.

In addition to traditional sources of legitimacy, authoritarian monarchies benefit from ruling families' strong ties throughout society and ability to mobilize diverse networks of support, similar in many ways to the role ruling parties play in single party dictatorships. Those regimes with large and engaged ruling families—what Michael Herb (1999) has called **dynastic monarchies**—tend to be the most resilient. According to Herb, dynastic monarchies are durable because:

> ruling families have formed themselves into ruling institutions. [They] have developed mechanisms to distribute and redistribute power among their shaykhs and princes, without drawing outsiders into family disputes. At the same time, these families preserve their tight grip on power and maintain multitudinous contacts within their societies.

Non-dynastic monarchies, in contrast, more closely resemble personalist dictatorships where the king rules with a narrower set of cronies at his side. The non-dynastic monarchies in Egypt (1952), Iraq (1958), Libya (1969), Afghanistan (1973), and Iran (1979) crumbled when faced with domestic opposition.

Similarly, monarchies depend on their ability to foster cross-cutting coalitions within society—what Yom and Gause (2012) define as 'historical alliances linking different social constituencies to the ruling family' (p. 81). These coalitions expand the number of citizens who have a vested interest in the continuation of the regime and are willing to counter opponents during crises. In Morocco, for example, the monarchy used economic payments, policy guarantees, and nationalist appeals to secure the interests of the business class, agricultural elites, and religious authorities. Such partnerships enabled the Alaouites to weather postcolonial unrest (Gause, 2011). Moreover, and also like single party regimes, dynastic monarchies have institutionalized leadership transitions. The process of selecting a leader from among the family ranks requires aspiring rulers to build consensus and bargain among various family factions. Family members who occupy key positions within the state bureaucracy assert a right to determine succession and have the resources to defend that right. Ultimately, members of ruling families who are not in direct competition for the lead post have incentive to bandwagon together as a family when succession disputes arise. **Bandwagoning** assures that the family does not split, which could threaten the dynastic monopoly on state power (Herb, 1999).

Blended regimes and changes over time

Not all regimes fit so neatly into one category. There are several dictatorships that combine elements of more than one of the categories we described. The Cuban dictatorship under Fidel Castro, for example, contained strong single party and personalist elements (Ezrow and Frantz, 2011). Fidel Castro seized power in the Cuban Revolution in 1959 and ruled Cuba for fifty years, along with the Communist Party of Cuba (PCC), before passing power to his brother Raúl in 2008. During his reign, Castro controlled, 'every key lever of power in Cuba, including the judiciary, and [was] responsible for every important appointment' (Palmer, 2005, p. 231). At the same time, Castro created the PCC after the revolution, and he relied heavily on the party to mobilize regime support. By the end of the 1970s, the PCC was institutionally strong enough that it resembled a typical communist party, permeating all elements of Cuban life. Similarly, the Egyptian regime (1952–2011) featured a significant role for the military, a fairly robust political party (the National Democratic Party), and charismatic leaders, including Gamal Abdel Nasser, Anwar Sadat, and Hosni Mubarak.

Not only do some regimes incorporate elements from more than one category, but the regime's classification may evolve over time. In particular, many dictatorships exhibit some level of personalism (Hadenius and Teorell, 2006). Dictatorships often experience periods during which the leader's power vis-à-vis the party, military, or royal family is stronger than others. These fluctuations are especially common following a leadership transition within the same regime, such as when a leader dies in office. In the Cuba example, the transition of power from Fidel to Raúl reduced the salience of the personalist element of the regime. Likewise, in Ethiopia, the transition of power from Meles Zenawi to Hailemariam Desalegan in 2012 diminished the personalist element of that regime. Desalegan struggled to fill the charismatic footsteps of his successor, and the ruling Ethiopian People's Revolutionary Democratic Front (EPRDF) has played a more significant role in decision-making post-Meles. However, in April of 2018 Desalegan resigned and was replaced by the far more charismatic leader, Abiy Ahmed. Ahmed has released political prisoners and unblocked censored websites, but has also created a personality cult around him, with taxi windscreens displaying his photo everywhere and t-shirts bearing his face selling out.

In addition to fluctuations that might occur given a leadership transition, fluctuations can also occur during a single leader's reign. This is likely to be most common in the first years of a new leader's tenure. In Egypt, for example, President Abdel Fattah el-Sisi seized power via coup in 2014. Initially, the military played an important supporting role for the president. Soon after, however, el-Sisi sought to diminish the military's influence on his regime and took a number of steps to consolidate his personal power. Today, el-Sisi most closely resembles a personalist dictatorship and relies on the military to implement his decisions, but the military does not exercise influence over those policies.

The mixed nature of some regimes can make it more difficult to generate theoretical expectations for their behaviour and the outcomes they produce. However, recognizing how regimes draw on various institutional arrangements and the way that regime characteristics shift over time can still give us analytic purchase on understanding their behaviour.

Conclusion

We often assume that all dictatorships fit the strongman mould. Vivid anecdotes and mental images of infamous and eccentric leaders such as Libya's Muammar al-Qaddafi and the former Zaire's Joseph Mobutu reinforce this perception. But as this chapter discussed, the reality is more nuanced. For almost seventy years, Chinese leaders have come from just one party, the Communist Party of China, and many have voluntarily left office after a maximum of two five-year terms (though this may be changing). Meanwhile, in North Korea, the Kim dynasty has ruled for decades, with each leader dying while in office and ensuring the passage of power from father to son amid a highly repressive system of political control (Svolik, 2012). There is in fact tremendous variation across these governments in terms of the segments of society they draw on to staff government offices, the procedures they use for making decisions, and the ways they handle the choice and transitions of leaders. As Barbara Geddes concluded, 'different kinds of authoritarian regimes differ from each other as much as they differ from democracy' (1999, p. 121). In the last twenty years, a significant amount of research has been done to open up the black box of autocracy.

A well-established body of political science research shows that whether leaders rule largely at their own discretion or face institutional constraints from a powerful party or influential military dramatically affects how decisions are made and the policies that result. For example, because elites in different institutional contexts use markedly different strategies to stay in office, regime survival rates differ systematically across autocracies. Likewise, the nature of the authoritarian regime affects the likely trajectory these regimes follow once the regime fails. We build on the framework presented in this chapter throughout the rest of the book to help explain how these authoritarian 'types' explain differences in the decisions and behaviour across autocracies.

Key Questions

1. What are the defining features of a totalitarian regime? What makes North Korea totalitarian?

2. Why do personalist regimes tend to perform so poorly economically compared to single party regimes?

3. Why are dynastic monarchies and single party regimes so resilient? What do these two regimes share in common?

4. What differentiates a personalist regime led by a military officer from a military regime?

5. How would you categorize China today? Xi Jinping has taken steps to increase his own power relative to the Chinese Communist Party. Is China still a single party regime? Why or why not?

6. Why have personalist regimes become more common since the end of the Cold War? What factors do you think are driving their rise?

Further Reading

Ezrow, N.M. and Frantz, E., 2011. *Dictators and Dictatorships: Understanding Authoritarian Regimes and Their Leaders*. Bloomsbury Publishing USA.
Dictators and Dictatorships provides an overview of the different types of dictatorships around the world, using categorical measures to distinguish between different regimes. The book also focuses on the regional trends, and why certain types of authoritarian regimes emerge in certain regions.

GANDHI, J., 2008. *Political Institutions under Dictatorship*. Cambridge University Press.

Political Institutions under Dictatorships explores the democratic institutions such as legislatures and political parties that authoritarian regimes use as a survival tool to prolong their rule. The book explains how institutions can neutralize threats from the opposition and are an important component to the operation of authoritarian regimes.

LINZ, J.J., 2000. *Totalitarian and Authoritarian Regimes*. Lynne Rienner Publishers.

Totalitarian and Authoritarian Regimes provides a through overview of how totalitarian regimes function and offers a clear typology to help distinguish between authoritarian and totalitarian rule.

SVOLIK, M.W., 2012. *The Politics of Authoritarian Rule*. Cambridge University Press.

The Politics of Authoritarian Rule looks at the threats that dictators face when they are in power, both from the masses (the problem of authoritarian control) and from their elites (the problem of authoritarian power sharing). Svolik also explains how authoritarian regimes are able to control the masses, using both co-optation and repression.

4

Dysfunctional Democracies and Hybrid Systems

> Thinking exclusively in terms of the opposition between democracy and authoritarianism threatens to trap democratic theorists within the two assumptions that this opposition implicitly contains: first, that when an authoritarian system collapses, democracy will naturally arise by default; and second, that if democracy fails to develop, authoritarian forces must be to blame ... the truth is that today authoritarianism survives best in the no-man's land between democracy and authoritarianism. (Ivan Krastev, 2011)

We began Chapter 2 by laying out examples of democracy and dictatorship. Sweden, Germany, and the United States, we said, are quite clearly democratic. And we identified North Korea and Turkmenistan as unequivocally authoritarian. When it comes to Turkey, Hungary, Poland, and Venezuela, however, we noted that things become less clear. In this chapter we turn our focus to this 'messy middle,' or those ambiguous systems that mix democratic characteristics with authoritarian tendencies. Since the end of the Cold War, there has been a substantial rise in the number of these **hybrid regimes**—the broad label used to describe countries combining democratic and authoritarian elements. In fact, hybrid regimes have proliferated to such an extent that scholars contend they are now 'the modal type of political regime in the developing world' (Schedler, 2006, p. 3; Brownlee, 2007). How should we think about these mixed systems? Do they behave more like dictatorships, or are they best viewed and addressed as countries going through the painstaking ups and downs of democratization?

A body of research published in the early 2000s concludes that hybrid regimes are best thought of as a distinct type of political system. But this was not always the case. It took some time before scholars recognized that the countries that sit between democracy and autocracy are not necessarily in transit and that this new mix of characteristics was a permanent feature of a growing number of governments. After the Cold War, in particular, there was a widely held assumption that countries experiencing movements away from autocracy were on a one-way path that would end in democracy. But the uptick in the number of countries that failed to advance much beyond holding sub-optimal elections led scholars to question this assumption. In 2002, Thomas Carothers captured this conceptual shift when he proclaimed that we had reached the end of the 'transitions paradigm', or the idea that all authoritarian regimes that fall will transition to a democracy. Rather than ushering in democracy, the collapse of many authoritarian regimes gave way to new forms of undemocratic rule. These countries were not on their way to democracy, but instead had adapted to the new post-Cold War reality by mimicking democratic rule. Perhaps most surprising has been the durability of some of these systems. A large body of research documents that the presence of pseudo-democratic institutions like elections and political parties in non-democratic contexts prolongs the life of these regimes (Gandhi, 2008; Gandhi and Przeworski, 2007; Levitsky and Way, 2010; Magaloni, 2006; Svolik, 2012).

In this chapter we delve into the messy middle and map the terrain between democracy and dictatorship. The goal is to highlight the wide variety of political systems today and underscore the rather astonishing frequency with which contemporary authoritarian regimes possess seemingly democratic features (Diamond, 2015). We identify the different types of hybrid systems that occupy this middle ground—focusing on electoral democracy, competitive authoritarianism, and hegemonic authoritarianism—and define their key characteristics. We then conclude the chapter by examining why hybrid systems have become more common in the post-Cold War era.

Mapping the terrain

In this section, we map the messy middle. In doing so, we seek to condense and simplify a large body of research examining this space. Since the 1990s, there has been an explosion of research and interest in understanding those countries that defy the binary democracy–dictatorship distinction. As a result, there has been a surge of often-conflicting approaches to classifying hybrid regimes. As David Collier and Steven Levitsky (1997) noted, 'the result [of this uptick in interest] has been a proliferation of alternative conceptual forms, including a surprising number of subtypes involving "democracy with adjectives"' (pp. 430–1). In addition to 'hybrid regimes', scholars have referred to these mixed systems as 'semi-authoritarianism' (Ottaway, 2003), 'competitive authoritarianism' (Levitsky and Way, 2002), 'electoral authoritarianism' (Diamond, 2015; Schedler, 2002), 'illiberal democracies' (Zakaria, 1997), 'flawed democracies', or, as Freedom House puts it, 'Partly Free'.

Our approach to mapping the terrain between democracy and dictatorship is consistent with scholars who view hybrid regimes as '**diminished subtypes**' of democracy and dictatorship (Collier and Levitsky, 1997). Diminished subtypes are cases that fall short of the root category (democracy and dictatorship for our purpose) because they lack one or more of the defining attributes of these root categories. In other words, diminished subtypes have fewer defining attributes of the prototypical type. Hybrid regimes, therefore, do not possess all of the attributes assigned to either democracy or dictatorship. Because they have missing attributes, hybrid regimes should be thought of as a distinct category, representing a different set of cases than the countries designated as democracies or dictatorships.

Figure 4.1 illustrates the spectrum of regimes we discuss in this chapter. As you can see from Figure 4.1, political regimes across the globe can be grouped into five categories: full democracy (or liberal democracy), full autocracy (or closed authoritarianism), and three diminished subtypes (**defective democracy, competitive authoritarianism,** and **hegemonic authoritarianism**). Since both competitive and hegemonic autocracies hold regular elections—albeit under conditions that are generally authoritarian—they are frequently grouped within a larger category that many researchers have termed '**electoral authoritarianism**'. It is important to note that these regime types are intended to serve as categories and do not necessarily represent a progression through which all regimes must pass as they move toward or away from democracy (Howard and Roessler, 2006).

At the far end of Figure 4.1 are *full democracies*, or liberal democracies. Liberal democracies, as Chapter 2 explained, not only hold regular and competitive elections

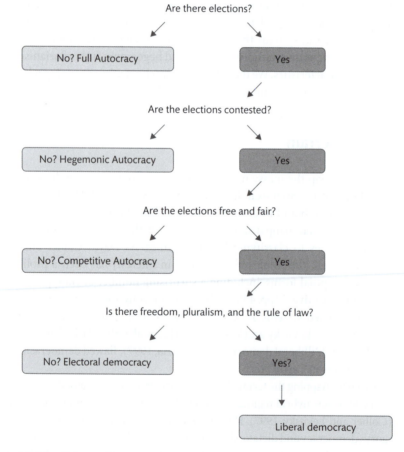

Figure 4.1 Classifying regimes.

Howard, M.M. and Roessler, P.G., 2006. 'Liberalizing Electoral Outcomes in Competitive Authoritarian Regimes'. *American Journal of Political Science*, *50*(2), pp. 365–81. © Midwest Political Science Association. By permission of John Wiley and Sons.

for all key positions of powers, but they also have other democratic attributes, including robust protections for political and civil liberties. They uphold the **rule of law**, are accountable to their citizens, and feature some degree of participation. Liberal democracies therefore do not fall within the grey zone.

At the opposite end of the spectrum are *full autocracies,* or closed authoritarian regimes. These are countries in which leaders are selected by small groups of elites from the ruling family, military, or political party rather than through national elections. Opposition political parties are banned, and incumbents rely heavily on repression to maintain control, including through heavy restrictions on the media and civil society. Like liberal democracies, closed autocracies are not hybrid regimes.

It is interesting to note that the number of closed autocracies has substantially declined since the end of the Cold War while hegemonic autocracies have become more prevalent. This is in large part due to the widespread adoption of institutions, such as elections, political parties, and legislatures across the full spectrum of political systems. Although elections existed in non-democratic settings prior to the 1990s, their use has become almost ubiquitous since that time. In 1970, for example, 59 per cent of autocracies held an election at least once every six years. As of 2008, 83 per cent hold an election at least once every six years (Kendall-Taylor and Frantz, 2015; Roessler and Howard, 2008). These figures underscore the fact that the vast majority of today's systems utilize seemingly democratic institutions, although they operate quite differently in non-democratic contexts, as we discuss at greater length in Chapter 5.

In the following subsections we discuss these categories of hybrid regime. We divide our discussion into two parts: those hybrid regimes that constitute diminished forms of democracy, and those that are best conceived as diminished forms of dictatorship. The boundaries between the various categories of hybrid regimes we discuss are blurry and often require difficult and disputable judgements (Diamond, 2015). Scholars have put much effort into debating the criteria used to distinguish between different types of hybrid regimes. Such debates and distinctions are crucial for comparative research that seeks to understand the causes and implications of the various regime types; the definitions that researchers use affects the results they get. For our purposes, however, we avoid being bogged down in these debates and rather focus on sketching the broad contours of the different types of hybrid regimes based on a range of perspectives scholars have provided (see the discussion in Box 4.2 of Singapore and Malaysia as examples of hybrid systems).

Defective democracies

As we discussed in Chapter 2, there are two general approaches to defining democracy: minimalist definitions, which focus on the occurrence of competitive elections; and maximalist definitions, which include a number of additional criteria that countries must meet in order to be considered full democracies. Defective democracies pass the minimalist threshold of democracy, but they fail to uphold all of liberal democracy's essential features. The most common label assigned to these countries is '**electoral democracy**' (Diamond, 2002; Schedler, 2002). Some scholars have also referred to them as **illiberal democracies** (Zakaria, 1997). Unlike competitive autocracies, which we discuss later, defective democracies hold free and fair elections, which put them closer to the democracy side of the spectrum. However, they do not adhere to more robust definitions of political and civil liberties, rule of law, accountability, and/or participation, making them a diminished subtype of democracy.

Defective democracies tend to fall short of democracy for several shared reasons. One of their most common shortcomings is a lack of robust protections for political and civil liberties. Countries such as Poland and Serbia, for example, would be classified as defective democracies because they perform well on electoral processes, but restrict civil liberties. Leaders in such systems come to power through competitive elections, but subsequently target journalists, increase state control over public broadcasters, harass and intimidate their political opponents, limit the activities of civil society organizations, and pursue majoritarian policies that are at odds with minority rights.

Another key feature of defective democracies is that they feature weak institutions. Political parties and legislatures, in particular, are typically not strong enough to provide an effective check on executive power. Political parties in defective democracies are often centred on charismatic leaders rather than being rooted in identifiable societal interests or cleavages. Weak party systems hamper democracy for a number of reasons (see Chapter 2)—they hinder the development of a stable opposition, political competition, and accountability. Weak parties also struggle to mobilize support or engage citizens in the political process. Countries with weak party systems often give rise to opportunistic leaders who can play fast and loose with democratic procedures, paving the way for greater authoritarianism, as in Peru under Alberto Fujimori and Venezuela under Hugo Chávez.

Not only do defective democracies tend to have weak party systems, but they also often suffer from weak legislatures. In many defective democracies, popular elected officials bypass their parliaments and rule by presidential decree, eroding basic constitutional practices (Zakaria, 1997). In other cases, popular officials enjoy extensive support in parliament, enabling them to pass laws that entrench the party's hold on power. In other words, leaders can exploit the legal process and pass legislation that impinges on freedom of speech and assembly, diminishing levels of liberty within the country. Moreover, many legislators in defective democracies lack political experience and expertise in policymaking. These legislatures struggle to constrain the executive, raising the risk that leaders abuse power.

Influential work by Guillermo O'Donnell (1994) labelled those systems that lack institutions that can effectively check executive power as **delegative democracies**. Delegative democracy is essentially another name for defective democracy. O'Donnell described delegative democracies as countries that 'rest on the premise that whoever wins election to the presidency is thereby entitled to govern as he or she sees fit, constrained only by the hard facts of existing power relations and by a constitutionally limited term of office' (p. 59). Delegative democracies, therefore, meet the minimum standards for democracy but have strong presidents and weak horizontal accountability, or 'checks and balances'. Leaders of these systems view checks and balances, particularly legislatures and judiciaries, as unnecessary encumbrances to their 'mission' and therefore make efforts to marginalize these bodies (O'Donnell, 1994). According to O'Donnell, these systems make quick, unconstrained decisions, which lead to gross miscalculations. Delegative democracies are prone to breakdowns and function poorly. Much of O'Donnell's work on delegative democracy is based on Latin America, where there has historically been a number of countries with strong presidents, but that were prone to instability, including Brazil after military rule, Ecuador, and Peru.

Another characteristic of defective democracy is a weak civil society. A robust civil society is important because it enables people to hold the government accountable, serves as a check on government power, and broadens public engagement in the political process. Many new democracies, in particular, have underdeveloped civil societies as a result of their experience under dictatorship. Authoritarian governments either thwarted the development of an independent civil society, or, in the case of communist dictatorships, co-opted civic organizations in ways that eroded public trust in those organizations. Civil societies also tend to be weak in those democracies where exclusive ethnic, family, or friendship-based networks persist post-transition. Such polarized and restrictive societal structures impede the development of interpersonal trust that is a necessary foundation of civil society and ultimately, democracy.

Finally, defective democracies often emerge where governments struggle to deliver. In these cases, the government's inability to meet citizen expectations of what democracy should deliver can lower political participation and stunt civil society development. New democracies that overpromise and/or create unrealistic expectations about what democracy can deliver (and on what timeline) often suffer from large swaths of citizens disenchanted with the system. This disappointment, in turn, can raise public apathy, increasing a government's vulnerability to being taken over by non-democratic forces (Howard, 2002). Public disappointment with democracy has been evident across several fragile democracies. A 2001 Latinobarometer survey of Latin American countries revealed, for example, that 21 per cent of respondents felt that the form of government made no difference.[1] In the 1997 parliamentary elections in Chile where voting is compulsory, almost a third voted for no one (Payne, 2002). Likewise, South Africa also suffers from low voter turnout and high levels of apathy among its youth (Runciman, 2016). With little enthusiasm for democracy or its institutional processes, citizens struggle to hold their governments accountable resulting in diminished forms of democracy.

Diminished dictatorship

Just as scholars have theorized about defective democracies, so too have they recognized that a growing number of countries have evolved from our historical conception of dictatorship. Dictatorships of the past seized power violently, ruled through the use of mass arrests, firing squads, and other forms of brutal intimidation, and faced little opposition from those they ruled. But these are no longer useful models for understanding

---

[1]   http://www.latinobarometro.org/lat.jsp (accessed 21 June 2019).

contemporary authoritarian systems. Today, most authoritarians hold regular elections, allow multiple political parties to operate and compete, and claim to uphold the rule of law. It is critical to note, however, that these seemingly democratic institutions function very differently in authoritarian versus democratic settings. In today's dictatorships, pseudo-democratic institutions are not intended to give people a voice in the political process or protect them from the whims of state power. Instead the façade of democracy serves *authoritarian* purposes, ultimately reinforcing incumbents' hold on power (see Chapter 6 on authoritarian durability).

Diminished dictatorships are distinct from closed autocracies because they hold regular elections and feature many of the trappings of democracy, such as political parties and legislatures. They also differ from defective democracies in that their elections do not meet international standards of freedom or fairness. Because they feature elections, however, the two forms of diminished dictatorship we discuss—competitive autocracies and hegemonic autocracies—are together referred to as **electoral authoritarian systems** (Schedler, 2002). According to Schedler, these systems play 'the game of multiparty elections ... yet [they] violate the liberal-democratic principles of freedom and fairness so profoundly and systematically as to render elections instruments of authoritarian rule rather than instruments of democracy' (Schedler, 2006: 3).

The hybrid system type that sits closest to full autocracy is '**hegemonic authoritarianism**' (Howard and Roessler, 2006). Although hegemonic authoritarian systems hold regular elections, the electoral process is not competitive. In many cases, these systems ban opposition parties from participating in elections, as in China, such that voters do not have a real choice. In other cases, incumbents allow an opposition to compete, but these candidates have no positive prospect of winning because they are prevented from accessing state-owned media coverage, banned from holding political rallies, or routinely harassed and jailed (Munck, 2006). Sometimes opposition candidates and parties boycott elections in these environments. Understanding they will not be able to compete fairly, opposition actors view their participation as giving unwarranted legitimacy to an election. Put simply, electoral outcomes in hegemonic autocracies are never in doubt.

There are two indicators that can help us discern hegemonic from competitive autocracy. The first is the incumbent's vote share (Diamond, 2015; Roessler and Howard, 2008). In hegemonic autocracies, leaders win by fantastic margins. Countries such as Tunisia under Zine al-Abidine Ben Ali (1987–2011) and Uzbekistan under Islam Karimov (1991–2016) were hegemonic autocracies. In Tunisia, Ben Ali consistently won re-election during his twenty-three-year tenure with vote margins over 90 per cent. Likewise, Karimov won all four of the presidential elections he held until he died in office in 2016 by 87 per cent or more. A second indicator of dominance is the ruling party's control of the legislature. In hegemonic autocracies, the ruling party wins almost all of the seats. In hegemonic autocracies such as Singapore under the People's Action Party, Egypt under Mubarak, and Tunisia under Ben Ali, ruling parties received over 80 per cent of legislative seats (Diamond, 2015).

To some observers, hegemonic autocracies differ very little from closed autocracies. As we noted, the primary distinction between these two system types is that hegemonic autocracies hold elections while closed autocracies do not. However, given the wide-spread adoption of elections across non-democratic systems, this distinction has become less meaningful. Elections have become an accepted way of life in most autoc-racies and actually serve to make dictatorships more durable (Geddes, 2006; Gandhi and Przeworski, 2007; Gandhi, 2008; Magaloni, 2008; Pepinsky, 2014).

More meaningful, perhaps, than the distinction between full and hegemonic dicta-torship is the distinction between hegemonic and '**competitive authoritarian**' systems (Levitsky and Way, 2002). Political scientists Steven Levitsky and Lucan Way (2002) define competitive autocracies as those systems where 'formal democratic institutions are widely viewed as the principal means of obtaining and exercising political author-ity' but where 'incumbents violate those roles so often and to such an extent . . . that the regime fails to meet conventional minimum standards for democracy' (Levitsky and Way, 2002, p. 52). In other words, competitive autocracies fall short of democracy, but they maintain pseudo-democratic institutions that offer an important channel through which the opposition may periodically challenge, weaken, and occasionally even defeat autocratic incumbents (Levitsky and Way, 2002).

Semi-competitive elections are a defining feature of competitive autocracies. Authoritarian incumbents in these countries still manipulate the pre-electoral environ-ment. They typically leverage their control of state resources, bias the media coverage, and harass—sometimes violently—opposition candidates and activists (Levitsky and Way, 2002). In fact, competitive authoritarian systems engage in tactics that severely tilt the playing field in their advantage, creating an uphill battle for opposition challengers. Nevertheless, competitive autocracies differ from hegemonic systems because there is still some uncertainty about the election outcome. In some cases, incumbents in com-petitive autocracies win elections by modest margins. In Kenya, for example, long-time president Daniel Arap Moi (1978–2002) won presidential elections in 1992 and 1997 by bare pluralities (with only around 30 per cent of the overall vote each time). And in some cases, opposition forces have managed to defeat autocratic incumbents or their hand-picked candidates. Leaders or their designates in competitive autocracies lost elections in Nicaragua in 1990, Zambia in 1991, Malawi and Ukraine in 1994, Albania in 1997, and Ghana in 2000, and Kenya in 2002 (Levitsky and Way, 2002). In hegemonic autocracies, in contrast, incumbent candidates or parties have never lost an executive election in which they participated (Howard and Roessler, 2007, p. 9).

 Box 4.1: **Pseudo-opposition**

The outcome of Egypt's 2018 Presidential election was never in doubt. Incumbent candidate Abdel Fattah el-Sisi won in a landslide victory with 97 per cent of the vote. These results were unsurprising not least because Sisi's only opponent, Moussa Moustafa Moussa, was a vocal sup-porter of Sisi until his abrupt decision to stand for election. During the election campaign Moussa told one interviewer that he was 'not here to challenge the president' (The Guardian, editorial).

Moussa was what many observers call the '**pseudo-opposition**'. A pseudo-opposition is defined as opposition parties and candidates that the incumbent regime approves and allows to participate in the political process with the understanding that they will not threaten the regime. The regime allows them to operate because they view the façade of competition as adding legitimacy to their election. By allowing some opposition members to participate in the election and banning others, it also allows autocratic governments to divide the opposition such that it cannot mount a cohesive challenge. Not only does this divide and rule tactic create suspicion among the opposition about who is in the pocket of the regime, but it also divides the votes of the discontented, preventing any one candidate from making a strong showing in an election.

The existence of a pseudo-opposition is not unique to Egypt. In fact, it is quite common in dictatorships. In Mexico under the PRI, for example, the Authentic Party of the Mexican Revolution (PARM) and the Party of the Cardenist Front of National Reconstruction (PFCRN) were archetypal pseudo-opposition parties. They endorsed PRI candidates and helped legitimize elections for the PRI. By participating in the electoral process, they undermined the inclination of serious opposition parties such as the National Action Party (PAN) to boycott the elections (Crespo, 2004). Likewise, in authoritarian South Korea, Chun Doo Hwan created loyal opposition parties in order to co-opt potential challengers (Solinger, 2001). In more liberal systems these parties may be given a degree of independence and a limited voice in public affairs in return for loyalty to the ruling party.

The pseudo-opposition is not to be mistaken with genuine opposition, of course. In the case of Taiwan, there were some pseudo-opposition parties that the authoritarian KMT regime brought with it from the mainland. These parties differed, however, from the real opposition that emerged in the late 1970s, originally known as Tang-wai movement. This movement genuinely challenged KMT rule and eventually became the Democratic Progressive Party (DPP). The DPP won the presidential election in 2000 and currently holds power under the leadership of Tsai Ing-wen.

Even beyond elections, competitive autocracies have other meaningful democratic institutions that create 'arenas of democratic contestation' (Levitsky and Way, 2002). Competitive autocracies, for example, feature legislatures that, while weak, can become focal points of opposition activity. Opposition forces in competitive autocracies can use the legislature as a public platform from which to denounce the government. In Peru, despite the fact that opposition parties exerted little influence over the legislative process between 1995 and 2000, anti-Fujimori legislators used congress (and media coverage of it) as a place to air their views (Levitsky and Way, 2002).

Competitive autocracies also have judiciaries that tend to be relatively independent. According to Levitsky and Way (2002), 'Governments in competitive authoritarian regimes routinely attempt to subordinate the judiciary, often via impeachment, or, more subtly, through bribery, extortion, and other mechanisms of co-optation . . . Yet the combination of formal judicial independence and incomplete control by the executive can give maverick judges an opening' (p. 56). For example, Malaysia's Federal Court overthrew the conviction of opposition leader Anwar Ibrahim in 2004 on the grounds that it violated due process. Likewise, Pakistan's Supreme Court remained active and assertive under Pervez Musharraf's military government from 1999–2008 (Gilley, 2010).

Finally, competitive authoritarian systems also allow for some limited press freedoms. Independent media outlets in these countries are not only legal, but often influential. These outlets can play a critical watchdog role by investigating and exposing government abuses of power. In contrast to hegemonic autocracies, which seek to exercise complete state control over media or systematically repress the space, competitive autocrats use more subtle tactics, such as vague laws that encourage self-censorship and enable them to selectively target their most vocal critics. They employ bribery and the targeted allocation of state advertising and manipulate debts and taxes owed by media outlets. In Venezuela under Hugo Chávez, for example, journalists were regularly harassed, intimidated, and subject to fines and censors. The government used legislation to control news content, increased the number of government-run TV channels, and complicated the efforts of critical media outlets to renew their licences. Nonetheless, the media was often able to be quite critical of the former president.

In Chapter 5 we discuss the effects of regime type on a host of factors, including economic growth, political stability, levels of terrorist activity, and corruption. However, we note here that the differences between hegemonic and competitive authoritarian regimes affect how each regime type tends to fall from power. In competitive autocracies, elections provide the potential to unseat unpopular incumbents. Though it typically requires the right confluence of factors and some time for an opposition to gain experience, elections can be a viable mechanism for change. In hegemonic autocracies, in contrast, institutions do not provide such an outlet. The lack of opportunities to express citizen preferences through institutional mechanisms in hegemonic systems means that people view the street as their most likely avenue for change. In other words, the death or violent overthrow of the president is a more likely means of succession than the ballot box. In hegemonic autocracies, there were two transitions to democracy between 1995 and 2006. In both cases (Indonesia in 1999 and Georgia in 2004) the transitions occurred because of mass demonstrations.

 Box 4.2: **Hybrid systems in Singapore and Malaysia**

Singapore and Malaysia are two examples of hybrid systems. Both of these systems feature democratic institutions (such as elections and a parliament) but prior to Malaysia's 2018 general election—which we discuss shortly—there had not been any alternation in the party of power in decades. In Malaysia, the Prime Minister came from the United Malays National Organisation (UMNO) party (part of the Barisan Nasional coalition) from 1963 to 2018. In Singapore, the Prime Minister has been from the People's Action Party (PAP) since 1959.

Though it is too soon to tell how events will unfold in Malaysia given the opposition's electoral victory in 2018, we describe features of both systems leading up to this point. In both systems, citizens enjoy some civil liberties and media freedom, albeit only to a limited extent. NGOs exist, though they have to be registered. In both systems, some freedom of press, speech, and religion is permitted, but Internal Security Acts are in place that allow dissidents to be detained without a trial. In Singapore, the PAP has extensive control over the media. The Ministry of Information and Arts nominates individuals who control Singapore Press Holdings, which owns local newspapers and scrutinizes foreign publications. Likewise, in Malaysia, the UMNO was linked to the New Straits Time Press Holdings, which owns the major newspapers. The UMNO also forbid certain topics to be discussed in the media and purged editors who were overly critical of the government (Rodan, 2004). Despite their strict control over traditional media, in both countries citizens can access the Internet and foreign media.

Both countries also hold elections where the opposition has won seats, but never a majority (again, in the case of Malaysia, this was true up until 2018). In both, the government uses tactics that heavily skew the electoral field to its advantage. In addition to controlling the information environment, both governments gerrymander electoral districts in order to preserve their control (Schedler, 2002). Malaysia's electoral districts are drawn such that the UNMO's rural support base is given more representation while the urban areas that have a large concentration of ethnic Chinese and generally support the opposition have less representation. Both governments also engage in clientelist practices—rewarding supporters while withholding benefits from those that do not support the government. In Malaysia, the UNMO promised villagers improvements to roads, clinics, and schools in exchange for votes (Case, 2007) and offered free health care for poor rural voters. Likewise, Singapore's government has threatened to deny funding to improve public housing in areas where the opposition won.

When characterizing the hybrid nature of the Malaysian and Singaporean systems, it is useful to compare them to Japan. Japan's electoral politics have also been dominated by one party, the Liberal Democratic Party (LDP). The LDP has held a majority in the parliament for all but four years (1993–97) since 1955. One crucial difference between these systems, however, is that unlike in Malaysia and Singapore, Japan's electoral playing field is considered free and fair and citizens enjoy full civil liberties and political rights.

Malaysia's 2018 general election highlights one of the key features of competitive autocracies: although the electoral playing filed is heavily skewed in favour of the incumbent government, there is still some positive probability that the opposition can win. In May 2018, the Barisan Nasional coalition was defeated after more than sixty years in power. Its defeat came at the hands of the opposition coalition Pakatan Harapan (the Alliance of Hope), led by 92-year-old Mahathir Mohamad. Mahathir was formerly prime minister of Malaysia (1981–2003) but defected from the UNMO and came out of retirement to challenge his former party. Mahathir's opposition alliance won 115 seats, over the 112-seat threshold required to form a government. Some political observers argued that the opposition victory was not surprising given that the UMNO has become increasingly unpopular—losing seats in each of the last two elections in 2008 and 2013—and has been dogged by accusations of corruption and the mismanagement of funds. Nonetheless, it was a historic victory and underscores the fine line that competitive authoritarian systems must walk in order to maintain control.

The spread of hybrid regimes

Hybrid regimes are not unique to the post-Cold War era. Several countries, such as Mexico under the PRI (1929–2000), and Argentina under Perón (1946–55), mixed democratic institutions with authoritarian tendencies. Although hybrid systems are not a new phenomenon, their numbers have grown dramatically during what Samuel Huntington famously called the '**Third Wave**' of democratization. This wave began in the mid-1970s and picked up steam with the collapse of the Soviet Union in the late 1980s and early 1990s (for more on the waves of democracy see Chapter 11 and the Conclusion). It has been during this Third Wave, however, that many transitions— perhaps even the majority—resulted in hybrid regimes. What explains the rapid rise of these mixed regimes? How was the Third Wave different than the previous waves of democratization? We highlight three factors that help account for the rise of hybrid regimes: the *process* through which the Third Wave of democratization unfolded and the *economic* and *international context* in which these transitions occurred.

Third Wave democratic transitions occurred differently than previous waves of democratization. Historically, the onset and consolidation of democracy followed long periods of state building, including the development of the rule of law, civil society, and institutions of horizontal accountability. First Wave democracies, for example, developed a modern state before universal suffrage was introduced; they democratized with the benefit of having institutional foundations in place. As the experiences of the United Kingdom, the United States, and the Scandinavian countries illustrate, the rule of law and political order were firmly entrenched before universal suffrage was expanded. In contrast, Third Wave regimes 'democratized backwards' (Rose and Shin, 2001). They introduced competitive elections before building a strong and modern state. Many leaders undergoing transitions during the Third Wave, therefore, faced a double challenge: they had to simultaneously complete the construction of a modern state while competing with their critics in free elections (Rose and Shin, 2001, p. 336). For many governments this dual challenge proved insurmountable and the number of countries with neither a strong state nor consolidated democracy ballooned.

The notion that democratization must follow a specific particular sequence—often referred to as the sequencing debate—is compelling. However, scholars and policymakers hotly debate the merits and the implications of the argument (Carothers, 2007, Mansfield and Snyder, 2007). We will discuss the 'sequencing debate' in greater depth in Box 11.3 of Chapter 12. However, we note here that despite some evidence that capable states enhance the likelihood of successful democratic consolidation, we have also seen democracy survive in poor countries with limited state capacity (Haggard and Kaufman, 2016). Moreover, we still lack sufficient evidence that allows us to reject the possibility that the causal arrow may run in the other direction: from democratic accountability to enhanced state capacity (Fortin, 2012).

The second factor accounting for the spread of hybrid regimes is the economic context in which Third Wave transitions occurred. First Wave transitions took place predominately in wealthy and industrialized societies. Industrialization was instrumental in weakening a landed class that monopolized wealth and had little interest in promoting political or economic equality, while simultaneously strengthening the middle classes that are more likely to demand and sustain democracy (Huber et al., 1993). The historical record has shown that consolidated democracies have survived in wealthy and industrialized countries, as the experience of Australia, New Zealand, and Japan show (Cheibub et al., 1996). Moreover, there is strong empirical evidence that democracy is more likely to endure in wealthier countries than in poorer ones (Przeworski et al., 2000; Svolik, 2008). Przeworski et al. (2000) famously show that no democracy has ever failed above a per capita GDP of $6,055, Argentina's level in 1975.

The Second Wave of democratization also occurred under economic conditions that were more favourable than the Third Wave. The Second Wave occurred in the aftermath of World War II when Allied occupation promoted the adoption of democratic institutions in countries such as Germany, Italy, and Japan. In the wake of the war, there was a massive reconstruction process through the **Marshall Plan** that entailed large injections of capital into Europe. As a result, and helped by the expanding world economy, the Second Wave countries achieved strong economic growth rates shortly after the transition to democracy (O'Donnell, 1994). Positive economic growth, in turn, contributed to government stability, citizen satisfaction, and the strength and resilience of most democracies that took root during this period.

The Third Wave of democracy, in contrast, happened amid a more challenging economic environment and in countries at lower levels of economic development. Many of these transitions took place in developing countries not yet at the wealth threshold that makes democracy more likely to stick. During the early part of the Third Wave in the 1970s and 1980s, worldwide economic troubles severely affected transitions in countries such as Spain, Portugal, Greece, Argentina, Bolivia, Brazil, Ecuador, and Peru. The democratic regimes that initially emerged not only inherited serious socio-economic difficulties from their authoritarian predecessors, but economic hardship made it difficult for them to fulfil citizen expectations. Transitions later in the Third Wave also corresponded with challenging economic conditions. The end of the Cold War meant that countries lost external support from their Soviet or Western backers. Deep economic crises deprived these governments of the resources needed to orchestrate an effective transition to democracy. Governments in Africa and the former Soviet Union, in particular, struggled to pay their bureaucrats, soldiers, and police (Levitsky and Way, 2015). The result was a wave of countries that lacked the capacity to engineer political change in either direction.

In other words, hybrid regimes often emerge by default. Some countries were too weak to take the steps necessary to consolidate democracy. Others lacked the capacity required to impose a fully authoritarian system. In such cases, political competition survives not because leaders are especially democratic or because institutions or societal actors are particularly strong. Instead, weak democracies remained because governments were too fragmented and the state too weak to impose authoritarian rule in the post-Cold War era where democracy was the standard of legitimacy.

For example, in Ukraine, Leonid Kravchuk attempted to shut down parliament in early 1994 in order to avoid early presidential elections. His inability to control the police and security services, however, forced him to back down—resulting in elections and Ukraine's first electoral turnover. Similarly, the high degree of pluralistic competition in Russia under Boris Yeltsin in the 1990s was not simply a function of Yeltsin's relatively liberal values but also because of his lack of capacity to assert control (Way, 2005). The decline of pluralism under Putin, in contrast, was in large part because of Putin's ability to consolidate state power in the early 2000s. Putin targeted pockets of power and brought them under state control, including the oil and gas industry and regional governments. With greater state capacity, Putin was able to consolidate his personal power. In sum, the rise of hybrid regimes has been a product of a growing number of weak states, which are often unable to move decisively toward democracy or dictatorship and therefore combine elements of both.

Finally, changes in the geopolitical environment also played an important role in fuelling the uptick in hybrid regimes in the 1990s. The end of the Cold War meant that numerous states faced economic hardship as their external financial support from the Soviet Union or the United States dried up. In many cases, the loss of economic assistance and international backing plunged countries into crises and conflict (Dorff, 1996). The end of the Cold War, therefore, unleashed tremendous political volatility across the globe as corrupt and ineffective states beset with religious or ethnic polarization struggled to stand on their own. Territorial disputes, armed ethnic conflicts, and civil wars erupted across the former Soviet Union, Africa, and beyond, including in countries such as Tajikistan, the former Yugoslavia, Haiti, and Somalia. The end of the Cold War, in other words, gave rise to a record number of weak and failing states.

Moreover, against this backdrop of instability and state fragility, the pressure to adopt democratic norms and institutions dramatically increased. The ideological defeat of **communism** led many to view democracy as 'the only game in town' (Linz and Stepan, 1996). Authoritarian regimes, therefore, began to suffer from a legitimacy problem in a new world where democratic values were now widely accepted. Donors, international organizations, and other powerful states also became more active in supporting democracy. In this new international environment, established authoritarian regimes faced domestic and international pressure to adopt, or at least mimic, more formal democratic institutions.

Weak and volatile states, however, provide inhospitable conditions for democracy to flourish. For one, research shows that political transitions that are accompanied by violence are much less likely to usher in democracy than peaceful ones (Celestino and Gleditsch, 2013). At an even more basic level, disputes or uncertainty about the definition of the nation and the boundaries of the state also complicate the emergence and consolidation of democracy. In his seminal study, Dankwart Rustow (1970) argued that democracy is unlikely to develop and, if it does, thrive if there is continuing contestation over who is a member of the nation, and if the state is unable to define and defend its borders and exert authority within them. The confluence of a growing number of weak and fragile states, combined with the widespread adoption of democratic institutions during Third Wave transitions, led hybrid systems to proliferate.

In sum, Third Wave democratizers faced significantly different domestic and international factors at the time of their transitions than did those countries that democratized earlier. Against this backdrop, we summarize three specific pathways that Levitsky and Way (2002) identify through which hybrid regimes emerge: **authoritarian decay**, authoritarian breakdown that is followed by a diminished version of autocracy, and **democratic decay**. We write in greater depth about many of these themes throughout this book, such as in our discussion of authoritarian breakdown (Chapter 7), democratic consolidation (Chapter 11), and changes in the way that democracies are falling apart (Chapter 14). Here, however, we briefly sketch the primary pathways to hybridism identified in the literature.

Pathway 1: Authoritarian decay

Authoritarian rulers often adopt limited liberalizing reforms to appease the opposition and/or strengthen support for their own governments (Haggard and Kaufman, 2016). Describing this dynamic in the context of African politics, van de Walle (2003) posited that the 'turn to multiparty competition [in the 1990s] amounted to little more than an erstwhile authoritarian ruler donning the garb of democracy and tolerating regular elections as a successful strategy for holding on to power' (p. 307). Such actions, however, become a slippery slope and many autocrats have found that once they set such change in motion, the process becomes hard to control and even more difficult to reverse. Navigating small-scale liberalization can be especially perilous when leaders are making concessions in the face of challenges arising from fiscal crises, weak state capacity, and international pressure. A confluence of factors can create a 'perfect storm for dictatorship' (Levitsky and Way, 2015, p. 50). The result is often 'pluralism by default,' in which political competition increases because governments lack even rudimentary means to suppress opposition challenges. Although openings in these systems emerge, the weakness of opposition movements still mean that transitions fall short of democracy.

Authoritarian decay has been a common pathway to hybridism across much of sub-Saharan Africa. Economic crisis and international pressure compelled many established autocrats to call multiparty elections, but transitions often fell short of democratization (Levitsky and Way, 2002). In Tanzania, for example, pressure from donors led to limited liberalization when long-time President Julius Nyerere (1964–85) stepped down from power in 1985. Despite the movement away from autocracy, the party of power, Chama Cha Mapinduzi (CCM), maintained its dominance.

Pathway 2: Authoritarian breakdown gives way to new diminished dictatorship

This pathway to hybridism occurs when an authoritarian regime collapses but is replaced by a lesser version of the previous regime (Carothers, 2002). In these cases, new governments lack the capacity to consolidate authoritarian *or* democratic rule. **Civil society and political parties are too weak to support democracy**, and years of authoritarian rule often mean that there are few, if any, democratic traditions to build on. Although elections are held, the legacies of the authoritarian system persist.

This path was followed by post-communist countries such as Armenia, Croatia, Romania, Russia, Serbia, and Ukraine, as well as by Haiti after 1994 (Levitsky and Way, 2002). As we discussed, after the collapse of the Soviet Union, Russia became a hybrid regime. Russian politics initially became competitive in the early 1990s not because Yeltsin presided over a democratic transition, but rather because political disarray left him unable to control his own security forces, bureaucracy, and regional governments.

Pathway 3: Democratic decay

Just as dictatorships can grow less intense, so too can democracies degrade over time. During the last twenty years, there has been a steady stream of **democratic backsliding**— what Guillermo O'Donnell (1994) called the 'slow deaths' of democracy—that have given rise to hybrid systems (See Chapter 14 for an in-depth discussion on changes in how democracies are breaking down). O'Donnell characterized these 'slow deaths' as 'a progressive diminution of existing spaces for the exercise of civilian power and the effectiveness of the classic guarantees of liberal constitutionalism'. There are a wide variety of events and dynamics that can gradually weaken democracy. Some of the most common incidences include: episodes of state violence or weakness that enable a government or leader to subvert the rule of law; the rise of a dominant party that suffocates electoral competition; a government's subversion of electoral institutions that ultimately affect the honesty of vote counting; a government's abuse of state resources, including the media, that violate minimum standards of electoral fairness and equal opportunity; and the introduction of exclusionary citizenship laws that violate democratic norms of inclusiveness (Schedler, 2002).

Democratic decay occurs more frequently in new democracies than more fully established ones (although they too are not immune). Democratic decay, therefore, typically happens when electoral democracies give way to competitive autocracies. Democratic decay was a pathway to competitive authoritarianism in Venezuela under Hugo Chávez, Russia under Vladimir Putin, and Turkey under Recep Erdoğan. The case of Nicaragua illustrates how it can happen. In Nicaragua, democratization occurred in 1990 with the election of centrist candidate Violeta Chamorro. The years that followed were difficult and unstable, however, and subsequent leaders were charged with large-scale corruption. In 2007, Daniel Ortega gained the presidency in relatively free and fair elections, but he later eroded respect for democratic norms and practice. In 2014, Nicaragua's national assembly voted to remove presidential term limits, enabling Ortega to remain in power indefinitely. As Freedom House noted in its 2018 country report, 'President Ortega has consolidated all branches of government under his party's control, limited fundamental freedoms, and allowed unchecked corruption to pervade the government.'[2] Most observers today for these reasons consider Nicaragua to have transitioned to a competitive form of dictatorship.

Conclusion

One of the defining features of post-Cold War politics has been the rise of hybrid regimes, or those regimes that look democratic in form but continue to rely on authoritarian tendencies to survive. This is in large part because, as this book will emphasize, the breakdown of authoritarianism often does not usher in democracy. More often than not, an outgoing dictatorship gives rise to a new authoritarian system, or some sort of hybrid regime. In those cases in which democratization does occur, the resulting democracy tends to be fragile and its consolidation is by no means guaranteed. In many cases, those countries meeting the minimum requirements of democracy frequently remain in the grey zone, lingering short of full democracy.

In this chapter we examined these ambiguous systems and identified the most common approaches scholars use to think about and categorize this 'messy middle'. Some of these mixed systems sit quite close to the democratic side of the political spectrum. They hold regular, competitive elections, allow multiple political parties to participate,

---

[2] https://www.refworld.org/docid/5a8aedf6fd.html (accessed February 22, 2019).

and permit these parties to hold seats in the legislature. But despite the trappings of democracy, many of them fall short of more substantive definitions of democracy.

There are also a number of countries that more closely resemble dictatorship than democracy, but that nonetheless have adopted several democratic features, such as elections, parties, and legislatures. In the immediate aftermath of the Cold War, there was tremendous optimism that the widespread uptake of democratic institutions we observed in these places meant that democracy was on the march. With time, however, it became clear that these 'democratic' gestures did not necessarily mean that these countries were on their way to democracy. Instead, authoritarian regimes have learned to co-opt seemingly democratic institutions for their own purpose.

The prevalence of hybrid regimes complicates today's political picture. In particular, it is becoming more difficult for observers to assess the implications of seemingly liberalizing measures on a country's political trajectory. What should we make, for example, of the political reforms that have occurred in Uzbekistan after long-time President Islam Karimov died in office in 2016? His successor, Shavkat Mirziyoyev, has taken several steps to move the country away from the hegemonic autocracy that existed under his predecessor. Should these moves be viewed as the start of a process that will democratize Uzbekistan? Or will they simply serve to consolidate Mirziyoyev's control and enhance the durability of his regime? Likewise, how should we interpret political reforms in Saudi Arabia, including giving women the right to vote in local elections in 2015? Despite these reforms, it appears that the de facto power of elected political representatives remains minimal and real authority remains monopolized by a small group of male members of the royal family. The introduction of more participatory elections, in other words, was likely not a sign of democratization, but instead served to enhance the durability of the regime.

As this chapter has shown, the vast variation among political systems that we see today requires that we update the way we think about democracy and dictatorship.

Key Questions

1. What are the benefits of using continuous measures of political systems rather than categorical measures? What are the advantages of having 'democracy (or autocracy) with adjectives'?

2. Pick one or more of the following countries: Bolivia, Ghana, Hungary, Russia, South Africa, Serbia, and Tanzania. Determine how you would categorize the country(s). What factors did you consider in your decision?

3. What factors explain why there are so many hybrid systems today? What things will be most likely to determine the proportion of hybrid regimes in the next ten years?

4. How do you define democratic decay? What factors make democratic decay difficult to identify?

5. What are the key differences between defective democracies and competitive authoritarian regimes? Imagine you are a citizen living in one of these types of regimes. What would be the advantages and disadvantages of living in these types of systems?

Further Reading

LEVITSKY, S. and WAY, L.A., 2010. *Competitive Authoritarianism: Hybrid Regimes after the Cold War.* Cambridge University Press.

Competitive Authoritarianism provides important typology of authoritarian regimes, conceptualizing a new form of autocracy that held relatively competitive elections, but that never lost power. The book also demonstrates that authoritarian regimes that had greater economic and social ties to the West were more likely to break down and democratize.

O'DONNELL, G.A., 1994. 'Delegative Democracy'. *Journal of Democracy*, 5(1), pp. 55–69.

This article offers a new conceptualization of flawed democracy, drawing from experience in Latin America. The article demonstrates how high levels of presidential power at the expense of other institutions lead to instability and undermine the rule of law.

OTTAWAY, M., 2003. *Democracy Challenged: The Rise of Semi-authoritarianism.* Carnegie Endowment for International Peace.

Democracy challenged offers an in-depth explanation of what semi-authoritarian regimes are, and how they challenge policymakers. The book also explains why the notable theories of democratic transitions that inform democracy promotion strategies have failed to be effective.

SCHEDLER, A., 2006. *Electoral Authoritarianism: The Dynamics of Unfree Competition.* Lynne Rienner.

Electoral Authoritarianism offers an overview of how competitive authoritarian regimes stay in power while still holding elections. It summarizes the key research on regime trajectories, explains how this is impacted by regime dynamics, and lays out the strategies of these regimes.

5

The Consequences of Democracy and Authoritarian Regimes

So far we have focused on defining different types of political systems. We discussed how to distinguish democracy from autocracy and the rising prevalence of **hybrid regimes**, or those governments that combine democratic practices with authoritarian tendencies. These definitions are important for theoretical and methodological reasons. And, as we discuss in this chapter, they also have practical importance. Democracy, autocracy, and hybrid systems constitute very different ways of organizing politics—of selecting leaders, processing conflict, and making and implementing decisions. As we will make clear, differences in a country's institutional arrangements lead to vastly different political, economic, security, and social outcomes.

Understanding the differences that regime type fosters is important given current debates within Western governments and societies about the importance of supporting democracy, both at home and abroad. Since **9/11** (when the United States was hit by a massive terrorist attack by the terror network Al Qaeda in 2001), and particularly in the wake of the Arab Spring, enthusiasm for democracy support has waned among many established Western democracies. The spread of conflict, including in Syria, Libya, Yemen, and Ukraine; fragile governance in Afghanistan and Iraq; and sustained threats from terrorist groups, such as the so-called Islamic State, have shifted Western focus to security and stability. For example, U.S. concerns over counter-terrorism, intelligence sharing, basing, and overflight rights, along with the perception that autocracy equals stability, are currently topping democracy and human rights considerations. The election in 2016 of U.S. President Trump, who has lavished praise on authoritarian leaders and openly questioned the notion that the United States should stand up for democracy and human rights, has also raised questions about its commitment to supporting these values.

In short, the last decade has seen Western policymakers regularly prioritize stability and security concerns over cultivating respect for democratic principles and practices.

Declining enthusiasm for democratic development has not been confined to the West. Many citizens in non-democracies have also tempered their interest in democratization. The rise of violent extremism and sectarian conflict in the Middle East has fed into a broader narrative, fuelled by authoritarian-directed **propaganda**, that democracy leads to chaos and the breakdown of security. In the Middle East, many citizens appear more willing to trade political and civil liberties for the promise of averting the turmoil that grew out of the Arab Spring. Moreover, autocratic leaders have stepped up their efforts to highlight the polarization of U.S. politics as evidence that democracy does not work. In China, for example, the main state-run news agency Xinhua argues that the Chinese system of governance leads to 'social unity' rather than the divisions that it claims are unavoidable consequences of Western democracy. Chinese state media hold up Trump's America as an example of what Xinhua refers to as 'the endless political backbiting, bickering and policy reversals, which are the hallmarks of liberal democracy'.[1]

The debate about the trade-offs between democracy and autocracy is not new. Since World War II, a number of prominent scholars and policymakers have argued that autocracy has a number of advantages over democracy, particularly in low-income countries. These voices posit that democracy in such contexts breeds economic stagnation and civil unrest. The impressive rise of China and the strong growth performance of many past autocracies, including the '**Asian Tigers**' in South Korea, Taiwan, and Singapore, and Chile under Agosto Pinochet, further popularized the notion that autocracy is beneficial (and even desirable) in certain settings. Although the end of the Cold War and subsequent rise in the number of democracies worldwide temporarily softened deliberations about democracy's merits, the debate is back. Growing global turmoil and resurgent authoritarian powers have sharpened the discourse and raised the salience of these discussions.

The debate about the importance and efficacy of democracy is not purely academic either. The momentum of any one side in this argument has implications for how the West approaches international affairs, including its support for political and economic development in the developing world. It is therefore important to understand and articulate what we know about the benefits and shortcomings of democracy relative to authoritarianism. Are there compelling reasons to prioritize the development of democracy? If so, what are they? The goal of this chapter is to present the research that should shape our thinking on these timely and important conversations.

Perhaps not surprisingly, there is a long tradition of scholarship examining the effects of democracy on a country's economy, security, and society. Scholars from disciplines including international relations, comparative politics, political theory, economics, development, and sociology have studied the implications of regime type. Many have set forth arguments about the *intrinsic* value of democracy. Nobel Prize-winning economist Amartya Sen, for example, argues that democracy is a universal value. For Sen, not only should people be afforded freedom in human life, but the practice of democracy

---

[1] The Economist, 'America and China: Barbarian Outreach', 11–17 November 2017.

is critical because it 'gives citizens an opportunity to learn from one another and helps society to form its values and priorities' (Sen, 1999, p. 10).

Though the arguments about democracy's *intrinsic* value are important and compelling, in this chapter we focus on the evidence that people marshal in making more *instrumental* claims about what democracy can (and cannot) deliver. In other words, our emphasis here is not on the value of democracy itself, but whether it is a means to other more measurable outcomes. To that end we specifically discuss the consequences of democracy for a government's propensity to fight wars, likelihood of experiencing internal conflict (or civil war), levels of terrorism, economic growth and development, corruption, and human rights. In the next section we highlight two key themes that emerge from scholarship on the implications of regime type that you will see repeated through the chapter. We then turn to more in-depth discussions of democracy's effect on key outcomes of interest.

Key themes

Much research examining the implications of regime type is contested. With the exception of the democratic peace theory—which posits that democracies do not go to war with other democracies (and that we discuss at greater length)—research on the consequences of regime type has yielded conflicting results. Some of the inconsistency in the empirical analysis stems from differences in research design and the measurement of key variables across studies. This variation makes it hard to evaluate competing claims and has contributed to a good deal of confusion with respect to how regime type affects a host of outcomes of interest. In the last ten years, however, research on the consequences of regime type has evolved and there are two key takeaways we wish to highlight.

First, studies that use a continuous approach to disaggregating political systems show that hybrid regimes, or those countries that sit in the middle of the autocracy–democracy spectrum, perform less well than either their fully democratic or fully authoritarian counterparts in a number of areas. The countries in the 'messy middle' are particularly vulnerable to insecurity, including from repression, terrorism, and prospects for internal conflict (Boswell and Dixon, 1990; Muller and Weede, 1990; Hegre, 2001; Fearon and Laitin, 2003). They are also the least durable (Gurr, 1974; Gates et al., 2006; Knutsen and Nygard, 2015) and accordingly most volatile regime type (Epstein et al., 2006). Full autocracies and consolidated democracies have internally consistent institutional arrangements, which create a self-enforcing equilibrium. The inconsistency and incoherence created by hybridism, in contrast, creates challenges in terms of security. Hybrid systems lack the benefits of democracy that encourage citizen satisfaction and therefore stability, such as avenues for citizens to participate and articulate their preferences. At the same time, they do not have the concentrated power and repressive capacity that facilitates control and stability in full autocracies.

Some scholars and policymakers have interpreted the 'messy middle' argument to mean that political liberalization—or movements from autocracy towards greater democracy—will unleash political violence and deteriorate government performance.

Political liberalization, the argument goes, disrupts the institutional procedures of a transitioning state. Samuel Huntington (2006), for example, argued that the process of democratization is associated with mass mobilization, which can trigger violence if the political institutions are not prepared to accommodate this level of participation. The instability surrounding the **Arab Spring** has given this view greater credence in the minds of many. Protesters" efforts to topple long-standing dictators in Egypt, Libya, Yemen, and Syria unleashed instability and violence that continue to plague the Middle East and North Africa. Indeed, full autocracies rarely become mature consolidated democracies overnight. Transitioning countries typically pass through the messy middle where mass politics mixes with authoritarian elite politics—generating a view that democratization produces instability.

We offer a note of caution when drawing such sweeping conclusions. Making the argument that political liberalization triggers instability requires disentangling it from hybridism (Hegre, 2001). Our discussion in Chapter 4 underscored that not all countries that are categorized in the middle range of democracy indicators should be considered 'in transition', as many become entrenched in a more permanent state of hybridism. Likewise, some countries in the messy middle may be backsliding from democracy to autocracy. In other words, countries that lie in the mid-range of the democracy–autocracy spectrum include hybrid regimes, liberalizing states, and backsliding states. We can reasonably expect the behaviour of these types of states to differ. Recent studies seeking to disentangle these dynamics find little empirical support for the notion that democratization raises a country's risk of civil war. Empirical studies show that democratizing countries have only a marginally higher share of conflict onset during the transition compared to years without transitions (Gleditsch and Ruggeri, 2010). Before making broad conclusions about the risks associated with political liberalization, more research is needed. For example, are some liberalization processes—perhaps those that occur 'organically' and without international intervention or that occur gradually—less likely to lead to instability?

Second, studies that use a categorical approach to disaggregate political systems (such that democracies lie in one category and dictatorships in the other) find that democracies outperform dictatorship on almost every indicator examined. Democracies are less likely to fight inter-state wars against other democracies (Levy, 1988). They are less likely to employ repression against their citizens than autocracies, and civil wars in democracies are comparatively less lethal (Davenport, 2007; Gleditsch, Hegre, and Strand, 2009). Most recent research indicates that democracies grow their economies at a rate that is at least on par with dictatorships and that the growth they produce is of higher quality—both less volatile and more likely to benefit the people they govern. This suggests that societies that feature free and fair elections are safer and more prosperous, and their citizens enjoy a higher quality of life.

The superior performance of democracy relative to dictatorship raises a number of critical questions and implications. How should policymakers approach full dictatorships, such as those in the Middle East or Central Asia? If, as some research suggests, movement towards hybridism ups the chance of internal conflict and insecurity, should political liberalization be avoided? Should we reinforce the dictators in office to lessen the chance of turmoil? Or is this view short-sighted? If democracy delivers better outcomes for the people living under these regimes and enhances a country's prospects for prosperity over the long-term, should we work to encourage democratic development to avoid repeated cycles of instability?

These issues are neither easy to address nor straightforward in their response. A host of additional factors, including national security interests, culture, and past (in)experience with democracy often further complicate the picture. However, here we present the cutting-edge research that should shape our thinking on these important questions. We provide a more in-depth discussion of the research on the effects of regime type on a state's conflict propensity, levels of terrorism, economic and human development, corruption, and human rights.

Regime type and conflict

Inter-state war

One of the most important and broadly agreed upon findings in political science is that democracies almost never go to war with other democracies (Doyle, 1986; Maoz and Russett, 1993; Russett, 1994). Known as the '**democratic peace**', the idea originated in the work of the eighteenth-century philosopher Immanuel Kant. Since that time the empirical evidence in support of the democratic peace has been so consistent that the finding comes as close to the only 'empirical law' as anything we have in international relations (Levy 1988). Although there is disagreement about *why* it works, academics share the belief that the effect of system type *is* causally meaningful: there is something about the internal makeup of democratic states that keeps them from fighting one another.

The democratic peace is not only theoretically significant, but also has important practical applications. If the argument is correct, then the spread of democracy across the globe should dramatically reduce the incidence of inter-state conflict. Several U.S. presidents, from Woodrow Wilson to Bill Clinton, used the idea of the democratic peace to justify their efforts to enlarge the sphere of democratic rule. And indeed the rise in the number of democracies during the third wave of democratization has been accompanied by a decline of inter-state conflict, particularly after the end of the Cold War.

Scholars have proposed several explanations for why democracy reduces the chance of conflict between these like-minded states. The first group of explanations is *normative*, meaning they stem from the values and behavioural norms associated with democracy. Proponents of these explanations start from the premise that citizens in democracies are normatively opposed to violence. Writing in 1795, for example, Kant posited that citizens are more conflict averse than leaders, because it is the people who tolerate the direct costs of fighting. Because citizens have more influence over policy in democracies compared to autocracies, democratic states should be less inclined toward war. According to Kant, 'If . . . the consent of the citizens is required to decide whether or not war is to be declared, it is very natural that they will have great hesitation in embarking on so dangerous an enterprise. For this would mean calling down on themselves all the miseries of war ... But under a constitution where the subject is not a citizen, and which is therefore not republican, it is the simplest thing in the world to go to war' (1991, 100).

In the past few decades, scholars refined the initial argument that democracies are inherently more peaceful than autocratic states. It turns out that democracies actually fight as many wars as non-democracies; it is only when they interact with one another that peace emerges. The underlying ideas are that people in democracies solve domestic disagreements without resorting to violence, and their leaders are accustomed to the negotiated trade-offs of shared power. Because democracies expect other democracies to externalize these same peaceful norms, they trust that they will not be attacked by other democracies and shape their behaviour accordingly (Doyle, 1986; Maoz and Russett, 1993; Risse-Kappen, 1995; Russett, 1994). When democracies engage with authoritarian states, in contrast, they are willing to set aside their aversion to violence or their respect for other points of view, because they lack faith that the other side will share these common values. As stated by Maoz and Russett (1993, p. 625), 'when a democratic state confronts a nondemocratic one, it may be forced to adapt to the norms of international conflict of the latter lest it be exploited or eliminated by the nondemocratic state that takes advantage of the inherent moderation of democracies'.

Shared democracy might also reduce the risk of conflict because democratic citizens are morally averse to attacking fellow democracies (Doyle, 1983; Tomz and Weeks, 2013). According to this view, people in democracies are morally reluctant to overturn policies that citizens of other democracies have chosen freely. Coercively interfering with another democracy would, by this argument, count as an illegitimate assault on the freedom and self-determination of individuals. In contrast, democratic publics might have fewer moral qualms about using force to reverse the will of a dictator who has imposed foreign and domestic policies without popular consent.

There are several criticisms of normative explanations for the democratic peace. One of the most common critiques is the observation that history is replete with examples of democratic states following policies at odds with the normative argument. Several democracies have, for example, pursued imperialistic policies or initiated wars against weak non-democracies. These actions are hard to reconcile with the normative perspective that posits that democracies only resort to realist strategies when confronted by a non-democratic opponent who threatens their existence (Bueno de Mesquita et al., 1999).

Other scholars, therefore, have advanced *structural* theories of the democratic peace. Proponents of this perspective hold that democracies are more deliberate in their decision making than autocracies because democratic institutions slow the mobilization process for war. Democratic leaders have to secure the support of a variety of stakeholders such as the legislature, political bureaucracies, and key interest groups. Democratic constraints, therefore, preclude unilateral action by leaders, reduce the likelihood of a surprise attack (Russett, 1994), and prolong the mobilization process, providing diplomats with time to pursue non-military solutions to disputes.

Structural theories also posit that democratic institutions reduce the risk of war between democracies because they provide transparency and allow leaders to credibly signal their intentions, which lower the chance of escalation and avoidable military conflict (Fearon, 1994; Schultz, 2001). Democratic leaders can more credibly signal their preferences than autocrats because they face greater **audience costs**, or the risk that citizens can and will punish leaders—ultimately by removing them from office—for backing down from public threats. When a leader's threats are credible, it facilitates diplomats' ability to negotiate a settlement. Such credibility also reduces the prospects that an adversary will miscalculate, including by taking additional escalatory steps that can spiral unnecessarily into military conflict.

A final category of explanations of the democratic peace centre on **deterrence** (Bueno de Mesquita et al., 1999; Reiter and Stam, 1998). Proponents of this perspective contend that democracies are unattractive targets because they are more effective at fighting wars than autocracies. Democratic leaders may be more likely to be ousted from office in the event of an unsuccessful war than autocrats, who can rely more heavily on the provision of patronage to their key backers to make up for any discontent over a failed foreign adventure (Bueno de Mesquita, 1999). Democratic leaders therefore expend more effort in war fighting than their authoritarian counterparts. For this reason, democracies are simultaneously unlikely to be chosen as targets by other democrats—who recognize other democracies as more formidable adversaries than autocracies—and unlikely to wage wars against democracies because they are less certain of winning.

While the democratic-peace hypothesis is widely accepted, there is still controversy concerning the possibility that the *process* of democratization may trigger war. In 2005, Mansfield and Snyder argued that democratizing countries are more war prone than full democracies. They contend that leaders in democratizing states unleash nationalist forces to smooth the transition away from autocracy and reassure elites that their interests will be protected. According to Mansfield and Snyder, '**nationalism** is an ideology with tremendous appeal for elites whose privileges are threatened. It can be used to convince newly empowered constituencies that the cleavage between the privileged and the masses is unimportant compared to the **cleavages** that divide nations, ethnic groups, or races' (p. 2). The uptick in nationalism, in turn, triggers aggressive international behaviour. Numerous scholars, however, have questioned the validity of their results (McFaul, 2007; Narang and Nelson, 2009). Michael McFaul (2007), in particular, underscores that it is not democratization per se, but instead, 'failed democratic transitions under very special circumstances [that] lead to war some of the time' (p. 161).

Beyond examining differences in conflict propensity across the binary democracy–autocracy divide, scholars studying authoritarianism have argued that certain categories of autocracies are more belligerent than others. In particular, research shows that **personalist dictatorships** are the most conflict prone of any other regime type (Kendall-Taylor, Frantz, and Wright, 2017). As the adventurism of Saddam Hussein, Idi Amin, and Kim Jong-un suggests, the lack of accountability that personalist leaders face translates into an ability to take risks that dictators in other systems simply cannot afford. For this reason, personalist dictatorships are more likely than other regime types to be involved in inter-state conflict and initiate conflicts with democracies (Reiter and Stam, 1998).

Part of the reason for these dynamics is that personalist dictatorships generate the fewest audience costs of any political system (Weeks, 2008). Democratic leaders are accountable to the majority of the voting age public. And within other authoritarian settings, single party leaders are accountable to the ruling party, military rulers the military, and monarchs the extended royal family. Personalist leaders, in contrast, rely on a very small clique of family or loyal friends to maintain control. With such minimal restraint from elites and the public, they have substantial latitude to initiate provocations without the risk of being punished for their words or actions. Moreover, personalist leaders are also prone to receive incomplete or inaccurate information because their 'yes men' fear reprisal for passing less than optimal news. Equipped with skewed perceptions of reality, personalist dictators are the most prone to miscalculation and other policy mistakes that raise the risk of war (Frantz and Ezrow, 2011).

The experience of Russia demonstrates the connection between personalism and aggressive foreign policy (Kendall-Taylor et al., 2016). Though Putin's involvement in Crimea in 2014 and Syria in 2015 may have been based on strategic concerns, because Putin faces few constraints on his power, he is able to take on much more risk to achieve strategic goals. Along with greater control over political elites in Russia, Putin also has almost total control over the media. This ensures that the public only hears a specific narrative of foreign affairs. The public's lack of access to alternative information and Putin's eliminatation of any voices that might oppose him have facilitated his ability to pursue the foreign policy of his choosing.

The personalization of politics in China under Xi Jinping also underscores a similar cause for concern. During his time in power as President and General Secretary of the Communist Party, Xi has sidelined his political opponents by using an aggressive anti-corruption campaign targeting potential political rivals. This campaign and a number of other recent actions have enabled Xi to amass a great deal of power, comparable to Mao Zedong. As a result of Xi's growing power, China has pursued an increasingly aggressive posture in the South China Sea. Research on the perils of personalism suggest that if Xi continues to personalize the Chinese political system, he will likely engage in more aggressive action and rhetoric in the South China Sea (Kendall-Taylor et al., 2016).

Intra-state war

While the frequency of inter-states wars has declined during the last several decades, the number of internal armed conflicts has risen, with a particular uptick since 2010. In 2015, for example, there were fifty armed-conflicts between governments and rebel groups— the second highest number of conflicts in a given year since data are available.[2] The highest number of internal conflicts (fifty-two) occurred in 1991, during the upheaval that accompanied the end of the Cold War and communism's collapse. Intra-state wars clearly entail significant violence and devastation for the countries and citizens experiencing them. The particularly brutal civil war in Syria, for example, has killed upwards of 400,000 people since the war started in 2011. Even beyond human life, internal conflict and its aftermath corrode virtually every aspect of society: law and order, human rights, socio-economic development, education, basic health services, and the environment.

---

[2] Uppsala Conflict Data Program (UCDP).

Not only are internal conflicts devastating for the countries they take place in, they also pose a significant challenge for the international community. The **United Nations** and other multilateral institutions tasked with addressing violence, such as the **African Union** (AU) and the **Organization of American States** (OAS), are struggling to fulfil their mandates. More specifically, the growing number of internal conflicts, combined with a multitude of competing priorities and agendas, has meant that global demand for peacekeeping is exceeding global willingness and capacity to provide monetary or operational support for peace operations. Moreover, the rise in intra-state conflict is producing an unprecedented surge of refugees. The **United Nations High Commissioner for Refugees** (UNHCR) reported that at the end of 2015 the number of displaced people reached 65.3 million, or 1 out of every 113 people on earth.[3] Today, the number of refugees has reached the highest level in history, even surpassing post-World War II numbers, when the world was struggling to come to terms with one of the most devastating events in history.

Given the upward trend in the number of intra-state wars and their very significant implications, what do we know about how regime type affects the prevalence of these events? There is broad consensus that hybrid regimes, or those countries that mix democratic institutions with authoritarian tendencies, are most susceptible to internal war (see e.g. Hegre 2001; Muller and Weede, 1990). The relationship between regime type and internal conflict, therefore, resembles an inverted 'U-shape' in which a state's likelihood of internal war is highest at middling levels of democracy. Full democracies afford opportunities for groups to pursue their aims by nonviolent political means, and hence provide plausible substitutes for violence. Full autocracies also experience relatively few intra-state wars because they respond to dissent with harsh repression, making it difficult for insurgents to organize and mobilize. Hybrid regimes, in contrast, feature enough repression to create grievances that induce groups to take action and enough openness that such groups can organize and engage in activities against the government. Some studies have questioned this finding on methodological grounds (Vreeland, 2008), but subsequent research addressing this concern still finds an inverted U-shaped relationship between levels of democracy and internal war onset (Gleditsch and Ruggeri, 2010). In other words, due to the simultaneous weakness of both democratic and repressive institutions, hybrid systems are more prone to internal conflict than full democracies or full autocracies.

Regime type and terrorism

Since 9/11 one of the primary arguments of Western democracy advocates has been that democratization will stem a country's production of terrorists and terrorist groups. As democracy spreads, the thinking goes, discontented citizens will have more constructive outlets for political grievances and opportunities to express their views through the

---

[3] https://www.unhcr.org/news/press/2016/6/5763ace54/1-human-113-affected-forced-displacement-hits-record-high.html. Accessed 22 February 2019.

political process, alleviating their need to use violence to achieve their goals (Crenshaw, 1981; Eubank and Weinberg, 1994; 1998; 2001; Eyerman, 1998; Li, 2005). U.S. President George W. Bush made this logic explicit in a speech in 2005. 'When a dictatorship controls the political life of a country, responsible opposition cannot develop, and dissent is driven underground and toward the extreme. And to draw attention away from their social and economic failures, dictators place blame on other countries and other races, and stir the hatred that leads to violence.' U.S. President Barak Obama shared these views. His administration's National Strategy for Counterterrorism stated in 2011 that 'promoting representative and accountable governance is a core tenet of U.S. foreign policy and directly contributes to our counterterrorism goals' (White House 2011, pp. 4–5).

Does greater democraticness make a country less likely to produce or experience terrorism? The prevailing wisdom from academic literature indicates no. In fact, a majority of empirical studies published in the last fifteen years generally shows that democracies experience more terrorism than autocracies (Eubank and Weinberg, 1994, 2001; Weinberg and Eubank, 1998; Pape, 2003; Chenoweth, 2010). However, a number of recent studies suggest that the relationship between regime type and terrorism is somewhat more nuanced. In keeping with one of the key themes in this chapter, there is some evidence that the relationship between regime type and terrorism is non-linear, with hybrid regimes and new democracies experiencing more terrorism than full autocracies or full democracies. We discuss these findings in greater detail.

According to most scholars, **terrorism** is 'the threatened or actual use of illegal force and violence by a non-state actor to attain a political, economic, religious, or social goal through fear, coercion, or intimidation' (Global Terrorism Database).[4] Potential terrorists hold policy preferences that differ from the state and are commonly more extreme than those of the general population (Lake, 2002). Because they cannot mobilize broad support for their positions and are weak relative to states they oppose, terrorists seek political change by targeting the civilian population with violence. In many ways, terrorism may be viewed as one part of a larger repertoire of political contention (Chenoweth, 2013; Ash, 2016).

There are a number of explanations for why democracies are more prone to terrorist activity than autocracies. The first argument suggests that democratic norms and institutions create a more permissive environment for terrorism than closed authoritarian systems. Democracies are likely to experience more frequent terrorist attacks because greater executive constraints and preservation of individual rights provide a more hospitable environment for terrorism than is found in more repressive environments (Li, 2005; Pape, 2003). Democratic freedoms, such as freedoms of movement, association, and expression, provide opportunities for groups to form, operate, recruit, and coordinate terrorist activities without fear of intrusion from the governments they oppose. Moreover, expansive and secure civil liberties hinder democratic governments' ability to suppress discontented groups. The political and civil liberties that democracies extend to their citizens mean that there are greater restrictions on policing, as well as legal frameworks that make it more difficult to convict terrorists, lowering the costs

---

[4] https://www.start.umd.edu/gtd/using-gtd/ (accessed 22 February 2019).

of conducting terrorist activities. Autocrats, in contrast, have nearly unlimited discretion to target and repress potential terrorists.

Likewise, freedom of the press—a core feature of democracies—creates incentives for terrorists to target such states. This is because market-driven media companies are the most enthusiastic in reporting about violent events, providing free publicity to terrorist groups and exacerbating the fear these groups intend to create (Crenshaw, 1981; Hoffman, 2006; Gadarian, 2010). Democracies place fewer restrictions on the media and often produce more sensationalist news coverage, which might provide more extensive attention to terrorist events than would occur in closed authoritarian settings.

Not only do the institutional features of democracies make them more vulnerable to terrorist activity, but terrorists may also be more likely to target them because democracies are more likely to make concessions. Democracies are more accountable and responsive to domestic pressures for policy change, making them more likely to modify policy as a result of violence (Ezrow, 2017). Moreover, democratic publics are unlikely to tolerate the costs imposed by suicide terrorist attacks and more likely to push for changes in state policy that will lessen the likelihood of future attacks (Pape, 2003). Although voters may not share the policy preferences of terrorist groups, terrorist attacks can lead to changes in government policy consistent with terrorist goals. For example, one of the stated intentions of Al Qaeda prior to the 2001 attacks was removal of U.S. troops from Saudi Arabia. Nearly all U.S. troops were removed by 2003.

Research on regime type and terrorism has recently moved beyond the dichotomous classification of regime type. A number of studies now suggest that the relationship between democracy and terrorism is nonlinear (Kurrild-Klitgaard et al., 2006; Abadie, 2006; Chenoweth, 2010). Consistent with the 'messy middle' argument we discussed, these studies show that it is neither the freest nor the most repressive states that experience the most terrorism, but rather those in the middle of this spectrum. This implies that countries experiencing political transitions from autocracy to democracy are particularly prone to terrorism (Chenoweth, 2010). Political transitions may heighten opportunity, unleash long-standing grievances, and trigger competing terrorist organizations to compete with one another for influence in a newly democratic environment (Chenoweth, 2010). Similarly, there is evidence that new democracies are especially vulnerable to terrorism (Eyerman, 1998; Piazza, 2013). Terrorist organizations view new democracies as fragile and less capable of countering their actions (Eyerman, 1998). Also, in the earliest days of democracy, groups with grievances may maintain their previous approach of using violence to achieve their objectives. It takes time for such groups to recognize the utility of eschewing armed struggle in favour of nonviolent political engagement through democratic institutions. Advanced democracies, in contrast, generally do not suffer from high levels of terrorism unless they interfered in other countries' affairs through military intervention or occupations, in which case such countries often become targets of transnational terrorism (Chenoweth, 2013; Pape, 2003; Savun and Phillips, 2009).

It is important to note in closing this section that the types of countries most likely to experience terrorism may be changing (Chenoweth, 2013). Although consolidated democracies still experience several hundred attacks per year, this figure is lower than in past decades, indicating that robust democracies are indeed becoming more immune to terrorism over time. Only a very few advanced democracies (such as Israel) continue to experience high numbers of terrorist acts. Instead, factionalized democracies (such as India), partial autocracies (such as Algeria and Pakistan), and occupied countries (such as Iraq and Afghanistan) have become the most frequent targets. This change is an interesting and important puzzle for scholars to explore. Future research will need to examine what explains the shift from terrorism in democracies to terrorism in semi-democratic and non-democratic contexts, especially after 9/11.

Regime type and economic performance

Since the 1950s, a number of prominent scholars have maintained that authoritarian regimes are better equipped than democracies to promote growth and development. The logic is that authoritarian regimes are free from constraints from both the legislature and their citizens, allowing them to pursue unpopular but growth-inducing economic policies. China's impressive growth record since the late 1970s has fanned support for the merits of authoritarian-led economic development. Likewise, the rapid economic growth of several East Asia autocracies (e.g. South Korea, Singapore, and Taiwan), Chile under Augusto Pinochet, and Rwanda under Paul Kagame have further popularized the argument that strong, technocratic governance, insulated from the chaos of democratic politics is the best way to pursue growth. Many politicians, therefore, have come to view the 'authoritarian advantage' as an unfortunate fact of life and often use this premise as part of the justification for supporting dictatorship in the developing world. The implication is that democracy is a luxury that countries can afford only after the difficult task of development is complete.

Despite these popularly held views, the overall body of theoretical and empirical research examining the effect of regime type on growth is actually quite contested. Starting in the 1950s, the message was that autocracies outperform democracies (Huntington, 2006). Subsequent research, however, found that autocracies have no economic advantage (Diamond, 2008; Tsebelis, 2002; Przeworski et al., 2000; La Porta et al., 1999; Barro, 1996). Still others studies have concluded that democracy has a positive effect on economic outcomes, particularly when its indirect effects on growth—through democracy's positive effect on education, health, and life expectancy, for example—are taken into account (Knutsen, 2012; Baum and Lake, 2003). Here we present the arguments made for and against democracy as a growth stimulus and evaluate the competing claims.

The authoritarian advantage

A large body of research posits that authoritarian regimes are better equipped to drive economic growth and development. These arguments generally stem from the notion that is easier for autocrats to pursue growth-maximizing policies because they do not face the same pressure for re-election as their democratic counterparts. Instead, authoritarian leaders are insulated from inefficient public demands, are able to impose publicly unpopular programmes, and can avoid the policy paralysis that often plagues democratic decision-making.

Broadly speaking, economic growth requires capital accumulation. In a poor economy, growth cannot occur unless factories are built, infrastructure developed, education improved, and innovation spurred. These advancements require high levels of investment, which in turn require that resources be diverted from current consumption to saving and investment. One of the most common arguments that proponents of this view make is that authoritarian regimes can resist popular demands for redistribution and consumption that slow down growth (Huntington, 2006; Haggard and Kaufman, 1997). According to the theory, autocrats have the latitude to pursue policies that advantage the wealthiest segments of societies. Democracies, in contrast, redistribute income to provide consumption resources to the majority of citizens, who have elected the government to serve their interests. Because the rich have a higher propensity to save than poorer citizens, dictators' ability to shift resources to the wealthy stimulates capital accumulation, and thus investment and growth.

Not only are autocracies better able to avoid redistribution to their poorer citizens, they can also deflect pressure from particularistic interests, such as labour unions and large firms (Alesina and Rodrik, 1994; Persson and Tabellini, 1994). In contrast, democracies—especially those that recently transitioned—have weak institutions that are unable to resist demands from special interest groups, leading to policies that are inconsistent with the broader public interest (Huntington, 2006). Democratic leaders may be willing to sacrifice growth, for example, in order to satisfy specific business sectors or pivotal voting blocs. Similarly, groups like labour unions are expected to have a higher demand for immediate consumption and will use their political power to raise wages, tax capital, and engage in other redistributive policies that inhibit profits and therefore investment. Rodrik (1999) provides empirical evidence that democracies pay higher wages, which in turn is assumed to decrease the return to capital and thus lower the incentives for private investment. In other words, because authoritarian leaders are unconcerned with winning elections, they are immune to the short-sightedness of the electorate and free to resort to the politically unpopular measures—such as suppressing labour and paying lower wages—that are required to marshal the resources needed to spur growth-enhancing investment (Przeworski and Limongi, 1997).

Finally, dictatorships may have more capacity than democracies to drive growth. Proponents of this view argue that autocrats can implement policies more efficiently because they are free from the political gridlock that slows democratic decision-making (March and Olsen, 1995). Because a smaller number of people in power reach decisions more quickly and more certainly, outside investors may also view these countries as attractive investment destinations. Moreover, autocracies' repressive capacity allows their governments to assert greater control over labour and labour markets, use coercion to break traditional economic patterns, and direct economic policies.

Researchers have noted that some forms of authoritarianism are better suited for growth than others. In particular, **single party dictatorships** such as China, Taiwan, and Singapore tend to produce more solid economic outcomes. Personalist dictatorships such as Robert Mugabe's Zimbabwe or Mobutu's Congo, in contrast, are the most erratic and feature prominently at the bottom of the growth charts (Frantz and Ezrow, 2011). Thanks to limited constraints on decision-making, personalist leaders generally have the latitude to change their minds on a whim, producing volatile economic policies. Moreover, personalist regimes are the most corrupt. Strongman dictatorships, more so than any other type of government, depend on the distribution of financial incentives to maintain power (Bueno de Mesquita et al., 2005). These governments, therefore, tend to pursue more self-enriching and predatory policies that weaken growth outcomes in these countries.

It is important to note that the scholars and experts who assert an authoritarian advantage over democracies in promoting growth do not necessarily deny the inherent values of democracy (Halperin et al., 2009). Rather, the key is timing. These scholars argue that authoritarian governments are better suited to drive growth and that once a country achieves a basic level of development, a transition to democracy becomes more viable. This process is known as **modernization theory**, which we discuss in greater depth in Chapter 10. Modernization theory posits that the urbanization, expanded literacy, and broadened middle class that growth brings enables democracy to develop (Lipset, 1959). Proponents of this view, therefore, view dictatorship as generating development, and development as leading to democracy.

Democracy promotes growth

A similarly substantial body of literature argues that democracy produces better development outcomes than autocracy. Proponents of this view argue that political and economic freedoms are mutually reinforcing. Democracy safeguards the private sphere, maximizes economic freedom, stimulates investment, and its free flow of ideas allows for the most efficient allocation of resources. In other words, these studies suggest that democratic processes and free and open political environments create conditions necessary to motivate citizens to work, save, and invest (Sirowy and Inkeles, 1990).

Underlying this perspective is the idea that democratic institutions provide checks and balances that curtail the abuse of power that can derail growth (North, 1990; Halperin et al., 2009). This runs counter to arguments that dictators are insulated from special interests and therefore are more capable of making long-term decisions that benefit the whole of society. The behaviour of numerous autocrats such as the Democratic Republic of Congo's Joseph Mobutu, Iraq's Saddam Hussein, or Zimbabwe's Robert Mugabe underscores that unaccountable leaders frequently do not have the public interest at heart. Instead, rulers with discretionary power tend to set up distortionary policies that benefit a small set of insiders at the expense of the general population (e.g. Acemoglu and Robinson, 2006; Bratton and van de Walle, 1994). These leaders are also are more reliant on patronage to sustain their rule than democratic leaders are. Aside from directly draining state resources, the prevalence of patronage networks in dictatorships stunts the independence and productivity of the private sector, reducing their growth potential.

Not only do democratic institutions check abuses and control the quality of policymaking, they also create stability and certainty that is advantageous to growth. Although we know from the previous section that fully authoritarian regimes experience civil wars at similar rates as their fully democratic counterparts, democracies are likely to provide other sources of certainty that encourage investment. In particular, the institutionalized nature of politics in democracies relative to autocracies increases predictability in the former. According to Douglas North (1990), 'The major role of institutions in a society is to reduce uncertainty by establishing a stable ... structure to human interaction' (p. 6). By better securing property rights and facilitating contract enforcement, democracies may raise the returns to investment. Although authoritarian regimes are also fully capable of protecting property rights and upholding the rule of law, history shows that they are less inclined to do so. Rather than serve as sources of stability, many autocrats wield institutions like legislatures, judiciaries, and the **rule of law** as tools for retaining their own hold on power.

Democracy's clear mechanisms for succession also foster continuity. Even if an authoritarian regime adheres to consistent policy objectives during its tenure, there may be little continuity between that regime and its successor. As Mancur Olson (1993) noted, the stability of even durable autocrats is limited to a single lifetime. When an authoritarian regime collapses, it is often followed by an entirely different one, characterized by a new set of rules and procedures. In democracies, in contrast, although political parties may change, the overall political framework remains intact.

Democracies' dispersion of authority also enables them to learn and adapt more readily than autocracies. Those political systems in which power is more widely dispersed have higher probabilities of accepting good, novel projects under uncertainty than hierarchical organizations, stimulating innovation and growth (Sah and Stiglitz, 1986). Democracies protect civil liberties, allowing for the free and open debate necessary for debunking bad ideas and spurring new ones (Halperin et al., 2009). In autocracies, leaders restrict civil liberties and the more general diffusion of information, both from abroad and within the country, to lower threats to their own political survival. This stymies the spread of economically productive ideas and technologies, even if the regime wants technological change and economic growth to take place. Several studies have found empirical support for the positive effect of democracy on technological change and productivity growth (Przeworski et al., 2000; North et al., 2009). In sum, political **pluralism** acts to release energies and foster conditions conducive to change, entrepreneurial risk, and economic development (Sirowy and Inkeles, 1990).

Finally, many studies have shown that democracy has positive, indirect effects on economic growth. The extra public expenditure brought about by popular and electoral pressures promotes the delivery of public goods that enhance human capital, such as education, health, and life expectancy. These factors have a positive effect on growth (Tavares and Wacziarg, 2001; Baum and Lake, 2003; Barro and Sala-i-Martin, 2004). Thus, while dictatorship may increase investment in physical capital (although there is large variation among different dictatorial regimes in this area), democracy increases the accumulation of human capital indirectly encouraging growth.

Evaluating the arguments

As we have shown, there are a plethora of arguments and empirical studies that produce conflicting conclusions about the effect of regime type on growth.[5] Many of the discrepancies result from differences in the statistical methods, control variables, countries included in the samples, and time periods under consideration. Given the disagreement in the research, how should we interpret the results?

First and foremost, we feel it is safe to say that there is not sufficient evidence to claim that democracy is detrimental to development. The most systemic empirical studies give no real support to the claim that political rights undermine economic performance. In their study based on a sample of more than 4000 country-years from 1950 to 1990, for example, Przeworski et al. (2000) concluded, '[i]n the end total output grows at the same rate under the two regimes' (p. 179). This conclusion is supported by Doucouliagos and Ulubasoglu's (2008) meta-analysis, which finds that, 'there is indeed a zero direct effect of democracy on growth' (p. 63). In other words, there is no economic basis for supporting authoritarianism, even in low-income countries.

Even if we remain agnostic about democracy's effect on growth, there is broad consensus that democracies produce higher *quality* growth. More specifically, growth in democracies is less volatile, both between countries (Rodrik, 2008; Besley and Kudamatsu, 2008) and within countries over time (Rodrik, 2008). For instance, it is clear that several autocracies such as China, Taiwan, and Chile have produced high levels of economic growth. However, there have been an equal (if not greater) number of autocracies that have been associated with economic devastation. According to Przeworski et al. (2000), 'For every developmental miracle, there have been several dictatorships that have engaged in grandiose projects that have ended in ruin, or else dictatorships that have simply stolen and squandered' (p. 4). Simply put, democracies are better equipped than autocracies to avoid disastrous economic outcomes. The probability of any country experiencing a 10 per cent decline in annual per capita GDP from 1960 to 2005 was 3.4 per cent; for democracies, specifically, it was less than one per cent (Halperin et al., 2009). Democracies avoid the alternating patterns of booms and busts often found in autocracies. Dictatorships that experience high growth for some period tend to eventually revert to the mean or even experience disastrous economic crises, as the records of countries such as Nigeria, Iraq, Romania, and Ecuador highlight. Democracies, in contrast, are more likely to undergo a stable pattern of moderate gains and small declines.

In sum, it is clear that both democratic and authoritarian regimes have the capacity to implement pro-growth policies. The economic growth records of countries such as China, Singapore, and Rwanda underscore the potential for autocracies to produce quite spectacular economic success, but it is important to avoid drawing generalizations

---

[5] Doucouliagos and Ulubasoglu (2008) conducted a comprehensive meta-analysis of 84 studies published prior to 2006 on democracy and growth. Based on the 483 regressions included in these studies, the authors found that 15 per cent of the estimates were negative and statistically significant, 21 per cent were negative and statistically insignificant, 37 per cent of the estimates were positive and statistically insignificant, and 27 per cent were positive and statistically significant (Doucouliagos and Ulubasoglu, 2008, p. 63).

from a handful of cases. At a minimum, it appears that democracy is not detrimental to growth. And, as we discuss in the following section, democracy produces a number of other benefits for the citizens living in them too.

Regime type and quality of life

Economic growth is not the only way to evaluate development and is in many ways an inadequate indicator of socio-economic progress. How does regime type affect a government's capacity to satisfy people's basic needs, such as access to food and clean water, the way economic benefits are distributed throughout society, and the quality of government services like health care and education? While conclusions about regime type's effect on economic growth are contentious, the research on democracy and development is more conclusive: most studies find that democracies provide a better quality of life for their citizens than autocracies.

First, democracies spend more on public goods such as education, health care, and social security than non-democracies. One study, for example, finds that democratically-elected politicians in Africa are more responsive than their authoritarian counterparts to the demands of rural groups that form the majority of citizens in most African countries (Stasavage, 2005). More specifically, contested elections led leaders to spend more on education and prioritize primary schools over universities. The focus on primary relative to university spending benefits the rural majority as this tends to be the only formal schooling they receive. Additional research has found similar patterns in Latin America where democracies have also spent more on education and health than autocracies (Segura-Ubiergo, 2007). Likewise using an innovative data set of night lights visible from satellites, scholars have even found that democratization is associated with a substantial increase in electrification (Min, 2008).

Democracies' focus on the needs of the majority translates into substantive differences in the welfare of the people living under them. Citizens in democracies live longer, healthier, and more productive lives, on average, than those in autocracies (Przeworski et al., 2000; Halperin et al., 2009). Consider, for example, differences in **infant mortality rates** across regime type. Social scientists consider the infant mortality rate to be a useful indicator of societal welfare because it serves as a window into how governments provide for the economic and social well-being of their citizens. Democracies significantly outperform autocracies on this metric at every level of income (Navia and Zweifel, 2003). One innovative study, for example, examined the survival probabilities of infants born to the same mothers before and after their country underwent a democratic transition (Kudamatsu, 2012). It found that infant mortality fell by 1.2 percentage points, or 12 per cent of the sample mean, after democratization. The study concluded that infant mortality rates declined after democratization because of improvements in public health service delivery, not an increase in affluence.

It is important to note that some scholars question democracy's positive effect on infant mortality rates. Ross (2006), for example, contends that previous studies produced overly optimistic conclusions about the effects of democracy on infant mortality rates as a result of selection bias arising due to missing data from high-performing autocracies. Once missing data problems are accounted for, he argues, there is no significant relationship between democracy and infant mortality rates. Democracies do maintain the edge over autocracies in education and health spending, but some studies suggest that the benefits of these policies do not seem to translate into lower infant mortality rates.

In a variety of ways, democracy appears particularly beneficial for the poor and women. Democracies pay higher manufacturing wages than autocracies; growth in democracies, therefore, allows workers—who tend to be poor—to capture a larger percentage of economic expansion (Rodrik, 1999). This is especially advantageous for women, who are disproportionately employed in manufacturing sectors. According to Przeworski et al. (2000), women living under autocracy, 'participate in gainful activities at the same rate as they do in democracies, and as workers, get lower wages ... they also have more children, see more of them die, and are themselves more likely to die in childbirth' (p. 271). The higher wages and services that democracies deliver even translate into greater calorie consumption among the poorest segments of society (Blaydes and Kayser, 2011).

Why might democracies perform better on these dimensions? First, in democracies voters can hold their governments accountable for their choices and actions. In his influential work on the relationship between governance and **famine**, Amartya Sen (1999) finds that famine has never occurred in any independent and democratic country with a relatively free press. This is, in part, because the democratic electoral process allows citizens to penalize governments that allow famines to occur; political leaders, in turn, are strategic and seek to avert famines. According to Sen:

> Famines kill millions of people in different countries in the world, but they don't kill the rulers ... if there are no elections, no opposition parties, no scope for uncensored public criticism, then those in authority don't have to suffer the political consequences of their failure to prevent famines. Democracy, on the other hand, spreads the penalty of famines to the ruling groups and political leaders. (p. 180)

The political and civil liberties that democracy affords largely determine the extent of accountability in a political system and greater respect for these principles benefits development (Sen, 1999). Freedom of the press, for example, enables the media to report on policy disasters, like famines, drawing these issues into the public discourse. Where citizens lack information about government performance, in contrast, they are unable to hold politicians to account (Keefer and Khemani, 2004).

Overall, democracy entails greater levels of accountability than dictatorship, leading them to produce superior outcomes. Even in authoritarian settings, however, more accountability can enhance policy outcomes. In China, for example, informal accountability structures increased public goods provision (and thus human development), even in the absence of democracy (Tsai, 2007). In those villages where solidarity groups existed—groups based on shared moral obligations or shared interest—the provision of public goods improved. These groups served to enhance public goods provision by spreading information about the performance of local officials. Because local officials are sensitive to this information given that it affects their moral standing in the community, this form of accountability creates incentives similar to elections. Likewise, there is also evidence that local elections in China benefit local citizens. Local elections may shift the tax burden from households to enterprises (Zhang et al., 2004), and direct elections of a village's leader may increase public goods investment in the village (Luo et al., 2007).

The last explanation for the observed variation in developmental outcomes across democracies and dictatorships focuses on the incentive structures created by each type of system (Bueno de Mesquita et al., 2005). According to this line of thinking, all leaders seek to maintain power and will pursue a set of policies designed to sustain support among the group of backers whose support they need to retain office (their 'winning coalition'). Leaders can use private goods, such as cash payoffs, or public goods, such as access to health and education, to satisfy their key constituents. Those who depend on a relatively narrow set of backers to keep them in office, as in autocracies, engender loyalty through patronage and other private payoffs. Democratic leaders, in contrast, (in theory) require the support of 51 per cent of the public, making private payoffs a prohibitively expensive strategy to pursue. Democratic leaders, therefore, shift their strategy to the provision of public goods, which benefit everyone in society. In other words, as the number of supporters a leader must satisfy to remain in power grows, the more likely it is that he or she will use public versus private payoffs.

Despite the large number of studies suggesting that democracies enhance education, public goods, health care, and other development outcomes of interest, research is ambiguous about democracy's effect on inequality. Although the theoretical motivations we outlined in this section suggest that democracy should improve inequality, the empirical evidence is mixed. While there are a number of studies that show that democracy reduces inequality (Acemoglu and Robinson, 2000; Muller, 1988; Moon, 1991; Rodrik, 1998), there are also several compelling studies that find no statistically significant effect (Sirowy and Inkeles, 1990; Bollen and Jackman, 1985; Deininger and Squire, 1998; Gasiorowski, 1997).

Why might democracy fail to mitigate inequality?

Democracy may not enhance the distribution of wealth in those countries if the middle class is able to disproportionately capture the benefits of the democracy relative to the poor. Ross (2006), for example, shows that although democracies spend more money on education and health than non-democracies, these perks seem to accrue to middle- and upper-income groups. Ross argues that in some settings, political competition binds rulers to constituencies that are relatively well-off, subsidizing access to health and education services for those who could otherwise use their own resources. Likewise Nelson (2007) explains, 'in democracies, pro-poor reallocation of resources across levels of service and among regions may be particularly difficult politically ... middle class demand for more and better education and health services is virtually unlimited' (p. 27). In sum, although democracies re-allocate income and invest in their citizens, the more politically active middle class tend to benefit more than the poor, which can reinforce inequality in these countries.

Regime type and corruption

Corruption is the misuse of office for private gain. The 'gains' may accrue to the individual official or to the groups or parties he or she belongs to. Corruption can take the form of **bribery**, **embezzlement**, the intentional misappropriation of assets, or **nepotism**. Corruption can be further disaggregated into grand corruption and petty corruption. **Grand corruption** refers to major abuses of power that take place at the national level of government, such as an official who rigs the bidding process for state contracts in order to gain kickbacks for personal gain. **Petty corruption** is the abuse of power at the local level, such as an official requiring a relatively small bribe or favour in return for some good, a basic service that the official should provide for free, or other opportunity.

The scale and cost of corruption is difficult to assess, but the World Economic Forum in 2016 estimated that each year the cost of corruption amounts to roughly 5 per cent of the world's GDP, including about $1 trillion in bribes. Moreover, empirical studies have consistently demonstrated that the poor are disproportionately burdened by corruption, because they pay the highest percentage of their income in bribes. For example, in Paraguay, the poor pay 12.6 per cent of their income to bribes while high-income households pay 6.4 per cent (The World Bank, 2018). Corruption also discourages these citizens from accessing health services and education if they cannot afford to pay bribes that are requested. And embezzlement and the diversion of public funds for personal gain reduce the government's resources available for development and poverty reduction spending.

In addition to economic and quality of life considerations, corruption has important security ramifications. Corruption is a tool that countries such as Russia and China use to gain international influence. Russia, for example, leverages corrupt relationships with politicians and prominent economic actors in the Balkans and parts of Eastern Europe to acquire political influence in those countries. These relationships also harm Western businesses, which are unable to compete in some environments because of their inability to pay bribes and engage in corrupt practices. Finally, corruption can facilitate crime and terrorism. Corruption among security forces and border guards can help the movement of drugs and illicit weapons across borders. Likewise, security sector corruption can compromise the capacity of these services to manage threats posed by insurgents and terrorist organizations.

Given the significant costs of corruption, what can we say about its relationship to regime type? Corruption directly benefits those groups or individuals participating in it, including through personal enrichment and the ability to gain political support. These potential benefits are attractive to many politicians and people, regardless of whether they live in a democracy or autocracy (Drury et al., 2006). Is there anything systematic we can say about the prevalence of corruption?

Before delving into this, it is important to briefly discuss how scholars measure corruption. The broad scope of corruption makes it difficult to quantify. Researchers struggle with what to include in such a measure and face challenges gathering objective data. Corruption is carried out, in most cases, away from the public eye and cannot be observed in public records. Two of the most widely used measures of corruption,

Transparency International Corruption Perceptions Index and the World Bank's corruption index, therefore, rely instead on *perceptions* of corruption. Both of these indices aggregate information from a number of sources that include country risk ratings produced by business consultancies, surveys of international or domestic business people, and polls of country inhabitants. Both groups aim to reduce measurement error by averaging different sources and use similar (and overlapping) sets of inputs. In sum, the data do not measure corruption itself but rather opinions about its prevalence. Because measures of corruption are imperfect and indirect, we must therefore use caution when we draw inferences from most research on the subject (Treisman, 2007).

So how does regime type affect corruption? The current consensus indicates that democracy has a non-linear effect on corruption—democratization may increase corruption in the short run, but corruption declines over time as democracy deepens (Montinola and Jackman, 2002; Treisman, 2000, 2007). This is particularly true for countries with a free press (Adsera et al., 2003; Brunetti and Weder, 2003; Chowdhury, 2004). Press freedom exposes corruption to voters, who, equipped with this information, can punish corrupt politicians in the polls. The consolidation of democratic institutions—including independent judiciaries and social attitudes and norms—enable citizens to expose corruption, make it an issue of political importance, and facilitate recourse ranging from public hearings to voting corrupt officials out of office.

 Box 5.1: **Shining light on kleptocracy**

A **kleptocracy** is a government that uses its power to exploit its people and resources for the personal gain of officials. The primary objective of kleptocratic leaders is to maximize their own personal enrichment and structure the political and economic system to serve these ends (Lundahl, 1997). Foreign aid is often embezzled. Extracted resources go directly into the leaders' pockets. There are unfortunately numerous examples of kleptocratic regimes. In Indonesia, the Suharto family was so parasitic that researchers estimate that they amassed a fortune worth more than $15 billion (Robertson-Snape, 1999). After a decade in power, Liberia's president Samuel Doe accumulated a fortune equivalent to half of the country's annual domestic income (Reno, 2000). Sani Abacha (1993–98) of Nigeria stole $4 billion in less than five years by awarding contracts to front companies, accepting huge bribes and stealing money directly from the treasury. Family members and friends then transferred the money abroad (Goldsmith, 2004).

Few leaders embody kleptocratic rule more than Joseph Mobutu of Zaire (today's Democratic Republic of Congo). Robert Rotberg writes, 'What set Mobutu apart from other neo-patrimonial rulers was his unparalleled capacity to institutionalize kleptocracy at every level of the social pyramid and his unrivalled talent for transforming personal rule into a cult and political clientelism into cronyism. Stealing was not so much a perversion of the ethos of public service as it was its raison d'etre' (Rotberg, 2003, 31). Mobutu acquired over $8 billion by siphoning off Zaire's various resources—a figure that exceeded the recorded annual economic output of the country (Reno, 2000). In the 1970s, 15–20 per cent of the operating budget of the state went directly to Mobutu. In 1977 alone, Mobutu's family took $71 million from the National Bank for personal use (Leslie, 1987, p. 72).

Kleptocracies only exist in authoritarian regimes. Although corruption is certainly present in democracies, as we note elsewhere in this book, democratic institutions make corruption on such a grand scale unlikely. Press freedom, the presence of a political opposition, and a relatively free legislature and judiciary can call public attention to transgressions and prosecute officials who abuse public office. Moreover, an informed public has the opportunity to use relatively free and fair elections to vote out potentially kleptocratic leaders before they have the chance to undermine the system.

In addition to a country's time under democracy, levels of economic development also influence democracy's ability to mitigate corruption. Democracy may reduce corruption but only in economies that have already crossed a GDP per capita level of approximately U.S.\$2,000 (Jetter et al., 2015). For poorer nations, democratization may actually increase corruption. Consistent with this, democratic India has done no better than China at checking corruption and may have fared worse given its modest level of economic development (Sun and Johnston, 2009). Underdevelopment, the argument goes, reflects a scarcity of legitimate alternatives for gain, and pervasive vulnerability to exploitation. Just establishing elections and other institutional hardware is not enough to create the accountability required to curb corruption.

A body of case study evidence lends credence to the notion that democracy has a non-linear effect on corruption. In Latin America, for example, the wave of democratization that swept across the continent starting in the late 1970s initially led perceptions of corruption to rise (Weyland, 1998). Democratization dispersed political power and incorporated more institutions into decision-making processes, effectively increasing the number of actors demanding bribes. Under authoritarian rule citizens could get by bribing officials in the federal government; under democracy, however, state and municipal governments and legislators in Congress also demanded their share. A study notes, for example, that in Brazil the 'commissions' that public officials extorted rose from about 8 to 12 per cent of a contract's value under the **military regime** to between 15 and 20 per cent under democracy (Weyland, 1998). A number of other scholars have noted similar dynamics in countries ranging from Russia (Mohtadi and Roe, 2003), Turkey (Mohtadi and Roe, 2003), Indonesia (McLeod, 2005; Robison and Hadiz, 2004) and Thailand (Ammar, 1997; Case, 2002; Hicken, 2001; Pasuk and Baker, 1998; Rock 2000).

Relative to established democracies, however, authoritarian regimes tend to be more corrupt. Autocrats are far more reliant than their democratically-elected counterparts on the distribution of patronage in order to secure loyalty (Bueno de Mesquita et al., 2005). This is particularly true for personalist dictatorships (Chang and Golden, 2010). In a study of highly personalized dictatorships in Africa, 'neo-patrimonial regimes' differ fundamentally from other types of autocracies in their extraordinary reliance on the exchange of material rewards for political support (Bratton and van de Walle, 1997). Likewise, corruption in those autocracies with leaders who are uncertain about their longevity in office is likely to be especially severe. Autocrats with short time horizons will be the most predatory and seek to maximize the personal benefits of holding power while their access to such opportunities last (Wright, 2008). To summarize, while transitions to democracy can lead corruption to proliferate, fully consolidated democracies are less corrupt than autocracies.

Regime type and repression

Repression is defined as a form of socio-political control used by authorities against those within their territorial jurisdiction to deter specific activities and beliefs perceived as threatening to political order (Goldstein, 1978). The particular magnitude or combination of repressive activities that governments use varies across time, space, and context, but all governments use some form of repression (Davenport, 2007). Although all governments use it, a robust body of research shows that repression is far more prevalent—in both severity and incidence—in dictatorships than in democracies (Poe and Tate, 1994; Poe, Tate, and Keith, 1999; Davenport and Armstrong, 2004; Vreeland, 2008). Scholars have referred to the robust body of empirical evidence showing democracy's pacifying effect as the '**domestic democratic peace**', mirroring the international relations research on interstate war. In autocracies, repressive leaders cannot be voted out of office, meaning that repressive leaders in these systems often go unpunished. Moreover, because they are not popularly elected and exclude large swaths of the population from decision-making, dictators must substitute force for legitimacy as a means of obtaining public acquiescence to regime decisions.

Repression comes in many forms, each of which serves a distinct purpose for the regime (Frantz and Kendall-Taylor, 2014; Fein, 1995; Davenport, 2007a). Broadly speaking there are two categories of repression: civil liberty or empowerment rights repression (i.e. censorship, restrictions on assembly) and **personal integrity rights repression** (i.e. torture, disappearances, political imprisonment). Dictators use civil liberties restrictions to make it harder for the political opposition and public to mobilize anti-regime activity. **Physical integrity rights violations**, in contrast, are more focused and tend to target specific individuals or groups that threaten the regime. Most dictators use a mixture of both. Moreover, in addition to state-sponsored repression, some authoritarian regimes permit (or even direct) non-state actors, including thugs, vigilantes, mercenaries, and secret death squads to perpetrate violence against regime dissidents. These irregular actors enable regimes to further stifle dissent while giving the regime plausible deniability about their involvement (Rudbeck et al., 2016).

In addition to the fact that democracies repress less because repressive leaders can be voted out of office, there are additional reasons that democratic leaders rely less on repression than their authoritarian counterparts. First, democratic institutions—including elections, a free and open media, and checks and balances—raise the cost of using repression to stifle dissent (Davenport, 2007; Linz, 2000). Of all aspects of democracy, scholars have argued that executive constraints have the greatest pacifying influence on democratic leaders (Bueno de Mesquita et al., 2005). Autonomous courts, for example, can constrain state behaviour by resisting the state's attempts to suppress dissent, including by raising the likelihood of litigation against abusive leaders (Mitchell et al., 2013; Powell and Stanton, 2009). Independent media, for its part, raises the likelihood that human rights violations will be exposed.

Second, democracies are likely to have less need to use repression because they possess alternative pathways of control, such as participation in the political system, that are absent or constrained in autocracies. Finally, some scholars have emphasized how democratic norms of compromise and negotiation reduce repression because they provide a 'realistic way to accommodate demands with a minimum of conflict' (Henderson, 1991, pp. 123–4). Democratic processes and decision-making, in other words, provide a non-coercive way to manage conflict before grievances mount and invite repression.

While full democracies clearly repress less than autocracies, some research argues that the relationship between regime type and repression is non-linear (Fein, 1995; Gartner and Regan, 1996). Some scholars have argued that there is 'more murder in the middle', positing that hybrid and transitioning systems are more repressive than either full autocracies or consolidated democracies (Fein, 1995; Regan and Henderson, 2002). This argument is based on a widely held view that repression is largely a response to dissent. The more dissent a government faces, including protests, riots, terrorism, and other challenges to state authority, the higher state repression is likely to be (Davenport, 1995; 2000; Gartner and Regan, 1996; Poe and Tate, 1994). Hybrid regimes, the argument goes, face more regime-threatening dissent than either full democracies (which channel dissent in less threatening ways) or full autocracies (which have effectively quashed mobilization). A recent study, however, disputes this argument. This study argues that dissent is endogenous to repression; the state acts to prevent dissent from ever occurring, and groups often self-censor in the very anticipation of repression. Once this strategic interaction is accounted for, the study finds that dissent has no effect on levels of repression (Ritter and Conrad, 2016).

Rather than an inverted U-shape between regime type and repression, a growing body of research suggests instead that there is a threshold effect (Bueno de Mesquita et al., 2005; Davenport and Armstrong, 2004). At low levels of democracy, including in new or weakly institutionalized democracies, democratic institutions are unlikely to have much effect on repression. Above a certain level of democratic development, however, democracy reduces repression. In other words, movement along the autocracy–democracy spectrum does not lower levels of repression until a certain level of democracy has been reached.

Although it is difficult to pinpoint the democratic threshold above which human rights improve, it is clear that full democracies do a better job of protecting the rights of their citizens than autocracies. Moreover, research shows that regime type is among the most important determinants of repression levels (Hill and Jones, 2014; Davenport and Appel, 2014). Among all the variables scholars have examined—including economic development, population size, and international constraints arising from human rights treaties and NGO activity—democracy has one of the substantively largest effects on repression (Hill and Jones, 2014). This relationship is significant because it underscores the importance of democracy for protecting human rights.

Conclusion

In the seventy years since the end of World War II, the United States and the West have fostered a global order dominated by states that are liberal, capitalist, and democratic. They have promoted the spread of democracy to strengthen global norms and rules that constitute the foundation of our current international system. However, despite the steady rise of democracy since the end of the Cold War, over the last decade or so we have seen dramatic reversals in respect for democratic principles across the globe. A 2015 Freedom House report stated that the 'acceptance of democracy as the world's dominant form of government—and of an international system built on democratic ideals—is under greater threat than at any point in the last 25 years'.

In this chapter, we examined why democratic decline matters. We examined the effects of democracy on a range of outcomes, including the propensity for countries to fight wars, internal conflict, terrorism, economic growth, quality of life, corruption, and repression. Two key themes were woven throughout this chapter. First, hybrid regimes, or those countries that sit in the middle of the autocracy-democracy spectrum, perform less well than either their fully democratic or fully authoritarian counterparts in a number of areas. The countries in the 'messy middle' are particularly vulnerable to insecurity, including from repression, terrorism, and prospects for internal conflict. Second, research suggests that democracies outperform dictatorship on almost every indicator we examined. Democracies are less likely to employ repression against their citizens than autocracies and experience less terrorism. Most recent research indicates that democracies grow their economies at a rate that is at least on par with dictatorships and that the growth they produce is of higher quality—both less volatile and more likely to benefit the people they govern.

In conclusion, we believe that the academic record demonstrates that even after we set democracy's intrinsic value aside, government is better when it is more democratic. Although democratic decision-making can be slower, this process is more likely to weigh risks, thereby avoiding volatile and ruinous policies. When something is going wrong, democratic leaders hear about it and have incentives to take action. If democracy recedes in the face of growing pressure from authoritarian powers like China and Russia, it would have important effects on the outcomes we discussed in this chapter.

Key Questions

1. What is meant by the 'messy middle'? Why are systems found in the middle of the democracy–autocracy spectrum more susceptible to conflict?

2. What factors might make democracies more vulnerable to terrorist activity than autocracies? What factors might increase their resilience to such attacks?

3. Does autocracy promote economic growth in the developing world? How should we interpret the tremendous authoritarian-led growth in China and the Asian Tigers?

4. Is there a democratic advantage when it comes to dealing with poverty and inequality?

5. Should policymakers give greater emphasis to developing democracy in the Middle East? Lay out your best arguments for and against encouraging democracy in this region.

6. How would widespread democratic decline—in either the number of democratic states or their influence in the international system—affect the current international order? What would change?

Further Reading

DAVENPORT, C., 2007. *State Repression and the Domestic Democratic Peace*. Cambridge University Press.
State Repression and the Domestic Democratic Peace argues that in most cases, democracies are less repressive. The book does caution that not all types of repression are reduced. While human rights violations tend to decrease with the onset of democracy, restrictions on civil liberties are not uniformly alleviated by democracy.

PRZEWORSKI, A., ALVAREZ, M.E., CHEIBUB, J.A., and LIMONGI, F., 2000. *Democracy and Development: Political Institutions and Well-being in the World, 1950–1990* (Vol. 3). Cambridge University Press.
Democracy and Development tests some of the critical questions of the chapter: are democracies better at encouraging growth and how does economic growth affect regime type. The book argues that economic development does not always lead to democracy, but democratic governance is more likely to stick in wealthy countries. Surprisingly the book also claims that democracies are no better than autocracies at fostering economic growth, but democracies are better at encouraging GDP/capita growth.

TSEBELIS, G., 2002. *Veto Players: How Political Institutions Work*. Princeton University Press.
Veto Players advances a new understanding of how governments are structured by focusing not on whether the governments are democratic or not, but on the number of veto players. The book argues that the number of veto players impacts politics and has important consequences for stability.

PART II

Political Dynamics of Autocracies

In Part I of this book we defined democracy and authoritarianism. One of the main takeaways of Chapter 3, where we focused on autocracies, is that authoritarian regimes are not one and the same. There are differences in the way that autocracies are organized, the segments of the society they draw on for support, and the way they make decisions. These differences affect the incentive structures of political actors in these countries, and ultimately the behaviour and outcomes they produce. In Part II of this book, we delve deeper into the political dynamics of autocracies. We will discuss authoritarian pillars of stability (Chapter 6), the factors that increase their prospects for instability and collapse (Chapter 7), and the patterned way that these regimes unravel (Chapter 8).

Understanding the political dynamics of autocracy is critical for several reasons. First, globalization has meant that the domestic politics of states are highly intertwined. What happens in one country—a financial crisis or instability, for example—influences politics far beyond its borders. The civil war in Syria, for instance, created significant ripple effects, including the migration crisis that has strained European democracies. Because of the interconnected nature of today's world, it is crucial that we understand the factors that drive politics inside the world's autocracies. These aren't just academic exercises—they have significant political, economic, and security implications for the world's democracies.

Understanding the political dynamics of autocracy is also critical for protecting democracy. While it is true that much of the crisis facing liberal democracy emanates from the current challenges inside these systems, autocracies have also become a more formidable challenge. Authoritarian regimes are surviving longer in power and have grown more emboldened and brazen in their efforts to shape events beyond their borders. Protecting democracy, therefore, will also require an offensive mind set. But to engage effectively, Western actors require an accurate understanding of the internal dynamics at play in these regimes. Without an understanding of how autocracies function and the way their tactics have evolved, Western actors interested in supporting democracy will be less effective. Staying abreast of what makes contemporary autocrats—both those in power and those aspiring to it—behave as they do is fundamental to developing strategies to engage and interact with such regimes, and to counter autocracy's resurgence.

Before delving into the political dynamics of these countries, we define several key concepts that we use throughout Part II. We define authoritarian *regime* and the key dynamics we focus on in Part II—*authoritarian survival* and *authoritarian breakdown (or regime change)*.

Authoritarian regime. An authoritarian *regime* is the ruling group—though not necessarily the same individuals—that controls the government and uses the same basic rules for choosing leaders and policies (Geddes et al., 2014). Barbara Geddes and her colleagues (2014) define a regime as the 'rules that identify the group from which leaders can come and determine who influences leadership choice and policy' (Geddes et al. 2014, p. 314). Our focus on regimes is intentional. As we discussed in Part I of this book, using the regime (rather than just distinguishing authoritarianism from democracy) enables researchers to more accurately gauge authoritarian stability and collapse (ibid.). A country may be continuously authoritarian, but experience a regime change that is accompanied by volatility or violence that policymakers must navigate. Likewise, a country may be continuously authoritarian, but be governed by dramatically different types of regimes that require different policy responses, as in Iran with the transition in 1979 from the monarchy to the authoritarian system led by a Supreme leader and a group of Muslim clerics—a system still in place today. By focusing on the regime, scholars and policymakers can better understand the dynamics of autocracies.

Authoritarian survival. Authoritarian survival refers to the number of years a given regime maintains power. As we discuss in Chapter 7, there is significant variation in the duration of these regimes. We will examine the tools and approaches that autocrats use to maintain their regime in power.

Authoritarian breakdown (or regime change). Authoritarian breakdown occurs when an authoritarian regime loses power. Authoritarian breakdown is different than and should be distinguished from the exit of an authoritarian leader. Authoritarian regimes frequently last well beyond any individual leader. Since WWII, only about 45 per cent of leadership changes in autocracies led to regime failure (Geddes et al., 2014). In the remaining 55 per cent of cases, the regime elite coalesced around a new leader and the regime persisted intact. The Chinese Communist regime, for example, has had five leaders during the almost seventy years it has been in power. In North Korea, the Kim dynasty has ruled since 1912, with Kim Il-Sung and Kim Jong-Il each dying while in office and ensuring the passage of power from father to son. Today, Kim Jong-Un upholds the same highly repressive rules and policies.

Regime change versus democratization. Authoritarian breakdown must also be distinguished from democratization. Sometimes authoritarian breakdown ushers in democracy. These transitions are often vivid and memorable moments, as in Tunisia during the **Arab Spring** or the **Colour Revolutions** that occurred in Georgia, Ukraine, and Kyrgyzstan in the early 2000s. But more often than not, the failure of one authoritarian regime gives rise to another autocracy. Since World War II, fewer than half of all authoritarian breakdowns resulted in democracy (Geddes et al., 2014).

Until recently, most political science studies on the political stability of autocracies used democratization as the primary indicator of authoritarian breakdown. Using democratization as the only measure for regime breakdown, however, has important consequences for our understanding of the political dynamics in these settings. For example, what if we want to know the effect of economic crisis on the stability of authoritarian regimes? If we use democratization as our primary measure of regime failure, we would seriously underestimate autocratic vulnerability to economic crisis (Geddes et al., 2014). This is because economic crisis can some-times spur democratic transitions, but it can also trigger autocracy-to-autocracy transitions. In other words, we would only be able to gauge the effect of economic crisis on democratization and not its effect on the stability of a given regime. By clearly defining and measuring the pro-cesses we are most interested in as researchers, we gain more accurate insights into the political processes we seek to understand.

Regime change versus liberalization. Importantly, we are also clear in the chapters that fol-low to distinguish between regime change and political liberalization. Political liberalization refers to changes to a political system that make its politics more participatory (high levels of effective enfranchisement) and competitive (a level playing field for the competition). Some studies use the term 'regime change' when describing what is really political liberaliza-tion occurring within an authoritarian regime, such as when Joseph Mobutu of Zaire (today's Democratic Republic of Congo) legalized multiple political parties in 1990. Though this event was heralded as a movement towards greater democracy in the country, the Mobutu regime remained intact. It did not collapse until a few years later in 1997 when an insurgency led by Laurent Kabila forced it out. For some outcomes of interest, such as civil liberty protection and respect for human rights, it is important to know when a country moves towards greater 'democraticness'. Looking at political liberalization, however, does not tell us anything defini-tive about a country's prospects for regime change. In some cases, political liberalization signals the beginning of regime change and a country's transition to democracy. In a large number of cases, however, liberalization simply means greater participation and contestation within the same regime apparatus. And, as we discuss in what is to come, greater participation and con-testation can actually prolong the survival of authoritarian incumbents.

We now delve into a discussion of the political dynamics of autocracies.

6

The Durability of Autocracy

Many authoritarian regimes in power today have been around for decades. The People's Action Party, for example, has controlled Singapore since its independence in 1965. The Chinese Communist Party has been in power for even longer, approaching nearly seven decades of rule. And the monarchy in Oman has governed for more than two hundred years. Of course, not all authoritarian regimes have this staying power. Cambodia's Pol Pot and the Khmer Rouge ruled for only four years. Similarly, the Turkish military's reign in the 1980s lasted just three years. This variation in longevity raises the question: what makes some authoritarian regimes more durable than others?

Durability differs not only across regimes, but also over time. Since the end of the Cold War authoritarian regimes have grown more durable with post-Cold War autocracies lasting in power longer than their Cold War predecessors. From 1946 to 1989, the average duration of an authoritarian regime was twelve years. Since the end of the Cold War this number has almost doubled to an average of twenty years. Today, the typical authoritarian regime has been in power for twenty-five years.[1] Iran's theocratic regime, for example, has ruled for nearly four decades since the Shah was toppled in the Iranian Revolution in 1979. The Cuban regime has maintained power since 1959, even riding out the leadership handoff from Fidel Castro to his brother Raul in 2008 and the changeover to a non-Castro (long-time party man Miguel Diaz-Canel) in 2018. Learning from the mistakes—and successes—of their predecessors and peers, today's autocracies are altering their tactics in ways that increase their longevity.

In this chapter, we identify sources of authoritarian durability. We first identify the domestic groups that influence authoritarian survival—namely, the elite, opposition,

---

[1] Data on dictatorships come from Barbara Geddes, Joseph Wright, and Erica Frantz, 'Autocratic Breakdown and Regime Transitions: A New Data Set', Perspectives on Politics 12, no. 2 (2014) pp. 313–31, who code autocratic regime start and end dates from 1946 through 2010. Their data set also includes information on the type of dictatorship, the mode of entry, and the type of transition.

and public. After discussing the relationship of these groups to regime durability, we outline the two primary strategies that autocracies use to maintain control, **repression** and **co-optation**, and the benefits and risks of each. We then highlight other factors that research has shown to enhance regime durability, including regime type, state capacity, a country's access to natural resource wealth, and whether the regime was born out of a revolutionary struggle.

Authoritarian constituents and their role in stability

No authoritarian leader rules alone. Even the most personalized and repressive dictators cannot survive in office without the backing of a core support group (Bueno de Mesquita et al., 2005). In autocracies, the stakes of losing support are high. While defeated democratic leaders can retire quietly or even make a repeated run for political office, members of ousted authoritarian governments are frequently jailed, exiled, or killed (Svolik, 2009, 2012). To maintain a firm grip on power, authoritarian regimes must maintain some support among three primary constituencies—the elite, the opposition, and the broader public.

The elite

Dictatorships that command support from a broad swath of elites—including individuals from an autocrat's inner circle, the government, and the security services—tend to be the most durable. A strong and coherent elite is better able to resist bottom-up pressure to reform and less likely to collapse because of internal fissures or divisions. In contrast, regimes that fail to elicit elite buy-in or that allow ambitious members of the inner circle to develop independent bases of support are shorter-lived. A robust body of academic research shows that regime insiders pose the greatest threat to a dictator's rule. Empirical analysis finds that regime insiders ousted 205 of the 316 authoritarian leaders (or two-thirds of all autocrats) that held office between 1946 and 2008 and lost power through non-constitutional means (Svolik, 2012). [2] Dictators therefore seek to maintain the unity and cohesion of their elite by ensuring the perceived benefits of supporting the regime outweigh the cost of defection.

Not only do authoritarian regimes benefit from a cohesive political elite, but loyal security forces are critical to regime survival. As Geddes et al. (2014) show, about one-third of all authoritarian regimes from 1946 to 2010 were ousted via **coups**—the most common way that autocracies end. Many coups are carried out by senior military officers who are part of the regime's inner circle. Durable autocracies, therefore, must secure the backing of these actors to maintain power. A loyal security apparatus is unlikely to make attempts or support the efforts of others to depose an incumbent regime through a coup; it is also more willing to protect a regime in the face of widespread citizen unrest (see Box 6.1).

---

[2] Non-constitutional means include any exits from office that did not follow a natural death or a constitutionally mandated process, such as an election, a vote by a ruling body, or a hereditary succession.

Box 6.1: **The security services and authoritarian durability**

As we noted in the text, the loyalty of the security services is a key pillar of authoritarian stability. Given the importance that these actors play in the survival of autocracies, how do we know which security services are likely to be loyal? Political science research suggests that the loyalty of the security services is shaped by two often-related factors: *the social composition* of the regime and its military and the *professionalism of the security apparatus* (Bellin, 2012, Gause, 2011).

Security actors who are motivated by ethnic/sectarian or familial ties are the most loyal because these officials see their fate as closely tied to that of the leader. Those security services that are led by family members of the regime leader or that are largely composed by members from the incumbent's ethnic group are therefore more willing to follow orders to employ violence to maintain control.

In contrast, professionalized security actors—namely those that serve in a security sector governed by rules, with established paths of career advancement and recruitment, and where promotion is based on performance, not politics—have an identity separate from the state. These officials can typically envision a career regardless of the specific leader in power, rendering them less willing to pursue actions, such as cracking down on protesters, which could tarnish their standing with prospective leaders and the public.

The outcomes of protests during the **Arab Spring** demonstrate the importance of the social composition and professionalism of the security apparatus (Bellin, 2012; Gause, 2011). Egypt and Tunisia, two countries that experienced regime breakdown, are two of the most ethnically homogeneous societies in the Arab world and both have relatively professionalized militaries. The Tunisian military was small and removed from politics. The Egyptian army lacked familial ties to Hosni Mubarak and his family. In these two cases, security actors realized that their institutions could play an important role under new regimes and thus were willing to abandon the regime in the face of protests. In contrast, in several countries where security actors stood firm and regimes remained in place (at least initially), such as Bahrain, Libya, and Syria, security services had close ties to the incumbent regime through familial and/or sect connections.

The opposition

In addition to managing the elite, authoritarian regimes must also contend with individuals who actively oppose the regime. Political opposition in autocracies may take a number of forms, including formalized political parties, **civil society** organizations, social movements, charismatic leaders with small groups of backers, and even armed groups. The opposition can threaten an authoritarian regime's hold on power if these groups gain enough strength and/or resources to rival that of the incumbent regime (Dahl, 1971; Rustow, 1970). If the regime comes to view the opposition as a credible threat, it may be willing to grant concessions, such as greater political and civil liberties, in an effort to stave off the challenge. In some cases, such limited openings can enable the opposition to gain momentum. If enough concessions are made and power becomes evenly distributed between the regime and the opposition, a stalemate occurs in which it is difficult for any one faction to monopolize control or exert its preferred course of action on the other. To navigate out of the stalemate, an authoritarian regime may come to view competitive elections as a viable pathway out. Competitive elections, in turn, can threaten an autocracy's hold on power.

In order to avoid this cycle, authoritarian regimes seek to ensure that they clearly maintain the upper hand relative to the opposition. In fully authoritarian regimes, the power imbalance between the regime and opposition is extreme and incumbents provide little space for opposition to exist. In hybrid regimes, governments tolerate or are unable to reign-in opposition competition. The ability of authoritarians to maintain power in hybrid regimes, therefore, depends decisively on their ability to ensure the playing field remains sufficiently tilted in their favour and that the opposition is unable to present a cohesive challenge to the regime.

The public

Authoritarian regimes must also maintain the support of at least a subset of the population to maintain power. The basis of an authoritarian regime's public support is often referred to as a **social contract,** or an implicit agreement between members of society and the regime over the exchange of some mix of social benefits in return for compliance. Social contracts vary by country, but they often include considerations including economic performance, political stability, or ideological, religious, or tribal legitimacy. A country's historical experience shapes citizen expectations of what their government should deliver. For example, the social contract in Tajikistan, which experienced civil war from 1992 to 1997 and has faced decades of low economic development, is likely to differ significantly from public expectations in petroleum-rich Saudi Arabia.

Public support enhances regime stability because it is difficult for challengers to unseat autocracies that enjoy high levels of popularity, regardless of whether this support is genuine or partly manufactured (Dimitrov, 2009). Some degree of public support enhances regime durability in two ways. First, public support reduces a regime's coup risk. Members of the elite or security services will only be willing to stage a coup if they think the public (or at least some significant segment of it) will broadly welcome their action. In other words, the erosion of popular support or overt public displays of dissatisfaction with the government increases the risk of coups (Welch, 1970; Finer, 2017). By ensuring the loyalty of some segments of society, autocracies can affect the decision calculus of would-be-coup plotters and reduce the incidence of coups.

Public support can also enhance regime endurance by reducing the risk of wide scale protest. Throughout history, the public's ability to overthrow autocracies has been limited. Regime-ending protests have been relatively rare because, in contrast to elites, citizens do not control weapons, personnel, or other political resources. Citizens' power stems exclusively from their numbers. However, as we discuss at greater length in Chapter 8, protests are ousting a rising proportion of autocrats in the post-Cold War era. In many instances, the regime goes down with the ousted leader. The growing threat of protest helps explain why we see authoritarians such as Vladimir Putin and Xi Jinping seeking to popularize narratives about the so-called risks of U.S.-backed attempts to unseat unfriendly dictators and tighten restrictions on political and civil liberties. As authoritarian regimes come to view the public as an increasing threat to their power, they are pursuing measures to make it harder for people to organize and threaten their hold on power.

Box 6.2: **Authoritarian tactics**

The absence of a viable alternative to the incumbent regime is a key source of authoritarian durability. If elites and citizens cannot envision a future under different leadership, they have little choice but to acquiesce to the current regime. Autocrats frequently use the following tactics to pre-emptively weaken challengers from the elite, opposition, and public to prevent the emergence of an alternative and maintain their control:

Divide and rule

Authoritarian regimes seek to use fissures within society—including inter-ethnic or geographic divisions—to create opposing factions they play off one another. Such '**divide and rule**' strategies make it difficult for opponents to coordinate, which prevents the emergence of a unified or cohesive challenge to the regime. Many leaders, such as Libya's Muammar Qaddafi and Kenya's Jomo Kenyatta and Daniel Arap Moi pitted tribal groups against one another to maintain their power (Black, 2000; Fox, 1996). In addition to exacerbating existing fissures, authoritarian leaders also seek to manufacture them. As we discuss later in this chapter, autocrats enable some opposition groups to participate in elections while banning others from participation. Because members of the opposition cannot be certain who receives support from the regime, this divide and rule strategy creates suspicion and distrust among the opposition and prevents their formation of a unified front.

Elite rotation

Authoritarian leaders may also regularly shuffle high-level government officials to ensure that no one individual is able to establish a personal following or base of support (Migdal, 1988). This practice also enables leaders to breed loyalty among their inner circle. By creating a system characterized by uncertainty and vulnerability, public officials come to realize they depend on and are indebted to the leader for their selection and maintenance of power. This was a favoured tactic of Zaire's Mobutu. A New York Times correspondent wrote in 1988, 'Every six months or so, Mr. Mobutu shuffles the Cabinet, with some ministers moving up, others put on the street and a few put in jail on graft or nepotism charges . . . the shuffling makes it hard for anyone to become a recognized rival to the President.'[3] Similarly, Acemoglu et al. wrote that Zairian government officials were 'constantly reminded of the precariousness of tenure by the frequency of office rotation, which simultaneously fuels the hopes of those Zairians anxiously waiting just outside the portals of power' (2004, p. 168).

Promoting based on loyalty, weeding out competence

Authoritarian leaders often promote regime officials based on loyalty rather than competence and may sideline their most capable advisors to prevent the emergence of skilful and/or ambitious challengers. Georgy Egorov and Constantin Sonin (2011) underscore that, 'while incompetent ministers are not completely unusual in democratic countries, most historians and political scientists would agree that dictatorships are especially marred by incompetence' (p. 904).

Such preference for loyalty is most pronounced in personalist dictatorships, which lack strong political parties or militaries that can incorporate and harness skilled bureaucrats in a manner less threatening to the regime. In the **personalist dictatorship** under Rafael Trujillo in the Dominican

---

[3] Steven Greenhouse, *New York Times*, 24 May 1988.

Republic, for example, loyalty was the key criterion for political appointments. Vice President Jacinto Bienvenido Peynado was appointed 'due to his loyalty and the fact that he preferred leisure to power' (Crassweller, 1966). In a more extreme case, Cambodia's Pol Pot was so fearful of potential rivals that he executed anyone with a higher education or public service experience upon his assumption of power (Kiernan, 2004).

Although these tactics help leaders prevent the emergence of political rivals, they also create liabilities for authoritarian leaders. As discussed in Chapter 5, autocrats who make promotions based on loyalty rather than competence and who actively remove experienced and competent individuals from important positions tend to receive inaccurate or incomplete information that can lead to policy miscalculations. Former Philippine government officials who served under Ferdinand Marcos reported that, 'loyalty dictated that they would not state anything to contradict Marcos' (Hawes, 1995, p. 158). Another study argues that personalist authoritarian leaders are the most likely to be involved in inter-state wars in part because these leaders receive inaccurate information that raises the risk of war (Weeks, 2012).

Emphasizing security threats

Authoritarian regimes use a country's recent experience with instability or threats to security to justify repressive tactics. The military regime in South Korea under Park Chung Hee (1963–79) used the threat from North Korea to justify martial law. Similarly, Ferdinand Marcos (1965–86) used threats of an insurgency in the south to implement martial law in the Philippines and Peru's Alberto Fujimori used the Shining Path insurgency to justify his more repressive measures. The political psychology literature suggests that dictators are wise to pursue this approach. Studies show that when individuals feel threatened—from a fear of outsiders, physical threats, or destabilizing change, for example—they prefer strong and decisive leaders willing to use force to restore or maintain order (Feldman and Stenner, 1997; Feldman, 2017).

Purges

Political purges are defined as the removal of elite members through violent means, including execution, imprisonment, or exile. Purges can be used to eliminate political enemies that threaten an autocrat's power. Purges also dissuade future challengers by sending a clear message to other elites as to the risk of their ambitions. By removing members of the inner circle, purges enable leaders to reduce the size of the ruling coalition and concentrate power and benefits in a remaining group of supporters (de Mesquita, 2005). Saddam Hussein, for example, executed most members of his elite support group in 1979, replacing them with new supporters. Of those executed, most had been among his most intimate associates (Ezrow and Frantz, 2011). The great purge in the Soviet Union in the 1930s saw hundreds of potentially threatening government officials purged in order to eliminate challenges to Stalin's rule (Egorov and Sonin, 2011).

Academic research suggests that purges are most likely to occur early in a leader's tenure, although not before a new autocrat has established control (Bueno de Mesquita and Smith, 2017). Leaders such as Uganda's Idi Amin, Zimbabwe's Robert Mugabe, and China's Mao Zedong carried out their purges relatively early in their tenures and all the purges petered out as the leaders aged. Of course there are exceptions. For example, Turkish Prime Minister Erdoğan—in power since 2003—used a failed coup attempt in July 2016 to dismiss or suspend more than 140,000 Turkish workers who were believed to be critical of his government. Exceptions notwithstanding, purges *tend* to be most common in the first several years after a leader assumes power.

Research is divided, however, on the effect of a country's coup risk on the timing of purges. Some studies suggest that purges are more likely to occur when a leader perceives that the risk of a coup is rising. Dictators are more inclined to purge strong and competent officers to diminish capabilities to organize a coup (Stepan, 1971; Finer, 2017; Belkin and Schofer, 2003; 2005; Roessler, 2011). A recent study, however, contradicts this claim. Using data on 438 military purges in 111 authoritarian countries from 1969 to 2003, a 2017 study finds that dictators are more willing and able to purge regime officials when they perceive their coup risk is low (Sudduth, 2017). This is because purges can trigger a backlash, prompting the elite to seek to remove the leader. In Pakistan, for example, just hours after Prime Minister Sharif dismissed powerful army Chief Gen. Pervez Musharraf in 1999, Musharraf and his remaining military supporters ousted Sharif in a coup. A dictator may therefore prefer to purge when he senses that the security services' capacity to retaliate is low.

Although purges have been a common tactic in autocracies, little empirical work has tested the effectiveness of the tactic. Using cross-national statistical analysis, another study finds that purges *increase* the risk of coups in autocracies (Bove and Rivera, 2015). They suggest that elite fears of being the target of repression lead some actors to pre-emptively seek to oust the incumbent. Another work however, finds that purges can enhance regime stability in post-conflict environments (Braithwaite and Sudduth, 2016). This study finds evidence that military purges reduce a country's risk of reverting to civil conflict.

Authoritarian survival strategies

Autocrats, like all politicians, seek to maintain power. This can be particularly hard for dictators who typically cannot rely on electoral legitimacy to defend their rule and face a constant threat of overthrow from their elite, opposition, and public. To mitigate these threats, dictators have two broad tools at their disposal: repression and co-optation. Each of these tools serves a distinct purpose for the regime. But each also generates risks. In determining their plan for maintaining power, dictatorships weigh the costs and benefits of both tools. In this section, we discuss the benefits and risks of a regime's use of repression and co-optation.

Repression

Repression is perhaps the most obvious tool that dictatorships use to maintain power and is a defining feature of authoritarian governance. Repression is defined as a form of socio-political control used by authorities against those within their territorial jurisdiction to deter specific activities and beliefs perceived as threatening to political order (Goldstein, 1978). Unlike in democracies where governments that rely heavily on repression can be voted out of office, autocrats have little to no electoral accountability and repressive regimes often go unpunished. Dictatorships are therefore far more repressive than their democratic counterparts (Davenport and Armstrong, 2004; Poe and Tate, 1994; Poe, Tate, and Keith, 1999; Vreeland, 2008).

Repression comes in many forms (Davenport, 2007; Fein, 1995). The political science literature lacks consensus on how best to categorize different types of repression. Many empirical studies, such as those examining causes and implications of repression, divide repressive strategies into two broad bins: *civil liberty or empowerment rights repression* (i.e. censorship, restrictions on assembly), which typically affects the population at large, and **physical integrity rights** *repression* (i.e. torture, disappearances, political imprisonment), which generally affects specific individuals. Most dictators use a mixture of both. Researchers quantify these forms of repression using human rights reports and government records that document state coercion within countries over time.

Other scholars take a different approach to disaggregating repression and instead distinguish between 'high intensity' and 'low intensity' repression (Levitsky and Way, 2002). High intensity repression involves visible and more blatant actions, such as the use of violence against well-known opposition leaders or large groups of protesters, or the outright theft of elections. Low intensity repression, in contrast, is subtler and includes measures such as surveillance, detainment, and use of the tax police and libel suits to target the opposition. Low intensity coercion enables autocracies to weaken the opposition before it becomes too strong and signal to citizens the bounds of acceptable behaviour. Levitsky and Way (2002) note that a leader's mix of these forms of repression depends in large part on the capacity of the state. Low intensity coercion requires extensive state scope, such as a well-trained state service that penetrates most of society. High intensity coercion, in contrast, demands a cohesive and loyal security apparatus, willing and able to use force to protect the regime.

The empirical record indicates that repression is an effective strategy for prolonging regime survival. Put differently, the more repressive the dictatorship, the lower the risk of overthrow (Escriba-Folch, 2013). Repression works as a survival tool in several ways. Most directly, regimes can prolong their rule by eliminating their most threatening opposition through political imprisonment, disappearances, and extra-judicial killings. In the Middle East, such targeted repression also weakens the opposition because the threat of state violence requires opposition actors to focus primarily on survival, rather than developing clear demands or policy agendas (Bellin, 2004).

Repression also works as a survival tool because it increases the costs of opposing the dictatorship, making disloyalty a less attractive option. In autocracies, citizen *perceptions* of a regime's willingness and ability to use force can be just as important as the government's actual repressive capacity. No autocratic government wants to be in the position of having to give the order to use force against protesters for fear that the security service will defect, which would spell the end of the regime. Regimes, therefore, go to great lengths to convince citizens of their capacity to put down anti-regime activity. In Russia, for example, President Putin created a new Presidential Guard in April 2016—a powerful structure comprised of more than 180,000 interior ministry troops plus special police units. Just a few months earlier, Putin signed into law a bill allowing agents from the **Federal Security Service** (FSB) to open fire on crowds, possibly without warning. These measures affect citizens' willingness to participate in anti-regime activities by raising the perceived costs of their actions.

Finally, repression reduces anti-regime activity by making collective action more difficult. Most importantly, high levels of repression limit the extent to which citizens are willing to make their true opinions about the regime public. This acts as a deterrent against dissident activities because most individuals will only participate in protests if they believe others will do the same (Tucker, 2007). Because citizens in repressive regimes do not openly voice dissatisfaction with the regime for fear of government retaliation, it makes collection action hard to orchestrate. As a result, repressive autocracies experience fewer protests and other acts of civil disobedience relative to more permissive regimes (Kricheli et al., 2011).

A dictatorship's use of repression, however, does not come without costs (Gartner and Regan, 1996). Repressive measures can breed popular discontent and decrease political legitimacy, increasing the chances that isolated acts of resistance will more easily escalate into destabilizing civil unrest (Lichbach, 1987; Moore, 1998). Similarly, in some cases, indiscriminate repression can actually serve to elicit a backlash against the state and strengthen opposition (Francisco, 1995; Kalyvas, 2006). Dictatorships, therefore, must factor in the capacity of their security services when contemplating the use of repression. Effective coercive apparatuses can deploy violence in a controlled way, ensuring that state repression does not go beyond specified targets and limits. In states with limited coercive capacity, however, autocratic governments can overreact to regime threats and take actions that actually serve to strengthen anti-regime activity and raise the risks of overthrow.

Moreover, repression makes individuals less inclined to convey information about levels of social discontent to the dictator out of fear of reprisal. Ronald Wintrobe (1998) termed this predicament the 'dictator's dilemma', because the more dictators repress citizens to deter efforts to oust them, the less information dictators have about such efforts (Wintrobe, 1998). Repression, therefore, reduces the amount of information available to dictators, complicating their ability to rule. Dictators in highly repressive regimes sometimes operate from a faulty understanding of economic and/or political trends within their countries, raising the risk of policy miscalculations or other missteps that can weaken the broader regime's hold on power.

Lastly, in order to increase levels of repression, dictatorships must allocate sufficient power to the security services, which, in the end, may constitute the greatest threat of all to their rule (Wintrobe, 1998). Armed with greater resources, the same individuals hired to protect the regime may at any moment turn against it.

Co-optation

In addition to repression, autocracies seek to prolong their political survival by co-opting support for their regime (Gandhi, 2008; Gandhi and Przeworski, 2006, 2007; Geddes, 2006; Magaloni, 2008; O'Donnell, 1979; Wintrobe, 1998). Co-optation, as we use it here, refers to a regime's efforts to engender loyalty, often by tying strategically relevant actors or groups to the regime elite (Gerschewski, 2013).

Co-optation is an effective way to maintain power for a number of reasons. First, under dictatorship, it is a very real possibility that a generous leader will be replaced with a more repressive one. This possibility offers individuals, especially those who do particularly well under the current leadership, a powerful motive to support it (Wintrobe, 1998). Doling out benefits, whether in the form of lump sum payments, positions of power, or policy influence, gives individuals a vested interest in the continuation of the dictator's survival and the regime's more broadly.

Second, the use of co-optation decreases the likelihood that isolated episodes of discontent will escalate into the type of large-scale civil unrest that can trigger the dictatorship's collapse (Kuran, 1991). Small scale protests over particularistic issues, such as student protests over poor facilities or civil servants complaining about salary arrears, are relatively frequent events in autocracies, but are rarely destabilizing. Co-optation, rather than repression, can enable leaders to maintain control without creating high levels of overall social discontent that in turn allow low-level protests to spread or gain momentum.

Third, the opposition's decision over whether to 'accept' the regime's offer of co-optation often divides it, increasing the coordination costs associated with challenging the regime (Magaloni and Kricheli, 2010). In most autocracies, for example, there are 'opposition' groups that are closely associated with the incumbent regime. These groups, sometimes called the '**pseudo-opposition**' are often funded by the government or receive perks in exchange for compliance with the government line. By creating these relationships and permitting the pseudo-opposition to function, incumbent regimes can create a façade of multiparty democracy and simultaneously sow fissures within the opposition that make it hard for regime opponents to mount a cohesive challenge.

Finally, co-optation can be an effective deterrent against efforts by the elite to unseat the dictator. By 'purchasing' the support of key sectors of the population, dictators can convey to rivals that they are legitimately popular and that citizens will view any efforts to unseat them unfavourably (Geddes, 2006). In the post-Soviet space, for example, it has been the 'popular autocrats' in Azerbaijan, Kazakhstan, and Russia—those regimes that can use natural resource wealth to buy the support of the electorate—that have proven to be most resilient (Dimitrov, 2009).

Autocrats can co-opt support for their regimes in several ways. A leader's distribution of **patronage**, or financial incentives provided in exchange for regime loyalty, is among the most common tool in autocracies' arsenal of survival tactics. Regimes can use such 'gifts' to establish control over recipients and induce them to behave in ways that they might not otherwise, inculcating their loyalty over time (Wintrobe, 1998). A leader's distribution of patronage is effective not only for ensuring the loyalty of the elite (Bueno de Mesquita et al., 2005), but also of other influential segments of society (Stokes et al., 2013; Wantchekon, 2003). For example, in Azerbaijan and Kazakhstan, governments fund the media, NGOs, artists, and intellectuals. In return, newspaper publishers publish exclusively pro-government stories, and opera singers, painters, poets, and intellectuals are called upon for public endorsements at politically opportune times, such as during election campaigns. The regime's distribution of financial resources reduces the number of prominent individuals who openly challenge government policies and advocate for reform. (Kendall-Taylor, 2011).

There are several risks, however, associated with a regime's reliance on patronage. First, purchasing the support of key segments of society requires that a regime have steady access to resources to sustain the practice. Those regimes that rely disproportionately on patronage may have a greater risk of breakdown in times of economic stagnation or decline. Second, the distribution of resources is not a credible guarantee of long-term support for the regime. In a study of the effects of targeted social spending in Brazil, for example, empirical research showed that while the recipients of government benefits were more likely to vote for the incumbent party in the proximate election, the loyalty of these recipients diminished over time (Zucco, 2013). Moreover, once an individual has received a gift from the regime, there is nothing to guarantee that the recipient will not use the transfer to strengthen his own coalition and seek the regime's overthrow (Magaloni, 2008).

To mitigate the problems that arise from a strategy based on distributing financial incentives, dictatorships have also learned to use political institutions to co-opt their opponents. A large body of political science research shows that an autocracy's use of institutions—namely elections, political parties, and legislatures—prolong their durability (Gandhi, 2008; Gandhi and Przeworski, 2007; Geddes, 2005; Magaloni, 2008). These institutions in authoritarian settings are often referred to as **pseudo-democratic institutions** because they mimic those found in democracies, but do not function in the same ways. Elections in autocracies, for example, do not typically serve as a mechanism for citizens to select their leaders, and legislatures do not meaningfully constrain executive power. Although many observers view pseudo-democratic institutions as little more than 'window dressing', these institutions shape the relationships between dictators and their ruling coalitions in ways that enhance the resilience of authoritarian regimes. We discuss them in detail in what follows.

Elections

Elections have become routine in contemporary autocracies. In 1970, only 59 per cent of autocracies regularly held elections (one at least every six years). As of 2008, that number increased to 83 per cent (Kendall-Taylor and Frantz, 2015). Although elections occasionally catalyse regime-ending protests (a topic we discuss in the next chapter), the empirical record shows that, on the whole, authoritarian regimes that hold elections last longer in office than those that do not (Geddes, 2005). Authoritarian elections serve several functions that enable incumbent regimes to solidify their support among the elite, opposition, and public.

Authoritarian elections enable incumbents to deter potential rivals by signalling the regime's strength (Geddes, 2005; Magaloni, 2006). Autocratic governments, even those that are certain to win uncompetitive elections, allocate significant resources to election campaigns, including funding billboards, banners, and parades. They go to such great lengths in the run-up to elections because massive victory margins and high voter turnout convey a sense of insurmountable regime dominance that deters potential challengers.

Although many dictators may seek to win elections without using excessive fraud (to avoid the risk of triggering protests), even fraudulent tactics can buttress regime strength (Simpser, 2013). A regime's ability to mobilize state resources, such as monopolizing the media, paying bribes, and pressuring state-run university students and employees to vote, discourage would-be rivals by demonstrating the unevenness of the electoral playing field and the difficulty challengers would face attracting sufficient support to unseat the incumbent (Geddes, 2005).

Elections also enable authoritarian regimes to maintain elite cohesion (Geddes, 2005; Blaydes, 2008). Elections institutionalize competition for power and resources, which helps mitigate potentially destabilizing elite disagreements or rivalries (Lust-Okar, 2006). Autocracies, for example, can use the insights they gain from the electoral process to more objectively reward those individuals who successfully turn out the vote (Blaydes, 2010; Lust-Okar, 2006). In Egypt, for example, Hosni Mubarak rewarded ruling party candidates that defeated Muslim Brotherhood candidates with appointed government posts (Blaydes, 2010). Authoritarian regimes use elections to motivate the elite to advance the regime's goal of winning them and ensure that the most competent and committed individuals remain associated with the regime.

In addition to managing the political elite, elections in autocracies provide incumbents with an opportunity to weaken the political opposition. In autocracies, the regime sets the rules for who can compete (Lust-Okar, 2004). Dictatorships pursue a 'divide and rule' strategy in which they allow some opposition parties or candidates to participate in the election while disqualifying other (typically more popular) opposition parties or candidates from running. Authoritarian incumbents in the Ivory Coast, Kenya, and Zambia, for example, used nationality clauses to prevent many opposition candidates and parties from running in elections. In the Middle East, several Islamic parties have been banned from competing. And in Iran, the Guardian Council's vetting process is so strict that it ensures that potentially threatening candidates are unable to run. In these ways, autocrats use elections to undermine opposition unity, complicating any group's ability to mount a cohesive challenge.

Authoritarian regimes also use elections to boost public support. Political science studies demonstrate that many authoritarian regimes manipulate the economy in the run-up to elections to increase their popularity, including by ratcheting up public spending on social benefits and subsidizing goods such as bread and fuel to make them temporarily cheaper just before the election (Kendall-Taylor, 2012). Spikes in government spending ahead of elections also occur in democracies where candidates need popular support to win competitive elections. In authoritarian settings, however, popular support is a means of deterring rivals. Although autocratic incumbents can use fraud to ensure their electoral victory, their ability to mobilize supporters and secure massive numbers of real votes can influence their rivals' perceptions of how difficult it would be to attract enough backers to unseat them (Schedler, 2006).

Finally, elections provide authoritarian regimes with an important source of information that they can use to calibrate their policies or approach to maintaining control (Ames, 1970; Brownlee 2007; Magaloni, 2006). Autocratic governments (particularly those that rely heavily on repression) often receive inaccurate or incomplete information. The elite are reluctant to pass along negative news and citizens are unwilling to convey their true preferences, making it hard for them to gauge the public mood. The results of multiparty elections, therefore, provide a source of objective information about regime popularity and opposition strength. In the case of the Partido Revolucionario Institucional (PRI) in Mexico, this knowledge proved instrumental in ensuring the longevity of the regime. The PRI used electoral results to identify where the party lacked support and needed to focus additional resources to win votes (Magaloni, 2008).

Parties and legislatures

Like elections, political parties and legislatures are a common feature of contemporary autocracies. Although the vast majority of dictatorships have long incorporated at least one political party, they have increasingly adopted multiple political parties and feature legislatures. As of 2008, 84 per cent of autocracies allowed multiple political parties and a legislature (Kendall-Taylor and Frantz, 2015). As with elections, political parties and legislatures prolong the durability of autocracies (Gandhi and Przeworski, 2008; Geddes, 2005). Since the end of the Cold War, dictatorships with multiple political parties and a legislature lasted fourteen years longer in office than those without these institutions (nineteen years versus five, on average) (Kendall-Taylor and Frantz, 2015).

Political parties have been a standard feature in autocracies because they enable regimes to mobilize support. Autocrats use political parties to spread the regime's ideology or policy views and distribute (or withhold) benefits to citizens in villages and neighbourhoods—extending the regime's reach far beyond the capital city (Geddes, 2005). Magaloni (2006) shows, for example, that in Mexico, the PRI distributed benefits such as land, medicines, scholarships, and fertilizer to supporters while opponents were systematically refused these material benefits. Authoritarian parties tend to be particularly effective at trapping poor rural constituents into supporting the regime because these citizens depend most heavily on state transfers for their livelihood. Dictators also use parties to help win elections. These networks can mobilize voter support, organize public rallies, and carry out electoral fraud such as ballot stuffing, which requires the coordination of a mass organization (Brownlee, 2007). An authoritarian political party, in other words is, 'an instrument by which the dictatorship can penetrate and control the society' (Gershenson and Grossman, 2001).

In addition to mobilizing regime support, authoritarian parties enhance regime durability by providing citizens with a vested interest in perpetuating the regime. Authoritarian parties give members benefits, including jobs, preferential access to schooling for their children, and access to lucrative government contracts (Geddes, 2005). Political parties, in other words, provide citizens a pathway for upward mobility. They draw motivated citizens into the regime rather than having them challenge it externally.

Similarly, legislatures also incentivize potential opponents to participate within the system by providing perks and some policy influence in exchange for compliance (Gandhi and Przeworski, 2006; Reuter and Robertson, 2014). In a study using data from Russian regional legislative elections, Ora John Reuter and Graeme Robertson (2014) found that those regions where opposition elites held legislative leadership positions (and therefore had opportunities to profit from their positions) experienced fewer protests than those regions where the opposition was excluded. Legislatures, in other words, enable regimes to distribute financial perks to the opposition in exchange for agreement to refrain from mobilizing constituents. Similarly, in Jordan, King Hussein allows the Muslim Brotherhood (MB) and its political party, the Islamic Action Front, to participate in the system, rather than exclude it. The palace gives the MB space to operate, including delegating some influence over education and social policies with the expectation that the MB respects the authority of the king and the continuity of the monarchy in return.

Authoritarian parties and legislatures also enhance regime durability by providing institutional forums that stabilize the dictator–elite relationship. Carles Boix and Milan Svolik (2013) argue that political parties and legislatures enhance authoritarian durability because they provide for regular interactions between leaders and their inner circle that enable each side to monitor the actions of the other. These repeated interactions, in turn, help alleviate the secrecy that often characterizes authoritarian governance and prevent unnecessary and destabilizing elite defections. Consistent with this argument, there is empirical evidence that elected authoritarian legislatures decrease a country's risk of coups (Bove and Rivera, 2015). These institutions enable the regime to make policy concessions that satiate the elite and help mitigate intra-elite conflicts—decreasing the incidence of coups and prolonging regime durability.

Finally, like elections, parties and legislatures convey information that enables autocracies to identify and address potential sources of discontent. Parties can monitor citizen behaviour through cells that reach schools, places of employment, and neighbourhoods. They can collect information about who joins the party and who does not, enabling the regime to identify who to reward with patronage or administer with repression. Similarly, legislatures allow groups to convey their demands to the government without these demands appearing as acts of public resistance. The regime, in turn, can calibrate its response. For this reason, Jennifer Gandhi (2008) describes legislatures as allowing dictators to 'control bargaining' and her research shows that autocracies with multiparty legislatures are more responsive to society, produce more public goods, and perform better economically than noninstitutionalized regimes.

Other sources of authoritarian durability

In addition to repression and co-optation, political science research has identified a number of other factors that affect authoritarian durability. We review the most widely discussed factors here.

Authoritarian regime type

Some *types* of autocracies are more durable than others: military dictatorships are the shortest lived while single party regimes tend to last longest in office (Geddes, 1999, 2003). Monarchies have also proven durable—on par with single-party dictatorships—but there is relatively less empirical research on the comparative durability of these regimes. Regime type affects the longevity of autocracies because structural differences across governments, including the composition of the groups that staff governments offices, the segments of society they draw on for support, and the procedures they use to make decisions, create different incentives for leaders and elites, in turn affecting the endurance of regimes.

Military dictatorship

Unlike civilian politicians who value maintaining power above all else, the military elite prioritizes military efficacy and unity. Disagreements about how to respond to governance challenges and elite rivalries, therefore, tend to be particularly destabilizing in **military dictatorships**, because elite divisions have the potential to divide the military, pitting one military faction against another (Geddes, 2003). Rather than risk a civil war-like scenario, military officers respond to political factionalism by returning to the barracks. Moreover, military leaders can envision a life beyond politics given that they can expect to continue their careers (and receiving paychecks) as military officers, which lowers the costs of leaving office. Regime officials in other types of autocracies, in contrast, expect a far worse fate. For these reasons, military dictatorships carry within them 'the seeds of their own destruction' and are the least durable form of dictatorship (ruling for an average of nine years) (Geddes, 2003, p. 131).

Although military dictatorships rarely last long, certain factors can prolong the tenure of these regimes. Military regimes are more durable, for example, in those countries where the civilian leadership is viewed as incompetent, making military dictatorship a relatively more attractive option, as was the case in Thailand and Nigeria. Military regimes are also more durable in those countries where conflict and/or instability can be used to justify military rule, as in Pakistan, where the military used ongoing conflict with India to validate its political activism. Finally, military regimes are more durable when they have the support of foreign actors. Many of Latin America's military regimes—such as Brazil's military dictatorship that ruled for more than twenty years (1964–85)—endured with the support of the United States during the Cold War.

Importantly, when they do collapse, military regimes are the most likely of all dictatorships to democratize. This is largely because they frequently step down from power before conditions in the country have reached a crisis level. Military regimes often negotiate orderly transitions, rather than cling to control at all costs, making democracy easier afterwards (for more on pacted transitions see Chapter 8). For these reasons, about 60 per cent of military regimes democratize when they fall from power (Geddes et al., 2014).

Single party dictatorship

Single party dictatorships tend to be the longest-lasting form of autocracy (lasting on average for twenty-three years). Factions and elite fissures in single party regimes are common, but unlike in military regimes they are rarely destabilizing. Party elites understand that they are all better off in power, which provides strong incentive to resolve policy differences and competition over leadership positions (Geddes, 1999). Single party regimes are also resilient to succession and economic crises—two factors that raise the risk of authoritarian breakdown. The party structure provides an institutional channel for managing succession, which makes these regimes well equipped to navigate leadership transitions (Kendall-Taylor and Frantz, 2016). Often times this is handled through internal party elections, which as the chapter has previously stated can add to the longevity of a regime. Single party regimes have also been remarkably resilient even in the face of long, severe economic decline (Geddes 1999). These regimes can rely on other methods of control, such as party ideology or co-optation through the party structure, to ride out economic challenges.

When single party regimes do collapse, they transition to a new dictatorship more frequently than they democratize; in fact, democratization has only occurred in about 40 per cent of cases (Geddes et al., 2014). Even in those places where transition to democracy did transpire, the democracy has been of low quality, such as in Eastern Europe. This may be because institutionally entrenched authoritarian parties leave in place long-lasting legacies, potentially deteriorating the quality of the democracy that follows (Loxton and Mainwaring, 2018).

Personalist dictatorship

The behaviour of elites in **personalist dictatorships** largely mirrors that of single party elites (Geddes, 1999). Like single party officials, members of personalist ruling cliques calculate that they can 'hang together, or hang separately' and therefore have strong incentive to continue supporting the regime and its leader. However, personalist regimes tend to be less durable than single party regimes (lasting on average fifteen years in office), because they are more vulnerable to collapse following the leader's departure. Leaders in personalist dictatorships often marginalize or purge potential rivals and dismantle institutions that might constrain their power. These regimes, therefore, often collapse with the departure of the founder. Moreover, personalist autocracies are the most reliant of any regime type on the distribution of patronage to sustain their rule. Economic crises or deep structural economic reforms—events that disrupt the patronage on which these governments depend—often spell the end of them.

When personalist regimes fall from power, their departures are often violent. Personalist rule provides few institutional channels for negotiation over rules and power sharing. Instead, it gives rise to all-or-nothing power struggles. These leaders, therefore, most often cling to power in the face of domestic challenges, often resulting in violent and protracted transitions (Geddes et al., 2014). Recent events in Iraq, Libya, and Syria illustrate this dynamic. Personalist dictators also create environments that are not conducive for democracy once these leaders fall from power. Personalist dictators actively dismantle institutions and isolate competent individuals out of fear for their own survival. In doing so, the country is devoid of any institutional framework and expertise to build off of. As a result, personalist regimes tend to be followed by new dictatorships, such as in the case of Uganda when Milton Obote was followed by Idi Amin, and then again by Milton Obote, or in Guinea when Ahmed Sékou Touré was followed by Lansana Conté.

Monarchic dictatorship

As we noted in Chapter 3, political science research long asserted that monarchy was incompatible with modern political order. **Monarchies** were considered 'an anachronism in the modern world of nations' (Hudson, 1977, p. 167) and researchers largely overlooked these regimes. Then the Arab Spring erupted. Protests toppled leaders in four authoritarian republics (Tunisia, Egypt, Yemen, and Libya) while the eight Arab monarchies stood firm. As a result, scholars have reenergized their efforts to better understand the sources of durability in monarchies.

Some suggest that the exceptional legitimacy that many monarchies enjoy enhances the resilience of these regimes (Schlumberger, 2010). While other types of autocracies must manipulate elections or inflate national security imperatives to remain in power, monarchic rule is buttressed by traditional religious and tribal legitimacy, which induces exceptionally loyal support from citizens. The structure of monarchies also increases their durability. Those monarchies with large ruling families, like in Saudi Arabia, tend to be especially long-lived (Herb, 2004). Large ruling families function like political parties in single party dictatorships and are capable of penetrating society to distribute patronage and provide channels for citizen–regime consultation. Monarchies with small ruling families, in contrast, operate more like personalist regimes with less familial collaboration and greater dependence on the discretion of the monarch. Finally, most monarchies have access to oil and gas resources, which also enhances their durability (Brownlee et al., 2013; Stepan et al., 2014). Oil and gas wealth provides these governments with revenue needed to forestall and contain challenges to the regime. We discuss the relationship between natural resource wealth and regime durability at greater length below.

In addition to domestic sources of durability, Middle Eastern monarchies have also benefited from U.S. and Western support (Stepan et al., 2014; Yom and Gause, 2012). Monarchs with powerful foreign allies have a lower cost of using repression because international responses to human rights abuses in these countries are often muted. External supporters have also buttressed regime durability by providing these governments with additional economic and coercive resources. During the **Arab Spring**, for example, external support from Saudi Arabia reinforced regional monarchies' efforts to resist citizen uprisings. Riyadh distributed economic resources to some of the poorer kingdoms, and Saudi troops directly intervened in Bahrain to assist with the crackdown on protesters.

Like personalist dictatorship, when monarchies do collapse they are unlikely to democratize. In the post-1945 period, democracy replaced monarchy in only one country: Nepal in 1991, where the king agreed to a transition to constitutional monarchy, and again in 2006, after a brief return to unconstitutional monarchy. Because the total number of monarchic dictatorships is small to begin with, any assertions about their tendencies have to be tentative. That said, thus far the ouster of monarchies has rarely led to democracy and arguably left most people in the countries once ruled by them worse off, as the experiences of Yemen and Afghanistan illustrate.

State capacity

Numerous political science studies examine authoritarian durability through the lens of state capacity. **State capacity** can be defined as the state's ability to, 'penetrate society, regulate social-societal relations, extract resources, and appropriate or use resources in determined ways' (Migdal, 1988, p. 4). As this definition makes clear, state capacity is a multifaceted concept that encapsulates a number of distinct state functions. Given the complexity of the concept and the difficulty in operationalizing it, there is no consensus on how to measure state capacity. Although studies vary in terms of the specific components of state strength they emphasize, the central message to emerge is that a strong state is better suited for maintaining authoritarian rule (Slater and Fenner, 2011; Way, 2005). Moreover, not only do strong states prolong authoritarianism, but state capacity also is critical to the durability of democracy. Research suggests, however, that while building state capacity is likely to extend the life of an autocracy, it also raises the chances that should a transition occur, democracy will be more likely to emerge and endure.

Studies on authoritarian state capacity have emphasized four key components: the state's ability to repress opposition, co-opt citizen support, access and control economic resources, and register its citizens. Because we discussed repression and co-optation in a previous section, we focus here on the latter two factors.

Authoritarian regimes that can effectively extract revenue from their economies are likely to last in office longer than those that do not have access to or control over financial resources. Beyond facilitating a regime's ability to co-opt support through actions such as paying soldiers or wooing voters with handouts, autocracies' ability to collect revenue provides them with stores of capital they can use to ride out or pre-empt crises (Slater and Fenner, 2011). The *scope* of an authoritarian regime's control over economic resources also affects its durability (Way, 2005). Extensive state control over economic activity enables authoritarian regimes to cultivate the loyalty of state employees, limit the size of the private sector (which produces income that can be used to fuel opposition activity), and minimize the number of non-state organizations that citizens might come to view as an alternative to the government. Moreover, citizens' dependence on the state for services gives autocrats a 'wider menu of punishment options', providing the government with opportunities to sanction anyone demonstrating opposition sympathies (Slater and Fenner, 2011, p. 23).

The capacities of authoritarian regimes to penetrate, monitor, and collect information about citizens and organizations also prolong the tenure of these regimes (Slater and Fenner, 2011). A regime's ability to conduct national censuses, compile local voter lists, and maintain birth registries, school rolls, and economic data provides valuable information states can use to enhance social control. Those authoritarian regimes that can make their citizenry more 'legible' can not only effectively target coercion and co-optation, but such information can enhance their policies. By having a strong pulse on domestic social and economic dynamics, governments can calibrate policy choices and responses to citizen demands in ways that enhance regime performance and therefore public support for the regime.

Natural resource wealth

Closely related to state capacity, a regime's access to natural resource wealth increases the durability of authoritarianism. Not only do natural resource abundant countries tend to be authoritarian (Beblawi and Luciani, 1987; Ross, 2004), but they also tend to be highly durable political systems (Wright et al., 2015; Smith, 2004, Ulfelder, 2007). Often referred to as **rentier states**—or countries that derive a substantial proportion of their national income from natural resource-related revenue—these autocracies have easy access to income that enables them to more effectively co-opt and repress their citizens, making them more resistant to collapse than their resource poor counterparts.

Resource-rich governments can rely on natural resource rents as their primary source of income and use the income to buy political support and avoid having to tax their citizens. Because they do not pay taxes, citizens in these countries, in turn, have little incentive to make demands on the regime, dampening domestic democratizing pressure. Natural resource revenue also provides dictatorships with income they can use to ride out a crisis. During the Arab Spring, for example, the oil-rich monarchies were able to stave off widespread protests by purchasing public support, while their resource poor counterparts collapsed in the face of mass unrest (Brownlee et al., 2013). Just days after Ben Ali fled Tunisia and a week before the onset of Egypt's revolution, Kuwait's oil-rich government announced a grant of U.S.$3,500 to every citizen and a year's worth of free staples such as sugar, cooking oil, and milk. Likewise, Saudi Arabia announced an $80 billion package of public-sector wage hikes, unemployment payments, increased college stipends, and investments in low-income housing (Brownlee et al., 2013). Oil revenue enabled these governments to grant concessions to their citizens and diminish pressure for regime change or meaningful reform.

Natural resource wealth also increases authoritarian durability by enabling autocracies to invest in their security apparatus, enhancing the capacity and loyalty of security actors (Ross, 2004). In addition to their ability to use concessions to stave off protests, the oil-rich Arab states were also better able to fund their coercive forces. Oil-rich Saudi Arabia, Kuwait, Oman, and UAE, for example, deployed cohesive military responses to protesters that ensured regime continuity (Brownlee et al., 2013). Natural resource-rich countries also experience fewer coups (Wright et al., 2015). This is because natural resource income allows governments to sustain higher-levels of military spending relative to non-resource endowed countries, which enhances military support for the regime.

Revolutionary regimes

Revolutionary regimes, which include dictatorships like those in the Soviet Union, China, Cuba, Iran, North Korea, and Vietnam, are remarkably durable (Levitsky and Way, 2013). **Revolutionary regimes** are regimes that emerge out of sustained, ideological, and violent mass mobilization, and whose establishment is accompanied by significant efforts to transform state and social structures (Huntington, 2006; Skocpol, 1979; Levitsky and Way, 2013).

Revolutionary regimes tend to be so enduring because they face little domestic opposition to their rule (Levitsky and Way, 2013). The violence that accompanies revolutions eliminates both immediate rivals to the new regime and alternative centres of power that could mobilize against it. These new regimes also use any post-revolutionary conflict as cause to eliminate remaining organizations that could compete for power. In Iran, for example, the Islamic government's ruthless campaign against the

Mojahedin-e-Khalq and other insurgent groups in the years immediately following the fall of the Shah resulted in the defeat of nearly all effective opposition.

Revolutionary regimes also have strong and cohesive political parties that provide a foundation for enduring rule (Levitsky and Way, 2013). Military struggle breeds strong organizational structures and can inject military-style discipline into governing institutions. In Zimbabwe, 'military commandism' remained deeply ingrained in ZANU-PF structures long after the guerrilla struggle ended in 1979. Revolutionary leaders also enjoy substantial legitimacy, which they can use to unify the party and ride out crises. In China, for example, the generation of the Long March (1934–35) strongly supported a crackdown on the pro-democracy protests in 1989 and possessed the authority to unify the party behind such a strategy.

Finally, revolutionary regimes benefit from highly capable security services and are relatively immune from coups (Levitsky and Way, 2013). Years of military struggle create a security cadre with experience in sustained, high intensity coercion that they are often willing to employ to sustain the regime. The security forces in these countries also tend to be led by officers who participated in the revolutionary struggle and that fully support the revolutionary ideology, making them unlikely to seek to overthrow the political leadership. In Cuba, for example, there was 'almost total overlap' between the ruling civilian and military elites.

Revolutionary legacies are not permanent. Steven Levitsky and Lucan Way (2013) note in their study that the passing of the revolutionary generation creates challenges for these regimes. Some revolutionary government such as China, Vietnam, and Mozambique were able to navigate the transition away from the revolutionary transition. The key to stability in these cases has been the regime's ability to create a new narrative about the basis of their legitimacy. In China, for example, the communist party has shifted its basis of legitimacy from the revolution to its ability to deliver economic growth. Those countries unable to transform the legitimacy narrative face greater prospects of failure.

Conclusion

There tends to be a widespread assumption that authoritarianism is inherently unstable and that it is just a matter of time before a given autocracy collapses. But as we noted at the outset of this chapter, many contemporary authoritarian regimes are quite durable. In fact, some of today's most challenging dictatorships have proven to be especially enduring, including North Korea (sixty-nine years), Iran (thirty-eight years), and Russia (eighteen years). Moreover, authoritarian regimes are learning and adapting their survival tactics in ways that have made them even more robust in the post-Cold War era. In this chapter we identified those factors that contribute to authoritarian durability. Being able to articulate what keeps these regimes in power is important for understanding the political dynamics at play in the countries they govern. Any erosion in the pillars of authoritarian stability, for example, suggests that a country's prospects for regime breakdown have grown.

Understanding authoritarian survival dynamics also provides valuable insight into democratization. In particular, the factors we identified in this chapter can help illuminate those countries where authoritarian regimes are least entrenched and therefore that might be most ripe for political change. Moreover, this chapter highlighted that political institutions such as parties, elections, and legislatures enhance authoritarian durability. Political observers, therefore, should not necessarily view a regime's adoption of these institutions as a step towards democratization. On the contrary, as we discussed in this chapter, mimicking democracy has become an effective approach to strengthening authoritarian rule.

Key Questions

1. If you were assessing a particular regime's prospects for maintaining power, what factors would you measure?

2. How do the elite affect authoritarian durability? How might the relative importance of this factor be changing over time?

3. What are the benefits and risks of a leader's reliance on co-optation and repression?

4. China is currently one of the longest-lasting regimes in the world; how would you explain its durability?

5. What factors explain why the monarchies in the Middle East are so stable and resilient?

Further Reading

FRANTZ, E. and KENDALL-TAYLOR, A., 2014. 'A Dictator's Toolkit: Understanding How Co-optation Affects Repression in Autocracies'. *Journal of Peace Research*, *51*(3), pp. 332–46.
This article offers a clear overview of how dictators maintain themselves in power and lays out all of the key tools that they have used both historically and today.

GERSCHEWSKI, J., 2013. 'The Three Pillars of Stability: Legitimation, Repression, and Co-optation in Autocratic Regimes'. *Democratization*, *20*(1), pp. 13–38.
This article provides an understanding of what makes authoritarian regimes stable. The article focuses on three areas as the title suggests: how authoritarian regimes foster legitimacy, who they co-opt, and how they repress their citizens.

SVOLIK, M.W., 2009. 'Power Sharing and Leadership Dynamics in Authoritarian Regimes'. *American Journal of Political Science*, *53*(2), pp .477–94.
This article argues that the dynamics of power sharing in authoritarian regimes. The article explains why some dictators last longer than others, looking at the strategic behaviour of the dictator and the ruling coalition.

7

Authoritarian Instability
and Breakdown

Forecasting the failure of authoritarian regimes is difficult. Many long-standing and seemingly stable autocracies have unraveled in a matter of weeks. No one predicted, for example, that the **self-immolation** of Mohamed Bouazizi, a Tunisian fruit vendor, would trigger protests in 2011 causing President Ben Ali to flee the country. After fifty-five years in power, the Tunisian autocracy fell in just twenty-seven days. Likewise, few people expected that perceptions of fraud in Georgia's 2003 legislative elections would precipitate the protests that became known as the Rose Revolution and the collapse of the autocracy there. After all, fraudulent elections in authoritarian regimes are a common occurrence. And the self-immolation of the Tunisian fruit vendor was certainly not the first event of its kind.

Not only are regime-destabilizing protests hard to anticipate, but **coups**—the most common way autocracies fall—are equally difficult to foresee. Secrecy is critical for coup conspirators, particularly given the dire consequences of being discovered. Regime officials uncovered coup plots in Togo, Haiti, and Iran all of which resulted in the execution of the planners. Given the stakes, coup plotters confine their plans to the smallest necessary circle of accomplices, which makes the coming of a coup difficult for outside observers to see.

Just as some autocracies end with little warning, other regimes that appear to be on their last legs limp along for years. They ride out economic decline that most observers believe will spell the end of the regime or are able to withstand heightened periods of domestic turmoil. In the 2008–09 period, Zimbabwean President Robert Mugabe oversaw a period of severe economic turmoil as the country's economy contracted by more than 50 per cent. Poverty and unemployment rates reached 80 and 94 per cent, respectively.[1] Many observers anticipated that this would certainly bring about the end of the Mugabe regime. But in spite of the country being on the brink of collapse, Mugabe and his party ZANU-PF weathered the storm. It was not until years later, when Mugabe made the mistake of firing his first vice president, Emmerson Mnangagwa, in 2017 to possibly make room for his wife Grace to be his successor, that Mugabe fell from power. On the 15th of November the National Army placed Mugabe under house arrest and several days later ZANU-PF sacked him as party leader, giving him an ultimatum to resign, which he eventually agreed to.

Given the difficulty of forecasting authoritarian breakdown, how should we think about these critical moments? In this chapter we identify the factors that increase the prospects of authoritarian regime failure. We base this discussion primarily on political science studies that use statistical methods to identify and measure the impact of factors that increase a regime's risk of collapse. It is important to note that the emergence of one or more of the factors discussed in this chapter does not automatically mean that an autocracy will collapse. Instead, the emergence of the factors we outline tell us that a regime's *odds* of failure have risen. History shows that some autocracies that experience these events will be able to ride them out.

Moreover, the emergence of any one of these risk factors in isolation is rarely destabilizing. In-depth accounts of the downfall of specific authoritarian regimes shows that it is most often a confluence of risk factors that bring down regimes. For example, an economic crisis increases an authoritarian regime's risk of failure. However, the presence of an economic crisis alone rarely topples an autocracy. Instead, economic decline tends to generate widespread social dissatisfaction that makes it more difficult for a regime to weather additional stress. Poor economic performance coupled with other risk factors, such as a corruption scandal or a natural disaster, tends to be particularly destabilizing in autocracies. Economic decline therefore raises a regime's risk of collapse, but we often do not observe authoritarian breakdown until one or more other factors generate additional stress on the regime.

As we mentioned in the introduction to Part II, conceptualizing authoritarian breakdown as just those transitions from autocracy to democracy provides an incomplete picture of this dynamic. In fact, about half of the time that an autocracy collapses, it is succeeded by a new one (Geddes et al., 2014). In this chapter, therefore, we focus on the **regime** as the unit of analysis so that we do not underestimate the frequency of authoritarian regime breakdown by ignoring those that occur when one authoritarian regime replaces another.

We start this chapter by discussing the most common factors that academic research has shown to increase an authoritarian regime's risk of falling from power. Though the timing of authoritarian breakdown is hard to anticipate, this chapter is intended to enhance understanding of the underlying conditions and possible triggers that make autocracies most vulnerable to collapse.

---

[1] IMF (2009), 'Public Information Notice: IMF Executive Board Concludes 2009 Article IV Consultation with Zimbabwe'. http://www.imf.org/external/np/sec/pn/2009/pn0953.htm (accessed 2 June 2019).

What factors increase the risk of autocratic breakdown?

In Chapter 6, we addressed authoritarian durability. We identified three main constituencies that all authoritarian regimes must appease to some degree to maintain power: the regime elite (including the security services), the opposition, and the public. Each of these groups continually evaluates their support for the incumbent regime. As long as the benefits of supporting it outweigh the costs of defection, the regime is likely to persist. But what factors affect the cost–benefit calculus of these groups?

This section identifies the conditions that empirical political science research has shown influence an authoritarian regime's vulnerability to breakdown. These things undermine authoritarian control by one of two ways. First, these factors may undermine the regime by decreasing the elite's, the opposition's, and/or the public's perceived benefits of supporting the regime. Second, these factors may also weaken the regime by lowering these groups' perceived costs of defection or of making their opposition to the regime public.

It is important to underscore that problems in dictatorships may persist for years without leading to breakdown. Authoritarian regimes can and often do persist in the face of elite divisions, poor socio-economic conditions, corruption, and demographic challenges such as **youth bulges**. Such *long-term factors* increase a regime's risk of collapse by reducing a government's resilience to other *short-term factors* that often initiate its downfall. These short-term 'triggering events' include economic crises, fraudulent elections, and natural disasters. In this chapter we discuss both. To be clear, the long-term risk factors we discuss influence the underlying foundations of the regime and make regime survival more difficult. However, there is almost always a more proximate short-term factor that precipitates a regime's demise, and that precise trigger is often unexpected.

Elite divisions and defections

As discussed in Chapter 6, the regime elite have traditionally posed the greatest threat to authoritarian leaders. In some cases, elite-infighting simply precipitates a change in the top leadership and the incumbent regime persists. This was the case in Tunisia when President Zine al-Abidine Ben Ali ousted his predecessor President Habib Bourguiba in 1987. Ben Ali was a member of Bourguiba's inner circle, serving as the Minister of the Interior and then Prime Minister. Ben Ali conspired with others in the inner circle to have the 86-year-old Bourguiba declared unfit to rule, and the same general group went on to lead the regime. In other cases, however, elite infighting and disagreements can lead individuals to defect and ultimately spell the end of the regime. In this section we focus on the latter and examine how elite divisions can trigger authoritarian regime breakdown.

Writing in 1986, Guillermo O'Donnell and Philippe Schmitter asserted that, 'there is no transition whose beginning is not the consequence—direct or indirect—of important divisions within the authoritarian regime itself' (p. 19). Elite divisions in autocracies most commonly arise between regime 'hardliners', who defend the status quo and oppose liberalization, and 'soft-liners', who advocate for reform. Soft-liners are not inherently pro-democracy, but rather see reform as necessary to ensure the regime's long-term survival. Samuel Huntington (1991) identifies several reasons why some members of a ruling coalition come to embrace reform. Soft-liners might emerge because: they view the costs of staying in power via repression and co-optation as outweighing the benefits; they see the opposition as a credible threat and calculate that concessions to the opposition reduce their risk of being overthrown, or at least improve their fates should the regime collapse; they believe that pro-democratic international actors will reward reform, potentially adding legitimacy or needed economic assistance that can keep the regime afloat; they conclude that they can remain in power even with a loosening of controls; or they come to view democracy as normatively preferable to continued dictatorship.

As discussed in Chapter 6, the emergence of elite divisions is more destabilizing in some types of autocracies than others. Military regimes are especially vulnerable to elite factionalism. Should tensions emerge within the elite in **military regimes**, the ruling group often prefers to leave power and return to the barracks than to govern as a divided force (Geddes, 2003). Empirical research supports this insight, revealing that military regimes are far less likely to withstand crises and splits in the ruling group than other forms of dictatorship are (Geddes et al., 2014).

Government officials in **single party** and **personalist autocracies**, in contrast, have more incentive to resolve policy differences and competition over leadership positions. Although elite divisions are less likely to bring down these types of regimes, they do occasionally precipitate regime breakdown. The defection of prominent regime officials to the opposition can breathe new life into opposition movements and improve citizen perspectives of the opposition as a viable alternative to the incumbent regime. In Sri Lanka, for example, President Mahinda Rajapaksa was ousted in elections after nearly a decade in office (2005–15). He was defeated by Maithripala Sirisena, a long-time loyalist who suddenly defected from Rajapaksa's own political party. Sirisena's departure spurred additional defectors who then focused the electoral campaign on Rajapaksa's vulnerabilities, especially allegations of corruption, which eroded his support base and ultimately resulted in the regime's collapse. Similarly, in Kenya, the decision of high-level regime officials, including Mwai Kibaki, to defect from long-time President Daniel Arap Moi's regime (1978–2002) and form the National Rainbow Coalition, was a key factor in the breakdown of Kenya's authoritarian system.

Elite splits have also contributed to the breakdown of personalist dictatorships. In Georgia, a high-level elite defection from President Eduard Sheverdnadze's personalist authoritarian regime played a key role in fueling the Rose Revolution and authoritarian breakdown in 2003. Shevernadze's government was divided between conservative elements of the political establishment and a group of young reformers, led by Mikheil Saakashvili. Dissatisfied by the slow pace of reform, Saakashvili split from the regime in 2001 and created a new opposition party, the United National Movement (UNM). Saakashvili's defection increased the credibility of Georgia's opposition movement and led citizens to view UNM as a viable alternative to the incumbent regime.

Economic factors

Case study analyses of authoritarian breakdown frequently point to economic factors as a primary cause of a regime's demise (Haggard and Kaufman, 1997). Economic explanations for the collapse of dictatorships can be grouped into two types: long-term factors focused on *levels* of development, which increase a regime's underlying vulnerability to breakdown, and those centred on *acute changes* in economic conditions, which can serve as a more proximate trigger for regime failure.

Modernization theory is the most prominent, although contested, theory linking *levels* of economic development to authoritarian breakdown (for more on modernization theory and the effect of economic factors on democracy, see Chapter 10). Modernization theory has ebbed and flowed in its popularity among academics and practitioners since the 1950s. The theory posits a direct, causal relationship between economic development and democracy (Lipset 1959). Modernization theorists argue that economic development sets off a process of social change that undermines autocracy and ultimately produces democracy. The basic logic is that higher levels of development create a vibrant middle class that is less dependent on the state for its advancement, better educated, more urban, more mobile, and therefore more capable of pressing the state for political change (Lipset, 1959). In this way, the process of modernization transforms social life and political institutions in ways that make democracy increasingly likely to emerge.

Modernization theorists frequently highlight the experience of countries such as South Korea and Taiwan, which democratized after years of economic growth. Both countries experienced long spells of authoritarian rule, but a growing middle class led to a more vocal opposition. Taiwan's democratization process was gradual and ultimately culminated with the 2000 election of an opposition candidate, Chen Shui-ban. South Korea's democratization took place after the military regime stepped down from power in 1988, following mass protests (for more on these cases see Box 10.1 in Chapter 10).

Despite the strong positive correlation between economic development and democracy, some scholars question whether economic development *causes* democratization. Economic development seemed to spur on democratization in South Korean and Taiwan. But for every South Korea and Taiwan, there is a Singapore and China. In these countries, impressive economic growth and the presence of a middle class have not caused their long-running single party regimes to break down. Instead, higher levels of development may actually provide these types of regimes with the resources required to sustain their rule. Greater development bolsters state strength by building the state's repressive capacity (Fearon and Laitin, 2003) and reducing the economic deprivation of average citizens that might lead them to push for change (Goldstone et al., 2010).

Even today scholars continue to debate the effects of economic development on democratization. Several recent studies lend new support to modernization theory's basic premise that development causes democratization (Miller, 2012; Treisman, 2015). However, these new studies suggest that the effect of development on democracy is conditional—greater development increases the risk of authoritarian breakdown and the emergence of democracy only when other dynamics are present within a regime. Specifically, economic development spurs democratization, but only after executive turnover. This dynamic is a complex one. On the one hand, greater development provides authoritarian leaders with greater resources to perpetuate themselves in power and thus makes executive turnovers less likely. Simultaneously, development makes democracy more likely to endure in the unstable periods following such transitions. Treisman (2015) underscores that the relationship between development and democracy creates a dilemma for dictators:

> Supporting economic growth increases their personal survival odds. But the higher develop-ment level it produces over time makes it harder to deliver the state to a son or trusted aide. While prolonging their own tenure, they unintentionally hasten their regime's demise. (p. 928)

Establishing that development *causes democratization* is clearly tricky. That said, there is evidence that higher levels of wealth make democracy more viable should a transition occur (Przeworski et al., 2000). As Adam Przeworski summarized in 2011, 'I do not think that economic development necessarily leads to democracy but only that, once established, democracy survives in developed countries.'[2]

The second category of explanations linking economic conditions to authoritarian breakdown focuses on ***changes*** in economic conditions, particularly economic crisis. Numerous studies have shown that economic crises increase the risk of regime failure (Epstein, 1984; Gasiorowski, 1995; Markoff, 1990; Pepinsky, 2009; Remmer, 1991).[3] It is notable that the effect of economic crisis on regime stability is not limited to authori-tarian settings (Linz, 1978; O'Donnell, 1978). A body of academic research has shown that economic crises are equally as destabilizing in democratic settings, especially at lowers levels of development, as they are in autocracies (Svolik, 2015, Przeworski et al., 2000). Economic crises, therefore, delegitimize incumbent governing groups, regardless of their regime type.

In authoritarian settings, economic crises increase the risk of breakdown by under-mining the regime's standing with the elite, opposition, and public (Geddes et al., 2018). Economic downturns tend to be particularly destabilizing for those regimes that seek to justify their existence by pointing to their ability to generate strong economic growth. Periods of economic decline can weaken elite support by reducing the resources available to sustain corruption or other privileges that individuals expect in return for loyalty. Less access to the perks of office changes the elite cost–benefit calculus that determines whether they will continue to support the regime. As the benefits of loyalty decline, the elite become more likely to defect and openly challenge the regime. Economic crises also create or exacerbate splits within the ruling coalition by generating disagreement about how best to address the crisis. These conflicts can widen the gap between regime hardliners, who prefer to stay the course and increase repression to sustain the system, and other elite who view reform as a more viable option for maintaining power. Moreover, an economic crisis can weaken the military and security services' loyalty to the regime, making these individuals less likely to defend the regime in the event of a mass uprising or other external threat.

Economic crises can also threaten regime stability by enhancing the viability of the political opposition. Economic deterioration, for example, weakens the political bargain

---

[2] 'Przeworski: "No Democracy without Free, Competitive Elections"', Afronline.org, 04 December 2011, https://www.afronline.org/?p=14539 (accessed 11 December 2018).

[3] Oil-rich countries seem to be more immune to booms and busts (Smith, 2006).

that rulers forge with segments of the private sector. In particular, Stephen Haggard and Robert Kauffman (1997) suggest that economic crises undermine the confidence of the business elite in the ability of the regime to manage crises effectively, leading them to align with moderates in the opposition. The increasing efficacy of the opposition, fuelled by financial and other support from the business elite, combined with the growing popularity of an opposition promising change, has the potential to bring down an incumbent autocracy.

Finally, economic crises can decrease public perceptions of a regime's legitimacy and foment popular discontent. Citizens are less willing to support the status quo if they evaluate that it is threatening their ability to be gainfully employed or put food on the table. As an economic crisis fuels citizen discontent, it increases the prospects that people will be willing to challenge the regime. Dawn Brancati (2016), for example, finds that economic crises make pro-democracy protests more likely to occur. Moreover, such crises often affect domestic perceptions—real or perceived—of a regime's ability to repress. If domestic actors perceive that a regime's ability to repress has declined, possibly stemming from its inability to pay the security services, domestic actors are likely to be more willing to overtly challenge it.

The fall of the PRI in elections in 2000 illustrates how a number of the factors we discuss in this chapter—namely economic decline, elite divisions, and corruption—converged and contributed to authoritarian breakdown (see Box 7.1).

  Box 7.1: **Autocratic breakdown in Mexico: The fall of the PRI**

Mexico's Institutional Revolutionary Party (PRI) ruled as a single party dictatorship for seventy years (1929–2000). Most accounts of the collapse of the PRI regime in Mexico focus on economic factors. Mexico's economic troubles began in 1982 when Mexico, like many other Latin American countries, suffered a major debt crisis. After borrowing large sums of money during a period of strong growth fuelled by high oil prices in the 1970s, Mexico was unable to service its debt in the face of rising interest rates in the United States and Europe. As a result, the Mexican government was forced to adopt a number of economic measures, including the privatization of state-owned enterprises, which depleted the PRI's access to the resources it needed to sustain its **patronage system** (Greene, 2010). Economic liberalization also broke the state's monopoly on the distribution of economic benefits, a tool it long used to maintain loyalty. As a result, local actors independent of the PRI were able to benefit from new economic relationships. The PRI, therefore, grew less capable of rewarding and punishing dependent citizens, which weakened loyalty to the regime (Diaz-Caveros, Magaloni, and Weingast, 2003).

Disagreements about how to address Mexico's growing economic challenges also exacerbated elite divisions and weakened the regime. Observers cite the defection of one of the PRI's key members, Cuauhtémoc Cárdenas, and his creation of the Democratic Revolutionary Party (PRD) in 1988 as a critical catalyst for the regime's demise. Cardenas's departure spurred additional defections, which contributed to the PRI's declining popularity and legitimacy (Shirk, 2000).

Finally, corruption also took a toll on regime resilience. Pervasive corruption enabled local officials to use their positions of power to extract resources rather than provide services (Bailey, 2006). Some scholars contend that the PRI's long-time political dominance eroded the regime's incentive to provide reliable services, such as electricity and clean water, or address other development problems (Norris, 1999). Instead, the PRI expended resources to win elections and reward loyal constituents rather than provide the services that would generate a broader base of public support. In these ways, growing public dissatisfaction with corruption also contributed to the PRI regime's demise in Mexico.

After almost seventy years in power, the PRI was ultimately defeated in elections in 2000.

Country	% under 18
Niger	56.9%
Uganda	55%
Chad	54.6%
Angola	54.3%
Democratic Republic of Congo	52.6%
Mozambique	52.1%
Tanzania	51.6%
Burundi	50.9%
Cameroon	49.1%
Eritrea	49%
Republic of Congo	48.8%

Source: UN. Autocracies classified by Geddes, Wright, and Frantz (2018).

Figure 7.1 Autocracies with highest percentage of population under 18.

Burton, J. '30 Countries with The Youngest Populations in The World' World Atlas https://www.worldatlas.com/articles/thepl-youngest-populations-in-thepl-world.html (accessed 21 March 2019).

Based on this data from here: https://population.un.org/wpp/Download/Standard/Population/.

Youth bulge

The existence of a '**youth bulge**', or a high proportion of individuals ages 15 to 24 relative to the total adult population, is another factor that increases the risk of authoritarian breakdown (to see a list of autocracies with the highest percentage of population under 18, see Figure 7.1). A youth bulge can lead to authoritarian breakdown because large youth cohorts are often drawn to new ideas and more willing to challenge existing forms of authority (Goldstone, 2001; Huntington, 1996). Moreover, young people are more easily mobilized and willing to take on the risk associated with challenging dictatorships because they have fewer responsibilities stemming from family and career (Collier, 2000).

Two factors—youth unemployment and an expansion in education—increase the likelihood that a large youth population will lead to authoritarian breakdown (Huntington, 1963). The rapid growth of a country's youth can increase unemployment if the number of people entering the labour market exceeds economic growth. In these situations, the youth cohort tends to bear the brunt of unemployment and economic hardship. Studies find that youth are three times more likely to be unemployed than other age groups and account for 40 per cent of total global unemployment (Brainard and Chollet, 2007). Youth bulges are also associated with high poverty rates among this segment of the population—young people make up almost 60 per cent of the world's poor (Mansbach and Rhodes, 2008, p. 335).

High youth unemployment combined with recent educational advances tends to be an especially volatile combination. Research shows that individuals with higher educational attainment consistently exhibit a greater propensity to participate in political activities, ranging from voting or discussing politics, to more public forms of mobilization such as protests (Putnam, 1995; Sondheimer and Green, 2010). Moreover, when there is a mismatch between the rising expectations of an increasingly educated and active labour force and their economic realities, it tends to create high levels of discontent and instability. According to Huntington (1963, p. 48), 'The higher the level of education of the unemployed ... the more extreme the destabilizing behaviour which results.'

Youth bulges can elevate the risk of authoritarian breakdown by raising the chance of violent conflict. Countries experiencing youth bulges equivalent to 35 per cent or more of the population are three times more likely to experience internal violence than countries with age structures that resemble the median developed country (Urdal, 2006). From 1970 to 2007, 80 per cent of all outbreaks of conflict occurred in countries where 60 per cent or more of the population was younger than 30 (Zakaria, 2011). Similarly, there is evidence that youth bulges are linked to revolution (Moller, 1968, Goldstone, 2001, 2002). A number of major revolutions, including the English Revolution of the seventeenth century and the French Revolution of the eighteenth century, and most twentieth century revolutions in developing countries occurred where exceptionally large youth bulges were present (Goldstone, 2001, 2002). Iran, for example, went through a youth bulge right before the revolution that toppled the Shah in 1979.

Most recently, scholars have focused on the role of youth in the **Arab Spring** (Austin, 2011; Richards et al., 2013). In 2011, about 60 per cent of the Middle East and North Africa's population was under 30—twice the rate of North America. Moreover, the Arab world had recently experienced a significant expansion in education, and youth unemployment was staggeringly high, as Figure 7.2 demonstrates. Unemployment in the region averaged at least 10 per cent, the highest regional rate of joblessness in the world. For the region's young people, however, the unemployment rate was four times the average (Knickmeyer, 2011). Likewise, data measuring the average years of schooling in the population aged 15 and over between 1980 and 2010 showed a significant increase in the Arab world, and in Tunisia, Egypt, and Libya in particular (Barro and Lee, 2010). Inadequate economic opportunities for an increasingly young and educated populace, combined with factors such as a significant rise in food prices, played a major role in fuelling the Arab Spring and the breakdown of three long-standing autocracies (Campante and Chor, 2012).

Youth bulges do not always produce revolution and violence. The West experienced a demographic bulge in the decades after World War II. Rather than fuel instability, this cohort, known as 'the baby boomers', became an engine for high levels of economic growth. China and India, likewise, have a large cohort of young workers that contribute to their economic strength. In the absence of economic growth and employment opportunities, however, a large youth population can make for mass discontent (Zakaria, 2011) and increase the risk of authoritarian breakdown.

Armenia	37.6%
Botswana	33.3%
Egypt	33.4%
Gabon	39.7%
Iraq	36.1%
Jordan	34%
Libya	48.1%
Mozambique	41.4%
Namibia	49.9%
Oman	50.8%
Swaziland	52.8%
Syria	31.5%
Yemen	38.8%
World	13.6%

Figure 7.2 Autocracies with the highest youth unemployment in the world (15–24).

Source: World Bank. Autocracies classified by Geddes et al. (2018).

Unemployment, youth total (% of total labour force ages 15–24) (modelled ILO estimate) https://data.worldbank.org/indicator/sl.uem.1524.zs (accessed 21 March 2019).

Corruption

Corruption can be broadly defined as the abuse of public office for illegitimate private gain (e.g. Shleifer and Vishny, 1993). Academic studies show that authoritarian regimes are more corrupt than democracies (Treisman, 2000). But how does corruption affect authoritarian vulnerability to collapse? Qualitative, area-studies research ascribes a critical role to political corruption in explaining political outcomes (Rose-Ackerman, 1999). However, the effect of corruption on authoritarian breakdown remains contested. Some academic studies indicate that corruption enhances the durability of autocracies, while others suggest it increases their risk of breakdown.

On the one hand, corruption can stabilize autocracies by enabling authoritarian regimes to purchase the support of key segments of society (Fjelde and Hegre, 2014). The idea is that political corruption reinforces a regime's monopolization of power. In Ukraine under Leonid Kuchma, for example, the regime used corruption, including blackmail, to systematically secure compliance (Darden, 2001). Kuchma had control over government jobs, which he would provide to loyalists. And substantial amounts of the state payroll were used to ensure that Kuchma had widespread support (D'Anieri, 2003). In these ways, corruption can enhance the durability of authoritarian regimes.

On the other hand, corruption can increase the risk of authoritarian breakdown by eroding government legitimacy and decreasing economic performance. Importantly, corruption can reduce public trust in the government's capacity to address citizens' demands (Della Porta, 2000, p. 205). Exposure to corruption erodes belief in the political system and reduces interpersonal trust (Seligson, 2002). Corruption has also been cited as a reason for why military coups were staged in countries such as Pakistan, Nigeria, Thailand, and South Korea, because this lowered the legitimacy of the regime (Finer, 2017, Nordlinger, 1977). Weakened government legitimacy and public trust make such governments less resilient in the face of additional stressors.

There is also strong consensus, based on considerable empirical evidence, that corruption has negative economic consequences (Mauro, 1997). Poor economic performance, in turn, increases social discontent that can serve as fodder for anti-regime activity. Although some early studies viewed corruption as a necessary evil that could 'grease the wheels' and enhance economic performance in developing counties (Huntington, 2006), most recent work refutes the claim. Economists have now mounted significant empirical evidence suggesting that corruption lowers growth and investment (Mauro, 1997), and increases income inequality, primarily by decreasing income growth for the poor (Gupta et al., 1998).

Given the analytic disagreement, how should we evaluate competing claims about the role of corruption on authoritarian breakdown? We see corruption as raising a dictatorship's baseline risk of instability. Corruption on its own, however, including pointed revelations of high-level corruption, is unlikely to trigger breakdown. Instead, most case study evidence of authoritarian breakdown highlights corruption as one of many factors that converge to bring down a regime. Corruption and corruption scandals are likely to be most destabilizing when other factors such as poor economic performance, high unemployment, or a surge in domestic prices have already eroded regime resilience.

Electoral fraud

Some authoritarian regimes hold elections that are free of massive **electoral fraud** and win. But in many autocracies, particularly competitive authoritarian regimes, **electoral manipulation** and other malpractices are common (Birch, 2011; Donno and Roussias, 2012; Schedler, 2002). Electoral fraud can take on a number of forms, including ballot box stuffing, multiple voting, voter intimidation, or the falsification of counts. It is important to highlight that electoral fraud is not always (or even most frequently) carried out by the incumbent, but at the level of individual polling stations by a machinery consisting of political operatives, party members, and state employees. Ashlea Rundett and Milan Svolik (2016) show that the incumbent lacks full control over the political machinery and these actors rarely deliver the amount of fraud that the incumbent requires (they either oversupply or undersupply fraud). Even popular incumbents preside over seemingly unnecessary fraud.

Moreover, as we discussed in the previous chapter, elections increase the durability of autocracies. Even fraudulent elections can reinforce a regime's hold on power. Autocrats may use fraud not just to win the election, but to shore up their control over subordinates in the bureaucracy (Gelbach and Simpser, 2015), to increase their bargaining power, and reduce their need to share rents or compromise on policy (Simpser and Donno, 2012). Fraud also enables regimes to deter future challenges. By delivering a fraudulent supermajority, authorities signal their monopoly on the political system and convince opposition candidates that any challenge to the regime would clearly be futile (Simpser and Donno, 2012; Wedeen, 2008).

Most of the time, fraudulent elections are met with acquiescence by the opposition and public. But history has shown that perceptions of fraud can trigger revolutionary protests (Magaloni, 2010; Tucker, 2007). Citizen perceptions of fraud can galvanize anti-incumbent sentiment and serve as a focal point around which the opposition can more easily mobilize mass dissent and coordinate their activities (Donno, 2013; Shirah, 2015). In these ways, a fraudulent election can enable citizens to overcome collective action problems associated with protesting against an unpopular regime. Perceptions of electoral fraud were the trigger for each of the protests that became known as the '**Colour Revolutions**', which ultimately unseated incumbent authoritarian leaders in Georgia in 2003, Ukraine in 2004, and Kyrgyzstan in 2005.

Given that **electoral fraud** is such a common occurrence, how can we anticipate when it is likely to be accepted versus when it will spark anti-regime protests and authoritarian breakdown? As we noted at the outset of this chapter, it is difficult to anticipate with foresight which triggering events are likely to elicit public backlash. However, academic research provides some insight into the question.

Examples of cases of electoral fraud that have led to authoritarian breakdown

United opposition. First, the presence of a united opposition increases the risk that fraud will trigger mass mobilization and elevate the chance of authoritarian breakdown (Bunce and Wolchick, 2010; Magaloni, 2010). Using game theory, Beatriz Magaloni (2010) shows how divided oppositions enable authoritarian leaders to extend their rule via fraud. In a simple model with an incumbent autocracy and two opposition groups, one opposition group's acceptance of the incumbent's use of electoral fraud enables the incumbent to survive. This is because one group's acceptance of the results sends mixed signals to the public about the acceptability of the election, diminishing the prospects for collective action. Magaloni (2010) argues, for example, that mass protests never developed against Mexico's ruling PRI in 1988 after a likely stolen presidential election, because one opposition faction accepted the results, thus muddying a potential signal to the population. In this way, the absence of opposition unity can diminish the chance that fraud will be contested.

Elite divisions and defections. Fraudulent elections are also more likely to lead to authoritarian breakdown when they precipitate elite divisions, particularly in the security apparatus, over how to respond (Magaloni, 2010). Citizens can overpower authoritarian regimes if protests induce the armed forces and other regime insiders to switch sides. In the case

Country	Year	Result
Philippines	1985	Ferdinand Marcos ousted from power
Peru	2000	Alberto Fujimori forced to resign
Yugoslavia	2000	Slobodan Milošević forced out and arrested
Georgia	2000	Eduard Shevardnadze resigned
Kyrgyzstan	2005	Askar Akayev ousted from power
Cote d'Ivoire	2010	Violence followed by opposition candidate Alassane Ouattara's forces taking control over the country, ousting Laurent Gbagbo from power

Figure 7.3 Examples of cases of electoral fraud that have led to authoritarian breakdown.

of Georgia, the security forces were poorly paid (or in some cases had not been paid in months), weak, and underequipped after years of fighting off secessionist regions in the early 1990s. In the face of mass demonstrations, President Eduard Shevardnadze declared a state of emergency and began to mobilize troops and police near his residence in Tbilisi. However, the armed forces refused to support the government. Similarly, in Serbia in 2000 and Kyrgyzstan in 2005, the security services were also vastly underpaid, which probably contributed to their decision to step aside in the face of public resistance.

It is important to note that authoritarian governments have become highly attuned to the threat posed by outright electoral fraud. This threat, in turn, has led dictatorships to adapt their approach to manipulating elections. Rather than utilize blatant forms of vote fraud, such as ballot box stuffing, they now pursue subtler forms of electoral malpractice. In particular, they seek to skew the playing field in the run-up to elections in ways that make it difficult for the opposition to compete (Levitsky and Way, 2010). For example, today's dictatorships often restrict the opposition's access to the media and financial resources to fund their campaigns and limit the opposition's access to public spaces to hold rallies. There is evidence that while electoral fraud as a whole has not diminished, open fraud on election day has decreased (Bermeo, 2016). As one U.S. diplomat noted, 'today, only amateurs steal elections on election-day'.[4] By shifting their electoral tactics, autocratic incumbents increase their ability to retain power without resorting to the kinds of blatant abuse that can threaten authoritarian breakdown.

Natural disasters

Scholars have recently begun to examine the impact of natural disasters on authoritarian stability. Natural disasters do not directly cause political change, but they can act as catalysts that put into motion changes that can destabilize dictatorships (Pelling and Dill, 2006, 2010). There are few cross-national empirical studies on the relationship between natural disasters and authoritarian breakdown. However, Alejandro Quiroz Flores and Alistair Smith's (2013) article is a notable exception. Their study shows that natural disasters do in fact truncate autocratic survival. They argue that natural disasters erode public support for the government over time by: 1) facilitating anti-regime collective action; and 2) exposing regime incompetence.

First, natural disasters can destabilize dictatorships by incentivizing anti-regime protest. More specifically, natural disasters force together large numbers of people and such physical proximity helps overcome barriers to collective action. Autocracies appear attuned to this threat. For instance, when Cyclone Nargis struck Myanmar in 2008, the military junta sought to prevent survivors from seeking assistance in larger towns and villages. Within a week of the disaster the army also began forcibly dispersing survivors from makeshift camps, schools, and monasteries (Flores and Smith, 2013).

---

[4] Diplomat quoted in Brian Klaas, 'Bullets over Ballots: How Electoral Exclusion Causes Coups d'Etat and Civil Wars' (PhD diss., Oxford University, 2015), p. 2.

For this reason, authoritarian regimes are most vulnerable to collapse in the face of natural disasters that occur in urban rather than rural settings (ibid.). Disasters that afflict the capital city or other densely populated urban areas are more likely to stimulate protest than those in rural or remote areas. In China, the government only half-heartedly assisted the remote province of Qinghai after an earthquake in 2010 and suffered few political consequences for its inaction. But when an earthquake hit Sichuan in 2008, the Chinese government—wary of protest in this politically and economically powerful centre—undertook relief operations that won the approval of much of the international community.

Second, natural disasters have occasionally proved destabilizing when they serve to expose regime incompetence or corruption. In Nicaragua, for example, a massive earthquake in Managua in 1972 exposed the corruption of the Somoza family, which had ruled for decades with an iron fist. In the wake of the earthquake it was revealed that the regime stole funds donated by the international community, which created widespread public anger. The earthquake also weakened elite support for the regime. Many sectors of the economy, such as the manufacturing sector, were hit hard by the earthquake, causing these groups to withdraw their support for the regime (Olson, 2000). The regime also excluded key business elite from the reconstruction boom. As a result of the earthquake and how it was dealt with, the Sandinista party, a revolutionary movement, became a more visible threat to the Somoza regime (Midlarsky and Roberts, 1985).

External factors

Our discussion of authoritarian breakdown so far has focused on domestic dynamics and events that raise a regime's vulnerability to failure. However, academic research shows that authoritarian breakdown is also more likely in the wake of changes in the international environment (for more on international factors, see Chapter 12). Foreign-imposed regime change represents an extreme example of how external factors can cause authoritarian breakdown. In this section, however, we focus on more moderate external forces such as **foreign aid, sanctions**, and **diffusion**. These factors can alter the balance of power between regimes and opposition forces and change domestic actors' perceptions about what is possible.

Discerning which external factors are most likely to destabilize autocracies has important policy implications. Since the end of the Cold War, the international community has largely favoured democratization. For example, it has used economic sanctions to punish leaders that deviate from the democratic course and supported election monitoring and assistance to improve the quality of elections. These factors likely contribute not just to democratization, but also to democratic consolidation. In this section we focus on how sanctions, foreign aid, and diffusion contribute specifically to authoritarian breakdown. We look at the effects of external factors on democratic development and consolidation more fully in Part III.

Foreign aid and sanctions

The effect of foreign aid and sanctions on a dictatorship's risk of breakdown is debated in academic and policy circles. Numerous studies have shown that aid and sanctions do not destabilize autocracies and may in fact help sustain them. For example, dictators can scapegoat the sanctioning country or countries, and use the heightened perception of external threat to rally elite and public support for the regime. In the last ten years however, research has evolved to offer more nuanced insights. Most recent studies suggest that both aid and sanctions can be effective foreign policy tools, especially under certain circumstances. We briefly summarize the literature here beginning with the effects of foreign aid.

A large body of research suggests that foreign aid has no effect on democratization (Knack, 2004) and might even prolong the tenure of authoritarian regimes (Bueno de Mesquita and Smith, 2010; Ahmed, 2012). Take Egypt, for example. Egypt has received more Western foreign aid than any other dictatorship since the Camp David Accords. And yet Mubarak's regime remained afloat for decades and democracy failed to take root in the wake of the Arab Spring. According to scholars in this camp, foreign aid functions like other sources of unearned income, such as oil revenue, which governments can exploit to keep themselves in power. Dictatorships can use aid to pay off political challengers, fund repression or electoral campaigns, avoid taxing important support groups (Ahmed, 2012), and/or by actually providing development that enhances government legitimacy (Morrison, 2009). Along with Egypt, numerous long-time autocracies have benefited from large amounts of foreign aid. Notable examples include the Mobutu regime in Zaire, the Marcos regime in the Philippines, the Duvalier regime in Haiti, and the Somoza regime in Nicaragua.

Despite the often-vocal arguments about the inefficacy of aid, the evidence linking aid—especially from Western countries since the end of the Cold War—to authoritarian durability has not stood up to scrutiny (see Dunning, 2004; Bermeo, 2011, 2016). Instead, several studies over the last decade find that in many circumstances, foreign aid *can* increase a country's prospects for democratization (and hence its risk of authoritarian breakdown).

These studies suggest that aid is more likely to lead to democratization in some *types* of autocracies than others (Wright, 2009; Escriba-Folch and Wright, 2015). More specifically, they show that aid can be especially effective in single party autocracies. According to Wright:

> the promise of future aid, contingent on democratization, only provides an incentive for democratization for political leaders who expect to remain in office after democratization occurs. If dictators with large distributional coalitions (found in single party regimes) are more likely to win power in a democratic election, then aid to dictators with larger coalitions provides an incentive to democratize while aid to dictators will small coalitions (in personalist and military regimes) offers no such incentive. (p. 554)

The international environment has also affected the efficacy of aid over time. In particular, some research suggests that aid increases a country's likelihood to transition to democracy, but that this has only been the case in the post-Cold War era when donors' threats of aid withdrawal have been most credible (Dunning, 2004; Wright, 2009; Bermeo, 2011). These findings suggest, however, that China's rise and Russia's global activism are likely to affect foreign aid's effect on democratization, rendering it less effective. China and Russia present themselves as viable alternatives to the West, which could reduce the credibility of Western donor's threats to withdraw aid. Similarly, a growing swath of countries today are using the threat of moving closer to Russia and China to water down the democracy and human rights conditions that have historically been associated with Western aid.

Similarly, Nancy Bermeo (2011) suggests that contextual factors determine the effect of aid on democratization. She provides evidence that the intent of the donor determines aid's efficacy. During the period from 1992 to 2007, aid from democratic donors was associated with an increase in the likelihood of a democratic transition. During the same period, aid from authoritarian donors exhibited a negative relationship with democratization. Future research will be needed to test whether China's rise—and the increasing aid and investment it delivers, including through its Belt and Road Initiative—will have a negative impact on respect for democratic norms and practices.

The effect of international sanctions on authoritarian breakdown is equally contested. Sanctions have been one of the most commonly used tools of Western countries to affect the behaviour of autocracies, especially in the post-Cold War era. Yet the persistence of authoritarian regimes in the face of sanctions in countries ranging from Cuba, Iran, and North Korea has led scholars to question their efficacy. Several studies indicate that while sanctions may be effective against democracies, they are unlikely to succeed when imposed against autocracies (Lektzian and Souva, 2007; Marinov, 2005; Nooruddin, 2002). Sanctions can stabilize authoritarian rule by enabling governments to capture the rents associated with sanctions, which they can use to pay off political supporters. Autocracies may also be better positioned to resist sanctions than democracies because they can pass the costs of sanctions off onto the general public, who have little influence over policy outcomes or leadership retention (Allen, 2008). Sanctions can also strengthen autocracies if the regime manages to incorporate their existence into its legitimation strategy (Grauvogel and von Soest, 2013). Such a **rally-round-the-flag effect** occurs most often in cases where comprehensive sanctions targeting the entire population are imposed on regimes that enjoy strong claims to legitimacy and have only limited linkages to the sanction sender.

Other studies suggest some types of sanctions can be effective in destabilizing autocracy. For example, costlier sanctions appear to increase the likelihood of success (Dashti- Gibson, Davis, and Radcliff, 1997; Lektzian and Souva, 2007). The reason is based on 'punishment theory', which contends that the economic harm caused by sanctions directly translates into political pressure on a leader to comply. Sanctions that lead to a certain level of deprivation will induce citizens to challenge the regime. In addition to costly sanctions, democratic sanctions, or those sanctions that explicitly aim to promote democracy, appear to increase levels of democracy in targeted authoritarian countries (von Soest and Wahman, 2015).

Similar to investigations into the effectiveness of aid, part of the reason for the mixed findings on the effectiveness of sanctions lies in the aggregation of authoritarian regimes into a single category. Research shows that some types of authoritarian regimes are more vulnerable to sanctions than others. More specifically, sanctions are likely to be most effective in authoritarian settings when they target personalist autocracies (Escriba-Folch and Wright, 2010). Of all types of dictatorships, personalist regimes are the most reliant on economic rents to maintain their support coalition. If sanctions can disrupt the regime's ability to maintain its patronage system, they are likely to increase the risk of regime failure. The use of sanctions also makes personalist regimes more likely to use repression, which also delegitimizes and therefore further destabilizes the regime (Escriba-Folch and Wright, 2010). U.S. sanctions imposed on the Dominican Republic provide an example of successful sanctions targeting a personalist regime. After years of supporting President Rafael Trujillo, the United States decided to restrict sugar imports in 1952 (Hall, 2000).[5] This put the Trujillo regime in a difficult spot, as the sanctions constrained resources and undermined its support, ultimately leading to the regime's downfall (Kirshner, 1997).

Joseph Wright and Abel Escriba-Folch note, however, that while sanctions can desta-bilize personalist dictatorship, a new autocratic regime rather than a democracy most often follows. In Uganda, for example, the United States imposed sanctions against Idi Amin's rule. In 1978, the Carter Administration signed into law a ban of Uganda's coffee trade, the rents of which comprised a significant source of income for the Amin regime. The U.S. sanctions had a devastating effect on Uganda's economy and ultimately set off a chain of events that led to Amin's ouster less than six months later.[6] Amin's departure did not pave the way for democracy, however. Instead, after a short provisional period, a former dictator, Milton Obote, returned to power.

Diffusion

In the most general terms, **diffusion** is defined as anything that spreads, including an innovative idea, product, policy, institution, or repertoire of behaviour. Political scien-tists and sociologists have focused extensively on how protests and democracy spread across countries. Using sophisticated quantitative techniques and spatial models, this research finds strong support for the idea that democratization in one country increases the likelihood of democratization in neighbouring states (Brinks and Coppedge, 2006; Gleditsch and Ward, 2006). Diffusion can increase a country's risk of authoritarian breakdown gradually, by creating pressure on authoritarian governments in democratic neighbourhoods to transition to democracy, or by serving as a more immediate catalyst for regime change.

Gradual diffusion is often referred to as the **neighbourhood effect**. This line of research grew out of a recognition that countries with similar political system types tend to cluster geographically. Several political science studies do in fact suggest that regime type tends to converge within a region over time (Brinks and Coppedge, 2006; Gleditsch and Ward, 2006). Kristian Gleditsch and Hugh Ward (2006), for example, show that between 1951 and 1998 a country's chance of transitioning to democracy was

---

[5] The United States has issued sanctions on mostly authoritarian regimes. For example, in 2001 85 per cent of U.S. sanctions were targeted at regimes that were 'not free' or 'partly free' (Kaempfer et al., 2004).

[6] https://foreignpolicy.com/1980/03/15/when-sanctions-worked/ (accessed 3 June 2019).

almost zero when its neighbours were predominantly authoritarian. In contrast, when 75 per cent of a non-democracy's neighbours were democratic, its chance of democratization rose to approximately 10 per cent. Although this seems like a modest increase in a country's prospects for democracy, it is important to remember that democratization is a rare event. When viewed in this light, a 10 per cent increase resulting from the regime type of neighbouring states is substantively quite large. Moreover, this research shows that the pressure for convergence—and therefore the risk of authoritarian breakdown—is highest when the difference in regime type between a country and its neighbours is especially pronounced.

While the neighbourhood effect is likely to shape a country's longer-term risk of authoritarian breakdown, more acute diffusion, or the spread of regime threatening protests can provide a more immediate challenge to authoritarian stability. The Colour Revolutions in Eurasia, for example, clearly illustrate the diffusion dynamic. Many researchers credit the Serbian Bulldozer revolution that overthrew Slobodan Milošević in 2000 as the genesis of the protests that swept across Eurasia in the early 2000s. While the Serbian protesters may have drawn inspiration from the fall of Marcos in the Philippines in 1986, the Serbs popularized a model of revolution—mass mobilization in the wake of contested elections—that spread to Georgia in 2003, Ukraine in 2004, and Kyrgyzstan in 2005. More recently, the wave of protests that swept the Arab world drew inspiration from the successful mobilization that first ousted Ben Ali in Tunisia in 2011. In each of these cases, the success of the protest changed domestic actors' calculus about what is possible.

If protests unseat an autocracy, which of its neighbours should we expect to be the most vulnerable to diffusion effects? First, diffusion requires that potential adopters are aware of the original protest and the tactics employed (McAdam, Tarrow, and Tilly, 2001). Knowledge of the event and tactics can spread through a number of transmission channels, including mass information like news media and the Internet, relational and social networks, and brokerage (McAdam, Tarrow, and Tilly, 2001). Brokerage, or the proactive linking of previously unconnected individuals or groups, played an important role in the Colour Revolutions. For example, activist youth and student groups, especially the Serbian group Otpor, set out to train counterparts in other countries such as Ukraine (Kuzio, 2006). This sharing of best practices served as an important driver of diffusion.

Second, not only do adopting citizens have to be aware of the protests, but they must also view them as relevant to their own social situation (Strang and Meyer, 1993). Perceptions of similarity can arise as a result of any number of factors, including shared histories, similar institutional arrangements, or shared grievances. In the case of the Arab Spring, for example, similarities in culture, religion, language, demographic pressures, and grievances across the Middle East and North Africa raised the likelihood that citizens in nearby countries would view ongoing protests as relevant to their own situation and seek to emulate the process.

Recent research, however, offers a slightly more nuanced perspective on diffusion, viewing it as a highly conditional process (Houle et al., 2016). Rather than seeing diffusion as the spread of democracy across borders, quantitative research suggests that the spread of democracy is contingent first on the collapse of existing regimes. Economic or political crises must first trigger an authoritarian breakdown. Diffusion then influences whether the new regime is democratic or authoritarian. Put differently, diffusion has only a conditional effect on democratization, requiring the preceding condition of autocratic breakdown. This helps to explain the outcome of the Arab Spring, where there was a clear regional and temporal clustering of regime breakdown (Egypt, Libya, Syria, Yemen), but very little diffusion of democracy apart from the political transition in Tunisia (Conroy-Krutz and Frantz, 2017).

Before we conclude this section, it is important to note that just as protests and opposition tactics can spread, so too can repertoires of repression and other counter-tactics (Beissinger, 2007). We elaborate on counter-diffusion in Chapter 12 (focusing on international factors). We note here, however, that research has acknowledged that the processes of democratic diffusion can also work in reverse and create conditions that promote autocracy (Ambrosio, 2010; Cameron and Orenstein, 2012).

Conclusion

In this chapter, we discussed the factors that empirical political science research has shown to increase an authoritarian regime's vulnerability to breakdown. As we mentioned at the outset of the chapter, anticipating authoritarian breakdown is hard. There is little agreement about what precisely will cause an autocracy to fall, and even less consensus about how to anticipate the timing of such an event. Instead, authoritarian breakdown should be thought of as a dynamic process that results from the interaction of multiple long-term and short-term factors. We focused our discussion on *long-term structural factors*, such as elite divisions, socio-economic conditions, corruption and demographics, which affect a country's vulnerability to breakdown. We also identified several *short-term factors*, such as economic crisis, fraudulent elections, and natural disasters, which can provide more immediate triggers of regime failure.

It is important to remember, however, that in addition to the factors we discuss in this chapter, human motivations, decisions, and reactions can play a critical role in accelerating or eluding authoritarian breakdown. The role of the individual is difficult to analyse and nearly impossible to quantify in a meaningful way across countries or over time. But in reality, government officials can and often do take measures to mitigate regime vulnerabilities. Likewise, opposition members or the public can respond to events in ways that exacerbate regime vulnerabilities. In other words, human agency also plays a critical role in the process of authoritarian breakdown. This likely explains why so many risk factors may persist for years without bringing down an authoritarian regime, and conversely why so many seemingly stable regimes can fall apart so quickly.

In the next chapter we build on our discussion of risk factors for authoritarian breakdown by identifying *how* autocracies fall apart. In particular, we focus on the most common pathways of authoritarian collapse, including coups, protests, elections, and civil wars.

Key Questions

1. Why is the difference between 'authoritarian breakdown' and 'democratization' significant?

2. How does economic crisis affect an authoritarian regime's risk of breakdown?

3. What are the primary external factors that affect authoritarian regime stability? In your opinion, *should* outside actors ever seek to destabilize authoritarian regimes? What factors did you consider in developing your response?

4. What were the most significant causes of the Arab Spring? Which other regimes or regions are most vulnerable to a wave of protests? Why?

5. What factors or conditions increase the likelihood that elite divisions will occur? When are elite divisions likely to lead to regime change?

6. Pick a current autocracy—such as Russia, China, Zimbabwe, or North Korea—and discuss how the regime could break down. Posit a scenario, or a series of events, that could result in authoritarian breakdown in the country you selected. What signs would you look for to indicate that the country you selected was becoming less stable?

Further Reading

HUNTINGTON, S.P., 2006. *Political Order in Changing Societies.* Yale University Press.
   Political Order's central thesis is that contrary to previous works, economic growth and development does not always lead to stability, but may actually have the opposite effect. States that are seeing their institutions decaying may face growing instability during periods of change and reform.

MAGALONI, B., 2006. *Voting for Autocracy: Hegemonic Party Survival and Its Demise in Mexico.* Cambridge University Press.
   Voting for Autocracy explains how the PRI regime in Mexico was able to hold elections continuously during its eight decades in power and still maintain itself in power. The book also explains the factors that impacted the PRI's eventually fall in 2000.

O'DONNELL, G., SCHMITTER, P.C., and WHITEHEAD, L., 1986. *Transitions from Authoritarian Rule: Southern Europe* (Vol. 1). JHU Press.
   This edited volume offers interesting case studies on how authoritarian regimes in Italy, Greece, Spain, Turkey, and Portugal transitioned from authoritarian rule. The book also offers what prospects each case had to democratize.

TUCKER, J. A. (2007). 'Enough! Electoral Fraud, Collective Action Problems, and Post-communist Colored Revolutions'. *Perspectives on Politics*, 5(03), 535–51.
   This article focuses on the post-communist Colour Revolutions and demonstrates how electoral fraud can serve as a trigger to mobilize opponents of authoritarian regimes to action.

8

Autocratic Transitions

In Chapter 7, we identified the factors that political science research shows increase the risk of authoritarian breakdown. For political observers and policy analysts, knowing that factors such as economic decline, elite divsions, and youth bulges raise an autocracy's risk of breakdown is useful because it helps us focus our analytic attention on the factors that matter most. However, only understanding the triggers of instability tells us relatively little about *how* these regimes actually fall apart.

To illustrate, we explained in Chapter 7 that economic decline raises the risk of authoritarian regime failure. But economic decline can lead to authoritarian regime failure in a number of ways. For example, economic decline can provide military leaders with an opening to mount a coup, or it can generate social discontent that fuels regime-ending protests. Likewise, elite divisions raise a regime's prospects of breakdown, but highly factional dictatorships have unraveled in different ways. In Togo, ethnic-based factionalism motivated a group of army officers to stage a coup to oust Togo's independence leader and first president, Sylvanus Olympio (Decalo, 1990; Roessler, 2011). But factionalism can also lead authoritarian incumbents to actively exclude competing factions from the government, raising the risk of insurgency. In Chad in 1990, then-President Hissène Habré accused his ethnic Zaghawa Army Chief, Idriss Déby, of plotting a coup, leading Déby to flee the country. Déby tapped into social discontent over Habré's sustained targeting of ethnic Zaghawa to mobilize an insurgency that eventually overthrew the Habré regime (Roessler, 2011). In short, there can be several ways that the risk factors we identified in the previous chapter can bring down an autocracy.

In this chapter, we discuss the patterned pathways of authoritarian breakdown. We highlight the factors that increase the prospects that a particular pathway will emerge and the likelihood that its emergence will bring down the regime. Elections and widespread protests, for example, are relatively common in autocracies. We put forth the factors that help us gauge whether these events are likely to be regime threatening.

We also show how the mode of regime failure influences a country's subsequent political trajectory. Some modes of exit like **coups** rarely lead to democratization, while other pathways, like peaceful protest, are more likely to usher in democracy.

We close this chapter by switching gears to discuss a different type of political transition: the departure of the regime's leader. Here, we overview the pathways of authoritarian *leader* failure. Importantly, we explain how authoritarian *leader* exits influence the chance that the *regime* falls with the leader.

Pathways of authoritarian regime transitions

We begin this chapter by focusing on *the pathways* through which authoritarian *regimes* break down. We base this discussion on regime failure data from all of the 280 authoritarian regimes that ruled between 1946 and 2010 (Geddes et al., 2014). These data are categorical in that they group political systems into two groups: democratic and authoritarian. For those that are authoritarian, they measure the start and end dates of each authoritarian regime. This enables researchers to capture when authoritarian breakdown results in the establishment of a new authoritarian regime or a democracy.

Authoritarian regime exits fall into two general categories. Authoritarian regimes break down as a result of **top-down processes** initiated by regime insiders, such as military coups and elections. For example, Muamar Qaddafi, then a 27-year-old junior army officer, brought down the Libyan monarchy in coup in 1969. And elections have unseated several long-standing dictatorships, including in Senegal in 2000 and more recently in the Gambia in 2016.

Authoritarian regimes also break down as a result of **bottom-up pathways**, including protests or insurgencies. The protests known as the 'Colour Revolutions' that swept across the former Soviet Union led to authoritarian breakdown in Georgia, Ukraine, and Kyrgyzstan in the early 2000s. And insurgencies have ended numerous dictatorships, most notably in Somalia in 1991.

In addition to the top-down and bottom-up pathways we discuss, there are a few other ways that autocracies fail. Foreign invasions, for example, have toppled authoritarian regimes. The French intervention in Central African Republic in 1979 removed the regime led by Jean-Bédel Bokassa and a U.S.-led coalition removed the Iraqi regime led by Saddam Hussein in 2003. However, data show that these other modes of change have been relatively infrequent. In this section, we focus our discussion on top-down and bottom-up pathways to regime failure because they are far and away the most common ways that dictatorships unravel. We also highlight, where relevant, changes over time in the way that authoritarian regimes are falling from power.

Top-down paths to regime breakdown

Authoritarian regimes most frequently break down through top-down processes. Coups and elections, the most common type of top-down transitions, account for more than 60 per cent of all authoritarian breakdowns (Geddes et al., 2018). Since the end of the

Cold War, however, this has declined slightly to 48 per cent, largely due to the steep decline in regime-ending coups.

Coups are classified as a top-down form of exit, because they are almost always carried out by 'insiders', frequently senior military officers who are part of the regime's inner circle or disgruntled junior officers affiliated with it (Finer, 2017). Elections are also considered a top-down path to regime breakdown because they require regime insiders to agree to hold a contest that is free and fair enough that an incumbent can actually lose it (Kendall-Taylor and Frantz, 2014).

Coup d'etat

Coups are the most common pathway to authoritarian breakdown. From 1946–2010, coups toppled approximately one-third of all authoritarian regimes (Geddes et al., 2018). That said, coups have declined in frequency since the end of the Cold War (Marinov and Goemans, 2014). Whereas coups comprised 47 per cent of authoritarian regime failures during the Cold War, this number has declined to just 12 per cent since.

A **coup** is defined as the illegal removal of a leader from power, planned and plotted by a small but critical segment of the state. Given that the use or threat of force is necessary to take power, military or security services are always involved. However, the extent of security service involvement varies. **Palace coups**, for example, are driven primarily by civilian elites, although they must have the backing of either the military or security services to be successful.

One reason that coups have been such a common mode of authoritarian breakdown is that they are relatively easy to orchestrate. Of all the ways that dictatorships fall apart by force, coups require the cooperation of the fewest individuals. In many cases, they are planned and implemented by just a handful of officers. Lower level officers and soldiers who participate in coups tend to obey orders given by the officers who organize the plot and may not even know the purpose of their activities until the action is over. Coups also unfold quickly. Military units, typically within a day or two, arrest key members of the leadership group, seize control of executive buildings to establish physical authority, take over media outlets to control the flow of information, and position soldiers on the streets to maintain order. Coup conspirators may also shut down or take over telecommunications or transportation nodes, such as telephone activities and airports, and deploy military troops to block movements of non-cooperative military units to prevent a countercoup.

Although coups are easier for regime opponents to orchestrate relative to other methods of seizing power, they are nonetheless risky. About half of all coups fail (Singh, 2014). Moreover, the consequences for coup plotters of a failed attempt are severe. Participants in failed coup are most often killed, jailed, or exiled. Coup conspirators, therefore, must carefully evaluate their chances of success and should only attempt a coup when the expected rewards of the coup and its probability of success are greater than the costs of failure. Political science research has identified a number of factors that enhance coup plotters' perceptions of their likelihood of success and, consequently, the likelihood of a coup. We discuss three of these factors: economic conditions, political instability, and grievances of military officers.

Broadly speaking, volatile and uncertain political and economic conditions increase the chances of a coup. Such environments signal weak executive leadership, providing would-be coup plotters with incentive and justification for their actions. Poor governance also eases the decision of the rest of the military to cooperate with a coup and minimizes public opposition. Low levels of development, in particular, raise a regime's coup risk. Low-income countries are twenty-one times more likely to experience a coup than are rich countries, where successful coups almost never occur (Londegran and Poole, 1991). Poor countries may lack effective institutional checks on the military's power, making the military more likely to see a coup as a viable option. Likewise, income distribution affects a country's prospects for a coup (Houle, 2016). Inequality heightens distributional conflicts between the elite and the masses, raising the risk of conflict and political volatility. At the same time, unequal countries tend to have stronger militaries, because they face greater threats from the public (Svolik, 2012). These two factors together—heightened distributional conflict and enhanced military capacity—lead to a heightened coup risk.

There is also evidence (although it has been debated) that economic *crisis* increases the chance of a coup (Fossum, 1967; Galetovic and Sanhueza, 2000; Johnson et al., 1983; Needler, 1966; Nordlinger, 1977; O'Kane, 1981). Economic factors convey information about the strength and popularity of a regime. Economic decline can signal government incompetence and undermine regime legitimacy, enhancing regime opponents' perceptions that a coup will be successful. The military may also regard the civilian government as incompetent, reasoning that a military take-over is necessary to help discipline the government and stimulate economic growth. In Latin America, for example, the military viewed its role as protecting the middle class and often stepped in to protect this cohort from perceived government transgressions (Huntington, 2006; O'Donnell, 1973; Tusalem, 2010). Though some studies have found no statistically significant relationship between coups and economic crisis (Powell, 2012; Svolik, 2013), newer research suggests that this is largely due to differences in how economic crisis is measured (Kim, 2016). Once more accurate measures are used, economic crises are found to increase the chance of a coup.

In addition to economic uncertainty, political volatility also raises a country's coup risk. Political instability, such as protests, strikes, institutional gridlock, and internal conflicts provide an especially informative signal of regime weakness and create uncertainty about the staying power of the incumbent regime (Casper and Tyson, 2014). Potential plotters, therefore, become more willing to accept riskier coup attempts than they would under more stable domestic conditions (Casper and Tyson, 2014; Bell and Sudduth, 2017; Johnson and Thyne, 2018). Militaries also view political turmoil as requiring intervention to restore public order (Welch and Smith, 1974). For many countries in the developing world, citizens view the military (and not just the police) as responsible for providing public order (Huntington, 1995). Finally, political upheaval makes international actors less likely to punish coup leaders (Johnson and Thyne, 2018). Coup leaders who take power amid mass protests can claim to be responding to the will of the people, reducing the risk of international sanction and therefore raising coup plotters' willingness to seize control.

Recent coups (within the last five to six years), and those autocratic incumbents that themselves seized power via coup, also raise a country's risk of experiencing a subsequent coup. (Londegran and Poole, 1990; Bienen and Van de Walle, 1989). Known as a 'coup trap', a previous coup raises the risk of a subsequent coup because it demonstrates that the collective action problem inherent in organizing such an event can be overcome. Coups—successful or failed—also disrupt established relationships among political elites in ways that raise the future probably of another coup. According to Jay Ulfelder, 'these disruptions increase elites' uncertainty about the intentions of their potential rivals, and the proximity of the last attempt may lead them to overestimate the likelihood of the next one. In a kind of self-fulfilling prophecy, this intensification of uncertainty strengthens incentives to try to seize power' (Ulfelder, 2012). Countries that have frequent coups may also have populations that have become accustomed them, and see coups as an acceptable means of leadership turnover (Finer, 2017). The coup trap dynamic helps explain the recurrence of coups in countries such as Nigeria, Benin, and Thailand.

Finally, corporate interests and officer grievances also motivate coups. Military leaders may stage a coup, for example, if they fear the government is impinging on the military's organizational interests, such as cutting the military budget or interfering in military promotions (Thompson, 1973; Needler, 1975; Nordlinger, 1977). Cuts to the Kenyan military budget caused junior officers to stage a (failed) coup attempt in 1982 (Diangá, 2002). Similarly, in Ghana, Kofia Busia's decision to cut the military's budget by 10 per cent triggered a coup there in 1972. Personal factors, such as individual ambition or fears of demotion can also inspire coups (Decalo, 1990). In Uganda, then-army commander Idi Amin preemptively ousted Milton Obote in 1971 because of Amin's fears that he was going to be arrested. In Nigeria, as well, Ibrahim Babangida, the Chief of the Army Staff staged a coup against President Muhammadu Buhari in 1985, due to concerns that he was about to be charged with corruption.

Coup plotters will only attempt a coup if they calculate that the benefits of ousting the incumbent and the probability of success surpass the costs of failure. Incumbent governments—both authoritarian and democratic—take a number of steps to reduce the likelihood of a coup (see Box 8.1).

 Box 8.1: **Coup proofing**

Scholars have termed the actions governments take to protect themselves from a coup, '**coup proofing**'. Several studies have found that while coup-proofing strategies mitigate a country's coup risk, they have the unintended consequence of reducing the military's capacity to fight (Reiter and Stam, 1998; Biddle and Long, 2004). We identify several examples of the most common coup proofing tactics:

• *Overpaying the security services*: Governments use military expenditures, such as higher salaries, a larger budget, or state of the art weaponry, to 'buy' the loyalty of the armed services and signal that the regime is taking military interests into account (Huntington 1991; Powell, 2012). The security services, in turn, may be motivated to protect the incumbent regime, as they cannot be certain that a subsequent regime will treat them as favourably.

- *Counter-balancing:* Governments seek to create 'numerous, mutually suspicious rival forces that check and balance one another' (Belkin and Schofer, 2003, p. 596). This is most frequently done by dividing power between a conventional military service and a parallel service charged with regime protection. Examples of rival units include the National Guard in Saudi Arabia or the Islamic Revolutionary Guard Corps in Iran. Although counterbalancing is a frequent coup-proofing tactic, the creation of a new service can backfire and increase the risk of a coup by exacerbating perceptions of favouritism or fueling concerns that institutional equities are under threat.

- *Elite shuffling*: Governments try to rotate the elite, particularly in the military or security services, to prevent any one individual from developing a support base he or she could use to challenge the incumbent leader (Pollack, 2002).

- *Ethnic or familial favouritism*: Incumbent leaders post family members or allies from ethnic or regional groups in positions of power in the military and security services. These personal ties and connections decrease the likelihood of disloyalty to the leader.

- *Shadow commands*: Political leaders seek to assign non-military personnel to military commands units to retain oversight. Communist leaders, for example, often placed party members in military command units.

Elections

Elections are the second mode of top-down authoritarian breakdown. Elections lead to authoritarian breakdown when an authoritarian incumbent or his or her chosen successor lose to the opposition or choose not to run. It is important to note that elections can also provide a catalyst for other modes of authoritarian breakdown, particularly protests, which we discuss at greater length. About one-quarter of authoritarian regimes have ended at the ballot box (Geddes et al., 2018). Whereas coups that oust authoritarian regimes have decreased in frequency since the Cold War, regime-ending elections have dramatically increased. Elections toppled 21 per cent of authoritarian regimes during the Cold War, but 36 per cent of them since it ended.

As we discussed in Chapter 6, elections have become commonplace in autocracies. Since the end of the Cold War, the proportion of dictatorships holding elections rose from just over 70 per cent in 1989 to about 85 per cent in 2010. Overall, elections enhance the durability of autocracies. However, they do occasionally dislodge authoritarian regimes. In Senegal, for example, Abdou Diouf was ousted in elections in 2000 by Abdoulaye Waye, a long-time opposition leader. Diouf accepted the election results and peacefully left office, bringing an end to the authoritarian regime that had ruled Senegal for forty years. More recently, Yahya Jammeh of the Gambia was forced to step down after twenty-two years in office when Adama Barrow defeated him in elections in December 2016.

Although elections have ousted several authoritarian incumbents, this is still an infrequent phenomenon. Autocrats lose a very small proportion of elections they contest. So what factors increase the risk that elections lead to authoritarian breakdown?

First, elections are likely to be most destabilizing in hybrid regime. More specifically, elections are more likely to lead to regime change in competitive autocracies, compared to full autocracies. Between 1987 and 2006 one-third of executive elections in competitive authoritarian regimes resulted in non-incumbent victories. In contrast, fully authoritarian regimes never lost executive elections they participated in (Roessler and Howard, 2008). Intuitively, this makes sense. Full autocracies tend to be more blatant and excessive in their efforts to ensure incumbent victory, including their harassment of opposition leaders, and their control of the media and other institutions like electoral commissions.

Second, elections are more likely to unseat dictators when the incumbent does not run in the election (Howard and Roessler, 2006). Authoritarian incumbents may choose not to contest elections for several reasons, including term limits or poor health. In these cases, authoritarian leaders often identify a chosen successor to compete on the regime's behalf. The autocrat's decision about a successor, however, can elicit elite backlash and create elite splits that often prove to be destabilizing. If such elite disagreements and infighting are made public, it can increase public perceptions of regime weakness, making the opposition appear to be a viable option. Elite splits also create uncertainty among the elite that their future is secure, reducing their propensity to engage in fraud to secure the election for fear of future reprisal. In Kenya, for example, Daniel Arap Moi's decisions to honor his term limits and not contest the 2002 election led to the breakdown of the Kenya African National Union (KANU) regime, which had been in power for thirty-nine years. Moi's designation of Uhuru Kenyatta, the son of Kenya's first President, as his successor and KANU candidate prompted the defection of his Vice President Mwai Kibaki, who went on to lead an opposition coalition that won the election. Of course, this is not always the case. In Kazakhstan, President Nursultan Nazarbayev stepped down as President in 2019 after almost thirty years in power. His put forth a hand-picked successor, Kassym-Jomart Tokayev, who contested and won the country's elections (although not without widespread protests).

Two additional factors we addressed in Chapter 7 are also particularly relevant for gauging how elections will pan out in authoritarian regimes: economic crisis and opposition cohesion. Economic crises not only undermine incumbent legitimacy, but economic hardship reduces government resources necessary for the regime to execute an effective electoral campaign. Fewer resources diminish the incumbent regime's ability to maintain elite loyalty, co-opt opposition leaders, and employ security services to harass the opposition and voters. In Mexico, many analysts view Mexico's 1994 peso crisis as an important factor eventually contributing to the PRI's electoral defeat that ended the regime's seventy-one-year reign in 2000.

Opposition cohesion also becomes particularly salient during electoral periods (Howard and Roessler, 2006). Marc Howard and Philip Roessler (2006) identify four reasons that opposition cohesion increases the risk of incumbent defeat. First, opposition unity concentrates anti-regime votes. Rather than spreading votes across multiple opposition candidates, a unified opposition may accumulate enough votes to defeat an incumbent. Second, opposition cohesion renders an autocrat's divide and rule strategy less effective. When the opposition is united, it is more difficult for the regime to play factions off one another. Third, opposition cohesion can limit repression and manipulation during elections. If the police, army, and bureaucrats calculate that the opposition is sufficiently organized that it can credibly challenge the ruling party, they are likely to be less willing to employ illegal practices to benefit the incumbent. The viability of an opposition victory raises the risk that corrupt practices would be punished should a new regime come to power. Finally, a united opposition increases the chances that the public will view the movement as a viable alternative to the incumbent leader. When citizens view the opposition as viable, they are more likely to vote against the regime.

Opposition cohesion has also played a role in those cases in which elections catalyze anti-regime protests that ultimately bring down dictatorships. In the Philippines, for example, Ferdinand Marcos held a snap election in 1986 amid escalating public discontent over sharply declining economic conditions and rumours that he was positioning his wife Imelda and his children to succeed him. The opposition united behind Corazon Aquino, the widow of prominent opposition leader Benigno Aquino who was assassinated in 1983. When it was clear that the elections results were rigged in favour of Marcos, the opposition joined together in what became known as the People Power Revolution that ultimately led Marcos to flee the country (Smith, 2005).

 Box 8.2: **Pacted transitions**

A pacted transition is a process of authoritarian breakdown that occurs through a series of negotiated agreements between an outgoing authoritarian regime and an incoming democratic government. Pacted transitions have tended to occur when the balance of power between supporters and opponents of the authoritarian regime was relatively equal and uncertain. In these moments of parity, the regime elite conclude that the costs of repression are greater than the costs of toleration. They therefore opt to negotiate power-sharing arrangements with the opposition. O'Donnell et al. (1986) have described these pacts as an 'explicit but not always publicly explicated or justified, agreement among a select set of actors which seeks to define rules governing the exercise of power on the basis of mutual guarantees for the vital interests of those entering into it' (p. 37). Pacted transitions have occurred most frequently in the breakdowns of military regimes, including in Brazil and Uruguay.

Pacted transitions tend to produce durable democracies (Karl, 1990). This is in part because pacts reduce the uncertainty that characterizes political transitions (O'Donnell et al., 1986). Pacts make democracy more palatable for the authoritarian elite because they mitigate concerns about wealth redistribution and/or guarantee key elites a role in the future system. The ensuing democracies tend to be durable because the elites of the old regime help shape the new rules of the game and are therefore more committed to upholding them. Pacted transitions are by no means the only pathway to democracy. McFaul (2002) argues, for example, that successful democratic transitions in the post-Soviet period did not follow the pacted path. Regardless, they do constitute one process through which authoritarian regime have transitioned out of power.

Bottom-up paths to regime breakdown

Relative to the top-down pathways of authoritarian breakdown, bottom-up modes of exit have been less frequent. As we discuss, these forms of forced regime breakdown have been less common because they are more difficult to orchestrate relative to coups. Protests and insurgencies together accounted for one-quarter of all authoritarian regime failures between 1946 and 2010. That said, bottom-up regime failure has grown more frequent since the end of the Cold War; protests and insurgencies account for 33 per cent of all regime breakdowns in the post-Cold War era.

Protests

Protest is the most common bottom-up mode of authoritarian breakdown; protests brought down 17 per cent of all regimes that have collapsed (Geddes et al., 2018). However, protests have begun to unseat a slightly larger proportion of regimes (20 per cent) in the post-Cold War period. This is in line with research on authoritarian *leader* exits, which shows that protests are increasingly unseating authoritarian leaders (Kendall-Taylor and Frantz, 2014). Kendall-Taylor and Frantz (2014) show that popular revolts now pose a growing threat to autocratic leaders—a topic we return to later in the chapter.

Though they are growing more common, protests are difficult to effectively engineer. In comparison to coups, for example, which require the coordination of only a handful of individuals, a revolt capable of bringing down an incumbent entails the mobilization of tens of thousands of citizens. The organization and mobilization of this many people is challenging in any setting. But the closed and repressive nature of autocracies severely complicates the process.

In particular, a dynamic academics have called '**preference falsification**' helps explain why anti-regime protests in authoritarian settings are so rare, particularly in more repressive environments (Kricheli et al., 2011; Kuran, 1991). In simplest terms, preference falsification is the idea that individuals seek to convey preferences and opinions that are socially acceptable. In autocracies, high levels of repression make it costly for citizens to display any discontent, which in turn leads most citizens to believe that support for the regime is the most socially acceptable stance. This means that a majority of the population, even a vast one, may want change, but most citizens stay silent. Preference falsification impedes protests because most citizens will only join one if they believe that a sufficient number of their fellow citizens will do the same.

This is why the occurrence of a '**triggering event**' is so critical for the precipitation of a widespread protest. A triggering event may be something expected, such as an election, or something entirely unanticipated, such as the Tunisian fruit vendor who set himself on fire. Triggering events are important for initiating the protest process because they provide a focal point for mobilization. Triggering events can also be critical catalysts if they signal to a large number of citizens the extent of public discontent or reveal previously unknown information about regime weakness. Once the information that the triggering event conveys is in the public domain, it becomes difficult for the regime to defend its viability.

Political science theories on '**information cascades**' provide a framework for understanding how a triggering event can catalyze a widespread protest (Lotan et al., 2011). In most countries, dissidents and other hardcore anti-regime elements are always prepared to voice their discontent with the regime. A cascade of mass mobilization begins, however, when a triggering event shifts the decision calculus of a new group of ordinary citizens who, now equipped with the new information, decides to protest. The actions of this new group of activists reduces the cost of political action for the next group, who are now willing to express their opposition to the regime publicly. Those citizens with more extreme anti-regime views are likely to mobilize early on, while moderates join in later. The key, however, is that citizens' willingness to protest is affected by their perceptions of what their fellow citizens are likely to do. As their perceived costs of protesting decline, a wave of protest is likely to swell.

Not all widespread protests are sufficient to force an authoritarian incumbent to step down. History is ripe with (often brutal) examples of authoritarian regimes that are able to ride out such movements. Recent examples of authoritarian regimes that were able to withstand large-scale popular resistance include Belarus after its 2010 presidential election, Russia following parliamentary elections in 2011 and 2012, and Algeria and Jordan on the heels of the Arab Spring. So what enables some protests to topple long-standing authoritarian regimes, while the authorities more easily contain others?

When it comes to the success of protests, academic research has suggested that two inter-related factors matter most: the size of the protest and the tactics employed. Protests are most likely to reach a regime-threatening size when participants use non-violent tactics. Non-violent movements lower the barriers to participation and avoid alienating citizens hesitant to associate with more extreme or dangerous tactics (Celestino and Gleditsh, 2013; Stephan and Chenoweth, 2008; see Box 8.2). Large, broad-based, non violent protests have the potential to precipitate regime change because they often prompt elite defections that spell the end of the regime. Non-violent protests create fissures within the regime between those officials who advocate forcefully ending the protests and those that view concessions as their preferred approach. Moreover, large non-violent protests raise the costs for leaders contemplating the use of force. It is much more difficult to justify repression against normal citizens with moderate demands than against smaller, more radical groups. Police and soldiers are also more likely to identify with dissidents that cannot be easily labelled as extreme. In the case of East Germany, the chief of the East German police, Erich Mielke warned Communist Party leader Erich Honecker that they could not beat up hundreds of thousands of people (Przeworski, 1991).

 Box 8.3: **Case study: Burkina Faso**

Blaise Compaoré resigned and fled Burkina Faso on 31 October 2014. He had been in power for twenty-seven years. Just days earlier, women armed with wooden spoons took to the streets to protest the government's announcement that the legislature would vote on—and likely pass—a constitutional amendment to extend presidential term limits. The women's efforts were the latest instalment of pro-democratic protests that had been building for months against Compaoré's pursuit of a term limit extension. The security services dispersed that day's crowd with tear gas. But the following day, the protesters' ranks swelled. Tens of thousands of Burkinabe citizens gathered in the capital city, Ouagadougou, and other towns throughout the country. As the protests grew, so did activist demands. What began as an effort to prevent the extension of presidential term limits grew into a movement calling for Compaoré's resignation.

Compaoré initially rejected protester calls to resign. But signals from the military that they would not use force against the people emboldened the protesters. On 30 October, activists set fire to parliament and other government buildings forcing legislators to postpone their vote. That night Compaoré offered a concession to the protesters and announced on a private TV station (the national television building had been looted) that he was withdrawing the amendment and would hand over power at the end of his term to a democratically-elected successor. But it was too little too late. Sensing their momentum, on 31 October the protesters marched to the presidential palace. The Presidential Security Regiment reportedly informed Compaoré they would not shoot on the unarmed protesters approaching. Later that day, Compaoré resigned and fled the palace with his entourage in a convoy heading south where a French helicopter evacuated him to Cote d'Ivoire.

Compaoré's ouster represented a significant change in the way that leaders have historically left office in Burkina Faso. Each of the country's previous five presidents were overthrown in coups. As we discuss later in this chapter, when autocrats are ousted in coups, democracy is unlikely to follow. Each of the country's coups did indeed usher in a new authoritarian leader or system. The protests that dislodged Compaoré, however, created an opportunity for democratization. After a year-long political transition, Roch Marc Christian Kabore was elected president in November 2015 in free and fair elections. Burkina Faso's break with the old system led Freedom House to revise its ranking of the country to 'Partly Free'. Burkina Faso will continue to face a number of challenges, including poor socio-economic development and terrorist threats, that can impede democratic consolidations, but the ouster of Compaoré at the hands of the people created an opportunity for meaningful political change in a long-time autocracy.

There are of course examples of violent protests that led to authoritarian breakdown. In Iran, several thousand people were executed or killed in the 1978–79 Iranian Revolution when the Shah was overthrown (Bill, 1982). Similarly, about a thousand people died in the Romanian Revolution that resulted in the execution of Nicolae Ceauşescu and his wife Elena in 1989 (Siani-Davies, 2007, 281). However, statistical studies show that violent movements are less likely to succeed, when holding other factors constant (Celestino and Gleditsh, 2013). Violent protest tactics make it easier for governments to justify violence to preserve state security against credible threats.

A government's response to protest also plays a role in determining whether the regime will endure the challenge. However, it is nearly impossible to gauge with foresight whether repression or concessions will be most effective. In the face of widespread protests, a regime's use of **repression**, such as forcefully dispersing protesters or restricting media, can raise the cost of protesting and put an end to the confrontation. As we discussed in Chapter 7, however, the use of repression can also elicit backlash. Attempts at repression can enhance sympathy for protesters, alienate the public, increase foreign support for protesters, and spur regime divisions. Likewise, a regime's use of concessions, such as willingness to enact policy reforms, can take the steam out of protests. In other cases, the same policies create a sense of opportunity and lead protesters to escalate their demands. Once citizens are in the streets, protest dynamics are extremely fluid making it difficult to gauge the trajectory of the conflict.

Box 8.4: **State failure**

State failure occurs when a government is unable to project its authority over at least half of its territory. Failed states are unable to fulfil basic state functions such as providing security, controlling borders, offering basic administrative services, and enforcing laws and regulations (Ezrow and Frantz, 2013). States most often collapse because of, or in conjunction with other forms of political instability. Insurgencies, for example, can lead to state failure. In such environments, countries can lapse into failed state status until the incumbent government or rebel forces that defeat the government are able to consolidate control. Examples of failed states that resulted from insurgency include Syria after the Arab Spring and Afghanistan in the 1970s, when the government was unable to suppress the armed opposition that coalesced against it.

States can also fail as a result of a more gradual process of disintegration. In these cases, the state fails to enforce its authority even in the absence of a rival claimant, resulting in widespread lawlessness and disorder. Somalia under Siad Barre (1969–91) is one of the most notable cases of this form of state failure. For years, Barre deliberately weakened his security services, pitted clans against one another, and appointed cronies to positions of power. As his regime became increasingly unpopular, Barre inflamed clan rivalries to distract the public from regime corruption and poor economic performance. The Ogaden War, a conflict Barre waged against Ethiopia in 1977 in an attempt to reclaim the disputed Ethiopian region Ogaden, also weakened the Somali army substantially and led to military spending that crippled the economy. As the clans became increasingly well-armed, militias carved out territory and the military was unable to defend the state. Barre eventually lost control and Somalia entered a prolonged period of state failure.

Insurgency

Insurgency (sometimes referred to as internal conflict) is the second bottom-up pathway to authoritarian breakdown, making up 8 per cent of authoritarian regime failures (Geddes et al., 2018). Insurgency has also increased in frequency since the end of the Cold War, now making up 13 per cent of all authoritarian regime failures.

This mode of breakdown occurs when political challengers use sustained political violence to overthrow the government. Insurgencies are difficult to orchestrate, take a long time to execute—they last an average of a decade (Fearon and Laitin, 2003)—and the costs for participants are high. Furthermore, insurgency is unlikely to be successful. Insurgent groups only secure outright victories against governments in about a third of cases (Fearon, 2007). By contrast, about half of all coup attempts are successful (Powell and Thyne, 2011). Moreover, the chance of death, injury, and hardship is much greater for participants in insurgencies than for participants in coups or popular uprisings. In other words, insurgency is rarely the strategy of choice when an army exists that could lead a coup; it is used when no other strategy is feasible (Geddes et al., 2018). For these reasons, insurgencies have been a relatively less common pathway to authoritarian breakdown, though they do on occasion dislodge authoritarian regimes, such as in Cote d'Ivoire in 2011, Liberia in 1990, and Cambodia in 1975.

Scholars studying the onset of insurgencies have grouped risk factors into two categories—those based on 'greed' and those based on 'grievance' (Collier and Hoeffler, 2004). Studies focused on the former find that autocracies that are rich in 'lootable' resources such as diamonds, minerals, and drugs have an elevated risk of an insurgent movement (Lujala et al., 2005; Ross, 2004). The presence of these types of resources makes controlling territory a more attractive endeavour and provides political challengers with a source of income to fund their efforts. Some studies have also argued that grievances, including discontent with economic conditions or a history of conflict that fosters lingering resentment against the government or hostility between groups, raise the risk of insurgency (Berdal et al., 2000; Collier and Hoeffler, 2004). Countries with resources also may not distribute the resource wealth evenly, which can serve as a driver for the formation of violent groups.

More recently, scholars have focused on grievances that coincide with ethnic or regional divides (Wimmer et al., 2009). In particular, those authoritarian regimes that exclude ethnic groups from power are at greater risk of being ousted in an insurgency. Large ethnic groups (and those with concentrated settlement patterns in particular) that are excluded from power or are under-represented in government are more likely to seek to seize power from an authoritarian regime. Authoritarian incumbents will risk excluding ethnic groups from power-sharing arrangements if they view the group as posing an immediate and credible threat to their political survival. While excluding powerful groups is a dangerous game and increases the likelihood of future violent resistance, rulers calculate that this distant threat from society is preferable to an existential one from within the regime. In other words, governments trade an immediate coup risk for a more distant threat of insurgency (Roessler, 2011).

Not only does ethnic exclusion facilitate the organization of insurgency, but it also weakens the regime's counterinsurgency capabilities (Roessler, 2011). Ethnic exclusion erodes a regime's relationships with parts of society making excluded groups more willing to support or enable an insurgent movement. Moreover, given the geographic concentration of many ethnic groups, exclusion forfeits a government's control of terrain, which provides insurgents with invaluable space from which to organize and launch military operations. The most recent conflict in Yemen illustrates the repercussions of ethnic exclusion. The Houthis, a rebel group in Northern Yemen, had complained of being disenfranchised and excluded from the government for decades under the authoritarian government led by former president Ali Abdullah Saleh (1978–2012).

In Box 8.4 we outline the most widely discussed factors that raise a country's risk of internal conflict.

 Box 8.5: **Risk factors for civil war**

The prevention of civil war is an important policy priority. Because violent conflict is highly politicized, with supporters of each side advancing their own self-serving 'explanations', it is problematic to rely on the public discourse to assess the forces driving conflict. Gaining a sense of the causes of internal conflict is therefore particularly well suited to statistical analyses of global data that highlight those factors most often associated with its onset. In addition to the greed and grievance arguments we discuss in this chapter, the political science literature has highlighted the following factors as raising a country's risk for civil war:

- *Exclusion from power*: Groups that lose out in the struggle for state power are more fertile breeding grounds for organizations that challenge the government. Given nationalist principles of political legitimacy, feelings of resentment will be widespread and can be channelled into successful collective action (Cederman et al., 2010). The power balance between the peripheral group compared to the centre (measured as the demographic size of the groups), is a strong predictor of ethno-nationalist conflict. Civil wars occur, therefore, when peripheral contenders to the government are powerful enough to challenge the centre and are sufficiently motivated to do so (Buhaug, Cederman, and Rod, 2008).

- *Ethnic groups that recently experienced a loss of relative power*: Negative emotions are especially likely to be aroused following loss of power and prestige, suggesting that leaders of ethno-nationalist organizations will be most likely to resort to violence if they have recently experienced a loss of relative power. They can channel the resentment of their constituencies and mobilize to 'reverse a reversal' (Cederman et al., 2010).

- *Large ethnic groups*: Successful mobilization requires both motivation and organizational capacity. Larger excluded ethnic groups are particularly suited to challenge a government because they can draw on their superior numbers to recruit fighters and have a larger potential resource pool to sustain an organizational infrastructure. The political claims of larger ethnic groups also enjoy more **legitimacy**. Given the principles of representation that underlie the nation state, the exclusion of large sections of the population from power is more scandalous than the exclusion of smaller groups (and minority-ruled states are among the least legitimate political systems in the modern world) (Cederman et al., 2010; Cederman et al., 2009a).

- *Outside support:* The availability of external assistance alters power dynamics in ways that embolden secessionist leaders. All else being equal, minorities with outside patronage should be more likely than those without it to advance extreme claims against the centre (Cederman et al., 2009b; Jenne 2007). Moreover, the presence of external kin who could potentially offer support is more likely to increase the risk of conflict when the excluded minority is relatively large (Cederman et al., 2009b).

Trajectories of authoritarian regime change

In the early part of the 'Third Wave' (1974–89) many instances of authoritarian breakdown led to democratization. In many ways, the experiences of countries such as Portugal, Spain, Argentina, Brazil, Poland, and Hungary—cases in which authoritarian openings evolved into full democratic transitions—shaped our thinking about what happens when autocracies fail (Levitsky and Way, 2015). In each of these examples, when an authoritarian regime collapsed, a democracy replaced it. These experiences have led many political observers to conflate authoritarian breakdown with democratization. This assumption is misguided, however, and not supported by the empirical record. Historically, most authoritarian breakdowns have not brought democracy, but rather renewed dictatorship.

Here, we briefly summarize how the type of authoritarian regime transition influences what happens next.[1] The key takeaway is that neither top-down pathways nor bottom-up pathways guarantee democracy will result afterwards.

Among top-down pathways, regime transitions that occur via elections are far more likely to lead to democratization than those that occur via coups. In 90 per cent of cases, regime-change elections led to a transition to democracy, compared to only 9 per cent of regime-change coups. This is perhaps unsurprising. Elections signal a regime willing to cede power through peaceful means. Such conditions bode well for democratic politics. Coups, by contrast, represent a breach of the rules. They should therefore be less likely to set the stage for democracy. Although there is evidence that regime-change coups are more likely to lead to democracy since the end of the Cold War than they were during it, the probability is still greater that a regime change coup will result in dictatorship than democracy (Derpanopoulos et al., 2016).

Looking at bottom-up pathways, regime changes that happen through popular uprisings are far more likely than insurgencies to usher in democracy. A majority of regime-change protests (61 per cent) led to a transition to democracy. On the one hand, this should give reform-oriented protestors some hope when such revolutions occur. The '**Colour Revolutions**' that swept through the post-Soviet space in the early 2000s, for example, ushered in greater democracy in Georgia, Kyrgyzstan, and Ukraine. Although most of those advances have since been rolled back in Kyrgyzstan and Ukraine (and to a lesser extent in Georgia), these revolutions did—at least initially improve the democratic credentials of those places. On the other hand, this still means that nearly 40 per cent of the time we see new dictatorships result instead, as occurred following the Iranian revolution in 1979.

Turning to insurgencies, the evidence reveals that only 18 per cent of these regime change events lead to democracy. Even worse, in nearly a quarter (23 per cent) of cases, regime-change insurgencies lead to state failure. The violence that accompanies an insurgent effort makes democratic politics difficult (Celestino and Gleditsch, 2013).

Pathways of authoritarian leader transitions

The previous section focused on pathways of authoritarian *regime* breakdown. In this section, we shift our focus to authoritarian *leaders* and explain how dictators exit office and how the mode of exit affects subsequent political dynamics. As we discussed in the introduction to Part II, dictators are not synonymous with the regimes they lead. This section gives us insight into how a particular country's political dynamics are likely to unfold once an authoritarian leader leaves office—an especially volatile time that tends to garner widespread interest and speculation. In particular, we show that some types of leadership transition are more likely to be associated with regime change than others. Throughout this discussion, we base our insights from research by Andrea Kendall-Taylor and Erica Frantz (2014) and the evidence they provide.

---

[1] The data we use to summarize how the type of authoritarian regime transition influences what happens next comes from Geddes, Wright, and Frantz (2018).

Table 8.1 Regime trajectories following selected forms of authoritarian leader transitions: 1946–2012[2]

Type of leader exit (% of all leader exits)	Likelihood of regime failure in the next year	Likelihood of regime failure in the next five years
Coup (32%)	59%	70%
Election (2%)	77%	85%
Protest (7%)	88%	94%
Insurgency (3%)	88%	94%
Foreign intervention (2%)	91%	91%
Death in office (16%)	13%	24%

Table 8.1 summarizes what happens to the regime when an authoritarian leader leaves power, based on the mode of exit. It shows that when bottom-up actions like protests and insurgencies topple authoritarian leaders, the ramifications for the political system are much greater than when they exit via coups or elections. In 88 per cent of cases in which authoritarian leaders have fallen victim to protests, the authoritarian regime has been swept away with them within the year. This number jumps to 94 per cent if we expand the timeframe to five years.

Likewise, insurgencies that successfully dislodge an incumbent leader often usher in significant political change. By their nature, insurgent movements are changed-based organizations. The rebel groups almost always seek to take over the central government or political control of a region of the country (Fearon, 2007). Moreover, because these groups also typically aspire to orchestrate some degree of societal transformation, once they assume power they frequently seek to remake the state. Members of the insurgent group assume the key levers of power and install a new ruling party comprised of the insurgent cadre. The new ruling party typically eliminates immediate rivals and alternative power centres, including the military (Levitsky and Way, 2013). For these reasons, insurgencies that topple authoritarian leaders frequently bring about a wholesale turnover in the ruling regime as well. Unsurprisingly, the same is true of foreign interventions that oust authoritarian leaders, which—like insurgencies—typically have fundamental political change as their goal.

In contrast, when coups oust autocratic leaders, regime change is less likely. In 40 per cent of cases, the same general system remains intact (although this number declines to 30 per cent if we look at the five-year period afterwards). In the cases where the regime remains intact, the coup simply serves to shuffle the regime's top leadership. This is particularly common in military dictatorships. Coups that simply change the top leadership have been so common in these settings that observers view them as analogous to votes of no confidence in parliamentary regimes (Geddes, 2003). In Argentina's military

---

[2] There are a number of other ways that dictators exit office that we do not discuss here. About a third of authoritarian leaders leave power as a result of other dynamics including enforced term limits, resignations, and consensus decisions of regime actors such as a politburo or military junta. And about 4% are assassinated. As Kendall-Taylor and Frantz (2014) document, these types of leadership transitions usually do not propel regime collapse.

dictatorship, for example, President Roberto Viola was overthrown in a coup in December 1981 by the Commander in Chief of the Army, Leopoldo Galtieri. Though Viola was tossed out, the regime persisted until 1983, when the military was forced to step down after its defeat in the Falklands War. The data suggest, in other words, that when a coup unseats an authoritarian leader, we cannot assume that the regime will collapse too.

About a quarter of authoritarian regimes survive when an election unseats their leader; looking five years after the election, however, this number declines to 15 per cent. Elections that bring about autocratic leadership transitions are therefore slightly less destabilizing than protests or insurgencies, but still events that are nearly always associated with regime collapse. Regimes typically fall in the face of such elections because the leadership group has chosen to loosen their grip on power (for reasons discussed earlier).

Finally, natural death in office is the most unlikely type of authoritarian leadership transition to bring about regime collapse (see Box 8.6). In the vast majority of cases where autocrats die in office, even looking five years after, the regime persists. This is largely because—unlike other forms of autocratic leader exit—natural death in office is not politically motivated (Kendall-Taylor and Frantz 2014). When an autocratic ruler dies in office, of natural causes while in power, he or she leaves behind a populace and an elite that, up to that point, had opted to support rather than challenge the leader. When the leader dies, therefore, we usually see the key actors rally around a new successor to ensure continued access to the perks of power.

 Box 8.6: **Death of a dictator in office**

Death in office is a relatively common way that autocrats exit office. From 1946 to 2012, seventy-nine autocrats died while still in power, representing 16 per cent of all autocrats who have ever left office during this time. Prominent examples include: Venezuela's Hugo Chávez; North Korea's Kim Jong-Il; the USSR's Joseph Stalin; Kenya's Jomo Kenyatta; and Yugoslavia's Tito.

Perhaps surprisingly, a dictator's death in office infrequently precipitates regime change (Kendall-Taylor and Frantz, 2016). In 87 per cent of cases in which a leader dies in office, the regime—or the group in power and rules for governing—remains intact the following year. Even five years after the leader's passing, the same regime remains in power in 76 per cent of cases. The extent of stability following a leader's death in office is particularly remarkable when compared to other forms of leadership transition in autocracies, which lead to regime change within a year in about half of all cases (54 per cent) and regime change within five years in about two-thirds of them (63 per cent). Moreover, in the rare cases that regimes do collapse in the wake of a leader's death, the emergence of a new dictatorship is the likely outcome.

Why is death in office such a unique form of leadership transition? Most forms of leadership transition have political motivations and are based on the decisions or actions of political actors. Death in office is the exception. When a sitting dictator dies of natural causes, he or she leaves behind an elite and populace that—up to that point—had chosen to support rather than challenge the leadership. Whereas many leadership transitions signal a disgruntled elite and citizenry, the same is not necessarily true when a leader dies in office. When a dictator dies, elites have incentives to coalesce around a new successor as opposed to engage in political bickering and infighting. To act otherwise would endanger their privileged access to power.

This is not to say that regime instability and political change never follow a dictator's death. Kendall-Taylor and Frantz (2016) found that recent experience with protests or coups and a lack of a strong political party or other institutionalized succession mechanism (such as a politically active military or royal family) increase the risk that a leader's death will be followed by instability. For example, 22 per cent of highly personalized dictatorships (or those regimes lacking strong parties or a military) collapse when the leader dies compared to 6 per cent of institutionalized dictatorships. Although instability risk in the face of a leader's death in highly personalized settings is comparatively higher, the prospects still remain low. Even when institutional channels for handling succession are weak, the elite have strong incentives to rally around a new leader. Death in office, it turns out, is a surprisingly inconsequential form of leadership exit for broader regime stability.

The evidence we provide in this section reveals the varied regime trajectories that occur following an authoritarian leader transition. These trends provide us with a baseline understanding of what *tends* to happen. These patterns, therefore, should inform our understanding of what is likely to come in an authoritarian regime should an incumbent leader lose power.

Conclusion

This chapter focused on how authoritarian leaders and regimes fall from power. Broadly speaking, authoritarian regimes are displaced by either top-down or bottom-up dynamics. Elections and coups are the most common top-down pathways, while protests and insurgencies are the most frequent bottom-up pressures that topple dictatorships. Together, these four pathways account for the vast majority of authoritarian regime failures. Beyond describing the pathways of regime failure, we highlighted the factors that increase the prospects that a particular pathway will actually bring down the regime. Elections and protests, for example, are relatively common in autocracies. We identified the factors that research suggests affects whether these events are likely to be regime ending.

There were several themes that were woven through this chapter. The first is that when an autocracy falls, democracy does not necessarily follow. In some cases, as in Malaysia in 2018, long-time autocracies can give way to democracy. In May 2018, the Barisan Nasional coalition was defeated at the ballot box after more than sixty years in power. Its defeat came at the hands of the opposition coalition, the Alliance of Hope, led by 92-year-old and former Prime Minister Mahathir Mohamad. As we discussed, elections infrequently bring down an authoritarian regime, but when they do democracy almost always follows. But as we also emphasized, we should not expect all authoritarian regime transitions to be so smooth. For every Malaysia there are just as many countries where the downfall of one autocracy gives rise to another. At the extreme end of the spectrum, as in Somalia in 1991, regime change can be highly destructive, creating an environment that makes it difficult for democracy to succeed.

Since WWII, fewer than half of all authoritarian breakdowns resulted in democracy (Geddes et al., 2014).

We also emphasized the difference between authoritarian leaders and regimes. Here too we showed that the type of leadership exit influences the future trajectory of the regime. A leader's natural death in office, for example, rarely leads to authoritarian regime change. In contrast, protests and insurgencies that dislodge authoritarian leaders nearly always do. These findings equip political observers to more effectively gauge how highly uncertain political events in a particular country will develop. In particular, these data provide us with the baselines odds that certain outcomes will unfold.

In the next section of the book we turn our focus away from authoritarian regimes and focus on movements away from autocracy. In Part III of this book we address the key drivers of democracy, focusing on the factors and theories that research show influence a country's prospects for democratization and democratic consolidation.

Key Questions

1. What are the different pathways of authoritarian regime transitions? Which pathway is more common: top-down or bottom-up? Why?

2. What factors make coups more likely to occur? What factors make insurgency more likely to happen? Why are coups more likely to be successful compared to insurgencies?

3. From an autocrat's perspective, what are the risks and benefits of coup-proofing?

4. What factors increase the risk that elections will lead to authoritarian breakdown? Can you think of an example of where elections led to the breakdown of the regime?

5. How does preference falsification explain why protests are so rare?

6. How do triggering events catalyse protests? What is an example where this has happened?

7. Which pathway of authoritarian leadership transition is most likely to lead to regime change? Why is this the case? Can you give an example of where a leader was ousted and the regime stayed intact?

8. The Colour Revolutions and Arab Spring have underscored the threat that protests pose to authoritarian regimes. Do you think that protests will continue to unseat a growing number of autocracies? Or are autocrats taking steps to counteract the trend?

Further Reading

DANAHAR, P., 2013. *The New Middle East: The World after the Arab Spring*. Bloomsbury Publishing.
  The *New Middle East* explains how the history of the Middle East helps explain why there was so much turmoil during the Arab Spring, and why the movement for democratic change dissolved into chaos.

KENDALL-TAYLOR, ANDREA and FRANTZ, ERICA. 'When Dictators Die'. *Journal of Democracy*, 27(4), pp. 159–71.

This article looks at all authoritarian leaders that died in office between 1946 and 2012 to uncover trends in what tends to happen. The article shows that death in office infrequently destabilizes authoritarian regimes and tends to be a remarkably unremarkable event.

SINGH, N., 2014. *Seizing Power: The Strategic Logic of Military Coups*. JHU Press.

Seizing Power offers a new explanation for why military coups happen. Instead of focusing on economic factors, the book lays out how the credibility of the coup plotters in the eyes of other officers impacts whether the military allows it to succeed or not.

WRIGHT, J. and ESCRIBÀ-FOLCH, A., 2012. 'Authoritarian Institutions and Regime Survival: Transitions to Democracy and Subsequent Autocracy'. *British Journal of Political Science*, 42(2), pp. 283–309.

This article explores how authoritarian parties and legislatures affect regime survival. The article argues that legislatures are stabilizing for dictators, but parties can be destabilizing.

PART III

Drivers of Democracy

In Part I and Part II, we explained how to differentiate democracy from autocracy, and how researchers make sense of the growing number of regimes that fall in between. We also explored the political dynamics inside autocracies, focusing on how authoritarian regimes maintain power, and why and how they break down. We have emphasized that when an authoritarian regime falls, democracy does not necessarily follow. More often than not, the fall of one autocracy gives rise to another (Geddes et al., 2014). Given that democratic transitions are relatively infrequent, what are the factors that increase the prospects that democracy will emerge? And when it does emerge, what enables democracy to persist and deepen?

In Part III we address these dynamics. We discuss the factors that are conducive to democracy—both for encouraging its onset and its consolidation. We cover a number of important questions. For example, why do some democracies survive—and even thrive—while others revert to dictatorship after only a brief democratic spell? What structural factors are relevant for stable democracy? Does a country have to develop a 'democratic culture' for democracy to emerge and endure? Why do some democracies deteriorate over time? We build our discussion around four key themes: culture and history (Chapter 9), economic factors (Chapter 10), institutions (Chapter 11), and international factors (Chapter 12). We discuss these factors separately, but it is important to note that they frequently interact with one another. For example, countries with high inequality at the time of democratization may create exploitative and inefficient institutions, which subsequently perpetuate or exacerbate existing class divisions, making it hard for democracy to survive.

We also want to emphasize that the factors we discuss in Part III drive movements both toward and away from democracy. In other words, the academic literature has largely treated **democratic consolidation** and **democratic backsliding** as opposite sides of the same coin. For example, high levels of economic development support democracy's development. Low levels of development raise the risk that democracy will fail. For this reason, the factors we discuss in Part III should be understood as *drivers of democracy*—they can strengthen democratic consolidation when they are present or working in the positive, but can weaken it when they are absent or working in a negative direction.

Before delving into the drivers of democracy, we define democratization, democratic consolidation, and democratic backsliding. Each of these foundational concepts have been widely theorized, studied, and tested. Our next discussion, therefore, doesn't even begin to scratch the surface of the scholarship dedicated to these processes. Nonetheless, we briefly lay out the contours of these dynamics. Each of the factors we discuss throughout Part III, to varying degrees, affect a country's prospects of democratization, consolidation, and backsliding.

Democratization

Democratization is a process through which a leadership group takes office following free and fair elections. At the most fundamental level, democratization often occurs because the elite calculate that the costs of suppressing their opponents exceeds the cost of tolerating them. In some cases, the opposition grows strong enough to force the government into a political stalemate, making democratic elections the most viable pathway forward. Democracy can also emerge as a result of elite splits when one portion of the leadership calculates that its interests are best served by liberalizing and ultimately democratizing.

Regardless of how the transition occurs, we emphasize that democratization requires that the authoritarian regime must fail. Moreover, the factors that destabilize the autocracy (the focus of Chapter 7) may not necessarily encourage the subsequent choice to establish democracy. Research suggests, therefore, that these two processes should be thought of as distinct (Kennedy, 2010; Miller, 2012). Democratization should also be distinguished from liberalization. Liberalization consists of any change to a country's political system that make its politics more participatory (high levels of effective enfranchisement) and competitive (a level playing field for the competition). A country can liberalize without democratizing.

Democracy can emerge under a wide range of conditions. Transitions to democracy have followed wars, economic crises that undermined the resources and legitimacy of authoritarian rulers, and peaceful decisions on behalf of the incumbent to step down. It is perhaps unsurprising then, that the academic literature is replete with competing interpretations and disagreements about its causes. Generally speaking, however, the explanations for democratization fall into two broad categories. The first group of explanations emphasizes *structural factors*—conditions like economic development, levels of inequality, or international alliances that make it more likely for democratization to start and succeed. The second approach eschews the possibility of systemic causality and instead views political transitions as highly fluid and contingent processes (O'Donnell and Schmitter, 1986). These theories emphasize the importance of *agency*, including the decisions and actions of elites, mass social movements, and international interventions at the time of transition. We address both types of explanations in Part III of this book, but our focus is predominately on the structural factors that increase a country's likelihood of democratization.

Democratic consolidation

Democratic consolidation is the process that occurs after a democratically-elected government has taken power. Once a country transitions to democracy, what makes democracy persist? History has shown that a vast number of democratic experiments fail. A majority of the democracies that formed from 1955 to 2007, for example, returned to authoritarian rule—usually within twenty years of the onset of democracy (Ulfelder and Woodward, 2010; Svolik, 2008; Svolik, 2015; and see Przeworski et al., 2000; Hadenius and Teorell, 2007; Kapstein and Converse, 2008; Ulfelder and Woodward, 2010). There are several reasons why new democracies are particularly vulnerable to collapse. Holding a free and fair election is relatively straight forward, but it takes far more time to build other effective institutions and routinize desirable patterns of behaviour that make democracy endure. For example, new democracies must establish their general authority with the public, draft new constitutions, establish competitive party systems, reassert civilian control over the military, and deal with other challenges that a legacy of authoritarian rule creates (Huntington, 1995). In this chapter we discuss the factors that increase the prospects of democratic consolidation. But how do we know consolidation has occurred?

The democracies we observe in power fall into two categories: democracies that are not consolidated, where at any moment we might see reversion to dictatorship, and consolidated democracies, where the risk of democratic breakdown is low. Time in office at least partially influences the likelihood of a new democracy becoming an old one. One study finds, for example, that between 1955 and 2003, just seven democracies older than fifteen years reverted to dictatorship (Ulfelder and Lustik, 2007). Time in office matters, in part, because it allows leaders, elite, and other stakeholders to become accustomed to the democratic rules of the game. As Adam Przeworksi famously wrote, 'democracy is consolidated when under given political and economic conditions a particular system of institutions becomes the only game in town' (1991, p. 26).

Identifying when democracy has become 'the only game in town', however, is often difficult and subject to debate. Some scholars have focused on the procedural aspect of consolidation and consider consolidation complete once a country has passed the 'two turnover test', or the completion of two successive peaceful transfers of power through competitive elections. Most scholars, however, recognize that consolidation is a complex process. It typically involves many false starts, misjudgements, detours, and setbacks. For these reasons, many researchers emphasize the importance of behavioural consolidation (Diamond, 1999; Linz and Stepan, 1996). Larry Diamond (1994) defined democratic consolidation as:

> the process by which democracy becomes so broadly and profoundly legitimate among its citizens that it is very unlikely to break down. It involves behavioral and institutional changes that normalize democratic politics and narrow its uncertainty. This normalization requires the expansion of citizen access, development of democratic citizenship and culture, broadening of leadership recruitment and training, and other functions that civil society performs. But most of all, and most urgently, it requires political institutionalization. (p. 15)

At the heart of this definition is the idea that a democracy is consolidated when its odds of failure substantively decline. Indeed, most scholars associate democratic consolidation with a qualitative change in the political process, which in turn greatly improves the odds that a democracy will survive (Acemoglu and Robinson, 2006; O'Donnell et al., 1986; Putnam, 1993; Przeworski, 1991; Rustow, 1970; Weingast, 1997; Diamond, 1999; Svolik, 2008). In the chapters that follow, we examine the factors that research suggests increase the odds that democracy will survive. Some argue that consolidation is dependent on a country's **political culture**, others emphasize the importance of economic distribution, and others highlight the role of the formal structure of government. The chapters to come will arbitrate these varying viewpoints and perspectives.

Democratic backsliding

While the research on democratic consolidation has been vast, there has been relatively less work focused on how democracies erode. The focus on democratic consolidation makes sense in that the uptick in democratization after the Cold War increased interest in understanding what would make these transitions stick. Research on consolidation became particularly salient given the growing propensity for many of the Third Wave democratizers to get 'stuck' somewhere short of full democracy. However, studies examining the reverse process—transitions *from* democracy, or democratic backsliding—have been largely absent (Waldner and Lust, 2018).

In this book, we define democratic backsliding as deterioration in the quality of democracy. It takes place through a series of discrete changes in the rules and informal procedures shaping electoral competition, respect for political and civil liberties, and government accountability (Lust and Waldner, 2015). Many scholars use democratic backsliding to refer to regime change, or outright reversions to autocracy. However, it is important to recognize that democratic backsliding may not necessarily lead to the breakdown of democracy. Instead, democratic backsliding often entails the degradation of citizens' rights and engagement with the state. Understanding democratic backsliding, therefore, requires that we recognize that it can occur in smaller increments or degrees of change than in the case of regime change (Aleman and Yang, 2011; Erdmann, 2011).

Not only does the endpoint of democratic backsliding vary, but the way that democracies deteriorate has changed over time (Bermeo, 2016; Kendall-Taylor and Frantz, 2016). We discuss changes in the way that democracies breakdown at length in Part IV. We note here, however, that the mode of democratic backsliding has changed. Prior to the end of the Cold War, democracies tended to end by rupture—the result of sudden and clear-cut decisions by either military or civilian leaders to suspend the democratic rules of the game and to engineer an immediate transition to authoritarian rule. Today, such sudden and clear-cut breaks with democracy are far less frequent. Instead, democracy is more likely to breakdown at the hands of democratically-elected leaders who very slowly and gradually roll back democracy. The factors we examine in Part III affect the prospects of whether a democracy will consolidate or erode.

Predicting the course of new democracies is a hard. Democratic consolidation is a complex, long-term, and dynamic process. Moreover, many countries defy our best-informed expectations about democracy's durability. Some countries, like Hungary, seem ideally situated to endure, but nonetheless experience significant deterioration in their quality. Other democracies, like Indonesia since the late 1990s, have persisted, despite a very inhospitable political and economic profile. Nonetheless, our goal in Part III is to review the extensive literature and to isolate those factors that seem to have the most explanatory power in determining the deepening and erosion of democracy.

9

Cultural, Social, and Historical Drivers of Democracy

Some observers of Russian politics assert that democracy is unlikely to take root in Russia. They point to the country's lack of positive historical experience with democracy and the population's long-held preference for order and strong, decisive leadership. Likewise, some political analysts have argued that democratic decline in Turkey—which accelerated after a failed coup attempt against Recep Tayyip Erdoğan in 2016—is unsurprising. These observers posit that Turkey's lack of experience with democracy, the prevalence of Islam, and Turkish appreciation for a strong military create 'cultural' preferences that are inhospitable for democracy. But perhaps the most frequently trotted out socio-cultural argument about (the lack of) democracy occurs in reference to Islamic culture in the Middle East. Many commentators have suggested that Islamic traditions and 'Arab exceptionalism' (or historical and economic forces specific to Arab societies, where Muslims constitute a majority) reinforces authoritarianism and precludes democracy (Huntington, 1996; Teorell, 2010).

These types of socio-cultural and historical theories of democracy have held considerable sway in academic and policy circles. In the 1990s, for example, the notion of 'Asian exceptionalism' gained considerable traction as a justification for the persistence of authoritarianism in East Asia. The central premise of Asian exceptionalism was that Asian cultural values were incompatible with democracy. One of the greatest champions of this argument was Singaporean Prime Minister Lee Kuan Yew (1959–90), whose authoritarian style of governance was widely credited with enabling Singapore's exceptional economic transformation. Lee regularly argued that Asian societies lack a concept of the individual in anything like the Western sense (Zakaria, 1994). He and others asserted that Asian values were less supportive of freedom and more concerned with order and discipline than Western values. The uniqueness of Asian cultural values, according to this argument, required these societies to be faithful to their own system of political priorities, which did not include the same adherence to liberal values and human rights found in Western civilizations.

Are these arguments valid? To what extent do culture and history shape a country's prospects for democracy? Do countries have to have certain 'preconditions' present for democracy to emerge?

We examine these questions in this chapter. We begin with a discussion of culture as a driver of democracy. Despite the popularity of cultural theories of democracy, there is little empirical evidence to support them. Next, we highlight that although research does not support the notion that cultural factors *cause* democratization, there is some evidence indicating that culture—as expressed through values, attitudes, and beliefs—affects the *persistence* of stable democracy. Once democracy has emerged (for other more structural reasons) democracy is most likely to deepen and endure where elites gradually adopt a values-based commitment to the rules of the democratic game.

Beyond culture, we also examine in this chapter several historical drivers of democracy. In particular, we focus on the most widely discussed social and historical drivers in the academic literature, including state identity and boundaries, ethnic cleavages, and historical experience with democracy and dictatorship. For each of the drivers, we examine how they influence both democratization and democratic consolidation.

Cultural drivers of democracy

A large body of research has examined whether and how a country's culture and values shape its potential for democratization and democratic consolidation. **Political culture** can be broadly defined as 'a people's predominant beliefs, attitudes, values, sentiments, and evaluations about the political system of its country, and the role of the self in that system' (Diamond, 1994). Theories of political culture seek to explain political outcomes by way of these attitudes, beliefs, norms, and rituals, which are widely shared and have deep emotional resonance (Lust and Waldner, 2015). Culture can produce political outcomes directly by forming political preferences, or indirectly by shaping behaviour like trust and cooperation (or alternatively zero-sum competition) that then affect subsequent outcomes. Because culture cannot be measured directly, scholars generally define political culture as the aggregation of individual attitudes and behaviours within a society or region. They measure these attitudes and behaviours in different ways, including ethnographic observation and surveys of citizens, which they then use as a proxy for culture. In many studies, scholars use survey data to 'operationalize' culture.

Scholars have advanced a number of different arguments about the relationship between culture and democracy. These views range from those that posit that culture exerts no causal power with regard to democracy, to those contending that some cultures and religions are simply incompatible with it (Przeworski, 1998). Scholars in the latter group contend that political culture predetermines political structures and behaviour, and is unlikely to change substantively over time (Almond and Verba, 1963; Inglehart, 1988, 1990). In between these two poles is a 'weakly culturist view' that holds that a democratic culture is required for democracy to emerge and endure, but that *any* society has the potential to develop these preferences and attitudes 'since traditions are malleable, subject to being invented and reinvented' (Dahl et al., 2003, p. 181).

In this section, we review arguments about the relationship between culture and democracy. As this body of literature has progressed, political scientists have gained greater confidence in the assertion that culture is an inadequate explanation for the emergence of democracy. There is relatively more support, however, for the argument that political culture affects the *persistence* of stable democracy. Still, even this view is contested. Supportive public attitudes may facilitate the deepening of democracy, but such attitudes are not a sufficient safeguard. As political developments in countries such as Turkey, Hungary, and Poland suggest, elites can undermine democracy from the top down even when the public retains a favourable attitude toward it.

Culture and the quality of democracy

The central premise of early studies in this field was that a democratic political culture is a requisite for democracy (Lipset, 1959). These scholars argued that the absence of a particular set of public values and beliefs, such as support for the principles of civil liberties and the rule of law, obstruct the emergence of democracy and, if democracy emerged, would prevent democracy from rooting deeply (Diamond et al., 1990). This body of research examined a wide range of factors thought to shape political culture and a country's disposition towards democratic rule. Some early studies, for example, suggested that those cultures that stressed high levels of attachment to the nuclear family were more likely to be authoritarian, whereas cultures that were less obedient were more likely to be democratic (McClelland, 1961; Banfield, 1958). Other research examined the role of religion and argued that Western, mostly Protestant democracies with a focus on individuality functioned better than the Catholic democracies in Latin America, which focused on the intermediating authority of the Church (Lipset, 1959, 1990). A final strand of research focused on cultural traits such as trust, which was considered to be an essential building block of a vibrant **civil society** (Pye and Verba, 1965). This argument posited that a lack of social trust hindered the creation of public organizations that are necessary for democratic development.

In testing these ideas and arguments, many studies unearthed a positive correlation between a 'civic culture' and democraticness (Almond and Verba, 2015; Inglehart, 1988; Putnam, 1994). One of the foundational works in this field was *The Civic Culture,* published by Gabriel Almond and Sidney Verba in 1959 (2015). This was the first study to use cross-national survey data to understand how public attitudes and values affect levels of democracy across countries. Using survey data from the United States, the United Kingdom, Germany, Italy, and Mexico, Almond and Verba found that countries with a **'civic' culture**—defined as high levels of interest in politics, individual and collective engagement in the political process, and respect for the rule of law—are more likely to adopt and sustain democracy over time than are countries without such a civic culture. Subsequent research built on the idea that a civic culture is critical for democracy, but emphasized the importance of citizen preferences for self-expression, which they defined as the belief in one's ability to influence political decisions (Inglehart, 1988; Inglehart and Welzel, 2005). According to Ronald Inglehart, democracy is not attained or reinforced solely by making changes to institutions or through elite pacts; its 'survival depends also on the values and beliefs of ordinary citizens' (2000, p. 96).

Despite the allure of such arguments, many political scientists are sceptical that culture is a driver of democracy. Political scientists have identified three general concerns with these arguments and research. First, political culture changes very gradually over time. As a result, many political scientists find cultural explanations too slow-moving to satisfactorily explain the political changes that give rise to, or undercut, democracy (Conroy-Krutz and Frantz, 2017). In other words, because culture tends to be static it is difficult to see how it explains the emergence of democracy in a given country at a given time.

This is not to say that culture does not change. As the 'weakly culturist' camp argues, cultural attitudes toward democracy can gradually shift over time. The reorientation of the Catholic Church's position on democracy underscores this point. Catholicism was long regarded as culturally antithetical to democracy. Catholicism emphasized vertical bonds of authority, which fuelled **clientelism**, and was seen as centralized, hierarchical, and hostile to dissent. Scholars highlighted differences between the development of democracy in North America (highly Protestant) and the prevalence of authoritarianism in Latin America (predominately Catholic) as evidence of their claims (Lipset and Lakin, 2004). The Third Wave, however, discredited this conventional wisdom given the numerous democratic transitions that occurred in Catholic countries, including in Southern Europe and Latin America. Many scholars, including Huntington, credited the Catholic Church's evolving stance on social justice and human rights as facilitating the spread of civic 'values' and, hence, democracy. In the 1960s, the Second Vatican council joined intellectuals and activists among the ordinary clergy and laity in endorsing democratic structures and the principle of religious freedom for all. Since that time, Catholic Popes have promoted democracy as a protector of human rights (Philpott, 2004). The role of religious organizations in democratization is discussed further in Box 9.1.

In sum, cultural elites can change the direction of cultural values, but even so such changes are typically so slow that it is hard to show that they were the specific cause of political change in a given country at a particular time.

 Box 9.1: **Religious organizations and democratization**

In a number of dictatorships, religious organizations played an important role in bringing about democratization. The Catholic Church applied pressure on Poland's authoritarian government to democratize in the 1980s. Religious groups also played a role in democratization in several countries in Africa. Catholic bishops wrote a letter to long-time autocrat Hastings Banda of Malawi critical of his rule, just prior to his stepping down from power. Though Zimbabwe remains authoritarian, the Council of Churches initiated a National Constitutional Assembly which led to the Zimbabwean government's defeat in the first post-independence referendum in 1997 (Dorman, 2002).

At the same time, there are also instances of religious organizations that choose to support the authoritarian status quo. While the Catholic Church in Chile was a defender of human rights, the

Catholic Church in Argentina legitimized the military dictatorship and was complicit in its human rights violations. In Brazil, the Church made a deal with the military and remained silent amid abuses, only speaking out against them in the latter stages of military rule. In Uruguay, as well, the Church spoke out initially, but soon afterwards was silenced (Goldfrank and Rowell, 2012). Likewise, in South Africa, the Catholic Church included among its higher ranks supporters and perpetrators of apartheid. It also failed to support Archbishop Desmond Tutu in his bid to win international sanctions against the regime (De Gruchy, 2005).

Given the opposing roles that religious organizations have played in supporting democracy, can we make any generalizations about the role of the church and democratization? Research suggests that a key factor influencing whether religious organizations will help or hinder democratization is the autonomy of the church from the state (Philpott, 2007). Where religious groups are autonomous from the government—meaning the church maintains its authority over the choice of its officials, to set its policies, and carry out its activities—they are more likely to criticize repressive governments and work towards undermining them. Where, instead, they are dependent on the regime for resources and/or need it to maintain privileged positions, they may be more likely to turn a blind eye to abusive governments.

Another common criticism of cultural explanations is that it is difficult to establish the direction of causality (Coppedge, 2012; Hadenius and Teorell, 2005). Is it that certain cultures or historical experiences produce attitudes and values that are conducive to democracy? Or is it the experience of living in democracy that gradually engenders those attitudes and values? Several studies note the correlation between democratic values and democraticness but argue that these values are an outcome of democracy, not the cause of it (Hadenius and Teorell, 2005; Jackman and Miller, 1996; Dahlum and Knutsen, 2017). One study argues that the presence of most civic attitudes does not have a significant impact on subsequent changes in levels of democracy (Muller and Seligson, 1994). They find that measures of civic culture like interpersonal trust are, instead, a product of a country's experience with democracy. The reality is likely a combination of both views: attitudes can influence democratic political behaviour, and democratic structures, in turn, can influence attitudes (Almond, 1990).

Finally, the more deterministic cultural arguments are often criticized on methodological grounds. For example, scholars often highlight that studies documenting correlations between specific historical or cultural traits and levels of democracy exclude some unobserved factor that actually drives the result, such as high levels of development or elite bargaining (Coppedge, 2012). The idea is that once you take these factors into account, the strong correlation between cultural/historical factors and democracy would disappear. Similarly, the mechanisms or pathways through which historical and cultural explanations affect democratic outcomes are often underdeveloped in the research (Conroy-Krutz and Frantz, 2017). Further complicating matters, some scholars question whether survey-based measurement of individual psychological attitudes—the most common ways these studies are operationalized—is a valid measure of culture to begin with (Lust and Waldner, 2015).

In sum, the most widely accepted accounts of the emergence of democracy are not cultural. Instead, political scientists are much more supportive of the structural accounts we discuss throughout Part III, including changes in economic, institutional, and international structures. In fact, many political science scholars explicitly reject the idea that there must be a prior consensus on democratic values among the elite and people for a democratic transition to occur. Although mass demands for democracy and opposition strength shape the choices that elites face, the emergence of democracy often stems from the strategic choices of a relatively small number of political actors (Diamond, 1994).

Culture and the persistence of democracy

Although research does not support the notion that cultural factors influence whether democracy will emerge, there is some evidence indicating that culture affects the *persistence* of stable democracy. The central argument in this literature is that once democracy has emerged (for other more structural reasons) it is most likely to deepen and endure where both elites and the people gradually adopt greater commitment to the rules of the democratic game. Research by Michael Burton, Richard Gunter, and John Higley (1992), for example, argues that authoritarianism will be more likely to give way to stable democracy where there is gradual acceptance by 'major dissidents and hostile elites' of the legitimacy of a democratic political system (in Diamond 1994, p. 5). Larry Diamond similarly notes, 'we observe during democratic consolidation the emergence of an elite political culture featuring moderation, accommodation, restrained partisanship, system loyalty, and trust' (p. 5).

In addition to normative change at the elite level, research on democratic consolidation also focuses on the attitudes of the people. These studies emphasize that the attitudes, beliefs, and behaviour of citizens shape prospects for stable democracy. This research underscores, in particular, the importance of legitimacy. When citizens view a democratic political system as legitimate, democracy is more likely to endure. Legitimacy can be generated in part through a democracy's performance over time. Those governments that deliver on citizen expectations of economic performance and stability, especially in the immediate aftermath of a transition from authoritarianism, are likely to be perceived as legitimate. In addition to this **'performance legitimacy'**, governments also derive legitimacy from their ability to acquire and exercise political power in a way that accords with citizen values regarding the content of particular laws, rules and customs (Gilley, 2006). Bruce Gilley (2006) argues that this type of **'cultural' legitimacy** aids the durability of democracy in several ways. Governments that are perceived as legitimate are able to inspire citizens' compliance, which allows them to spend less on coercion. In contrast, elite doubts about legitimacy undermine self-esteem, which creates splits that accelerate the breakdown of regimes.

The historical record shows, however, that many democracies endure even amid low levels of such legitimacy or positive public support for the regime. Some studies have highlighted, therefore, that while the legitimacy of the system matters, so too does the presence of viable alternatives to the incumbent government. Even if citizens do not view their government as legitimate, the government may nonetheless persist if there is not another option for citizens to back. Richard Rose and William Mishler (1998), for example, examine the effect of citizen attitudes on democratic development using survey data across a number of post-Communist societies. They found that democracy was most durable when citizens not only viewed democracy as the best form of government, but when citizens determined that their own democracy was preferable to the alternatives, even considering the failures and shortcomings of the current system. In other words, democracies will only last if citizens view their system as a better form of governance than the autocratic alternatives.

In addition to legitimacy, research has also highlighted the importance of a civic culture for sustaining a vibrant and durable democracy. Civic culture generates **social capital**—that is, the ability for individuals to cooperate and function effectively within groups—which facilitates the collective action needed for a healthy democracy. The notion that participatory cultures are more prone to sustain democracy stems from the ideas of Alexis de Tocqueville, who observed in the early nineteenth century that U.S. citizens had a proclivity to join civic associations. So-called 'neo-Tocquevillians' subsequently argued that societies that are association-orientated tend to have higher levels of social capital, which in turn facilitates trust in fellow citizens, which in turn creates conditions conducive to democracy. In particular, if citizens have the capacity to organize in groups, they will be better positioned to challenge powerful actors and pressure for democracy.

Much research has built on the early ideas of Tocqueville and underscored the importance of participation and social capital for sustaining democracy. In his classic study, 'The Social Requisites of Democracy', Seymour Lipset noted that 'the chances for stable democracy are enhanced to the extent that groups and individuals have a number of cross-cutting, politically relevant affiliations' (1960, pp. 88–9). Decades later, influential research by Robert Putnam (1993, 2000) showed that higher levels of associational activity in Northern as compared to Southern Italy helped explain why democracy in the north not merely endured but outperformed democracy in the south. According to Putnam, group membership—whether in political associations or bowling clubs—creates social capital that builds norms of social trust. Social trust, in turn, facilitates coordination and cooperation that is needed for a 'democratic' approach to the satisfaction of popular demands. The implication is that citizen membership in groups such as sports clubs, cooperatives, mutual aid societies, cultural associations, and voluntary unions can improve the performance and survival of democratic regimes.

Despite the attractiveness of these ideas, however, recent research has shown that social capital and citizen participation do not automatically translate into sustainable democracies. On the contrary, there are many forms of 'uncivil society' in which governments channel high levels of citizen participation toward undemocratic or illiberal ends and in ways that sustain authoritarian rule (Jamal, 2009; Rossteutscher, 2010; Jamal and Nooruddin, 2010). For example one study notes that the Weimar Germany was marked by high levels of involvement in civil society (Berman, 1997a). Rather than promote democracy, as neo-Tocquevillian theory would predict, however, Berman demonstrates how the Nazis leveraged pre-existing, apolitical organizations to control and undermine democracy. Other researchers have echoed this point, noting that some civil society groups organize violence and promote hate speech (Varshney, 2001). In these cases, social capital allows groups to reach new audiences and more effectively pursue their objectives, but those objectives may be inimical to open and tolerant democratic norms and practices.

One final caveat to our discussion on the importance of citizen support for democratic government and civic participation is that these factors, on their own, are not sufficient guardrails for democracy. As we will discuss at length in Chapter 14, the way that democracies are failing is changing. Today, leaders are coming to power in free and fair elections and then taking gradual steps to dismantle democratic constraints on executive power. In many cases, democratic backsliding is occurring in countries with relatively robust civil society sectors, such as in Poland, and in countries where elected leaders have strong public support, such as in Hungary under Prime Minister Viktor Orbán. Although citizens in these countries may view electoral politics and democracy as the best form of government, elite actors have still been able to weaken democratic institutions and norms from the top down.

In the next section, we turn our attention to discuss a number of social and historical factors that influence a country's prospects for democracy.

 Box 9.2: **Women and democracy**

The level of women's political empowerment and access to leadership across the globe has steadily and significantly improved. According to the Varieties of Democracy (**V-Dem**) dataset, women have seen improvements in a number of areas, including the number of female journalists, property rights for women, and how power is distributed by gender. The number of female parliamentarians has seen an especially significant increase. Currently, 23.8 per cent of parliaments around the world are filled by women. In 1998, by comparison, the global average was 12.7 per cent. The voting gap between men and women has also shrunk considerably such that it is now almost insignificant (Coffé and Bolzendahl, 2010). Likewise, women are also just as likely as men to sign a petition or donate to a political campaign. However, gender gaps persist in other types of political participation. Men are more likely to engage in collective forms of political participation such as going on strike, demonstrating, and contacting political officials and party members (Inglehart and Norris, 2003; Marien et al., 2010). And men still dominate political parties and ballot lists. In fact, only 15 per cent of the world's population lives in societies where political power is evenly distributed between genders. It is also important to note that the data suggest that the progress that women have made has begun to plateau. The V-Dem data show that 2017 was the first year in seventy years that the global level of women's political inclusion and empowerment did not improve.[1]

IMPACT OF FEMALE POLITICAL PARTICIPATION

Studies demonstrate that a larger presence of women in parliament translates into a host of positive outcomes. More female parliamentarians in Africa, for example, led to high levels of female political participation and engagement (Barnes and Burchard, 2013). Likewise, research in

[1] By political inclusion and empowerment, the dataset examines civil liberties for women, and women's civil society and political participation (such as voting and collective action).

Scandinavia found that greater representation of women in parliaments improved gender equality and the quality of democracy (Sainsbury, 2001). Beyond enhancing women's rights, greater levels of female participation in government also leads to increases in spending for health care, education, and other family and social policies (Bolzendahl and Brooks, 2007; Childs and Withey, 2004; Karam and Lovenduski, 2005) and lower levels of corruption (Dollar et al., 2001). In Rwanda, which has the highest percentage of women in parliament, issues such as education and healthcare are now raised more easily and more frequently than before (Devlin and Elgie, 2008). Likewise, there is evidence that a greater number of female council leaders in villages in West Bengal, India led to higher education levels for girls and better outcomes for girls (Beaman et al., 2012).

Women's participation also can play an important role in conflict prevention and resolution, as experiences in Liberia and Sierra Leone illustrate (Adebajo, 2002). Consistent with this, the UN notes that conflict-afflicted countries have very low levels of women in parliament and ministerial positions compared to the world average (Kumalo, 2015). For these reasons, there is increasingly greater support for involving women in peacebuilding (Chinkin and Charlesworth, 2006).

WOMEN'S RIGHTS AND DEMOCRACY

Many studies have examined the important relationship between women's rights and democratization (Wang et al., 2017). A dataset that examined the state of democracy in 177 countries from 1900 to 2012 revealed that democratization was more likely to occur when governments afforded greater rights to both men and women (For more on the best and worst countries for women in parliament, see Tables 9.2 and 9.3). Women's civil liberties are particularly important because they enable women to organize during the transition process, which has been historically important in sparking protests in initial phases of democratization. Greater women's rights, including freedom to move, discuss politics, and to hold material and immaterial assets—is also critical to the establishment of electoral democracy (Wang et al., 2017).

On the flip side, countries that democratize also have higher levels of female representation over time (Fallon et al., 2012). Greater levels of freedom of speech and assembly have led to higher levels of political participation in Ghana, for example. A shift from one-party to multi-party elections also leads to greater levels of participation by women (Tripp, 2001). Not surprisingly, the most democratic countries in the world are the most gender inclusive. As Table 9.1 demonstrates, Scandinavian countries stand out for their inclusiveness and the quality of their democracies, whereas countries in the Middle East are far less gender inclusive and also far more authoritarian.

Table 9.1 Women in national parliaments

Women in national parliaments	1998	2008	2018
Global average	12.7%	18.2%	23.8%
Nordic countries	36.7%	41.4%	41.4%
Americas	15.4%	21.6%	28.9%
Europe (including Nordic countries)	15%	19.3%	27.6%
Europe (excluding Nordic countries)	12.7%	19.3%	26.3%
Asia	14.1%	18.3%	19.8%
Africa	11.4%	17.1%	23.7%
Arab States	3.5%	9.7%	18%

Table 9.2 25 best countries for women in national parliaments[2]

Country	Lower House %	Upper House %
Rwanda	61.3%	38.5%
Cuba	53.2%	N/A
Bolivia	53.1%	47.2%
Mexico	48.2%	49.2%
Sweden	47.3%	N/A
Namibia	46.2%	23.8%
Costa Rica	45.6%	N/A
Nicaragua	44.6%	N/A
South Africa	42.7%	35.2%
Senegal	41.8%	N/A
Finland	41.5%	N/A
Spain	41.1%	36.8%
Norway	40.8%	N/A
New Zealand	40%	N/A
Timor-Leste	40%	N/A
France	39.7%	32.2%
Mozambique	39.6%	N/A
Argentina	38.8%	41.7%
Ethiopia	38.8%	32%
North Macedonia	38.3%	N/A
Iceland	38.1%	N/A
Belgium	38%	43.3%
Ecuador	38%	N/A
Serbia	37.7%	N/A
Denmark	37.4%	N/A

Table 9.3 25 worst countries for women in national parliaments[3]

Country	Lower House %	Upper House %
Papua New Guinea	0%	N/A
Yemen	0.3%	2.7%
Oman	1.2%	16.5%
Haiti	2.5%	3.6%
Kuwait	4.6%	N/A
Lebanon	4.7%	N/A
Sri Lanka	5.3%	N/A
Thailand	5.4%	N/A
Nigeria	5.6%	6.4%
Iran	5.9%	N/A

[2] For countries over one million in population.
[3] For countries over one million in population.

Country	Lower House %	Upper House %
Benin	7.2%	N/A
Central African Republic	8.6%	N/A
Mali	8.8%	N/A
Belize	9.4%	15.4%
Botswana	9.5%	N/A
Qatar	9.8%	N/A
Japan	10.2%	20.7%
Gambia	10.3%	N/A
Democratic Republic of Congo	10.3%	4.6%
Cote d'Ivoire	11%	12.1%
Myanmar	11.3%	12.1%
Congo	11.3%	18.8%
Ukraine	11.6%	N/A
Mauritius	11.6%	N/A
Sierra Leone	12.3%	N/A

Social and historical drivers of democracy

In addition to culture, several social and historical factors that are related to culture—namely state identity and boundaries, ethnic cleavages, and past experience with democracy and dictatorship—also influence a country's prospects for democratization and the consolidation of democracy. We discuss the relationship between each of these factors and democracy in what follows.

State boundaries, citizen identity, and democracy

In his seminal study published forty years ago, Dankwart Rustow (1970) argued that democracy is unlikely to develop and thrive if the public and elite cannot agree on the boundaries of the state. Robert Dahl (1989) reached the same conclusion emphasizing that democratic consolidation is not possible without an agreement on the proper boundaries of a political unit. In addition to consensus over geographic boundaries, agreement over whom—or what groups—constitute the state is also critical for establishing conditions conducive to democracy. In their influential work on democratic consolidation, Juan Linz and Alfred Stepan (1996) reinforce the importance of these dynamics for democracy, arguing;

> in a modern polity, free and authoritative elections cannot be held, winners cannot exercise the monopoly of legitimate force, and citizens cannot effectively have their rights protected by a rule of law unless a state exists. In some parts of the world, conflicts about the authority and domain of the polis and the identities and loyalties of the demos are so intense that no state exists. No state, no democracy. (p. 14)

Put simply, disagreements over borders, secession, or which groups should be considered part of the nation make stable democracy unlikely to emerge and difficult to sustain.

Consensus about political boundaries and the formation of groups that share a common identity facilitate democracy because such agreement makes it easier for people to mobilize in large numbers to demand more rights from the state. In other words, such consensus facilitates the collective action needed to agitate for democratic rules and norms. A state's inability to exert its authority throughout its territory or disputes over which groups count as citizens obstruct the state from effectively providing public goods for everyone, leading people to grow dissatisfied with the 'output' of democracy. In extreme cases, the exclusion of groups creates incentives for the political losers or the military to violate or terminate the rules of the game, directly threatening democratic survival and political order. Thus, democracy is unlikely to consolidate if there is contestation over the borders of the state and membership in the nation.

We briefly discuss two factors—ethnic heterogeneity and colonial legacies—that research has discussed as potentially complicating boundary drawing and the determination of political membership. These two factors pose challenges for democratic consolidation.

Ethnic cleavages

A number of political observers have noted that establishing and maintaining democracy in ethnically fragmented countries is more difficult than in homogenous ones (Linz and Stepan, 1996; Diamond, 2015). Political theorist Robert Dahl, for example, worried that high levels of ethnic diversity would make democracy less likely, particularly in countries where one ethnic group can plausibly aspire to dominate a state. Writing in the wake of the Soviet Union's collapse, political scientist Donald Horowitz argued that the democratic trajectory of countries in the region were shaped by the diversity of each country. Democracy progressed furthest where there were few serious **ethnic cleavages**, such as in Hungary, the Czech Republic, and Poland, and more slowly or not at all in more deeply divided societies, such as Bulgaria, Romania, and the former Yugoslavia. Freedom House President Adrian Karatnycky captured the sentiment of this perspective when he concluded in 2002 that, 'democracy has been significantly more successful in mono-ethnic societies than in ethnically divided and multi-ethnic societies' (Karatnycky, 2002, p. 107). But why might these cleavages have such an adverse effect on democracy?

First, some scholars contend that ethnic divisions create political incentives that favour an autocratic status quo, thereby thwarting the emergence of democracy (Lijphart, 1977; Dahl, 1971; Rabushka and Shepsle, 1972; Horowitz, 1993). The idea is that ethnic differences divide society, often privileging one ethnic group over others, making compromise and consensus difficult. As Donald Horowitz (1993) explains:

> democracy is about inclusion and exclusion, about access to power, about the privileges that go with inclusion and the penalties that accompany exclusion. In severely divided societies, ethnic identity provides clear lines to determine who will be included and who will be excluded. Since the lines appear unalterable, being in and being out may quickly come to look permanent. (p. 18)

In ethnically exclusive autocracies, incumbent powers will be resistant to changes that have the potential to bring their ethnic opponents to power. Even ethnic-minority opponents of the incumbent regime may oppose democratization out of fear that changes to the status quo could leave them worse off.

The incentive to resist democratization may be particularly strong in those autocracies that are governed by a minority ethnic group. For the ruling minority group, the costs of democratization are extremely high. Democratization threatens the existing order and puts at risk the minority group's status within society, the division of wealth, opportunities for education, cultural expression, chances for upward mobility, the representation of interests within the state, and even how citizenship is defined (Beissinger, 2008). Syria serves as a sobering example of this dynamic. Since Hafez al-Assad took power in 1970, Syria has been dominated by the Alawites, a group that comprises just 11 per cent of the Syrian population. The Alawites historically had been repressed under Ottoman rule. Under French rule, however, the Alawites rose to prominence in the army when the colonial administration used divide-and-rule tactics to control Syria. The French encouraged the Alawites to join the Syrian armed forces to serve as a counterweight to the Sunni majority, which was much more hostile to French rule. This minority–majority dynamic and the al-Assad family's desire to protect the future fate of the Alawite minority is one factor contributing to Bashar al-Assad's violent and ruthless resolve to cling to power and crush any 'democratic' opposition to his regime.

 Box 9.3: **Civic versus exclusionary nationalism**

In a speech to French lawmakers in July 2018, French President Emmanuel Macron identified rising nationalism as a top challenge for France and the European Union. Just months earlier he addressed the U.S. Congress warning of the dangers of pursuing a nationalist agenda. Macron's comments echo the concerns of many observers who view the rise of nationalism—evident in examples such as U.S. President Trump's 'make America great again' slogan, Turkish President Erdoğan's strident Islamic nationalism, and India's influential radical *Hindutva* (Hindu nationalist) groups—as dangerous to democracy. While it is true that leaders have harnessed nationalism to undermine democracy—often violently—research also shows that nationalism can be *beneficial* to democracy. This research emphasizes that not all nationalism is alike. It comes in different forms, namely civic nationalism and exclusionary nationalism, each with very different consequences for democracy. We discuss these two types of nationalism here.

When we think about nationalism, we are most likely to think of **exclusionary nationalism**—a form of nationalism that excludes minority groups that do not share common bonds, often on the basis of race, religion, or culture. Exclusionary nationalism has posed challenges for democratic rule in a number of places. In the past, governments in Romania, Serbia, and Slovakia, for example, capitalized on perceived threats from national minorities to promote exclusionary policies and legitimize regime closure (Snyder and Vachudova, 1997). More recently, Fidesz in Hungary has used nationalism to justify efforts to monopolize control over politics. Exclusionary nationalism can also help sustain dictatorship, as exemplified by authoritarians such as Russian President Putin and the Chinese Communist Party.

While exclusionary nationalism can be detrimental to democracy, **civic nationalism** can aid democratic development (Ipperciel, 2007; Wimmer, 2018). Civic nationalism is based on citizenship and appeals to principles and universal values, such as freedom and equality. Research by Andreas Wimmer suggests that this brand of nationalism is most likely to emerge when governments are able to reach across regional and ethnic divides to 'integrate ethnic majorities and minorities into an inclusive power arrangement' (Wimmer, 2018, p. 1). Three factors can facilitate the creation of such inclusive political alliances: a government's ability to provide public goods equally across the country, which builds support for the national government rather than leaders of ethnic communities; the presence of an established civil society early in the nation building process, which allows the government to leverage the sector's diverse networks to broaden its political support; and a shared medium of communication, so that people can easily talk or write to one another (Wimmer, 2018). Civic nationalism can serve as a 'glue' that binds citizens together, as they work in concert in the pursuit of a common good.

Unfortunately, the surge of nationalism we see today is predominantly exclusionary. In Europe, for example, nationalism is deeply intertwined with populism as ethnic nationalists 'mine race and history to create a politics that sacrifices individual liberty to the will of the majority' (The Economist).[4] These nationalist currents are creating strong headwinds for democracy today. Moreover, the effects of today's nationalism are being felt beyond domestic politics, shaping external relations between states. This new nationalism paints international affairs in pessimistic and zero-sum terms, portraying global interests as being in competition with national ones. If this type of nationalism continues to gain traction, it could not only threaten democracy, but also raise the risk of inter-state conflict.

Second, ethnic divisions not only obstruct the onset of democracy, but once democracy emerges these fissures make democracy difficult to sustain. At a fundamental level, ethnic heterogeneity creates tension between state building and democratization (Brubaker, 1996). State building entails efforts through which leaders seek to create a state that is 'of and for' the nation. In homogenous societies there is less conflict between state building and democratization because most of a state's population identifies with one subjective idea of the nation (Linz and Stepan, 1996). In more ethnically diverse societies, in contrast, ethnic divisions complicate politics by making it more difficult for a multitude of groups to reach a consensus about the fundamentals of a democratic system.

Rigid ethnic cleavages also make democracy difficult to sustain because they create natural fault lines that opportunistic politicians can activate to advance their own political ambitions. In divided societies, political parties and other organizations coalesce more readily around ethnic than other identities. Political entrepreneurs therefore have an incentive to play on such divisions to facilitate their consolidation of power. These leaders can instigate an 'us versus them' narrative as a means to gain popular legitimacy. Political competition in fragmented democratic countries, in other words, has the potential to devolve into a process of 'ethnic outbidding' as leaders seek to maximize support and legitimacy from voters in their respective ethnic in-group (Rabushka and Shepsle, 1972).

This form of exclusionary ethnic nationalism raises the risk of instability and civil war—factors that bode poorly for democracy. Research published by Central Intelligence

---

[4] https://www.economist.com/christmas-specials/2017/12/19/whither-nationalism (accessed 7 June 2019).

Agency's Political Instability Task Force supports the notion that, unlike 'inclusive' cultures, sharply polarized societies are at greater risk of such instability. The Task Force shows that weak democracies (closest to what we have called electoral democracies) *with political factionalism*—defined as a pattern of sharply polarized and uncompromising competition between blocs pursuing parochial interests at the national level—are the most unstable of any other regime type (Goldstone et al., 2010). The authors find that these weak democracies have relative odds of instability over thirty times greater than for full autocracies, other things being equal, and elevated risk for the onset of civil wars and adverse regime changes. Although not explicitly about a country's ethnic makeup, the zero-sum political competition that such polarization captures is often centred on ethnic and religious divisions. In sum, ethnic and religious polarization raises the risk of instability and violence, and this can quickly undermine the open politics associated with democracy (see also Montalvo and Reynal-Querol, 2005).

Despite the long-held belief that ethnic cleavages are bad for democracy, some scholars have argued that it is not ethnic diversity *itself* that is inherently bad for democracy (Fish and Brooks, 2004; Beissinger, 2008). Rather, it is the deliberate politicization of exclusionary cultural cleavages and deliberate efforts to delegitimize cultural differences that hurts democratic prospects. Ethnic diversity may also affect democratization's chances *indirectly*, by interacting with and influencing other factors that dim democracy's prospects such as lowering economic growth and governmental performance, weakening civil society, or altering institutional design. Research has shown, for example, that ethnic fractionalization leads governments to spend less on public goods (Alesina et al., 1999) and is a key factor accounting for slow growth in Africa (Easterly and Levine, 1997). When governments spend less on public goods and produce suboptimal growth outcomes, democratic governance can fall short of citizen expectations, leading to less public support for democracy.

Understanding if ethnic cleavages have a direct or indirect effect on democracy is not just an academic question. If it is not ethnic fragmentation itself that undermines democracy, then there may be institutional solutions and other types of interventions that can mitigate ethnic heterogeneity's negative effects on things such as growth and government performance, raising the prospect for democracy. Moreover, if ethnic heterogeneity itself is not responsible for poor political outcomes, it also discredits an argument made by many a dictator seeking to justify repressive rule. Indeed, few excuses for authoritarianism are trotted out more frequently than the claim that factionalized societies need a strong hand to preserve the peace.

In sum, ethnic and religious polarization complicate democracy, but more research is needed to determine the mechanisms through which these divisions influence democratization and democratic consolidation.

Legacies of colonialism

Colonial legacies are the second factors that can complicate boundary drawing and the determination of political membership. Indeed, some empirical research suggests that countries once occupied by a colonial power face long-lasting diminished prospects for democracy (Bernhard et al., 2004). This is in part because colonialism often amplified ethnic polarization making it especially difficult for governments to reach national consensus on the identity of the citizenry as well as national boundaries. These effects were especially pronounced in countries colonized by European powers, especially in Africa. Until the twentieth century, borders in Africa were highly fluid and political systems were diverse. The Berlin Conference of 1884–85 further accelerated the 'scramble for Africa' as the major European powers including France, Great Britain, and to a lesser extent Spain, Germany, Belgium, Italy, and Portugal raced to expand their influence on the continent. National borders were drawn to suit the needs of the colonial powers, negating the realities of African identities and autonomous African perceptions of the world (Prah, 2004, p. 6). According to Larry Diamond, 'some large ethnic groups were split between colonial states, while others with little in common, save in some instances a history of warfare and enmity, were drawn together into the new state boundaries'.

In many countries, colonial powers also pursued policies that deliberately amplified ethnic divisions. To maintain control over indigenous populations, colonial powers often used **divide and rule policies**, which heightened ethnic identities. Colonial powers also established a form of exclusionary politics in which a very narrow coalition of ethnic elites controlled access to state structures and resources. These 'divide and rule' tactics set in motion many of the ethnic dynamics we referenced in our previous discussion of ethnic heterogeneity, including sowing the seeds of the internal conflicts that make democracy more difficult to establish and sustain. Through these interactions, colonial powers often built or reinforced an extensive system of ethnically based patron-client networks that continue to serve as an important aspect of politics in many post-colonial countries (Berman, 1998).

In addition to complicating the settlement of boundaries and a consensus over who constitutes the state, the legacy of colonialism affects a country's prospects for democracy through three additional pathways: economic development, the relationship between the state and civil society, and the quality of institutions. We discuss these three drivers of democracy in other parts of the book, but we wish to briefly note here that colonialism has an indirect and lasting effect on a country's prospects for democracy. Empirical research shows, for example, that colonialism is associated with underdevelopment (Frank, 2018). Low levels of devolvement, in turn, can hamper a country's prospects of developing and sustaining democracy.

In the final section of this chapter, we discuss how a country's prior experience with democracy and dictatorship matters for its future prospects for democratization and consolidation. As you will see, time under democracy can make it more likely to re-emerge in the future. However, certain aspects of authoritarian rule often endure well beyond a democratic transition and can complicate consolidation.

Previous experience with democracy and dictatorship

Time under democracy

In assessing the probability of democratization and democratic consolidation, some scholars posit that a country's previous experience with democracy matters (Donno and Russett, 2004). As Samuel Huntington (1991) argued, 'longer and more recent experience with democracy is more conducive than is a shorter and more distant one' (pp. 270–1). Of the countries that transitioned to democracy during the **Third Wave**, for example, those with prior democratic experience have generally been more stable than those that had to construct democratic institutions for the first time. The empirical evidence supports these arguments. Prior experience with democracy facilitates democracy down the road (Escriba-Folch and Wright, 2015).

Why might having prior experience with democracy raise a country's future prospects for returning to and sustaining it? Importantly, earlier experience with democracy reduces uncertainty about the new regime, thus mitigating anxiety among elites that are wary about what democracy may bring. Democratic interludes also frequently leave in place institutional foundations that re-democratizing states can leverage. For example, judicial precedents may exist for interpreting the constitution and restraining executive power. Those in the security sector may have experience upholding the rule of law and protecting civil liberties. And local governments and autonomous agencies may be better prepared to help new democracies make the transition because they have done it before. Even in those cases where incumbent government officials did not have direct experience serving in the previous democracy, time under democracy can instill norms like accommodation and compromise that sustain democracy once it re-emerges. In sum, previous experience with democracy raises a country's prospects for re-democratization and facilitates democratic consolidation because these countries do not have to start the process from scratch.

Uruguay's experience highlights how previous experience with democracy can facilitate the re-emergence and consolidation of democracy (Higley and Gunther, 1992). Uruguay had long been one of the most stable democracies in Latin America. The country's two main political parties, the Blancos and Colorados, competed and alternated in power for decades. In 1973, however, Uruguay's military defied expectations about the stability of consolidated democracy and seized control in a military coup that ushered in twelve years of military rule. Uruguay's long experience with democracy, however, created inhospitable soil for authoritarianism. Many citizens viewed the military regime as illegitimate, for example, hindering the regime's ability to institutionalize its rule (Diamond, 1994). The Blancos and Colorados continued to operate in opposition and, along with other institutions that persisted from the democratic period like trade unions and social movements, they continued to press the military regime to reinstate democracy. In 1984, Uruguay transitioned back to democracy and the country's democratic foundations paved the way for a relatively smooth transition. Tellingly, Uruguay has remained democratic since it re-established democracy.

Authoritarian legacies

In addition to prior experience with democracy, a country's experience with authoritarianism or autocracy can also shape its prospects for democracy. There are several pathways through which a country's authoritarian legacy can persist and influence the quality of democracy in a newly transitioned regime. For example, citizens in weak or dysfunctional democracies occasionally grow nostalgic for their time under authoritarian rule. Such nostalgia is most likely to emerge when the new democracy is unable to meet citizens' economic expectations, especially if people remember the autocratic period as being relatively more prosperous. Studies of Eastern Europe, for example, have shown that many people remain nostalgic about the authoritarian past (Neundorff et al., 2017). They associate the authoritarian period with stability, predictability, security, and employment. Such sympathy for authoritarianism makes citizens less willing to stand up to elite transgressions or other threats to the new democracy, which can degrade democratic quality over time.

Another pathway through which a country's authoritarian legacy can influence the sustainability of the democracy that follows it is through the persistence of **authoritarian enclaves**. Authoritarian enclaves are durable pockets of authoritarian practice at odds with the democratic regime's political norms (Gilley, 2010; Magaloni and Sanchez, 2006). Authoritarian enclaves may emerge within institutions such as the military, legislature, or courts or through social actors not fully willing to adhere to democratic rules (Garretón Merino, 1995; Magaloni, 2006). While authoritarian enclaves can be found at the national level, they are also prevalent at sub-national levels of government, particularly in rural areas (Montero, 2010). For example, local leaders may choose not to enforce the rule of law in their jurisdiction, compromise the secret ballot, or take advantage of fiscal resources to build clientelist networks.

The persistence of authoritarian enclaves tends to be most problematic in those countries emerging from military dictatorship. Empirical research by Milan Svolik (2008) underscores this dynamic by showing that new democracies with a military past are the most likely to backslide. More specifically, he shows that a military past has a large, negative, and independent effect on the persistence of authoritarian enclaves and, thus, a democracy's susceptibility to reversals. Other scholars have similarly noted that a military legacy is particularly bad for democracy (Cheibub, 2007). Initially, this finding might appear to contradict empirical research we discussed in Chapter 3 that showed that military regimes are the most likely type of dictatorship to transition to democracy. However, these two findings are not inconsistent. Instead, the research suggests that military regimes are both the most likely to transition to democracy *and* to face significant challenges in consolidating and deepening democracy once it emerges.

Military rule poses a particular challenge for democratic consolidation because the military often maintains substantial bargaining power in particular 'enclaves' within the new democracy. The military uses its influence to ensure that safeguards are in place to protect its financial interests, autonomy from civilian leaders, and immunity from prosecution. Where it can, the military may also seek to dictate who can run for office and hold important cabinet positions that shape the types of policies that are implemented.

The case of Chile illustrates how a legacy of military rule, enduring in particular enclaves, can complicate democratic development. Chile transitioned to democracy in 1990 when long-time dictator Augusto Pinochet lost a referendum on his leadership and stepped down. The first post-Pinochet government, led by President Patricio Aylwin, encountered several authoritarian strongholds. It inherited a cohesive bloc of Pinochet-appointed senators, a largely autonomous armed forces free from civilian control, and a legacy of unresolved cases of human rights violations left behind by the military regime (Garretón Merino, 1995). According to Manuel Garreton, these

authoritarian enclaves create challenges for new democracies because they 'make it difficult for social and political actors to emerge and express their alternative proposals'
(p. 155). In these ways, the legacy of authoritarian rule can influence the quality of the
democracy that emerges afterwards.

Finally, the political parties that exist under authoritarianism frequently survive the
transition to democracy and also serve as a carrier of the authoritarian legacy. Empirical
research shows that not only do these former autocratic ruling parties frequently survive, but they often prosper within democracy (Grzymala-Busse, 2002; Loxton, 2015).
Former ruling parties enter democracy with significant advantages in organization,
membership, and brand recognition, particularly if they are still in power at the moment
of the democratic transition (Langston, 2017). In many cases, these authoritarian parties
are the most professionalized and experienced parties in the political system. Moreover
they often carry over reserves of autocratic power, including clientelist networks, state
and military allies, control of the media, monetary resources, and mass support (Birch,
2003; Langston, 2017). As Joy Langston (2017, p. 200) argues, 'almost all authoritarian
parties are better positioned than their upstart opposition party rivals when the transition to democracy begins and ends'.

Although there have been cases in which formerly authoritarian parties did not hinder democracy, including in Mexico, Taiwan, and South Korea, the empirical record
suggests these cases do not represent the norm. Instead, authoritarian parties negatively impact democratic survival and quality. In Nicaragua, for example, the Sandinista
National Liberation Front and ex-revolutionary leader Daniel Ortega regained power
in the 2006 election after a sixteen-year absence. Ortega's tenure has featured state
dominance of the media and widespread abuse of the courts to abolish term limits
and disqualify opposition candidates. These parties may erode democracy because they
have experience ruling undemocratically and may be eager to manipulate the rules to
re-establish dominance. As Terry Lynn Karl (1990) argues, autocratic influence over
democratic design can produce a 'frozen', elite-dominated democracy. Legacy authoritarian parties may also erode democracy if, after electing a clear representative of the
autocratic past, voters feel that the system and their fellow citizens are turning away
from democracy and are unwilling to oppose violations of democratic norms and practices (Seligson and Tucker, 2005).

More research is needed to trace how authoritarian legacies affect the quality of
democracy. What seems clear, however, is that a country's authoritarian past can cast a
shadow on a new democracy. As Rachel Riedl (2014, xv) argues, 'democratization is not
a tabula rasa: legacies from the past, specifically authoritarian strategies for maintaining
power, play a major role in determining how democracy operates'.

Conclusion

Understanding the extent to which cultural, social, and historical factors shape a
country's prospect for democracy has important policy implications. Those that view
culture as pliable, for example, believe that democratic institutions can function in all

cultural environments. Efforts to create conditions conducive to democracy are therefore a worthwhile endeavour. Those that see some cultures as inherently undemocratic, in contrast, argue that we must accept that some cultures are compatible with only various forms of authoritarianism. Political scientists have so far not been able to produce an authoritative answer to this debate. This is in large part because the evidence required to adjudicate between these different cultural arguments is hard to come by (Przeworski,1998). Nonetheless, as this body of literature has progressed, political scientists have gained greater confidence in the assertion that culture alone is an inadequate explanation for the emergence or sustainability of democracy.

Although empirical research does not support the notion that cultural factors cause democratization, there is some evidence indicating that culture—as expressed through values, attitudes, and beliefs—affects the persistence or stability of democracy. Once democracy has emerged (for other more structural reasons) democracy seems most likely to deepen and endure where elites gradually adopt a values-based commitment to the rules of the democratic game. However, recent developments including the erosion of democracy in places such as Hungary and Poland—which observers viewed as having safely crossed the threshold into consolidated democracy—underscore that elite attitudes can change. Although countries may feature relatively robust civil societies and citizens may view democracy as the best form of government, these attributes and attitudes do not always prevent elite efforts from weakening democracy from the top down.

In addition to culture, we covered the most widely discussed social and historical drivers in the academic literature, including state identity and boundaries, ethnic cleavages, and historical experience with democracy and dictatorship. For example, the empirical research on the relationship between ethnic diversity and democracy suggests that ethnic diversity hinders democracy, but serious questions about the robustness of this claim remain. However, there is relatively more robust evidence that a long history of democratic rule is conducive to engendering and preserving democracy in the long term.

In the next section we shift our focus from domestic drivers of democracy to a number of external factors that shape a country's prospects for democracy. In particular, we discuss how changes in the international environment in the last decade in particular are creating conditions more conducive to autocracy.

Key Questions

1. Why are most political science scholars sceptical that culture is a driver of democracy?

2. What is the relationship between social capital and the quality of democracy?

3. What is the relationship between ethnic diversity and democracy?

4. How does past experience with democracy and autocracy affect a country's future prospects for democracy?

5. What do you think are the prospects of democracy taking root in an Islamic and ethnically divided Middle East? Do you think the region is incompatible with democracy or, given the right conditions, can democracy emerge? What do you see as the key catalysts and the primary barriers to democratization in the Middle East?

Further Reading

ALMOND, G.A. and VERBA, S., 2015. *The Civic Culture: Political Attitudes and Democracy in Five Nations.* Princeton University Press.

The *Civil Culture* is a seminal work in understanding the role of political culture in fostering democracy and democratic consolidation. The book undertook a comparative cross-national survey of five countries (the United States, the United Kingdom, Germany, Italy, and Mexico) and quantified the ideals and attitudes that are the most supportive of democracy.

INGLEHART, R. and WELZEL, C., 2005. *Modernization, Cultural Change, and Democracy: The Human Development Sequence.* Cambridge University Press.

Modernization, Cultural Change and Democracy demonstrates how modernization is impacting people's values and their behaviour, and bringing coherent cultural changes that are actually conducive to democratization.

TEORELL, J., 2010. *Determinants of Democratization: Explaining Regime Change in the World, 1972–2006.* Cambridge University Press.

Determinants of Democratization provides an overview of the key factors that foster democratization. The book argues that economic prosperity and peaceful protests are important, but that elite dynamics is also a critical factor in the short term for explaining regime breakdown and democratization.

10

Economic Drivers of Democracy

Wealthy democracies do not become dictatorships. This assertion—backed by robust empirical support—has been a pillar of our contemporary understanding of democracy and dictatorship (Diamond, 2008). Although political scientists debate whether wealth *causes* democracy, virtually all agree that should democracy emerge, it is more likely to endure in wealthier rather than poorer countries (see also Boix and Stokes, 2003; Bollen and Jackman, 1985; Dalh, 1989; Lipset, 1959). In their highly influential book, *Democracy and Development*, Adam Przeworski and his co-authors found that since 1950 no democracy has failed when non-oil per capita income exceeds about $6,000 (in 1985 constant prices adjusted for purchasing power parity). This was the income level of Argentina in 1985, the year before a coup toppled President Isabel Perón and ended democracy. Since then, democracy has never failed in a country more affluent than Argentina in 1985. In short, the conventional wisdom has long held that high levels of wealth and development make democracy 'sticky'.

Recent developments in Turkey, however, challenge this conventional wisdom (Brownlee 2016). Turkey is a relatively developed country—far wealthier than Argentina was at the time of its coup. Moreover, since Erdoğan came to power in 2003, the Turkish economy has grown substantially, and the middle class has more than doubled in size (Brownlee, 2016). Yet despite Turkey's relative affluence, democracy has deteriorated such that conditions have fallen below the minimum threshold of democracy. In 2018, Freedom House changed Turkey's rating from 'party free' to 'not free'. (For more on Turkey's democratic decline, see Chapter 14). Of course, Turkey's path to democracy has been volatile. The country experienced military **coups** in 1960, 1971, and 1980. But in each of these cases Turkey's level of development was significantly below the wealth threshold that we think democracy needs to survive.

Democratic failure in Turkey raises a critical question: how should we think about the role of economic factors in democratic development? If wealth did not safeguard Turkey's democracy, should we assume that democracy is secure in other developed countries, such as Hungary and Poland where per capita GDP is just above Turkey's? Although Hungarian Prime Minister Viktor Orbán and Poland's Law and Justice Party have sought to roll back democratic norms and practices, political observers have assumed that their countries' relatively high levels of wealth and strong ties within the European Union would limit the extent of democratic decline. But is this still a safe assumption? Likewise, perhaps we should be more concerned than we are about democracy's well-being in other democracies with GDP per capita similar to Turkey, like Romania and Brazil. Would Brazil's level of development be enough to safeguard the country's democracy if the populist president Jair Bolsonaro, who assumed office in January 2019, attempts to roll it back?

In this chapter we examine the relationship between economic factors and democracy. Of all the different explanations for democratic development, arguments about the salience of economic factors are the most strongly supported by empirical evidence. We begin with a discussion of **modernization theory** (see also Chapter 7) and highlight the disagreement about whether wealth *causes* democracy or simply makes it more likely to endure. Despite this dispute, most scholars agree that development is good for democracy. We therefore examine the pathways through which economic development affects democracy, including via education levels, the middle class, organized labour, and values and beliefs. In addition to *levels* of development, research also shows that *changes* in economic growth influence democracy. Economic crises can be destabilizing, especially for young democracies. Finally, we discuss research on economic inequality and democracy, which is inconclusive in its findings about whether a relationship between the two exists.

Economic development

There is a robust body of research showing a strong, positive relationship between economic development and democracy (Lipset, 1959; Burkhart and Lewis-Beck, 1994). The richer the country, the more likely it is to be democratic. Figure 10.1 illustrates this relationship. It lists the twenty richest and poorest countries (and autonomous territories) in 2017 and their political system type. The countries with the highest per capita income tend to be democratic (with the notable exception of a handful of oil-rich states and Singapore). The countries with the lowest per capita income levels, however, feature far more autocracies. The positive correlation between democracy and development that we see in Figure 10.1 holds across the full sample of countries and over time. Przeworski et al. (2000), for example, find that they can correctly predict the political system type of more than 75 per cent of the 4,126 annual country observations in their 1950 to 1990 data sample just by looking at per capita income.

While scholars recognize that there is a strong, positive correlation between development and democracy, they disagree about why. Economic development might make

Top 20 richest countries and autonomous territories

Country	PPP	Political system
1. Qatar	$127,000	Autocracy
2. Luxembourg	$104,000	democracy
3. Singapore	$87,000	Autocracy
4. Brunei	$76,000	Autocracy
5. Kuwait	$71,000	Autocracy
6. Norway	$69,000	democracy
7. Ireland	$69,000	democracy
8. United Arab Emirates	$67,000	Autocracy
9. Switzerland	$59,000	democracy
10. Hong Kong	$58,000	democracy
11. United States	$57,000	democracy
12. Saudi Arabia	$55,000	Autocracy
13. Netherlands	$51,000	democracy
14. Bahrain	$50,000	Autocracy
15. Sweden	$49,000	democracy
16. Iceland	$49,000	democracy
17. Australia	$48,000	democracy
18. Germany	$48,000	democracy
19. Taiwan	$48,000	Democracy
20. Austria	$48,000	Democracy

Top 20 poorest countries

Country	PPP	Political system
1. Central African Republic	$652	Autocracy
2. Democratic Republic of Congo	$773	Autocracy
3. Burundi	$814	Autocracy
4. Liberia	$855	Democracy
5. Niger	$1,107	Democracy
6. Malawi	$1,134	democracy
7. Mozambique	$1,215	Autocracy
8. Guinea	$1,265	Democracy
9. Eritrea	$1,410	Autocracy
10. Madagascar	$1,505	Democracy
11. Comoros	$1,529	autocracy
12. Togo	$1,550	Autocracy
13. South Sudan	$1,657	Autocracy
14. The Gambia	$1,667	Autocracy
15. Sierra Leone	$1,672	Democracy
16. Guinea-Bissau	$1,730	democracy
17. Burkina Faso	$1,782	democracy
18. Haiti	$1,784	democracy
19. Afghanistan	$1,919	democracy
20. Ethiopia	$1,946	autocracy

Figure 10.1 Per capita income levels (PPP) and political system type, as of 2017.

Source: IMF and Geddes, Wright, and Frantz (2018).

democracy more likely to emerge. Or conversely, we could also observe the same correlation between democracy and development if democracy emerges for any number of other reasons (including by chance), but is more likely to survive in wealthier countries (Przeworski et al., 2000). The earliest modernization theorists, including Seymour Lipset (1959), argued in support of the former—that economic development increases a country's likelihood of transitioning to democracy. Lipset's argument was simple: 'democracy is related to the state of economic development. The more well-to-do a nation, the greater the chances it will sustain democracy' (Lipset, 1959, p. 31). Contemporary proponents of this view concede that modernization will not *automatically* lead to democracy. They argue, however, that over the long term, the development process—including industrialization, urbanization, education, communication, mobilization, and a general accumulation of other social changes—make it impossible for leaders to maintain the extent of political control autocracy requires. Several studies provide empirical support for these views (Bollen and Jackman, 1985; Diamond, 1992). Economist Robert Barro, for example, concluded in a comprehensive empirical study in 1997 that 'increases in various measures of the standard of living forecast a gradual rise in democracy. In contrast, democracies that arise without prior economic development . . . tend not to last' (p. 160).

However, a number of influential studies support the second view—they argue that development does not *cause* democracy, but rather make it more likely to endure (Przeworski et al., 2000; Acemoglu et al., 2008). Proponents of this view argue that transitions to democracy are largely random—they occur for a whole host of reasons that differ across countries making any generalizations impossible to draw. For example, Göran Therborn (1977) emphasizes that many European countries democratized because of wars. Likewise, Przeworski et al. (2000) contend that 'Some dictatorships have fallen in the aftermath of the death of a founding dictator, such as Franco, uniquely capable of maintaining the authoritarian order. Some have collapsed because of economic crises, and some because of foreign pressure, and perhaps some for purely idiosyncratic reasons' (p. 89). Regardless of what precipitates the transition, democracy is more likely to 'stick' in more affluent countries.

As we noted at the outset of this chapter, wealthy democracies do not become dictatorships (see Diamond, 2008). And as Przeworski et al. (2000) put forth, no democracy with a per capita income greater than about $6,000 has failed (p. 98). Democratic failure in countries we now consider to be wealthy, such as Greece and Uruguay, occurred when these countries still had income below the $6,000 threshold. In the latter instance, though Uruguay is considered developed today, when its military seized power in 1973 its per capita income was under $1,500. Moreover, just as wealth makes democracy likely to endure, so too does its absence make democracy more likely to fail (Przeworski et al., 2000). The implication, therefore, is that wealth is a necessary condition for democracy to survive.

Relatively recently, studies have put forth that the relationship between democracy and development is more nuanced, as we discussed in Chapter 7. Development increases the chance of democracy, but only under specific conditions (Miller, 2012; Treisman, 2015). These arguments contend that greater development enhances the prospects of democratic transition conditional on the occurrence of a leadership transition. Should democracy emerge following such a transition, greater wealth also makes democracy more likely to endure the unstable period that typically comes afterwards.

How should we interpret these different explanations for the relationship between democracy and development? We believe it is safe to say that development plays an important and positive role in democratic development. Policies designed to promote economic growth and development are likely to create conditions conducive to the survival of democracy, should it emerge. Whether or not such development affects the timing of a democratic transition is likely to be debated for some time. At a minimum, however, such policies are likely to make democracy sticky. In other words, supporting development in autocracies is likely to make these countries more resilient to the numerous challenges they will face should democratization occur, thereby raising the prospects that the transition will endure (Svolik, 2015).

It is important to highlight, however, that efforts to enhance growth and development in autocracies do not come without costs. As we discussed in Chapter 6, economic growth makes autocracies more durable. When the economy is growing, authoritarian regimes have greater resources to secure the loyalty of their elite and security services, to placate the public, and fund the **repression** of the opposition and discontented citizens. For outside actors, therefore, efforts to encourage economic growth and development come with a trade-off—these efforts might initially strengthen the position of an incumbent dictator, but over time, they raise the likelihood that democracy will last once it emerges.

Given the importance of economic development for democratic consolidation, we briefly discuss the most frequently identified explanations for why greater wealth helps sustain democratic rule. Generally speaking, each of these explanations describes different causal sequences, or pathways, through which development increases the relative preferences of citizens and/or elites for democracy over dictatorship. The pathways are inter-related and taken together help explain the observed positive relationship between development and democracy.

The spread of education

Rising development tends to occur in conjunction with improvements in education. A body of research shows, in turn, that there is a direct, positive relationship between education and democracy (Lipset, 1959; Bourguignon and Verdier, 2000; Glaeser et al., 2007; Papaioannou and Siourounis, 2008). Studies argue that expanding levels of education—as measured by variables such as literacy, school enrolment rates, and years of schooling—fosters democracy by increasing participation and activism (Glaeser et al., 2007). Education builds the social capital, trust, and norms that make responsible political participation easier (Huang et al., 2009; Glaeser et al., 2007; Alesina and Ferrara, 2000). Education also fosters democracy by facilitating the formation of intermediary organizations, increasing people's access to media that can shape their political views and expose them to the ideas and experiences of other democracies, and by engendering less extreme and more tolerant preferences (Lipset, 1959b). In sum, scholars argue that higher education is correlated with democracy and that more highly educated democracies are more stable than less educated ones (Glaeser et al., 2007).

It is important to note that a lack of education does not prevent democracy. India, for example, transitioned to democracy with a literacy rate of about 18 per cent. India has remained a democracy since 1951 despite the fact that its literacy rate today stands at just 72 per cent. Likewise, high literacy rates or improvements in those rates do not guarantee democratization. There are many authoritarian regimes, including in the former Soviet Union, that have near perfect literacy rates yet have either struggled to consolidate democracy or remain staunchly authoritarian.

In addition to influencing levels of democracy across countries, education also affects political attitudes toward democracy within a given country (Glaeser et al., 2007). According to Almond and Verba (1963, 1989) 'The uneducated man or the man with limited education is a different political actor from the man who has achieved a higher level of education' (p. 315). There are several examples that demonstrate the extent to which education can shape individual preferences for democracy. Across countless authoritarian regimes, for example, dictators find significantly less support among their more educated voters (Geddes and Zaller, 1989; Magaloni, 2006). In Robert Mugabe's Zimbabwe, it was the better-educated (and wealthier) individuals who pressed for reform. The less educated, in contrast, were most open to manipulation and intimidation by the Mugabe regime (McGreal, 2001).

Similar trends can also be observed in democracies. Research has shown that education levels are a significant predictor of support for populist parties and leaders (Inglehart and Norris, 2017). Less educated voters are more likely to see multicultural societies as a threat to their way of life and therefore are more likely to support populist parties and leaders than more educated voters (Warwick, 1998; Lubbers, 2001; Lubbers et al., 2002). In his early work on modernization theory, Lipset (1959) summed up the relationship between education and democracy. He examined data gathered by public opinion research agencies that questioned people in different countries with regard to their belief in various democratic norms of tolerance for opposition, their attitudes toward ethnic or racial minorities, and with regard to their belief in multi-party as against one-party systems. Lipset concluded that, 'the most important single factor differentiating those giving pro-democracy responses to others has been education. The higher one's education, the more likely one is to believe in democratic values and support democratic practices' (p. 79).

Role of a middle class

Another factor that some researchers view as linking development and democracy is the middle class. Some scholars argue that development fosters the development of a more robust middle class, which then puts pressure on the government for the freedoms that democracy provides. Perhaps one of the best-known scholars to emphasize this is Barrington Moore. In his *Social Origins of Dictatorship and Democracy* (1966), Moore studied the development trajectories of England, France, the United States,

Germany, Japan, China, and Russia and famously concluded, 'No bourgeois, no democracy'. According to Moore, democracy materialized in England, France, and the United States because the urban bourgeoisie emerged as the most powerful political and economic actor. The aristocracy in these countries either did not oppose the bourgeoisie's democratizing efforts or was destroyed by this group in a bourgeois revolution.

Some scholars view the relationship between development, the middle class, and democracy as direct: socio-economic modernization gives rise to the middle class, which in turn spearheads democratization in a nondemocratic society (Dahl, 1971; Nie et al., 1969; Walsh et al., 2004). Proponents of this view argue that the middle class holds different political preferences than the upper class. The upper class has abundant economic resources and close **clientelist** ties with political elites that lead them to support an authoritarian status quo. They oppose democratization in large part because it would threaten to redistribute their wealth. The middle class, in contrast, has limited economic resources and lacks connections to powerful patrons in the government. Out of self-interest, the middle class supports a democratic system that would protect their individual rights and moderate private properties from potential encroachment by the government and the upper class (Chen and Lu, 2011; Glassman, 1995, 1997). The middle class is also more likely than the poor to push for democracy, because the middle class has more leisure time and education, which enables it to participate in public affairs more effectively than the poor (Mills and Wolfe, 2000)

In contrast to a direct and linear relationship between development, the middle class, and democracy, other scholars see it as a process that is highly contingent and fraught with conflict, negotiations, and occasionally setbacks (Acemoglu and Robinson, 2000; Dickson, 2003; Hattori and Funatsu, 2003; Rueschemeyer et al., 1992). Proponents of this view argue that the middle classes (see Figure 10.2 on the middle class around the world) do not necessarily support democracy in principle: like everyone else, they are self-interested actors who want to protect their property and position (Fukuyama, 2012). Instead, the middle-class view of democracy is dependent upon domestic socio-political and socio-economic conditions, which vary across countries. The extent to which the middle class will agitate for democracy has to do with a host of factors such as the economic dependence of the middle class on the state, its perception of its own well-being, its own class cohesiveness, relationships with other socio-economic classes, and its views of the potential for or recent experience with political instability (Chen and Lu, 2011).

Country	Number of middle class
North America	350 million
Europe	650 million
Asia	500 million
Sub-Saharan Africa	30 million
World	2 billion

Figure 10.2 Middle class in the world.

Source: OECD, 2010; figures are approximate.

For example, if a country's middle class is highly dependent on an authoritarian state for employment and income, then it is likely to favour the status quo and resist democratization. If these conditions were to change—potentially as a result of privatization and other efforts to reduce the state's role in the economy—then the middle-class orientation towards democracy would also change.

China is an important example where the rise of a middle class has not (yet) brought democracy. The expectation in the West has been that giving China a stake in global institutions such as the World Trade Organization would bind it to the rules-based system that has been in place since the end of World War II. The West expected that economic integration would encourage China to develop a market economy and that, as it grew wealthier, its people would demand democracy. China has not developed a fully market economy, but its impressive growth rates have spawned a growing middle class. By 2030, the middle class in China is forecasted to make up 74 per cent of the population (Chen, 2013). By 2020 the ranks of China's middle class are likely to outnumber the total population of Europe.

Despite the growth of China's middle class, pressure to democratize has not materialized. Why? For one, many Chinese remember the bloody Cultural Revolution of the 1960s and have a deeply held fear of chaos. More recent events like the Arab Spring have hardened these concerns. The middle class therefore has perhaps not been willing to push for democratic freedoms and rights because of its concerns about triggering instability. China's middle class may also feel threatened by the redistributive demands of the poor. As a result, it may support an authoritarian government that protects its class interests. Finally, high repression and fear raise the costs for anyone sympathetic to regime change, creating a formidable barrier against collective action. For these reasons, the growth of China's middle class has not led to democracy as many modernization theorists would have expected. However, some observers contend that China's middle class might still play an important role in pressuring for political change. Despite the factors that currently limit middle-class activism, several studies and commentaries document discontent among these segments of Chinese society (Economist Special Report, 9 July 2016). For example, many among the middle classes want more autonomy in their personal lives and are anxious about protecting their private property and assets in a country with weak regulation and rule of law. Although the Chinese middle class is not likely to rise up and fight for democracy any time soon, it is looking for change. Only time will tell if modernization theory's expectations about the power of the middle class will come to pass in China.

Role of organized labour

Although the middle classes have featured prominently in modernization theory, some scholars argue that a robust middle class alone is not enough to ensure that democratization and consolidation will occur. Instead, influential research has argued that it is organized labour (rather than the middle class) that has consistently championed democracy and served as the critical catalyst. Consequently, some research argues that strong labour movements make democratic outcomes more likely (Rueschemeyer et al., 1992).

In their seminal research on democratization in Western Europe, North America, Latin America, and the Caribbean, Rueschemeyer, Stephens, and Stephens (1992) argue that democracy is most likely to emerge and deepen in those societies that have experienced massive industrialization and capitalist development. They argue that this is because these processes transform class structures, strengthening the working and middle classes and weakening the landed upper class. According to the authors, the middle classes were generally supportive of democracy and the rule of law but opposed extending these rights to or including the lower classes. The threat perception of the upper and middle classes was crucial in determining whether a country would transition to democracy and, if it did, whether it would consolidate. In those cases where the upper and middle classes felt that popular pressure threatened their interests, they opposed introducing democracy or actively sought to support authoritarian alternatives where it was already established. In sum, from this viewpoint it was the working classes, and not the middle classes, whose actions were decisive in establishing and maintaining democracy.

Other studies have highlighted the role of the working classes in democratization and consolidation but emphasize that it is the interaction of the working class with the political elite that matters most. For some, democratization is a multi-faceted process in which the working classes and political elites must negotiate and compromise (Collier, 1999). Przeworski and Wallerstein (1982), for example, see democracy as emerging from 'class compromise'. They assert that such a compromise can emerge when 'workers consent to the institution of profit and capitalists to democratic institutions through which workers can effectively press claims for material gains' (p. 215). In sum, a number of scholars believe the working class plays an important role in democratic development; they disagree, however, about the relative importance of the various groups in the democratization and consolidation process.

In Box 10.1 we discuss the how economic development supported democratization in South Korea and Taiwan.

 Box 10.1: **Case studies: South Korea and Taiwan**

South Korea and Taiwan are two frequently cited examples of how development can foster democracy. Both countries developed under dictatorship, during which time export-led economic growth led to a rapid rise in the size of the middle class and dramatic improvements in education and human capital. Thus, economic growth was not only spectacular, but it was equitably distributed, which limited the elites' perceived costs of democracy. Growth and development were certainly not the only factors that spurred democratization. In addition to rapid development, scholars have noted that a number of additional factors present in both South Korea and Taiwan contributed to democratization, including a history of repeated elections, the presence of an opposition party or opposition politicians, charismatic opposition leaders, international pressure, and party splits (Slater and Wong, 2013; Solinger, 2001). Despite the influence of these additional factors, there is broad consensus that economic development played a critical role in the countries' transitions to democracy.

When the Korean War ended in 1953, South Korea was devastated by the war and deeply impoverished, in part because a majority of industry was located in the North. President Syngman Rhee remained president of South Korea, although he was widely regarded as authoritarian and corrupt. He stepped down from office in 1960 amid widespread protests after accusations of vote fraud in an election for vice president. After two years of rule under Yun Posun, military strongman Park Chung Hee seized power in a military coup. Park ruled from 1962 until his assassination in 1979. Beginning during his tenure, South Korea embarked on a process of rapid industrialization. High growth led per capita income to quadruple from 1975 to 2005, and literacy rates rose from 22 per cent in 1945 to almost 100 per cent today. These spectacular changes spurred social changes that made authoritarian rule increasingly difficult to maintain. In particular, citizen participation rose dramatically as urbanization and the rising capacity of labour unions and student groups enabled them to assert their interests (Cotton, 1989; Chu, 1998). The mobilization of the *minjung* movement, a broad-based coalition of middle-class activists, workers, church leaders, and students, highlights how South Koreans increasingly began to lobby against the state's repressive and authoritarian tactics.

Against this backdrop of modernization and widespread participation, citizens grew dissatisfied with the high levels of repression of the military regime of Park's successor, Chun Doo Hwan, and waged large-scale and sustained protests. A series of large demonstrations eventually led to the June 1987 announcement that the next president would be elected by direct popular vote—for the first time in twenty-six years. Given divisions within the opposition, Chun's hand-picked successor, General Roh Tae Woo, won the election with just 36.5 per cent of the vote. Though Roh's election was a setback, South Korea did not turn its back on democracy. It initiated a number of reforms to the electoral system in the 1990s. New laws placed limits on campaign spending and the government passed amendments requiring provincial governors, city mayors, and county chiefs to be directly elected (Solinger, 2001). In 1997, five years after the country's direct election, there was alternation in power, and the civilian opposition (led by Kim Dae Jong) won the presidential election.

Since South Korea's transition to democracy, the country has deepened democracy in a number of key respects, despite challenges stemming from the Asian Financial Crisis and corruption scandals surrounding former President Park Geun-hye.

Taiwan was also a poor country with a complex political situation. It was run by the Republic of China (ROC), led by Chiang Kai-shek, a Chinese mainlander who fled China after his Nationalist Party (Kuomingtang or KMT) lost to Mao Zedong's Communist Party. Chiang's rule was supposed to be temporary, but the ROC never left the island. Mainlanders controlled the government and ruled over the native Taiwanese in an oppressive manner. Unlike South Korea, which is homogenous, Taiwan has both native Taiwanese and Chinese mainlanders, the latter of which comprise 14 per cent of the population.

But just like South Korea, Taiwan experienced spectacular growth rates. Driven by its mission to eventually retake the mainland, the KMT prioritized economic growth and national security. Land reform initiated during the late 1940s broke the landlord class, paving the way for more equitable economic development and giving the regime considerable autonomy from traditionally dominant classes (Slater and Wong, 2013). The government also invested in education, human capital, and technology, spurring an export-led growth strategy. The economy grew an average of 9 per cent a year from 1952 to 1961. By the 1970s the government expanded its investments and targeted heavy industry, infrastructure, and advanced technologies. Education reform and growing per capita income meant that Taiwan developed a better educated and wealthier population who grew dissatisfied with authoritarian rule.

In the mid-1970s, the Tang-wai opposition movement formed (becoming the Democratic Progressive Party (DPP) in 1986) and began to pressure the KMT to democratize. Though labour in Taiwan was not as unionized and robust as in South Korea, it was still involved in the movement for democracy. Small entrepreneurs were also active in pro-democracy efforts (Chu, 1998). In addition to internal pressures, international pressure also mounted for the regime to pursue reforms. Taiwan was expelled from the United Nations in the early 1970s. When the United States normalized relations with China in 1979, Taiwan's already precarious international standing was dealt another debilitating blow. The KMT's post-war mission to reclaim China no longer enjoyed superpower support. To make matters worse, the KMT was increasingly chastised by the international community for its authoritarian practices (Slater and Wong, 2013).

By 1975, Chiang Ching-kuo, the son of Chiang Kai-shek took over after his father's death and started to bring more native Taiwanese into key political posts alongside a new generation of elites from the mainland. Changes were made to the electoral laws and legislation increased the number of seats in the National Assembly, leading to more political diversity in the legislature. As the country became more prosperous, Chiang Ching-kuo took actions before his death to broaden the ROC political system (Scalapino, 1993). Most important was his decision to lift martial law in 1987 and eliminate the ban on opposition parties. This enabled the DPP to officially form and contest elections for the first time (Solinger, 2001). In 2000, the DPP won the presidency, signifying Taiwan's transition to democracy.

Though Taiwan and South Korea have faced numerous challenges, democracy in both countries appears robust with few signs of potential **backsliding**. But as the chapter notes, this may not be surprising given that both countries have also maintained strong economies. South Korea staved off a major financial crisis in 1997 and a 2017 corruption scandal, but managed to keep its democracy intact (Financial Times, 2017). In Taiwan, in spite of threats from mainland China, democracy appears to be the only game in town. A 2018 survey demonstrated that 70 per cent of Taiwanese were willing to fight to defend their nation's democratic way of life if China attempted to annex it by force, while 94 per cent claimed that living in a democratic society is important (Cole, 2018).

Changes in beliefs and values

The former President of Tanzania, Julius Nyerere, stated that, 'Democracy means much more than voting on the basis of adult suffrage every few years; it means (among other things) attitudes of toleration and willingness to co-operate with others on terms of equality' (Nyerere, 1998, p 27). These values—tolerance, equality, and others such as trust—are a foundation of democratic governance. Some scholars argue that modernization fosters their emergence. Put differently, they put forth that modernization changes people's beliefs and values in ways that make democracy more likely to develop and endure (Inglehart and Welzel, 2005). The value change that development produces, therefore, is another factor posited to link development and democracy.

In their influential research on modernization theory Ronald Inglehart and Christian Welzel (2005, 2009) assert that, other things equal, 'high levels of economic development tend to make people more tolerant and trusting bringing more emphasis on self-expression and participation in decision-making' (Inglehart and Welzel, 2009, p. 36).

Although factors such as political leaders and country-specific events shape levels of democracy, Inglehart and Welzel contend that economic development is also critical because it processes produce liberal or freedom-oriented values that increase mass demands for democratic institutions and more responsive elite behaviour. These attitudinal changes are closely related to education and the middle class. Some scholars who have highlighted the importance of the middle class, for example, argue that the middle class is important for democracy because these people rarely support extremist policies and are more tolerant of differences (Bollen and Jackman, 1985; Diamond, 1992; Lipset, 1960).

Subsequent research has found little empirical support for Inglehart and Welzel's key finding, however (Conroy-Krutz and Frantz, 2017). Once factors such as sample selection bias, country-specific effects, and the endogeneity of values to democracy are considered, liberal and freedom-oriented values do not enhance democracy levels or democratization chances, and neither do they stabilize existing democracies (Dalhum and Knutsen, 2017). Instead, there is even some evidence that the causal arrow runs in the other direction. A country's experience with democracy may 'teach' citizens to become more supportive of these types of values. In other words, time under democracy is associated with a learning process, which in turn explains the observed correlation between freedom-oriented values and democracy.

Economic inequality

In addition to levels of wealth, research has also suggested that the way that wealth is distributed within a country affects levels of democracy. The findings from this body of work parallel those from the modernization literature—namely scholars disagree about whether inequality affects the onset of democracy but widely agree that greater equality supports consolidation (Diamond, 1994; Solt, 2008). Theoretically, inequality should have cross-cutting effects on the likelihood that democracy emerges. Greater inequality raises the incentives for disadvantaged groups to press for more open and competitive politics. Yet the wider the income disparity in society, the more elites have to fear from a democratic transition and the more vigorously they will seek to repress challenges from below (Haggard and Kaufman, 2012; Houle, 2009). As we discuss shortly, research has produced conflicting empirical results. Some studies argue that inequality inhibits democratization. Others suggest inequality can encourage the onset of democracy, that it has a non-linear effect, or that it has no net effect at all. As we noted, however, there is broad consensus across multiple studies that once democracy emerges, economic equality is conducive to its deepening and survival (Houle, 2009).

Studies arguing that inequality *hinders* democratization are based on a fundamental assumption that economic elites are threatened by democratic reforms because they fear that a politically empowered citizenry will redistribute their wealth. This body of research shares much in common with our previous discussion about the relationship between the middle class and democracy. Highly unequal societies have a small and underdeveloped middle class, which means there are few actors willing and able to push for democratic reform. Most recently, Carles Boix (2003) found empirical support for the view that inequality makes democratization less likely. His research suggests that in addition to inequality, the nature of a country's economic assets—whether assets can easily be moved out of the country or are immobile—also shapes the elite calculus about the costs of democracy. Democratization will be unlikely in those countries with high inequality and immobile assets. In very unequal societies, the redistributive demands of the worse-off citizens on the wealthy are particularly intense. As a result, the wealthy have a strong incentive to oppose democracy, which would enable the majority of the population to impose heavy taxes on them. The prevalence of highly immobile types of capital amplifies upper class support for the authoritarian status quo. Unable to shift assets abroad to escape the threat of high taxes, capital owners grow more resolute in their efforts to block democracy (p. 3).

The ability of elites to shift assets abroad is not just determined by the nature of their assets, but also by the extent of an autocracy's integration into financial markets. Research underscores that those autocracies that are integrated into global financial markets are more likely to democratize, even amid high levels of inequality, because the country's elites can diversify their asset portfolios (Eichengreen and Leblang, 2008; Freeman and Quinn, 2012). Asset diversification decreases both elite stakes in and collective action capacity for opposing democracy. This finding suggests that in a country such as Russia, the elite will have strong incentive to protect the authoritarian status quo. Russia has high levels of inequality and, given mounting Western **sanctions** against the political elite, is being cut out of Western financial markets. Facing high costs of redistribution and few options to mitigate those costs by moving their money abroad, the Russian elite are likely to strongly oppose democratization.

On the opposite side of the argument, a body of research claims that rising income inequality *fosters* democratization. Ben Ansell and David Samuels (2010, 2014) argue that democratization will be most likely when disenfranchised economic groups within society begin to grow and demand more from the state. As these disenfranchised groups accumulate assets and wealth, they leave behind the poorer segments of society, generating greater societal inequality. Moreover, these upwardly mobile groups seek to curb the power of the autocratic state and gain credible commitments that their new-found income and assets will not be confiscated. According to Ansell and Samuels (2014), 'democracy is about fear of the autocratic state, not fear of the poor' (p. 2). In other words, upwardly mobile groups have greater incentive to protect their new status from the predation by the government and therefore push for democratic safeguards. The authors underscore, however, that this argument applies to income inequality and not land inequality. Because land is more or less fixed in supply, high land inequality means the elite will be wary of higher taxation or even expropriation of their fixed assets under democracy (Ziblatt, 2008).

Finally, qualitative studies have produced conflicting results, suggesting that the relationship between inequality and democratization is non-linear, or that inequality has no systematic effect on a country's propensity to transition. Using in-depth cases studies of Singapore, South Africa, the United Kingdom, and Argentina, Daron Acemoglu and James Robinson (2000, 2006) argue that the relationship between inequality and democracy resembles an inverted U-shaped curve. Democratization is unlikely in authoritarian governments with low levels of inequality because the demand for it is tempered. It is equally unlikely at high levels of inequality because high inequality increases the incentives for authoritarian elites to repress political demands for redistribution. At moderate levels of inequality, however, democratic transitions are most likely. Another study using qualitative research examining Third Wave transitions (1980–2000) argues that inequality has little explanatory power (Haggard and Kaufman, 2012). It finds that just more than 50 per cent of the democratic transitions during this period conformed to the causal mechanisms specified in the distributive conflict models. In other words, about half of the Third Wave transitions to democracy occurred without the presence of distributional conflict.

Though research has been largely inconclusive about the relationship between inequality and democratization, most scholars agree that social equality facilitates democratic consolidation (Houle, 2009). Put differently, inequality raises a country's risk of backsliding from democracy to dictatorship. Data show that those democracies that are able to reduce levels of inequality last an average of eighty-four years. Those democracies where inequality grows, in contrast, survive just twenty-two years (Houle, 2009, p. 43). In countries in Central America such as Guatemala, El Salvador, and Honduras, high levels of inequality have made it difficult for democracy to deepen. Economic inequality makes democracy fragile because it creates incentives for elites to subvert it so that they can capture a larger share of the country's wealth (Tilly, 2003). In unequal democracies, redistribution is more extreme than in equal societies, making democracy costlier for elites. Indeed, research shows that high levels of inequality in a democracy raise the likelihood of coups (Houle, 2016).

The relationship between inequality and democracy is an important one and adds additional nuance to the expectations that modernization theory produces. Specifically, work on inequality suggests that democracy *can* survive in relatively poor countries *if* income is distributed equally. In his research, Christian Houle (2009) underscores that since World War II many poor countries where wealth was distributed relatively equally, perhaps most notably India, have successfully established and sustained democracy. At the same time similarly poor but economically unequal countries, such as Nigeria, Peru, and Turkey, have oscillated between dictatorship and democracy. The key difference between these two groups, Houle asserts, is that inequality made it difficult for the latter group to sustain democratic regimes. Similarly, other scholars have noted that high levels of inequality in Latin America have posed challenges for democratic consolidation there (Karl, 2000) (for more on this relationship between inequality and regime type, see Figure 10.4). Costa Rica and Uruguay have experienced relatively stable periods of democratic consolidation, perhaps in large part because they are two of the more economically equal societies in Latin America. South Africa is considered to be a success story of democratization, but persistent inequality continues to cause high levels of social and political instability, challenging the quality of its democracy (Sisk, 2017).

Inequality is clearly not just an issue plaguing the developing world, and research shows that inequality in developed democracies erodes their democratic quality as well. This dynamic is particularly concerning given that inequality has been rising in all of

Country	GINI Index	Per capita income
1. Norway	.235	$70,665
2. Iceland	.24	$73,092
3. Sweden	.254	$53,248
4. New Zealand	.33	$36,254
5. Denmark	.275	$56,335
6. Canada	.316	$40,409
7. Ireland	.30	$68,604
8. Switzerland	.295	$80,837
9. Finland	.256	$42,611
10. Australia	.336	$56,135

Figure 10.3 Most democratic countries in the world, GINI index and per capita incomes (nominal).

Source: Economist Democracy Index, OECD, IMF.

the world's upper and middle-income democracies since at least the 1980s. Greater inequality concentrates power in the hands of the rich, which is readily converted into greater political influence. Studies show, for example, that elected representatives are more responsive to the demands of the rich, including in the United States (Bartels, 2016). Robert Dahl and others theorized that as a result of their frustration and resentment, poorer citizens do not press for more political and economic equality, but instead become disengaged from politics (Dahl, 1971; Pateman, 1971). Numerous studies support this claim by documenting the negative effects of inequality on a range of political activities. Inequality has been found to reduce interest in politics, views of government responsiveness, and participation in elections (Boix, 2003; Goodin and Dryzek, 1980; Solt, 2004).

The data in Figure 10.3 illustrate the relationship between inequality and the quality of democracy. (Here we use a continuous measure of political system type to capture

Country	Economic inequality	Political system
South Africa	.634	flawed democracy
Botswana	.605	flawed democracy
Namibia	.613	flawed democracy
Haiti	.608	hybrid system
Suriname	.576	flawed democracy
Zambia	.571	hybrid system
Lesotho	.542	flawed democracy
Swaziland	.515	authoritarian
Brazil	.513	flawed democracy
Colombia	.511	flawed democracy

Figure 10.4 Economic inequality and political system type.

Source: World Bank, Economist Democracy Index.

differences in 'levels' of democraticness, given the emphasis in the literature on demo-cratic quality.) Those countries with the lowest inequality, as measured by the GINI coefficient, are all full democracies. In contrast, high inequality has been a barrier to democratic deepening.

Economic growth

As we did in our discussion of authoritarian breakdown in Chapter 7, we distinguish here between *levels* of development and *acute changes* in economic conditions. In addi-tion to levels of economic development, scholars posit that changes in economic growth rates and inflation affect democratic development. Economic recessions, for example, are one of the most robust predictors of the breakdown of democracy (Przeworski and Limongi, 1997; Przeworski et al., 2000; Svolik, 2008, 2015). One study finds that between 1848 and 2008, a democracy was more than twice as likely to revert to dictatorship during an economic decline than during a period of economic growth (Svolik, 2008). Likewise, another study finds that most democratic failures are accompanied by some economic crisis: in twenty-eight out of thirty-nine instances of democratic failure, there was a drop in income during at least one of the two preceding years (Przeworski et al., 2000). Economic crises have precipitated democratic backsliding in several countries in Latin America. Democracy weakened in Ecuador after a severe economic downturn led to a coup to oust the maligned leader Jamil Mahuad in 2000. The rise of autocrat Alberto Fujimori in Peru and the 1973 coup that ousted democratically-elected leader Salvador Allende from power in Chile were also both preceded by an economic crisis (Harmer, 2011).

Economic crises are especially dangerous for young and poor democracies; when democracies break down, nine in ten do so before they are twenty years old and/or when their annual GDP per capita is less than $4,900 (Svolik, 2013). More consolidated democracies, in contrast, tend to be more immune to such downturns. In consolidated democracies, an economic crisis may lead to low levels of public satisfaction with the incumbent government, but not necessarily fuel public dissatisfaction with the way democracy works. For example, the global financial crisis beginning in 2008 hit Ireland and Iceland hard, but both governments were able to weather the storm (Cordero and Simón, 2016).

Why would an economic crisis in a democracy lead to breakdown? After all, unlike in a dictatorship, voters in a democracy have the opportunity to remove those leaders that deliver poor economic results. Milan Svolik (2013) articulates an argument linking economic decline with democratic failure. He argues that in new democracies, popular dissatisfaction with the performance of individual politicians turns into doubts about the value of democracy as a political system. Because newly democratic politicians do not have established reputations, voters are quick to conclude that 'all politicians are crooks'. Politicians, in turn, respond by conforming to these expectations and act like crooks even if most of them may be willing to perform well in office if given the appropriate incentives. Once a new democracy descends into the trap of pessimistic expectations, even voters who are initially optimistic about the ability of elections to motivate accountable behaviour rationally conclude that their particular democracy cannot deliver governance that is more responsive than that under a dictatorship. Citizens grow unwilling to defend democracy against attempts to subvert it, thus eliminating a key check on politicians or parties with authoritarian ambitions.

Just as economic troubles can undermine democracy, so too can positive economic performance sustain it, even in less developed countries (Cheibub et al., 1996). Democracies are more likely to survive when they grow at a faster rate (e.g. more than 5 per cent annually) than when they grow at a slower one. According to one study (Cheibub et al., 1996), poor democracies (those with per capita income under $1,000) are expected to last less than five years if their income falls, compared to 12.5 years if their income grows. In sum, economic growth is particularly important for sustaining democracy, especially if democracy emerges in developing countries.

Clientelism

In the final section of this chapter, we discuss how perverse economic incentives can obstruct democratic consolidation. Under dictatorship, many regimes rely, in part, on the distribution of **patronage** to maintain support. Patronage can be dispensed in many forms, including cash hand-outs, public sector employment, access to public services like housing or healthcare, and preferential access to lucrative state contracts. Regardless of the form patronage takes or how it is distributed, the underlying logic is straightforward: politicians (the patrons) supply benefits in return for the recipient's (the client's) support. This process enables autocrats to create political subservience and socio-economic dependence on the regime (Grzymala-Busse, 2008; Wintrobe, 2000). Political systems that are based on this logic—the exchange of political goods and services for votes—are often called clientelist systems. Particularly in personalist dictatorships, such as Georgia under Eduard Shevardnadze (1995–2003) and Kyrgyzstan under Askar Akayev (1990–2005), clientelist networks are deeply entrenched and serve as the lifeblood of the political system.

When new democracies emerge in these settings, clientelist networks are difficult to dismantle—especially the underlying culture of patronage-based politics. Both Georgia and Kyrgyzstan experienced democratic transitions following protest movements in 2003 (the Rose Revolution) and 2005 (the Tulip Revolution). Clientelist legacies in both countries however, have obstructed their democratic development. Not only do elites become accustomed to using political office for personal gain, but their political experience and approach to politics is informed by these patterns of contingent exchange. Citizens also grow used to this pattern of politics and come to expect politicians to provide patronage (Shefter, 1994). Despite the transition to democracy, clientelism remains a familiar tool for building loyal networks of supporters.

Definitions of **clientelism** emphasize four elements (Hicken, 2011). First, clientelist exchanges are based on personal relationships. Although these networks may be complex and 'reach from the summits of national politics down to the municipal level'

(Kitschelt, 2000, p. 849), they are at their core highly personal in nature. Second, clientelism is conditional—a quid pro quo. It is rooted in the regular exchange of resources for votes. Third, definitions of clientelism emphasize the asymmetry between client and patron. In some cases, the power imbalance is severe; clients, especially poor rural ones, have few opportunities to withdraw from the relationship. Patrons have tools to enforce client compliance, such as social ostracism and the withholding of benefits. Clients, in contrast, have few options to force a patron to honour his or her commitment. Doing so requires a large number of clients to coordinate their threats to withdraw support. Finally, clientelist exchanges are repeated and ongoing. The iterative nature of these relationships allows politicians to observe which voters keep their promises and which can be swayed, enabling them to calibrate the size of their offers (Kitschelt and Wilkinson, 2007; Stokes, 2007). Such repeated interactions also create trust between the parties over time.

Clientelism is distinct from other forms of political exchange, such as pork barrel politics or populist promises to redistribute resources to marginalized segments of society (Hicken, 2011). All of these tactics are carried out with electoral considerations in mind: politicians expect that the benefits they hand out will help them win elections. The primary distinction between clientelism and these other political tactics, however, is the nature of the targeted groups. **Pork barrel** politicians and populists make promises to entire groups or constituencies. Importantly, no member within the targeted group can be excluded from the benefit on the basis of a lack of support for the politician or party. Clientelism, in contrast, is more individualized and particular. Clientelist states structure their networks in ways that allow patrons to target benefits to individuals or small groups of voters and monitor their political support. Allen Hicken (2011) uses an example from Singapore to illustrate clientelism's targeted nature. In the 1980s, the Singapore government changed its vote-counting system to allow the government to tally and report votes at the ward level, which in Singapore roughly equates to an apartment block. As the vast majority of Singaporeans live in public housing, the change gave the government access to detailed data about the distribution of its support. The ruling People's Action Party subsequently tied housing services to support for the regime. Apartment complexes that supported the opposition could expect to be last on the list for upgrades and improvements (Tremewan, 2016). Similarly, in Nigeria (see Box 10.2) deeply engrained clientelism and corruption are considered major factors hindering democratic development.

 Box 10.2: **Case study: Clientelism and corruption in Nigeria**

The armed forces ruled Nigeria—Africa's most populous country—for a large share of the country's history following its independence from Great Britain in 1960. In 1999, the country began to transition away from military rule. That year, Nigerians voted for the first time in sixteen years and brought Olusegun Obasanjo, a former military officer who led a military dictatorship from 1976–79, to power in free and relatively fair elections. Although Nigeria has regularly held elections since 1999, the People's Democratic Party (PDP) monopolized politics until 2015. That year, the political opposition (led by Muhammadu Buhari) won the presidential election for the first time in Nigerian history. Although the quality of Nigeria's elections has improved, the country is still considered a defective democracy in large part because of the persistence of corruption and clientelism.

Nigeria has a number of features that academic research suggests make it difficult for democracy to deepen, including an ethnically heterogeneous population, natural resource wealth, and low economic development. In addition to (or perhaps related to) these 'structural features', high levels of clientelism have hindered Nigeria's democratic development. The durability of the PDP, for example, rested in large part on the party's access to oil revenue, which provided it with income flows needed to fund its clientelist networks. Rather than developing programmatic parties, leaders have opted to compete for power based on personal relationships built on benefits and loyalty. Political elites vie to control the spoils of office and use them to enrich members of their ethnic groups and ultimately to sustain their power. To win office, politicians rely on powerful **Godfathers** or **Big Men** who sit atop vast patronage networks (Olarinmoye, 2008). The Godfathers in Nigerian politics are brokers who work between the political parties and the voting public for a profit. Having no political interests, they are focused on their own self-enrichment. To help ensure electoral victories they interfere in electoral processes. Every level of Nigerian politics has its relevant Big Men and their supporters (Fagbadebo, 2007).

Corruption has also been pervasive, particularly in the oil and security sectors (Freedom House, 2018). Transparency International, a corruption watchdog, ranked Nigeria as the 148th most corrupt country out of 180 countries. Beginning under **military rule**, oil revenue has been diverted to private accounts and questionable contracts awarded to companies owned by government cronies. The military elites circumvented the mechanisms intended to promote accountability and focused on accumulating wealth (Agbiboa, 2012). Throughout the military's rule, corruption became 'institutionalized and assaulted every facet of the country's political and socio-economic life' (Aiyede, 2008 p. 39). According to Ilufoye Ogundiya (2009), 'political corruption has remained a major obstacle to national progress in Nigeria. Corruption is indeed the major explanation for the seemingly insolvable problem of poverty, diseases, hunger and general acute development tragedy in Nigeria' (p. 289).

In addition to the economic inefficiencies that clientelism and corruption create, these factors have also stunted Nigeria's democratic progress. Like other countries, corruption has undermined Nigerians' interpersonal trust and faith in government and hindered collective action and the development of civic behaviour. Political participation in Nigeria is low in large part because citizens do not perceive they can make a difference. Because elite relationships rather than public need tend to drive national policymaking, public dissatisfaction with the political system is high. According to a 2017 survey, 58 per cent of Nigerians are not satisfied with the way democracy is working in their country (Wike et al., 2017).

Numerous Nigerian leaders have sought to tame corruption, although 'most of them that came in as physicians have come out as patients' (Ogundiya, 2009, p. 289). Former President Olusegun Obasanjo, for example, embarked on a fight against corruption by implementing civil service reform and promoting more technocrats within the government. President Muhammadu Buhari (2015–) has also sought to make corruption a priority and campaigned for office on the promise that he would reduce graft and improve transparency. Despite his efforts, Nigeria's democracy remains vulnerable. The culture of clientelism and corruption persists at the state and local level and continues to impede the effective functioning of political institutions.

Clientelism has profound negative implications for the quality of democracy and how citizens view their government (Hicken, 2011). Stokes (2005), for example, argues that clientelism undermines democratic accountability. Rather than voters holding parties and politicians responsible for their performance, parties and politicians hold voters accountable for their vote. As a result, voters in clientelist systems are, on average, more cynical and disillusioned than their counterparts in non-clientelist settings (Kitschelt and Wilkinson 2007, Kitschelt et al., 2010). Clientelism also hinders political party development, which impedes democratic development. In particular, clientelist leaders do not invest in the development of programmatic political parties, defined as parties that compete based on a policy platform. Instead, leaders in clientelist systems compete based on charisma and their own individual networks. The failure to build programmatic parties is detrimental to democracy because these parties produce lower electoral volatility, lower party-system fragmentation, and higher levels of party–system institutionalization (Kitschelt et al., 2010).

Clientelism also distorts economic incentives. Empirical research shows that clientelist governments underprovide public goods and are more corrupt (Keefer, 2007). Such governments are less interested in providing public goods because they cannot exclude non-supporters from enjoying the benefits of these services. Instead, they spend a greater proportion of their budgets on targeted expenditures, such as jobs and public works projects (Keefer, 2007). As a result, clientelist systems are associated with large public sectors and public sector inefficiency (Gimpelson and Treisman, 2002; Grzymala-Busse, 2008; Hicken and Simmons, 2008). Finally, numerous studies have found a strong link between clientelism and corruption, or perceptions of corruption (Hicken, 2011). Matthew Singer (2009) contends that clientelism may drive corruption in three ways. First, clientelism—or certain forms of clientelist exchange such as vote buying—may be illegal. Second, by undermining the ability of citizens to hold public officials accountable, clientelism may foster a culture of impunity and make it difficult to punish individuals for corrupt behaviour. Third, the demand for resources to support clientelist exchange may increase the incentives of politicians to raise funds through illicit means.

In sum, those new democracies that emerged from autocracies with deeply entrenched clientelist networks are likely to struggle to overcome these practices. Clientelism constitutes significant barriers to democratic consolidation.

Conclusion

This chapter has focused on the relationship between economic factors and democracy. Although it remains unclear whether economic development causes democracy, there is broad consensus that wealth sustains democratic systems. Likewise, research is inconclusive about whether inequality influences democratization, but there is strong agreement that inequality is detrimental to the quality and duration of democracy.

Economic recessions are also one of the most robust predictors of the breakdown of democracy. Severe financial crises are especially problematic. On the eve of the Great

Depression in 1929, for example, Germany was one of the world's leading industrial powers, the labour force was well educated, and communications and mass media were extensive. Germany rated highly on all of the most robust economic indicators that scholars posit to be conducive to stable democratic systems. And yet, just four years after the crash of the New York stock exchange in 1929, Adolf Hitler seized power and obliterated German democracy.

The German example is extreme, but it underscores the fragility of democracy. A severe global financial crisis, akin to but more significant that the 2008–09 global financial crisis, could further fuel the flames of xenophobia and authoritarianism. Already public support for populist parties and leaders has been on the rise across Europe without the presence of major economic hardship in these countries. It could take just one major event—such as a major global trade war or economic default in Italy—to trigger such a global financial crisis. As this chapter has outlined, that would create socio-economic conditions inhospitable to democracy.

Finally, we would like to conclude this chapter where we began it—with the example of democratic decline in Turkey. Turkey is one of the most affluent countries in recent times to experience democratic failure. Scholars are likely to debate whether Turkey debunks our long-standing conventional wisdom that economic development safeguards democracy for some time. Certainly if democratic backsliding gives way to democratic failure in Hungary and Poland it would trigger a major re-evaluation of our understanding of development's relationship with democracy. As we will discuss at length in Chapter 14, democracies are dying differently today than they have historically. Although economic development is likely to remain an important guardrail for democracy, time will tell whether it continues to provide the guarantee that we long assumed it would.

Key Questions

1. Summarize the different explanations for the positive correlation between development and democracy. Which view do you find to be most valid and why? What evidence would you need to see to determine which view you think is correct?

2. Why does a robust middle class not always lead to democracy?

3. What is the relationship between economic inequality and democracy? Can a country with high levels of inequality, such as South Africa, be truly democratic?

4. Why is patron-clientelism so detrimental to the consolidation of democracy? Can a country be corrupt and still democratic? Why or why not?

5. Do you think the case of democratic failure in Turkey—a country at a relatively high level of economic development—is an aberration? Or does the fact that Erdoğan was able to dismantle Turkish democracy amid economic conditions long expected to safeguard democracy signal a shift in contemporary politics? Why or why not?

6. Does the degree of economic development achieved in Taiwan and South Korea explain the timing of their movements toward democracy?

7. How might economic developments affect China's political development? What do you see as the prospects that Beijing's slower growth could destabilize the regime? Conversely, if China continues its strong economic growth, what might lead the middle class to demand greater rights?

Further Reading

ACEMOGLU, D. and ROBINSON, J.A., 2006. *Economic Origins of Democracy and Dictatorship*. Cambridge University Press.

The Economic Origins of Dictatorship explores when dictatorships don't survive. The book offers a framework for understanding how democracies emerge and consolidate based on how costly it is to repress and what incentives exist for elites to maintain it. Economic factors come into the analysis in helping to comprehend the challenges elites face in maintaining stability.

RUESCHEMEYER, D., STEPHENS, E.H., and STEPHENS, J.D., 1992. *Capitalist Development and Democracy*. University of Chicago Press.

Capitalist Development and Democracy disputes the argument that a middle class is sufficient precondition for democracy to take place. The books argues, drawing largely from research in Latin America, that it is not only the middle class that is important but also organized labour, as there are many cases of where the middle class has allied with elites.

WINTROBE, R., 2000. *The Political Economy of Dictatorship*. Cambridge University Press.

The Political Economy of Dictatorship starts from the vantage point of dictatorships, and argues that dictatorships are rational and concerned with their own survival. As such they have rational strategies for accumulating and sustaining themselves in power. Based on this, the book offers an explanation for why and when a dictator will resort to repression.

11

Institutional Drivers of Democracy

In the former Soviet space (excluding the Baltics), some countries are more open and less authoritarian than others. Ukraine, Georgia, Moldova, and Kyrgyzstan, for example, have enjoyed relatively greater political and civil liberties—and even periods of nascent democracy. Freedom House rated Ukraine as 'Free' shortly after the country's Orange Revolution in 2004–05. In contrast, Russia, Azerbaijan, Belarus, and the other Central Asian countries have been far more closed. What accounts for this difference? The former Soviet states share a number of common features like their communist history and high levels of corruption, making these factors poor candidates for explaining the political divergence. Economic factors also have little explanatory power, as some of the poorest countries like Georgia and Kyrgyzstan have been among the relatively more democratic. Instead, some scholars have emphasized the importance of institutions for explaining the different levels of freedom within the region. The relatively more open counties have parliamentary systems, while the more authoritarian countries have presidential systems (Hale 2016, 2011). When power is vested in a president rather than divided between a president and prime minister, the argument goes, it facilitates a president's expansion of executive power.

Do the negative effects of presidentialism apply beyond the former Soviet space? More broadly, do institutions matter for the development and survival of democracy? If so, which institutional arrangements are best suited to promote democracy's consolidation and durability? In this chapter we address these questions and examine how the institutional design of new democracies affect their political evolution. By institutions, we are referring to formal political institutions, including political parties, electoral systems, and state design (namely federal versus unitary states). As we will show, institutions can play a particularly critical role in the consolidation and sustainment of democracy because they structure and constrain political behaviour.

Institutions encourage effective democracy through three pathways (Lust and Waldner, 2015). First, democratic institutions can increase vertical accountability and representativeness, making governments more responsive to citizens, and citizens more likely to view their government as legitimate. Effective institutions, therefore, diminish incentives to support antidemocratic movements. Second, institutions may affect horizontal accountability, serving as key constraints on executive power. Strong and resilient institutions make it more difficult for elected leaders to subvert democracy from within. Finally, institutions may affect government performance. When they work well, institutions reduce the chances of political stalemate and crisis that leaders can use to justify antidemocratic actions.

As we emphasize throughout this chapter, there is no one-size-fits-all institutional blueprint that assures democratic stability. Although presidential systems facilitated autocracy in the former Soviet space, political science research indicates that this dynamic cannot be generalized across all political systems. According to the latest research, presidentialism is not inherently inferior to parliamentary government if the goal is to maximize the quality or persistence of democracy (Cheibub and Limongi, 2002; Kapstein and Converse, 2008; Houle, 2009). In other words, it is not necessarily the choice of institutions that matters. Instead, what the research overwhelmingly suggests is that institutions will facilitate democracy when they effectively constrain executive power. The creation and maintenance of alternative centres of power, including representative assemblies, judiciaries, and the media, that check the power of governing officials is particularly important for the consolidation and durability of democracy. Moreover, simply establishing such institutions by no means guarantees that they will have the capacity to constrain the leadership in reality. The strength and quality of the institutions must also be taken into account. Institutions with *de jure* powers do not necessarily wield *de facto* influence.

Though there is a lack of robust support showing that any particular institutional design enhances democracy, there is a large body of empirical political science research that discusses the advantages and drawbacks of particular institutional choices. By understanding the trade-offs associated with particular institutional choices, policymakers can choose those institutions that best address the specific challenges of transitioning states. We turn now to address this body of research focusing specifically on the way that political parties, electoral rules, and government systems (such as presidentialism and parliamentarism) and state design (unitary versus federal), impact the likelihood of stable democracy.

Though most of this chapter addresses how institutions affect a country's prospects for **democratic consolidation** (or **backsliding**) we conclude the chapter by examining the relationship between institutions and democratization. This section builds on our previous discussion of the role of institutions in autocracies and highlights why the adoption of political institutions, such as parties and elections does not always lead to democratization. Most countries in the world have adopted these types of institutions, and yet democratization more often than not has not followed suit. As we discussed in Chapter 6, the presence of 'democratic' institutions in dictatorships should not necessarily be viewed as a precursor to democratization. In fact, the presence of these institutions is likely to perpetuate authoritarian rule, rather than signal its demise.

Box 11.1: 'Great man' theory and democracy

There is a long-standing debate about whether democracy emerges because of deep structural dynamics, or as a result of the choices and actions of individuals. This debate in many ways centres on a discussion about the relative causal power of agency versus structure. Agency refers to the capacity of an actor to realize his or her intentions (Hay, 2002, 94). Structure refers to the setting or context that the actor is constrained by, in this case the political institutions, norms, and practices that impact political behaviour. While the primary focus of this chapter is on the role of institutions in democratic consolidation, such an approach ignores the role of agency: how individuals build and opt for these institutions in the first place. For this reason, 'great man' theories of democracy have held particular sway. Such theories argue that 'great men', by virtue of their privileged position or noteworthy talents, have the ability to shape the course of events in meaningful ways. Even when structural conditions make different paths more probable, the preferences and choices of particular leaders can overcome challenges and have a significant impact on outcomes.

Some accounts of democratization in India and South Africa, for example, have placed great importance on the role of 'great men'. India in particular possessed many structural features that made democracy appear unlikely, including ethnic, religious, and linguistic diversity, and high levels of poverty and low literacy rates. Yet despite these factors, India's post-independence leadership was able to overcome these odds and play a decisive role in establishing democracy. India's first prime minister, Jawaharlal Nehru, pursued a number of actions that were critical, such as allowing dissent within the ruling Congress Party and supporting institutional checks on his power. These choices set important precedents for Indian democracy that constrained the choices available for subsequent leaders (Varshney, 1998).

Similar arguments are made about democracy in South Africa. South Africa's first post-apartheid president, Nelson Mandela, made a number of choices that set the way for stable democracy. For one, he championed the institutionalization of the African National Congress over elevating his own personal power. By choosing not to seek a second term, Mandela also eschewed the **hyper-presidentialism** so often seen elsewhere in Africa. Importantly, Mandela was instrumental in pursuing a strategy of reconciliation with the former apartheid regime, appealing for calm and forgiveness rather than vilifying his opponents.

These cases illustrate instances in which the preferences and behaviours of individuals paved the way for democratic consolidation. That said, while arguments focusing on agency are persuasive and leaders' preferences and personalities might matter at key junctures, it is 'only through the establishment of durable institutions that their decisions might have long-lasting legacies' (Conroy-Krutz and Frantz, 2017, p. 48). The role of structure, in other words, cannot be ignored. In this chapter, we discuss the institutions that structure the incentives facing leaders and that therefore shape a country's prospects for establishing and maintaining democracy.

Political parties

Political parties play a vital role in the establishment and proper functioning of democracy. Writing in 1942, E.E. Schattschneider highlighted the fundamental role of political parties in democracy positing that, 'modern democracy is unthinkable save in terms of the parties' (p. 1). In this section we outline the vital functions that political parties play in the development and sustainment of democracy. We also discuss how political parties in established democracies are changing and how their shortcomings may be creating conditions more conducive to democratic backsliding.

First and foremost, political parties enable representation and accountability—two factors that are critical for establishing and sustaining effective democracy. Political parties facilitate representation and accountability through the multitude of functions that they fulfil within the mass population, as organizations, and in government (Dalton et al., 2011). Within the mass population, parties simplify choices for voters, thereby reducing the policy complexity of modern government into a small number of options that voters can understand. Parties convey information to citizens about government performance, making it is easier for citizens to evaluate incumbents and synthesize the key positions and qualifications of political candidates (Downs, 1957). Parties are also important vehicles for citizen mobilization, which is required if ordinary individuals are going to organize to challenge the leadership or advocate for specific positions (Mainwaring, 1998). Parties motivate the citizenry to vote and get involved in the political process, instilling in them 'a vested interest in the system' (Diamond and Gunther, 2001, pp. 7–8).

At the organizational level, parties recruit and train potential political leaders and candidates for political office, socializing them into the norms and values of democratic governance (Dalton et al., 2011). Political parties also help aggregate and articulate citizen preferences and inject these preferences into the political sphere. Once these preferences are articulated, they can more effectively guide policy if and when party leaders are elected to office.

Finally, at the government level, parties organize the work of government (Dalton et al., 2011). Once in government, parties possess a comprehensive set of policy objectives for which they have an electoral mandate. The party in government, or a coalition of parties, will then move to implement policies and organize the administration to that end. Moreover, parties help prevent government crises, which have on occasion served as a justification for nondemocratic actions. In Latin America, for example, those countries with weak parties have been unable to legislate coherent policies, making them more prone to crises (Levitsky and Cameron, 2003). By promoting a cohesive message and disciplining party members who break from it, strong political parties can pave the way for more predictable and stable government.

In addition to facilitating representation and the functioning of democracy, political parties also constrain incumbents, providing an important check on executive power. Political parties that are not in office form the basis of the opposition. Opposition parties use the legislature to check the power of the executive by seeking to reduce the resources available to officeholders and to enlarge the rights available to those out of power. They can also help ensure that the courts are not stacked with biased judges and oversee the implementation of policies. Over time, in both new and revived democracies, conflict between the governing and opposition parties helps establish democratic norms and rules (Lipset, 2000).

Which party systems are most likely to encourage democratic consolidation and the persistence of effective democracy? To function effectively, political parties must be firmly aligned with and rooted in identifiable societal interests and cleavages. These linkages provide parties with a base of support among a significant segment of the population that they need to survive electorally. Those party systems that are not aligned with deep societal interests, in contrast, tend to be far less effective in driving democracy. These party systems are instead driven by strong personalities or elite interests. Their lack of ties to a strong public constituency hinders the development of a stable opposition and political competition because it becomes more difficult for the public to hold leaders to account. Party systems that lack linkages to societal interests also struggle to mobilize support bases or engage citizens in political processes. Moreover, highly personalized parties tend to have short time horizons and decision-makers are easily co-opted by incumbent leaders, creating excessive fragmentation in parliaments. Excessive fragmentation, in turn, hinders the formation of stable majorities needed for effective government.

The experience of Pakistan illustrates how weak parties can stymie democratic consolidation. According to Freedom House, Pakistan has a thriving and competitive multiparty system. Democracy continues to remain weak, however, in part given the highly personalized nature of the country's two main political parties, the Pakistan People's Party (PPP) and the Pakistan Muslim League-Nawaz (PML-N). Both parties have struggled to establish strong linkages with identifiable societal interests, and instead are instruments of powerful families, the Bhuttos and Sharifs respectively. Both families have a history of corruption, and until recently have faced few repercussions for such activities. Even beyond Pakistan's two main political parties, the country's other political parties also rely on charismatic leadership, and tribal and community loyalties play a powerful role in determining voters' choices. These party dynamics—along with factors such as the strength of the Pakistani military—has precluded democratic consolidation; Freedom House continues to classify Pakistan as a hybrid regime.

Although strong political party systems generally facilitate the development and persistence of democracy, occasionally strong parties can threaten democracy. Strong political parties tend to be most threatening in new democracies where incumbent parties grow strong relative to other institutions that are tasked with checking executive control (for more on the strength of dominant party systems see Chapter 3). Ukraine offers an example of this dynamic. In 2010, Viktor Yanukovych was elected president as the head of the Party of Regions (PoR). PoR was viewed as being well organized and cohesive (especially relative to other Ukrainian parties) and was more than simply a personal machine for Yanukovych. In particular, the party membership included a number of wealthy oligarchs from Eastern Ukraine, which provided Yanokovych with the resources he needed to consolidate control. Yanukovych's formal powers were limited when he stepped into office. However, he leveraged the monetary and organizational capacity of the PoR to buy off and neutralize competing centres of power. Yanukovych gradually eroded Ukrainian democracy which ultimately crossed the line into autocracy in 2012 amid parliamentary elections that the international community heavily criticized. In sum, strong political parties are critical for the functioning of effective democracy, but they must also be balanced by alternate centres of power to prevent these parties from expanding executive power.

Western political parties and democratic decline

Strong, cohesive, and stable political parties have long been a defining feature of Western democracy. In recent decades, however, there have been frequent claims that traditional political parties are in decline in established democracies, or at the very least experiencing significant change. For example, research shows that voters are less inclined to identify with political parties than at any time since public opinion polling was developed, and party membership is in precipitous decline in these countries. Numerous observers have claimed that the weakening of political parties is giving rise to populist-fuelled democratic backsliding, including in well-established democracies (Levitsky and Ziblatt, 2018)—a topic we also address in Chapter 14.

Several scholars and political observers attribute the strain we see today in Western democracy as resulting, in part, from the declining importance of political parties in Western democratic systems. Dominant parties long counted on deep divides in Western societies—divisions between church and state, a landed elite and a bourgeoisie class, and capitalists and workers—to deliver a reliable and durable source of votes. The post-industrial revolution, however, led to fundamental changes in Western societies in the 1960s that weakened the bonds between citizens and parties. The political left, in particular, began to drift away from workers to focus on the culturally liberal and degree-holding middle class. The emergence of so-called post-materialist issues—a cleaner environment, equal status for women and minorities, improvements in education and culture, a more permissive morality (particularly in regard to familial and sexual issues), and a greater emphasis on rights—introduced new sources of social and political cleavage, giving rise to new parties and rearranging the bases of support of older ones (Clark et al., 1993).

This evolution in the political landscape of established democracies is producing de-alignment, or an erosion of bonds between citizens and the traditional parties (Garzia et al., 2018). Between 2004 and 2015, the average share of the vote going to traditional mainstream parties in Europe dropped by 14 points to 72 per cent. Meanwhile, the share of the vote going to new populist challengers, whether on the left or the right, more than doubled to 23 per cent. The centre-left, in particular, has experienced record losses, and in several political systems, the combined share of the vote going to the traditional mainstream parties has reached record lows. In Germany, for example, in regional elections in 2018, the social democrats saw their worst electoral performance since 1933. The far-right Alternative for Germany (AfD) and the Green Party, in contrast, have seen their vote shares rise.

The **de-alignment** (see further Box 11.2) in Western democracies is fragmenting political systems, leading to higher rates of electoral volatility and clearing the way for an assortment of new challengers. In *How Democracies Die*, Steven Levitsky and Daniel Ziblatt (2018) argue that where democracies have broken down, existing political parties have failed to serve as effective gatekeepers, allowing extreme political challengers to enter mainstream political competition. In numerous cases, de-alignment created space for political outsiders to emerge, including Hugo Chávez in Venezuela, Alberto Fujimori in Peru, and Adolf Hitler in Germany. Once these political outsiders gained traction with some segments of the public, traditional political parties looking to stem their declining vote share sought to forge alliances with these leaders to boost their popular support. As Levitsky and Ziblatt note, the mainstream political parties and leaders mistakenly believe they can co-opt these leaders into their ranks and control their future actions. Instead, their efforts to co-opt the charismatic outsiders gave these insurgents legitimacy, paving the way for the erosion of democracy from within.

 Box 11.2: **Realignment versus de-alignment**

With the rise of Trump and other right-wing populist parties, political observers have speculated Western democracies are undergoing a realignment of their party systems. **Realignment** occurs when there is a sharp but durable shift in the electorate, affecting the partisan balance and signifying enduring changes to the party coalition (Mair, 1984). Realignments can take place when there has been a major change in policy or strong external factors that shape electoral support. These factors can affect the extent to which voters support each party. For the most part, realignments are infrequent. For example, a major realignment in the United States occurred in the election in 1800, when the Jeffersonian Republicans defeated the Federalists.

While realignment constitutes a major shift in public support for existing political parties, de-alignment is a decline in the importance of parties to citizens. De-alignment is a sign that parties have weakened, and they are often accompanied by an increase in support for Independent candidates and/or anti-system candidates. De-alignment can be indicative of high levels of voter apathy, but it does not necessarily mean that partisanship has been completely abandoned. Some view a de-alignment as a natural precursor to a realignment, because partisan alignments have to be weakened first for a realignment to eventually take place (LeDuc, 1985). However de-alignments can occur without producing major partisan shifts (Carmines, 1991).

At the extreme end of de-alignment is party system collapse. Party system collapse takes place when a large percentage of voters completely disengage with parties in the system. New political parties emerge in the vacuum and different configurations of inter-party competition take place. Party system collapse took place in both Peru and Venezuela, giving rise to anti-party candidates, Alberto Fujimori and Hugo Chávez, respectively (Dietz and Myers, 2007).

Consider Hugo Chávez's rise to power and the subsequent degradation of democracy in Venezuela. Venezuelan democracy was long dominated by two parties, the centre-left Democratic Action (AD) and the centre-right Social Christian Party (COPEI). These parties alternated in power for more than thirty years, making Venezuela a model of democracy in an authoritarian neighbourhood. In the 1980s, however, declining oil revenues ushered in a prolonged economic crisis that led to a precipitous drop in living standards and raised dissatisfaction with the political system. In addition to economic crisis, two additional factors undermined Venezuela's mainstream parties, paving the way for Chávez's rise. First, high levels of corruption discredited the AD and COPEI, prompting a precipitous decline in party identification. Voter anger made individuals more willing to tolerate the risk of voting for a political outsider (Seawright, 2012). Second, Venezuela's two parties converged toward the centre, making it hard for voters to distinguish between them ideologically. Many Venezuelans voters, therefore, did not feel that either party could represent their interests, pushing voters out to the extremes and making them more likely to support an alternative presidential candidate. The decline of Venezuela's parties created the space for Chávez's rise.

Chávez ultimately won the presidency in free and fair elections in 1998. After coming to power, he began to slowly dismantle executive constraints and expand his personal power. By 2005 the country had crossed the threshold to dictatorship. Venezuela therefore is a paradigmatic case of the incremental erosion of democracy, characterized not by a single dramatic event such as a military coup but, rather, by a sequence of steps that cumulatively represent an erosion or breakdown of democracy (Mainwaring, 2012). Although there is no single cause of the collapse of Venezuelan democracy, the erosion of the country's major political parties clearly played a role. Once fragmented, the parties were unable to prevent the expansion of Chávez's powers, including his ability to rule by decree. Chávez likewise sought to keep political parties weak through activities such as banning public financing of political parties, knowing that they could pose a challenge to his rule (Corrales and Penfold-Becerra, 2007).

As this discussion illustrates, the erosion of political parties creates fertile conditions for the emergence of charismatic politicians who may or may not be committed to the democratic rules of the game. Absent strong political parties to weed out extreme politicians, political outsiders with little experience in politics can emerge. Because they are unrestrained by a cohesive party, the result is often ineffective government and, in some cases, undemocratic behaviours (Levitsky and Cameron, 2003).

Electoral systems

As the previous section explained, political parties are critical to democratic consolidation. But what are the institutional choices available to (new) democracies that hope to build strong parties and ensure representation? A country's choice of electoral system can shape democratic dynamics. Electoral systems are the rules that translate votes into seats. Although, once established, electoral systems remain fairly constant, occasionally political crisis within an established democracy may lead to momentum for electoral system change. Whether in new democracies emerging from authoritarianism or crisis, or in established democracies reforming their electoral system, the choice of electoral system affects political life and a country's prospects for democratic stability (Reynolds et al., 2008).

There are three broad categories of electoral systems: proportional representation, plurality/majoritarian, and mixed systems. In what follows, we discuss proportional representation and majority systems and the arguments that scholars make linking them with democratic consolidation (or fragility).

Proportional representation

Proportional representation systems are electoral systems where seats are distributed proportionally based on the number of votes received. Countries such as Belgium, Israel, and Italy all have proportional representation systems. The vast majority of proportional representation systems use some sort of threshold that establishes a baseline percentage of the vote that a party needs to gain a seat in the legislature. With proportional representation, coming in first is not required to receive representation; a party simply needs enough votes to pass the threshold. Proportional representation systems are designed to reduce the disparity between a party's share of the national vote and its share of the parliamentary seats; if a major party wins 40 per cent of the votes, it should win approximately 40 per cent of the seats, and a minor party with 10 per cent of the votes should also gain 10 per cent of the legislative seats (Reynolds et al., 2008).

Some scholars argue that proportional representation systems are superior to majoritarian systems for maintaining democratic stability (see, for example, Lijphart, 1977). Scholars holding this view posit that such systems are better for ensuring that a wide variety of citizens feel that their views are represented in government, minimizing the likelihood that disgruntled groups will work to subvert the government and lessening the chance of conflict (Blais and Carty, 1990; Lijphart, 1977; Powell and Powell, 2000). Indeed, both women and minority groups have better representation in proportional representation systems. With proportional representation, individual voters are also more likely to vote for the party that more closely aligns with their preferences rather than vote strategically for a party that is the lesser of two evils. **Gerrymandering**, or the manipulation of the boundaries of an electoral district to favour a particular party, and other forms of electoral manipulation are also less influential with proportional representation systems (Lijphart and Grofman, 1984).

PR systems are common in new democracies, especially those which face deep societal divisions. In these environments, the inclusion of all significant groups in the legislature can be an important condition for democratic consolidation. Failing to ensure that both minorities and majorities have a stake in developing political systems can derail democratic development.

In sum, proponents of proportional representation argue that because citizens are more likely to feel that their views are represented in the political process, the chance of conflict or instability erupting is lower.

Critics argue, however, that proportional representation systems create a platform for more extreme views to enter government. These systems create incentives for parties to court extreme voters rather than moderate ones and gives a stage in the legislature to extremist parties of the left or the right. Relatedly, PR systems may facilitate the hardening of ethnic and extremist positions (Roeder and Rothchild, 2005). Critics also charge that PR can lead to a destabilizing fragmentation of the party system. By expanding the number of electorally viable parties, proportional representation systems increase the chance of democratic gridlock or collapse: with too many parties, it becomes difficult to reach compromise and govern effectively. A final criticism is that some proportional systems may have a threshold (or a minimum percentage of votes that a party must gain in order to be awarded seats) that could be designed with the intention of excluding groups. This was the case when Turkey imposed a 10 per cent threshold to prevent the power of minority groups such as the Kurds (Gumuscu, 2013). Thus, there are different variations of PR that may have the same exclusionary effects of majoritarian systems.

Majoritarian systems

Majoritarian systems (also referred to as single-member district plurality, winner-take-all, or first-past-the-post) are electoral systems in which the candidate with the most votes in a district wins the seat. Countries such as Pakistan, the United Kingdom, and Ghana all have majoritarian systems. Majoritarian systems usually lead to dominance of two large parties, because smaller parties have to coalesce into permanent coalitions in order to remain competitive.

Some scholars argue that majoritarian systems are preferable to proportional representation systems for ensuring democratic stability. Because parties need to have a wide appeal under such systems to win the majority of votes in individual districts, extremist and fringe parties—which can threaten democracy—are disadvantaged (Powell, 1982; Huntington, 2006; Sartori, 2005). Parties are instead forced to be broad-based and representative of many interests, building bridges across diverse social groups. As an example of this, many countries that are known for accommodating diverse populations, such as the United States, India, and Canada, have majoritarian electoral systems (Reilly, 2005). In order to win, parties operating under majoritarian rules also have to offer the electorate a coherent programme for governing and prove their ability to garner a majority. Another advantage is that majoritarian systems may be better at being responsive, since there are individual leaders that must respond to their constituents. Legislators may have to be more accountable to their constituents because they are directly responsible to them (Hoffman, 2005).

There are also a number of drawbacks of majoritarian systems. Majoritarian systems tend to exclude smaller parties, under-represent minorities, and exclude women from the legislature. Evidence across the world suggests that women are less likely to be elected to the legislature under plurality/majority systems than under PR ones. Majoritarian systems also amplify the phenomenon of 'regional fiefdoms' where one party wins all the seats in a province or area. Moreover, these systems can leave a large number of wasted votes that do not go toward the election of any candidate, and they may be unresponsive to changes in public opinion since a pattern of geographically concentrated electoral support means that one party can maintain control in the face of a substantial drop in overall popular support (Reynolds et al., 2008). Another possible issue is that some studies have shown (see Blais and Aarts, 2006; Powell 1982) that voter turnout is lower in majoritarian systems than in proportional systems. The logic behind this is that voters in proportional systems may feel that they can vote for parties that they support, and their vote won't be wasted in the way it would by voting for a candidate outside of the two dominant parties.

As this discussion makes clear, there are persuasive reasons to expect both types of electoral system to be helpful (and harmful) to democratic consolidation. A review of the literature on the effects of electoral systems on democratic stability, finds little evidence suggesting that we should favour one system over the other. In divided societies, PR systems are likely to fare best, but that is not necessarily the case in other contexts (Lust and Waldner, 2015). In sum, the choice of electoral rules matters for a number of outcomes (such as propensity for conflict), but democratic stability is not one of them.

System of government

The system of government refers to the way in which executives are selected. As we noted in the introduction, there are two general types of government systems: presidential systems and parliamentary systems. A large body of literature has examined the impact of the type of government system on democratic consolidation and stability. For many years, most studies in the literature argued that parliamentary systems were more conducive to stable democracy, but recent evidence suggests a more complicated story. Here, we review the major arguments on both sides before closing with a summary of the evidence supporting them.

Presidential systems

In **presidential systems**, citizens directly elect the executive (the president), who is both the head of government and head of state. The executive and legislative branches are distinct, each with their own powers. Typically, the president cannot introduce legislation and is not a voting member of the legislature. The president usually has a fixed term of office and presidential elections are generally held at scheduled intervals.

As mentioned, most early research on the impact of government system type on democratic stability emphasized the dangers of presidentialism (Ackerman, 2000; Linz, 1990; Linz and Valenzuela, 1994). Scholars have put forth a number of arguments that underpin their concerns. First, presidents are more likely to lack experience and proper qualifications than prime ministers. Because the president is directly elected rather than vetted through the legislature, there is a greater propensity in presidential systems to have leaders that lack political experience but that are charismatic in the eyes of voters. In parliamentary systems, in contrast, all contenders for the prime ministership are members of the legislature who typically have substantial political experience and have worked their way up party ranks. Moreover, it is more difficult to unseat poorly performing presidents than prime ministers, who can be removed by votes of no confidence. Other than cases in which presidents may be impeached for violating laws, it is difficult to remove presidents outside of national elections (Linz and Valenzuela, 1994). The rigidity of presidential systems, therefore, can lead to the breakdown of democracy by incentivizing actors such as the military to use force to remove unpopular or poorly-performing leaders.

Critics also argue that presidential systems can weaken democracy because they have the potential to give way to personalism. As O'Donnell writes, presidential systems are more likely to become 'delegative democracies', or democracies with low levels of horizontal accountability (1994). Because the executive branch wields its own independent powers, this weakens the influence of the legislature. Would-be autocrats can leverage this weakness and consolidate control in their own hands, pushing the country into personalist dictatorship. Moreover, leaders may even have incentive to concentrate power in presidential systems. Disagreements between the legislature and executive may give way to policy paralysis and gridlock, giving reason for the president to bypass the legislature and rule by decree.

Parliamentary systems

In **parliamentary systems**, by contrast, the legislature elects the executive (typically referred to as a prime minister). The prime minister is the head of government; the head of state is typically a separate position and in some cases is ceremonial. The prime minister remains the head of government so long as he/she maintains the confidence of the legislature. Should the legislature pass a no confidence vote, legislative elections are called and a new prime minister is selected. In parliamentary systems, the legislative and executive branches are combined and power is not separated between them.

Proponents of parliamentary systems point to a number of reasons why they are better for democracy than presidential systems (O'Donnell et al., 1986; Linz and Valenzuela, 1994; Linz, 1990). For one, they are more flexible in the face of changing circumstances given that elections are not fixed. When prime ministers (or their governments) become unpopular or implement poor choices, the legislature can call early elections, allowing such crises to be resolved through constitutional means (Lijphart, 2004, pp. 101–4).

Advocates of parliamentary systems also argue that the chance of concentration of power in the hands of the leadership is minimized by the fact that power does not rest in the hands of a single individual (Lijphart, 1985). Rather, the power of the prime minister is contingent upon maintaining the confidence of the legislature. It is easier to pass legislation in parliamentary systems as well, preventing the kind of gridlock that can lead to executive grabs for power. Whereas in presidential systems there are no guarantees that supporters of the leader will have a majority in the legislature, in parliamentary systems the prime minister must maintain a majority of the legislature's support to get selected to the position, typically giving the prime minister and his/her government a mandate to direct policy.

Though the bulk of the literature suggests that presidentialism is harmful for democratic stability, the empirical record reveals a far more complicated story. Initially, a number of studies found evidence that presidential democracies were more unstable than parliamentary democracies (see Easter, 1997; Frye, 1997; Linz and Stepan, 1996). Subsequent research has challenged this finding, however (Lust and Waldner, 2015, p. 26). First, many of these studies compared parliamentary democracies in richer countries with presidential democracies in poorer countries. Lower levels of development, therefore, rather than presidentialism may have been driving the initial findings. Second, some studies show that the type of dictatorship in place prior to democratization is the critical factor driving the connection between presidentialism and democratic instability (Cheibub, 2007). Democracies emerging from military rule are more unstable than those emerging from civilian rule; because they are also more likely to be presidential, we see presidentialism associated with a higher chance of democratic breakdown. Indeed, Svolik (2015) finds that though presidentialism does not influence whether new or transitional democracies revert to dictatorship, it does lessen the likelihood that democracy will stabilize in the years to come.

To summarize, it is clear that there is a correlation between presidential systems and less stable democracies, but whether this is due to the nature of presidentialism itself or other confounding factors is less certain. The time frame under analysis also appears to matter. For new and transitional democracies, presidentialism does not appear to impact the chance of democratic collapse. As the number of years of democracy accumulate, however, presidentialism appears to lessen the chance that the democracy will survive in the years to come. Because of the complexity of the relationship between government system type and democratic consolidation, we should be careful before drawing firm conclusions that one type is superior to the other.

Federal versus unitary states

Another institutional choice involves the decision to establish a **federal** versus a **unitary** state. Federalism is the division of power to both the national (federal) government and local governments. Whereas in a unitary system the national government is ultimately supreme, in a federal system some powers lie exclusively in the domain of local governments. With the exception of about a dozen countries, most countries in the world have unitary systems. Those countries with federal systems tend to be larger and more populous (e.g. the United States, Brazil, and Russia), likely because their greater size makes devolution of powers more desirable.

Some scholars argue that federal systems are superior to unitary systems for democratic consolidation, particularly in diverse societies. The logic is that federalism provides greater independence to groups and reduces the number of issues on which the national government has to intervene to resolve. By dispersing power, federalism makes it easier to manage conflict, while also increasing political participation and improving efficiency (Brumby and Galligan, 2015). Proponents of federalism posit that enhancing group autonomy in this way facilitates democratic consolidation (Lijphart, 2004; Diamond, 1999; Horowitz, 1993).

Other scholars, however, express concerns about federalism in new democracies. They argue that by reinforcing territorial identities that are based on ethnic terms, federalism has the potential to stoke or harden tensions (Bunce and Watts, 2005; Kymlicka, 1998). It may also incentivize the rise of regional parties supportive of secessionist conflicts (Brancati, 2006). And it could lead to centre–periphery struggles that undermine democracy.

There are logical arguments on both sides of the federalism debate, and perhaps it is for this reason that the record is mixed. Some new democracies have succeeded under federalism (e.g. Mexico), while others like Iraq have faced challenges (see further Box 11.3). The cross-national empirical research reflects this mixed record and shows that there is little substantive relationship between federalism and the durability of democracy in developing countries (Hadenius, 1994). Rather, whether federalism is desirable for a new democracy likely depends on the specific environment of the country in question. And as we emphasized previously, the critical dynamic is whether the institutional arrangements put in place can effectively constrain the chief executive.

Box 11.3: **Federalism in Iraq**

Proponents of federalism argue that it guarantees minority rights and reduces incentives for conflict. However, power sharing systems that allow local groups to have their own autonomy may also magnify the salience of communal identities, which make it harder for cross-cutting cleavages to be established. In Iraq's case, federalism has led to instability and hardened sectarianism rather than serve as a safety valve to guarantee minority rights (Anderson and Stansfield, 2010). Why did federalism fail to lead to a stable democracy in Iraq?

After the U.S. invasion of Iraq in 2003, the United States' Coalition Provisional Authority was tasked with devising the country's institutions post-Saddam Hussein. This was a complicated assignment from the outset, due to a variety of demographic and historical challenges. Ethnically, Iraq is a mix of approximately 20 per cent Kurds (who for the most part are geographically concentrated together) and 80 per cent Arabs. Though the vast majority of Iraqis are Muslim, roughly 60 per cent are Shiites and 40 per cent are Sunnis. Because Saddam Hussein was a Sunni Arab, Sunni Arabs were favoured under his rule.

In light of this setting, the natural choice from the United States' perspective was to choose a federal system that would give regions of Iraq substantial autonomy. Though federalism sounded good on paper, opinion polls revealed that a strong majority of Iraq's population did not support such a system. Almost 80 per cent favoured a unified state (BBC News, 2004). Many worried that a federal system would lead to the partitioning of the country, fueling sectarianism even further.

In spite of the lack of local support for a federal system, the 2005 Constitution stipulated an extreme version of federalism, resulting in a de facto partitioning of the country (Kane et al., 2012). It allowed Iraq's governorates to form a federated region, where local laws would have priority over federal laws. This severely weakened the power of the central government. The provinces could mostly ignore the central government on many important issues, and it was nearly impossible for it to impose taxes. Tensions quickly rose over the management of Iraq's sizeable oil and gas revenues, as well, and how they would be shared. Disputes also broke out between the Kurdish Regional Government and the central government over budget allocations and contested territory (Le Billon, 2015).

At first blush, a federal system seemed like the preferable choice for post-Saddam Hussein Iraq. But the implementation of an extreme form of federalism in an already weak state made the central government even more impotent and illegitimate. It was so hollowed out that it could not offer much support to the regions, let alone help create a national identity. The lack of consensus over how power is shared and distributed in Iraq continues to be a contentious issue that challenges the stability of its democracy.

Consociationalism

In addition to the decision to create a federal versus a unitary state, some scholars and policymakers have advocated for a **consociational** approach to democracy in countries that feature significant ethnic, religious or other cleavages—an issue that is often salient in post-conflict and newly democratizing states. Consociational democracy is essentially a democracy that allows for significant power sharing—or the ability to access positions of power—among the country's various factions (Lijphart, 1985). In some cases, executive power is shared by majority parties. The presidency of Bosnia and Herzegovina, for example, is a three-member body representing the Serbs, Croats, and Bosniaks, which collectively serves as head of state. Consociational approaches have also been used in other post-conflict environments like Northern Ireland (Nagle, 2011; Nagle and Clancy, 2012), South Africa (Lijphart, 1998), and most recently in Burundi (Lemarchand and Niwese, 2007). The goal is to give diverse communities representation, which in turn is expected to foster greater political stability (McGarry, 2008).

One of the key advocates of consociationalism, Arend Lijphart, defines consociationalism in terms of four characteristics. The first is grand coalition, which means that all political leaders of all the segments of the society jointly govern the country. An extraordinary majority is needed for important decisions such as amending a constitution. A grand coalition is a form of power sharing because it includes representatives of all of the relevant social groups in the executive decision-making process. All parties gain from cooperation because it helps maintain order and peace (O'Leary, 2013, 2). Some previous research has demonstrated that Lijphart's grand coalition decreases the risk of ethno-nationalist civil war substantially (Cederman, Wimmer, and Min, 2010).

In addition to a grand coalition, Lijphart argues in favour of a minority veto which enables communities to block a policy that might jeopardize their interest within the system. This gives a minority group a sense of security.

Lijphart also advocates a proportional system, which applies not only to the electoral system but also to the 'composition of the public service and to the allocation of public funds' (1999, p. 15). This helps to ease competition over state resources, which can help ensure a fair and just democratic system. Parity representation can take place at the executive level, as in Belgium, or across the state such as in Lebanon. Proportional systems are supposed to serve as a guarantee for representation.

The final characteristic is segmental autonomy, which means that decision-making authority is delegated to the separate groups to the extent possible. Segmental autonomy can be applied differently, depending on whether groups have concentrated settlement patterns or are more evenly distributed throughout the country. Federalism can be applied when groups are geographically concentrated such as in the Kurdish region of Iraq. In cases where a given group is scattered, cultural autonomy can be applied by providing funding for specific groups and allowing groups to maintain their linguistic, religious, and cultural heritage (Lijphart, 2004, p. 105).

Although consociationalism may be the most expedient way to get conflict to end and has been applied effectively in cases such as Northern Ireland, South Africa, and Belgium, critics nonetheless claim that it can obstruct democracy. This is in large part because consociational arrangements freeze identities and interests, which can lead to political instability and undermine democratic consolidation (Byrne, 2001). Moreover, power sharing institutions 'empower ethnic elites from previously warring groups, [and] create incentives for these elites to press radical demands once the peace is in place'. This dynamic can increase polarization and/or make it difficult to reach consensus, which can also threaten democracy (Roeder and Rothchild, 2005, p. 56).

Box 11.4: **Constitutional design: The case of Tunisia**

For new democracies, the collapse of the old regime often results in a period of uncertainty with many consequential decisions to be made. One of the more pressing of these is the choice of a constitution (Landau, 2012). While the laws laid out in the constitution are certainly important, so too is the adaptability of these laws. Some scholars argue that a rigid constitution, which allows for judicial review, is best for new democracies (Lijphart, 2004). Others, by contrast, posit that an easily amendable constitution is preferable because it allows for more flexibility to adjust to changing contexts and social norms (Albert, 2015). There is no 'one-size-fits-all' constitutional model, of course. The case of Tunisia illustrates the pressures on new democracies in producing a constitution and what key lessons can be learned.

The Tunisian Constitution, which was adopted in January 2014, has been universally praised as a significant achievement in the country's path to democratization (Blaisdell, 2016). Observers have lauded its progressive commitments to curtailing executive power, as well as its protection of human rights and women's rights in particular. Examples include the gender-sensitive wording used in the constitution and the assurance that both men and women have the right to work, vote, and stand for election (Charrad and Zarrugh, 2014).

That said, there are some criticisms of Tunisia's Constitution. One particular concern is that it may be too rigid for a country still in transition. As an example, the president can only be removed through impeachment, which requires two-thirds support from the parliament (Pickard, 2014). There are also concerns about the eternity clauses that have been put in place (Bell et al., 2017. Though these unamendable provisions serve as a guarantee to parties that their interests will be safeguarded, they forever close off avenues for constitutional change and make it more difficult to compromise further down the line (Suteu, 2017).

Others criticized the process of constitution making in Tunisia. The country was put under a lot of pressure to do things quickly, forcing the drafters to write the constitution—an incredibly complex process—in a matter of months. Moreover, the largest political party, Ennahda (a moderate Islamic party), dominated the drafting committee, upsetting other committee members (Stepan, 2012). This led to compromises that benefited the Islamists and gave them greater influence, such as their ability to impose Islam as the state religion (Netterstrøm, 2015).

Other critics took issue with the fact that no official role was granted to Tunisia's many constitutional law experts to ensure that modern constitutional practices were implemented. Although hundreds of conferences, seminars, and other meetings were organized, constitutional law experts were only consulted on an ad hoc basis. Many declined to take part, expressing concerns that the scope of their involvement was too ambiguous. There were also concerns that key constitutional law experts were not permitted to take part in the process (Gluck and Brandt, 2015).

Later stages of the process were more inclusive, however. After the National Constituent Assembly (NCA) presented the first draft of the constitution to the public in August 2012, it launched an outreach campaign that included public meetings with interest groups and debates broadcast on television. The United Nations Development Programme supported a dialogue between the members of the NCA and hundreds of civil society organizations, as well. Though the NCA was under no obligation to listen to these groups, some key changes took place after the first draft that reflected hopes for more checks and balances (Gluck and Brandt, 2015). Still, some observers criticized the fact that the constitution was adopted through a two-thirds majority vote in the parliament as opposed to a referendum. In spite of this, in the end the government made efforts to reach out to and consult the public, which helped secure greater legitimacy and support for the constitution. As the speaker of the Tunisian parliament declared, the Tunisian Constitution 'without being perfect, is one of consensus' (Kottoor, BBC News, 2014).

Political institutions and democratization: A double-edged sword

Up until this point our discussion of institutional design has focused on the effect of institutions on democratic consolidation and backsliding. Before we conclude this chapter, we wish to briefly highlight the relationship between institutions and transitions to democracy.

As we have discussed through the first part of this book, contemporary autocracies are evolving. The twenty-first century autocrat is not the same as his pre-Cold War predecessor. Of course there are enduring similarities and tried and true tactics that have persisted over time. But authoritarian regimes are learning and adapting in important ways. One important change we see today in authoritarian regimes is their widespread adoption of seemingly democratic institutions, such as local and national elections, referendums, political parties, and legislatures (Gandhi, 2008; Schedler, 2006). Although the presence of these institutions in authoritarian settings is not altogether a new phenomenon, there has been a substantial uptick in autocrats' adoption of institutions since the end of the Cold War (Kendall-Taylor and Frantz, 2015).

At first glance, it would appear that the growing presence of democratic institutions in dictatorships would make these countries more likely to transition to democracy. The presence of democratic institutions, it would seem, should create space the opposition can use to grow and develop, and provide an outlet people can use to make their political preferences known, facilitating collective action. Authoritarian regimes, however, have learned to co-opt institutions for their own purposes. Rather than increase the likelihood of democratization, the presence of these **pseudo-democratic institutions** actually prolongs an authoritarian regime's time in power (Gandhi, 2008; Gandhi and Lust-Okar, 2009; Geddes, 2005; Smith, 2005). By pseudo-democratic institutions we are referring to institutions that do not properly function for the purpose they are intended. We should therefore be cautious before interpreting the adoption and/or deepening of pseudo-democratic institutions in dictatorships as a sign that democratization is around the corner.

Although pseudo-democratic institutions extend the life of an authoritarian regime, these institutions also make it more likely that once an autocracy collapses, democracy will follow (Kendall-Taylor and Frantz, 2015; Howard and Roessler, 2006). Put differently, those countries that utilize pseudo-democratic institutions are more likely to democratize upon their collapse than those regimes where these institutions are absent. Since the end of the Cold War, 70 per cent of institutionalized dictatorships democratized upon their collapse (38 out of 54), compared to 61 per cent of those that lacked these institutions (11 out of 18). Young autocracies with institutions are especially likely to democratize. Institutionalized dictatorships that fall from power during their first decade democratize at a rate of 77 per cent. Even among dictatorships that lack pseudo-democratic institutions, the chance of democratization is significantly higher during the first decade in power (69 per cent) than after it (33 per cent).

Institutions in autocracies might increase their prospects of transitioning by providing pro-reform actors with important experience and resources in the pre-transition era. Institutions also have the potential to disperse political power in ways that allow for greater pluralism after democratic openings occur. For example, Lindberg (2006) finds that regularly holding elections, even if highly flawed, can increase a country's prospects for democratization. He argues that *de jure* competitive elections can create a set of institutions, rights, and processes that alter incentive structures in ways that are conducive to greater democratic strength over time. The opposition also learns strategies for competition and mobilization and is better able to pursue a more level playing field and push to expand civil liberties as it improves its ability to navigate regime institutions. Ultimately, this can result in a slow transformation of the old regime into a more democratic one. Elections also provide an opportunity for key factions within the regime elite to defect. Outside of Africa, however, scholars have found little evidence that repeated elections lead to democratic change (McCoy and Hartlyn, 2009; Lust-Okar, 2009). Looking at the Middle East, for example, Lust-Okar (2009) shows that elections actually work to dampen pressures for democracy.

In sum, institutions in authoritarian regimes are a double-edged sword: they increase the durability of an authoritarian regime, but once the autocracy collapses, it has a greater chance of democratizing than less institutionalized authoritarian regimes.

Conclusion

This chapter examined the relationship between institutions and democratic development. We began by looking at the importance of political parties for democratic consolidation. We noted that political parties are a critical component of democracy, but we highlighted the importance of striking the right balance between well-institutionalized and cohesive parties, and those that are able to dominate the political system (hegemonic parties). After explaining the importance of political parties, we focused on institutional choices such as majoritarian versus proportional system, parliamentary versus presidential systems, unitary versus federal systems, and consociationalism.

The central message to emerge from this chapter is that there is no institutional blueprint that countries can follow that will put them on the path towards democratic consolidation. The reality is far more complicated. What works well in one setting may aggravate or amplify existing societal challenges in another. Instead, the key to deepening and safeguarding democracy is building strong institutions with the strength and capacity to check executive power. Examples include a well-developed and autonomous judicial system, an independent media, and a pattern of respect for election results and term limits. Where institutions and norms of behaviour are weak or disregard the rule of law, in contrast, they do very little to actually structure behaviour. Governing groups intent on harassing their opponents or stealing elections, for example, can do so with little resistance. Likewise, leaders in these settings can use the law and selectively apply it to target the opposition—through libel suits aimed at journalists critical of the government, and prosecution of tax violations aimed at businesses that fund opposition.

In sum, where institutions are weak, the risk of democratic breakdown will be higher relative to those countries with strong and effective institutions. Because weak institutions create fewer constraints on behaviour, leaders can have an outsized impact and their political preferences have greater potential to shape the political trajectory of their country. Those leaders seeking to enhance their own personal power, for example, will encounter fewer roadblocks in their efforts to do so. Where institutions are robust, by contrast, the individual preferences of the governing group matters less, and the future of democracy is more secure.

Key Questions

1. How do parties affect democratic consolidation? Can you have stable democracy without well-functioning parties? Why or why not?

2. Technological change and social media in particular allow leaders to bypass political parties and communicate directly with voters. How do you think these changes will affect political parties and their role in a functioning democracy?

3. What type of electoral system is better for fostering stable democracy? What are the strengths and weaknesses of each system?

4. Is presidentialism harmful to democratic consolidation? Why or why not?

5. Should Iraq have chosen federalism? What challenges did Iraq face that a unified system would be unlikely to resolve either?

6. What lessons that can be learned from Tunisia's constitution-making process? Overall, can we say it was a success? Why or why not?

Further Reading

CHEIBUB, J.A., 2007. *Presidentialism, Parliamentarism, and Democracy*. Cambridge University Press.

LIJPHART, A., 1977. *Democracy in Plural Societies: A Comparative Exploration*. Yale University Press.

POWELL, G.B. and POWELL JR, G.B., 2000. *Elections as Instruments of Democracy: Majoritarian and Proportional Visions*. Yale University Press.

12

International Drivers of Democracy

Most scholars agree that democratic transitions tend to cluster in time and space. Samuel Huntington was the first to refer to this phenomenon as 'waves of democracy'. The most recent and widely analysed wave, the **Third Wave**, began in 1974 when Portugal's dictatorship collapsed in the 'Carnation Revolution'. At that time, there were only forty-six democracies in the world, representing just 30 per cent of the world's independent states. Portugal's transition subsequently catalysed democratization in some thirty countries over the next fifteen years, including in right-wing dictatorships in Southern Europe, military juntas in Latin America, and single party regimes in East Asia. Then came the collapse of the Soviet Union in 1989. The end of the Cold War gave new momentum to democracy's march, including a series of democratic transitions in Eastern Europe and sub-Saharan Africa. Although scholars generally agree that the Third Wave has crested (if not begun to recede), the number of democracies in the world today remains near historic highs.

Democracy's remarkable run since 1974 has in many ways fuelled complacency about its progress and endurance. We have come to assume that the international *zeitgeist*, or 'spirit of the times' will facilitate and sustain democracy. In the twenty-five years following the Cold War's end this was a safe assumption. Democracy, it seemed, had triumphed and secured its status as the world's preferred form of governance. Momentum appeared to be squarely on democracy's side. In the last ten years, however, it has become clear that this logic no longer applies. Research by Freedom House underscores how the international tides have changed—the democracy watchdog has documented that respect for democratic norms and principles have declined for the last thirteen consecutive years.

Adding additional concern to the trend captured by Freedom House data is the often-overlooked aspect of the **democracy-in-waves** metaphor: both of the previous two waves of democracy were followed by reverse waves during which large shares of the democratic gains were lost. The first wave of democracy—which occurred over the course of almost one hundred years spanning the American and French Revolutions—ended around 1926 when Mussolini's rise set off widespread democratic decline. Democracies fell in countries ranging from Estonia, Germany, Greece, and Spain, to Argentina, Brazil, and Japan. Similarly, the democratic gains accrued during the second wave of democracy, which occurred in the aftermath of WWII, were significantly eroded in the 1960s and early 1970s by a substantial uptick in military interference in the political process. The rise **of military dictatorships** was most prevalent in Latin America, but also spread to Greece, Pakistan, the Philippines, and Indonesia.

What accounts for this observed clustering of democracy over time? Why is it that democracies are more prevalent in some regions than others? To address these questions, we shift our attention away from the domestic drivers of democracy we have focused on thus far, such as economic development and political institutions, and examine the international forces that shape democratic development. As we will see throughout this chapter, international dynamics influence the balance of power among domestic actors, which can shape a country's prospects for the onset and deepening of democracy (Gunitsky, 2014). In fact, a large and growing body of research underscores that factors taking place outside a country's borders have played a significant and under-examined role in regime change and democratic development.

In this chapter we discuss these external factors including diffusion, foreign intervention, linkages (like trade and cross-cultural contacts), and foreign aid. We begin by discussing how the structure of the international system affects democratic development worldwide. One of the key takeaways of this chapter is that geopolitics matter. When the international system is led by a single democratic power—as has been the case since the end of the Cold War—the democratic super-power and its partners can use trade, aid, and other linkages to encourage the onset and consolidation of democracy. Once competing authoritarian regimes emerge, however, these dictatorships can use the same tools in ways that dilute democratic leverage. Competition between democratic and authoritarian great powers, in other words, enables other countries to play great powers off one another, ultimately making it easier for governments to sustain hybrid or authoritarian systems.

In our view, the rise of geopolitical competition has been a key driver of the declining respect for democratic norms and practices we see today. As was previously noted, international dynamics since the end of the Cold War have strongly supported democracy. The particulars of the immediate post-Cold War era—namely the collapse of an authoritarian superpower and the dissolution of its empire, a period of unchallenged U.S. dominance, and a widely shared commitment to free trade and liberal values—converged to propel democracy forward.

But the post-Cold War system is changing. Today, democratic nations are in retreat in the realm of geopolitics. The United States, the architect of the liberal post WWII international system, has called into question its commitment to free trade and democracy. Meanwhile, the influence of several authoritarian countries, especially China and Russia, is rising. Given the tectonic shift currently underway, we focus much of this chapter's discussion on how the mechanisms that favoured democracy are now working in reverse, creating conditions more conducive to the spread of authoritarianism. While the traditional democracy literature tends to focus on the positive progression of democracy, in this chapter we emphasize those international forces that are working to advance autocracy.

Geopolitics and the international order

Political science research demonstrates that the structure of the international system affects the number of democratic countries in the world at any given time (Gunitsky, 2014; Boix, 2011). These studies show that the waves to and from democracy coincide with shifts in the distribution of power among key states in the international system. When the Soviet Union's power rose early in the Cold War, for example, authoritarianism spread. Toward the end of the Cold War, when the United States and Western Europe gained the advantage and ultimately triumphed, democracies proliferated. In other words, research shows that the global distribution of power, and whether that power is held by democratic or authoritarian regimes, explains the relative frequency of democratic versus authoritarian systems.

Empirical research shows that when a single democratic country dominates the international system, the number of democracies in the world peaks. Research by Carles Boix (2011) argues that democratic hegemons have tended to favour the spread of democracy, in part, because of their principled commitment to human rights. But it is the absence of an alternative great power that enables democracies to more assertively support democracy. Democratization is messy, and a dominant democratic state must be willing to accept the risks that its efforts to promote democracy could result in a less reliable or even unfriendly regime. A democratic power will be more willing to assume such risk when there is no competing power present to capitalize on and support a more antagonistic regime (Boix, 2011).

As the democratic hegemon, the United States played a critical role in advancing democracy during the Third Wave. As Larry Diamond (2008) notes, the Third Wave did not just happen. The United States and European democracies played a key part, making a 'heavy investment … in support of the democratic parties' (p. 5). The United States used a variety of tools, including direct military intervention, to aid democratic transitions and protect existing fragile democracies all across the globe (Kagan, 2016). Samuel Huntington estimated that in the aftermath of the Cold War, U.S. support was 'critical to democratization in the Dominican Republic, Grenada, El Salvador, Guatemala, Honduras, Uruguay, Peru, Ecuador, Panama, and the Philippines' and 'a contributing factor to democratization in Portugal, Chile, Poland, Korea, Bolivia, and Taiwan'. International activism on the part of the United States and its democratic partners helped to build a broad, if not universal, consensus that was favourable to democracy and less sympathetic to authoritarian forms.

Just as the number of democracies rises with a democratic hegemon, so too does the number of democracies decline when authoritarian great powers dominate the system. Dominant authoritarian powers support authoritarianism because even seemingly inconsequential democratic states may be used as a base to spread democratic ideas and to support a democratic movement within the authoritarian great power (Boix, 2011). Moreover, when the global hegemon is authoritarian (or a coalition of autocracies holds most global power) then the dynamics we discuss throughout this chapter such as the diffusion of norms and linkages through trade and aid work to spread autocracy.

The reverse wave that occurred after World War I illustrates the dynamics that occur with the rise of authoritarian powers. **The Great Depression** and the rise of **fascist** Germany led to a significant decline in the number of democracies in the inter-war period. In Europe, the democratic great powers, France and Britain, were suffering the effects of the recent war, while the United States had largely withdrawn from international affairs. In the vacuum, Mussolini came to power in Italy in 1922 and Germany's Weimar Republic crumbled. While democracies were weakened, Europe's fascist regimes sought to present themselves as stronger and more capable of providing reassurance in troubled times (Kagan, 2016). They appealed effectively to nationalist, ethnic, and tribal sentiments. As political commentator Robert Kagan summarized, 'people tend to follow winners, and between the wars the democratic-capitalist countries looked weak and in retreat compared with the apparently vigorous fascist regimes and with Stalin's Soviet Union'.

In sum, 'politics follows geopolitics' (Kagan, 2016). Changes in the balance of power among leading states have a strong and statistically significant effect on the domestic evolution of regimes, even when accounting for other variables commonly associated with political development (Boix, 2011; Gunitsky, 2014). In the remainder of this chapter we discuss the pathways through which international actors and changes in the distribution of power between them create conditions that are more—or less—conducive to democracy.

Diffusion, diffusion-proofing, and autocracy promotion

In Chapter 7 we discussed how a democratic transition in one state raises the risk of democratization in a neighbouring or similar state—a process called **diffusion**. We defined diffusion as the transfer among countries of an innovative idea, product, policy, institution, or repertoire of behaviour (Koesel and Bunce, 2013). Scholars of diffusion have traditionally conceptualized it as a process whereby past events make future events more likely (Oliver and Myers, 2003; Strang, 1991). Regime-threatening protests in one country raise the risk of regime-threatening protests in neighbouring states or countries with similar grievances and internal dynamics. Similarly, the presence of democratic regimes in a region raises the likelihood that a neighbouring non-democracy will democratize. Our previous discussion about the effects of the structure of the international system is also a story of diffusion. Rather than regime type spreading in domino-like fashion, however, changes to the structure of the international system shift the institutional preferences and incentives of domestic actors in many states simultaneously (Gunitsky, unpublished manuscript).

As research on diffusion has progressed, however, it has become clear that diffusion is not a linear process. Past events do not always make future events more likely. Instead, democratic diffusion almost always triggers *resistance* to diffusion (Gunitsky, unpublished manuscript). In his work, Seva Gunitsky describes the life cycle of diffusion. Initially, the spread of a new tactic or norm strengthens actors pushing for reform and catches ruling groups off guard, unseating many governments before they have a chance to react. The early phases of diffusion also generate optimism about the prospects for regime change, and in some cases create powerful international pressure for democratic reform. But as diffusion advances, these same processes transform or fade away: the coalitions of actors pushing for reform dissolve as their disparate interests divide them; elites learn from the experiences of others and begin to repress, pre-empt, or co-opt challenges; the initial optimism of reform movements can give way to disappointment with results; and the international support for democratization associated with the early phases diminishes. In these ways, authoritarian elites learn to counter pro-democracy diffusion and enhance regime resilience.

Authoritarian leaders have strong incentive to learn and adapt their tactics to counter democratic diffusion. Since the end of the Cold War, pro-democracy diffusion has unseated twenty-one autocrats from office—including the democratic wave that swept across Eastern Europe at the end of the Cold War, Eurasia's Colour Revolutions, and the Arab uprisings. Democratic diffusion caught these governments off guard despite in many cases the long tenure of leaders, their considerable coercive powers, and their alliances with powerful international actors (Koesel and Bunce, 2013). Aware of the threat that protests have posed to their peers, autocrats are taking active measures to 'diffusion-proof' their regimes.

Russian and Chinese actions following the Colour Revolutions illustrate the way that autocrats are learning and responding (Koesel and Bunce, 2013). Both governments take the view that they are at risk of what they perceive as Western-backed regime change, and the repertoire of tactics they adopted demonstrates their understanding of diffusion dynamics. Following the **Colour Revolutions**, Russian and Chinese governments sought to control the information available about protests in other countries, framed the uprisings and outcomes negatively, and denied citizens the coordinative resources needed to carry out their own revolutions. For example, Russian and Chinese governments targeted the key constituencies that play a prominent role in protests, especially opposition groups, civil society associations, and youth. Beijing and Moscow targeted the first two groups with **repression**; in the case of youth, they have sought to co-opt younger generations through the creation of pro-government youth movements committed to promoting patriotism and defending the state (Koesel and Bunce, 2013).

Not only have Russian and Chinese government adapted their survival strategies to confront perceived external threats to their rule, but they are also working together to share 'best practices' for fending off Western democracy promotion and shore up at-risk dictatorships. In the remainder of this section we focus on this coordination and collaboration. These dynamics represent an important aspect of the international influences that shape democratic development. No longer is it sufficient to just talk about pro-democracy diffusion and democracy support as a key driver of democracy worldwide. Instead, autocrats are asserting themselves on the world stage and are colluding to counter democracy promotion, creating substantial headwinds for global democracy.

In what follows we discuss two forms of authoritarian coordination—direct and passive. We think of **direct collaboration** as those processes that result from proactive efforts by leading autocracies to broadcast their lessons learned and best practices to like-minded governments. It is a very intentional form of collaboration requiring networks and relationships, both at the government and non-government levels. **Passive collaboration**, in contrast, is more indirect and less deliberate. Other scholars have referred to passive collaboration as 'emulation' or 'demonstration effects'. In these cases, regime officials learn from the mistakes and successes of their peers and change their behaviour accordingly.

Direct authoritarian collaboration

Although it is not always apparent, authoritarian leaders collaborate. For example, in the wake of the Cold War, the widespread adoption of elections initially unseated several authoritarian regimes. Following the electoral defeat of Kenneth Kaunda in Zambia in 1991, however, African leaders proactively began to advise each other of how to hold competitive elections without being voted out of office (Bratton, 1998). Today, autocrats have figured out how to use elections to serve their own self-sustaining purposes.

More recently, there is substantial evidence indicating that autocracies such as Russia and China proactively seek to transmit their diffusion-proofing and other survival strategies to other leaders looking to shore up their domestic control. In some cases, Moscow and Beijing proactively push their preferred tactics for resisting external threats and maintaining domestic control to like-minded governments. In other cases, admiring leaders proactively seek out the support and advice of Russian and Chinese government officials (Ademmer and Borzel, 2013; Koesel and Bunce, 2013).

Authoritarian leaders often collaborate in times of crises. China, Russia, Saudi Arabia, and Venezuela, for example, have engaged in extensive efforts to prop up embattled autocratic regimes in their neighbourhoods. In addition to military intervention, which we address in the next section, autocracies have used a number of tools to support like-minded leaders. Elections are an especially critical juncture for many autocrats, and provide an important window for authoritarian collaboration (regarding collaboration in subverting election monitoring, see Box 12.1). Russia has been especially active in this regard, particularly in its efforts to back pro-Russian leaders during elections in post-Soviet states such as Belarus, Ukraine, and Kyrgyzstan. Beyond Russia, former Venezuelan President Hugo Chávez also provided electoral support to allies. As an example, Chávez openly backed the election of Nicaraguan leader Daniel Ortega in 2011. Chávez assisted Ortega financially with low interest loans on oil payments, which better enabled Ortega to fund social programmes, keep energy prices low, and eliminate opposition TV stations.

Box 12.1: **The rise of election monitoring and authoritarian efforts to mimic it**

Election monitoring is a key focus of international efforts to support democracy. Election observation has grown so prevalent that it has become an international norm, and it is rare for any country to hold an election without inviting international observers. Nearly 80 per cent of all national elections are now monitored (Hyde, 2011; Kelley, 2008). In many instances, especially in **hybrid systems**, governments allow election monitors to observe their elections because they seek the legitimacy observer missions can confer. The costs of refusing monitors are also so high these days that even many cheating governments have found it rational to invite them (Kelley, 2008). Those states accepting monitors are rewarded with greater investment, foreign aid, trade, military support, and membership into international organizations (Hyde, 2011). The most active election observation organizations are the **Organization for Security and Cooperation in Europe** (OSCE), the EU, the Organization for American States (OAS), and the African Union.

As election monitoring has increased, however, non-democracies have learned to adapt, developing new ways to co-opt the practice. In many cases, governments intent on cheating have crafted strategies to avoid the condemnation of observers. In particular, governments no longer wait until election-day to manipulate the process. Instead of easily observable practices such as ballot box stuffing, they manipulate the playing field well ahead of the vote using techniques that are less likely to be criticized and punished. In their research, Alberto Simpser and Daniela Donno (2012) argue that autocrats have learned to evade international scrutiny and instead resort to tactics of election manipulation that are more damaging to domestic institutions, governance, and freedoms, such as rigging courts and administrative bodies and repressing the media.

Not only have non-democracies adapted to evade detection, but they have also sought to mimic the practice of election monitoring in ways that serve their authoritarian interests. In particular, authoritarian regimes have created what Alexander Cooley has called 'zombie' election monitors, or monitors that try to look like democratic observers, but serve autocratic purposes by pretending that clearly flawed elections deserve clean bills of health (2015).

Examples of this phenomenon abound. The Russian-led **Commonwealth of Independent States** (CIS) has been especially active in this regard. In Kazakhstan, for example, after the Organization for Cooperation and Security in Europe (OSCE) denounced the 2012 parliamentary elections for not meeting basic standards, Kazakhstan invited elections monitors from the Inter-parliamentary Assembly of the Commonwealth of Independent States (IPA-CIS) to observe its 2014 Senate elections and received a glowing report (Kramerjan, 2012; Witte, 2014). Similarly, though the OSCE reported serious problems during Azerbaijan's 2013 presidential election, alternative organizations such as the Cooperation Council of Turkic-Speaking States provided a glowing assessment of the vote (Walker and Cooley, 2013). Authoritarian regimes are also noted for cooperating with each other on election observation missions. China, for example sent small teams to observe elections in Madagascar and Zimbabwe (Cooley, 2013).

Authoritarian regimes have used these zombie monitors to 'legitimize' their rule, or in the very least create confusion. As Cooley explains, regimes leverage zombie monitors to confuse and distract, sow uncertainty by promoting pro-government 'narratives', and boost the plausibility of government complaints that critical foreign observers are biased. **Zombie election monitors**, therefore, are a highly visible example of counter-diffusion, where autocrats have learned to co-opt a democratic practice and the success of early adopters has led other countries to emulate it.

The external support from fellow autocrats can play an important role in helping autocrats maintain power in these times of crisis. Scholars have highlighted, for example, that authoritarian collaboration was critical for stemming the **Arab Spring** in the Gulf region (Odinius and Kuntz, 2015). The **Gulf Cooperation Council** supported monarchies under stress to prevent similar uprisings in proximate regimes (Von Soest, 2015). Saudi Arabia, for example, sent 1,200 armed forces to Bahrain to quell the protests. In addition, the Kingdom dispensed at least $500 million to boost the Bahraini economy and made visible gestures of political support for the Bahraini regime (Hassan, 2014). Saudi support for Bahrain proved decisive for the Bahraini regime. From the Saudi perspective, such support was also critical for its own stability. The protests in Bahrain were the first in a monarchy raising the risk that the people in Saudi Arabia would identify closely with events in Bahrain and seek to emulate the protests. Bahraini protests were also in close proximity to Saudi oil fields increasing Riyadh's incentive to intervene to restore stability.

Increasingly, we are seeing indicators that authoritarian regimes are collaborating more closely outside times of crisis. Russia's effort to share its tactics for countering 'Colour Revolutions' is perhaps one of the clearest examples of such direct collaboration. In the wake of the **Colour Revolutions** and even more intently after the Russian protests surrounding Putin's return to the presidency in 2011–12, the Kremlin has proactively sought to educate other governments about the 'threat' of Colour Revolution and train them to counter it (McFaul and Spector, 2010). As one study shows, Russia has shared its techniques and laws aimed at suppressing dissent. Russia's laws, or versions of it, have been adopted in a number of other states, including China, Venezuela, Kazakhstan, Uzbekistan, Tajikistan, Belarus, Egypt, Ethiopia, Kenya, and Zimbabwe (Koesel and Bunce, 2013). Similarly, Russia and China share technologies aimed at monitoring dissent online. The Chinese and the Russians share technologies with each other and with other authoritarian states such as Kazakhstan, Belarus, and Venezuela that block the free flow of information and enhance the ability of the regime to monitor the exchange of information (Koesel and Bunce, 2013). The Kremlin, for example, shares its online surveillance technology (called SORM, or 'system for operational investigative measures') with several post-Soviet states. This technology enables governments to monitor online content, including the targeting of opposition leaders (Freedom House, 2017).

Perhaps most notably, however, China has increasingly begun to export surveillance technology. Under Chinese President Xi Jinping, the Chinese government has vastly expanded domestic surveillance, enhancing the government's control over its citizens. Often referred to as China's 'Digital Silk Road', Beijing now exports its surveillance know-how and equipment to a growing swath of countries. Aside from exporting its digital and technological practices, scholars have also highlighted how China pursues an active strategy of increasing its soft power around the world, especially in Africa and Latin America (Kurlantzick, 2007). Although much of China's efforts emphasize more indirect influence, including infrastructure projects and no-strings-attached foreign aid, Beijing also engages in direct collaboration through training programmes for foreign officials and government managers (Kurlantzick and Link, 2009). Joshua

Kurlantzick and Perry Link (2009, p. 24) note that these training programmes 'often involve discussions of how the [Chinese Communist Party] has managed to open its economy, keep the middle class on the side of the government, and avoid socio-political chaos like that experienced during the transition periods in Russia and many other developing countries'.

Before we move to discuss passive collaboration, it is important to address the intent behind authoritarians' sharing of best practices. The consensus among scholars is that autocrats do not engage in 'autocracy promotion' in the same way that Western countries promote democracy (Way, 2016). Authoritarian powers' motivations to support fellow autocrats are self-serving rather than driven by an ideological commitment to autocracy (Von Soest, 2015). Instead, autocracies such as Russia and China appear more concerned with blunting democracy promotion—which they see as a vehicle for the United States to spread its influence—than they are with spreading authoritarianism. Although these regimes might prefer to work with fellow strongmen, they tend to be most concerned with advancing national interests, including economic ties and stability in foreign relations (Carothers, 2009; Bader et al., 2010). In other words, today's autocrats are primarily interested in their own survival and in creating conditions that ensure that the West cannot impose its form of government on them and others like them (Ambrosio, 2010).

Russia's assertive actions and assault on Western democratic institutions since 2014 is an important caveat to this academic consensus. Russia's efforts to interfere in democratic elections, including in the 2016 U.S. presidential election and the 2017 French presidential election, cannot be understood simply as efforts by Moscow to blunt democracy promotion. Instead, since Russia's illegal annexation of Crimea in 2014, Russia has expanded the scope and intensity of its actions and proactively seeks to undermine Western democracy. The Kremlin measures Russian power in terms that are relative to the United States and the West. Therefore, the Kremlin views weakening these democratic systems as a way to enhance Russia's own influence. Although Russia likely does not seek to transform Western democratic institutions into authoritarian ones, its assertive actions should lead scholars to question the assumption that Russia merely seeks to blunt democracy promotion.

Passive collaboration

In the last section we discussed how autocrats deliberately share and spread their tactics. In addition to these proactive efforts, authoritarian best practices can also be spread through more passive and less intentional mechanisms. Social scientists have sometimes referred to what we call passive collaboration as 'emulation' or 'demonstration effects' (Bunce and Wolchik, 2007). In his study of autocratic diffusion and cooperation, Kurt Weyland (2017) defines passive diffusion as an 'uncoordinated, unilateral, predominantly horizontal process through which political, policy, or institutional innovations spread from an innovator ... to learners, imitators or emulators' (p. 1237).

One of the primary mechanisms through which passive diffusion occurs is through **norm change** (see Box 12.2). Normative shifts entail a change in the relative strength of 'dominant understandings' of what is deemed appropriate, pushing decision-makers to conform to goals and practices that are seen as socially legitimated (Lee and Strang, 2006, p. 886). Large geopolitical shifts, potentially including the changes underway in today's international order, alter perceptions about what constitutes a legitimate regime (Gunitsky, 2014). Changes in the balance of power send powerful signals about the relative strength and efficacy of different regime types, with the dominant powers becoming more attractive to would-be emulators (Gunitsky, 2014, p. 576). This was the story of the immediate post-Cold War era. As Steven Levitsky and Lucan Way (2002, p. 61) argue, 'Western liberalism's triumph and the Soviet collapse undermined the legitimacy of alternative regime models and created strong incentives for peripheral states to adopt formal democratic institutions.' Even countries that were autocratic became more compelled to present themselves as more democratic by holding 'elections'.

 Box 12.2: **Changing international norms and the spread of autocracy**

In a public speech in 2014, Hungarian Prime Minister Orbán praised **'illiberal democracy'** and declared the Western political model dead. After highlighting the success of Russia, China, Turkey, and Singapore, he declared that to be globally competitive, Hungary would have to 'abandon liberal methods and principles of organizing a society'. That Orbán was so willing to openly declare the end of liberal democracy underscores the notion that international norms are shifting. Political scientist Alexander Cooley identified three new norms—namely the prioritization of state security, civilizational diversity, and traditional values over **liberal democracy**—that now enjoy significant backing and are reshaping the international environment in ways that are conducive to the spread of autocracy. Research suggests that if these new norms gain traction, new actors will become more likely to internalize them in order to become respected members of international society (Finnemore and Sikkink, 1998). We briefly summarize them here.

- *Counter-terrorism and state security:* The single most powerful source of counter-norms has been the post- 9/11 turn towards counter-terrorism and state security. The 2001 terror attacks in particular set off an 'international state of emergency' that empowered governments to expand executive authority (Scheppele, 2004). Since 2001, many countries have used counter-terrorism narratives to justify their crackdown on civil society, especially laws restricting the foreign funding of NGOs. Concurrent with a global emphasis on counter-terrorism, the last two decades have also been marked by a high incidence of instability, including civil wars and large-scale protests. Events such as the Arab Spring have led many citizens to be more accepting of restrictions on their political and civil liberties in return for leaders' promises of stability. Most recently, Europe's migration crisis has breathed new momentum into the state security counter norm. European leaders, including in countries long assumed to be consolidated democracies, are using fears of migration and terrorism to roll back respect for democratic principles.

- *Civilization diversity:* Appeals to 'civilizational diversity' and the principle of non-interference in the domestic affairs of sovereign states form another class of emerging counter-norms. China has been especially proactive in this regard. Beijing regularly refutes liberal democracy's universalism and criticizes the political conditionality that international institutions adopt to advance universal democratic norms. Along with Russia, Beijing has sought to use regional organizations to help spread this counter-norm. For example, the Shanghai Cooperation Organization (SCO)—a regional security organization founded in 2001 by China, Russia, and four Central Asian states—emphasizes the importance of non-interference in other countries' affairs.

- **Traditional values:** Russian President Putin is leading a conservative movement to counter what he sees as a decadent and morally bankrupt West. He has sought to frame multiculturalism, radical feminism, and homosexuality as threatening to Russian society and further evidence of Western attempts to encroach on Russian values. Not only has Putin sought to protect Russian society from these 'deviant' forces, but he has also become a vocal advocate of policies protecting 'traditional values' abroad. Support for Putin's traditional-values agenda has been strongest along Russia's periphery, especially in Central Asia. However, elements of this agenda have been gaining traction in places such as Hungary as well. The EU and multiple human rights watchdogs have warned that introducing the concept of traditional values into the global discourse risks distorting interpretations of existing human rights norms and undermining their universality.

In a relatively short period, the leading autocracies have mounted a formidable challenge to democracies and their values. Although there is still no coherent ideological alternative to democracy—a factor many observers contend will limit autocracy's spread—these countries are advancing norms that have the potential to further undermine the West's normative appeal.

Scholars have emphasized that norms can change even absent an international shock and without the effort of a 'norm entrepreneur'. According to Ann Florini (1996, p. 375): 'An international norm may begin to spread in the absence of a norm entrepreneur if some states simply emulate the behaviour of some prestigious or otherwise well-known actor, even if the emulated actor is not attempting to communicate its behaviour.' States with a high level of prestige help set the tone about what is acceptable in the international system, which in turn facilitates the diffusion of norms and values (Ambrosio, 2010). A country's prestige is determined by a host of factors, such as military capability, economic strength, self-confidence, and recognized importance on the world stage. The point here is that prominent authoritarian powers can create conditions that are more conducive to autocracy even when they do not proactively seek to promote a coherent alternative ideology. In other words, autocracies do not have to engage in 'autocracy promotion' to weaken democracy. Powerful autocracies can inspire emulation, provide other states with 'cover from criticism' and confer credibility and/or immunity to countries following their lead (Elkins and Simmons, 2005, p. 7).

There is some evidence to suggest that Russia's return as a global power has begun to inspire like-minded leaders to look to President Putin as an emulation-worthy actor. More specifically, for Turkish President Erdoğan and Central and Eastern European leaders such as Hungarian Prime Minister Orbán, Putin's combination of authoritarian rule and anti-Western ideology has served as a model to emulate (Krastev, 2018). These leaders have adopted several tactics and narratives Putin has used to maintain his control in Russia. In Hungary, Orbán—like Putin—has emphasized the importance of stability over individual liberties, including scapegoating minorities and emphasizing the importance of conservative values. Like Putin, Orbán has also demonized the opposition and sought to centralize power in his own hands by undermining liberal checks and balances. It is, of course, difficult to demonstrate the extent to which these and other leaders consciously emulate Putin's tactics (Buzogány, 2017). At a minimum, however, Orbán's public statements suggest he appears to admire the strongman form of government in Russia.

Research on authoritarian collaboration will continue to evolve. Some commentators see changes in the geopolitical environment, active collaboration, and passive diffusion as playing an important role in deterring democratic development globally. Other scholars question whether these factors play a causal role (Brownlee, 2017). In his cross-national empirical study, political scientist Jason Brownlee argues that authoritarian powers have not precipitated an authoritarian resurgence, and he points to the high number of electoral democracies as evidence for his claim. Moreover, Brownlee finds that where we have seen democracies falter in the last two decades, they have done so for primarily domestic reasons and not because of any substantial outside influence by assertive autocracies.

In the end, it may well be that the truth lies somewhere in between these two views. We agree that contemporary authoritarian regimes are not driven by a missionary impulse to spread their form of government; they are predominately interested in supporting the specific policies and leaders (democratically chosen or not) that benefit their own national interests (Brownlee, 2017). Nonetheless and over time, the end result of today's geopolitical dynamics and the actions of assertive autocracies is that they are creating conditions that are detrimental to democracy. The international actions of authoritarian regimes reinforce other leaders' pre-existing autocratic tendencies by serving as a model for others to follow, providing them with alternative sources of aid and trade that dilute Western influence, and by conferring top cover and external legitimacy that bolsters their domestic standing. In sum, a rise of illiberal and authoritarian practices will provide other like-minded leaders with alternative sources of support that will facilitate their turn away from democracy and make it easier for existing autocracies to remain that way.

In the next section we shift gears and talk about a much more direct mechanism through which outside actors can influence democratic development—external imposition.

External imposition

The most direct way that outside actors can influence another state's regime type is through direct military intervention. Changes in the balance of power in the international system increase the likelihood that the rising power will intervene in the domestic affairs of other states (Gunitsky, 2014). Seva Gunitsky argues that by producing stark but temporary disparities in relative power, changes in the international order create windows of opportunity for rising hegemons to impose their regimes on other states. Shifts in the balance of power, he suggests, increase the legitimacy of the rising power's external actions while lowering the cost of foreign intervention. Rising powers have built military forces that facilitate their power projection. Moreover, significant changes in the balance of power often follow major wars, meaning that most rising hegemons have recently mobilized their military. Because the coercive power needed for intervention has already been built and mobilized, a new hegemon faces relatively low costs for foreign intervention.

Since the end of the Cold War, the United States and its democratic allies have intervened militarily—at least in part to empower democratic rule—in Panama (1989), Haiti (1994), Bosnia (1995), Yugoslavia/Kosovo (1999), Afghanistan (2001), Iraq (2003), and Libya (2011). Yet little is known about the implications of these types of actions. To date, the empirical record on whether such foreign interventions can raise a country's prospects for democracy is inconclusive. We briefly outline the different perspectives on foreign intervention's effect on democratic development.

A first group of scholars and policymakers is optimistic about the usefulness of military force for encouraging democracy. In the U.S. policy realm, **neo-conservatives** have been the most vocal proponents of using military force to promote democracy. Neo-conservatives contend that not only does the United States have a moral obligation to encourage democracy abroad, but doing so furthers U.S. national security interests by creating peaceful, like-minded states. Neo-conservative ideology, for example, significantly shaped George W. Bush's foreign policy agenda, most notably his belief that the United States could democratize Iraq. Democratization scholars that support this view have posited that foreign intervention can raise a non-democracy's prospects for political change through several pathways. Some contend that intervention may be necessary to dismantle and remove abusive political and military institutions that have become entrenched against popular pressure (Bermeo, 2009; Whitehead, 2009). Others argue that military defeat can discredit ruling elites or foster new elite bargains that favour democracy (Dogan and Higley, 1998). These views have found some empirical support. One study finds that foreign interventions have enhanced democracy, as measured by improvements along the POLITY democracy measure (Pickering and Kisangani, 2006).

The case of Panama offers an example of how external imposition can promote positive change. In December of 1989, the United States invaded Panama to oust military dictator Manuel Noriega as part of Operation Just Cause. Hundreds of Panamanians died in the operation and the UN General Assembly declared the invasion to be a violation of international law. Since the ousting of Noriega, Panama has successfully completed five peaceful transfers of power. Elections are competitive and regularly held and citizens enjoy a wide range of civil liberties. However, Panama faces high levels of corruption, growing socio-economic inequalities and weak judicial institutions. All of these issues remain impediments to democratic consolidation (Guevara-Mann, 2016; Pérez, 2017).

Other scholars are more pessimistic about the effects of foreign intervention on democracy. Although some in this camp concede that democratic interventions can spur a transition to democracy, they find that the target state ends up with weak democracy and an unstable political system (Gleditsch and Beardsley, 2004). Research suggests that this sub-optimal outcome may stem from the fact that most interventions have targeted countries that are poor (e.g. Afghanistan), resource-dependent (e.g. Iraq), and located in nondemocratic neighbourhoods—all factors that bode poorly for democracy. Other scholars in this camp argue that democratic interventions have no discernible effect on regime type. Bruce Bueno de Mesquita and George Downs (2006) show that despite the substantial investment of blood and treasure that some democracies have made in part to promote democracy, the targets of military intervention experience no meaningful degree of democratic improvement afterward.

The strongest pessimists, however, argue that regime-changing interventions adversely affect a country's prospects for democracy. The military action required to remove unfriendly leaders, they posit, creates violence and other conditions inhospitable for democracy. Likewise, foreign interventions can provoke a nationalist backlash against political institutions imposed from the outside (Mearsheimer, 2005), and/or weaken domestic institutions by cultivating dependency on external support (Fukuyama, 2004). Empirical analysis supports the pessimistic perspective, showing that foreign intervention rarely produces democracy. The evidence shows that over half of regime-toppling military interventions result in new dictatorships (Escriba-Folch and Wright, 2015). Such interventions are particularly unlikely to produce democracy when military actions target personalist dictatorships, such as those in Afghanistan (2001), Iraq (2003), and Libya (2011).

Finally, there is a group of scholars who view the effect of foreign intervention on democracy as contingent on other factors. One line of research sees the intentions and effort of the intervening state as decisive. These studies have found that interventions were more favourable for democracy when the objective of the intervention was explicitly to liberalize the target state (Meernik, 1996), when the United States took concrete actions to promote liberal reform, including supervising elections (Hermann and Kegley, 1998; Peceny, 1999), and/or where the U.S. and international community invested significant effort, including high troop levels and financial aid for state building (Dobbins, 2003; Brownlee, 2017). Similarly, some see the effects of foreign intervention on democracy as dependent on conditions in the target state. These studies emphasize many of the domestic drivers of democracy we have discussed, including development, inequality, and ethnic fragmentation. These studies produce evidence suggesting that foreign intervention can spur democracy in countries that are relatively developed, equitable, and homogenous.

Another study combines these perspectives and argues that both intervener actions *and* the presence of preconditions for democracy determine the success of foreign interventions (Downes and Monten, 2013). The authors argue that, on average, foreign intervention by a democracy has no effect on a target country's prospects for democracy. Foreign actions tend to be more successful, however, when interveners remove leaders and change institutions, but even then, these actions are not enough to overcome domestic impediments such as underdevelopment, domestic fragmentation, and inexperience with democracy.

Clearly democracies are not the only countries to use external intervention to advance their national interests. Authoritarian regimes also use military force in ways that affect democratic development, typically to shore up the control of a besieged authoritarian regime. During the Cold War, for example, the Soviet Union was quick to deploy the Red Army in any country that had a protest, such as during the Hungarian Revolution of 1956 and Prague Spring in Czechoslovakia in 1968. As we previously discussed, Saudi Arabia (with the support of the Gulf Coordination Council) sent troops into Bahrain during the Arab Spring to prevent the monarchy from falling (Gunitsky, 2014). Most recently, Russia and Iran deployed military force to support Bashar al-Assad and his regime in Syria. In the case of Russia, Moscow's decision to intervene was guided by its desire to advance a number of core national security interests, but key among them was the Kremlin's desire to push back against the United States and what Russia perceives as Washington's efforts to unseat unfriendly regimes. Although the Syrian civil war continues, Russian intervention was decisive in shifting battlefield dynamics in favour of the Assad regime.

In sum, academic research does not offer clear policy guidance for outside actors interested in advancing democracy. One area of relative consensus, however, is that domestic context matters: some countries are better candidates for democratization than others, and external efforts to bring about democratic change are more likely to work where those preconditions are present than where they are absent. Of course, many countries where Western actors would consider military intervention do not meet the enabling criteria. In those cases, outside actors may be better off employing non-forceful means—such as foreign aid, development assistance, and attempts to build civil society—to encourage democratic development. We now turn our discussion to examine the effect of these other international influences.

Linkage and leverage

Different countries face very different external constraints and opportunities for autocratic behaviour. In some cases, such as the Middle East, the external environment is extremely permissive, and outside actors apply little pressure for democratic reform. Other countries, however, face a great deal of scrutiny. In their influential book *Competitive Authoritarianism* (2010), Steven Levitsky and Lucan Way argue that the extent of a country's linkage with the West and Western leverage substantially shapes the external environment a country faces. **Western linkage** refers to the density of ties (economic, political, diplomatic, social, and organizational) and cross-border flows (of capital, goods and services, people, and information) among particular countries and the United States, the Euopean Union, and Western-dominated multilateral institutions. **Western leverage** refers to a governments' vulnerability to external democratizing pressure. Leverage is lowest in large, militarily capable states, with strategic allies in volatile regions, and in those countries where governments have support from alternative regional actors. Through their examination of about three dozen regime transitions, Levitsky and Way conclude that democracy is most likely to emerge and remain strong in those countries where the United States and West maintain extensive ties, and especially when those ties are combined with sufficient leverage (Levitsky and Way, 2005, 2006, 2010).

International actors may exert leverage in a variety of ways, including political con-ditionality and punitive sanctions, diplomatic pressure, and military intervention. As Levitsky and Way note, the impact of such measures (or even the threat of them) on authoritarian governments is greatest in regimes over which Western leverage is high. Leverage supports adherence to democratic norms and practices by raising the cost of bad behaviour, such as coup attempts, repression, electoral fraud, and other govern-ment abuses. When leverage is high, Western countries can credibly threaten to sanc-tion bad actors, withhold aid, or even intervene. According to the authors, however, Western leverage over electoral authoritarian systems is rarely sufficient to convince them to democratize.

Leverage is most effective when combined with extensive linkage to the West. Levitsky and Way argue that the density of linkages between the democratic West and other countries affect democratic development in four ways. First, in countries with extensive penetration by Western media and NGOs, dense communication flows, and widespread elite contact, it is more likely that government abuses will reverberate in Western capitals. Second, and closely related, the density of these networks raises the probability that the West will respond to the abuse. Third, extensive ties with the West create incentives for local actors to uphold the democratic rules of the game. Because egregious violations could threaten their country's standing within Western demo-cratic communities, domestic actors have an incentive to oppose government abuses. For businesses that depend on transnational economic activity, for example, norm-violating government behaviour risks triggering sudden shifts in trade or investment flows. Finally, linkages can make domestic pro-democracy groups more powerful. Ties to influential foreign actors can increase domestic groups' access to resources, provide them with valuable information and know-how, and help to protect some opposition groups from repression.

Levitsky and Way emphasize that linkages are rooted in a number of structural variables like colonialism, cultural, and historical factors, and especially geography. Countries located near the United States or the **European Union (EU)** generally have more economic interaction, a larger number of intergovernmental and inter-organizational connections, and higher cross-border flows of people and information than more geo-graphically distant ones. Western linkages have been strongest in Central Europe and Latin America, and weakest in Africa, Central Asia, and East Asia. In other words, a country's potential for creating extensive linkage with the West is difficult to change.

Two factors with the potential to change the ties that a given country shares with Western democracies is a shift in the distribution of power in the global system and a state's political will to play an active and leading role internationally. As we discussed earlier, the rise and fall of powerful democracies affects the frequency and quality of their interactions with other states. Rising powers can rapidly expand their networks of trade and patronage with many states at once, as the United States and EU did in the aftermath of the Cold War. Declining powers, in contrast, quickly lose their abil-ity to exercise influence beyond their borders (Gunitsky, 2014). The Soviet collapse, for example, disrupted patronage networks in many African states in the early 1990s, which both diminished the policy options available to elites and led citizens to question the legitimacy of pro-Soviet rulers (Decalo, 1992). As Gabon's ruler Omar Bongo proclaimed in 1990, 'The winds from the east are shaking the coconut trees in Africa' (Decalo, 1992, p. 7).

Just as strong linkages between other countries and Western democracies exert a strong pro-democracy force, so might the opposite be true—the growing influence and activism of authoritarian regimes could increase the frequency and quality of their interactions with other states. Rising ties among autocracies, in other words, has the potential to facilitate authoritarian efforts to sustain their repressive systems of rule. Several scholars have speculated, for example, that China's increasing ties to African states will hamper the long-term democratic prospects of these countries (Keenan, 2009; Lagerkvist, 2009). We note here, however, that recent research questions whether authoritarian ties actually enhance the durability of autocracies. One study examines the impact of Chinese engagement—including state visits, arms trading, aid projects, economic cooperation, and trade dependence—and finds that bilateral interactions with China have little effect on the longevity of authoritarian regimes (Bader, 2015).

Less is known about the potential influence of growing ties between autocracies and new or weak democracies. Will such connections dilute Western leverage? Will these relationships gradually weaken pro-democratic forces and strengthen the autocratic tendencies within regimes? Will these ties ultimately empower anti-democratic forces just as ties with democracies encouraged democratization? Future research is needed to answer these important questions.

Foreign aid

Economic aid and democracy support constitute part of the network of ties between states that we discussed above. These tools have been important pillars of U.S. foreign policy, particularly since the end of the Cold War. In the 1990s and 2000s, donors contributed hundreds of billions of dollars of aid worldwide. Today, more than $10 billion a year is spent on democracy assistance alone (Carothers, 2015). Nearly every Western government gives some aid for democracy building, and the number of political party foundations, private foundations, NGOs, and multilateral organizations operating in this space has proliferated (Carothers, 2015). But what do we know about the effectiveness of foreign aid as a policy instrument? Does **foreign aid** and democracy support improve the quality of democracy and/or reduce the risk of **backsliding**?

In this section we build on our discussion of foreign aid in Chapter 7, where we presented competing views on the effect of foreign assistance on democratization. As we noted, some scholars contend that foreign aid has done little to spur democratization, and may actually provide leaders with additional resources they can use to sustain their hold on power. Others argue that foreign financial support raises a country's likelihood of transitioning to democracy, especially if it comes from democratic states, it targets particular types of autocracies, it is conditional, and donors' threat of aid withdraw is credible (Dunning, 2004; Bermeo, 2016; Wright et al., 2015). But once a country transitions to democracy, what is the role of aid?

Unfortunately, the research on the effect of foreign aid on democratic consolidation is equally inconclusive. Some scholars argue that foreign aid has no effect or is detrimental to democratic development (Knack, 2004). According to this perspective, foreign aid functions like natural resource wealth—it provides governments with income that reduces incentive for taxation. Governments that do not depend on taxation, in turn, grow less accountable to their citizens. High levels of aid, in other words, can make recipient governments more accountable to foreign donors than to taxpayers. Other research has found that aid is harmful to democracy because it raises a country's coup risk. Foreign aid might increase country's coup risk through a number of mechanisms, including by making control of the government a more valuable prize (Grossman, 1992), worsening corruption, especially in ethnically diverse societies (Knack, 2004; Svensson, 2000); and by reinforcing executive dominance in new democracies (Bräutigam, 2000).

Finally, Thomas Carothers took a broad look at the state of the democracy aid community since the late 1980s and identified several shortcomings that continue to hinder the effectiveness of aid (Carothers, 2015). Although he notes that practitioners' approach to democracy aid has evolved, he highlights that the competing objectives among foreign aid providers, their propensity to focus aid on a limited circle of favoured NGOs in the capital city, and the tendency of some organizations to rely on a one-size-fits-all approach to programming are key factors that hinder aid's effectiveness.

Other scholars, however, produce evidence that foreign assistance encourages democratic consolidation. Studies suggest that aid can contribute to democratic consolidation through two general pathways (Finkel et al., 2007). First, it can affect levels of democracy *indirectly*, by transforming structural conditions that enhance the quality of democracy and its prospects for survival. Examples include assistance to improve education and increase per capita incomes. Aid can also affect democracy *directly*, by empowering agents (individuals, political institutions, and social organizations) that participate in the political process and that monitor government performance. This type of aid is referred to as democracy aid, and typically seeks to enhance *vertical* and *horizontal* accountability (Dietrich and Wright, 2014). Democracy aid targeting *vertical* accountability includes technical assistance targeting electoral processes, such as educating and empowering voters and supporting political parties, and the promotion of **civil society** organizations, including a free press, public interest NGOs, and civic-education initiatives. Democracy aid targeting *horizontal* accountability includes support for strengthening legislatures, judiciaries, and anti-corruption commissions that serve as checks on executive power.

Most of the research finding that aid positively influences democracy indicates that it is democracy aid rather than more general foreign aid that has the greatest impact. Steven Finkel et al. (2007) examine democracy support allocated by **USAID** and finds that these disbursements increase recipient countries' overall democracy levels. Simone Dietrich and Joseph Wright (2014) also show that democracy aid furthers democratic consolidation, by increasing the stability of multi-party systems and reducing the likelihood of electoral misconduct. They note, however, that democracy aid does not enhance the competitiveness of the opposition, underscoring that external support tends to work best when it does not necessarily threaten incumbent regimes. The finding that democracy aid is more effective than general aid has also been borne out in studies looking specifically at transitions to democracy: targeted democracy aid (and not general aid) is positively linked to democratization (Scott and Steele, 2011).

In addition to the type of aid, research also shows that the geopolitical environment in which such aid is disbursed influences its efficacy. In particular, empirical research demonstrates that foreign aid—especially democracy aid—was particularly effective in the aftermath of the Cold War (Dunning, 2004; Wright, 2009; Bermeo, 2011). The end of the Cold War meant that Western donors and international financial institutions increased their focus on promoting democracy and accountable government. Even more importantly, the end of the Cold War signalled that Western threats and conditions attached to foreign aid became more credible because powerful donors such as the United States no longer had to prioritize anti-Communism over democracy promotion. Likewise, recipient countries could no longer use the Soviet Union and the superpower rivalry to stave off reforms. The geopolitical context has also shaped how aid influences economic reform. David Bearce and Daniel Tirone (2010) similarly show that foreign aid promoted economic growth in recipient countries by facilitating economic reform, but only after 1990 when Western governments could more credibly threaten to curtail their aid if such reform was not forthcoming.

This body of research suggests that the rising assertiveness of Russia and China has the potential to render conditional aid and democracy support less effective. As Beijing and Moscow deepen their relationships with other autocracies and hybrid systems, they are more likely to be viewed by these states as viable alternatives to the United States and other Western countries. Already, sub-Saharan countries are learning from their Northern African counterparts how to play China, and to a lesser extent Russia, off the United States to reduce Western pressure for reform. More governments are learning from countries such as Egypt that they can threaten to move closer to China and Russia if Washington and Brussels push too hard for reform.

Shifting geopolitical dynamics are also fuelling several counter-norms that stigmatize conditional aid and democracy support. In just the past few years, dozens of governments across the globe have taken steps to block, limit, or denounce democracy and human rights support. Aid from the United States is sometimes the principal target, and USAID has been expelled from countries ranging from Bolivia to Russia. These norms not only suffocate domestic groups in the most closed societies, but even in more permissive environments external actors have begun to respond by diluting their programmes. Already, there is evidence that explores the nature of civil society assistance and finds that democracy promotion has grown more compliant. International NGOs increasingly aim to choose more regime-compatible projects to guarantee future funding (Scott and Steele, 2011). Moreover, practitioners now have to consider whether Western support for opposition members in many of these countries does more to hurt than help their prospects for success. Although most common in authoritarian settings, a widening swath of leaders has begun to use evidence of Western support to discredit domestic actors.

Many policymakers, scholars, and practitioners have registered the challenges surrounding democracy support today and begun to question the utility of foreign aid as foreign policy tool. Thomas Carothers (2015) counters such scepticism and notes, instead, that 'democracy aid is not facing an existential crisis so much as it is coming up against hard realities that are far from historically unusual when seen in a longer-term perspective'. He goes on to note that, 'for the foreseeable future, democracy aid will have to operate principally in countries rife with forbidding obstacles to democratization; powerholders in many places will resist and resent such aid; and alternative political models will vie hard for attention and influence' (p. 73). If democracy aid is to remain effective, practitioners will need to continue to update their approaches to respond to the changing geopolitical context and address the ways in which authoritarianism is evolving.

 Box 12.3: **The sequencing debate**

U.S. interventions in Iraq and Afghanistan and the upheavals in the Middle East revived a long-standing policy debate about the efficacy of U.S. efforts to promote democracy. Scholars and policymakers regularly debate when—and even whether—external actors should press for democratic reform. This debate is referred to as the 'sequencing debate.' It pits the 'sequentialists', or those that posit that outside actors should not push for democracy until after a strong state is established, against the 'gradualists', or those that believe that democracy support should not be contingent on preconditions (Carothers, 2007; Fortin, 2012; Fukuyama, 2012; Mansfield and Snyder, 2007; Rose and Shin, 2001). Here we summarize the opposing views of the sequencing debate.

TEAM A: THE SEQUENTIALISTS

The **sequentialists** argue that democracy will struggle to take root—or even worse, unleash violence and chaos—unless it is preceded by a strong state and the rule of law. Without a strong state, the leaders of new democracies are doomed to fail. Richard Rose and Don Chull Shin (2001) argue, for example, that in weak states leaders face a double challenge of 'completing the construction of the modern state while competing with their critics in free elections' (p. 336). In more extreme cases, scholars including Samuel Huntington caution that the rise of mass participation absent institutionalization leads to fragility, conflict, and breakdown. Edward Mansfield and Jack Snyder (1995, 2005) argued that states that democratize absent strong state institutions are conflict-prone, pointing to violence in former Yugoslavia and the former Soviet Union as evidence. Amy Chua (2004) similarly asserted that the simultaneous pursuit of democracy and market reform in countries with 'market-dominant minorities' leads to ethnic conflict and anti-market backlashes.

For sequentialists, efforts to push democracy in countries that are ill-prepared can and often do lead to bad outcomes, including illiberal leaders or extremists in power, nationalism, ethnic and other types of civil conflict, and interstate wars. The aftermath of the Arab Spring only underscored for many the risk of democratization absent pre-conditions. To prevent such results, adherents of this view believe that outside actors seeking to promote positive political change in a nondemocratic society should concentrate first on helping that state to achieve the rule of law and a well-functioning state. Only much farther down the road, when those preconditions are established, should outsiders push for elections and other democratic components.

TEAM B: THE GRADUALISTS

Although there is some evidence that capable states enhance the likelihood of successful democratic consolidation, scholars have emphasized that there have been a number of states that
democratized 'sequentially' but experienced conflict and instability (Berman, 2007a, 2007b).
Likewise, the historical record shows that numerous democracies were born and survived in poor
countries with limited state capacity. Indeed, it is difficult to reject the possibility that the causal
arrows run in the other direction: from democratic accountability to increases in the capability of
the underlying state (Fortin, 2012).

   The **gradualists** hold that the sequentialist argument rests on two faulty assumptions. According
to Thomas Carothers (2007), it is incorrect to assume 'that authoritarian leaders can and will act
as generators of rule-of-law development and state-building and that democratizing countries
are inherently ill-suited for these tasks' (p. 14). Authoritarian leaders have little incentive to build
strong state institutions or implement rules that constrain their exercise of power. Here Carothers
notes that the sequentialists get things backwards. He argues that, 'it is the lack of democracy—
that is, the persistence of autocracy in many countries—that is a fundamental obstacle to rule-of-
law development' (p. 16). Rather than waiting for preconditions to be met, gradualists advocate
that external actors should 'reach for the core element(s) now, but do so in iterative and cumula-
tive ways rather than all at once' (Carothers, 2007, p. 25). Building democracy is hard, but putting
some democratic practices in place can create space needed for deeper institutional reform. The
gradualists warn, however, that many contemporary autocrats are abusing the gradualist logic
and falsely portraying themselves as being on a pathway to more meaningful reform. These leaders disingenuously claim that their cosmetic reforms are intended to serve as incremental steps
on the path to democracy when in reality they just use this language to blunt pressure for change.

International organizations

The final external driver we address in this chapter is a country's participation in regional
and international organizations. Research shows that membership in these organizations
affects a country's prospects of democratization and consolidation (Pevehouse, 2002a,
2002b). Scholars argue that international organizations advance democracy by setting rules,
promoting values, and providing information, assistance, and enticements (Finnemore and
Sikkink, 1998; Schimmelfennig and Sedelmeier, 2002; Kelley, 2004). Empirical research
by Jon Pevehouse (2002) finds that democracies that join democratic regional organizations are more durable than those that do not. Pevehouse, along with Edward Mansfield
(2006), argues that regional organizations prolong democracy because new democracies
use their membership to bind elites to reform. Membership provides elites with strong
incentive to reform because it creates high political and economic costs for governments
that fail to comply with their international commitments. In addition, governments can
use resources created by the organizations to buy off uncooperative groups. In addition to
their binding function, regional organizations can encourage democracy through social
influence and persuasion, transmitting norms and values in ways that alter the target state's
belief systems and ensure that new norms and values are internalized (Kelley, 2004, p. 428;
Finnemore and Sikkink, 1998; Schimmelfennig and Sedelmeier, 2002).

The European Union is the classic example of how regional organizations can advance democracy. There is widespread consensus among scholars that EU enlargement contributed significantly to European economic recovery, peace and stability, and democratization following the Cold War. Of all the tools the EU had at its disposal, EU conditionality, or the promise of material incentives in return for reform, drove political change. More specifically, the desire of most Central and Eastern European countries to reap the benefits of EU membership, combined with the high volume and intrusiveness of the rules attached to its membership, gave the EU an unprecedented ability to reshape domestic institutions (Schimmelfennig and Sedelmeier, 2004). Research suggests that EU influence was greatest when Brussels offered full membership (rather than association or partnership) and when the domestic costs of implementing democratic reforms were relatively low (Schimmelfennig and Scholtz, 2008; Schimmelfennig and Sedelmeier, 2004). In other words, the benefits of EU membership were insufficient to motivate reform in those countries where the adoption of democratic rules would have undermined a regime's hold on power, such as Slovakia under the Mečiar government, or Croatia during the Tudjman regime. To summarize, although scholars would not claim that EU conditionality was more important than the domestic determinants of democratization, the incentives to join the EU were instrumental in overcoming domestic obstacles to further democratic reform.

Democratic backsliding in EU member states such as Hungary and Poland, however, has recently called into question the ability of regional organizations to sustain democracy. Scholars have highlighted a number of reasons why the influence of regional organizations declines post-accession. Some argue that international organizations are unable to prevent democratic reversions because they lack the ability to enforce state behaviour (Poast and Urpelainen, 2015). Studies specifically examining democratic decline in Europe argue that the EU has been ineffective at thwarting democratic backsliding because a combination of voting rules, member state preferences, and party politics have prevented it from using Article 7, its most severe sanction (Sedelmeier, 2017). Moreover, once authoritarian-inclined leaders roll back democracy in a member state of a regional organization, it makes it easier for other leaders to follow suit. Hungarian Prime Minister Orbán, for example, has made it clear that Hungary would not support sanctions targeting illiberal and undemocratic actions in Poland, which mitigates the threat of EU sanctions and creates a more permissive environment for the Poland's Law and Justice Party (PiS) and other like-minded regimes in the future.

Not only has it become an open question whether regional organizations will be able to defend democracy, but as with each of the international factors we have discussed so far, the effect of international organizations may now work to *reinforce autocracy* in several regions of the globe. In particular, authoritarian governments are establishing their own organizations that promote alternative norms, especially those seeking to make it illegitimate to criticize or interfere in the domestic politics of countries (Ambrosio, 2008). Several regional organizations emphasize regional stability, state sovereignty, and non-interference to a far greater extent than any democratic norms, if democracy is even discussed at all. In the case of the **Shanghai Cooperation Organization** (SCO), dominant member states Russia and China have sought to use the organization to de-legitimize anti-regime activities and democracy promotion through the use of key phrases such as 'stability' and 'diversity'. The SCO's norms and values are based upon preserving the non-democratic status quo in the region. Based on his in-depth study of the SCO, Thomas Ambrosio (2008) concludes, 'the SCO represents an additional strategy of authoritarian resistance to regional and global democratic trends' (p. 1341). The **Association of Southeast Asian Nations** (ASEAN) shares the SCO's commitment to state sovereignty and non-interference and purposefully emphasizes regime survival over the promotion of democratic norms. Ambrosio quotes international relations scholar Amitav Acharya who notes, 'the emergence of [ASEAN] was founded upon the common desire of its members, which had by then retreated significantly from their postcolonial experiments in liberal democracy, to ensure regime survival. This orientation was further institutionalized by ASEAN's doctrine of non-interference, which helped to shield its members from outside pressures toward democratization' (Acharya, 2003, p. 375).

Moreover, authoritarian collaboration is also apparent in the rules-based international organizations that have formed the backbone of the international order for the last seventy years. Like-minded leaders are coordinating their efforts in the **United Nations** (UN), the **International Monetary Fund** (IMF), and **World Bank** to advance their shared interests, including degrading these institutions' human-rights and democracy components. In the case of Internet governance, for example, Western democracies support an open, largely private, global Internet. Autocracies, in contrast, promote state control over the Internet, including laws and other mechanisms that facilitate their ability to censor and persecute dissidents. Already many autocracies, including Belarus, China, Iran, and Zimbabwe, have coalesced in the 'Likeminded Group of Developing Countries' within the United Nations to advocate their interests. Within the IMF and World Bank, autocracies—along with other developing nations—seek to water down conditionality or the reforms that lenders require in exchange for financial support. If successful, diminished conditionality would enfeeble an important incentive for governance reforms.

Conclusion

In this chapter, we added an additional layer to the way we have conceptualized democratic development. Up to this point, we have focused entirely on domestic drivers of democracy. In this chapter, however, we demonstrated that factors outside a state's border can also affect its prospects of transitioning to and sustaining democracy.

One of the key takeaways of this chapter is that geopolitics is a critical driver of democracy. When there is a single, strong democratic power, that country has tremendous leverage to use its foreign policy toolkit to encourage democracy. A democratic hegemon shapes the international norms of acceptable behaviour, and can use trade, aid, international organizations, and other linkages to create conditions that are conducive to democracy. The traditional democracy literature has tended to focus on demonstrating how these factors encourage the positive progression of democracy. However, the rise of assertive autocracies such as Russia and China and dysfunction and division in the West are altering the international scene. In today's geopolitical environment, the tools and mechanisms that long favoured democracy are now functioning in reverse: diffusion is working in ways that reinforce autocracy, China and Putin's model of autocracy are inspiring emulation, new norms are creating conditions more conducive to authoritarianism, and autocracies are establishing linkages that dilute Western leverage.

As we discussed in this chapter, authoritarians have adapted to changes in their external environment. Democracies, therefore, cannot afford to be complacent. To remain dominant, they must engage in the same process of learning and adaptation as their autocratic peers.

Key Questions

1. How do autocracies collaborate? Provide examples from current events.

2. Levitsky and Way argued that Western efforts to establish linkages with other countries could encourage and sustain democracy. Why do such linkages work? What is the potential for this dynamic to work in reverse—for greater authoritarian linkages to promote autocracy?

3. Should the United States and other Western democratic countries intervene in non-democracies to support human rights and democracy?

4. How might Russia and China undermine democracy? Even if they do not intend to export their models of authoritarianism, what are the different pathways that their actions could affect levels of democracy globally?

5. How can we distinguish between Russian efforts to interfere in democratic societies and Western efforts to support democracy abroad?

Further Reading

Diamond, L. 2008. *The Spirit of Democracy: The Struggle to Build Free Societies throughout the World*. Macmillan.
The Sprit of Democracy explains why democracy advances and how this process takes place. The book argues that many authoritarian regimes like Iran or China could democratize eventually but the book also highlights some of the challenges to building democracy in the world today, and why there has been a democratic recession in some previously democratic states like Venezuela.

Knack, S., 2004. 'Does Foreign Aid Promote Democracy?' *International Studies Quarterly*, 48(1), pp. 251–66.
As the article indicates, the question of whether or not foreign aid promotes democracy is explored. The article argues that there is no evidence that foreign aid does contribute to democracy.

Wejnert, B., 2014. *Diffusion of Democracy: The Past and Future of Global Democracy*. Cambridge University Press.
Diffusion of Democracy explores the causes of democratic diffusion and argues that networks between democratic states and authoritarian regimes are more important to democratization than foreign aid.

PART IV

Contemporary Challenges to Democracy

We began this book by asserting that democracy is in crisis. In the first three sections of the book we have explored this theme through a number of approaches and perspectives. In Part I, for example, we discussed the rise of hybrid regimes, or those countries mixing democratic elements with authoritarian tendencies. The increasing frequency with which countries become stuck between democracy and authoritarianism underscores the challenges to democratic development. In Part II we also addressed how authoritarian regimes are adapting and evolving, including by mimicking elements of democracy. As autocracies have grown more capable at maintaining power, they have become more assertive and a more formidable challenge to democracy. And in Part III, we discussed the drivers of democracy, noting throughout the difficulties that countries face in their efforts to consolidate democracy. We acknowledged, in particular, that the shifting geopolitical landscape is creating conditions more conducive to the spread of autocracy.

Absent from our discussion so far has been an explicit discussion of the challenges taking place inside today's Western democracies. Scholars and political observers have long recognized that new and weakly institutionalized democracies tend to be politically volatile—democracy frequently comes and goes. Put differently, we have come to expect that there will be episodes of democratic backsliding in hybrid settings. What has been so alarming, however, is that we are now observing democratic decay in countries we assumed had safely crossed the threshold into consolidated democracy and where democracy was unlikely to decline. In the last decade, it has become increasingly apparent that consolidated democracies—including in Western Europe and the United States—are facing a growing swath of challenges from within.

In Part IV of this book we discuss these challenges. We document two trends in particular. In Chapter 13 we discuss the rise of **populism**. We define populism and identify the conditions that have facilitated its rise. In Chapter 14 we discuss how populism threatens democratic rule. In particular we show that the way that democracy is breaking down has changed, and populist-fuelled **backsliding** now presents the primary way that democracies fall apart.

In addition to documenting and explaining the change, we detail the classic playbook that today's aspiring autocrats are using to initiate such grabs for power. We close in the Conclusion by looking forward and framing a discussion about democracy's future. We identify several factors, including technological change and the role of China, that we think will shape the future trajectory of global democracy.

13

The Rise of Populism and Its Impact on Democracy

Populism is not new. Although there has been a substantial uptick in support for popu-list parties and leaders in recent years, populism has long been a feature of democratic politics. Since Roman times, almost every type of government holding competitive elections has experienced some form of populism (Mounk, 2014). From Tiberius and Gaius Gracchus in the Roman Republic, to the Jacobins in Paris in the late eighteenth century, the United States People's Party in the late nineteenth century, and the Latin American populists from the 1930s until recently—populist movements have dotted the globe, featuring ambitious politicians who mobilize the masses in opposition to an establishment they depict as corrupt or self-serving. By the mid-twentieth century, populism had become commonplace.

But then, during an extended period of economic growth in the aftermath of World War II to the late 1970s, most Western democracies managed to push populism to the fringes of politics. On the right, populists occasionally featured in local or regional governments, but inevitably failed to gain traction in national elections. On the left, the countercultural protest movements of the 1960s and 1970s challenged the status quo but did not secure institutional representation until they subdued their more rad-ical elements. As political scientists Seymour Martin Lipset and Stein Rokkan (1967) famously observed, during the post-war years the party structures of North America and Western Europe were 'frozen' to an unprecedented degree. Between 1960 and 1990, Western democratic parties barely changed (Mounk, 2014).

Beginning in the 1990s, however, populist parties re-emerged on the political scene and their support has steadily grown. Since that time, populist movements in Europe and the United States have uprooted traditional party structures and forced ideas long regarded as extremist or unsavoury onto the political agenda. Brexit, the election of Donald Trump, and Marine Le Pen's appearance in the runoff of the French presidential elections in 2017 underscore just how pronounced the rise of populism has been. Even beyond the United Kingdom, the United States, and France, populist parties and their leaders have surged. The average vote share of populist parties in national and European parliamentary elections has more than doubled since the 1960s, from around 5.1 per cent to 13.2 per cent; their share of seats has tripled from 3.8 per cent to 12.8 per cent (Inglehart and Norris, 2016). The rapid rise of these parties led José Manuel Barroso (head of the European Commission from 2004 to 2014) to state in 2012 that his number one concern was the rise of populist movements in Europe (Stavrakakis and Katsambekis, 2014).

Since 2012, populist parties have shown few signs of cresting. In Germany, the radical-right populist party Alternative for Germany entered the Bundestag (the German parliament) in the 2017 federal election as the third largest party—outperforming the expectations of many political observers. In Italy, as well, the far-right League party and the anti-establishment Five Star Movement entered into a coalition and formed a new government in Italy in 2018. As of early 2019, far-right parties had a presence in twenty-three out of twenty-eight European parliaments.

Many political commentators have sounded the alarm bell about populism's rise and asserted that it poses a threat to liberal democracy. But is this true? This question is important to understand given that the forces driving populism have not abated. A number of deep structural changes—the declining importance of political parties, rising inequality, and values and identity changes, all of which we discuss in this chapter—have transformed how people interact with their governments and reduced governments' abilities to satisfy their citizens. Given the likely staying power of populist parties and movements, scholars, policymakers, and political actors must learn to address and manage the challenges that populism poses for the foreseeable future.

In this chapter we address these issues. In the first section, we define populism and describe the key attributes of populist leaders and their supporters. We then discuss the relationship between populism and democracy. We conclude the chapter by discussing the key drivers of contemporary populism.

What is populism?

Populism is difficult to define because it encompasses such a broad range of actors and ideas (Bale, 2012; Mudde, 2007). The term 'populist' has been used to characterize leaders and movements as varied as Juan Perón in Argentina, Marine Le Pen and the National Front in France, and the Syriza party in Greece. Scholars and political observers have argued that the expansive application of the term has rendered the concept of populism almost meaningless, such that it is too ambiguous to tell us anything useful about politics. So what is populism? How can a single concept encapsulate such different movements, leaders, parties, and governments with such radically divergent characteristics? In this section we define the core characteristics of populism, as well as the specific contours of the right-wing and left-wing variants of the phenomenon. We also discuss the traits of populist leaders and their supporters.

Populist ideology

Populism is chameleonic—it appears differently in different times and places (Taggart, 2000). Despite its variation, populist movements share several fundamental characteristics. At its core, populism is an ideology that separates society into two homogeneous and antagonistic groups: 'the pure people' and 'the corrupt elite' (Mudde, 2004). Moreover, populism makes moral distinction between these groups; it seeks to valorize and legitimize the people while denigrating the elite (Stanley, 2008). While all populist movements leverage this polarizing, anti-establishment framework, there is little consensus across movements about who constitutes 'the pure people' and 'the corrupt elite'. The definitions of these groups and the values they embrace differ depending on the characteristics of the power structures they seek to overturn. Where political elite culture is characterized by a commitment to liberal values of individualism, multiculturalism, and internationalism, for example, populism is likely to be shaped by its resistance to these ideas (Canovan, 1999 p. 3–4). In other words, definitions of these groups (the pure people and the corrupt elite) should be thought of as empty vessels, filled in differently by different actors (Mudde and Kaltwasser, 2013). See further Box 13.1.

 Box 13.1: **Populism as a 'thin ideology'**

Numerous scholars have characterized populism as a 'thin ideology', one that is unable to offer complex arguments and often varies based on the perceptions and needs of different societies (Freeden, 1998; Mudde and Kaltwasser, 2013; Stanley, 2008). Populism, for example, seeks to displace the political establishment, but does not offer specific ideas about what should replace it. 'Thick ideologies', in contrast, provide a holistic view of how politics, the economy, and society should be ordered. Because populism is amorphous and lacks the depth of other ideologies, populist leaders often draw on and pair their political platforms with elements of 'thick' ideologies. Populism, therefore, frequently appears in combination with the following 'thick' ideologies (Pauwels, 2011, p. 99):

- **Nationalism:** Nationalism advocates that the nation is the legitimate source of power and should govern itself free from external interference. It focuses on maintaining a national identity based on shared characteristics of culture, language, race, religion, and common ancestry. Nationalism cultivates a sense of belonging and membership that taps into people's emotions. In terms of domestic policy, nationalism is exclusive and seeks to promote and defend the interests of the majority, including against immigrant minorities and out of touch elite. In terms of foreign policies, nationalists espouse policies that put the nation first at the expense of relationships with other countries, such as advocating economic nationalism and protectionism or closing borders to immigration. Nationalism, therefore, is opposed to foreign rule by members of other nations, as in colonial empires, as well as to rulers who disregard the perspectives and needs of the majority (Wimmer, 2019).

- **Socialism:** Socialism advocates greater public/collective ownership and operation of the social means of production for the common good (Martin, 1911). Socialism is sometimes presented as an alternative to capitalism, where the means of production are privately held. Socialism aims to minimize inequalities through public control of industry and social services.

> • **Fascism**: Fascism is associated most closely with Europe between the world wars when movements bearing this name took power in Italy and Germany and wreaked havoc in many other European countries. Although fascists differed from country to country, they shared a virulent opposition to democracy and **liberalism**, as well as a deep suspicion of capitalism. They also believed that the nation—often defined in religious or racial terms—represented the most important source of identity. Fascist leaders, therefore, promised a revolution that would replace liberal democracy with a new type of political order devoted to nurturing a unified and purified nation under the guidance of a powerful leader (Berman, 2016).

Another core characteristic of populism is a belief that politics should be an expression of 'the general will' of the people (Mudde, 2004). Populism, therefore, assumes that a singular popular will exists, can be articulated, and should be privileged over the preferences of the elite. Contemporary European populists, for example, profess to serve the 'ordinary people' whose opinions they view as being overridden by elites, corrupt politicians, and vocal minorities (Canovan, 1999). Many European populists believe that free and fair elections do not sufficiently constitute representative democracy because the main parties do not provide individuals with a real choice (Mudde and Kaltwasser, 2013). Populists, therefore, aim to bypass the 'corrupt elite' and give a voice to the 'silent majority'. Seen in this light, populism centres on the belief that democratic institutions cannot express the true will of the people and advocates for a more pure form of democratic governance (Seligson, 2007).

Beyond these core characteristics, however, the concept of populism remains fairly indistinct. Scholars, therefore, have sought to provide additional clarity by articulating what populism is *not*. The concepts of **elitism** and **pluralism** are especially useful in this regard because they are essentially opposites of populism (Kaltwasser and Taggart, 2016; Mudde and Kaltwasser, 2012. Elitism is the belief that politics will be most constructive and beneficial for society when policies reflect the ideas of the elite, a select group of people with certain intrinsic qualities, high intellect, special skills, and/or experience. According to this perspective, the elite should be afforded greater influence and authority than 'the people'. Pluralism denies the homogeneity of both populism and elitism, seeing society as a heterogeneous collection of groups and individuals with often fundamentally different views and wishes (Mudde, 2004). Populism rejects both these perspectives, seeing politics as the expression of a homogenous general will of the people.

Although we have identified the characteristics common to all forms of populism, there are also important distinctions that differentiate its variants. Populism is typically separated into two subtypes, left-wing and right-wing. These subtypes differ on a number of dimensions, but particularly in terms of their level of inclusivity and in the way they define 'the people'. **Left-wing populism** tends to be more inclusive, demanding that politics be opened up to groups that have been discriminated against and whose voices have not been taken into account by the establishment, such as the poor. Left-wing populists, therefore, often define the people in terms of class (the downtrodden). They are frequently associated with movements that seek to build broad bases of mass support, often through their provision of material incentives, such as expansionary economic policies and the extension of social benefits. Left-wing populism has historically been most common in Latin America and includes leaders such as Juan Perón in Argentina and Hugo Chávez in Venezuela.

Contemporary left-wing populist movements have maintained their focus on socio-economic issues, particularly growing economic inequality, declining social mobility, and stagnating living standards. But left-wing populists have also emphasized additional social issues such as government and corporate corruption. In the United States, for example, the Occupy Wall Street movement rallied its supporters around the idea of the '99 per cent' of people struggling under the thumb of the elite one per cent. In Europe, left-wing populist movements, including Greece's Syriza and Spain's Podemos, seek to defend the traditional welfare state and reject austerity measures the EU imposed in the wake of the euro crisis. Even in Latin America today, scholars view corruption as the most likely mobilizer of future populist movements (O'Neil, 2016). See further Box 13.2.

 Box 13.2: **Populism in Latin America**

In the 1930s and 1940s, populism emerged in Latin America in response to political, socio-economic, and cultural exclusion. Populist leaders such as Juan Perón in Argentina and Getúlio Vargas in Brazil tapped into the mounting frustrations of ordinary citizens who had grown tired of their treatment under the system. Although many Latin American governments tried to combine liberal-inspired constitutions and elections with strong, highly personalized leadership, years of rapid urbanization and industrialization delegitimized the model.

Beginning in the early 2000s, populists re-emerged as a reaction to neo-liberalism and rising corruption. Populist leaders such as Hugo Chávez in Venezuela, Evo Morales in Bolivia, and Rafael Correa in Ecuador appealed to citizens using a dualistic and antagonistic discourse, pitting the people against the elites, the West, and globalization. In contrast to their predecessors, these populist leaders spurred on citizen revolutions through elections, rather than just through mass rallies or violence. All three enjoyed relatively high levels of support at various times during their presidencies and sustained themselves in power by winning elections. All three also sought to roll back democratic norms and practices. Correa stepped down in 2017 and the government that succeeded him eased the restrictions his administration had imposed on the media and civil society. At the time of writing, however, Morales remains in power in Bolivia, as does Chávez's successor, Nicolas Maduro in Venezuela.

As this chapter will discuss, many scholars see populism as creating challenges for democracy. A number of populist-fuelled leaders, including Chávez, Morales, and Correa, have weakened democratic institutions in ways that paved the way for **democratic backsliding** (Levitsky and Loxton, 2013; Mudde and Kaltwasser, 2012). But not all scholars of Latin American politics agree with this assessment. Ernesto Laclau (1977), for example, argued that populism is a process of political discourse that leads to the construction of popular political identities. Though society is split into two camps, he argues that populism enables citizens to challenge the inequities of the old order. Other scholars have noted that left-wing populism, or progressive populism, is vital to challenging more exclusive and inequitable forms of rule (Stavrakakis, 2017). Torbjörn Tännsjö (1992) calls populism the purest form of democracy.

Some scholars have taken a more nuanced perspective, suggesting that populism can be beneficial under certain circumstances. In particular, scholars have argued that left-wing populism can be helpful to democracy, but only when its leaders are not in power. They posit that when populists are the challengers, populism can strengthen democracy. These scholars cite instances in Latin America in which populist supporters have taken to the streets to protest political exclusion and corruption (De la Torre, 2016). When populist leaders are in office, in contrast, their influence on democracy can often be negative, as the examples of Correa, Morales, and Chávez underscore.

Like their leftist counterparts, **right-wing populism** also seeks to capitalize on public disenchantment and anxieties, and appeal to the common man. Right-wing populism, however, is exclusive in nature and advocates policies that protect the 'in group' at the expense of non-native groups, such as immigrants and ethnic minorities. Right-wing populists, therefore, have a cultural conception of 'the people' (i.e. the people as a nation). Right-wing populists portray 'outsiders' as threatening exclusive national cultures and local traditions and they reject notions of individual and social equality for these marginalized groups. Ideas of exclusion also carry over into economic policies. Whereas left-wing populists emphasize development and the creation of economic conditions that benefit 'the people', today's right-wing populists focus on protecting the economic rights of 'the people', which they consider increasingly threatened by outside forces (notably immigrants) (Mudde and Kaltwasser, 2013). Right-wing populism has been more common in Europe and includes leaders such as Geert Wilders and his Party for Freedom in the Netherlands, Viktor Orbán and his Fidesz party in Hungary, and Marine Le Pen and her National Front party in France (see further Box 13.3).

 Box 13.3: **Who are the right-wing populist parties in Europe?**

Support for populist parties in Europe has steadily grown since the 1990s. As we discuss in this chapter, recent economic hardship, the challenge of migration, and the apparent political failures of established parties have fuelled populism's rise. But despite the surge of popular support, it is important to remember that European populism has far deeper roots. One of the first parties to establish a doctrine of differentialist racism—or the idea that different cultures are not compatible and should not coexist within a nation—was the **National Front** in France, which was led by Jean-Marie Le Pen and formed in 1972. The party espoused a version of French nationalism that played on people's fears that Europeans faced extinction due to migration and low population growth rates. The National Front rose to prominence in the wake of mass immigration and growing unemployment by promising to return France to the mono-cultural glory of its past. The party gained national attention by 1984 and by 2002 Le Pen was the first National Front candidate to compete in the second round of the national presidential election. Though the National Front has never won a majority in the legislature, it received 13 per cent of the votes in the 2017 parliamentary election.

Here we review some of the major right-wing populist parties in Europe.

Western Europe

The *Swiss People's Party* (SVP) gained attention in the 1990s when it started to make impressive electoral gains in local and national elections. Its popularity was rooted in cultural intolerance, citing Islam as an obstacle to integration and proclaiming that multi-culturalism could not work. The party originally catered to farmers in rural areas, but under the leadership of Christoph Blocher changed its strategy to focus on defence of Swiss values and attacking European integration. It has been one of the dominant parties in Swiss politics and won a plurality of the votes in the 2015 elections. Austria has also seen the right-wing populist *Freedom Party of Austria* (FPO) gain popularity, winning 20 per cent of the vote in the 2013 election. In Germany, the *Alternative for Germany* (AfD) party (founded in 2013) won 4.7 per cent of the votes in the 2013 federal election and 12.6 per cent of the vote in the 2017 federal election. That year it secured ninety-four seats in the Bundestag, making it the third largest party.

Eastern Europe

In Eastern Europe, a number of right-wing populist parties have emerged and gained popularity. In the post-communist era in Hungary, *Fidesz* gained followers by increasing its anti-elitist, anti-immigration sentiment and emphasizing the importance of being an ethnic Hungarian. Concurrently, the Hungarian right has argued in the defense of national values while portraying the left as socialist, internationalist, and cosmopolitan. Elections became increasingly polarizing onwards, campaigns became much dirtier and more negative, and ordinary citizens felt the need to take sides in every realm of life (Palonen, 2009). More worrisome is the success of neo-fascist party *Jobbik* (an anti-Semitic and anti-Roma party), which has pushed the ruling Fidesz party even further to the right, spurring anti-migration policies. As Fidesz leader Viktor Orbán has eroded Hungarian democracy, he has increased cooperation with authoritarian governments, including Russia and China (Ostrow, 2014, p. 41). There are similar concerns about the democratic direction of Poland under the ruling *Law and Justice Party* which gained power in 2015, winning over half of the seats in both houses. Like their neighbours in Western Europe, the Fidesz and Law and Justice parties are increasingly Eurosceptic, particularly regarding European Union migration policy.

Scandinavia

Scandinavia has surprisingly seen the rise of far-right populist parties as well. The *Progress Party* of Norway formed a coalition with the Conservative Party in 2017 and holds 29 of 169 seats. The *Swedish Democrats* in Sweden won 62 out of 349 seats in 2018, becoming the third largest party in Sweden. The *Finns Party* or *True Finns Party* in Finland was part of the ruling coalition until members defected from the coalition in 2017. The *Danish People's Party* in Denmark gained 20 per cent of the votes in the 2015 election, its best showing to date. Many of these parties have gained support by focusing on issues of immigration and tackling challenges from immigration from Muslim countries in particular. In the 1980s, the Danish People's Party gained attention for wanting to make Denmark a Muslim-free zone.

Populist leaders

Our discussion so far has defined populism as a set of ideas. Numerous scholars, however, have argued that populism is best understood as a *political strategy* and focus on the characteristics of political leaders and their methods of winning and exercising power.

Weyland (2001), for example, defines populism as a 'political strategy through which a personalistic leader seeks or exercises government power based on direct, unmediated, un-institutionalized support from large numbers of mostly unorganized followers' (p. 14). Although scholars disagree about whether charismatic leadership and the ability to establish direct links with voters merely facilitate or actually define populism (Mudde, 2004), a discussion of these dynamics is useful for further elaborating the phenomenon.

Charisma tends to be (although is not always) an important characteristic of populist leaders (Roberts, 2007). Charisma is important because it enables populist leaders to create unusually strong connections to their followers. Paul Taggart (2000), for example, asserts that populism 'requires the most extraordinary individuals to lead the most ordinary of people' (p. 1). The highly personalized nature of populist leaders has led critics of populism to characterize populists as demagogues. They are frequently accused of opportunistically playing on popular emotions, making unrealistic promises to the people, and stoking an atmosphere of enmity and distrust toward the elite (Stanley, 2008).

In addition to charisma, populist leaders pursue a number of tactics designed to facilitate their direct connections with the 'common man' and legitimize their claims of speaking for 'the people'. Populist leaders seek to portray themselves as political outsiders with few links to the political establishment. In Latin America, leaders such as Alberto Fujimori of Peru, Hugo Chávez in Venezuela, and Lucio Gutiérrez in Ecuador never held elected office before winning the presidency. In many cases, however, populist leaders are not outsiders, but instead are individuals well connected to sections of the economic and political elite (Mudde, 2004). In the United States, for example, President Trump was a part of the economic elite before running for office. Nonetheless, he championed himself as a Washington D.C. outsider, demonized the corrupt establishment, and promoted theories that the system was 'rigged' against him.

Populist leaders also seek to connect directly with the people. For this reason, populists are commonly portrayed as speaking from balconies and moving their supporters with impassioned speeches (Taggart, 2000). Radio and television have often been used as a means of establishing direct and unmediated access to domestic audiences. Hugo Chávez, for example, previously connected with his supporters through a weekly chat show, called 'Aló Presidente', where he told stories, delivered long monologues, sang songs, and announced the nationalization of companies (Wallis, 2012). With the advent of social media, populist leaders have a platform to reach an even larger number of supporters (Bartlett, 2014; Waisbord and Amado, 2017). For example, Argentina's Cristina Fernández de Kirchner and Ecuador's Rafael Correa, regularly used Twitter. Social media offers a direct linkage to the people, helping populist leaders circumvent the traditional media and spread their messages directly (Engesser et al., 2017). In many instances the mainstream media, in turn, pick up the headline-grabbing tweets or other direct populist appeals, enabling populist parties and leaders to control the political narratives in their political systems.

In addition to direct appeals to the people, the content of populist rhetoric is also notable. Populists use emotional and direct language, including short, simple slogans that are directed at the 'gut feelings' of the people (Canovan, 1999; Inglehart and Norris, 2017; Taggart, 2000; Tarchi, 2002). Right-wing populists, in particular, appeal to xenophobia, if not overt racism to build support (Betz, 1993). Populists seek to offer simple solutions to complex problems that appeal to common sense. They advocate for transparency and denounce backroom deals, complicated procedures, and technicalities that only experts understand (Canovan, 1999). Many European populists, for example, have capitalized on mounting '**Euroscepticism**', or public criticism of the European Union, stemming in part from a belief that it is overly bureaucratic and removed from the voters. Populists claim that professional politicians seek excessively complex solutions to mask their efforts to line their own pockets, while populists instead look to find simple, direct solutions to the problems of ordinary people (Canovan, 1999).

Finally, populist leaders circumvent parties and other forms of institutional mediation to further facilitate their direct, personal ties to voters (Barr, 2009; Roberts, 2007). Elections, plebiscites, mass demonstrations, and opinion polls are crucial instruments with which populist leaders mobilize and demonstrate their broad appeal. Populist chief executives regularly invoke mass support to boost their influence and justify their actions (Weyland, 2001). Hungarian Prime Minister Orbán, for example, regularly points to his 'two-thirds revolution'—a reference to his party's 2010 electoral victory giving Fidesz two-thirds of the seats in parliament—as providing him with a mandate to enact his controversial reforms. Similarly, Chávez repeatedly claimed that Venezuela was the most democratic country in the world because he was constantly winning elections, and his rule was based on the 'will of the people'.

Populist supporters

While populist leaders have developed a number of tactics to help them win and maintain power, who are the individuals who support today's populists? What factors motivate voters to support these parties? Are there characteristics that are common across the voter bases of different populist parties? Answering these questions can help inform policy responses to populism's rise.

First and foremost, populist supporters tend to be dissatisfied with the functioning of democracy and feel they have been left behind and neglected by the establishment. According to Cas Mudde (2004), today's populist revolution is composed of 'hardworking, slightly conservative, law-abiding citizen[s], who, in silence but with growing anger, see [their] world being "perverted" by progressives, criminals, and aliens' (p. 557). Contemporary populist supporters, however, differ from those of past periods because they do not necessarily want to participate in politics in the ways that earlier populist movements envisioned. Rather than pursuing change through grassroots participation, today's populist supporter is looking for *leadership*. They want politicians who know the people and develop and implement policies that are in line with their preferences without having to take part in that process (Mudde, 2004).

Aside from their desire for strong, decisive leadership, contemporary populist supporters share several demographic traits. Today's supporters for right-wing populist in particular tend to be older, male, less educated, more religious, and members of the ethnic majority (Inglehart and Norris, 2017). Some studies suggest that education, in particular, is an important factor. Less educated individuals are more likely to see multicultural societies as a threat to their way of life and therefore more likely to support populist parties and leaders than are more educated voters (Lubbers, 2001; Lubbers et al., 2002; Warwick, 1998). In the United States, counties with the lowest education levels supported Trump while counties with higher education levels favoured Hilary Clinton. According to the Pew Research Center, 67 per cent of people without a college degree voted for Trump, while 28 per cent voted for Clinton—the largest education vote gap since 1980 (Friesen, 2016). It is important to note, however, that some studies of populism in Western Europe do not find support for the effect of education on support for populism. Teun Pauwels (2014) has shown, for example, that in Belgium, Germany, and the Netherlands education does not affect voter support for populism. Similarly, the relationship between education and support for left-wing populism is also inconclusive and some studies show that education exerts a positive effect on radical left voting. Generally speaking, in the case of left-wing populist movements, education levels tend to vary, as exemplified by the range of individuals supporting Spain's Podemos (Ramiro and Gomez, 2017).

Age also appears to be a particularly important predictor of populist support, with younger and older voters proving more likely to vote for populist parties than other generations (Inglehart and Norris, 2016). Although some studies argue that the effect of age on support for populism is best described as being U-shaped, other studies have found that support for populism is highest just among the older generations (Inglehart and Norris, 2016). It is notable, however, that in the French presidential election in 2017, the right-wing populist candidate Marine Le Pen received more support from young voters than any other age group. Approximately 45 per cent of 18- to 24-year-olds voted for Le Pen in the first round, compared to 20 per cent of voters over 65 (Kentish, 2017).

Perhaps surprisingly, economic factors are a less useful indicator of likely support for contemporary populist parties and leaders. At first blush, this appears inconsistent with widely held assertions that support for populism has been highest among the 'losers of globalization'. While such economic explanations are compelling at a macro-level, there is very little evidence that these factors actually drive individual voter choices. Instead, today's populist supporters tend to be small proprietors or self-employed workers rather than low-waged unskilled workers (Inglehart and Norris, 2017). Though unemployment is often linked to populist voting, empirical analysis by Inglehart and Pippa Norris (2017) finds that the effects of these economic factors on voting preferences are mixed and inconsistent in statistical models. Studies of left-wing populist movements also find that economic factors are poor predictors of backing for left-wing populists. Although poor voters constitute an important base of support for left-wing populists, such leaders have built diverse alliances, including among the urban classes (Roberts, 2003). In actuality, a number of populist leaders, such as Mario Vargas Llosa in Peru and Joaquín Lavín in Chile, received more votes from the more affluent sectors of society (Weyland, 2001). Likewise, in Venezuela, Chávez's rhetoric targeted the lower classes, but he also attracted substantial support from the middle classes by pursuing distributional policies that benefited these groups, such as lowering utility prices (Lupu, 2010).

Rather than voting based on economic issues, contemporary populist supporters tend to be most motivated by issues that cut across the economic left–right spectrum, such as the punishments of crimes, the restriction of immigration and asylum, and limiting the reach of the European Union (Ivarsflaten, 2005; Skocpol and Williamson, 2016). The empirical analysis by Inglehart and Norris (2017), for example, underscores the importance of cultural values for populist voters. They find that populist voters are not necessarily focused on the economy, but instead are best characterized by their anti-immigrant attitudes, mistrust of global and national governance, and support for authoritarian values. Such voters may want to feel part of a tribe that shares their identity and attitudes. In sum, most scholarly research suggests that the contemporary populist supporter cares most about cultural rather than economic issues.

It is important to note that although there appear to be factors that are common to voter bases across different populist parties, some research is ceptical that such generalizations can be drawn. Matthijs Rooduijn (2018), for example, examined the electorates of fifteen prototypical populist parties from eleven Western European countries and found little evidence of any unifying characteristics across different kinds of populist parties. Instead, he argues that 'the' populist voter does not exist.

Populism and democracy

Populism is not inherently anti-democratic. In some ways, it may be viewed as a corrective to the failures of democracy (Kaltwasser, 2012; Taggart, 2002). Populist parties and leaders see themselves as giving voice to popular grievances and advocating for issues that large portions of the population care about but that governments, mainstream parties, and media have ignored (Canovan, 1999). In the United States, The People's Party of the late 1800s helped usher in many progressive reforms, such as the income tax and corporate regulation, which made the United States a more humane society in the twentieth century (Kazin, 2016). Moreover, populism's (especially the left-wing variant's) approach to governing—mobilizing the public and using referendums and other popular initiatives—may be viewed as a more direct, participatory, and inclusive form of democracy, giving voice to new social groups and traditionally excluded sectors of society (Kaltwasser, 2013; Kazin, 1995).

Although not inherently anti-democratic, populism does run counter to the liberal democratic ideal that emphasizes the protection of rights. Problems arise when there are parts of the population that hold different views from the majority (Mudde and Kaltwasser, 2017). Populists look to place the needs of the majority or native group ahead of individual liberties and needs. They often advocate restrictions, especially on minorities, that limit individual rights in the name of reinforcing norms or national security. Populist perspectives on politics, therefore, often place them at odds with democracy.

The tension between populism and democracy is most pronounced once populists get into power (Mudde and Kaltwasser, 2017). The tactics that contemporary populist parties pursue to achieve their agendas can undermine democratic norms and practices. Today's populist parties, for example, extol the virtues of strong and decisive leadership, share a disdain for established institutions, and express deep distrust of perceived experts and elites. Moreover, the centrality of populist leaders and their direct rapport with the 'common man' transform them into something akin to infallible sovereigns, in that their decisions are unquestionable because they represent the people's will (Arditi, 2014).

Although views that populism poses a threat to democracy are widely held, the causal mechanisms linking populism to democratic decline remain poorly understood. In the remainder of this section we identify three ways that populism can undermine democracy.

Probably the greatest threat that populism poses to democracy arises from the relationship between populism and democratic institutions, such as parties, legislatures, and the media. Populists object to the idea that established, elite-run institutions should protect individual rights or constrain the general will of the people. The core message of populism is that the elite is corrupt and does not speak for the masses. Presidential candidates who win on the basis of such appeals, therefore, claim a mandate to reshape the political system and seek to dismantle the established institutions that might hinder their ability to deliver on their electoral promises (Levitsky and Loxton, 2013).

For one, populist movements empower charismatic leaders who promise to break with the political establishment and turn politics into a more personal experience (Canovan, 1999 p. 14). When populists seek to bypass traditional party structures, it can have a corrosive effect on democracy. As we discussed in Chapter 12, parties play a crucial function in democracies (Diamond and Gunther, 2001). Parties provide critical information about what candidates stand for, structure electoral choice, and frame policy alternatives. Parties help solve collective action problems by facilitating coordination and mobilizing public participation in the political process. Parties also serve as a bridge between executives and legislatures and help recruit and socialize political leaders (Randall and Svåsand, 2002).

In addition to undermining political parties, populist tactics have the potential to weaken other crucial institutions, such as independent judiciaries, free press, and civil society (Levitsky and Loxton, 2013). In more openly confrontational cases, populists might actually deliberately seek to weaken these institutions if they obstruct implementation of their policy agenda. Populist leaders maintain that once 'the people' have spoken, nothing should constrain the realization of their will. Their distrust for institutional procedures and the intricacies of the legislative process might give way to a discretional adherence to the rule of law that slips all too easily into authoritarian practices (Arditi, 2004). Populists can get away with undemocratic behaviour if their actions are perceived as representing the will of the people (Arditi, 2004).

Beyond weakening democratic institutions, the second way that populism can erode democracy is through its fostering of political polarization. Populism promotes antagonism between 'the pure people' and 'the corrupt elite'. The political struggle is conceived as a zero-sum game in which the gains of one collective identity are only possible with a loss of benefits of the other (Kaltwasser, 2013). This fragmentation becomes especially pronounced when populists harness other ideologies, such as nationalism, which can synchronize this competition with **ethnic divisions**. These cleavages, in turn, can cause political stalemate and dysfunction, which can undermine democracy by creating an excuse for incumbents to take undemocratic actions to overcome the paralysis. Similarly, political stalemate and dysfunction can further enhance public disenchantment with the performance of democratic institutions. Moreover, Latin America's experience with populism has shown that even when populists leave office, their noxious legacies linger. Moderate successors struggle to build trust in polarized societies. As the gaps between social groups widen, it becomes harder to forge compromises, the lifeblood of democracy (O'Neil, 2016).

Finally, populist leaders may use referenda to extend term limits. **Term-limit extensions** have become increasingly common in the post-Cold War period, including in democratic settings (Baturo, 2014). The removal of terms limits runs counter to democratic norms in a number of important ways. Key among them is the fact that removing term limits can convince the public that there are no institutional mechanisms to remove a leader from office, raising the risk that the opposition will resort to supporting non-democratic means to remove populist leaders. In Thailand, for example, Thaksin was a populist who won elections largely due to public support among rural voters. The Thai middle class realized he could not be beaten in an election and abandoned their democratic commitments. Thaksin was ousted in a coup in 2006 (as was his sister Yingluck in 2014).

The drivers of populism

The rise of contemporary populism is not a temporary crisis. Rather the spread of today's populism stems from a number of long-term dynamics that have changed how people interact with their governments and reduced governments' abilities to satisfy their citizens. In this section we discuss the underlying drivers of the rise of contemporary populism. These drivers fall into three broad categories: economic, including globalization and the economic stasis and inequality that has occurred along with it; the declining importance of political parties; and a cultural backlash against progressive values. These categories are in many ways intertwined and have all contributed to populism's rise to varying degrees in different environments.

Economic insecurity and rising inequality

Many political observers point to the 2007–08 global financial crisis and subsequent Eurozone crisis as catapulting populist parties and leaders into power in the United States and Europe. In the United States, households lost trillions in wealth as a result of the global financial crisis. In Europe, unemployment during the Eurozone crisis in countries such as Greece and Spain rose to 20 per cent and above. Populists exploited widespread citizen discontent and public perceptions that a 'greedy elite' caused what became the worst economic crisis since the Great Depression. In other words, many political commentators have suggested that recent economic crises created the conditions that allowed populism to take root.

While the global financial and Eurozone crises certainly contributed to populism's momentum, most scholars view the rise of populism as stemming from more fundamental economic changes. In particular, the typical citizen's living standard has declined in recent decades (Piketty and Saez, 2014; Mounk, 2014). This decline stands in stark contrast to the historical pattern since the start of the Industrial Revolution during which, except for brief moments of extreme crisis, the average citizen of a Western democracy enjoyed a higher standard of living than his or her parents. Instead, in most developed democracies today, median incomes have remained stagnant or declined over the past twenty-five years (Piketty and Saez, 2014). In the United States, for example, the Census Bureau reported a lower median household income in 2012 than in 1989. Similarly, in the United Kingdom, the average British worker has experienced a 10 per cent decrease in real wages since 2007 (OECD, 2017).

Concurrent with stagnating or declining real incomes for most people in the West, the real incomes of the wealthy are rising—a trend that has been accelerating since 1960 (Piketty and Saez, 2014). In the United States, for example, the top 10 per cent of the population accumulated half of all national income in 2012, compared to about 35 per cent of national income in 1960. And the trend is not confined to the United States: the share of overall income going to the one per cent has risen sharply in countries across the globe. In other words, the gains from globalization, technological advancements, and the rising mobility of capital and labour have been unevenly distributed. Moreover, the forces of globalization are changing the structure of Western economies in ways that create both winners and losers (Minkenberg and Perrineau, 2007). In the United States, for example, manufacturing and agriculture employed one in three workers just after World War II. Today, those sectors employ only one in eight (Thompson, 2012).

Stagnating living standards and rising inequality have contributed to a loss in citizens' perceived security (Beck, 1999; Giddens, 1990; Hacker, 2006).[1] Not only do average citizens make less money today relative to a generation ago, they are also a lot less certain about their future. Many individuals, therefore, have come to view the political establishment as failing to serve their interests. Moreover, academic research suggests that individual perceptions of declining security are conducive to in-group solidarity, conformity to group norms, and rejection of outsiders. Socially disadvantaged groups are most prone to blame ethnic minorities and migrant populations for deteriorating conditions, loss of manufacturing jobs, and inadequate welfare services (Betz and Meret, 2009). When threatened, individuals are likely to seek strong, decisive leaders to protect them from what are perceived as dangerous outsiders threatening jobs and benefits (Inglehart and Norris, 2016). In these ways, large-scale forces, such as technological innovation, demographic changes, and economic globalization have created fertile ground for populism's growth.

---

[1]   While it is true that rising inequality is leading to angst and frustration, whether or not populism rises in countries that are unequal is not conclusive. Populism has risen in countries that are unequal, but also in countries with high equality, such as in Sweden, Norway, Finland, and Denmark. The key factor, therefore, may not be levels of inequality, but *perceptions* of inequality and the government's ability to respond to these inequalities that matter most.

Declining importance of political parties

The rise of contemporary populism is also a result of a long-term, gradual decline in voters' attachment to traditional political parties and their perception of the waning importance these institutions play in the political process. This decline in political party attachment can be seen as a de-alignment. The post-industrial revolution, in particular, led to fundamental changes in European societies in the 1960s that weakened ties between individuals and communities. Because these ties historically played an important role in determining voters' attachment to political parties, their erosion promoted a decline in partisanship (Mair, 1984). For the centre-left, deindustrialization reduced the number of industrial workers who comprised its traditional electoral base. Social individualization also eroded the mass membership of traditional collective organizations, social networks, and mass movements that mobilized working class support for these parties (Keating 2013; Inglehart and Norris, 2017). On the right, a steep decline in religious observance and church attendance also diminished the support base of the centre-right. Along with weakening ties between individuals and their communities, the rising prominence of supranational institutions like the European Union eroded the importance of political parties. These structural changes reduced transparency in decision-making and empowered the executive branch to the detriment of parliaments, which in turn eroded the representative function of parties (Kriesi, 2014).

As their traditional constituencies shrank, many established political parties sought to maintain their vote share by broadening their electoral appeals. These parties, therefore, began to drift toward the ideological centre, particularly on economic policies, reducing the substantive differences between them. In the 1960s, for example, the difference between the left and the right was stark, with the left seeking to nationalize entire industries and the right seeking to minimize the role of government in the economy. Today, the differences are far less pronounced. Even beyond economics, political parties have become less distinct on a broad swath of issues. In Europe since the late 1980s, for example, Mudde (2016) asserts that mainstream parties increasingly converged on a new elite consensus—a common agenda that called for integration through the European Union, multi-ethnic societies, and neoliberal economic reforms.

Rising education levels and the spread of media technology have also reduced voters' perceptions of the importance of political parties, creating opportunities for more direct, personalist appeals to voters. With more political information available to a more educated electorate, citizens have become more self-sufficient in politics (Dalton, 1984; Inglehart, 1990; Mudde, 2004; Kriesi, 2014). The Internet and social media, for example, have assumed many of the informational functions that political parties used to play. Party leaders can now communicate directly with the public via the media and no longer need the party apparatus to get their messages to their constituencies (Kriesi, 2014). Moreover, changes in the media's coverage of politics, including persistent coverage of corruption scandals and other sensationalist stories, have made citizens more sceptical of political parties and the broader political establishment (Mudde and Kaltwasser, 2017).

Voters' detachment from traditional political parties and the convergence of political parties in ideological or policy terms has enabled populism to gain traction (Kriesi, 2014).

In Latin America, weak parties have been unable to mediate between citizens and the state. Populist leaders like Chávez in Venezuela and Fujimori in Peru emerged at a time when parties had ossified, and the mood was filled with dissatisfaction. Most parties in Latin America were not effective in incorporating the popular sectors. Only 21.9 per cent of the public in Latin America expressed confidence in political parties and 16 per cent claimed to be 'close' or 'somewhat close' to a party organization (Payne et al., 2002). Populist leaders have seized upon these openings created by the institutional vacuum and rising frustration to make direct connections with the population (Levitsky and Way, 2013).

Years of centrist policies in the United States and Europe also alienated large chunks of the population, leaving many voters to look for alternatives to the established parties. In the United States, support for third party movements has grown, as highlighted by Ross Perot's presidential candidacy in 1992 and 1996 and the Tea Party's explosion onto the political scene in 2009. Similarly, in France, voters were so dissatisfied with their traditional political options that none of the country's established parties made it to the run-off of the presidential election in 2017.

In sum, the decline of the importance and role of political parties in today's political environment has been a key driver of populism.

Values and identity challenges

In conjunction with declining living standards, rising inequality, and the demise of class-based parties, citizens in Western democracies have also had to deal with new challenges to their values and national identities. The post-industrial revolution precipitated not only a decline in partisanship, but also rising affluence that led citizens in Western societies to expand their interests. As more people grew up with secure economic and political conditions, they became less concerned with immediate needs and changed their priorities to focus more heavily on quality of life (Inglehart, 1971). A broad range of new parties emerged on the political scene in the 1960s and 1970s advocating for progressive social change, such as the Greens and Libertarian parties in countries such as Germany, the Netherlands, Belgium, Austria, Sweden, and Switzerland. Their party platforms no longer focused on social class and economic redistribution but were heavily based on post-materialist values such as tolerance of multi-cultural diversity, protection of minority rights, freedom of expression, secularism, racial and gender equality, flexible and fluid gender roles, and environmental protection.

This transformation of Western political culture, however, triggered a backlash—a 'silent counter-revolution', or a negative reaction among those citizens who felt threatened by the predominance of this new set of values (Ignazi, 1992). As discussed in the previous section, older, less educated, male citizens tend to more strongly support populist parties. This is in large part because these groups cling most strongly to traditional values and are most likely to view cultural change as threatening their livelihood and well-being. Particularly in contexts where the pace of value change is rapid, these citizens can become out of step with the changing culture, generating anger, resentment, and a sense of loss.

Immigration, in particular, has accelerated the pace of value change in Western democracies (Zakaria, 2016). In recent decades, Western societies have experienced a significant uptick in their influxes of foreigners. In 2015, there were around 250 million international migrants and 65 million forcibly displaced people worldwide. This stands in stark contrast to the vast majority of human history, when people were far less mobile. Europe has received the largest share of immigrants, approximately 76 million, and has therefore experienced the greatest backlash against their arrival. Large immigration flows from low-income countries with different cultures and religions stimulated a reaction in which much of the working class moved to the right, in defence of traditional values (Werts et al., 2013).

Conclusion

Many political observers have argued that Europe's populist surge has crested. They point to the defeat of Marie La Pen and the Nationalist Front in France's presidential elections in March 2017, Geert Wilders's and his Party for Freedom's (PVV) disappointing performance in legislative elections in the Netherlands in 2017, and even the less than expected gains in European parliamentary elections in 2019 as evidence that populism is losing steam. These perspectives, however, overlook populism's deep historical sources and underestimate the durability of today's populist appeals. Although Le Pen lost the presidential election, The National Front had its best electoral showing in France's political history. Moreover, Le Pen's support was especially strong among France's young voters suggesting that her positions on key policy questions are likely to resonate in the years to come. Likewise, in Germany, the radical-right populist party Alternative for Germany entered the German parliament as the third largest party—outperforming the expectations of many political observers.

The forces fuelling populism are not going away anytime soon. If anything, economic underperformance, disillusion with corruption, and dissatisfaction with government performance will continue to fan the flames of populism across the globe. A renewed wave of migration into Europe and even technological change brought by advances in artificial intelligence (AI) and automation that create new winners and losers could add fuel to these trends. That is why populism and the potential threat it poses to democratic development today should not be underestimated. In the next chapter we build on our discussion of populism and provide an in-depth examination of patterns in democratic breakdown.

Key Questions

1. Populist leaders often claim that populism is democratic. What is the case for populism being good for democracy, and what is the rebuttal? What challenges does populism create for liberal democracy?

2. What are the factors driving populism? What explains the Brexit vote and the election of Donald Trump in the United States? Why have populist movements gained attention in Europe?

3. What are the differences between left-wing and right-wing populist groups?

4. How would you characterize the populist voter? What is the typical populist voter looking for? Has the typical populist voter of today changed from the past?

5. Populism is described as having a thin ideology. Is that true? Have populist movements had any effect on policy?

6. In what ways have populist parties affected mainstream parties?

7. If a leader is well liked, does that make him or her populist? What distinguishes popularity from populism?

Further Reading

ALBERTAZZI, D. and MCDONNELL, D. eds., 2007. *Twenty-first Century Populism: The Spectre of Western European Democracy.* Springer.
Twenty-first Century Populism is an edited volume of the phenomenon of populism in Western Europe, and looks at the conditions that facilitate its emergence in different European countries such as France, Italy, the Netherlands, and Austria. The book also examines how much populism has affected mainstream politics.

MUDDE, C. and KALTWASSER, C.R., 2017. *Populism: A Very Short Introduction.* Oxford University Press.
Populism provides the reader with a short overview of how to best understand populism. The book illustrates the power of the ideology and how it polarizes society. The book offers insight into the attraction of populist leaders such as Silvio Berlusconi, Jean-Marie le Pen, Juan Perón, and Hugo Chávez.

MUDDE, C. and KALTWASSER, C.R., 2012. *Populism in Europe and the Americas: Threat or Corrective for Democracy?* Cambridge University Press.
Populism in Europe analyses the experience of populism in Europe and the Americas and argues that populism can threaten democracy, but in certain circumstances has helped democracy. The book points out the similarities between right- and left-wing populism and demonstrates how both forms of populism challenge liberal democracy.

MÜLLER, J.W., 2017. *What is Populism?* Penguin UK.
As the title suggests, *What is Populism?* provides a clear explanation of how to define and understand populism. The book argues that populism is actually a rejection of pluralism and could end up creating an authoritarian state that excludes individuals that don't fit into their ideal of who are proper citizens.

14

Changing Patterns of Democratic Backsliding and Breakdown

In Chapter 13, we discussed the rise of **populism** and the potential threat it poses to democracy. One of the key takeaways from that chapter is that while populism is not inherently anti-democratic, the tactics that today's populists are using to implement their agendas present a growing threat to democratic norms and practices. Today's populists share their predecessors' preference for strong and decisive leadership, disdain for established institutions, and distrust of perceived experts and elites. Their tactics, however, have evolved in ways that make contemporary populists a more formidable threat to democracy. Rather than orchestrating sudden and decisive breaks with democracy, which can elicit domestic and international condemnation, instead they are taking a slow and steady approach to dismantling democracy. This was the method Russia's Vladimir Putin, Venezuela's Hugo Chávez, and Turkey's Recep Tayyip Erdoğan took to consolidating power. Although new democracies and hybrid systems are particularly vulnerable to such populist-fuelled **backsliding**, even more fully consolidated democracies are susceptible.

In this chapter, we articulate the changes in the way that democracies are breaking down. In particular, we show that since the end of the Cold War, coups no longer present the greatest threat to democracy. Instead, there has been a rise in what we refer to as '**authoritarianizations**', or the slow dismantling of democratic norms and practices by democratically-elected leaders (Geddes et al., 2018). We focus in particular on identifying and describing the steps that contemporary populist parties and leaders are using to dismantle democracy. We then provide an in-depth look at two prominent cases of authoritarianization: Russia and Turkey. Finally, we conclude by discussing three key implications of the changing patterns in democratic breakdown.

Staying abreast of changes in how democracies fall apart is fundamental to developing strategies to engage and counter autocracy's resurgence. Previous research on democratic failure has tended to aggregate democratic breakdown into a single category of events (Svolik, 2008). However, the factors that lead to successful coups in democracies—historically the most common pathway to democratic collapse—are likely to be different from the factors that enable a leader to incrementally dismantle democratic institutions. A failure to understand that the modes of democratic breakdown are evolving leads to an outdated and incomplete understanding of how democratic decline occurs.

Democratic backsliding and breakdown

As we discussed in the introduction to this section, democratic backsliding refers to deterioration in the quality of democracy. It takes place through a series of discrete changes in the rules and informal procedures shaping electoral competition, respect for political and civil liberties, and government accountability (Lust and Waldner, 2015). Identifying whether a country is backsliding, therefore, requires that we examine changes in institutions and procedures in a number of domains, including the electoral arena, civil society, media, political institutions, and civil-military relations. The breadth of actors who might initiate backsliding is also diverse, ranging from democratically-elected leaders to military officers, or (less frequently) insurgents or foreign actors. In sum, the term democratic backsliding encapsulates a wide range of processes and agents.

Many scholars use democratic backsliding to refer to outright changes in political system type. However, we believe it is important to recognize that democratic backsliding can occur in small increments, requiring finer nuances or degrees of change than in the case of regime change (Aleman and Yang, 2011; Erdmann, 2011). In some cases, democratic backsliding does not lead to the breakdown of democracy, but it does degrade citizens' rights and their engagement with the state. For example, Hungarian Prime Minister Viktor Orbán and his Fidesz party's assault on the independence of the media and judiciary since 2010 represent backsliding within a political regime; Hungary (so far) remains a democracy but there are fewer restrictions on executive power and opportunities for citizens to hold the government accountable. But in other cases, democratic backsliding can lead to the outright breakdown of democratic governance and the emergence of an authoritarian regime.

Not only does the endpoint of democratic backsliding vary, but its mode and speed also differ across cases (Bermeo, 2016). Democratic backsliding can take place rapidly as a result of a military coup or blatant election-day voter fraud, both of which by most definitions result in the emergence of dictatorship. But it can also happen gradually through moves that undermine democracy, such as a government's strategic manipulation of elections to tilt the electoral playing field in its favour or stacking of the courts with loyalists. Such moves on their own degrade the quality of democracy but taken together can cumulate in democratic failure. As we discuss in greater detail in the next section, it is the latter pathway—the slow and gradual dismantling of democracy—that has become the more common way that democracies fall apart.

Despite democratic backsliding's frequency and the attendant consequences for citizens in countries where it occurs, there is limited understanding of the phenomenon or its contributing factors. Most research has focused instead on defining democracy and autocracy, the causes of democratic transitions, democratic consolidation, and authoritarian resilience. As organizations such as Freedom House continue to report on democracy's sustained decline across the globe, however, it is increasingly important for scholars to focus on and develop a better understanding of how and why democratic backsliding occurs.

The rise of authoritarianization

In 2012, a young Malian army officer, Amadou Sanogo, launched a **military coup** that ousted the country's democratically-elected President Amaadou Touré just one month ahead of the presidential election. The coup was a surprise to political analysts because President Touré had already announced his decision to abide by presidential term limits and was preparing to step down from office. The 2012 coup disrupted nearly twenty years of democratic rule in a historically turbulent corner of Africa. Relative to its neighbours in Senegal, Niger, and Cote d'Ivoire where leaders have sought to hang on to power past constitutional limits, Mali had served as a democratic exemplar.

Mali's coup, however, was notable for more than just the significant setback for democracy in East Africa that it represented. In fact, it was the first coup worldwide to bring down a democratically-elected regime in almost five years. From 1946–2010, coups accounted for 60 per cent of all democratic failures—by far the most common way that democratic failure has occurred (Kendall-Taylor and Frantz, 2016). But as scholars have documented, coups have become a less common mechanism of democratic failure in the post-Cold War era (Marinov and Goemans, 2014) Table 14.1 provides a summary.

From 1946 to 1999, 64 per cent of democracies failed because of coups (Kendall-Taylor and Frantz, 2016). At the height of their frequency in the 1960s, coups accounted for fifteen of the nineteen democratic failures in that decade. These coups took place in geographically diverse regions of the world, including in Greece (1967), Nigeria (1966), Brazil (1964), and Burma (1962). In the 1980s, coups were less frequent, but they still

Table 14.1 How democracies fail

Kind of seizure	1946–89	1990–2010
Coup	64%	36%
Authoritarianization	25%	50%
Insurgency	4%	9%
Foreign Imposed	7%	0%
Popular Uprising	0%	5%

Source: Geddes, Wright, and Frantz, 2018.

brought down all five of the democracies that failed that decade (Turkey, 1980; Ghana, 1981; Nigeria, 1983; Peru, 1988; and Sudan, 1989).

In the twenty-first century, however, coups have become much less likely to occur in democratic countries. The probability that any kind of coup would occur (successful or unsuccessful) reached a thirty-year low in 1995 (Bermeo, 2016). Although that probability rose slightly by 2010, it is still significantly less than in the 1960s. Moreover, the likelihood that a democracy was the target of a *successful* coup also declined markedly. Though this likelihood too has risen slightly in recent years, following coups that ousted democratically-elected leaders in Mali in 2012 and Egypt in 2013, the drop in the success rate of coups in democracies that began during the Cold War has not been reversed (Bermeo, 2016).

Instead, democracies are increasingly breaking down as a result of authoritarianization. Between 2000 and 2010, authoritarianization accounted for 40 per cent of all democratic failures, matching coups in frequency (Kendall-Taylor and Frantz, 2016). Since 2010, additional cases of this authoritarianization have occurred, including Erdoğan's gradual dismantling of democracy in Turkey and Daniel Ortega's incremental consolidation of power in Nicaragua. If current trends persist, populist-fuelled authoritarianization will soon become the most common way that democracies fail.

Authoritarianization occurs when democratically-elected incumbents initiate democratic breakdown. Sometimes, they happen at the hands of a dominant political party, as was the case in a number of African countries following the collapse of colonialism. In such instances, the party that led the independence movement won democratic elections and then subsequently consolidated control pushing the country toward dictatorship. Today, however, individual leaders more frequently initiate authoritarianizations. Occasionally, this happens quickly, as was the case in 1992 in Peru with President Alberto Fujimori's **autogolpe** (or self-coup, where the nation's leader assumes extraordinary powers). Usually, however, authoritarianization takes place gradually over the course of a number of years. The process starts slowly, and if a leader succeeds in several power grabs, he or she may accumulate enough power that regime officials will no longer be able to resist. This is because with each power grab, a leader's threat to eliminate noncompliant members of the inner circle becomes more credible, making regime officials less inclined to resist (Svolik, 2012). In other words, democratically-elected leaders look to gradually grab power from those institutions and individuals that have the potential to constrain their power.

This was the story of Venezuelan President Hugo Chávez. A career military officer and former coup leader with an anti-establishment populist message, Chávez rose to power through democratic elections in 1998. At the time of his election, Venezuela was the third-oldest democracy outside the advanced industrial democratic states, with strong democratic traditions and well-developed political institutions. Over the course of years, however, Chávez capitalized on oil-driven economic growth, rising public dissatisfaction with and alienation from the country's two dominant political parties, and his personal charisma to incrementally undermine political and civil liberties (Mainwaring, 2012). Chávez's path to dictatorship was a significant departure from the classic pattern of military coups observed so frequently in Latin America in earlier decades. Instead, Chávez blazed a new trail to dictatorship—one that has subsequently cleared the way for others, such as Nicaragua's Ortega.

As the number of democracies that have broken down as a result of authoritarianization has grown, the signposts and patterns of behaviour common across these cases have become increasingly clear. We identify the actions that today's leaders are taking to expand executive power and incrementally erode democracy.

Signposts of the slow dismantling of democracy

Framing public support and electoral 'mandates' as justification for undemocratic moves

Most leaders who gradually expanded executive control enjoyed relatively high levels of public support. Public support enables opportunistic leaders to accumulate power through legal channels, including by using legislative majorities or referenda to pass laws that facilitate their efforts. These leaders may also use existing courts in those cases where supporters of the executive have control. As political scientist Nancy Bermeo (2016) noted, 'the defining feature of executive aggrandizement [authoritarianization] is that institutional change is either put to some sort of vote or legally decreed by a freely elected official—meaning that the change can be framed as having resulted from a democratic mandate' (p. 11). Past scholarship has recognized the importance of legitimacy in the stability of authoritarian rule (Gerschewski, 2013; Schatz, 2006). Thus counter-intuitively, the public may offer support for leaders to attain more political power.

In Argentina, for example, Juan Perón was elected president in 1946 and leveraged his popularity to gradually consolidate control over the political system. More recently, Nicaraguan President Ortega has translated his high level of public support into expanded executive power. Ortega received 72 per cent of the vote in 2016 presidential election and his political party, the FSLN, holds a majority in the National Assembly, enabling it to pass laws without support from opposition parties. Similarly, in Hungary in 2010, Viktor Orbán's Fidesz party won two-thirds of the seats in parliament, an outcome that Orbán referred to as his 'two-thirds revolution'. Orbán has broadly interpreted his strong electoral outcome as giving him a mandate to increase executive power, including through constitutional change.

Attacking the media

Democratically-elected leaders looking to expand executive control seek to undermine media freedom in order to minimize journalists' ability to expose anti-democratic behaviour and amplify narratives that support their efforts to consolidate control. Although attacking the media and encouraging self-censorship is common in autocracies, this practice has become more prevalent in democracies. The pervasiveness of declining media freedom in democratic settings is highlighted by Freedom House's 2017 Freedom of the Press report, which found that 'press freedom worldwide deteriorated to its lowest point in thirteen years in 2016, driven by unprecedented threats to journalists and media outlets in major democracies' (p. 3).

Democratic leaders have used a number of tactics to undermine press freedom. First, populist-fuelled leaders have attacked the credibility of the independent and mainstream media through hostile rhetoric. Populists, in particular, seek to portray the media as part of the 'corrupt' political establishment and seek to discredit critical outlets. For example, in the run up to President Donald Trump's election and since taking office in 2017, he has labelled several media outlets as 'dishonest', '**fake news**', and 'enemies of the American people' in an effort to delegitimize information that is critical of his presidency. These types of actions can, over time, erode press freedom and remove an important constraint on executive power.

Democratically-elected leaders have also undermined the media's ability to act as a check on their power by increasing government control over public broadcasters. Peru's President Alberto Fujimori, for example, was democratically elected in 1990 but subsequently eroded democratic constraints on his power and emerged as a dictator following his 1992 *autogolpe*. As part of his efforts to expand his personal power, Fujimori corrupted much of the media. In the late 1990s, four of five private television networks and more than a dozen tabloid newspapers were on the state payroll (Levitsky and Loxton, 2013). In Poland, where the ruling Law and Justice Party has been criticized for its efforts to erode respect for democratic norms, the government has eroded media freedom by passing laws in 2016 that transferred authority over public media to government-appointed officials.

Finally, leaders intent on expanding executive power have shut down opposition journalists and media firms while raising the profile of media organizations under the control of regime insiders. In Hungary, Prime Minister Orbán is using financial tactics to reduce the number and reach of outlets that are critical of the government. In 2016, Orbán-connected businessmen bought up a number of independent outlets. Most notably, in October of that year, one of Hungary's oldest (sixty years) newspapers of record and a vocal government critic unexpectedly shut down. This paved the way for a Fidesz ally to seize control of the firm. Government agencies and private firms that wish to maintain good relations with the government also refrain from advertising with the independent media, making it difficult for these outlets to sustain their operations (Kornai, 2015). As a result, in Hungary under Orbán, media freedom and media access more closely represent what we usually see in an authoritarian regime (Ostrow, 2014).

Undermining judicial independence

Leaders seeking to slowly dismantle constraints on their control also undermine the separation of power between the executive and the judiciary. As discussed in Chapter 2 (Defining Democracy), judicial independence is critical for maintaining democracy because of its role in interpreting the constitution, protecting minority rights, and maintaining the rule of law (Linz and Stepan, 1996). With greater influence over the judiciary, leaders can use the courts and the semblance of the rule of law to remove barriers to their power and opportunistically target their opponents. In other words, these leaders can transform judicial authorities into instruments of prosecution, targeting opposition politicians, businesspeople, and independent media (Levitsky and Loxton, 2013). Those leaders that enjoy public support face fewer barriers to their efforts to erode judicial independence because they can use legislative majorities or referenda to pass laws that facilitate their efforts.

To increase influence over the judiciary, leaders typically seek to change its leadership —forcing out pre-existing judges and replacing them with loyalists. Leaders can do this in a number of ways, including by reducing the retirement age of judges and giving the executive or legislative branches the power to appoint high-level judges. In Poland, the Law and Justice Party came under significant criticism for its moves to curb the powers of the Constitutional Tribunal (TK) and interfere with the appointment of its judges. In Hungary, the government lowered the judicial retirement age of judges from 70 to 62, which forced hundreds of judges out of the courts (Kornai, 2015). Argentina's Carlos Menem also used a similar tactic, coaxing unfriendly judges from lifetime tenure with the promise of more prestigious posts (Chávez, 2007). In other cases, leaders can find ways of ousting unfriendly judges by accusing them of corruption. In the Philippines, Chief Justice Maria Lourdes Sereno was ousted in May of 2018 after President Rodrigo Duterte declared that she should be impeached (on the grounds that she had not declared her assets and liabilities). With Sereno out, Duterte was able install a loyalist (Villamor, 2018).

Leaders seeking to undermine judicial independence also make organizational changes to give the executive and legislative branches greater oversight and authority over the judiciary. In Hungary, for example, Orbán used his two-thirds legislative majority to change the constitution in 2010, including restructuring the judiciary in ways that gave the government greater influence. Similarly, in Turkey, the government passed legislation in 2014 giving the justice minister the power to directly appoint members to the High Council of Judges and to control the inspection board that disciplines judges. Within six months, more than 3,000 sitting judges had been removed.

Eroding civil society

The process of authoritarianization also requires that leaders weaken or restrict **civil society** to hinder the capacity of these groups to hold the government accountable or mobilize opposition to government efforts to expand control. Leaders often use national security arguments, including the threat of terrorism and instability, to justify their actions. Not only do these threats provide leaders with justification for their actions, but they also make citizens more willing to accept political and civil liberties restrictions in exchange for the promise of stability. Moreover, the trends fuelling populism—namely the growing swath of citizens who view cultural change as threatening their livelihood and well-being—also create an environment more permissive for opportunistic leaders to restrict civil society. Research suggests that as individual fears of societal change and external threats grow, so too does their preference for strong, decisive leaders who are willing to use force to maintain order (Feldman and Stenner, 1997).

Democratic leaders seeking to reduce constraints on their control rely predominately on legal means to selectively target those groups and individuals they view as threatening. In Hungary, for example, the government passed new legislation in 2017 requiring certain **NGOs**, including prominent U.S.-funded NGOs, to register as foreign-funded groups and indicate their foreign status on all media materials. Orbán argued that the new law will improve transparency and target money laundering and terrorism. Similarly, in Bangladesh, where Sheikh Hasina and her ruling Awami League have been gradually consolidating power, the government passed 'The Foreign Donations (Voluntary Activities) Regulation Act' in 2016, which made it more difficult for NGOs to obtain foreign funds and gave officials broad authority to deregister NGOs that make 'derogatory' comments about government bodies or the constitution.

Changing electoral laws to extend their rule

In many cases, democratically-elected leaders with autocratic ambitions ultimately seek to change the rules of how elections are run—including who gets to stand in them, who gets to vote, and how the votes are counted—such that it becomes difficult to remove the party or leader from power. In Hungary, for example, Fidesz saw its vote share decline from 52.7 per cent in 2010 to 44.9 per cent in 2014, yet its majority in parliament increased. This was largely because the government established an electoral system that favours the winning party and **gerrymanders** electoral districts.

Those leaders who enjoy enough public support may also be able to change or abolish term limits. Venezuela's Hugo Chávez used a referendum to abolish his term limits in 2009, for example. **Term-limit extensions** have become increasingly common; the average annual incidence of term-limit extensions has quadrupled in the post-Cold War period (Kendall-Taylor, Frantz, and Wright, 2017). Moreover, term-limit extensions in democratic countries (rather than those in countries that are already dictatorships) are rising. Today, 33 per cent of term limit extensions occur in democracies, up from just 8 per cent prior to 1989. In Nicaragua, for example, the National Assembly approved constitutional amendments in 2014 that paved the way for Ortega to win a third consecutive term in November 2016. In other words, changes to electoral laws and term limit extensions have become an increasingly common tactic to solidify the power that leaders gain through authoritarianization (see Box 14.1).

 Box 14.1: **Term limit extensions**

Changing term limits is not inherently anti-democratic. Leaders in many democracies have successfully pushed for term limit extensions. And in dictatorships, many leaders seeking to extend their time in office do so through nominally democratic processes, such as referenda, judicial rulings, or passing legislation amending a country's constitution. In Belarus, for example, President Alexander Lukashenko (in power since 1994) held a referendum in 2004 in which voters supported abolishing presidential term limits. More recently, in Rwanda, Paul Kagame passed a national referendum that enables him to stay in office until 2034. In Kazakhstan, the legislature was key to extending President Nazarbayev's time in office, as well. In 2007, it amended the constitution to lift the term limit on President Nazarbayev, who had been in power since the country's independence in 1991.[1]

Although not inherently anti-democratic, the rising frequency of term limit extensions threatens democratic development. Executive term limits play an important role in promoting **participatory democracy** and civil society development, because they enhance political competition, check abuses of power, and facilitate the development of political parties as opposed to specific leaders. When leaders alter term limits, it often becomes more difficult for the opposition to compete, and these changes frequently result in more personalized systems in which power is concentrated in the hands of the leader.

Leaders' efforts to contravene their term limits are not always successful, however, and can trigger instability, typically in the form of widespread protests. In Burkina Faso, the public opposed Blaise Compaoré's efforts to extend his term limits. Campaore's attempt to secure a term limit extension catalysed protests that ultimately led to his ouster in 2014. Burundi continues to face unrest after President Pierre Nkurunziza was controversially elected to a third term in 2015, violating the spirit of the Arusha Accords that ended Burundi's civil war in 1993 and heightening already troublesome ethnic tensions.

Though term limit enforcement is less frequent in dictatorships than in democracies, even in dictatorships term limits often exist and are enforced. New authoritarian regimes may agree to implement term limits to enhance their legitimacy and, perhaps more importantly, to make a leader's commitment to share power with other members of the elite more credible (Svolik, 2012). When a leader's commitment to share power is credible, it reduces the chances that the elite will take steps to preemptively oust the leader. If leaders are able to amass enough power relative to other members of the elite, however, term limits become difficult to enforce. Members of a dictator's inner circle must remain powerful and unified enough relative to the dictator to ensure a leader abides by such limits.

Case studies on authoritarianization

In this section we present two in-depth case studies of authoritarianization: Russia under Vladimir Putin and Turkey under Recep Tayyip Erdoğan. The case studies are useful for their ability to highlight the commonalities across countries, regardless of substantive differences in political and historical context. In many instances a leader's earliest efforts to consolidate control are dismissed by political observers as necessary to implement a popular leader's ambitious reform agenda. Once the evidence of a leader's intentions to dismantle democratic institutions becomes undeniable, however, it becomes more difficult for domestic and international actors to counter than if opposition were mobilized earlier in the process. These cases, therefore, illustrate how the signposts we discussed previously play out in specific countries. In doing so, these case studies are intended to provide additional context that can help analysts and observers interpret the early actions of opportunistic leaders in other democratic contexts.

---

[1] In a surprising move, Nazarbayev stepped down from the presidency in 2019, though he is likely to continue to wield significant influence over politics from behind the scenes.

Russia

No one would dispute that power in Russia today lies firmly in the hands of President Vladimir Putin. But his command over the political system was not always so sweeping. When Putin came to power in relatively free and fair elections in 2000, he inherited a nascent democracy that had taken a series of reforms in the aftermath of communism's collapse. Under Boris Yeltsin (1991–99), Putin's predecessor and Russia's first democratically-elected leader, Russia's political system featured competitive elections for parliament and the presidency, and mostly competitive elections for regional governors.[2] A wide range of political parties, including opposition communist and ultranationalist groups, and NGOs operated freely. Electronic and print media outlets not controlled by the state multiplied (McFaul and Stoner-Weiss, 2008). Yeltsin himself brought in Putin and other ex-KGB officers following Russia's disastrous default in 1998 as a form of protection, yet when Yeltsin resigned in 1999 most observers considered Russia to be a nascent democracy; Freedom House ranked Russia as 'partly free'.

During the course of his first four years in office, however, Putin began to reverse Russia's democratic trajectory and steadily concentrated power in his own hands. In a study on regime personalization in Russia, Alex Baturo and Johan Elkink (2016) find that Russia emerged as a personalist dictatorship by 2004. Freedom House had also downgraded Russia's ranking to 'not free' by 2005 focusing in particular on Putin's concentration of executive power. So how did Putin orchestrate authoritarianization in Russia?

High levels of public support for Putin provided a permissive environment for his efforts to dismantle Russia's fragile democracy. At the time he came to office, there was strong elite and public demand for a leader that would restore order and save Russia from the chaos it experienced following the collapse of the Soviet Union (Hill and Gaddy, 2013). The instability, unpredictability, and deprivation of the early 1990s reinforced for many Russians a belief that a more centralized state apparatus would be required to return Russia to a state that could be respected. Just as importantly, Putin benefited tremendously during his early years in office from high oil prices, a spate of terrorist attacks that enabled him to rally popular support, and success in containing an insurgency in the volatile North Caucasus. Against this backdrop, Putin maximized the power and influence of a robust presidential system that he inherited from Yeltsin following the latter's violent standoff with the legislature. Russia's 1993 constitution provides for a strong executive, and Putin leveraged those powers in ways that Yeltsin never could (Levitsky and Way, 2010).

As Putin sought to expand his presidential power, he carefully targeted those institutions and centres of power that could obstruct his ability to implement his reform agenda. The independent media was one of his first targets (McFaul and Stoner-Weiss, 2008). When Putin was elected, Russia had three television networks with national

---

[2] Some scholars consider Russia autocratic under Yeltsin as well (Geddes, Wright, and Frantz, 2018). Regardless of how Russia under Yeltsin is classified, however, the general consensus is that levels of democraticness have declined considerably under Putin.

reach: RTR (which was already state-owned), ORT, and NTV. Putin initially went after NTV owner Vladimir Gusinsky, who used his media holdings to shine light on alleged Kremlin wrongdoings. The Kremlin launched an investigation against Gusinsky for misappropriation of funds in relation to one of his companies, and ultimately arrested him in 2000. Shortly after Gusinsky was released from jail, he sold his media assets— eventually enabling NTV to be placed under government control—and left the country. Putin, along with Yeltsin-era holdovers, also targeted the de facto owner of ORT, billionaire Boris Berezovsky, who had been close to Yeltsin's family and who helped start Putin's party, but who became a vocal government critic as his standing with Putin began to wane. Under Kremlin pressure, Berezovsky surrendered his shares in ORT in part to another oligarch who was friendlier to the Kremlin. Today, the Kremlin controls all the major national television networks.

Another one of Putin's primary targets was regional government, which amassed significant power under Yeltsin. The Russian government's humiliating 'peace treaty' with Chechnya in 1996 gave the rebellious region de facto independence and highlighted a trend that saw several regions demand greater autonomy. This uneven decentralization empowered a number of regional officials and contributed to Russia's political disarray. Putin saw the trend as a threat to Russian governance—but also almost certainly saw the regions as constraining his efforts to recentralize state power (Hill and Gaddy, 2013). He therefore took a number of actions to rein in these competing centres of power. Among his very first initiatives after his inauguration in 2000, he created seven federal super-districts with appointed loyalists to bring regional legislation in line with federal legislation. Putin also strategically targeted some of the most problematic governors. Early in his term, Putin forced Primorsky Krai Governor Yevgeny Nazdratenko, a vocal critic of the government, to resign. Rather than repress Nazdratenko, Putin assigned him as Chairman of the lucrative Russian State Commission for Fisheries. This early move served as an important example to the elite that so long as they followed the new rules of the game (Nazdratenko ultimately voluntarily resigned), they would be protected (Hill and Gaddy, 2013).

Simultaneous with the creation of the federal districts, Putin emasculated the Federation Council (the upper house of Russia's parliament) through reforms that removed elected governors and regional legislative heads and replaced them with appointed representatives. These reforms effectively ended the governors' influence on federal policy. Although the Council resisted the plan, Putin threatened to open federal criminal investigations, forcing them to back down and approve the law. Finally, in 2004, Putin abolished elections for regional officials and replaced them with appointees. Putin took advantage of the Beslan School siege—a terrorist attack that ended with the death of at least 385 people, many of them children—to justify his claim that the terrorists attacked only because Russia was 'weak' and that the way to make it strong was to consolidate greater power in the Kremlin.

In addition to weakening the regions, Putin also set out to defang Russia's **oligarchs**, who many political observers long assumed would use their wealth and standing to constrain and even control Putin. In his first years in office, Putin struck a deal with these influential individuals in which Putin offered himself to the oligarchs as a protector

(Hill and Gaddy, 2013). The oligarchs' vast wealth in the 1990s and their ownership of the country's largest corporations was widely regarded as illegitimate (much of their wealth derived from the 'loans for shares' scheme—a shady process whereby political insiders obtained ownership of some of the state's largest assets as collateral for loans to the state). The oligarchs also required protection from one another—and ultimately looked to Putin to play that role—given their constant predation of each other's businesses. In return, the oligarchs were expected to grant the Kremlin greater access to their wealth (through taxation) and ultimately their loyalty.

In 2003, Putin effectively shifted the balance of power between himself and the oligarchs in his favour when he arrested and jailed Mikhail Khodorkovsky, the owner of oil giant Yukos and the wealthiest private businessman in Russia at the time. Despite most of the oligarchs' tacit understanding of their subordination to Putin, Khodorkovsky remained stubbornly independent-minded. His arrest, therefore, sent a powerful signal to the oligarchs about the risks associated with challenging Putin. Two other factors contributed to Putin's ability to rein in the oligarchs. First, Putin's assertion of control over Gazprom in 2001 provided him and the state with access to a large revenue source independent from the oligarchs, reducing his reliance on this group. Second, Putin also had considerable compromising information—or 'kompromat'—on the oligarchs, some of which he obtained during his time as **Federal Security Service** (FSB) head. Putin was able to use this information as leverage, also contributing to his ability to gain the upper hand vis-à-vis the oligarchs.

Putin's control over the media, the regional governorships, and the oligarchs enabled him to solidify his control over the legislature and weaken opposition political parties (McFaul and Stoner–Weiss, 2008). As early as 2003, Putin gained significant influence over the Duma, Russia's legislature, as the Kremlin's party, United Russia (UR), won a strong majority in the legislative elections that year. Putin used his control over the media to ensure constant positive coverage of UR party leaders (and negative coverage of opposition parties), financial support for UR from the oligarchs, and a near-unanimous endorsement by Russia's regional leaders to manufacture a strong UR outcome. Putin's control of these political resources also ensured that political parties not aligned with the Kremlin atrophied.

Even after 2004, Putin continued to consolidate control over the political system. In his second term (2004–08), Putin significantly undermined civil society—an effort he has continued to prioritize since returning to the presidency in 2012. The Kremlin has passed numerous laws giving the state the means to harass, weaken, and close down NGOs considered too political. A 2012 law required NGOs receiving funds from outside Russia to register as 'foreign agents' or pay significant fines. The Kremlin has also proactively funded its own cohort of regime-friendly NGOs, including youth groups such as Nashi, to proactively spread the regime's image and narrative.

In addition to weakening competing power centres, Putin also steadily installed loyalists, many from his early career in St. Petersburg and associates from the security services, in key positions of power (Treisman, 2007). Today, scholars estimate that Putin and a circle of 20–30 trusted advisors with ties to the military and security services make most of the decisions in Russia, and real power resides within an inner circle of just half a dozen individuals (Hill and Gaddy, 2013). Politics have become so personalized that the stability of the Russian system is largely contingent on Putin's own popularity.

Turkey

Turkish President Recep Tayyip Erdoğan has followed a similar trajectory to Putin, although the pace of authoritarianization in Turkey has been far more gradual than it was in Russia. Turkey's democratic decline has also not been as extensive as in Russia to date, as scholars and political observers continue to debate whether Turkey should still be considered a democracy. Political trends have been hard to characterize because some of the ruling Justice and Development Party (AKP's) changes initially made Turkey more democratic. Erdoğan and the AKP have, for example, decreased the military's outsized influence over politics and extended civilian control over the military. However, a number of scholars contend that since at least 2014 Turkey no longer meets the minimum threshold of democracy and should be viewed as an authoritarian system (Diamond, 2015; Esen and Gumuscu, 2016). The number of scholars viewing Turkey as a dictatorship grew following a 2016 failed coup; in 2018 Freedom House changed Turkey's rating from 'partly free' to 'not free'. In his time in office—first as Prime Minister (2003–14) and now as president (2014–present)—Erdoğan has dramatically expanded his informal and formal powers and consolidated his personal control of Turkey's media, business sector, and security apparatus.

Like Putin, Erdoğan's rise to power took place against a backdrop of political volatility. Since 1946, Turkey had experienced three military coups. In 2002, however, Erdoğan and his AKP received a governing majority that ended decades of unstable coalition rule. Erdoğan's success stemmed from his populist appeal—he promised to give voice to Turkey's conservative Islamic population. These citizens long felt relegated to the sidelines of public life in part because of policies pursued by Mustafa Kemal Atatürk, the founder of the Republic of Turkey who sought to create a secular state and deliberately marginalize the role of Islam.

Upon Erdoğan's victory, Turkey was heralded as an exemplar of a free-market, moderate Muslim-majority democracy. The AKP focused on political liberalization, economic modernization, and was looking to implement an **EU**-inspired structural reform programme. Given early success in delivering economic growth and investment and moving Turkey toward the European Union, the AKP has enjoyed relatively robust public support—the party has won every country-wide election since 2002.[3] The public support that stemmed from economic growth and the promise held by Erdoğan's ambitious reform agenda meant that domestic and international observers tended to downplay many of his early moves to consolidate power.

---

[3] In a notable turn of events, the ruling AKP lost control of Ankara and Istanbul, Turkey's capital and largest city, in local elections in 2019. The AKP claimed that there were irregularities in the Istanbul election and held a re-run of the election. Nonetheless, the opposition candidate from the Republican People's Party (CHP) won the second vote by an even larger margin than the original vote, delivering a surprising upset for Erdoğan's AKP and raising questions about the strength of Erdoğan's hold on power.

Beginning around 2007, Erdoğan embarked on a campaign to disempower the Kemalists (or individuals adhering to the founding ideology of Turkey established by Mustafa Kemal Atatürk) and the secular establishment that long dominated Turkish politics. Erdoğan first set out to end the secular military's grip on political institutions, which effectively gave military officers veto power over elected officials. For example, Erdoğan reduced the military's influence over the National Security Council by increasing its number of civilian members. He also removed the seats reserved for military officers on the Council of Higher Education and the Radio and Television Supreme Council. Moreover, Erdoğan and the AKP launched two court cases in 2008 and 2009—known as the Ergenekon and Balyoz cases—in which hundreds of retired and on-duty high-ranking military personnel were accused of and detained for planning an alleged military takeover against the AKP. Although Erdoğan's moves helped reduced the military's outsized influence over politics, many observers have been critical of how these efforts played out. They suggest that Erdoğan and the AKP used the trials to suppress opponents and critics of the AKP government. The government was also criticized for using undemocratic and illiberal measures throughout the trials, eroding respect for rule of law and fundamental human rights.

With the military effectively brought under control, Erdoğan subsequently sought to weaken the secular Kemalists' grip on the judiciary. In 2010, Erdoğan passed two dozen constitutional changes via national referendum. In many ways, the reforms were designed to enhance democracy by shifting the balance of power to elected officials (the democratically-elected AKP government) as opposed to appointed officials (secularist judges and bureaucrats who long dominated the Turkish state despite not holding elective office) (Turam, 2012). Ultimately, however, the reforms eroded judicial independence by giving the president the power to name fourteen of the seventeen Constitutional Court judges and shifting decisions about which parties are allowed to field political candidates from the courts to the AKP-dominated legislature. Again in 2014, the government passed legislation eroding the separation of power between the executive and the judiciary. The 2014 changes gave the justice minister the power to directly appoint members to the High Council of Judges and control the inspection board that disciplines judges. Within six months, more than 3,000 sitting judges were removed (Bermeo, 2016).

Also like Putin, Erdoğan moved early in his tenure to target the independent media. Besides creating AKP-friendly outlets, the AKP used political and financial pressure to punish and isolate its enemies. In 2009, for example, Erdoğan fined Dogan Media Group—a collection of newspapers and television channels critical of Erdoğan and owned by one of Turkey's biggest media tycoons—$2.5 billion for alleged tax evasion. At the time, public opinion was divided over whether Erdoğan was dutifully punishing a tax evader or intent on muzzling the press. In response to these measures, Dogan Media sold Milliyet and Vatan, two widely circulated and well-established newspapers, to businessmen with close ties to the AKP government. The European Commission's progress reports in 2009 and 2010 asserted that the fines on Dogan damaged freedom of the press in Turkey.

In addition to political and financial pressure on the media, the AKP government took a number of approaches to discipline the mainstream media, including intimidation; mass firings; legal pressure on journalists through defamation, criminal lawsuits, and antiterrorism laws; and imprisonment of journalists. The government has also created informal institutions to ensure positive coverage. For example, the government appoints pro-AKP managers and journalists to major TV stations and newspapers. These appointees serve as government representatives in their respective media companies and their presence allows them to supervise the internal operations of these stations and alter news content in line with government direction (Esen and Gumuscu, 2016). These practices have helped establish what has become a culture of censorship and self-censorship in Turkey (Esen and Gumuscu, 2016).

Perhaps gaining confidence from his early success in expanding executive control, Erdoğan accelerated his efforts to consolidate power after the Gezi Park protests in 2013. The demonstrations began as peaceful opposition to the urban development plan for Istanbul's Taksim Gezi Park, but escalated in response to the violent crackdown by police and broader concerns about the government's increasingly authoritarian tendencies. Amid differences within his cabinet about how to respond, Erdoğan used the opportunity to purge more liberal AKP members. This included then-President Abdullah Gül, who preferred a more conciliatory approach toward the protesters.

Perhaps the nail in the coffin for Turkish democracy, however, was a failed coup in July 2016. The harshness with which the Erdoğan and the AKP responded was a turning point in Turkish democracy. Erdoğan leveraged the coup attempt—which he referred to as a 'gift from god'—to crush the remaining opposition and facilitate his efforts to dominate Turkey's institutions. Erdoğan used new powers obtained through his declaration of a state of emergency to purge his regime of dissenting voices, including those from within the AKP, the military, the media, and the judiciary.

Throughout this period Erdoğan, like other aspiring autocrats, used threats (both real and manufactured) to justify his increasingly repressive measures. In Erdoğan's case, he used alleged threats from the 'deep state' and terrorism to rationalize his actions. The Turkish Government, for example, quickly blamed the failed coup on officers and civilians associated with Fethullah Gülen, an Islamic cleric and the spiritual leader of a transnational religious movement known as 'Hizmet' (Turkish for 'service'). Erdoğan and Gulen had been political allies after the AKP came to power, as they joined forces to rid the government and military of the Kemalists and secularists that they believed operated a 'deep state.' Following their success in weakening bureaucratic resistance to a more Islamist agenda, however, they turned against one another and embarked on an escalating series of attacks and counterattacks. Erdoğan used the failed coup to purge the Gulenist opposition; more than 160,000 state workers, soldiers, or others were suspended or dismissed from government jobs.

Ultimately, in April 2017, Erdoğan passed a referendum that expanded his powers as president and enabled him to stay in office potentially until 2029. In these ways, Erdoğan has transformed Turkey's decades-old parliamentary system into a heavily centralized presidential one where checks and balances have largely been eroded. As in Russia, the process of authoritarianization is likely to have significant implications that will live well beyond both Erdoğan and Putin. We now turn to a discussion of those implications.

Implications of authoritarianization

The changing nature of democratic breakdown creates a number of challenges to democratic development across the globe. In this section we identify three implications associated with the rise of authoritarianization.

First and foremost, and as the two case studies above suggest, the slow and gradual nature of populist-fuelled democratic backsliding makes it difficult to counter. Because it is subtle and incremental, there is no single moment that triggers widespread resistance or creates a focal point around which an opposition can coalesce. And in those cases in which vocal critics or organizations emerge, leaders can easily frame them as 'fifth columnists', 'agents of influence', or other provocateurs seeking to destabilize the system. Moreover, many leaders who have begun the process of authoritarianization enjoy substantial popular support. These leaders enjoy public support because they pursue populist policies and/or are well versed in using nationalist rhetoric to influence domestic audiences, tapping into frustrations and grievances. Populists, who distrust institutional checks on their power and are critical of the civil administration, political parties and the media, take advantage of their popularity and incrementally disassemble democratic institutions (in some cases using referenda to legitimize their authoritarian manoeuvres). And because they are elected on a platform of change, their early efforts to expand control are dismissed as necessary to implement ambitious reforms.

Second, not only is populist-fuelled authoritarianization difficult to counter, it is increasingly giving rise to 'personalist dictatorship', a unique form of autocracy we described in Chapter 3. Data show that just under half (44 per cent) of all instances of authoritarianization from 1946 to 1999 led to the establishment of personalist dictatorships. From 2000 to 2010, however, that proportion increased to 75 per cent (Kendall-Taylor and Frantz, 2016). In most cases, the populist strongmen rose to power with the support of a political party, but then proved effective in sidelining competing voices from within. This was the story not only in Turkey and Russia, but also with Chávez in Venezuela, Ortega in Nicaragua, and Fujimori in Peru. Even in countries where populist-fuelled threats to democracy have not fully evolved into autocracy, such as in Hungary and Poland, dominant leaders like Viktor Orbán and Jarosław Kaczyński have been able to personalize politics in their countries and enjoy a disproportionate share of power.

The rise of personalist dictatorships that authoritarianization is producing is cause for concern. As we discussed in Chapter 3, a robust body of political science research shows that such systems tend to produce the worst outcomes of any type of political regime: they typically pursue the most volatile and aggressive foreign policies, espouse the most xenophobic sentiments, are the most likely to mismanage foreign aid, and are the least likely to transition to democracy when they collapse. Today's populist movements, therefore, could very well be fueling the proliferation of the world's most problematic regimes.

Finally, the risk of authoritarianization is here to stay and is likely to put countries that we typically think of as stable democracies at risk. Recent political science research reinforces the idea that new democracies do indeed consolidate sometime between seventeen and twenty years after they are established (Svolik, 2008). However, the research shows that a declining risk of coups is the primary factor driving down a country's risk of democratic failure beyond this time frame. The threat of authoritarianization, it turns out, does not diminish over time. Venezuela is a case in point. When Chávez was elected in 2002, Venezuela was the third-oldest democracy outside of the industrialized West. Likewise, Hungary and Poland were long assumed to be fixtures within the democratic club but nonetheless have experienced significant declines in respect for democratic principles.

The staying power of populism will likely fuel this trend. As we discussed in the previous chapter, the forces fueling populism aren't going away anytime soon. Economic underperformance, disillusion with corruption, dissatisfaction with government performance, and new winners and losers resulting from technological change have the potential to fan the flames of populism across the globe. Democratic citizens, including those in established democracies in Europe and the United States, therefore, should hesitate before assuming that they are invulnerable to a populist-driven backslide. The tactics of today's populists might be subtle, but if left untamed, they will lead to grave consequences for global democracy.

Conclusion

This chapter provided an overview of how democracies backslide and break down and how these processes have evolved in the post-Cold War period. Historically, democratic breakdown was sudden and decisive. Today it occurs more gradually, making it difficult to discern exactly when the break with democracy happens. The more insidious process of democratic breakdown today, or as we refer to in this chapter, authoritarianization, is a major challenge to democratic development around the globe. We discussed the signposts and indicators of this process, as well as a number of examples, including Russia under Putin and Turkey under Erdoğan.

It is important to note that even advanced democracies are not immune. As we have discussed, countries such as Hungary and Poland—long considered fully consolidated democracies in the heart of Europe—have experienced a process of democratic decay. This is, in part, because many of the policies their leaders pursue that ultimately erode democratic quality are at least initially popular with their voters. The slow and incremental nature of contemporary democratic decline and the domestic popularity the leaders often enjoy make authoritarianization difficult to counter.

Though the emergence of new democracies still outpaces the emergence of new dictatorships, the rise of authoritarianization should give us pause. While it is true that democracy continues its reign as the most prevalent form of government worldwide and that citizens prefer it to the alternatives, current trends signal that authoritarianization will remain a significant challenge. The dynamics we discussed in this chapter, therefore, underscore one of the main themes we emphasize throughout this book: democracies are being strained not just by the actions of malign external actors, but increasingly face significant threats from within.

Key Questions

1. How has the mode of democratic breakdown changed over time? What accounts for this change?

2. How are leaders dismantling democracy today? Identify the indicators and explain how the actions that leaders are taking weaken democracy.

3. Why is it important for leaders to have popular support when they attempt a power grab? Can leaders centralize power today without some popular support in doing so?

4. Why do leaders target the media in the process of consolidating their rule?

5. Are there currently countries beyond those we focused on in this chapter where there are indicators of incremental democratic decline?

6. Does authoritarianization present a concern to the future of democracy? Why or why not?

Further Reading

BERMEO, N., 2016. 'On Democratic Backsliding'. *Journal of Democracy*, *27*(1), pp. 5–19.
This article provides a clear definition of what democratic backsliding is, using examples from Bangladesh and Turkey to demonstrate how backsliding takes place over time, and is often sanctioned by the public.

DIAMOND, L., PLATTNER, M.F. and WALKER, C. eds., 2016. *Authoritarianism Goes Global: The Challenge to Democracy*. JHU Press.
Authoritarianism Goes Global is a series of essays that looks at how countries such as China, Iran, Russia, Saudi Arabia, and Venezuela have developed tools and strategies to maintain their regimes, but also contain the spread of democracy. The book argues that these regimes have become more assertive in collaborating together to repress liberal forces in other societies and have fostered the emergence of authoritarian norms that challenge liberal democracy.

MECHKOVA, V., LÜHRMANN, A. and LINDBERG, S.I., 2017. 'How Much Democratic Backsliding?' *Journal of Democracy*, *28*(4), pp. 162–9.
This article provides a clear picture of whether or not there actually is a global democratic crisis, looking at data from the largest democracy database, the Varieties of Democracy Project. The article demonstrates the volatility taking place, which countries have been backsliding, and which countries have been able to overcome the global environment, and transition to democracy.

WALDNER, D. and LUST, E., 2018. 'Unwelcome Change: Coming to Terms with Democratic Backsliding'. *Annual Review of Political Science*, *21*, pp. 93–113.
This article acknowledges that while there is no clear theory to explain democratic backsliding, exploring theories of democratic transitions and breakdowns can shed light into what may impact democratic backsliding.

15

Conclusion: The Future of Democracy

This book has covered a large body of research on democracy, autocracy, and democratization within the context of contemporary global dynamics. One of the key messages to emerge is that democracy is under threat. Mounting problems within a number of long-lived democracies—many of which we have discussed in this book—have raised questions about democracy's future. Concurrently, we appear to be returning to a period of intense ideological competition between democracy and authoritarianism. China's rise is challenging Western hegemony and many now see Beijing as an increasingly viable alternative to the democratic West. As the strategic competition between democracies and authoritarian powers like China and Russia has intensified, levels of democracy across the globe have plateaued and possibly declined.

Democracy's lull has generated widespread concern among analysts and policymakers over democracy's global trajectory. A look back at the historical record underscores the validity of such concerns. During the last 100 years, democracy has experienced a series of ups and downs. Samuel Huntington referred to this ebb and flow as 'waves of democracy' (Huntington, 1991). He and subsequent researchers have provided compelling evidence that democracy does indeed cluster in time and space. As Chapter 12 explained, 'diffusion' theories indicate that a democratic transition in one country affects the likelihood of democratization in bordering states. The **Arab Spring** and **Colour Revolutions** provide vivid examples of the way that democratic movements seemingly spread across borders. Similarly, academic studies also find evidence of 'neighbourhood effects', or the idea that levels of democracy (or autocracy) tend to converge within regions.

As we discussed in Chapter 12, there have been three **waves of democratization**: a long slow wave from 1828 to 1926, a second wave from 1943 to 1964, and **a third wave** beginning in 1974. Although scholars debate the exact timing of the waves and whether the third wave has been one continuous wave or two shorter ones, there is broad agreement that levels of democracy ebb and flow in a wave-like dynamic. Democratic waves, therefore, have become a widely accepted metaphor for how we think about democratization dynamics.

The often-overlooked aspect of the democracy-in-waves metaphor, however, is the downward turn that historically occurs after democracy levels crest. In fact, both of the previous two waves of democracy were followed by a reverse wave during which a large share of the previous democratic gains was lost. The first wave of democracy ended in about 1926 when Mussolini's rise set off widespread democratic decline in countries ranging from Estonia, Germany, Greece, and Spain to Argentina, Brazil, and Japan. Similarly, the democratic gains accrued during the second wave that followed World War II were significantly eroded in the 1960s and early 1970s. During these two decades there was a substantial uptick in military interference in the political process, including the rise of military dictatorships in Latin America, as well as Greece, Pakistan, and Indonesia.

The democracy-in-waves framework raises a critical question: are we now sitting at the top of the third wave facing democracy's imminent decline? It remains true that the number of democracies in the world is higher today than in past decades and that the proportion of the world's population living under democratic rule has grown. However, the democracy-in-waves metaphor raises the very real possibility that we have reached the third wave's peak. Although we have yet to see a significant decline in the number of democracies in the world, a number of key trends suggest we could soon reach a tipping point that would usher in a period of authoritarian resurgence.

In this concluding chapter, we outline a number of factors that will potentially shape the future trajectory of democracy. We recognize that it is impossible to know with any certainty what lies ahead. The factors we discuss, however, are intended to shape discussion and debate about where democracy is going. After outlining these drivers, we end the book by summarizing the key takeaways from the material we have covered in this book.

The future of democracy

What will the state of democracy be in the next fifteen to twenty years? Such long-term thinking is hard, but important. It can help us identify the key assumptions that we hold about the future and the issues and decisions that are likely to be most consequential in the decades ahead. Such an exercise is also critical to the development of policies and actions that can help prevent the emergence of the most undesirable outcomes down the road.

The future of democracy will be determined by a number of complex, dynamic, and inter-related factors. As we look ahead, therefore, it is important that we avoid making straight-line projections about democracy's likely trajectory. In other words, we should not just observe current trends and extrapolate them neatly into the future. Political, social, and especially technological change is happening with unprecedented speed. The pace of change makes it difficult to grasp the full extent to which things might be different in the next two decades. Moreover, change is complex and often unfolds in cycles or shifts. Every decade (if not every year) we are surprised by social or technological upheavals that occur with seemingly little advanced warning. These 'wild card' type events have the potential to dramatically accelerate change or even outright alter the direction of political forces.

In this section we outline some of the driving forces that will likely play a role in shaping democracy's future. The factors we discuss are not intended to be an exhaustive list of the things that could potentially influence democracy's trajectory. Rather we identify four variables—global economic factors, instability and conflict, technological change, and China's development—that we view as particularly salient. The goal of this discussion is to stimulate thinking and debate about where democracy is headed and deepen and inform our understanding of the factors that are likely to matter most for the state of democracy in the years to come.

Global economic factors

Global economic conditions are likely to play a key role in democracy's trajectory. Currently, most economic forecasts indicate that the global economy will remain sluggish over the next several years. Low economic growth is apt to contribute to democratic backsliding in weakly consolidated democracies by making it difficult for new governments to meet citizen expectations of what democracy should deliver. It could also accelerate or trigger new episodes of democratic erosion in more fully consolidated democracies. Weak global growth would hurt the middle classes—which have seen their real incomes stagnate—and raise the salience of income inequality, thereby exacerbating conditions that feed illiberal **populism**. Consider, for example, how the 2008–09 global financial crisis and the Eurozone crisis contributed to the spread of populism in Europe. Although many of the economic currents that have fuelled populism's rise predate these crises, the economic challenges during these financial crises almost certainly hastened populism's momentum. The effects of the Eurozone crisis in Greece and Italy, for example, created conditions conducive to the rise of the Syriza party in Greece and the Five Star Movement and the League in Italy. Looking forward, many observers warn that Italy could be the epicentre of a new economic crisis, given the country's combination of high debt, weak banks, and erratic government (Ewing and Horowitz, 2018). An economic crisis in Italy would have the potential to wreak economic havoc on the West, further fuelling the rise of populism.

Cutting in the opposite direction, slow global growth or a new global financial crisis would also threaten the stability of autocracies. Economic downturns create or exacerbate rifts within the ruling elite about how best to address the situation. They often drive a wedge between reformists, who view the crisis as providing a window of opportunity for change, and hardliners who prefer to stay the course and may view repression as an effective tool for addressing social discontent stemming from the crisis.

Declining oil prices, in particular, could prove especially destabilizing in oil-dependent autocracies such as Saudi Arabia, Iran, and Russia. Any major progress in the development of renewable energy, such as solar energy, would likely force such regimes to make economic reforms that could weaken their hold on power. It is important to emphasize, however, that even where low oil prices and/or economic decline are sufficient to facilitate an autocracy's ouster, democracy does not necessarily follow.

Instability and conflict

Instability and conflict will also likely influence democracy's prospects. Many political analysts anticipate that global instability levels will continue to grow in the years to come. Instability and conflict—including terrorism, large-scale protests, and civil wars—provide leaders with justification to restrict political and civil liberties and repress political opposition. Already, leaders in countries including Russia, Kenya, and Egypt have used the threat of terrorism to restrict funding for non-government organizations. Such instability also creates public demand for a strong hand to rule the country (Chang et al., 2007). In the Middle East and North Africa, for example, instability surrounding the Arab Spring has led many citizens in the region to become more willing to exchange their political and civil liberties for the promise of stability. Developments including sustained or new conflict in the Middle East—possibly stemming from renewed instability in and around Syria or growing tension between Iran and Saudi Arabia—an uptick in terrorism in Europe, or conflict in the South China Sea could create conditions conducive to the spread and/or deepening of autocracy.

Conflict and instability also fuel migration, which can create challenges to democracy far beyond the country or countries in conflict. The war in Syria, for example, accelerated a wave of migration into Europe, which greatly contributed to the rise of many far-right populist parties and leaders that disavow liberalism. Global demographic trends are also likely to be an additional source of disruption, fuelling rising levels of migration. Working-age populations are shrinking in wealthy countries, but growing in developing countries, particularly in Africa. The increasing economic, employment, urbanization, and welfare pressures in developing countries are likely to continue to drive migration from the developing to the developed world. Although the influx of migrants enables these countries to sustain productivity and growth, it is also often seen by some citizens as threatening to national identities and values. Increasing levels of migration could therefore enable opportunistic leaders to use nationalism to boost their popularity, sowing conditions that are increasingly inhospitable to liberal democracy.

Technological change

Technology will have profound effects on democracy's trajectory, although the full extent of these effects is still not well understood. Already, changes in information communication technology (ICT) and social media have had significant—although countervailing—consequences. The same technologies that connect people and enable a free exchange of ideas, for example, are being used by authoritarians to deepen their grip internally, undermine basic human rights, spread illiberal practices beyond their borders, and erode public trust in open societies.

There are a number of reasons to be optimistic that technological change will favour democracy in the long run. First, there is some evidence that social media can produce a better-informed society and facilitate collective action in ways that enhance participation (Dimitrova et al., 2014). By spreading information, reinvigorating participation, and facilitating collective action, social media can enhance government accountability and give voice to marginalized communities or those seeking to reduce economic and political inequality. Secondly, technological advancements will continue to enhance efficiency and improve the health and welfare of citizens worldwide. Already, technology has helped lift millions of people out of poverty including by enabling companies, advocacy groups, charities, and local governments to more effectively deliver services. As more people grow accustomed to being economically secure, they could become less concerned with their immediate needs and have greater capacity to push for the types of changes that are conducive to democracy.

Conversely, technological change (and artificial intelligence (AI) in particular) also has the potential to facilitate an authoritarian resurgence. Many authoritarian regimes have already leveraged new technologies to sustain their rule by making it easier for them to track and suppress the opposition and control the information environment. New technologies will only increase the repressive capacity of these governments, enabling high levels of social control at a reasonable cost (Wright 2018). AI, for example, will allow repressive regimes to monitor, understand, and control their citizens far more closely than ever before. Using AI and big data, authoritarian regimes could predict (and subsequently control) potential dissenters similar to the way that Amazon or Google anticipate consumer behaviour and calibrate their advertising based on this understanding (Wright, 2018). Moreover, authoritarian governments would likely be far more effective as these regimes will draw on data in ways that are not allowed in liberal democracies.

Democracies will also be tested by technological change. Social media and ICTs are already transforming the media environment. Some of these changes stem from hostile external actors like Russia, which has supported the creation of 'troll factories' and other actors that seek to distort the information environment. But other changes are internal to democracies. ICTs and social media, for example, are fuelling political polarization as individuals expose themselves to like-minded points of view and avoid dissimilar perspectives, leading to more extreme and hardened opinions (Adamic and Glance, 2005; Van Alstyne and Brynjolfsson, 2005). Such polarization, along with disinformation and deep fakes—fake video and audio that appears convincingly real—will make it even more difficult to create a common base of knowledge from which society can operate. These developments may also erode the traditions of tolerance that underpin democracy.

Moreover, although new technologies will create new opportunities, they will also exacerbate divisions between winners and losers. Automation and artificial intelligence threaten to disrupt job markets and displace workers. If governments are unable to identify new services, sectors, and occupations to replace the jobs that automation and other technologies will eliminate—and to train workers to fill them—the forces that have fuelled populism will continue to rise.

Social media and new technologies are neither inherently democratic nor inherently undemocratic (Tucker et al., 2017). Rather, new technologies will constitute a space in which political interests battle for influence (see further Box 15.1). Much will depend on how established democracies and authoritarian regimes manage the rise of new technologies, including the ability to set standards and protocols, define ethical limits for research, and protect intellectual property rights. For this reason, looking out fifteen to twenty years, it is still unclear what the net effect of technological change on democracy's development will be.

Box 15.1: **Does social media facilitate or undermine democracy?**

Throughout the early 2000s there was widespread optimism that the Internet and social media would serve as a great democratizing force. New information technologies were expected to make it easier for citizens to monitor government abuses of power, provide exposure to democratic ideas and practices elsewhere, and facilitate social movements to oppose abusive regimes. Nowhere was this optimism more apparent than in the early days of the Arab Spring, where observers and academics alike widely documented the ways that new media contributed to the success of pro-democracy movements. Fast forward to the present day, however, and the optimism about the potential for social media to serve as a democratic panacea have dimmed. Authoritarian regimes have learned to harness the advantage of new information technology to monitor dissent, target opponents, and enhance their grip on power. Social media, we posit, is therefore best viewed as neutral—it is a tool that both pro-democratic and repressive forces can use to advance their disparate goals (Tucker et al., 2017). In this box, we briefly summarize some of the ways that new information technologies can advance and undermine democracy.

How social media can support democracy

- Creates new space for political discussion and debate
- Gives a voice to those whose views are normally excluded from political discussions in the mainstream media
- Facilitates collective action to oppose abusive regimes
- Exposes abuses of power; provides new means of holding governments accountable and pressing for wider political inclusion
    - Online mobilization can increase public and mainstream media attention (i.e. Tea Party and Black Lives Matter movements)

How social media can undermine democracy

- Fuels political polarization by allowing people to access information that is already consistent with their personal views
    - 'Slacktivism' reduces motivation to participate in social organizations and politics
    - Amplifies extreme and anti-system voices

How social media can support authoritarianism

- Autocrats can limit online dissent by blocking or suppressing unfavourable information and by encouraging self-censorship
- Facilitates the identification of noncompliant or citizens
- Facilitates the identification of sources of discontent that autocrats can quash before they gain momentum
- Readily spreads pro-regime narratives and drowns out regime opponents
- Propagates disinformation making it hard for citizens to assess government performance or actions
    - Online movements may mobilize protests, but unable to put sustained pressure on elites needed to consolidate democracy

China's development

China will be a significant wildcard. A sustained rise in China's international influence has the potential to spur a widespread authoritarian resurgence. Perhaps the most compelling evidence for this argument comes from a body of political science research that we discussed in Chapter 13, which demonstrates how the structure of the international system affects the number of democratic countries globally (Gunitsky, 2014; Boix, 2011). This research shows that when the world is dominated by a single democratic power, such as the United States in aftermath of the Cold War, the number of democracies increases. As authoritarian great powers emerge, however, the number of democracies in the world declines. If China's power and influence continues to rise, we should expect the number of autocracies in the world to grow with it.

While less likely, sustained instability or political change in China would have the potential to improve democracy's prospects, especially if such developments weakened the appeal or legitimacy of the Chinese model. China's democratization, in particular, could restore democracy's appeal worldwide. Currently, the Chinese Communist Party's (CCP) maintains a firm grip on power and has defied Western hopes that the country's remarkable economic growth would eventually usher in democracy, as modernization theory would predict. But authoritarianism in China is not inevitable. The CCP will continue to face challenges in satisfying the demands of its new middle classes for clean air, affordable houses, improved services, and continued opportunities. Drawing on evidence from Asia, research shows that strong, single-party regimes such as China's have chosen to democratize from a position of strength, not weakness (Slater and Wong, 2013). Such a scenario is particularly likely if the party both gauges that it is on the cusp of decline (possibly due to the prospect of sluggish economic growth or rising discontent from the growing middle class) and calculates that it has a chance of maintaining power through free and fair elections. In other words, such a transition would be apt to unfold in China should the party 'view democratic concession from a position of strength as the most viable choice to advance the party's fortunes' (Slater and Wong, 2013, p. 730).

Though there are currently no clear signs that the CCP is on the verge of decline, should the tides turn, the CCP could concede to democratization. If this were to unfold, it would likely boost the odds of democratic transitions elsewhere.

Implications of an authoritarian resurgence for the global order

It is impossible to forecast with any certainty democracy's future trajectory, as we discussed. The state of global democracy will be determined by a number of complex, dynamic, and inter-related factors. Based on current trends and future projections about the state of the global economy, levels of instability and conflict, technological change, and China's development, however, it appears that the risks of a widespread authoritarian resurgence have grown. Given these prospects, it is important to consider the implications of a rise in the number of autocracies worldwide. How would a wide-spread authoritarian resurgence affect today's global order?

Policymakers, analysts, and academics widely agree that the norms, values, laws, and institutions that have undergirded the international system and governed relation-ships between nations are being stretched and strained. As we have discussed at points throughout this book, widespread democratic decline would also accelerate changes in today's global order.

Before we conclude this chapter with an overview of the book's key themes and takeaways, we outline some of the implications of an authoritarian resurgence for the current global order. As in the previous section, our discussion of implications is not meant to be exhaustive. Rather we seek to stimulate debate and discussion about what a widespread authoritarian resurgence would mean for the United States, Europe, and elsewhere.

Rising authoritarian cooperation and influence

As we discussed in Chapter 5, domestic politics are a key determinant of the inter-national behaviour of states. In particular, countries with shared political systems are more likely to form alliances and cooperate than are countries with different political systems (Lai and Reiter, 2000). Democracies are more likely to form alliances and coop-erate more fully with other democracies, for example, than they are with autocracies. As the number of democracies in the world rose in the post-Cold War era, U.S. and Western influence rose with it. While the United States and other Western democra-cies find common cause with authoritarian partners on specific issues, the depth and reliability of such cooperation is limited. Consequently, further democratic decline could seriously compromise Western democracies' ability to form the kinds of deep partnerships that will be required to confront today's increasingly complex challenges. Global issues such as climate change, migration, and violent extremism demand the coordination and cooperation that democratic backsliding would put in peril. Put sim-ply, democracies would be less effective and influential actors if they lose their ability to rely on partnerships with other strong democratic nations.

Conversely, an increase in autocracies would provide a provide a broader platform for coordination among these states. An increase in authoritarianism could enable a growing number of regimes to overcome their divergent histories, values, and interests—factors that are frequently cited as obstacles to the formation of a cohesive challenge to the U.S.-led international system. Recent examples illustrate this. Democratic backsliding in Hungary and the hardening of Egypt's autocracy under Abdel Fattah el-Sisi have led to enhanced relations between these countries and Russia. Likewise, democratic decline in Bangladesh has prompted Sheikh Hasina and her ruling Awami League to seek closer relations with China and Russia, in part to mitigate Western pressure and bolster the regime's domestic standing. Although none of these burgeoning relation-ships have developed into highly unified partnerships, democratic backsliding in these countries has provided a stronger basis for cooperation among increasingly authoritar-ian countries.

Diluting Western influence in international institutions

Democratic decline would weaken Western efforts within international institutions, such as the United Nations, to advance issues such as Internet freedom and the responsibility to protect (R2P). In the case of Internet governance, for example, Western democracies support an open, largely private, global Internet. Autocracies, in contrast, promote state control over the Internet, including laws and other mechanisms that facilitate their ability to censor and persecute dissidents. Already many autocracies, including Belarus, China, Iran, and Zimbabwe, have coalesced in the 'Likeminded Group of Developing Countries' within the UN to advocate their interests.

Rising risk of instability and inter-state conflict

Violence and instability would also likely increase if more democracies give way to autocracy. International relations literature tells us that democracies are less likely to fight wars against other democracies, suggesting that inter-state wars would rise as the number of democracies decline (Oneal et al., 1996; Owen,1994). Moreover, within countries that are already autocratic, additional movement away from democracy, or an 'authoritarian hardening', would increase global instability. Highly repressive autocracies are the most likely to experience state failure, as was the case in the Central African Republic, Libya, Somalia, Syria, and Yemen. In this way, an authoritarian resurgence would significantly strain the international order because rising levels of instability would exceed the international community's ability to respond to the tremendous costs of peacekeeping, humanitarian assistance, and refugee flows.

Growing anti-Western sentiment

A rise in authoritarianism would contribute to rising anti-Western sentiment that could fuel a global order that is increasingly antagonistic to the West and its values. Most autocracies are highly suspicious of U.S. intentions, for example, and view the creation of an external enemy as an effective means for boosting their own public support. Russian President Vladimir Putin, Venezuelan President Nicolas Maduro, and Bolivian President Evo Morales regularly accuse the United States of fomenting instability and supporting regime change. This vilification of the United States is also a convenient way of distracting their publics from regime shortcomings and fostering public support for strongman tactics.

Taken together, the evidence indicates that an authoritarian resurgence would threaten global peace, cooperation, and stability—not to mention the negative impact it would have on the freedoms enjoyed by ordinary individuals. Even when we set ideological considerations aside, there is good reason for Western democracies to prioritize efforts to push back against the spread of authoritarianism. Though many of the threats to the current global order, such as China's rise or Russia's aggression, are influenced by things that largely fall outside of the international community's control, democracy is one domain where targeted actions can be influential.

Key themes of the book

At the outset of this chapter we raised the question of whether we are now sitting atop of the third wave of democracy, facing its imminent decline. Just fifteen years ago, this question would have been readily pushed aside. There was little consideration given to the possibility that a political system would emerge to challenge democracy's appeal or that democracy would deteriorate from within. Underpinning these assumptions was a strong belief in progress—that more and more societies would commit to individualism, to free trade and market economies, and to democracy. But today many experts are sounding the alarm bells. Democracies are facing mounting challenges from within, autocracies are evolving and adapting their survival strategies in ways that make them a more formidable challenge to democracy, and international developments, including the growing assertiveness of influential autocracies such as China and Russia, are trending in ways that are increasingly conducive to the spread of autocracy. This book was designed to provide insight into the political dynamics of democracy and authoritarianism and the trends that are shaping both the internal workings of these political systems and the ideological struggle between them.

We conclude by synthesizing the book's main insights and takeaways. In Part I of the book we defined democracy and authoritarianism. We began by exploring how scholars conceptualize democracy, and laid out the minimalist and maximalist definitions of democracy. Although there is no consensus on how to measure it, there are several key ingredients that scholars view as essential to democracy. Having a clear and consistent understanding of democracy's attributes is essential for tracking its development, including democratic consolidation and the identification of the early warning signs of its erosion.

Next, we moved to the other end of the spectrum—autocracies. Though past studies of authoritarian regimes glossed over the variation in authoritarian rule, more recent studies have opened up the black box to shed greater insight into these systems. In Chapter 3, we underscored that authoritarian regimes are not all the same and that understanding how they differ is important to making predictions about their behaviour and performance. In Chapter 4 we emphasized that a growing number of countries now fall somewhere between democracy and authoritarian regimes. These hybrid systems have become the most common form of political system around the world, in part because authoritarian governments see it in their interest to mimic democracy. While some of these hybrid systems are weak, dysfunctional, and flawed, others are trying to mask themselves as something they are not to maintain themselves in power. The goal of this chapter was to highlight the wide variety in political regimes today and to underscore the rather astonishing frequency with which contemporary authoritarian regimes possess seemingly democratic features.

Finally, we probed the consequences of regime type for a variety of important outcomes. As we discussed, democracy, dictatorship, and hybrid regimes constitute very different ways of organizing political lives—of selecting leaders, processing conflict, and making and implementing decisions. These differences in a country's institutional arrangements lead to vastly different political, economic, security, and social outcomes.

This chapter showed that fully consolidated democracies outperform dictatorship on almost every indicator we examined. Fully consolidated democracies are less likely to fight inter-state wars against other democracies, have lower prospects of civil war, and in the long-term, are generally more stable than full autocracies (Gates et al., 2006). They are less likely to employ repression against their citizens than full autocracies and experience less terrorism. Most recent research indicates that full democracies grow their economies at a rate that is at least on par with dictatorships and that the growth they produce is of higher quality—both less volatile and more likely to benefit the people they govern. In sum, societies that govern themselves with full respect for liberal democratic principles are safer, more prosperous, and more secure.

In Part II of the book, we turned our attention to the political dynamics of autocracies. As we discussed, authoritarian regimes do not perform evenly. There is tremendous variation in the durability of these regimes. In Chapter 6, we examined how authoritarian regimes stay in power. A central message is that autocracies have become savvier in terms of how they sustain their rule and more durable in the post-Cold War era. While authoritarian regimes of the past resorted to excessive uses of force, brutality, surveillance, and total control over information to maintain power, today's autocracies have learned that their chance being overthrow is lower if they adopt a subtler survival strategy. It is now common to see autocracies manipulate electoral victories rather than outright steal them, selectively restrict the media rather than fully censor it, and co-opt members of the opposition rather than push them underground. Moreover, those authoritarian regimes that are internally cohesive and use pseudo-democratic institutions to support their regime tend to be the most durable.

In spite of the rising durability of autocracies, no authoritarian regime is immune from being overthrown. However, forecasting the failure of authoritarian regimes is difficult. Many long-standing and seemingly stable autocracies have unravelled in a matter of weeks. Likewise, other regimes that appear to be on their last legs limp along for years. In Chapter 7, we discussed the factors that political science research shows can raise an autocracy's odds of failure. In particular, we discussed potential triggers of instability, including the role that elite splits, popular resistance, economic crisis, **diffusion**, and linkages with the West can have on the breakdown of authoritarian regimes. In Chapter 8, we discussed how an authoritarian regime actually breaks down. Examining the ways in which authoritarian incumbents are ousted is essential analysis because the way that dictators fall affects a country's subsequent political trajectory. Whether an authoritarian leader is ousted by a **coup**, protest, or insurgency affects the odds that the entire regime will fall with the leader or that democratization will occur.

In Part III of the book, we focused on drivers of democracy. We grouped these drivers into four thematic categories: economic, institutional, cultural, and international. In many instances, our review of contemporary political science research confirmed what our natural instincts would tell us about the factors likely to drive democracy. Democracies are more likely to survive in healthy economic environments, for example, in line with the robust positive correlation between democracy and levels of wealth. Likewise, democratic transitions do not occur in isolation, as discussed earlier in this chapter. Democratization in one country increases the prospects of democratization in others nearby. In other instances, however, our preconceptions of what might pave the way for democracy are not borne out by the evidence. For example, just because a dictatorship holds multi-party elections does not necessarily mean that it is any closer to democratizing. And just because citizens espouse and hold more democratic values does not necessarily boost the odds of a democratic transition or the longevity of democratic rule. Recent history has shown that elites can dismantle democracy from the top down, even amid strong public support for democracy.

Part IV of this book switched gears to assess the contemporary challenges to democracy. First, we began by discussing the rise of populism, which has become a defining feature of contemporary politics. We explained what populism is—distinguishing between far-left and far-right populism—and outlined how populism can affect liberal democracy. We then turned to look at how and why democracies backslide and break down and how the patterns of democratic collapse have evolved over time. We paid particular attention to the rise of authoritarianization, where democratically-elected incumbents dismantle democracy from within, often in a slow and gradual process. As we discussed, the gradual nature of democratic failure today makes it hard to discern when the break with democracy actually occurs, and its insidiousness poses one of the most significant threats to democracy in the twenty-first century.

This book recognized the vocal debates about the benefits and risks associated with democracy and its promotion abroad. We acknowledged that there is often a contentious environment surrounding democracy and efforts to support its development. This book has drawn on the full spectrum of academic research—ranging from seminal democracy studies to cutting edge research on democracy and authoritarian rule—to provide an objective overview to help us better understand and engage in these debates.

We conclude this book where we started—by sounding the alarm bell that democracy is in crisis. While it is true that new democracies continue to emerge at a rate that outpaces the emergence of new dictatorships, this rate has decreased. Around the globe we are seeing democracy decline in surprising and troubling places. Yet despite the challenges facing democracy and the deep dissatisfaction that many feel with their elected leaders, citizens around the globe still support and demand the freedoms that only democracy can provide. It's time for democratic citizens and leaders to do the innovative thinking and take the hard actions that will be required to restore liberal democracy's strength and appeal.

Glossary

9/11 September 11th, 2001 was the date that Al Qaeda, a global terror network, staged a terrorist attack on U.S. soil, hijacking four planes to crash into the Pentagon in Arlington, Virginia and the Twin Towers in New York City. Almost 3,000 people died in the attack, making it the single largest terrorist attack in history.

AFRICAN UNION A union of fifty-five countries in Africa that was launched in 2002 to replace the Organization for African Unity, which had been founded in 1963. It focuses on achieving unity, stability, and development in Africa.

ARAB SPRING A series of anti-government protests, uprisings, and revolutions that took place in North Africa and the Middle East from December 2010 until December 2012 in response to decades of corruption and authoritarian rule. In Tunisia, Egypt, Libya, and Yemen long-time dictators were ousted from power, sometimes violently, while Syria's uprising exploded into an ongoing civil war. Protests that took place elsewhere resulted in moderate reforms.

ASIAN TIGERS A group of countries in Asia—Singapore, Hong Kong, Taiwan, and South Korea—that are known for quickly industrializing and experiencing dynamic economic growth.

ASSOCIATION OF SOUTHEAST ASIAN NATIONS (ASEAN) A regional intergovernmental organization that consists of ten countries in Southeast Asia that cooperate on economic, political, and security issues.

AUDIENCE COSTS The political costs that a leader or regime suffers from their constituency if they escalate a foreign policy crisis and then have to back down from it. Democratic leaders typically face higher audience costs.

AUTOCRACY/AUTHORITARIAN REGIME A poitical regime in which power is concentrated in the hands of an individual, group, or party which seeks to maintain its authority by not permitting free and fair elections, and repressing citizens' civil liberties and political rights to minimize dissent.

AUTHORITARIAN DECAY Occurs when an authoritarian regime offers some limited political reforms.

AUTHORITARIAN ENCLAVES Durable pockets of authoritarian practice that are at odds with a new democratic regime's political norms.

AUTHORITARIANIZATION The process of a regime becoming increasingly authoritarian, such as by eliminating term limits and reducing civil liberties.

AUTO GOLPE The Spanish term for a self-coup. A self-coup takes place when an elected leader decides to dissolve the national legislature in order to assume extraordinary powers unlawfully.

BANDWAGONING Refers to a political actor aligning with a stronger actor in order to benefit from being part of a bigger alliance.

BOTTOM-UP PATHWAYS The processes of authoritarian breakdown that involve citizens rising up and applying pressure on the regime to step down.

BREXIT A referendum that took place in in the United Kingdom on 23 June 2016 in which 51.9 per cent of those of the public who participated voted to leave the European Union. The Brexit result is cited as an example of the rise of right-wing populism.

BRIBERY A type of corruption; the act of paying or offering a gift to an official or person in public office in order to influence their behaviour.

CATEGORICAL MEASURES The classification of different authoritarian regimes into distinct categories. This measurement is used by Barbara Geddes and her colleagues.

CIVIC CULTURE A term coined by Gabriel Almond and Sidney Verba. It describes a political culture in which citizens of a state have high levels of interest in politics, respect for the rule of law, and are most interested in being individually and collectively engaged in political processes. Almond and Verba argued that a civic culture is an important building block to sustaining democracy.

CIVIL SOCIETY Associational life that is outside the government, where groups of people come together to achieve collective political and social objectives.

CLIENTELISM/CLIENTELIST The asymmetrical relationship between a patron (or a person with power) and a client (or a person of lesser means). In these relationships the patron offers financial favours or patronage to the client in exchange for political loyalty.

COLOUR REVOLUTIONS A series of uprisings and revolutions that took place in the former Soviet Union and the Balkans in the 2000s.

COMMONWEALTH OF INDEPENDENT STATES A regional intergovernmental organization of ten former Soviet countries that aims to encourage economic, political, and security cooperation.

COMMUNISM A political and economic system where the means of production are controlled by the public, and there is no private ownership. In doing so, communism aims to create a classless society. Communist regimes were prevalent in Eastern Europe and East Asia during the Cold War but many have since reformed or fallen apart.

COMPETITIVE AUTHORITARIANISM A term most notably used by Steven Levitsky and Lucan Way to describe a hybrid regime that holds elections but where the incumbent has an enormous advantage. Though the elections are free of massive fraud, the regime represses civil liberties and the executive does not face checks and balances from other branches of government.

CONSOCIATIONALISM A political system in countries that have diverse ethnic/religious demographics under which power sharing takes place in order to foster greater political stability.

CONTINUOUS MEASURES Measurements of regimes that place them on a spectrum of authoritarianism and democracy. It assumes that how authoritarian or democratic a regime is can be a matter of degree.

CO-OPTATION The process of adding outsiders to a group in order to prevent these outsiders from challenging the status quo.

COUP A sudden seizure of power to oust a leader or regime through extra-legal means. It is usually staged by the security forces, though the security forces can be working at the behest of civilian leadership.

COUP-PROOFING The process of deliberately weakening the military in order to prevent it from staging a coup to oust the leader. Coup-proofing can also include creating a presidential guard that is formed for the sole purpose of the guarding the leader. Coup-proofed regimes emphasize regime security over national security.

COUP TRAP A cycle that a country faces when it has experienced a series of coups. Countries that have had coups are more likely to experience them in the future because the norms have developed that make coups more acceptable to the military, political elites, and the public.

CULTURAL LEGITIMACY Legitimacy achieved through exercise of political power in ways that concur with citizen values regarding laws, rules, and customs.

DE-ALIGNMENT The process of citizens losing their attachment to political parties.

DEFECTIVE DEMOCRACY Democracies that fail to uphold all of liberal democracy's essential features but meet the minimalist definition of democracy.

DELEGATIVE DEMOCRACIES As used by Guillermo O'Donnell, describes new democracies in which power is concentrated in the hands of an elected president, and, lacking adequate checks on the executive and deficiencies in the rule of law, fail to develop into fully representative democracies.

DELIBERATIVE DEMOCRACY A form of democracy in which decisions are made by discussion among free and equal citizens. It is assumed that decisions will evolve out of an argumentative process whereby citizens are able to deliberate on policies that affect them.

DEMOCRACY IN WAVES Refers to the idea that democracies appear in clusters during certain periods of time, such as after the end of World War II, or after the Cold War ended.

DEMOCRATIC BACKSLIDING The process of a democracy becoming increasingly less democratic, such as through the aggrandizement of the executive, the repression of civil liberties, and/or the refutation of the rule of law.

DEMOCRATIC CONSOLIDATION The process of a democratizing country becoming firmly democratic. This usually takes place once political elites and the public believes that the democracy is the best form of government.

DEMOCRATIC DECAY The process of democratic regimes becoming increasingly less democratic, such as through the rule of law deteriorating.

DEMOCRATIC PEACE The theory that democracies are less likely to engage in conflict with one another because they have checks and balances that slow down decision-making, publics that they have to answer to, and norms of resolving disputes peacefully and more transparently.

DETERRENCE The process of dissuading a political actor from engaging in an action which will change or affect the status quo. This usually only works when the actor wanting to change the status quo fears a reprisal.

DICTATORSHIP A dictatorship is a authoritarian regime in which power is concentrated in the hands of single individual, a single party, or an elite group of military officers, although the term dictatorship is often used to describe a regime in which a strongman is at the helm.

DIFFUSION The process of ideas and norms spreading from one country to another. Diffusion was most often used to explain why countries in a region democratize, but diffusion also has been used to spread authoritarian norms as well.

DIMINISHED SUBTYPES Cases that fall short of the root category; for example, lacking some of the defining attributes of democracy or autocracy.

DIRECT COLLABORATION Refers to authoritarian regimes directly working together to help stabilize their autocracies.

DIVIDE AND RULE POLICIES The process of pitting actors against one another in order to mitigate threats. This is common in personalist dictatorships where threats to their rule are common, and where opposing factions are played off one another.

DOMESTIC DEMOCRATIC PEACE The theory that democratic regimes are less likely to use repression because of the risk of being voted out of office.

DYNASTIC MONARCHIES A term used by Michael Herb to describe monarchies in which members of a ruling family are involved in political decision-making and governance, rather than having all power residing in the monarch. This form of monarchy is now prevalent in the Arab monarchies of the Persian Gulf.

ELECTORAL AUTHORITARIANISM A type of hybrid regime that holds elections, but where the outcomes are manipulated to largely favour the incumbent. With the exception of holding elections, the regime is otherwise authoritarian.

ELECTORAL DEMOCRACY A term commonly applied to regimes that hold free and fair elections but otherwise do not uphold all of liberal democracy's essential features, such as full civil liberties and the rule of law. See also illiberal democracy.

ELECTORAL FRAUD The process of illegally interfering in the outcome of an election. This includes activities such as buying votes, stuffing ballot boxes, improperly recording votes, and destroying ballots.

ELECTORAL MANIPULATION A type of electoral fraud whereby the outcomes are manipulated by behaviour that gives the incumbent (usually) an unfair advantage, such as offering voters inducements (e.g. food subsidy) to vote for a particular party or candidate.

ELITISM The theory that politics should be an expression of the moral and intellectually superior elites.

EMBEZZLEMENT A type of corruption that involves the theft or misappropriation of funds.

EUROPEAN UNION (EU) A political and economic union that created a single market among its European members and a standardized system of laws. As of publication the European Union had twenty-eight member states, although the UK Brexit vote may reduce this by one.

EUROSCEPTICISM Scepticism as to powers and goals of the European Union and the benefits of membership. Eurosceptics are against deepening integration among European Union states.

EXCLUSIONARY NATIONALISM A form of nationalism that excludes minority groups that do not share common bonds, often on the basis of race, religion, or culture.

FAKE NEWS A term used to delegitimize the media. It has largely been used by authoritarian regimes and populist-style leaders to question the accuracy of unflattering news stories.

FASCISM A right-wing, nationalist, and authoritarian system that is opposed to liberalism, diversity, and Marxism. Fascist movements were prominent in the early twentieth century.

FEDERALISM A system of government whereby regional and local governments exercise power alongside the national government. The United States, Canada, India, and Russia are notable examples of federal systems.

FEDERAL SECURITY SERVICE OF RUSSIA (FSB) The main security agency in Russia today, succeeding the Soviet Union's Committee of State Security (KGB). It is primarily tasked with counter-intelligence and internal and border security.

FOREIGN AID The voluntary transfers of resources from donors, NGOs, international organizations, and countries to other countries. Foreign aid is often used to induce states to engage in political reform but it is widely debated what impact this has.

GERRYMANDERING A form of electoral manipulation, where the boundaries of an electoral district are designed to favour a particular party or candidate.

GODFATHERS/BIG MEN Refers to powerful men that sit atop vast patronage networks and broker between the political parties and the voting public for a profit. Common in countries like Nigeria, they typically have no political interests beyond advancing their own financial gain.

GRADUALISM Gradualists argue that states should democratize slowly in order to prevent democratic breakdown. They are in disagreement with sequentialists who argue that the rule of law should be established before elections are held.

GRAND CORRUPTION A form of corruption that takes place at the top levels of government and may include the embezzlement of funds and the outright theft of revenues.

Grand corruption involves significant subversion of the political, legal, and economic system.

THE GREAT DEPRESSION A period in U.S. history of extreme economic despair that began when the stock market crashed in 1929 and ended in 1939. The depression hit other nations around the world and has been cited as a factor spurring authoritarianism in Europe and Latin America.

GULF COOPERATION COUNCIL (GCC) A regional intergovernmental political and economic union consisting of seven Arab monarchies that are located in the Persian Gulf. The union was formed in 1981 and aims to improve economic, political, and military coordination, but has suffered from tensions, most recently with Qatar.

HEGEMONIC AUTHORITARIANISM A type of authoritarian regime that holds elections in which the outcome is absolutely certain to favour the regime in power.

HORIZONTAL ACCOUNTABILITY The type of accountability that comes from the legislative and judicial institutions providing a check on the leadership in the executive.

HYBRID REGIMES Regimes that are somewhat authoritarian but have elements of democracy such as relatively free elections. A number of categories can be referred to as hybrid regimes, such as competitive authoritarian regimes and electoral authoritarian regimes.

HYPER-PRESIDENTIALISM Presidential systems that have a super-powerful president who does not have checks on his or her power.

ILLIBERAL DEMOCRACY A type of democracy that has free and fair elections but fails to uphold adequate civil liberties and the rule of law, and therefore does not qualify as a liberal democracy. The term was popularized by Fareed Zakaria.

INFANT MORTALITY RATES The figures of the number of infant deaths out of 1,000 births. Typically these rates are highest in poor countries, and these rates tend to be higher in authoritarian regimes.

INFORMATION CASCADES Refers to how information can spread after a triggering event which can help to catalyse a widespread protest and lead to authoritarian breakdown in some cases.

INTERNATIONAL MONETARY FUND (IMF) An international organization that provides loans for countries that are in debt in order to ensure that countries facing an international crisis are able to manage their balance of payments. The primary aims of the organization are to foster global monetary cooperation, promote free trade and economic growth, and ensure financial stability.

KLEPTOCRACY A regime or ruler that uses their power to steal public funds and resources; this constitutes an extreme form of grand corruption. Leaders such as the Duvaliers of Haiti, Ferdinand Marcos of the Philippines, and Joseph Mobutu of Zaire are noted kleptocrats who stole in the millions and in the latter case, billions.

LEFT-WING POPULISM A form of populism that is nationalistic, anti-elitist, anti-globalization, anti-corruption, and anti-capitalism. Contemporary left-wing populist movements focus on socio-economic issues, including economic inequality, social mobility, and stagnating living standards.

LIBERAL DEMOCRACY Refers to regimes that hold free and fair elections while also maintaining respect for civil liberties, political rights, and the rule of law.

LIBERALISM A political and moral philosophy which generally espouses, inter alia, support for democracy and the rule of law, individual and human rights, secularism, racial and gender equality, freedom of speech, and freedom of religion.

MAJORITARIAN ELECTORAL SYSTEMS Electoral systems in which the candidate with the most votes in a district wins a seat. Countries such as Canada, Pakistan, and the United Kingdom have majoritarian systems. Majoritarian systems tend to lead to fewer parties running because smaller parties have to coalesce into permanent coalitions to remain competitive.

MARSHALL PLAN A massive foreign aid plan initiated by the United States to help rebuild Western Europe after World War II and prevent Western Europe from falling to Communism. The plan was considered a success and regenerated the European economies.

MAXIMALIST DEFINITIONS OF DEMOCRACY Maximalist definitions of democracy view countries as democratic only if they satisfy a wide range of criteria including holding free, fair, and frequent elections, ensuring civil liberties, political rights, and the rule of law.

MILITARY REGIMES A form of government where the regime is led by military officers (the term 'military junta' is frequently used). Military regimes usually seize power from the existing regime in a coup. Military regimes were particularly prevalent across Latin America during the Cold War.

MINIMALIST DEFINITIONS OF DEMOCRACY Minimalists definitions of democracy view countries as democratic if they hold free, fair, and frequent elections. Minimalist definitions of democracy do not examine further the extent to which civil liberties and the rule of law are upheld.

MODERNIZATION THEORY A theory that the process of economic growth and industrialization would lead to the emergence of an educated middle class that would then advocate for democracy.

MONARCHY A form of government in which a single person is the head of the state, usually by inheritance from the previous monarch, although by election in some cases. The monarch may hold supreme authority, or may perform a legal and ceremonial role with limited or little poitical power. The monarch may also share power with an extended family (see Dynastic monarchies).

NATIONALISM An ideology that aims to build and maintain a single national identity and foster pride in national achievements.

NEIGHBOURHOOD EFFECT The theory that countries with similar political systems tend to cluster geographically. The neighbourhood effect has been used to explain why the propensity of being democratic was so low in regions that were largely autocratic.

NEO-CONSERVATIVISM A political movement originating from the United States that is anti-communist. Neo-cons are hawkish about foreign policy and want to aggressively promote democracy around the world, using force if necessary.

NEO-PATRIMONIAL REGIMES Political systems in which a patron stands atop of the state and disburses patronage to loyal followers, at the expense of a merit-based system or in accordance with the rule of law.

NEPOTISM A form of political corruption in which members of the governing regime grant opportunities or favour to family members, rather than on the basis of merit.

NON-GOVERNMENTAL ORGANIZATIONS (NGOs) Organizations that are usually non-profit and aim to make a positive economic, developmental, political, and humanitarian impact.

NORM CHANGE Shifts in the dominant understanding of what is or is not acceptable, and is important to understanding how diffusion takes place.

OLIGARCHY A power structure in which a small group of individuals (oligarchs) hold political power, their membership variously determined by nobility, wealth, family ties, military rank, etc. In current usage the term 'oligarch' is applied to describe individuals who have amassed a huge amount of wealth through their control of major businesses, and use their wealth to promote their own economic and political interests, often without formally being a member of the governing regime. Such individuals have been particularly notable in Russia and Ukraine.

ORGANIZATION OF AMERICAN STATES (OAS) An organization founded in 1948 to promote regional solidarity across the thirty-five member states in the Americas. It has worked to support democracy across Latin America.

ORGANIZATION FOR SECURITY AND COOPERATION IN EUROPE (OSCE) An intergovernmental organization consistent of fifty-seven participating states that originated in 1975 and aims to promote security and democracy.

PACTED TRANSITIONS Transitions from authoritarian rule that occur as a result of a pact or series of agreements between elites to allow for elections.

PALACE COUP A type of coup that is carried out by the political elites, and not by the military.

PARLIAMENTARY SYSTEMS Systems of government where the executive derives its legitimacy from the legislature. In contrast to presidential systems where the president is directly elected by the public, in parliamentary systems, it is the ruling party in the parliament that selects the prime minister.

PARTICIPATORY DEMOCRACY A theory of democracy which holds that democratic governance is most likely to thrive where citizens actively engage in politics and public life, working together to achieve collective goals.

PASSIVE COLLABORATION A form of cooperation among authoritarian regimes that is less overt compared to direct collaboration in matters such as the spread of authoritarian norms.

PATRONAGE Refers to government appointments or hiring of citizens by those in power in exchange for or as a reward for their loyalty, rather than on basis of merit or qualifications.

PERFORMANCE LEGITIMACY Legitimacy that is dependent on the performance of the regime in meeting citizen expectations, such as achieving strong economic growth or reducing unemployment.

PERSONAL INTEGRITY RIGHTS The respect for a person's physical and mental integrity. Examples of the violation of personal integrity rights include murder, torture, forced disappearances, and imprisonment of individuals for their political views.

PERSONALIST DICTATORSHIP An authoritarian regime in which an individual leader exercises power with little restraint, at their own discretion, and without reference to rules or commitment to an ideology.

PERSONALITY CULTS In a political context, wide-spread devotion or veneration directed to a leader, who has achieved a messianic, heroic, and idealized image through the use of propaganda, the mass media, and the ubiquitous imposition of objects bearing this person's face and name.

PETTY CORRUPTION A type of corruption that usually takes place when lower level civil servants or those that work for the state ask for bribes in exchange for their services.

PLURALIST DEMOCRACY Theory of democracy which holds that power should be dispersed through a society, and a wide range of interest groups should be involved in politics to ensure that many different interests are being heard and bargained.

POLITICAL CULTURE Encompasses the beliefs, attitudes, values and sentiments that citizens have about their country's political system, and how citizens feel about their role in the system.

POLITICAL PURGES The process of eliminating elites that may be politically or intellectually threatening to a regime. Purges either result in exile of these individuals or in their execution.

POLITICAL SYSTEM Refers to the broad type of government in power in a state. The two broad categories are identified as democracy and autocracy.

POLYARCHY A term defined by Robert Dahl to describe how democracies should perform in practice in order to satisfy the minimum requirements of a democracy. As Dahl sees it, polyarchy entails political contestation or elections, and inclusion or participation in the political system.

POPULISM Populism is an amorphous and thin ideology. Populist movements typically claim to represent the true will of the common people. Populism is noted for espousing a nationalist, anti-elitist, anti-intellectual agenda that resonates with the masses, who have usually felt disenfranchised and are looking for quick panaceas for complicated problems.

PORK BARREL Pork barrel policies are the appropriation of funding for localized projects that only benefit or serve their constituency at the expense of the general public. By guaranteeing their constituents these types of funding, legislators help ensure that they are re-elected. It is different than clientelism because the number of recipients is much larger.

PREFERENCE FALSIFICATION The theory that individuals seek to convey preferences and opinions that are socially acceptable. This is most notable in authoritarian regimes where individuals are usually cautious about expressing discontent.

PRESIDENTIAL SYSTEMS Systems of government that have an elected president who exercises power, and whose power is checked by other branches of government. In presidential systems, presidents do not need the support of the legislature to hold power.

PROPAGANDA Refers to the spread of biased information that is aimed at influencing an audience to further a specific agenda.

PROPORTIONAL REPRESENTATION An electoral system whereby the proportion of votes that parties/candidates receive most closely represents the proportion of seats that are allocated. Proportional systems tend to encourage the formation of more parties compared to majoritarian systems.

PROTECTIVE DEMOCRACY A theory of democracy which holds that the goal of democracy is to defend the rights of citizens from an intrusive state and other citizens.

PSEUDO-DEMOCRATIC INSTITUTIONS Institutions that are created by authoritarian regimes to provide the appearance of democracy but have no actual democratic function.

PSEUDO-OPPOSITION The pseudo-opposition is an opposition that is formed or cultivated by the incumbent authoritarian regime in order to provide the appearance that a legitimate opposition is allowed to exist and challenge the state.

RALLY-ROUND-THE-FLAG EFFECT A concept that explains why leaders enjoy high levels of popularity during and immediately after an international conflict or crisis.

REALIGNMENT The process where there is a sharp but durable shift in the electorate, affecting the partisan balance and signifying enduring changes to the party coalition.

RENTIER STATES Rentier states are states that derive a substantial portion of their revenues from the rent of resources, such as from oil, minerals, or gas. Rentier states often offer their citizens low taxes and other services which has the effect of depressing civil unrest or protest for regime change. Rentier state theory has been used to explain the durability of authoritarianism in oil-rich countries.

REPRESENTATIVE GOVERNMENT A form of government whereby citizens vote for individuals to represent their interests.

REPRESSION Repression is the use of violence against a political group or individuals for political reasons, most likely to prevent the overthrow of a regime.

REVOLUTIONARY REGIMES Regimes that emerge out of sustained, ideological, and violent mass mobilization, and whose establishment is accompanied by significant efforts to transform the state and social structures.

RIGHT-WING POPULISM A form of populism which is anti-elitist, anti-immigration and usually espouses exclusive forms of nationalism that opposes diversity and progressive laws.

RULE OF LAW The principle that all citizens including those in the government are considered equal before the law and are subjected to the same laws and legal standards.

SANCTIONS Forms of economic trade barriers, often used as a tool in international relations to compel regimes to change their behaviour. Sanctions have been used by democracies to force authoritarian regimes to reform.

SELF-IMMOLATION Self-immolation is an act of killing oneself as an act of political sacrifice and is considered to be a radical form of protest. The self-immolation of a street vendor, Mohamed Bouazizi, in Tunisia served as the catalyst for the country's revolution.

SEQUENTIALISM Sequentialists believe that elections should not be held in a state whch was previously authoritarian until the rule of law in a country is achieved. Sequentialists believe that there is an important sequence to achieving democratic consolidation, and building institutions before participation is extended is critical to achieving consolidation.

SHANGHAI COOPERATION ORGANIZATION (SCO) An organization that consists of eight member states including Russia, India, and China that aims to promote security along with greater political and economic ties. The organization formed in 2003 and plays an important role in shaping international politics.

SINGLE PARTY REGIMES Authoritarian regimes that are headed by a political party. The political party is therefore ultimately responsible for policymaking and decisions.

SOCIAL CAPITAL A building block of democracy, which entails the building of inter-personal trust and shared norms. Social capital enables individuals to coordinate and cooperate in order to form civil society groups to actively pressure to influence the government.

SOCIAL CONTRACT The social contract is an implicit agreement between members of society and their government over the exchange of some mix of social benefits in return for compliance.

SOCIALISM A system that advocates greater public/collective ownership and operation of the social means of production for the common good. Though socialism is sometimes presented as an alternative to capitalism, where the means of production are privately held, socialism does allow for some private enterprise.

STATE CAPACITY Refers to the strength and ability of the state to perform various functions of the state including providing administrative services, the rule of law, protection, and political representation.

STATE FAILURE The process of a state's institutions falling apart or not functioning. States that have failed are not able to provide their citizens with the minimal levels of security, administrative goods, the rule of law, or political representation.

TERM LIMIT EXTENSIONS Often used by authoritarian regimes and their leaders to prolong their time in power. Term limit extensions eliminate previous rules that dictated a limited number of years that incumbents could hold power before stepping down or holding elections.

TERRORISM Politically motivated violence that targets civilians with the purpose of making a psychological impact on a wide audience.

THIRD WAVE A term popularized by Samuel Huntington. The Third Wave was a period of democratization, that took place in the beginning in the 1970s in Southern Europe, Latin America, and Asia.

TOP-DOWN PROCESSES The processes of authoritarian breakdown that are initiated by the regime's elites.

TOTALITARIAN REGIMES Totalitarian regimes are extreme forms of authoritarian rule which rely heavily on ideology and propaganda to exert total domination over their citizens and require unconditional loyalty. Totalitarian regimes have extremely high levels of political repression and allow absolutely no dissent or political pluralism.

TRIGGERING EVENT A critical catalyst used to signal to a large number of citizens the extent of public discontent or reveal previously unknown information about regime weakness, which can then lead to widespread protests to topple an authoritarian regime.

UNITARY SYSTEMS Forms of governments that do not share power with regional or local governments. China, Japan, Saudi Arabia, and France are prominent examples.

UNITED NATIONS (UN) An intergovernmental organization that aims to maintain peace and security among nations. In addition to peacekeeping, the UN has a host of other agencies that offer support to nations around the world supporting peace and development. The UN was formed in 1945 and has 193 member states and two observer states.

UNITED NATIONS HIGH COMMISSIONER FOR REFUGEES (UNHCR) A programme of the United Nations that aims to protect refugees, stateless people, and those that have been internally displaced. The agency was created in 1950 to deal with the aftermath of World War II.

UNITED STATES AGENCY FOR INTERNATIONAL DEVELOPMENT (USAID) An independent agency of the U.S. government that offers civilian foreign aid and development assistance. Formed in 1961, it is one of the largest agencies in the world.

VERTICAL ACCOUNTABILITY Accountability that derives from citizen support of its leaders, and is demonstrated through elections.

WESTERN LEVERAGE The ability of Western countries to influence authoritarian regimes. The term was used by Steven Levitsky and Lucan Way to better explain how democratization takes place.

WESTERN LINKAGE Refers to the connections that Western countries may make with authoritarian regimes, such as cooperation in international organizations, economic linkages, and social linkages such as cultural exchanges.

WORLD BANK An international financial institution that offers loans to developing countries in order to help them improve their development and reduce poverty.

YOUTH BULGE Refers to countries that have a large percentage of the population that is young. Some studies look at the proportion of the population that is under 30, while others look at 18 and 15. Studies have demonstrated that countries with a large youth bulge may experience unrest.

ZOMBIE ELECTIONS MONITORS International groups that monitor elections in authoritarian regimes (though they have no track record in doing this), for the sole purpose of providing a stamp of approval that the elections are free and fair.

References

ABADIE, A. 2006. Poverty, Political Freedom and the Roots of Terrorism. *American Economic Review*, 96(2), pp. 50–56.

ACEMOGLU, D. and ROBINSON, J.A., 2006. *Economic Origins of Democracy and Dictatorship*. Cambridge University Press.

ACEMOGLU, D. and ROBINSON, J.A., 2000. Why Did the West Extend the Franchise? Democracy, Inequality, and Growth in Historical Perspective. *The Quarterly Journal of Economics*, 115(4), pp. 1167–1199.

ACEMOGLU, D., JOHNSON, S., ROBINSON, J.A., and YARED, P., 2008. Income and Democracy. *American Economic Review*, 98(3), pp. 808–42.

ACHARYA, A., 2003. Democratisation and the Prospects for Participatory Regionalism in Southeast Asia. *Third World Quarterly*, 24(2), pp. 375–390.

ACKERMAN, B., 2000. The New Separation of Powers. *Harvard Law Review*, pp. 633–729.

ADAMIC, L.A. and GLANCE, N., August, 2005. The Political Blogosphere and the 2004 US Election: Divided They Blog. In Proceedings of the 3rd International Workshop on Link Discovery (pp. 36–43). ACM.

ADEBAJO, A., 2002. *Building Peace in West Africa: Liberia, Sierra Leone, and Guinea-Bissau*. Lynne Rienner Publishers.

ADEMMER, E. and BÖRZEL, T.A., 2013. Migration, Energy and Good Governance in the EU's Eastern Neighbourhood. *Europe–Asia Studies*, 65(4), pp. 581–608.

ADSERA, A., BOIX, C. and PAYNE, M., 2003. Are You Being Served? Political Accountability and Quality of Government. *The Journal of Law, Economics, and Organization*, 19(2), pp. 445–490.

AGBIBOA, D.E., 2012. Between Corruption and Development: The Political Economy of State Robbery in Nigeria. *Journal of Business Ethics*, 108(3), pp. 325–345.

AHMED, F.Z., 2012. The Perils of Unearned Foreign Income: Aid, Remittances, and Government Survival. *American Political Science Review*, 106(1), pp. 146–165.

AIYEDE, E.R., 2008. The Role of INEC, ICPC and EFCC in Combating Political Corruption. In ADETULA, A.O., (ed.), *Money and Politics in Nigeria*. International Foundation for Electoral Systems, pp. 39–52.

ALBERT, R., 2015. Amending Constitutional Amendment Rules. *International Journal of Constitutional Law*, 13(3), pp. 655–685.

ALEMÁN, J. and YANG, D.D., 2011. A Duration Analysis of Democratic Transitions and Authoritarian Backslides. *Comparative Political Studies*, 44(9), pp. 1123–1151.

ALESINA, A., BAQIR, R., and EASTERLY, W., 1999. Public Goods and Ethnic Divisions. *The Quarterly Journal of Economics*, 114(4), pp. 1243–1284.

ALESINA, A. and LA FERRARA, E., 2000. Participation in Heterogeneous Communities. *The Quarterly Journal of Economics*, 115(3), pp. 847–904.

ALESINA, A. and RODRIK, D., 1994. Distributive Politics and Economic Growth. *The Quarterly Journal of Economics*, 109(2), pp. 465–490.

ALLAN, J. (ed.), 2003. *Inclusion, Participation and Democracy: What Is the Purpose?* (Vol. 2). Springer Science & Business Media.

ALMOND, G.A., 1990. *A Discipline Divided: Schools and Sects in Political Science* (Vol. 175). Sage Publications.

ALMOND, G. and VERBA, S., 1963. *The Civic Culture*. Little Brown.

ALMOND, G.A. and VERBA, S., 2015. *The Civic Culture: Political Attitudes and Democracy in Five Nations*. Princeton University Press.

AMBROSIO, T., 2008. Catching the 'Shanghai Spirit': How the Shanghai Cooperation Organization Promotes Authoritarian Norms in Central Asia. *Europe–Asia Studies*, 60(8), pp. 1321–1344.

AMBROSIO, T., 2010. Constructing a Framework of Authoritarian Diffusion: Concepts, Dynamics, and Future Research. *International Studies Perspectives*, 11(4), pp. 375–392.

AMES B. 1970. Bases of Support for Mexico's Dominant Party. *American Political Science Review* 64(1):153–167.

AMMAR, S., 1997. *Can a Developing Democracy Manage its Macro-economy?: The Case of Thailand*. School of Policy Studies, Queen's University.

ANSELL, B. and SAMUELS, D., 2010. Inequality and Democratization: A Contractarian Approach. *Comparative Political Studies*, 43(12), pp. 1543–1574.

ANSELL, B.W. and SAMUELS, D.J., 2014. *Inequality and Democratization*. Cambridge University Press.

ANDERSON, L. and STANSFIELD, G., 2010. Avoiding Ethnic Conflict in Iraq: Some Lessons from the Åland Islands. *Ethnopolitics*, 9(2), pp. 219–238.

ARAGONES, E. and SÁNCHEZ-PAGÉS, S., 2009. A Theory of Participatory Democracy Based on the Real Case of Porto Alegre. *European Economic Review*, 53(1), pp. 56–72.

ARENDT, H., 1963. *On Revolution*. Penguin Books.

ARENDT, H., 1972. *Crises of the Republic: Lying in Politics, Civil Disobedience on Violence, Thoughts on Politics, and Revolution* (Vol. 219). Houghton Mifflin Harcourt.

ARDITI, B., 2004. Populism as a Spectre of Democracy: A Response to Canovan. *Political Studies*, 52(1), pp. 135–143.

ARDITI, B., 2014. Insurgencies Don't Have a Plan—They Are the Plan. In DE LA TORRE, C. (ed.), *The Promise of Populism*. University of Kentucky Press, pp. 113–139.

ARMSTRONG, C.K., 2016. North Korea and the Education of Desire: Totalitarianism, Everyday Life, and the Making of Post-Colonial Subjectivity. In LÜDKE, A. (ed.), *Everyday Life in Mass Dictatorship*. Palgrave Macmillan UK, pp. 165–183.

ASH, K., 2016. Representative Democracy and Fighting Domestic Terrorism. *Terrorism and Political Violence*, 28(1), pp. 114–134.

AUSTIN, L. 2011. The Politics of Youth Bulge: From Islamic Activism to Democratic Reform in the Middle East and North Africa. *SAIS Review of International Affairs*, 31(2), 81–96.

BADER, J., 2015. China, Autocratic Patron? An Empirical Investigation of China as a Factor in Autocratic Survival. *International Studies Quarterly*, 59(1), pp. 23–33.

BADER, J., GRÄVINGHOLT, J. and KÄSTNER, A., 2010. Would Autocracies Promote autocracy? A Political Economy Perspective on Regime-type Export in Regional Neighbourhoods. *Contemporary Politics*, 16(1), pp. 81–100.

BAILEY, J.J., 2006. Perceptions and Attitudes about Corruption and Democracy in Mexico. *Mexican Studies/Estudios Mexicanos*, 22(1), pp. 57–81.

BALE, T., 2012. Supplying the Insatiable Demand: Europe's Populist Radical Right. *Government and Opposition*, 47(2), pp. 256–274.

BANFIELD, E. 1958., *The Moral Basis of a Backward Society*. Free Press.

BARNES, T.D. and BURCHARD, S.M., 2013. 'Engendering Politics: The Impact of Descriptive Representation on Women's Political Engagement in Sub-Saharan

Africa. *Comparative Political Studies, 46*(7), pp. 767–790.

BARR, R.R., 2009. Populists, Outsiders and Anti-establishment Politics. *Party Politics, 15*(1), pp. 29–48.

BARRO, R.J., 1996. Democracy and Growth. *Journal of Economic Growth, 1*(1), pp. 1–27.

BARRO, R.J. and LEE, J.W., 2010. A New Data Set of Educational Attainment in the World, 1950–2010. NBER Working Paper No. 15902. *National Bureau of Economic Research.*

BARRO, R.J. and SALA-I-MARTIN, X., 2004. Economic Growth. 2nd Edn. *MIT Press.*

BARTELS, L.M., 2016. *Unequal Democracy: The Political Economy of the New Gilded Age.* Princeton University Press.

BARTLETT, J. 2014. Populism, Social Media and Democratic Strain. In LODGE, G. and GOTTFRIED, G. (eds.), *Democracy in Britain: Essays in honour of James Cornford.* Institute for Public Policy Research, pp. 91–96.

BATURO, A., 2014. *Democracy, Dictatorship, and Term Limits.* University of Michigan Press.

BATURO, A. and ELKINK, J.A., 2016. Dynamics of Regime Personalization and Patron–Client Networks in Russia, 1999–2014. *Post-Soviet Affairs, 32*(1), pp. 75–98.

BAUM, M.A. and LAKE, D.A., 2003. The Political Economy of Growth: Democracy and Human Capital. *American Journal of Political Science, 47*(2), pp. 333–347.

BEAMAN, L., DUFLO, E., PANDE, R., and TOPALOVA, P., 2012. Female Leadership Raises Aspirations and Educational Attainment for Girls: A Policy Experiment in India. *Science, 335*(6068), pp. 582–586.

BEARCE, D.H. and TIRONE, D.C., 2010. Foreign Aid Effectiveness and the Strategic Goals of Donor Governments. *The Journal of Politics, 72*(3), pp. 837–851.

BEBLAWI, H. and LUCIANI, G., 1987. *The Rentier State* (Vol. 2 of *Nation, State and Integration in the Arab World*). Istituto Affari Internazionali.

BECK, U. 1999. *World Risk Society.* Polity Press.

BEER, C., 2009. Democracy and Gender Equality. *Studies in Comparative International Development, 44*(3), p.212.

BEETHAM, D., 2004. Freedom as the Foundation. *Journal of Democracy, 15*(4), pp. 61–75.

BEISSINGER, M.R., 2008. A New Look at Ethnicity and Democratization. *Journal of Democracy, 19*(3), pp. 85–97.

BEISSINGER, M.R., 2007. Structure and Example in Modular Political Phenomena: The Diffusion of Bulldozer/Rose/Orange/Tulip Revolutions. *Perspectives on Politics, 5*(02), pp. 259–276.

BELKIN, A. and SCHOFER, E., 2003. Toward a Structural Understanding of Coup Risk. *Journal of Conflict Resolution, 47*(5), pp. 594–620.

BELL, C., RODRIGUES, C., SUTEU, S., DALY, T., and SAPIANO, J., 2017. Constitution-Making and Political Settlements in Times of Transition. *University of Edinburgh School of Law Research Paper Series* 2016(23), pp. 1–133.

BELL, C. and SUDDUTH, J.K., 2017. The Causes and Outcomes of Coup during Civil War. *Journal of Conflict Resolution, 61*(7), pp. 1432–1455.

BELLIN, E., 2004. The Robustness of Authoritarianism in the Middle East: Exceptionalism in Comparative Perspective. *Comparative Politics, 36*(2), pp. 139–157.

BELLIN, E., 2012. Reconsidering the Robustness of Authoritarianism in the Middle East: Lessons from the Arab Spring. *Comparative Politics, 44*(2), pp. 127–149.

BERDAL, M.R., BERDAL, M., and MALONE, D. (eds.), 2000. *Greed & Grievance: Economic Agendas in Civil Wars.* Lynne Rienner Publishers.

BERMAN, B.J., 1998. Ethnicity, Patronage and the African state: The Politics of Uncivil

Nationalism. *African Affairs, 97*(388), pp. 305–341.

BERMAN, S., 1997a. Civil Society and the Collapse of the Weimar Republic. *World Politics 49*(3), pp. 401–429. ch. 9.

BERMAN, S., 2007a. Lessons from Europe. *Journal of Democracy, 18*(1), pp. 28–41.

BERMAN, S., 2007b. The Vain Hope for 'Correct' Timing. *Journal of Democracy, 18*(3), pp. 14–17.

BERMAN, S., 2016. The Lost Left. *Journal of Democracy, 27*(4), pp. 69–76.

BERMEO, N., 2009. Does Electoral Democracy Boost Economic Equality? *Journal of Democracy, 20*(4), pp. 21–35.

BERMEO, N., 2016. On Democratic Backsliding. *Journal of Democracy, 27*(1), pp. 5–19.

BERMEO, S.B., 2011. Foreign Aid and Regime Change: A Role for Donor Intent. *World Development, 39*(11), pp. 2021–2031.

BERNHARD, M., REENOCK, C., and NORDSTROM, T., 2004. The Legacy of Western Overseas Colonialism on Democratic Survival. *International Studies Quarterly, 48*(1), pp. 225–250.

BETZ, H.G., 1993. The Two Faces of Radical Right-wing Populism in Western Europe. *The Review of Politics, 55*(4), pp. 663–686.

BETZ, H.G. and MERET, S., 2009. Revisiting Lepanto: The Political Mobilization against Islam in Contemporary Western Europe. *Patterns of Prejudice, 43*(3–4), pp. 313–334.

BIDDLE, S. and LONG, S., 2004. Democracy and Military Effectiveness: A Deeper Look. *Journal of Conflict Resolution, 48*(4), pp. 525–546.

BIENEN, H. and VAN DE WALLE, N., 1989. Time and Power in Africa. *American Political Science Review, 83*(1), pp. 19–34.

BILL, J.A., 1982. Power and Religion in Revolutionary Iran. *The Middle East Journal, 36*(1), pp. 22–47.

BIRCH, S., 2003. *Electoral Systems and Political Transformation in Post-communist Europe.* Springer.

BIRCH, S., 2011. Post-Soviet Electoral Practices in Comparative Perspective. *Europe-Asia Studies, 63*(4), pp. 703–725.

BIRCHALL, F.T., 1934. Hitler Endorsed by 9 to 1 in Poll on his Dictatorship, but Opposition Is Doubled. *The New York Times.*

BLACK, C.R., 2000. *Deterring Libya: The Strategic Culture of Muammar Qaddafi.* AIR UNIV MAXWELL AFB AL.

BLAIS, A. and AARTS, K., 2006. *Electoral Systems and Turnout.* Acta politica, *41*(2), pp. 180–196.

BLAIS, A. and CARTY, R.K., 1990. Does Proportional Representation Foster Voter Turnout? *European Journal of Political Research, 18*(2), pp. 167–181.

BLAISDELL, M., 2016. Tunisian Exceptionalism or Constitutional Timing: A Comparison of Democratic Transitions in the Middle East. *Elements, 12*(2).

BLAYDES, L., 2006, August. Who Votes in Authoritarian Elections and Why? Determinants of Voter Turnout in Contemporary Egypt. In *Annual Meeting of the American Political Science Association. Philadelphia, PA, August.* 1–22.

BLAYDES, L., 2008, April. Authoritarian elections and elite management: Theory and evidence from Egypt. In *Princeton University Conference on Dictatorships.*

BLAYDES, L., 2010. *Elections and Distributive Politics in Mubarak's Egypt.* Cambridge University Press.

BLAYDES, L. and KAYSER, M.A., 2011. Counting Calories: Democracy and Distribution in the Developing World. *International Studies Quarterly, 55*(4), pp. 887–908.

BOBBIO, N., RYLE, M., and SOPER, K., 2005. *Liberalism and Democracy* (Vol.4) Verso.

BOIX, C., 2011. Democracy, Development, and the International System. *American Political Science Review, 105*(4), pp. 809–828.

BOIX, C., 2003. *Democracy and Redistribution.* Cambridge University Press.

BOIX, C. and STOKES, S.C., 2003. Endogenous Democratization. *World Politics, 55*(4), pp. 517–549.

BOLLEN, K.A. and JACKMAN, R.W., 1985. Political Democracy and the Size Distribution of Income. *American Sociological Review, 13*(4), pp. 438–457.

BOLZENDAHL, C. and BROOKS, C., 2007. Women's Political Representation and Welfare State Spending in 12 Capitalist Democracies. *Social Forces, 85*(4), pp. 1509–1534.

BOSWELL, T. and DIXON, W.J., 1990. Dependency and Rebellion: A Cross-national Analysis. *American Sociological Review, 55*(4), pp. 540–559.

BOURGUIGNON, F. and VERDIER, T., 2000. Oligarchy, Democracy, Inequality and Growth. *Journal of Development Economics, 62*(2), pp. 285–313.

BOVE, V. and RIVERA, M., 2015. Elite Co-optation, Repression, and Coups in Autocracies. *International Interactions, 41*(3), pp. 453–479.

BOVENS, M., CURTIN, D. and HART, P.T. (eds.), 2010. *The Real world of EU Accountability: What Deficit?* Oxford University Press.

BRAINARD, L., & CHOLLET, D. (Eds.). 2007. *Too Poor for Peace?: Global Poverty, Conflict, and Security in the 21st Century.* Brookings Institution Press.

BRAITHWAITE, J.M. and SUDDUTH, J.K., 2016. Military Purges and the Recurrence of Civil Conflict. *Research & Politics, 3*(1), p. 2053168016630730.

BRANCATI, D., 2006. Decentralization: Fueling the Fire or Dampening the Flames of Ethnic Conflict and Secessionism? *International Organization, 60*(3), pp. 651–685.

BRANCATI, D., 2016. *Democracy Protests.* Cambridge University Press.

BRATTON, M., 1998. Second Elections in Africa. *Journal of Democracy, 9*(3), pp. 51–66.

BRATTON, M. and VAN DE WALLE, N., 1994. Neo-patrimonial Regimes and Political Transitions in Africa. *World Politics, 46*(4), pp. 453–489.

BRATTON, M. and VAN DE WALLE, N., 1997. *Democratic Experiments in Africa: Regime Transitions in Comparative Perspective.* Cambridge University Press.

BRÄUTIGAM, D., 2000. *Aid Dependence and Governance* (Vol. 1). Almqvist & Wiksell International.

BRINKS, D. and COPPEDGE, M., 2006. Diffusion Is No Illusion: Neighbor Emulation in the Third Wave of Democracy. *Comparative Political Studies, 39*(4), pp. 463–489.

BBC News. 16 March 2004. Survey Finds Hope in Occupied Iraq. http://news.bbc.co.uk/1/hi/world/middle_east/3514504.stm. Accessed 13 June 2019.

BROWNLEE, J., 2007. *Authoritarianism in an Age of Democratization.* Cambridge University Press.

BROWNLEE, J., 2017. The Limited Reach of Authoritarian Powers. *Democratization, 24*(7), pp. 1326–1344.

BROWNLEE, J., 2016. Why Turkey's Authoritarian Descent Shakes Up Democratic Theory. *From Mobilization to Counter-Revolution, Washington Post,* March 23. https://www.washingtonpost.com/news/monkey-cage/wp/2016/03/23/why-turkeys-authoritarian-descent-shakes-up-democratic-theory/. Accessed 7 June 2019.

BROWNLEE, J., MASOUD, T., and REYNOLDS, A., 2013. Why the Modest Harvest? *Journal of Democracy, 24*(4), pp. 29–44.

BRUBAKER, R., 1996. *Nationalism Reframed: Nationhood and the National Question in the New Europe.* Cambridge University Press.

BRUMBY, J. and GALLIGAN, B., 2015. The Federalism Debate. *Australian Journal of Public Administration, 74*(1), pp. 82–92.

BRUNETTI, A. and WEDER, B., 2003. A Free Press is Bad News for Corruption. *Journal of Public Economics, 87*(7), pp. 1801–1824.

BRZEZINSKI, Z.K., 1962. *Ideology and Power in Soviet Politics*. Westport Press.

BUNCE, V.J. and WOLCHIK, S.L., 2010. Defeating Dictators: Electoral Change and Stability in Competitive Authoritarian Regimes. *World Politics*, *62*(1), pp. 43–86.

BUNCE, V. and WATTS, S., 2005. Managing Diversity and Sustaining Democracy: Ethnofederal versus Unitary States in the Post-communist World. *Sustainable Peace: Power and Democracy after Civil Wars*, National Council for Eurasian and East European Research.

BUNCE, V. and WOLCHIK, S.L., 2007. Transnational Networks, Diffusion Dynamics, and Electoral Revolutions in the Post Communist World. *Physica A: Statistical Mechanics and its Applications*, *378*(1), pp. 92–99.

BURKHART, R.E. and LEWIS-BECK, M.S., 1994. Comparative Democracy: The Economic Development Thesis. *American Political Science Review*, *88*(4), pp. 903–910.

BURTON, M., GUNTHER, R., and HIGLEY, J., 1992. Elites and Democratic Consolidation in Latin America and Southern Europe: An Overview. In HIGLEY, J., GUNTHER, R., and JOHN, H. (eds.), *Elites and Democratic Consolidation in Latin America and Southern Europe*. Cambridge University Press, pp. 323–48.

BUZOGÁNY, A., 2017. Illiberal Democracy in Hungary: Authoritarian Diffusion or Domestic Causation? *Democratization*, *24*(7), pp. 1307–1325.

BYMAN, D. and LIND, J., 2010. Pyongyang's Survival Strategy: Tools of Authoritarian Control in North Korea. *International Security*, *35*(1), pp. 44–74.

BYRNE, S., 2001. Consociational and Civic Society Approaches to Peacebuilding in Northern Ireland. *Journal of Peace Research*, *38*(3), pp. 327–352.

CAMERON, D.R. and ORENSTEIN, M.A., 2012. Post-Soviet Authoritarianism: The Influence of Russia in Its 'Near Abroad'. *Post-Soviet Affairs*, *28*(1), pp. 1–44.

CAMPANTE, F.R. and CHOR, D., 2012. Why Was the Arab World Poised for Revolution? Schooling, Economic Opportunities, and the Arab Spring. *Journal of Economic Perspectives*, *26*(2), pp. 167–168.

CANACHE, D., 2002. From Bullets to Ballots: The Emergence of Popular Support for Hugo Chavez. *Latin American Politics and Society*, *44*(1), pp. 69–90.

CANOVAN, M., 1999. Trust the People! Populism and the Two Faces of Democracy. *Political Studies*, *47*(1), pp. 2–16.

CARMINES, E.G., 1991. The Logic of Party Alignments. Journal of Theoretical Politics, *3*(1), pp. 65–80.

CAROTHERS, T., 1998. The Rule of Law Revival. *Foreign Aff.*, *77*, p. 95.

CAROTHERS, T., 2002. The End of the Transition Paradigm. *Journal of Democracy*, *13*(1), pp. 5–21.

CAROTHERS, T., 2007. The 'Sequencing' Fallacy. *Journal of Democracy*, *18*(1), pp. 12–27.

CAROTHERS, T., 2009. Democracy Assistance: Political vs. Developmental? *Journal of Democracy*, *20*(1), pp. 5–19.

CAROTHERS, T., 2015. Democracy Aid at 25: Time to Choose. *Journal of Democracy*, *26*(1), pp. 59–73.

CASE, W., 2002. Malaysia: Semi-democracy with Strain Points. In Case, W., *Politics in South East Asia*. Curzon.

CASE, W., 2007. Semi-democracy and Minimalist Federalism in Malaysia. In HE, B., GALLIGAN, B., and INOGUCHI, T. (eds.), *Federalism in Asia*. Edward Elgar Publishing, pp. 124–143.

CASPER, B.A. and TYSON, S.A., 2014. Popular Protest and Elite Coordination in a Coup d'état. *The Journal of Politics*, *76*(2), pp. 548–564.

CEDERMAN, L.E., BUHAUG, H. and RØD, J.K., 2009a. Ethno-nationalist Dyads and Civil War: A GIS-based Analysis. *Journal of Conflict Resolution*, *53*(4), pp. 496–525.

CEDERMAN, L.E., GIRARDIN, L., and GLEDITSCH, K.S., 2009b. Ethnonationalist Triads: Assessing the Influence of Kin Groups on Civil Wars. *World Politics*, 61(3), pp. 403–437.

CEDERMAN, L.E., WIMMER, A., and MIN, B., 2010. Why Do Ethnic Groups Rebel? New Data and Analysis. *World Politics*, 62(1), pp. 87–119.

CELESTINO, M.R. and GLEDITSCH, K.S., 2013. Fresh Carnations or All Thorn, No Rose? Nonviolent Campaigns and Transitions in Autocracies. *Journal of Peace Research*, 50(3), pp. 385–400.

CHANG, E. and GOLDEN, M.A., 2010. Sources of Corruption in Authoritarian Regimes. *Social Science Quarterly*, 91(1), pp. 1–20.

CHANG, Y.T., ZHU, Y., and PAK, C.M., 2007. Authoritarian Nostalgia in Asia. *Journal of Democracy*, 18(3), pp. 66–80.

CHARRAD, M.M. and ZARRUGH, A., 2014. Equal or Complementary? Women in the New Tunisian Constitution after the Arab Spring. *The Journal of North African Studies*, 19(2), pp. 230–243

CHÁVEZ, R.B., 2007. The Appointment and Removal Process for Judges in Argentina: The Role of Judicial Councils and Impeachment Juries in Promoting Judicial Independence. *Latin American Politics and Society*, 49(2), pp. 33–58.

CHEIBUB, J.A., 2007. *Presidentialism, Parliamentarism, and Democracy*. Cambridge University Press.

CHEIBUB, J.A. and LIMONGI, F., 2002. Democratic Institutions and Regime Survival: Parliamentary and Presidential Democracies Reconsidered. *Annual Review of Political Science*, 5(1), pp. 151–179.

CHEIBUB, J.A., PRZEWORSKI, A., LIMONGI NETO, F.P., and ALVAREZ, M.M., 1996. What Makes Democracies Endure? *Journal of Democracy*, 7(1), pp. 39–55.

CHEHABI, H.E. and LINZ, J.J. (eds.), 1998. *Sultanistic Regimes*. JHU Press.

CHEN, J., 2013. *A Middle Class without Democracy: Economic Growth and the Prospects for Democratization in China*. Oxford University Press.

CHEN, J. and LU, C., 2011. Democratization and the Middle Class in China: The Middle Class's Attitudes toward Democracy. *Political Research Quarterly*, 64(3), pp. 705–719.

CHENOWETH, E., 2010. Democratic Competition and Terrorist Activity. *The Journal of Politics*, 72(1), pp. 16–30.

CHENOWETH, E., 2013. Terrorism and Democracy. *Annual Review of Political Science*, 16, pp. 355–378.

CHINKIN, C. and CHARLESWORTH, H., 2006. Building Women into Peace: The International legal framework. *Third World Quarterly*, 27(5), pp. 937–957.

CHILDS, S. and WITHEY, J., 2004. Women Representatives Acting for Women: Sex and the Signing of Early Day Motions in the 1997 British Parliament. *Political Studies*, 52(3), pp. 552–564.

CHOWDHURY, S.K., 2004. The Effect of Democracy and Press Freedom on Corruption: An Empirical Test. *Economics letters*, 85(1), pp. 93–101.

CHU, Y.W., 1998. Labor and Democratization in South Korea and Taiwan. *Journal of Contemporary Asia*, 28(2), pp. 185–202.

CHUA, A., 2004. *World on Fire: How Exporting Free Market Democracy Breeds Ethnic Hatred and Global Instability*. Anchor.

CLARK, T.N., LIPSET, S.M., and REMPEL, M., 1993. The Declining Political Significance of Social Class. *International Sociology*, 8(3), pp. 293–316.

CLAWSON, R.A., KEGLER, E.R., and WALTENBURG, E.N., 2001. The Legitimacy-conferring Authority of the US Supreme Court: An Experimental Design. *American Politics Research*, 29(6), pp. 566–591.

COLLIER, P. 2000. Doing Well Out of War. In BERDALE, M.R. and MALONE, D. (eds.), *Greed and Grievance. Economic Agendas in Civil Wars*. Lynne Rienner Publishers, pp. 91–112.

COFFÉ, H. and BOLZENDAHL, C., 2010. Same Game, Different Rules? Gender Differences in Political Participation. *Sex Roles*, 62(5–6), pp. 318–333.

COLE, W.M., 2018. Poor and Powerless: Economic and Political Inequality in Cross-national Perspective, 1981–2011. *International Sociology*, 33(3), pp. 357–385.

COLLIER, R.B., 1999. *Paths toward Democracy: The Working Class and Elites in Western Europe and South America*. Cambridge University Press.

COLLIER, P. and HOEFFLER, A., 2004. Greed and Grievance in Civil War. *Oxford Economic Papers*, 56(4), pp. 563–595.

COLLIER, D. and LEVITSKY, S., 1997. Democracy with Adjectives: Conceptual Innovation in Comparative Research. *World Politics*, 49(3), pp. 430–451.

CONROY-KRUTZ, J. and FRANTZ, E., 2017. *Theories of Democratic Change II*. USAID.

COOLEY, A., 30 January 2013. The League of Authoritarian Gentlemen. *Foreign Policy*, 30. https://foreignpolicy.com/2013/01/30/the-league-of-authoritarian-gentlemen/ Accessed 7 Jun 2019.

COPPEDGE, M., 2012. *Democratization and Research Methods*. Cambridge University Press.

CORDERO, G. and SIMÓN, P., 2016. Economic Crisis and Support for Democracy in Europe. *West European Politics*, 39(2), pp. 305–325.

CORRALES, J. and PENFOLD, M., 2015. *Dragon in the Tropics: Venezuela and the Legacy of Hugo Chávez*. Brookings Institution Press.

CORRALES, J. and PENFOLD-BECERRA, M., 2007. Venezuela: Crowding out the Opposition. *Journal of Democracy*, 18(2), pp. 99–113.

COTTON, J., 1989. From Authoritarianism to Democracy in South Korea. *Political Studies*, 37(2), pp. 244–259.

COX, G.W., 2009. Authoritarian Elections and Leadership Succession, 1975–2004. 1–21.

CRASSWELLER, R.D., 1966. *Trujillo: The life and Times of a Caribbean Dictator*. Macmillan.

CRENSHAW, M., 1981. The Causes of terrorism. *Comparative politics*, 13(4), pp. 379–399.

CRESPO, J.A., 2004. The Party System and Democratic Governance in Mexico. *Policy Papers on the Americas*, 15(2), pp. 21–45.

DAHL, R.A., 1989. *Democracy and its Critics*. Yale University Press.

DAHL, R.A., 1973. *Polyarchy: Participation and Opposition*. Yale University Press.

DAHL, R.A., SHAPIRO, I., and CHEIBUB, J.A. (eds.), 2003. *The Democracy Sourcebook*. MIT Press.

DAHLUM, S. and KNUTSEN, C.H., 2017. Democracy by Demand? Reinvestigating the Effect of Self-expression Values on Political Regime Type. *British Journal of Political Science*, 47(2), pp. 437–461.

DALTON, R.J., 1984. Cognitive Mobilization and Partisan Dealignment in Advanced Industrial Democracies. *The Journal of Politics*, 46(1), pp. 264–284.

DALTON, R.J., FARRELL, D.M. and McALLISTER, I., 2011. *Political Parties and Democratic Linkage: How Parties Organize Democracy*. Oxford University Press.

DALTON, R.J., SIN, T.C., and JOU, W., 2007. Understanding Democracy: Data from Unlikely Places. *Journal of Democracy*, 18(4), pp. 142–156.

D'ANIERI, P. 2003. Leonid Kuchma and the Personalization of the Ukrainian Presidency. *Problems of Post-Communism*, 50(5), pp. 58–65.

DARDEN, K. A. 2001. Blackmail as a Tool of State Domination: Ukraine under Kuchma. *E. Eur. Const. Rev.*, *10*, p. 67.

DASHTI-GIBSON, J., DAVIS, P., and RADCLIFF, B., 1997. On the Determinants of the Success of Economic Sanctions: An Empirical Analysis. *American Journal of Political Science*, 41(2), pp. 608–618.

DAVENPORT, C., 1995. Multi-dimensional Threat Perception and State Repression: An Inquiry into Why States Apply Negative Sanctions. *American Journal of Political Science*, 39(3), pp. 683–713.

DAVENPORT, C., 2000. Understanding Illiberal Democracies, Liberal Autocracies, and Everything in Between: A Cross-National Examination from 1972–1996. *World Democratization 2000-Rethinking Democracy in the New Millennium*. paper prepared for World Democratization 2000—Rethinking Democracy in the New Millennium Conference, University of Houston, Houston, TX, 16–19 February 2000).

DAVENPORT, C., 2007. *State Repression and the Domestic Democratic Peace*. Cambridge University Press.

DAVENPORT, C. and APPEL, B., 2014. Stopping State Repression: An Examination of Spells, 1976–2004. APSA Annual Meeting Paper.

DAVENPORT, C. and ARMSTRONG, D.A., 2004. Democracy and the Violation of Human Rights: A Statistical Analysis from 1976 to 1996. *American Journal of Political Science*, 48(3), pp. 538–554.

DECALO, S., 1990. *Coups and Military Rule in Africa: Motivations and Constraints*. Yale University Press.

DECALO, S., 1992. The process, Prospects and Constraints of Democratization in Africa. *African Affairs*, 91(362), pp. 7–35.

DE GRUCHY, J.W., 2005. *The Church Struggle in South Africa*. Fortress Press.

DEININGER, K. and SQUIRE, L. 1998. New Ways of Looking at Old Issues: Inequality and Growth. *Journal of Development Economics*, 57(2), pp. 259–287.

DE LA TORRE, C., 2016. Populism and the Politics of the Extraordinary in Latin America. *Journal of Political Ideologies*, 21(2), pp. 121–139.

DELLA PORTA, D., 2000. Social Capital, Beliefs in Government, and Political Corruption. In PHARR, S.J. and PUTNAM, R.D. (eds.), Disaffected Democracies: What's Troubling the Trilateral Countries. Princeton University Press, pp. 202–228.

DE MESQUITA, B. and SMITH, A., 2017. Political Succession: A Model of Coups, Revolution, Purges, and Everyday Politics. *Journal of Conflict Resolution*, 61(4), pp. 707–743.

DE MESQUITA, B.B., SMITH, A., MORROW, J.D., and SIVERSON, R.M., 2005. *The Logic of Political Survival*. MIT Press.

DE MESQUITA, B.B. and DOWNS, G.W., 2006. Intervention and Democracy. *International Organization*, 60(3), pp. 627–649.

DE MESQUITA, B.B., MORROW, J.D., SIVERSON, R.M., and SMITH, A., 1999. An Institutional Explanation of the Democratic Peace. *American Political Science Review*, 93(4), pp. 791–807.

DE MESQUITA, B.B. and SMITH, A., 2010. Leader Survival, Revolutions, and the Nature of Government Finance. *American Journal of Political Science*, 54(4), pp. 936–950.

DE MONTEQUIEU, C. 1989, *Montesquieu: The Spirit of the Laws*. Cambridge University Press.

DERPANOPOULOS, G., FRANTZ, E., GEDDES, B., and WRIGHT, J., 2016. Are Coups Good for Democracy? *Research & Politics*, 3(1), p. 2053168016630837.

DEVLIN, C. and ELGIE, R., 2008. The Effect of Increased Women's Representation in

Parliament: The Case of Rwanda. *Parliamentary Affairs, 61*(2), pp. 237–254.

DIAMOND, L., 1999. *Developing Democracy: Toward Consolidation.* JHU Press.

DIAMOND, L., 1992. Economic Development and Democracy Reconsidered. *American Behavioral Scientist, 35*(4–5), pp. 450–499.

DIAMOND, L., 2002. Elections without Democracy: Thinking about Hybrid Regimes. *Journal of Democracy, 13*(2), pp. 21–35.

DIAMOND, L., 2015. Facing up to the Democratic Recession. *Journal of Democracy, 26*(1), pp. 141–155.

DIAMOND, L., 2015. *In Search of Democracy.* Routledge.

DIAMOND, L. 2008. *The Spirit of Democracy: TheSstruggle to Build Free Societies throughout the World.* Macmillan.

DIAMOND, L.J., 1994. Toward Democratic Consolidation. *Journal of Democracy, 5*(3), pp. 4–17.

DIAMOND, L. and GUNTHER, R. (eds.), 2001. *Political Parties and Democracy.* JHU Press.

DIAMOND, L., LINZ, J.J., and LIPSET, S.M. (eds.), 1990. *A Politics in Developing Countries.* Lynne Rienner Publishers, p. 9.

DIAMOND, L.J. and MORLINO, L., 2004. An Overview. *Journal of Democracy, 15*(4), pp. 20–31.

DIAMOND, L. and MORLINO, L. (eds.), 2005. *Assessing the Quality of Democracy.* JHU Press.

DIANGÁ, J.W., 2002. *Kenya 1982, the Attempted Coup: The Consequence of a One-party Dictatorship.* Pen Press.

DIAZ-CAYEROS, A., MAGALONI, B., and WEINGAST, B.R., 2003. Tragic Brilliance: Equilibrium Hegemony and Democratization in Mexico. Hoover Institution, Stanford University, pp. 1–41.

DICKSON, B.J., 2003. Threats to Party Supremacy. *Journal of Democracy, 14*(1), pp. 27–35.

DIETRICH, S. and WRIGHT, J., 2014. Foreign Aid Allocation Tactics and Democratic Change in Africa. *The Journal of Politics, 77*(1), pp. 216–234.

DIETZ, H.A. and MYERS, D.J., 2007. From Thaw to Deluge: Party System Collapse in Venezuela and Peru. *Latin American Politics and Society, 49*(2), pp. 59–86.

DIMITROV, M.K., 2009. Popular Autocrats. *Journal of Democracy, 20*(1), pp. 78–81.

DIMITROVA, D.V., SHEHATA, A., STRÖMBÄCK, J., and NORD, L.W., 2014. The Effects of Digital Media on Political Knowledge and Participation in Election Campaigns: Evidence from Panel Data. *Communication Research, 41*(1), pp. 95–118.

DOBBINS, J.F., 2003. America's Role in Nation-building: From Germany to Iraq. *Survival, 45*(4), pp. 87–110.

DOGAN, M. and HIGLEY, J. (eds.), 1998. *Elites, Crises, and the Origins of Regimes.* Rowman & Littlefield.

DOLLAR, D., FISMAN, R., and GATTI, R., 2001. Are Women Really the 'Fairer' Sex? Corruption and Women in Government. *Journal of Economic Behavior & Organization, 46*(4), pp. 423–429.

DONNO, D., 2013. Elections and Democratization in Authoritarian Regimes. *American Journal of Political Science, 57*(3), pp. 703–716.

DONNO, D. and ROUSSIAS, N., 2012. Does Cheating Pay? The Effect of Electoral Misconduct on Party Systems. *Comparative Political Studies, 45*(5), pp. 575–605.

DONNO, D. and RUSSETT, B., 2004. Islam, Authoritarianism, and Female Empowerment: What Are the Linkages? *World Politics, 56*(4), pp. 582–607.

DORFF, R.H., 1996. Democratization and Failed States: The Challenge of Ungovernability. *Parameters, 26*(2), p. 17.

DORMAN, S.R., 2002. 'Rocking the Boat?': Church-NGOs and Democratization in Zimbabwe. *African Affairs*, *101*(402), pp. 75–92.

DOUCOULIAGOS, H. and ULUBAŞOĞLU, M.A., 2008. Democracy and Economic Growth: A Meta-analysis. *American Journal of Political Science*, *52*(1), pp. 61–83.

DOUGLAS, S., 2005. Referendum: Hitler's 'Democratic' Weapon To Forge Dictatorship. *Executive Intelligence Review*, *4*.

DOWNES, A.B. and MONTEN, J., 2013. Forced to be free?: Why foreign-imposed regime change rarely leads to Democratization. *International Security*, *37*(4), pp. 90–131.

DOWNS, A., 1957. An Economic Theory of Political Action in a Democracy. *Journal of Political Economy*, *65*(2), pp. 135–150.

DOYLE, M.W., 1983. Kant, Liberal Legacies, and Foreign Affairs. *Philosophy & Public Affairs*, *12*(3), pp. 205–235.

DOYLE, M.W., 1986. Liberalism and World Politics. *American Political Science Review*, *80*(4), pp. 1151–1169.

DRURY, A.C., KRIECKHAUS, J., and LUSZTIG, M., 2006. Corruption, Democracy, and Economic Growth. *International Political Science Review*, *27*(2), pp. 121–136.

DUNNING, T., 2004. Conditioning the Effects of Aid: Cold War Politics, Donor Credibility, and Democracy in Africa. *International Organization*, *58*(2), pp. 409–423.

EASTER, G.M., 1997. Preference for Presidentialism: Post-communist Regime Change in Russia and the NIS. *World Politics*, *49*(2), pp. 184–211.

EASTERLY, W. and LEVINE, R., 1997. Africa's Growth Tragedy: Policies and Ethnic Divisions. *The Quarterly Journal of Economics*, *112*(4), pp. 1203–1250.

THE ECONOMIST, 9 July 2018. The New Class War. https://www.economist.com/special-report/2016/07/09/the-new-class-war. Accessed 19 November 2018.

THE ECONOMIST, 3 November 2011. Education in South Korea: Glutted with Graduates. https://www.economist.com/blogs/banyan/2011/11/education-south-korea. Accessed 24 July 2019.

EGOROV, G. and SONIN, K., 2011. Dictators and Their Viziers: Endogenizing the Loyalty–Competence Trade-off. *Journal of the European Economic Association*, *9*(5), pp. 903–930.

EICHENGREEN, B. and LEBLANG, D., 2008. Democracy and Globalization. *Economics & Politics*, *20*(3), pp. 289–334.

ELKINS, Z. and SIMMONS, B., 2005. On Waves, Clusters, and Diffusion: A Conceptual Framework. *The Annals of the American Academy of Political and Social Science*, *598*(1), pp. 33–51.

ELLNER, S. and SALAS, M.T. (eds.), 2006. *Venezuela: Hugo Chávez and the Decline of an 'Exceptional Democracy'*. Rowman & Littlefield Publishers.

ELSTER, J. (ed.), 1998. *Deliberative Democracy* (Vol. 1). Cambridge University Press.

ENGESSER, S., ERNST, N., ESSER, F., and BÜCHEL, F., 2017. Populism and Social Media: How Politicians Apread a Fragmented Ideology. *Information, Communication & Society*, *20*(8), pp. 1109–1126.

EPSTEIN, E.C., 1984. Legitimacy, Institutionalization, and Opposition in Exclusionary Bureaucratic-Authoritarian Regimes: The Situation of the 1980s. *Comparative Politics*, *17*(1), pp. 37–54.

EPSTEIN, D.L., BATES, R., GOLDSTONE, J., KRISTENSEN, I. and O'HALLORAN, S., 2006. Democratic Transitions. *American Journal of Political Science*, *50*(3), pp. 551–569.

ERDMANN, G., 2011. Decline of Democracy: Loss of Quality, Hybridisation and Breakdown of Democracy. In *Regression of Democracy?* (pp. 21–58). VS Verlag für Sozialwissenschaften.

ESCRIBÀ-FOLCH, A., 2013. Repression, Political Threats, and Survival under Autocracy. *International Political Science Review*, *34*(5), pp. 543–560.

ESCRIBÀ-FOLCH, A. and WRIGHT, J., 2010. Dealing with Tyranny: International Sanctions and the Survival of Authoritarian Rulers. *International Studies Quarterly*, *54*(2), pp. 335–359.

ESCRIBÀ-FOLCH, A. and WRIGHT, J.G., 2015. *Foreign Pressure and the Politics of Autocratic Survival.* Oxford Studies in Democratizat.

ESEN, B. and GUMUSCU, S., 2016. Rising Competitive Authoritarianism in Turkey. *Third World Quarterly*, *37*(9), pp. 1581–1606.

ETZIONI, A., 1995. *Rights and the Common Good: The Communitarian Perspective.* St. Martin's Press.

EUBANK, W.L. and WEINBERG, L., 1994. Does Democracy Encourage Terrorism? *Terrorism and Political Violence*, *6*(4), pp. 417–435.

EUBANK, W. and WEINBERG, L., 2001. Terrorism and Democracy: Perpetrators and Victims. *Terrorism and Political Violence*, *13*(1), pp. 155–164.

EWING, J. and HOROWITZ, J. October 12, 2018. Why Italy Could Be the Epicenter of the Next Financial Crisis. *New York Times.* https://www.nytimes.com/2018/10/12/business/italy-debt-crisis-eu-brussels.html Accessed 25 February 2019.

EYERMAN, J., 1998. Terrorism and Democratic states: Soft Targets or Accessible Systems. *International Interactions*, *24*(2), pp. 151–170.

EZROW, N., 2017. *Global Politics and Violent Non-state Actors.* Sage.

EZROW, N.M. and FRANTZ, E., 2011. *Dictators and Dictatorships: Understanding Authoritarian Regimes and Their Leaders.* Bloomsbury Publishing USA.

EZROW, N.M. and FRANTZ, E., 2013. *Failed States and Institutional Decay: Understanding Instability and Poverty in the Developing World.* Bloomsbury Publishing USA.

FAGBADEBO, O., 2007. Corruption, Governance and Political Instability in Nigeria. *African Journal of Political Science and International Relations*, *1*(2), pp. 028–037.

FALLON, K.M., SWISS, L., and VITERNA, J., 2012. Resolving the Democracy Paradox: Democratization and Women's Legislative Representation in Developing Nations, 1975 to 2009. *American Sociological Review*, *77*(3), pp. 380–408.

FARNSWORTH, S.J., 2003. *Political Support in a Frustrated America.* Greenwood Publishing Group.

FEARON, J.D., 1994. Domestic Political Audiences and the Escalation of International Disputes. *American Political Science Review*, *88*(3), pp. 577–592.

FEARON, J.D., 2007. Iraq's Civil War. *Foreign Affairs*, *86*(2) pp. 2–16.

FEARON, J.D. and LAITIN, D.D., 2003. Ethnicity, Insurgency, and Civil War. *American Political Science Review*, *97*(1), pp. 75–90.

FEIN, H., 1995. More Murder in the Middle: Life-integrity Violations and Democracy in the World, 1987. *Human Rights Quarterly*, *17*, p.170.

FELDMAN, S., 2017. Authoritarianism, Threat, and Intolerance. *At the Forefront of Political Psychology: Essays in Honor of John L. Sullivan.* Routledge.

FELDMAN, S. and STENNER, K., 1997. Perceived Threat and Authoritarianism. *Political Psychology*, *18*(4), pp. 741–770.

FINER, S., 2017. *The Man on Horseback: The Role of the Military in Politics.* Routledge.

FINKEL, S.E., PÉREZ-LIÑÁN, A., and SELIGSON, M.A., 2007. The Effects of US Foreign Assistance on Democracy Building, 1990–2003. *World Politics*, *59*(3), pp. 404–439.

FINNEMORE, M. and SIKKINK, K., 1998. International Norm Dynamics and Political Change. *International Organization*, *52*(4), pp. 887–917.

FISH, M.S. and BROOKS, R.S., 2004. Does Diversity hurt Democracy? *Journal of Democracy*, *15*(1), pp. 154–166.

FISHER, E., 2004. The European Union in the Age of Accountability. *Oxford Journal of Legal Studies*, 24(3), pp. 495–515.

FJELDE, H. and HEGRE, H., 2014. Political Corruption and Institutional Stability. *Studies in Comparative International Development*, 49(3), pp. 267–299.

FLORES, A.Q. and SMITH, A., 2013. Leader Survival and Natural Disasters. *British Journal of Political Science*, 43(4), pp. 821–843.

FLORINI, A., 1996. The Evolution of International Norms. *International Studies Quarterly*, 40(3), pp. 363–389.

FORTIN, J., 2012. Is There a nNecessary Condition for Democracy? The Role of State Capacity in Post-communist Countries. *Comparative Political Studies*, 45(7), pp. 903–930.

FOSSUM, E., 1967. Factors Influencing the Occurrence of Military Coups d'etat in Latin America. *Journal of Peace Research*, 4(3), pp. 228–251.

FOX, R., 1996. Bleak Future for Multi-party Elections in Kenya. *The Journal of Modern African Studies*, 34(4), pp. 597–607.

FRANCISCO, R.A., 1995. The Relationship between Coercion and Protest: An Empirical Evaluation in Three Coercive States. *Journal of Conflict Resolution*, 39(2), pp. 263–282.

FRANK, A.G., 2018. The Development of Underdevelopment. In Frank, A.G., *Promise of Development*. Routledge, pp. 111–123.

FRANTZ, E., 2018. Authoritarian Politics: Trends and Debates. *Politics and Governance*, 6(2), pp. 87–89.

FRANTZ, E. and EZROW, N.M., 2011. *The Politics of Dictatorship: Institutions and Outcomes in Authoritarian Regimes*. Lynne Rienner Publishers.

FRANTZ, E. and KENDALL-TAYLOR, A., 2014. A Dictator's Toolkit: Understanding How Co-optation Affects Repression in Autocracies. *Journal of Peace Research*, 51(3), pp. 332–346.

FREEDEN, M., 1998. Is Nationalism a Distinct Ideology? *Political Studies*, 46(4), pp. 748–765.

Freedom House, 2017. https://freedomhouse.org/report/freedom-world/freedom-world-2017. Accessed 8 June 2019.

Freedom House, 2018. https://freedomhouse.org/report/freedom-world/freedom-world-2018 Accessed 8 June 2019.

FREEMAN, J.R. and QUINN, D.P., 2012. The Economic Origins of Democracy Reconsidered. *American Political Science Review*, 106(1), pp. 58–80.

FRIEDMAN, M., 2009. *Capitalism and Freedom*. University of Chicago Press.

FRIEDRICH, C., and BRZEZINSKI, Z. 1956. *Totalitarianism, Dictatorship and Autocracy*. Harvard University Press.

FRIESEN, J. November 9, 2016. The Data behind Trump's Win. *The Globe and Mail.* https://beta.theglobeandmail.com/news/world/us-politics/white-voters-education-swing-states-the-data-behind-trumpswin/article32784716/?ref=http://www.theglobeandmail.com& Accessed 7 June 2019.

FRYE, T., 1997. A politics of Institutional Choice: Post-communist Presidencies. *Comparative Political Studies*, 30(5), pp. 523–552.

FUKUYAMA, F., 2012. The Future of History: Can Liberal Democracy Survive the Decline of the Middle Class? *Foreign Affairs*, 91(1), pp. 53–61.

FUKUYAMA, F., 2004. The Imperative of State-building. *Journal of Democracy*, 15(2), pp. 17–31.

GADARIAN, S.K., 2010. The Politics of Threat: How Terrorism News Shapes Foreign Policy Attitudes. *The Journal of Politics*, 72(2), pp. 469–483.

GALETOVIC, A. and SANHUEZA, R., 2000. Citizens, Autocrats, and Plotters: A Model and New Evidence on Coups d'état. *Economics & Politics*, 12(2), pp. 183–204.

GALSTON, W., 1992. New Familism, New Politics. *Family Affairs*, 5(1–2), pp. 7–9.

GANDHI, J., 2008. *Political Institutions under Dictatorship*. Cambridge University Press.

GANDHI, J. and LUST-OKAR, E., 2009. Elections under Authoritarianism. *Annual Review of Political Science*, 12, pp. 403–422.

GANDHI, J. and PRZEWORSKI, A., 2007. Authoritarian Institutions and the Survival of Autocrats. *Comparative Political Studies*, 40(11), pp. 1279–1301.

GANDHI, J. and PRZEWORSKI, A., 2006. Cooperation, Cooptation, and Rebellion Under Dictatorships. *Economics & Politics*, 18(1), pp. 1–26.

GANGL, A., 2003. Procedural Justice Theory and Evaluations of the Lawmaking Process. *Political Behavior*, 25(2), pp. 119–149.

GARRETÓN MERINO, M.A., 1995. Redemocratization in Chile. *Journal of Democracy*, 6(1), pp. 146–158.

GARTNER, S.S. and REGAN, P.M., 1996. Threat and Repression: The Non-linear Relationship between Government and Opposition Violence. *Journal of Peace Research*, 33(3), pp. 273–287.

GARZIA, D., FERREIRA DA SILVA, F., and DE ANGELIS, A., 2018. Partisan Dealignment and the Personalization of Politics in West European Parliamentary Democracies, 1961–2016. Center for the Study of Democracy.

GASIOROWSKI, M.J., 1995. Economic Crisis and Political Regime Change: An Event History Analysis. *American Political Science Review*, 89(4), pp. 882–897.

GASIOROWSKI, M.J., 1997. Political Regimes and Industrial Wages: A Cross-national Analysis. In MIDLARSKY, M.I. (ed.), *Inequality, Democracy, and Economic Development*, Cambridge University Press, pp. 244–267.

GATES, S., HEGRE, H., JONES, M.P., and STRAND, H., 2006. Institutional Inconsistency and Political Instability: Polity Duration, 1800–2000. *American Journal of Political Science*, 50(4), pp. 893–908.

GAUSE III, F.G., 2011. Why Middle East Studies Missed the Arab Spring: The Myth of Authoritarian Stability. *Foreign Affairs*, 90(4), pp. 81–90.

GEDDES, B., 2003. *Paradigms and Sand Castles: Theory Building and Research Design in Comparative Politics*. University of Michigan Press.

GEDDES, B., 2006. Stages of Development in Authoritarian Regimes. In TISMANEANU, V., HOWARD, M.M., and SIL, R. (eds.), *World Order after Leninism*. University of Washington Press, pp. 149–170.

GEDDES, B., 1999. What Do We Know about Democratization after Twenty Years? *Annual Review of Political Science*, 2(1), pp. 115–144.

GEDDES, B., 2005, September. Why Parties and Elections in Authoritarian Regimes? In *Annual Meeting of the American Political Science Association*, Washington D.C., pp. 456–471.

GEDDES, B., WRIGHT, J., and FRANTZ, E., 2014. Autocratic Breakdown and Regime Transitions: A New Data Set. *Perspectives on Politics*, 12(2), pp. 313–331.

GEDDES, B., WRIGHT, J., and FRANTZ, E., 2018. *How Dictatorships Work: Power, Personalization, and Collapse*. Cambridge University Press.

GEDDES, B. and ZALLER, J., 1989. Sources of Popular Support for Authoritarian Regimes. *American Journal of Political Science*, 33(2), pp. 319–347.

GEHLBACH, S. and KEEFER, P., 2011. Investment without Democracy: Ruling-party Institutionalization and Credible Commitment in Autocracies. *Journal of Comparative Economics*, 39(2), pp. 123–139.

GEHLBACH, S. and SIMPSER, A., 2015. Electoral Manipulation as Bureaucratic Control. *American Journal of Political Science*, 59(1), pp. 212–224.

GERSCHEWSKI, J., 2013. The Three Pillars of Stability: Legitimation, Repression, and Co-optation in Autocratic Regimes. *Democratization*, *20*(1), pp. 13–38.

GERSHENSON, D. and GROSSMAN, H.I., 2001. Co-option and Repression in the Soviet Union. *Economics & Politics*, *13*(1), pp. 31–47.

GIDDENS, A. (1990). *The Consequences of Modernity*. Stanford University Press.

GILL, G., 1984. Personality Cult, Political Culture and Party Structure. *Studies in Comparative Communism*, *17*(2), pp. 111–121.

GILLEY, B., 2010. Democratic Enclaves in Authoritarian Regimes. *Democratization*, *17*(3), pp. 389–415.

GILLEY, B., 2006. The Meaning and Measure of State Legitimacy: Results for 72 Countries. *European Journal of Political Research*, *45*(3), pp. 499–525.

GIMPELSON, V. and TREISMAN, D., 2002. Fiscal Games and Public Employment: A Theory with Evidence from Russia. *World Politics*, *54*(2), pp. 145–183.

GLAESER, E.L., PONZETTO, G.A., and SHLEIFER, A., 2007. Why Does Democracy Need Education? *Journal of Economic Growth*, *12*(2), pp. 77–99.

GLASSMAN, R.M., 1995. *The Middle Class and Democracy in Socio-historical Perspective* (Vol. 10). Brill.

GLASSMAN, R., 1997. *The New Middle Class and Democracy in Global Perspective*. Springer.

GLEDITSCH, K.S. and BEARDSLEY, K., 2004. Nosy Neighbors: Third-party Actors in Central American Conflicts. *Journal of Conflict Resolution*, *48*(3), pp. 379–402.

GLEDITSCH, K. and RUGGERI, A., 2010. Political Opportunity Structures, Democracy, and Civil war. *Journal of Peace Research*, *47*(3), pp. 299–310.

GLEDITSCH, K.S. and WARD, M.D., 2006. Diffusion and the International Context of Democratization. *International Organization*, *60*(04), pp. 911–933.

GLEDITSCH, N.P., HEGRE, H., and STRAND, H., 2009. Democracy and Civil War. In MIDLARSKY, M.I. (ed.), *Handbook of War Studies III: The Intrastate Dimension*. University of Michigan Press, pp. 155–192.

GLUCK, J. and BRANDT, M., 2015. Participatory and Inclusive Constitution Making. *United States Institute of Peace*, *105*, pp. 1–40.

GOETZ, A. and JENKINS, R., 2004. *Reinventing Accountability: Making Democracy Work for Human Development*. Springer.

GOLDFRANK, B. and ROWELL, N., 2012. Church, State, and Human Rights in Latin America. *Politics, Religion & Ideology*, *13*(1), pp. 25–51.

GOLDSMITH, A.A., 2004. Predatory versus Developmental Rule in Africa. *Democratization*, *11*(3), pp. 88–110.

GOLDSTEIN, R.J., 1978. *Political Repression in Modern America from 1870 to the Present*. GK Hall & Company.

GOLDSTONE, J.A., 2002. Population and Security: How Demographic Change Can Lead to Violent Conflict. *Journal of International Affairs*, *56*(1), pp. 3–21.

GOLDSTONE, J.A., 2001. Toward a Fourth Generation of Revolutionary Theory. *Annual Review of Political Science*, *4*(1), pp. 139–187.

GOLDSTONE, J.A., BATES, R.H., EPSTEIN, D.L., GURR, T.R., LUSTIK, M.B., MARSHALL, M.G., ULFELDER, J., and WOODWARD, M., 2010. A Global Model for Forecasting Political Instability. *American Journal of Political Science*, *54*(1), pp. 190–208.

GOODIN, R. and DRYZEK, J., 1980. Rational Participation: The Politics of Relative Power. *British Journal of Political Science*, *10*(03), pp. 273–292.

GRAUVOGEL, J. and von SOEST, C., 2013. Claims to Legitimacy Matter: Why Sanctions Fail to Instigate Democratization in

Authoritarian Regimes. *German Institute of Global and Area Studies*, (23).

GREENE, K.F., 2010. The Political Economy of Authoritarian Single-party Dominance. *Comparative Political Studies*, *43*(7), pp. 807–834.

GROSSMAN H. I. 1992 Foreign Aid and Insurrection. *Defense Economics 3*: 275–288.

GRZYMALA-BUSSE, A.M., 2002. Redeeming the Communist Past: The Regeneration of Communist Parties in East Central Europe. Cambridge University Press.

GUEORGUIEV, D.D., 2014. *Retrofitting Communism: Consultative Autocracy in China* (Doctoral dissertation, UC San Diego).

GUEVARA-MANN, C. 2016. Panamá: luces y sombras en torno a la institucionalidad Democrática. *Revista de ciencia política (Santiago)*, *36*(1), pp. 259–285.

GUMUSCU, S., 2013. The Emerging Predominant Party System in Turkey. *Government and Opposition, 48*(2), pp. 223–244.

GUNITSKY, S., 2014. From Shocks to Waves: Hegemonic Transitions and prove coro per concerto con Southbank Sinfonia-Democratization in the Twentieth Century. *International Organization, 68*(3), pp. 561–597.

GUPTA, S., DAVOODI, H. and ALONSO-TERME, R., 1998. *Does Corruption Affect Inequality and Poverty. Washington DC: IMF working paper*. WP/98/76.

GURR, T.R., 1974. Persistence and Change in Political Systems, 1800–1971. *American Political Science Review*, *68*(4), pp. 1482–1504.

GRZYMALA-BUSSE, A., 2008. Beyond Clientelism: Incumbent State Capture and State Formation. *Comparative Political Studies*, *41*(4–5), pp. 638–673.

HABERMAS, J., 1979. History and evolution. *Telos*, *1979*(39), pp. 5–44.

HACKER, J.S., 2006. *The Great Risk Shift: The Assault on American Jobs, Health Care, and Retirement and How You Can Fight Back*. New York: Oxford University Press.

HADENIUS, A., 1994. The Duration of Democracy: Institutional vs Socio-economic Factors. *Sage Modern Politics Series*, *36*, pp. 63–63.

HADENIUS, A. and TEORELL, J., 2006. *Authoritarian Regimes: Stability, Change, and Pathways to Democracy, 1972–2003*. Helen Kellogg Institute for International Studies, pp. 1–35.

HADENIUS, A. and TEORELL, J., 2005. Cultural and Economic Prerequisites of Democracy: Reassessing Recent Evidence. *Studies in Comparative International Development*, *39*(4), pp. 87–106.

HADENIUS, A. and TEORELL, J., 2007. Pathways from Authoritarianism. *Journal of Democracy*, *18*(1), pp. 143–157.

HAGGARD, S. and KAUFMAN, R.R., 2016. Democratization During the Third Wave. *Annual Review of Political Science*, *19*, pp. 125–144.

HAGGARD, S. and KAUFMAN, R.R., 2012. Inequality and Regime Change: Democratic Transitions and the Stability of Democratic Rule. *American Political Science Review*, *106*(3), pp. 495–516.

HAGGARD, S. and KAUFMAN, R.R., 1997. The Political Economy of Democratic Transitions. *Comparative Politics*, *29*(3), pp. 263–283.

HALE, H.E., 2011. Formal Constitutions in Informal Politics: Institutions and Democratization in Post-Soviet Eurasia. *World Politics*, *63*(4), pp. 581–617.

HALE, H.E., 2016. 25 Years After the USSR: What's Gone Wrong? *Journal of Democracy*, *27*(3), pp. 24–35.

HALL, M. R. (2000). *Sugar and Power in the Dominican Republic: Eisenhower, Kennedy, and the Trujillos* (No. 13). Greenwood Publishing Group.

HALPERIN, M., SIEGLE, J., and WEINSTEIN, M., 2009. *The Democracy Advantage: How Democracies Promote Prosperity and Peace*. Routledge.

HAMILTON, A., MADISON, J., and JAY, J., 2003. In BALL, T. (ed.), *The Federalist, with the Letters of 'Brutus'.* Cambridge University Press.

HARMER, T., 2011. *Allende's Chile and the Inter-American Cold War.* University of North Carolina Press.

HASSAN, S., 2014. Political Non-governmental Organizations: Ideals and Realities. In *Democracy in Malaysia.* Routledge, pp. 212–229.

HATTORI, T. and FUNATSU, T., 2003. The Emergence of the Asian Middle Classes and Their Characteristics. *The Developing Economies*, 41(2), pp. 140–160.

HAWES, GARY. 1995. Marcos, His Cronies, and the Philippines' Failure to Develop. In JOHN RAVENHILL (ed.), *Singapore, Indonesia, Malaysia, the Philippines and Thailand.* Edward Elgar Publishing.

HAWKINS, K.A., 2010. Who Mobilizes? Participatory Democracy in Chávez's Bolivarian Revolution. *Latin American Politics and Society*, 52(3), pp. 31–66.

HAY, C., 2002. *Political Analysis: A Critical Introduction.* Macmillan International Higher Education.

HE, B. and THØGERSEN, S., 2010. Giving the People a Voice? Experiments with Consultative Authoritarian Institutions in China. *Journal of Contemporary China*, 19(66), pp. 675–692.

HELD, D., 2006. *Models of Democracy.* Polity.

HELD, D., 1999. The Transformation of Political Community: Rethinking Democracy in the Context of Globalization. In SHAPIRO, I., HACKER-CORDÓN, C., and HARDIN, R. (eds.), *Democracy's Edges*, Cambridge University Press, pp. 84–111.

HENDERSON, C.W., 1991. Conditions Affecting the Use of Political Repression. *Journal of Conflict Resolution*, 35(1), pp. 120–142.

HERB, M., 1999. *All in the Family: Absolutism, Revolution, and Democracy in Middle Eastern Monarchies.* SUNY Press.

HERB, M., 2004. Princes and Parliaments in the Arab world. *The Middle East Journal*, 58(3), pp. 367–384.

HERMANN, M.G. and KEGLEY JR, C.W., 1998. The US Use of Military Intervention to Promote Democracy: Evaluating the Record. *International Interactions*, 24(2), pp. 91–114.

HIBBING, J.R. and THEISS-MORSE, E., 2002. *Stealth Democracy: Americans' Beliefs about How Government Should Work.* Cambridge University Press.

HICKEN, A., 2001. Parties, Policy and Patronage: Governance and Growth in Thailand. In CAMPOS, J.E.L. (ed.), *Corruption: The Boom and Bust of East Asia.* Ateneo University Press, pp. 163–182.

HICKEN, A., 2011. Clientelism. *Annual Review of Political Science*, 14, pp. 289–310.

HICKEN, A. and SIMMONS, J.W., 2008. The Personal Vote and the Efficacy of Education Spending. *American Journal of Political Science*, 52(1), pp. 109–124.

HIGLEY, J. and GUNTHER, R. (eds.), 1992. *Elites and Democratic Consolidation in Latin America and Southern Europe.* Cambridge University Press.

HILL, D.W. and JONES, Z.M., 2014. An Empirical Evaluation of Explanations for State Repression. *American Political Science Review*, 108(3), pp. 661–687.

HILL, F. and GADDY, C., 2013. Putin Personality Disorder. *The Brookings Institution.* https://www.brookings.edu/opinions/putin-personality-disorder/ Accessed 7 June 2019.

HOFFMAN, A.L., 2005. Political Parties, Electoral Systems and Democracy: A Cross-national Analysis. *European Journal of Political Research*, 44(2), pp. 231–242.

HOFFMAN, B., 2006. *Inside Terrorism.* Columbia University Press.

HOROWITZ, D.L., 1993. Democracy in Divided Societies. *Journal of Democracy*, 4(4), pp. 18–38.

HOULE, C., 2009. Inequality and Democracy: Why Inequality Harms Consolidation but Does Not Affect Democratization. *World Politics*, 61(4), pp. 589–622.

HOULE, C., 2016. Why Class Inequality Breeds Coups but Not Civil Wars. *Journal of Peace Research*, 53(5), pp. 680–695.

HOULE, C., KAYSER, M.A., and XIANG, J., 2016. Diffusion or Confusion? Clustered Shocks and the Conditional Diffusion of Democracy. *International Organization*, 70(4), pp. 687–726.

HOWARD, M.M., 2002. The Weakness of Post-communist Civil Society. *Journal of Democracy*, 13(1), pp. 157–169.

HOWARD, M.M. and ROESSLER, P.G., 2006. Liberalizing Electoral Outcomes in Competitive Authoritarian Regimes. *American Journal of Political Science*, 50(2), pp. 365–381.

HUANG, J., VAN DEN BRINK, H.M., and GROOT, W., 2009. A Meta-analysis of the Effect of Education on Social Capital. *Economics of Education Review*, 28(4), pp. 454–464.

HUBER, E., RUESCHEMEYER, D. and STEPHENS, J.D., 1993. The Impact of Economic Development on Democracy. *Journal of Economic Perspectives*, 7(3), pp. 71–86.

HUDSON, M.C., 1977. Arab Politics: The Search for Legitimacy. Yale University Press.

HUNTINGTON, S.P., 1996. Democracy for the Long Haul. *Journal of Democracy*, 7(2), pp. 3–13.

HUNTINGTON, S.P., 1991. Democracy's Third Wave. *Journal of Democracy*, 2(2), pp. 12–34.

HUNTINGTON, S.P. 2006. *Political Order in Changing Societies*. Yale University Press.

HUNTINGTON, S.P., 1963. Power, Expertise and the Military Profession. *Daedalus*, 92(4), pp. 785–807.

HUNTINGTON, S.P., 1995. I. Reforming Civil-Military Relations. *Journal of Democracy*, 6(4), pp. 9–17.

HUNTINGTON, S.P. and MOORE, C.H., 1970. *Authoritarian Politics in Modern Society: The Dynamics of Established One-party Systems*. Basic Books (AZ).

HYDE, S.D., 2011. *The Pseudo-Democrat's Dilemma: Why Election Observation Became an International Norm*. Cornell University Press.

IGNAZI, P., 1992. The Silent Counter-revolution: Hypotheses on the Emergence of Extreme Right-wing Parties in Europe. *European Journal of Political Research*, 22(1), pp. 3–34.

INGLEHART, R., 1988. The Renaissance of Political Culture. *American Political Science Review*, 82(4), pp. 1203–1230.

INGLEHART, R., 1971. The Silent Revolution in Europe: Intergenerational Change in Post-Industrial Societies. *American Political Science Review*, 65(4), pp. 991–1017.

INGLEHART, R., 1990. *Values, Ideology and Cognitive Mobilization in New Social Movements*. Taylor & Francis, pp. 43–66.

INGLEHART, R., NORRIS, P., and RONALD, I., 2003. *Rising Tide: Gender Equality and Cultural Change Around the World*. Cambridge University Press.

INGLEHART, R. and NORRIS, P., 2016. Trump, Brexit, and the Rise of Populism: Economic Have-nots and Cultural Backlash.

INGLEHART, R. and NORRIS, P., 2017. Trump and the Populist Authoritarian Parties: The Silent Revolution in Reverse. *Perspectives on Politics*, 15(2), pp. 443–454.

INGLEHART, R. and WELZEL, C., 2009. How Development Leads to Democracy: What We Know about Modernization. *Foreign Affairs*, 88(2), pp. 33–48.

INGLEHART, R. and WELZEL, C., 2005. *Modernization, Cultural Change, and Democracy: The Human Development Sequence*. Cambridge University Press.

IPPERCIEL, D., 2007. Constitutional Democracy and Civic Nationalism. *Nations and Nationalism*, 13(3), pp. 395–416.

IVARSFLATEN, E., 2005. The Vulnerable Populist Right Parties: No Economic Realignment Fuelling Their Electoral success. *European Journal of Political Research*, *44*(3), pp. 465–492.

JACKMAN, R.W. and MILLER, R.A., 1996. A Renaissance of Political Culture? *American Journal of Political Science*, *40*(3), pp. 632–659.

JAMAL, A.A., 2009. *Barriers to Democracy: The Other Side of Social Capital in Palestine and the Arab World*. Princeton University Press.

JAMAL, A. and NOORUDDIN, I., 2010. The Democratic Utility of Trust: A Cross-national Analysis. *The Journal of Politics*, *72*(1), pp. 45–59.

JENNE, E., 2007. *Ethnic Bargaining: The Paradox of Minority Empowerment*. Cornell University Press.

JETTER, M., AGUDELO, A.M., and HASSAN, A.R., 2015. The Effect of Democracy on Corruption: Income is Key. *World Development*, *74*, pp. 286–304.

JOHNSON, J. and THYNE, C.L., 2018. Squeaky Wheels and Troop Loyalty: How Domestic Protests Influence Coups d'État, 1951–2005. *Journal of Conflict Resolution*, *62*(3), pp. 597–625.

JOHNSON, T.H., SLATER, R.O., and MCGOWAN, P., 1983. Explaining African Military Coups d'État, 1960–1982. *American Political Science Review*, *78*(3), pp. 622–640.

KAEMPFER, W.H., LOWENBERG, A.D., and MERTENS, W., 2004. International Economic Sanctions against a Dictator. *Economics & Politics*, *16*(1), pp. 29–51.

KAGAN, R., 2016. This is How Fascism Comes to America. *The Washington Post*, 18.

KALTWASSER, C.R., 2012. The Ambivalence of Populism: Threat and Corrective for Democracy. *Democratization*, *19*(2), pp. 184–208.

KALTWASSER, C.R. and TAGGART, P., 2016. Dealing with Populists in Government: A Framework for Analysis. *Democratization*, *23*(2), pp. 201–220.

KALYVAS, S.N., 2006. *The Logic of Violence in Civil War*. Cambridge University Press.

KANE, S., HILTERMANN, J.R., and ALKADIRI, R., 2012. Iraq's Federalism Quandary. *The National Interest*, *118*, pp. 20–30.

KAPSTEIN, E.B. and CONVERSE, N., 2008. *The Fate of Young Democracies*. Cambridge University Press.

KARAM, A. and LOVENDUSKI, J., 2005. Women in Parliament: Making a Difference. In BALLINGTON, J. and KARAM, A. (eds.), *Women in Parliament: Beyond Numbers*. IDEA International Publication, pp. 187–210.

KARATNYCKY, A., 2002. Muslim Countries and the Democracy Gap. *Journal of Democracy*, *13*(1), pp. 99–112.

KARL, T.L., 1990. Dilemmas of Democratization in Latin America. *Comparative Politics*, *23*(1), pp. 1–21.

KARL, T.L., 2000. Economic Inequality and Democratic Instability. *Journal of Democracy*, *11*(1), pp. 149–156.

KAZIN, M., 1995. The Agony and Romance of the American Left. *The American Historical Review*, *100*(5): pp. 1488–1512.

KAZIN, M., 2016. Trump and American Populism: Old Whine, New Bottles. *Foreign Aff.*, *95*, p.17.

KEATING, M. (ed.), 2013. *Crisis of Social Democracy in Europe*. Edinburgh University Press.

KEEFER, P., 2007. Clientelism, Credibility, and the Policy Choices of Young Democracies. *American Journal of Political Science*, *51*(4), pp. 804–821.

KEEFER, P. and KHEMANI, S. 2004. Democracy, Public Expenditures and the Poor. World Bank, Policy Research Working Paper, 3164, pp. 1–45.

KEENAN, P.J., 2009. Curse or Cure? China's Investments in Africa and Their Effect on

Human Rights. *Berkeley J. Int'l Law*, *27*, pp. 84–126.

KELLEY, J., 2008. Assessing the Complex Evolution of Norms: The Rise of International Election Monitoring. *International Organization*, *62*(2), pp. 221–255.

KELLEY, J., 2004. International Actors on the Domestic Scene: Membership Conditionality and Socialization by International Institutions. *International Organization*, *58*(3), pp. 425–457.

KENDALL-TAYLOR, A., 2011. Instability and Oil: How Political Time Horizons Affect Oil Revenue Management. *Studies in Comparative International Development*, *46*(3), p. 321.

KENDALL-TAYLOR, A., 2012. Purchasing Power: Oil, Elections and Regime Durability in Azerbaijan and Kazakhstan. *Europe–Asia Studies*, *64*(4), pp. 737–760.

KENDALL-TAYLOR, A. and FRANTZ, E., 2014. How Autocracies Fall. *The Washington Quarterly*, *37*(1), pp. 35–47.

KENDALL-TAYLOR, A., FRANTZ, E., and WRIGHT, J., 2017. The Global Rise of Personalized Politics: It's Not Just Dictators Anymore. *The Washington Quarterly*, *40*(1), pp. 7–19.

KENDALL-TAYLOR, A. and FRANTZ, E., 2015. How Democratic Institutions Are Making Dictatorships More Durable. *Bloomberg View,* p. 2015. accessed 7 September 2018.

KENDALL-TAYLOR, A., FRANTZ, E., and WRIGHT, J., 2016. The New Dictators. *Foreign Affairs*. https://www.foreignaffairs.com/articles/2016-09-26/new-dictators. Accessed 7 June 2019.

KENDALL-TAYLOR, A. and FRANTZ, E., 2016. When Dictators Die. *Journal of Democracy*, *27*(4), pp. 159–171.

KENDALL-TAYLOR, A. and SHULLMAN, D., 2 October 2018. How Russia and China Undermine Democracy: Can the West Counter the Threat?, *Foreign Affairs*. https://www.foreignaffairs.com/articles/china/2018-10-02/how-russia-and-china-undermine-democracy. Accessed 7 June 2019.

KENNEDY, R., 2010. The Contradiction of Modernization: A Conditional Model of Endogenous Democratization. *The Journal of Politics*, *72*(3), pp. 785–798.

KENTISH, B., 7 May 2017. Nearly Half of Young French Voters Backed Marine Le Pen, Projections Suggest. *The Independent*. http://www.independent.co.uk/news/nearly-half-young-french-voters-marine-le-pen-emmanuel-macron-french-election-2017-a7723291.html

KIERNAN, B., 2004. *How Pol Pot Came to Power: Colonialism, Nationalism, and Communism in Cambodia, 1930–1975.* Yale University Press.

KIM, N.K., 2016. Revisiting Economic Shocks and Coups. *Journal of Conflict Resolution*, *60*(1), pp. 3–31.

KIM, S.S. (ed.), 2001. *The North Korean System in the Post-Cold War Era.* Macmillan.

KIRSHNER, J., 1997. The Microfoundations of Economic Sanctions. *Security Studies*, *6*(3), pp. 32–64.

KITSCHELT, H., 2000. Linkages between Citizens and Politicians in Democratic Polities. *Comparative Political Studies*, *33*(6-7), pp. 845–879.

KITSCHELT, H., HAWKINS, K.A., LUNA, J.P., ROSAS, G., and ZECHMEISTER, E.J., 2010. *Latin American Party Systems.* Cambridge University Press.

KITSCHELT, H. and WILKINSON, S.I. (eds.), 2007. *Patrons, Clients and Policies: Patterns of Democratic Accountability and Political Competition.* Cambridge University Press.

KLAAS, B., 2018. *The Despot's Accomplice: How the West is Aiding and Abetting the Decline of Democracy.* Oxford University Press.

KNACK, S., 2004. Does Foreign Aid Promote Democracy? *International Studies Quarterly*, *48*(1), pp. 251–266.

KNICKMEYER, E., 2011. The Arab World's Youth Army. *Foreign Policy*, *27*, p.170.

KNUTSEN, C.H., 2012. Democracy and Economic Growth: A Survey of Arguments and Results. *International Area Studies Review*, *15*(4), pp. 393–415.

KNUTSEN, C.H. and NYGÅRD, H.M., 2015. Institutional Characteristics and Regime Survival: Why Are Semi-Democracies Less Durable Than Autocracies and Democracies? *American Journal of Political Science*, *59*(3), pp. 656–670.

KOESEL, K.J. and BUNCE, V.J., 2013. Diffusion-proofing: Russian and Chinese Responses to Waves of Popular Mobilizations against Authoritarian Rulers. *Perspectives on Politics*, *11*(3), pp. 753–768.

KORNAI, J., 2015. Hungary's U-turn: Retreating from Democracy. *Journal of Democracy*, *26*(3), pp. 34–48.

KRAMERJAN, A., 16 January 16, 2012. Western Monitors Criticize Election in Kazakhstan. *New York Times*. https://www.nytimes.com/2012/01/17/world/asia/observers-criticize-kazakhstans-election.html Accessed 7 June 2019.

KRASTEV, I., 2011. The Age of Populism: Reflections on the Self-enmity of Democracy. *European View*, *10*(1), pp. 11–16.

KRASTEV, I., 2018. Eastern Europe's Illiberal Revolution: The Long Road to Democratic Decline. *Foreign Affairs*, *97*(3), pp. 49–56.

KRICHELI, R., LIVNE, Y., and MAGALONI, B., 2011. Taking to the Streets: Theory and Evidence on Protests under Authoritarianism.

KRIESI, H., 2014. The Populist Challenge. *West European Politics*, *37*(2), pp. 361–378.

KUDAMATSU, M., 2012. Has Democratization Reduced Infant Mortality in Sub-Saharan Africa? Evidence from Micro Data. *Journal of the European Economic Association*, *10*(6), pp. 1294–1317.

KUDAMATSU, T.B.M., 2008. Making Autocracy Work. *Institutions and Economic Performance*, pp. 452–510. HELPMAN, E. (ed.), 2009. Harvard University Press.

KUMALO, L. 26 May 2015. Why Women Should Have a Greater Role in Peacebuilding. *World Economic Forum* https://www.weforum.org/agenda/2015/05/why-women-should-have-a-greater-role-in-peacebuilding/ Accessed 12 February 2019.

KURAN, T., 1991. Now Out of Never: The Element of Surprise in the East European Revolution of 1989. *World Politics*, *44*(1), pp. 7–48.

KURLANTZICK, J., 2007. *Charm Offensive: How China's Soft Power Is Transforming the World.* Yale University Press.

KURLANTZICK, J. and LINK, P., 2009. China: Resilient, Sophisticated Authoritarianism. In Freedom House, *Undermining Democracy: 21st Century Authoritarians*, Freedom House, pp. 13–28.

KURRILD-KLITGAARD, P., JUSTESEN, M.K., and KLEMMENSEN, R., 2006. The Political Economy of Freedom, Democracy and Transnational Terrorism. *Public Choice*, *128*(1–2), pp. 289–315.

KUZIO, T., 2006. Civil Society, Youth and Societal Mobilization in Democratic Revolutions. *Communist and Post-Communist Studies*, *39*(3), pp. 365–386.

KYMLICKA, W., 1998. Is Federalism a Viable Alternative to Secession? In In P. LEHNING (ed.), *Theories of Secession.* Routledge, pp. 111–150.

LACLAU, E., 1977. *Ideology and Politics in Marxist Theory.* Verso.

LAGERKVIST, J., 2009. Chinese Eyes on Africa: Authoritarian Flexibility versus Democratic Governance. *Journal of Contemporary African Studies*, *27*(2), pp. 119–134.

LAI, B. and REITER, D., 2000. Democracy, Political Similarity, and International Alliances, 1816–1992. *Journal of Conflict Resolution*, *44*(2), pp. 203–227.

LAKE, D.A., 2002. Rational Extremism: Understanding Terrorism in the Twenty-first Century. *Dialogue IO*, *1*(1), pp. 15–28.

LANDAU, D., 2012. Constitution-Making Gone Wrong. *Alabama Law Review*, 64(5), pp. 923–980.

LANGSTON, J.K., 2017. *Democratization and Authoritarian Party Survival: Mexico's PRI.* Oxford University Press.

LA PORTA, R., LOPEZ-DE-SILANES, F., SHLEIFER, A., and VISHNY, R., 1999. The Quality of Government. *The Journal of Law, Economics, and Organization*, 15(1), pp. 222–279.

Le BILLON, P., 2015. Oil, Secession and the Future of Iraqi Federalism. *Middle East Policy*, 22(1), pp. 68–76.

LeDUC, L., 1985. Partisan Change and Dealignment in Canada, Great Britain, and the United States. *Comparative Politics*, 17(4), pp. 379–398.

LEE, C.K. and STRANG, D., 2006. The International Diffusion of Public-sector Downsizing: Network Emulation and Theory-driven Learning. *International Organization*, 60(4), pp. 883–909.

LEKTZIAN, D. and SOUVA, M., 2007. An Institutional Theory of Sanctions Onset and Success. *Journal of Conflict Resolution*, 51(6), pp. 848–871.

LEMARCHAND, R. and NIWESE, M., 2007. *Mass Murder, the Politics of Memory and Post-genocide Reconstruction: The Cases of Rwanda and Burundi.* United Nations University Press.

LESLIE, W.J., 1987. *The World Bank and Structural Transformation in Developing Countries: The Case of Zaire.* Lynne-Rienner Press.

LEVI, M., SACKS, A. and TYLER, T., 2009. Conceptualizing Legitimacy, Measuring Legitimating Beliefs. *American Behavioral Scientist*, 53(3), pp. 354–375.

LEVITSKY, S. and CAMERON, M.A., 2003. Democracy without Parties? Political Parties and Regime Change in Fujimori's Peru. *Latin American Politics and Society*, 45(3), pp. 1–33.

LEVITSKY, S. and LOXTON, J., 2013. Populism and Competitive Authoritarianism in the Andes. *Democratization*, 20(1), pp. 107–136.

LEVITSKY, S.R. and WAY, L.A., 2012. Beyond Patronage: Violent Struggle, Ruling Party Cohesion, and Authoritarian Durability. *Perspectives on Politics*, 10(4), pp. 869–889.

LEVITSKY, S. and WAY, L.A., 2010. *Competitive Authoritarianism: Hybrid Regimes after the Cold War.* Cambridge University Press.

LEVITSKY, S. and WAY, L., 2013. The Durability of Revolutionary Regimes. *Journal of Democracy*, 24(3), pp. 5–17.

LEVITSKY, S. and WAY, L., 2005. International Linkage and Democratization. *Journal of Democracy*, 16(3), pp. 20–34.

LEVITSKY, S. and WAY, L.A., 2006. Linkage Versus Leverage. Rethinking the International Dimension of Regime Change. *Comparative Politics*, 38(4): pp. 379–400.

LEVITSKY, S. and WAY, L., 2015. The Myth of Democratic Recession. *Journal of Democracy*, 26(1), pp. 45–58.

LEVITSKY, S. and WAY, L., 2002. The Rise of Competitive Authoritarianism. *Journal of Democracy*, 13(2), pp. 51–65.

LEVITSKY, S. and ZIBLATT, D., 2018. *How Democracies Die.* Crown.

LEVY, J.S., 1988. Domestic Politics and War. *The Journal of Interdisciplinary History*, 18(4), pp. 653–673.

LI, Q., 2005. Does Democracy Promote or Reduce Transnational Terrorist Incidents? *Journal of Conflict Resolution*, 49(2), pp. 278–297.

LICHBACH, M.I., 1987. Deterrence or Escalation? The Puzzle of Aggregate Studies of Repression and Dissent. *Journal of Conflict Resolution*, 31(2), pp. 266–297.

LIJPHART, A., 2004. Constitutional Design for Divided Societies. *Journal of Democracy*, 15(2), pp. 96–109.

LIJPHART, A., 1977. *Democracy in Plural societies: A Comparative Exploration.* Yale University Press.

LIJPHART, A., 1985. Non-majoritarian Democracy: A Comparison of Federal and Consociational Theories. *Publius: The Journal of Federalism, 15*(2), pp. 3–15.

LIJPHART, A., 1998. South African Democracy: Majoritarian or Consociational? *Democratization, 5*(4), pp. 144–150.

LIJPHART, A. and GROFMAN, B., 1984. *Choosing an Electoral System: Issues and Alternatives.* Praeger.

LINDBERG, S.I., 2006. *Democracy and Elections in Africa.* JHU Press.

LINZ, J.J., 1978. Non-competitive Elections in Europe. In *Elections Without Choice.* Palgrave Macmillan UK, pp. 36–65.

LINZ, J.J., 1990. The Perils of Presidentialism. *Journal of Democracy, 1*(1), pp. 51–69.

LINZ, J.J., 2000. *Totalitarian and Authoritarian Regimes.* Lynne Rienner Publishers.

LINZ, J.J. and STEPAN, A., 1996. *Problems of Democratic Transition and Consolidation: Southern Europe, South America, and Postcommunist Europe.* JHU Press.

LINZ, J.J. and VALENZUELA, A. (eds.), 1994. *The Failure of Presidential Democracy* (Vol. 1). JHU Press.

LIPSET, S.M., 1959. Democracy and Working-class Authoritarianism. *American Sociological Review, 24*(4), pp. 482–501.

LIPSET, S.M., 2000. The Indispensability of Political Parties. *Journal of Democracy, 11*(1), pp. 48–55.

LIPSET, S.M., 1960. *Political Man: The Social Basis of Modern Politics.* Doubleday.

LIPSET, S.M. and LAKIN, J.M., 2004. *The Democratic Century* (Vol. 9). University of Oklahoma Press.

LIPSET, S.M. and ROKKAN, S. (eds.), 1967. *Party Systems and Voter Alignments: Cross-national Perspectives* (Vol. 7). Free Press.

LONDEGRAN, J. and POOLE, K., 1991. Leadership Turnover and Unconstitutional rule. *Unpublished paper.*

LOTAN, G., GRAEFF, E., ANANNY, M., GAFFNEY, D., and PEARCE, I., 2011. The Arab Spring|the Revolutions Were Tweeted: Information Flows during the 2011 Tunisian and Egyptian Revolutions. *International Journal of Communication, 5*, p. 31.

LOXTON, J., 2015. Authoritarian Successor Parties. *Journal of Democracy, 26*(3), pp. 157–170.

LOXTON, J. and MAINWARING, S. (eds.), 2018. *Life after Dictatorship: Authoritarian Successor Parties Worldwide.* Cambridge University Press.

LUBBERS, M., 2001. *Exclusionistic Electorates: Extreme Right-wing Voting in Western Europe* (Doctoral dissertation, Radboud University Nijmegen).

LUBBERS, M., GIJSBERTS, M. and SCHEEPERS, P., 2002. Extreme Right-wing Voting in Western Europe. *European Journal of Political Research, 41*(3), pp. 345–378.

LUCE, E., 2017. *The Retreat of Western Liberalism.* Atlantic Monthly Press.

LUJALA, P., GLEDITSCH, N.P., and GILMORE, E., 2005. A Diamond Curse? Civil War and a Lootable Resource. *Journal of Conflict Resolution, 49*(4), pp. 538–562.

LUNDAHL, M., 1997. Inside the Predatory State. *Political Economy, 24*(1), pp. 31–50.

LUO, R., ZHANG, L., HUANG, J. and ROZELLE, S., 2007. Elections, Fiscal Reform and Public Goods Provision in Rural China. *Journal of Comparative Economics, 35*(3), pp. 583–611.

LUPU, N., 2010. Who Votes for 'Chavismo'? Class Voting in Hugo Chávez's Venezuela. *Latin American Research Review,* pp. 7–32.

LUST, E. and WALDNER, D., 2015. Unwelcome Change: Understanding, Evaluating, and Extending Theories of Democratic

Backsliding. *US Agency for International Development, 11.*

LUST, E., 2009. Competitive Clientelism in the Middle East. *Journal of Democracy, 20*(3), pp. 122–135.

LUST-OKAR, E., 2004. Divided They Rule: The Management and Manipulation of Political Opposition. *Comparative Politics*, pp. 159–179.

LUST-OKAR, E., 2006. Elections under Authoritarianism: Preliminary Lessons from Jordan. *Democratization, 13*(3), pp. 456–471.

MACPHERSON, C.B., 1977. *The Life and Times of Liberal Democracy.* Opus.

MACPHERSON, C.B., 1992. *The Real World of Democracy.* House of Anansi.

MAGALONI, B., 2008. Credible Power-sharing and the Longevity of Authoritarian Rule. *Comparative Political Studies, 41*(4–5), pp. 715–741.

MAGALONI, B., 2010. The Game of Electoral Fraud and the Ousting of Authoritarian Rule. *American Journal of Political Science, 54*(3), pp. 751–765.

MAGALONI, B., 2006. *Voting for Autocracy: Hegemonic Party Survival and Its Demise in Mexico.* Cambridge University Press.

MAGALONI, B. and KRICHELI, R., 2010. Political Order and One-party Rule. *Annual Review of Political Science, 13*, pp. 123–143.

MAGALONI, B. and SANCHEZ, A., 2006. An Authoritarian Enclave? The Supreme Court in Mexico's Emerging Democracy. In *Annual Meeting of the American Political Science Association*, Philadelphia, PA, pp. 1–39.

MAINWARING, S., 2012. From Representative Democracy to Participatory Competitive Authoritarianism: Hugo Chávez and Venezuelan Politics. *Perspectives on Politics, 10*(4), pp. 955–967.

MAINWARING, S., 1998. Party Systems in the Third Wave. *Journal of Democracy, 9*(3), pp. 67–81.

MAIR, P., 1984. Party Politics in Contemporary Europe: A Challenge to Party? *West European Politics, 7*(4), pp. 170–184.

MANDER, B. September 16, 2012. Venezuela: Up in Smoke. *Financial Times* https://www.ft.com/content/e0cdedba-fe4e-11e1-8228-00144feabdc0. Accessed 23 November 2018.

MANSBACH, R.W. and RHODES, E.J., 2008. *Global Politics in a Changing World: A Reader.* Cengage Learning.

MANSFIELD, E.D. and PEVEHOUSE, J.C., 2006. Democratization and International Organizations. *International Organization, 60*(1), pp. 137–167.

MANSFIELD, E.D. and SNYDER, J., 1995. Democratization and the Danger of War. *International Security, 20*(1), pp. 5–38.

MANSFIELD, E.D. and SNYDER, J., 2007. *Electing to Fight: Why Emerging Democracies Go to War.* MIT Press.

MANSFIELD, E.D. and SNYDER, J., 2005. Prone to Violence: The Paradox of the Democratic Peace. *The National Interest, 82*, pp. 39–45.

MAOZ, Z. and RUSSETT, B., 1993. Normative and structural causes of Democratic Peace, 1946–1986. *American Political Science Review, 87*(3), pp. 624–638.

MARCH, J.G. and OLSEN, J.P., 1995. *Democratic Governance.* Free Press.

MARIEN, S., HOOGHE, M., and QUINTELIER, E., 2010. Inequalities in Non-institutionalised Forms of Political Participation: A Multi-level Analysis of 25 Countries. *Political Studies, 58*(1), pp. 187–213.

MARINOV, N., 2005. Do Economic Sanctions Destabilize Country Leaders? *American Journal of Political Science, 49*(3), pp. 564–576.

MARINOV, N. and GOEMANS, H., 2014. Coups and Democracy. *British Journal of Political Science, 44*(4), pp. 799–825.

MARKOFF, J., 1990. Economic Crisis and Regime Change in Brazil: The 1960s and the 1980s. *Comparative Politics*, *22*(4), pp. 421–444.

MARTIN, J., 1911. An Attempt to Define Socialism. *The American Economic Review*, *1*(2), pp. 347–354.

MAURO, P., 1997. *Why Worry about Corruption?* (Vol. 6). International Monetary Fund.

MAYS, K. and GROSHEK, J., 2017. A Time-series, Multinational Analysis of Democratic Forecasts and Emerging Media Diffusion, 1994–2014. *International Journal of Communication*, *11*, pp. 429–451.

MCADAM, D., TARROW, S., and TILLY, C., 2003. Dynamics of Contention. *Social Movement Studies*, *2*(1), pp. 99–102.

MCCANN, J.A. and DOMINGUEZ, J.I., 1998. Mexicans React to Electoral Fraud and Political Corruption: An Assessment of Public Opinion and Voting Behavior. *Electoral studies*, *17*(4), pp. 483–503.

MCCLELLAND, D.C., 1961. *The Achieving Society*. Van Nostrand.

MCCOY, J. and HARTLYN, J., 2009. The Relative Powerlessness of Elections in Latin America. Democratization by Elections: A New Mode of Transition In S. LINDBERG (ed.), *Democratization by Elections: A New Mode of Transition*. The Johns Hopkins University Press, pp. 47–76.

MCEVOY, J. and O'LEARY, B. (eds.), 2013. *Power Sharing in Deeply Divided Places*. University of Pennsylvania Press.

MCFAUL, M., 2007. Are New Democracies War-prone? *Journal of Democracy*, *18*(2), pp. 160–167.

MCFAUL, M., 2002. The Fourth Wave of Democracy and Dictatorship: Noncooperative Transitions in the Post-communist World. *World Politics, 54*(2), pp. 212–244.

MCFAUL, M. and SPECTOR, R.A., 2010. External Sources and Consequences of Russia's 'Sovereign Democracy'. In BURNELL, P. and YOUNGS, R. (eds.), New Challenges to Democratization. Routledge, pp. 116–133.

MCFAUL, M. and STONER-WEISS, K., 2008. The Myth of the Authoritarian Model: How Putin's Crackdown Holds Russia Back. *Foreign Aff.*, *87*, p. 68.

MCGARRY, A., 2008. Ethnic Group Identity and the Roma Social Movement: Transnational Organizing Structures of Representation. *Nationalities Papers*, *36*(3), pp. 449–470.

MCGREAL, C., 2001. White Farmers Denounce ANC 'Land Grab:' South Africa is Accused of Following Zimbabwe's Example after a Farm is Returned to its Original Owners. *The Guardian*. https://www.theguardian.com/world/2001/mar/17/zimbabwe.chrismcgreal Accessed 7 June 2019.

MCLEOD, R.H., 2005. The Struggle to Regain Effective Government under Democracy in Indonesia. *Bulletin of Indonesian Economic Studies*, *41*(3), pp. 367–386.

MEAD, W.R., 2018. The Big Shift: How American Democracy Fails Its Way to Success. *Foreign Affairs*, *97* (3), pp. 10.

MEARSHEIMER, J.J., 2005. Hans Morgenthau and the Iraq War: Realism versus Neo-Conservatism, *open-Democracy*, 19 May.

MEERNIK, J., 1996. United States Military Intervention and the Promotion of Democracy. *Journal of Peace Research*, *33*(4), pp. 391–402.

MERKEL, W., 2004. Embedded and Defective Democracies. *Democratization*, *11*(5), pp. 33–58.

MIDLARSKY, M.I. and ROBERTS, K., 1985. Class, State, and Revolution in Central America: Nicaragua and El Salvador Compared. *Journal of Conflict Resolution*, *29*(2), pp. 163–193.

MIGDAL, J.S., 1988. *Strong Societies and Weak States: State–Society Relations and State Capabilities in the Third World*. Princeton University Press.

MILLER, M.K., 2012. Economic Development, Violent Leader Removal, and

Democratization. *American Journal of Political Science, 56*(4), pp. 1002–1020.

MILLS, C.W. and WOLFE, A., 2000. *The Power Elite* (Vol. 20). Oxford University Press.

MIN, B., 2008, April. Democracy and Light: Electoral Accountability and the Provision of Public Goods. In *Annual Meeting of the Midwest Political Science Association*, Chicago, IL.

MINKENBERG, M. and PERRINEAU, P., 2007. The Radical Right in the European Elections 2004. *International Political Science Review, 28*(1), pp. 29–55.

MITCHELL, S.M., RING, J.J., and SPELLMAN, M.K., 2013. Domestic Legal Traditions and States' Human Rights Practices. *Journal of Peace Research, 50*(2), pp. 189–202.

MODISE, L.J., 2017. The Notion of Participatory Democracy in Relation to Local Ward Committees: The Distribution of Power. *In die Skriflig, 51*(1), pp. 1–8.

MOHTADI, H. and ROE, T.L., 2003. Democracy, Rent Seeking, Public Spending and Growth. *Journal of Public Economics, 87* (3-4), pp. 445–466.

MOLLER, H. 1968. Youth as a Force in the Modern World. *Comparative Studies in Society and History, 10*(3): pp. 237–260.

MONTALVO, J.G. and REYNAL-QUEROL, M., 2005. Ethnic Polarization, Potential Conflict, and Civil Wars. *American Economic Review, 95*(3), pp. 796–816.

MONTERO, A.P., 2010. No Country for Leftists? Clientelist Continuity and the 2006 Vote in the Brazilian Northeast. *Journal of Politics in Latin America, 2*(2), pp. 113–153.

MONTINOLA, G.R. and JACKMAN, R.W., 2002. Sources of Corruption: A Cross-country Study. *British Journal of Political Science, 32*(1), pp. 147–170.

MOON, B.E., 1991. *The Political Economy of Basic Human Needs*. Cornell University Press.

MOORE, M., 1998. Death without taxes: Democracy, state capacity, and Aid Dependence in the Fourth World. *The Democratic Developmental State: Politics and Institutional Design, 86.*

MORRISON, K.M., 2009. Oil, Non-tax Revenue, and the Redistributional Foundations of Regime Stability. *International Organization, 63*(1), pp. 107–138.

MOUNK, Y., 2014. Pitchfork Politics: The Populist Threat to Liberal Democracy. *Foreign Aff., 93*, p. 27.

MUDDE, C., 2016. Europe's Populist Surge: A Long Time in the Making. *Foreign Aff., 95*, p.25.

MUDDE, C., 2007. *Populist Radical Right Parties in Europe* (Vol. 22, No. 8). Cambridge University Press.

MUDDE, C., 2004. The Populist Zeitgeist. *Government and Opposition, 39*(4), pp. 541–563.

MUDDE, C. and KALTWASSER, C.R., 2013. Exclusionary vs. Inclusionary Populism: Comparing Contemporary Europe and Latin America. *Government and Opposition, 48*(2), pp. 147–174.

MUDDE, C. and KALTWASSER, C.R., 2012. *Populism in Europe and the Americas: Threat or Corrective for Democracy?* Cambridge University Press.

MUDDE, C. and KALTWASSER, C.R., 2017. *Populism: a Very Short Introduction*. Oxford University Press.

MULLER, E.N. and SELIGSON, M.A., 1994. Civic Culture and Democracy: The Questions of Causal Relationship. *American Political Science Review, 88*(3), pp. 635–652.

MULLER, E.N. and WEEDE, E., 1990. Cross-national Variation in Political Violence: A Rational Action Approach. *Journal of conflict resolution, 34*(4), pp. 624–651.

MUNCK, G.L., 2009. *Measuring Democracy: A Bridge between Scholarship and Politics.* JHU Press.

MUNCK, G., 2006. *Monitoring Democracy: Deepening an Emerging Consensus*. University of Southern California.

Munck, G.L., 2016. What is Democracy? A Reconceptualization of the Quality of Democracy. *Democratization*, *23*(1), pp. 1–26.

Munck, G.L. and Verkuilen, J., 2002. Conceptualizing and Measuring Democracy: Evaluating Alternative Indices. *Comparative Political Studies*, *35*(1), pp. 5–34.

Murphy, T.A., 2004. Deliberative Civic Education and Civil Society: A Consideration of Ideals and Actualities in Democracy and Communication Education. *Communication Education*, *53*(1).

Nagle, J., 2011. Plying Nostrums or Exporting Peace Models? An Examination of the Contradictions Between the Northern Irish Peace Process and International Peacebuilding. *Democracy and Security*, *7*(2), pp. 160–183.

Nagle, J. and Clancy, M.A.C., 2012. Constructing a Shared Public Identity in Ethno nationally Divided Societies: Comparing Consociational and Transformationist Perspectives. *Nations and Nationalism*, *18*(1), pp. 78–97.

Narang, V. and Nelson, R.M., 2009. Who Are These Belligerent Democratizers? Reassessing the Impact of Democratization on War. *International Organization*, *63*(2), pp. 357–379.

Navia, P. and Zweifel, T.D., 2003. Democracy, Dictatorship, and Infant Mortality Revisited. *Journal of Democracy*, *14*(3), pp. 90–103.

Needler, M.C., 1975. Military Motivations in the Seizure of Power. *Latin American Research Review*, *10*(3), pp. 63–79.

Needler, M.C., 1966. Political Development and Military Intervention in Latin America. *American Political Science Review*, *60*(3), pp. 616–626.

Nelson, J.M., 2007. Elections, Democracy, and Social Services. *Studies in Comparative International Development*, *41*(4), pp. 79–97.

Netterstrøm, K.L., 2015. The Islamists' Compromise in Tunisia. *Journal of Democracy*, *26*(4), pp. 110–124.

Neundorf, A., Ezrow, N., Gerschewski, J., Olar, R.G., and R. Shorrocks. 'The Legacy of Authoritarian Regimes on Democratic Citizenship: A global analysis of Authoritarian Indoctrination, and Repression'. Presented at MPSA 2017, ECPR Joint Sessions 2017, EPSA 2017.

Nie, N.H., Powell, G.B., and Prewitt, K., 1969. Social Structure and Political Participation: Developmental Relationships, II. *American Political Science Review*, *63*(3), pp. 808–832.

Nooruddin, I., 2002. Modeling Election Bias in Studies of Sanctions Efficacy. *International Interactions*, *28*(1), pp. 59–75.

Nordlinger, E.A., 1977. *Soldiers in Politics: Military Coups and Governments*. Prentice Hall.

Norris, P. (ed.), 1999. *Critical Citizens: Global Support for Democratic Government*. Oxford University Press.

North, D.C., 1990. A Transaction Cost Theory of Politics. *Journal of Theoretical Politics*, *2*(4), pp. 355–367.

North, D.C., Wallis, J.J. and Weingast, B.R., 2009. *Violence and Social Orders: A Conceptual Rramework for Interpreting Recorded Human History*. Cambridge University Press.

Nyerere, J., 1998. *Africa Today and Tomorrow*. Taylor and Francis.

Odinius, D. and Kuntz, P., 2015. The Limits Of Authoritarian Solidarity: The Gulf Monarchies And Preserving Authoritarian Rule during the Arab Spring. *European Journal of Political Research*, *54*(4), pp. 639–654.

O'Donnell, G.A., 1994. Delegative Democracy. *Journal of Democracy*, *5*(1), pp. 55–69.

O'Donnel, G., 1973. Modernization and Bureaucratic Authoritarianism. *Studies in South American Politics*, 9.

O'DONNELL, G., 1978. Reflections on the Patterns of Change in the Bureaucratic–Authoritarian State. *Latin American Research Review*, 13(1), pp. 3–38.

O'DONNELL, G., 1979. Tensions in the Bureaucratic–Authoritarian State and the Question of Democracy. In COLLIER, D. and CARDOSO, F.H., 1979. *The New Authoritarianism in Latin America*. Princeton University Press, pp. 285–318.

O'DONNELL, G.A., 2004. Why the Rule of Law Matters. *Journal of Democracy*, 15(4), pp. 32–46.

O'DONNELL, G., SCHMITTER, P.C., and WHITEHEAD, L., 1986. *Transitions from Authoritarian Rule: Southern Europe* (Vol. 1). JHU Press.

OGUNDIYA, I.S., 2009. Political Corruption in Nigeria: Theoretical Perspectives and Some Explanations. *The Anthropologist*, 11(4), pp. 281–292.

OH, K. and HASSIG, R.C., 2004. *North Korea through the Looking Glass*. Brookings Institution Press.

O'KANE, R.H., 1981. A Probabilistic Approach to the Causes of Coups d'Etat. *British Journal of Political Science*, 11(3), pp. 287–308.

OLARINMOYE, O.O., 2008. Godfathers, Political Parties and Electoral Corruption in Nigeria. *African Journal of Political Science and International Relations*, 2(4), pp. 066–073.

OLIVER, P.E. and MYERS, D.J., 2003. Networks, Diffusion, and Cycles of Collective Action. In McADAM, M.D.D., (ed.) *Social Movements and Networks: Relational Approaches to Collective Action*, Oxford University Press, pp. 173–203.

OLSON, M., 1993. Dictatorship, Democracy, and Development. *American Political Science Review*, 87(3), pp. 567–576.

OLSON, M., 2000. *Power and Prosperity: Outgrowing Communist and Capitalist Dictatorships*. Basic Books.

ONEAL, J.R., ONEAL, F.H., MAOZ, Z., and RUSSETT, B., 1996. The Liberal Peace: Interdependence, Democracy, and International Conflict, 1950–85. *Journal of Peace Research*, 33(1), pp. 11–28.

O'NEIL, S.K., 2016. Latin America's Populist Hangover: What To Do When the People's Party Ends. *Foreign Aff.*, 95, p.31.

ORGANIZATION FOR ECONOMIC COOPERATION AND DEVELOPMENT. The United Kingdom in 2017. https://www.oecd.org/eco/surveys/United-Kingdom-2017-OECD-economic-survey-overview.pdf. Accessed 13 June 2019.

OSTROW, R., 2014. A deterioration of Democracy?: Corruption, Transparency, and Apathy in the Western World. *SAIS Review of International Affairs*, 34(1), pp. 41–44.

OTTAWAY, M., 2003. *Democracy Challenged. The Rise of Semi-authoritarianism*. Carnegie Endowment for International Peace.

OWEN, J.M., 1994. How Liberalism Produces Democratic peace. *International Security*, 19(2), pp. 87–125.

PALMER, M., 2005. *Breaking the Real Axis of Evil: How to Oust the World's Last Dictators by 2025*. Rowman & Littlefield.

PALONEN, E., 2009. Political Polarisation and Populism in Contemporary Hungary. *Parliamentary Affairs*, 62(2), pp. 318–334.

PAPADOPOULOS, Y., 2014. Accountability and Multi-level Governance: More Accountability, Less Democracy? In CURTIN, D., MAIR, P. PAPADOPOULOS, Y. (eds.), *Accountability and European Governance*. Routledge, pp. 112–131.

PAPAIOANNOU, E. and SIOUROUNIS, G., 2008. Economic and Social Factors Driving the third Wave of Democratization. *Journal of Comparative Economics*, 36(3), pp. 365–387.

PAPE, R.A., 2003. The Strategic Logic of Suicide Terrorism. *American Political Science Review*, 97(3), pp. 343–361.

PARSONS, T., 1970. Equality and Inequality in Modern Society, or Social Stratification Revisited. *Sociological Inquiry*, 40(2), pp. 13–72.

PASUK, P. and BAKER, C., 1998. *Thailand's Boom and Bust*. Silkworm Books.

PATEMAN, C., 1971. Political Culture, Political Structure and Political Change. *British Journal of Political Science*, 1(3), pp. 291–305.

PAUWELS, T., 2011. Measuring Populism: A Quantitative Text Analysis of Party Literature in Belgium. *Journal of Elections, Public Opinion and Parties*, 21(1), pp. 97–119.

PAUWELS, T., (2014). *Populism in Western Europe: Comparing Belgium, Germany and the Netherlands*. Routledge.

PAYNE, J.M., 2002. *Democracies in Development: Politics and Reform in Latin America* (Vol. 1). IDB Publications.

PAYNE, J.M, Zovatto, D.G., Carrillo Flórez, F., and Allemand Zavala, A., 2002. *Democracies in Development: Politics and Reform in Latin America*. Inter-American Development Bank and the International Institute for Democracy and Electoral Assistance, p. 138.

PECENY, M., 1999. *Democracy at the Point of Bayonets*. Penn State Press.

PELLING, M. and DILL, K., 2010. Disaster Politics: Tipping Points for Change in the Adaptation of Sociopolitical Regimes. *Progress in Human Geography*, 34(1), pp. 21–37.

PELLING, M. and DILL, K., 2006. Natural Disasters as Catalysts of Political Action. *Media Development*, 53(4), p.7.

PEPINSKY, T., 2007. Autocracy, Elections, and Fiscal Policy: Evidence from Malaysia. *Studies in Comparative International Development*, 42(1–2), pp. 136–163.

PEPINSKY, T. B. (2009). *Economic Crises and the Breakdown of Authoritarian Regimes: Indonesia and Malaysia in Comparative Perspective*. Cambridge University Press.

PEPINSKY, T., 2014. The Institutional Turn in Comparative Authoritarianism. *British Journal of Political Science*, 44(3), pp. 631–653.

PÉREZ, O.J., 2017. Panama: Democracy under the Shadow of Corruption. *Revista de Ciencia Política*, 37(2), pp. 519–540.

PERSSON, T. and TABELLINI, G., 1994. Representative Democracy and Capital Taxation. *Journal of Public Economics*, 55(1), pp. 53–70.

PEVEHOUSE, J.C., 2002. Democracy from the Outside-in? International Organizations and Democratization. *International Organization*, 56(3), pp. 515–549.

PHILPOTT, D., 2004. The Catholic Wave. *Journal of Democracy*, 15(2), pp. 32–46.

PHILPOTT, D., 2007. Explaining the Political Ambivalence of Religion. *American Political Science Review*, 101(3), pp. 505–525.

PIAZZA, J.A., 2013. Regime Age and Terrorism: Are New Democracies Prone to Terrorism? *International Interactions*, 39(2), pp. 246–263.

PICKARD, D., 2014. Prospects For Implementing Democracy in Tunisia. *Mediterranean Politics*, 19(2), pp. 259–264.

PICKERING, J. and KISANGANI, E.F., 2006. Political, Economic, and Social Consequences of Foreign Military Intervention. *Political Research Quarterly*, 59(3), pp. 363–376.

PITKIN, H.F., 1967. *The Concept of Representation*. University of California Press.

PLATTNER, M.F., 1998. Liberalism and Democracy: Can't Have One without the Other. *Foreign Affairs*, 77(2): pp. 171–180.

POAST, P. and URPELAINEN, J., 2015. How International Organizations Support Democratization: Preventing Authoritarian Reversals Or Promoting Consolidation? *World Politics*, 67(1), pp. 72–113.

POE, S.C. and TATE, C.N., 1994. Repression of Human Rights to Personal Integrity in the 1980s: A Global Analysis. *American Political Science Review*, *88*(4), pp. 853–872.

POE, S.C., TATE, C.N., and KEITH, L.C., 1999. Repression of the Human Right To Personal Integrity Revisited: A Global Cross-National Study Covering The Years 1976–1993. *International Studies Quarterly*, *43*(2), pp. 291–313.

POLLACK, K.M., 2002. Next Stop Baghdad? *Foreign Affairs*, *81*(2), pp. 32–47.

POP-ELECHES, G. and ROBERTSON, G.B., 2015. Structural conditions and Democratization. *Journal of Democracy*, *26*(3), pp. 144–156.

POPPER, K., 1945. The Poverty of Historicism, III. *Economica*, *12*(46), pp. 69–89.

POST, J.M., 1986. Narcissism and the Charismatic Leader–Follower Relationship. *Political Psychology*, *7*(4), pp. 675–688.

POWELL, G.B., 1982. *Contemporary Democracies*. Harvard University Press.

POWELL, G.B. and POWELL JR, G.B., 2000. *Elections as Instruments of Democracy: Majoritarian and Proportional Visions*. Yale University Press.

POWELL, J., 2012. Determinants of the Attempting and Outcome of Coups d'État. *Journal of Conflict Resolution*, *56*(6), pp. 1017–1040.

POWELL, E.J and STANTON, J. 2009. Domestic Judicial Institutions and Human Rights Treaty Violation. *International Studies Quarterly*, *53*(1), pp. 149–174.

POWELL, J.M. and THYNE, C.L., 2011. Global Instances of Coups from 1950 to 2010: A New Dataset. *Journal of Peace Research*, *48*(2), pp. 249–259.

PRAH, K.K., 2004. African Wars and Ethnic Conflicts: Rebuilding Failed States. In *Human Development Report 2004*.

PRZEWORSKI, A., 1998. Culture and Democracy. In *World Culture Report*. UNESCO.

PRZEWORSKI, A., 1991. *Democracy and the Market: Political and Economic Reforms in Eastern Europe and Latin America*. Cambridge University Press.

PRZEWORSKI, A., 2008. The Poor and the Viability of Democracy. In KRISHNA, A. (ed.), *Poverty, Participation, and Democracy*. Cambridge University Press, pp. 125–146.

PRZEWORSKI, A., ALVAREZ, M.E., CHEIBUB, J.A., and LIMONGI, F., 2000. *Democracy and Development: Political Institutions and Well-being in the World, 1950–1990* (Vol. 3). Cambridge University Press.

PRZEWORSKI, A. and LIMONGI, F., 1997. Modernization: Theories and Facts. *World Politics*, *49*(2), pp. 155–183.

PRZEWORSKI, A. and WALLERSTEIN, M., 1982. The Structure of Class Conflict in Democratic Capitalist Societies. *American Political Science Review*, *76*(2), pp. 215–238.

PUTNAM, R.D., 1995. Bowling Alone: America's Declining Social Capital. *Journal of Democracy*, *6*(1), pp. 65–78.

PUTNAM, R. D., 2000. *Bowling Alone: The Collapse and Revival of American Community*. Simon & Schuster.

PUTNAM, R. D., 1993. *Making Democracy work: Civic Traditions in Modern Italy*. Princeton University Press.

PYE, L.W. and VERBA, S., 1965. *Political Culture and Political Development*. Princeton University Press.

RABUSHKA, A. and SHEPSLE, K.A., 1972. *Politics in Plural Societies*. Stanford University Press, pp. 208–212.

RAMIRO, L. and GOMEZ, R., 2017. Radical-left Populism during the Great Recession: Podemos and Its Competition with the Established Radical Left. *Political Studies*, *65*(1_suppl), pp. 108–126.

RANDALL, V. and SVÅSAND, L., 2002. Party Institutionalization in New Democracies. *Party Politics*, *8*(1), pp. 5–29.

REGAN, P.M. and HENDERSON, E.A., 2002. Democracy, Threats and Political Repression in Developing Countries: Are Democracies Internally Less Violent? *Third World Quarterly*, *23*(1), pp. 119–136.

REILLY, B., 2005. Does the Choice of Electoral System Promote Democracy? The Gap between Theory and Practice. In ROEDER, P.G. and ROTHCHILD, D.S. (eds.), *Sustainable Peace: Power and Democracy after Civil Wars*. Cornell University Press, pp. 159–171.

REITER, D. and STAM, A.C., 1998. Democracy, War Initiation, and Victory. *American Political Science Review*, *92*(2), pp. 377–389.

REMMER, K. L. (1991). The Political Impact of Economic Crisis in Latin America in the 1980s. *American Political Science Review*, *85*(03), 777–800.

RENO, W., 2000. Shadow States and the Political Economy of Civil Wars. In BERDAL, M.R., BERDAL, M., and MALONE, D. (eds.), *Greed and Grievance: Economic Agendas in Civil Wars*. Lynne Rienner Publishers. pp. 43–68.

REUTER, O.J. and ROBERTSON, G.B., 2014. Legislatures, Co-optation, and Social Protest in Contemporary Authoritarian Regimes. *The Journal of Politics*, *77*(1), pp. 235–248.

REYNOLDS, A., REILLY, B., and ELLIS, A. (eds.), 2008. *Electoral System Design: The New International IDEA Handbook*. International Institute for Democracy and Electoral Assistance,

RICHARDS, A., WATERBURY, J., CAMMETT, M., & DIWAN, I. (2013). *A Political Economy of the Middle East*. Westview Press.

RIEDL, R.B., 2014. *Authoritarian Origins of Democratic Party Systems in Africa*. Cambridge University Press.

RISSE-KAPPEN, T., 1995. Democratic Peace—Warlike Democracies? A Social Constructivist Interpretation of the Liberal Argument. *European Journal of International Relations*, *1*(4), pp. 491–517.

RITTER, E.H. and CONRAD, C.R., 2016. Preventing and Responding to Dissent: The Observational Challenges of Explaining Strategic Repression. *American Political Science Review*, *110*(1), pp. 85–99.

ROBERTS, K.M., 2007. Latin America's Populist Revival. *SAIS Review of International Affairs*, *27*(1), pp. 3–15.

ROBERTS, K.M., 2006. Populism, Political Conflict, and Grass-roots Organization in Latin America. *Comparative Politics*, *38*(2), pp. 127–148.

ROBERTS, K.M., 2003. Social Correlates of Party System Demise and Populist Resurgence in Venezuela. *Latin American Politics and Society*, *45*(3), pp. 35–57.

ROBERTSON-SNAPE, F., 1999. Corruption, Collusion and Nepotism in Indonesia. *Third World Quarterly*, *20*(3), pp. 589–602.

ROBISON, R. and HADIZ, V., 2004. *Reorganising Power in Indonesia: The Politics of Oligarchy in an Age of Markets*. Routledge.

ROCK, M.T., 2000. Thailand's Old Bureaucratic Polity and Its New Semi-Democracy. In KHAN, M.H. and JOMO, K.S. (eds.), *Rents, Rent-Seeking and Economic Development: Theory and Evidence in Asia*. Cambridge University Press, pp. 182–206.

RODAN, G., 2004. *Transparency and Authoritarian Rule in Southeast Asia: Singapore and Malaysia*. Routledge.

RODRIK, D., 1999. The Asian Financial Crisis and the Virtues of Democracy. *Challenge*, *42*(4), pp. 44–59.

RODRIK, D., 1998. *Democracies and Economic Performance*. Harvard University. Fotocopia.

RODRIK, D., 2008. Second-best Institutions. *American Economic Review*, *98*(2), pp. 100–104.

ROEDER, P.G. and ROTHCHILD, D.S. (eds.), 2005. *Sustainable Peace: Power and Democracy after Civil Wars*. Cornell University Press.

Roessler, P., 2011. The Enemy Within: Personal Rule, Coups, and Civil War in Africa. *World Politics*, 63(2), pp. 300–346.

Roessler, P. and Howard, M.M., August, 2008. Electoral Dominance in Authoritarian Regimes. In *Annual Meeting of the American Political Science Association, Boston, MA*.

Roessler, P.G. and Howard, M.M., August, 2007. Measuring and Analyzing Post Cold War Political Regimes. In *Annual Meeting of the American Political Science Association, Boston, MA*.

Rooduijn, M., 2018. What Unites the Voter Bases of Populist Parties? Comparing the Electorates of 15 Populist Parties. *European Political Science Review*, 10(3), pp. 351–368.

Rose, G., 2018. Is Democracy Dying? *Foreign Affairs*, 9(3), pp. 1.

Rose, R. and Mishler, W., 1998. Negative and Positive Party Identification in Post-communist Countries. *Electoral Studies*, 17(2), pp. 217–234.

Rose, R. and Shin, D.C., 2001. Democratization Backwards: The Problem of Third-wave Democracies. *British Journal of Political Science*, 31(2), pp. 331–354.

Rose-Ackerman, S., 1999. Political Corruption and Democracy. *Conn. J. Int'l L.*, 14, p. 363.

Rosenfeld, M., 2000. The Rule of Law and the Legitimacy of Constitutional Democracy. *S. Cal. L. Rev.*, 74, p. 1307.

Ross, M., 2006. Is Democracy Good for the Poor? *American Journal of Political Science*, 50(4), pp. 860–874.

Ross, M.L., 2004. What Do We Know about Natural Resources and Civil War? *Journal of Peace Research*, 41(3), pp. 337–356.

Rossteutscher, S., 2010. Social Capital Worldwide: Potential for Democratization or Stabilizer of Authoritarian Rule? *American Behavioral Scientist*, 53(5), pp. 737–757.

Rotberg, R., 2003. *S State Failure and State Weakness in a Time of Terror*. Brookings University Press.

Rudbeck, J., Mukherjee, E., and Nelson, K., 2016. When Autocratic Regimes Are Cheap and Play Dirty: The Transaction Costs of Repression in South Africa, Kenya, and Egypt. *Comparative Politics*, 48(2), pp. 147–166.

Rueschemeyer, D., Stephens, E.H., and Stephens, J.D., 1992. *Capitalist Development and Democracy*. Cambridge University Press.

Runciman, C., 2016. The 'Ballot and the Brick': Protest, Voting and Non-voting in Post-apartheid South Africa. *Journal of Contemporary African Studies*, 34(4), pp. 419–436.

Russett, B., 1994. *Grasping the Democratic peace: Principles for a Post-Cold War World*. Princeton University Press.

Rustow, D.A., 1970. Transitions to Democracy: Toward a Dynamic Model. *Comparative Politics*, 2(3), pp. 337–363.

Sah, R.K. and Stiglitz, J.E., 1986. The Architecture of Economic Systems: Hierarchies and Polyarchies. *The American Economic Review*, 76(4), pp. 716–727.

Sainsbury, D., 2001. Gender and the Making of Welfare States: Norway and Sweden. *Social Politics: International Studies in Gender, State & Society*, 8(1), pp. 113–143.

Sartori, G., 2005. *Parties and Party Systems: A Framework for Analysis*. ECPR Press.

Scalapino, R.A., 1993. Democratizing Dragons: South Korea & Taiwan. *Journal of Democracy*, 4(3), pp. 70–83.

Schatz, E., 2006. Access by Accident: Legitimacy Claims and Democracy Promotion in Authoritarian Central Asia. *International Political Science Review*, 27(3), pp. 263–284.

Schedler, A., 1999. Conceptualizing Accountability. *The Self-restraining State: Power and Accountability in new Democracies*, 13, p. 17.

SCHEDLER, A., 2006. *Electoral Authoritarianism: The Dynamics of Unfree Competition.* Lynne Rienner.

SCHEDLER, A., 2002. The Menu of Manipulation. *Journal of Democracy*, *13*(2), pp. 36–50.

SCHEPPELE, K.L., 2004. Other People's Patriot Acts: Europe's Response to September 11. *Loy. L. Rev.*, *50*, p. 89.

SCHIMMELFENNIG, F. and SCHOLTZ, H., 2008. EU Democracy promotion in the European neighbourhood: Political Conditionality, Economic Development and Transnational Exchange. *European Union Politics*, *9*(2), pp. 187–215.

SCHIMMELFENNIG, F. and SEDELMEIER, U., 2004. Governance by Conditionality: EU Rule Transfer to the Candidate Countries of Central and Eastern Europe. *Journal of European Public Policy*, *11*(4), pp. 661–679.

SCHIMMELFENNIG, F. and SEDELMEIER, U., 2002. Theorizing EU Enlargement: Research Focus, Hypotheses, and the State of Research. *Journal of European Public Policy*, *9*(4), pp. 500–528.

SCHLUMBERGER, O., 2010. Opening Old Bottles in Search of New Wine: On Non-democratic Legitimacy in the Middle East. *Middle East Critique*, *19*(3), pp. 233–250.

SCHMITTER, P.C., 2000. Federalism and the Euro-polity. *Journal of Democracy*, *11*(1), pp. 40–47.

SCHMITTER, P.C. and KARL, T.L., 1991. What Democracy Is … and Is Not. *Journal of Democracy*, *2*(3), pp. 75–88.

SCHULTZ, K.A., 2001. *Democracy and Coercive Diplomacy* (Vol. 76). Cambridge University Press.

SCHUMPETER, J.A., 1942. *Socialism, Capitalism and Democracy.* Harper and Brothers.

SCHUMPETER, J.A. 1947. *Capitalism, Socialism and Democracy.* Harper.

SCOBELL, A., 2006. *Kim Jong Il and North Korea: The Leader and the System.* DIANE Publishing.

SCOTT, J.M. and STEELE, C.A., 2011. Sponsoring Democracy: the United States and Democracy Aid to the Developing World, 1988–2001. *International Studies Quarterly*, *55*(1), pp. 47–69.

SEAWRIGHT, J., 2012. *Party-system Collapse: The Roots of Crisis in Peru and Venezuela.* Stanford University Press.

SEDELMEIER, U., 2017. Political Safeguards against Democratic Backsliding in the EU: The Limits of Material Sanctions and the Scope of Social Pressure. *Journal of European Public Policy*, *24*(3), pp. 337–351.

SEGURA-UBIERGO, A., 2007. *The Political Economy of the Welfare State in Latin America: Globalization, Democracy, and Development.* Cambridge University Press.

SELF, A.J., 2008, Review of Ellner, S., *Rethinking Venezuelan Politics: Class, Conflict and the Chávez Phenomenon.* https://scholar.google.it/citations?user=p 0U9kBUAAAAJ&hl=fr#d=gs_md_cita-d&u=%2Fcitations%3Fview_op%3Dview_ citation%26hl%3Dfr%26user%3Dp0U9kB UAAAAJ%26citation_for_view%3Dp0U9k BUAAAAJ%3Ad1gkVwhDpl0C%26tzom% 3D-120. Accessed 25 July 2019.

SELIGSON, M.A., 2002. The Impact of Corruption on Regime Legitimacy: A Comparative Study of Four Latin American Countries. *The Journal of Politics*, *64*(2), pp. 408–433.

SELIGSON, M.A., 2007. The Rise of Populism and the Left in Latin America. *Journal of Democracy*, *18*(3), pp. 81–95.

SELIGSON, A.L. and TUCKER, J.A., 2005. Feeding the Hand that Bit You: Voting for Ex-authoritarian Rulers in Russia and Bolivia. *Demokratizatsiya*, 13(1), pp. 11–42.

SEN, A.K., 1999. Democracy as a Universal Value. *Journal of Democracy*, *10*(3), pp. 3–17.

SHEFTER, M., 1994. Party and Patronage: Germany, England, and Italy. *The State: Critical Concepts*, *3*, pp. 103–143.

SHIRK, D.A., 2000. Vicente Fox and the Rise of the PAN. *Journal of Democracy, 11*(4), pp. 25–32.

SHLEIFER, A. and VISHNY, R.W., 1993. Corruption. *The Quarterly Journal of Economics, 108*(3), pp. 599–617.

SIANI-DAVIES, P., 2007. *The Romanian Revolution of December 1989.* Cornell University Press.

SIMPSER, A., 2013. *Why Governments and Parties Manipulate Elections: Theory, Practice, and Implications.* Cambridge University Press.

SIMPSER, A. and DONNO, D., 2012. Can International Election Monitoring Harm Governance? *The Journal of Politics, 74*(2), pp. 501–513.

SINGER, M., 2009. Buying Voters with Dirty Money: The Relationship between Clientelism and Corruption. In *APSA 2009 Toronto Meeting Paper.*

SINGH, N., 2014. *Seizing Power: The Strategic Logic of Military Coups.* JHU Press.

SIROWY, L. and INKELES, A., 1990. The effects of Democracy on Economic Growth and Inequality: A Review. *Studies in Comparative International Development, 25*(1), pp. 126–157.

SISK, T., 2017. *Democratization in South Africa: The Elusive Social Contract* (Vol. 4838). Princeton University Press.

SKOCPOL, T. 1979. *States and Social Revolutions: A Comparative Analysis of France, Russia and China.* Cambridge University Press.

SKOCPOL, T. and WILLIAMSON, V., 2016. *The Tea Party and the Remaking of Republican Conservatism.* Oxford University Press.

SLATER, D. and FENNER, S., 2011. State Power and Staying Power: Infrastructural Mechanisms and Authoritarian Durability. *Journal of International Affairs, 65*(1), pp. 15–29.

SLATER, D. and WONG, J., 2013. The Strength to Concede: Ruling Parties and Democratization in Developmental Asia. *Perspectives on Politics, 11*(3), pp. 717–733.

SMITH, B., 2005. Life of The Party: The Origins of Regime Breakdown and Persistence under Single-Party Rule. *World Politics, 57*(3), pp. 421–451.

SMITH, B., 2004. Oil Wealth and Regime Survival in the Developing World, 1960–1999. *American Journal of Political Science, 48*(2), pp. 232–246.

SMITH, B., 2006. The Wrong Kind of Crisis: Why Oil Booms and Busts Rarely Lead to Authoritarian Breakdown. *Studies in Comparative International Development, 40*(4), pp. 55–76.

SNYDER, T. and VACHUDOVA, M., 1997. Are Transitions Transitory? Two Types of Political Change in Eastern Europe since 1989. *East European Politics and Societies, 11*, pp. 1–35.

SOLINGER, D.J., 2001. Ending One-Party Dominance: Korea, Taiwan, Mexico. *Journal of Democracy, 12*(1), pp. 30–42.

SOLT, F., 2004. Civics or Structure? Revisiting the Origins of Democratic Quality in the Italian Regions. *British Journal of Political Science, 34*(1), pp. 123–135.

SOLT, F., 2008. Economic Inequality and Democratic Political Engagement. *American Journal of Political Science, 52*(1), pp. 48–60.

SONDHEIMER, R.M. and GREEN, D.P., 2010. Using Experiments to Estimate the Effects of Education on Voter Turnout. *American Journal of Political Science, 54*(1), pp. 174–189.

STANLEY, B., 2008. The Thin Ideology of Populism. *Journal of Political Ideologies, 13*(1),

STASAVAGE, D., 2005. Democracy and Education Spending in Africa. *American Journal of Political Science, 49*(2), pp. 343–358.

STAVRAKAKIS Y., 2017. How Did 'Populism' Become a Pejorative Concept? And Why Is This Important Today? A Genealogy of Double Hermeneutics. POPULISMUS Working Papers No. 6. http://www. populismus.gr/wp-content/uploads/ 2017/04/stavrakakis-populismus-wp-6-upload.pdf Accessed 7 June 2019.

STEPAN, A., 1971. Brasil: los militares y la política.

STEPAN, A., LINZ, J.J., and MINOVES, J.F., 2014. Democratic Parliamentary Monarchies. *Journal of Democracy*, *25*(2), pp. 35–51.

STEPHAN, M.J. and CHENOWETH, E., 2008. Why Civil Resistance Works: The Strategic Logic of Nonviolent Conflict. *International Security*, *33*(1), pp. 7–44.

STOKES, S.C., 2007. Political Clientelism. In BOIX, C. and STOKES, S.C. (eds.), *The Oxford Handbook of Political Science*. Oxford University Press.

STOKES, S.C., DUNNING, T., NAZARENO, M. and BRUSCO, V., 2013. *Brokers, Voters, and Clientelism: The Puzzle of Distributive Politics*. Cambridge University Press.

STRANG, D., 1991. Adding Social Structure to Diffusion Models: An Event History Framework. *Sociological Methods & Research*, *19*(3), pp. 324–353.

STRANG, D. and MEYER, J.W., 1993. Institutional Conditions for Diffusion. *Theory and Society*, *22*(4), pp. 487–511.

STAVRAKAKIS, Y. and KATSAMBEKIS, G., 2014. Left-wing Populism in the European Periphery: The Case Of SYRIZA. *Journal Of Political Ideologies*, *19*(2), pp. 119–142.

STEPAN, A., 2012. Tunisia's Transition and the Twin Tolerations. *Journal of Democracy*, *23*(2), pp. 89–103.

STOKES, S.C., 2005. Perverse Accountability: A Formal Model of Machine Politics with Evidence from Argentina. *American Political Science Review, 99*(3), pp. 315–325.

SUDDUTH, J.K., 2017. Strategic Logic of Elite Purges in Dictatorships. *Comparative Political Studies*, *50*(13), pp. 1768–1801.

SUN, Y. and JOHNSTON, M., 2009. Does Democracy Check Corruption? Insights from China and India. *Comparative Politics*, *42*(1), pp. 1–19.

SUTEU, S., 2017. Eternity Clauses in Post-Conflict and Post-Authoritarian Constitution-Making: Promise and Limits. *Global Constitutionalism*, *6*(1), pp. 63–100.

SVOLIK, M., 2008. Authoritarian Reversals and Democratic Consolidation. *American Political Science Review*, *102*(2), pp. 153–168.

SVOLIK, M.W., 2013. Contracting on Violence: The Moral Hazard in Authoritarian Repression and Military Intervention in Politics. *Journal of Conflict Resolution*, *57*(5), pp. 765–794.

SVOLIK, M.W., 2012. *The Politics of Authoritarian Rule*. Cambridge University Press.

SVOLIK, M.W., 2009. Power Sharing and Leadership Dynamics in Authoritarian Regimes. *American Journal of Political Science*, *53*(2), pp. 477–494.

SVOLIK, M.W., 2015. Which Democracies Will Last? Coups, Incumbent Takeovers, And The Dynamic Of Democratic Consolidation. *British Journal of Political Science*, *45*(4), pp. 715–738.

TAGGART, P., 2000. *Populism*. Open University Press.

TAGGART, P., 2002. Populism and the Pathology of Representative Politics. In *Democracies and the Populist Challenge*. Palgrave Macmillan UK, pp. 62–80.

TÄNNSJÖ, T. 1992. *Populist Democracy: A Defense*. Routledge.

TARCHI, M., 2002. Populism Italian Style. In MENY, Y. and SUREL, Y., (eds.), *Democracies and the Populist Challenge*. Palgrave Macmillan, pp. 120–138.

TAVARES, J. and WACZIARG, R., 2001. How Democracy Affects Growth. *European Economic Review, 45*(8), pp. 1341–1378.

TEETS, J.C., 2013. Let Many Civil Societies Bloom: The Rise of Consultative Authoritarianism in China. *The China Quarterly, 213*, pp. 19–38.

TEORELL, J., 2010. *Determinants of Democratization: Explaining Regime Change in the World, 1972–2006.* Cambridge University Press.

TERCHEK, R.J. and CONTE, T.C., 2001. *Theories of Democracy. A Reader.* Rowman and Littlefield.

THERBORN, G. 1977. The Rule of Capital and the Rise of Democracy. *New Left Review* I/103, pp. 3–41.

THOMPSON, D.F., 2008. Deliberative Democratic Theory and empirical Political Science. *Annual Review of Political Science, 11*, pp. 497–520.

THOMPSON, D., 26 January 2012. Where Did All the Workers Go? 60 Years of Economic Change in 1 Graph. *The Atlantic.* https://www.theatlantic.com/business/archive/2012/01/where-did-all-the-workers-go-60-years-of-economic-change-in-1-graph/252018/ Accessed 7 June 2019.

THOMPSON, W.R., 1973. *The Grievances of Military Coup-makers* (No. 47). Sage Publications (CA).

TILLY, C., 2003. Inequality, Democratization, and De-democratization. *Sociological Theory, 21*(1), pp. 37–43.

TOMZ, M.R. and WEEKS, J.L., 2013. Public Opinion and the Democratic Peace. *American Political Science Review, 107*(4), pp. 849–865.

TRAUB, J., 19 February 2018. Selfishness Is Killing Liberalism. *The Atlantic.* https://www.theatlantic.com/politics/archive/2018/02/liberalism-trump-era/553553/ Accessed 20 February 2019.

TREISMAN, D., 2000. The Causes of Corruption: A Cross-National Study. *Journal of Public Economics, 76*(3), pp. 399–457.

TREISMAN, D., 2015. Income, Democracy, and Leader Turnover. *American Journal of Political Science, 59*(4), pp. 927–942.

TREISMAN, D., 2007. Putin's Silovarchs. *Orbis, 51*(1), pp. 141–153.

TREMEWAN, C., 2016. *The Political Economy of Social Control in Singapore.* Springer.

TRIPP, A. M., 2001. The Politics of Autonomy and Co-optation in Africa: The Ugandan Women's Movement. *Journal of Modern African Studies, 39*(1), pp. 101–128.

TRONVOLL, K. and MEKONNEN, D.R., 2014. *The African Garrison State: Human Rights & Political Development in Eritrea.* Boydell & Brewer Ltd.

TRUEX, R., 2014. The Returns to Office in a 'Rubber Stamp' Parliament. *American Political Science Review, 108*(2), pp. 235–251.

TSAI, K.S., 2007. *Capitalism without Democracy: The Private Sector in Contemporary China.* Cornell University Press.

TSEBELIS, G., 2002. *Veto players: How Political Institutions Work.* Princeton University Press.

TUCKER, J.A., 2007. Enough! Electoral Fraud, Collective Action Problems, and Post-Communist Colored Revolutions. *Perspectives on Politics, 5*(3), pp. 535–551.

TUCKER, J.A., THEOCHARIS, Y., ROBERTS, M.E., and BARBERÁ, P., 2017. From Liberation to Turmoil: Social Media and Democracy. *Journal of Democracy, 28*(4), pp. 46–59.

TUCKER, R.C., 1968. The Theory of Charismatic Leadership. *Daedalus, 97*(3): pp. 731–756.

TURAM, B., 2012. Are Rights and Liberties Safe? *Journal of Democracy, 23*(1), pp. 109–118.

TUSALEM, R.F., 2010. Determinants of Coup d'État Events 1970—90: The Role of Property Rights Protection. *International Political Science Review, 31*(3), pp. 346–365.

ULFELDER, J., 2012. The Coup Trap: Mali Edition. https://dartthrowingchimp. wordpress.com/2012/12/11/the-coup-trap-mali-edition/ Accessed 8 June 2019.

ULFELDER, J., 2007. Natural-Resource Wealth and the Survival of Autocracy. *Comparative Political Studies, 40*(8), pp. 995–1018.

ULFELDER, J. and LUSTIK, M., 2007. Modelling Transitions to and from Democracy. *Democratisation, 14*(3), pp. 351–387.

URDAL, H., 2006. A Clash Of Generations? Youth Bulges and Political Violence. *International Studies Quarterly, 50*(3), pp. 607–629.

VAN ALSTYNE, M. and BRYNJOLFSSON, E., 2005. Global Village or Cyber-Balkans? Modeling and Measuring the Integration of Electronic Communities. *Management Science, 51*(6), pp. 851–868.

VAN DE WALLE, N., 2003. Presidentialism and Clientelism in Africa's Emerging Party Systems. *The Journal of Modern African Studies, 41*(2), pp. 297–321.

VARSHNEY, A., 1998. *Democracy, Development, and the Countryside: Urban-rural Struggles in India*. Cambridge University Press.

VARSHNEY, A., 2001. Ethnic Conflict and Civil Society: India and Beyond. *World Politics 53*(3), pp. 362–398.

VERBA, S. and NIE, N.H., 1987. *Participation in America: Political Democracy and Social Equality*. University of Chicago Press.

VILLAMOR, F., 11 May 11 2018. Philippines' Top Judge Took On Duterte. Now, She's Out. *New York Times* https://www.nytimes.com/2018/05/11/world/asia/philippines-chief-justice-rodrigo-duterte.html.

VON SOEST, C., 2015. Democracy Prevention: The International Collaboration of Authoritarian Regimes. *European Journal of Political Research, 54*(4), pp. 623–638.

VON SOEST, C. and WAHMAN, M., 2015. Are Democratic Sanctions Really Counter-productive? *Democratization, 22*(6), pp. 957–980.

VREELAND, J.R., 2008. The Effect of Political Regime on Civil War: Unpacking Anocracy. *Journal of Conflict Resolution, 52*(3), pp. 401–425.

WAISBORD, S. and AMADO, A., 2017. Populist Communication by Digital Means: Presidential Twitter in Latin America. *Information, Communication & Society, 20*(9), pp. 1330–1346.

WALKER, C. and COOLEY, A., 2013. Vote of the Living Dead. *Foreign Policy*. https://foreignpolicy.com/2013/10/31/vote-of-the-living-dead/. Accessed 26 July 2019.

WALLIS, D., 8 January 2012. Chavez's 'Alo Presidente' Returns to Venezuelan TV. *Reuters*. https://www.reuters.com/article/us-venezuela-chavez-idUSTRE8070J620120108.

WALSH, K.C., JENNINGS, M.K. and STOKER, L., 2004. The Effects of Social Class Identification on Participatory Orientations towards Government. *British Journal of Political Science, 34*(3), pp. 469–495.

WANG, Y.T., LINDENFORS, P., SUNDSTRÖM, A., JANSSON, F., PAXTON, P., and LINDBERG, S.I., 2017. Women's Rights in Democratic Transitions: A Global Sequence Analysis, 1900-2012. *European Journal of Political Research, 56*(4), pp. 735–756.

WANTCHEKON, L., 2003. Clientelism and Voting Behavior: Evidence from a Field Experiment in Benin. *World Politics, 55*(3), pp. 399–422.

WARWICK, P.V., 1998. Disputed Cause, Disputed Effect: The Postmaterialist Thesis Re-examined. *Public Opinion Quarterly, 62*(4): pp. 583–609.

WAY, L., 2005. Kuchma's Failed Authoritarianism. *Journal of Democracy*, *16*(2), pp. 131–145.

WAY, L., 2016. Weaknesses of Autocracy Promotion. *Journal of Democracy*, *27*(1), pp. 64–75.

WEBER, M., 1978. *Economy and Society: An Outline of Interpretive Sociology* (Vol. 1). University of California Press.

WEBER, M., 1947. *The Theory of Social and Economic Organisation*. Free Press.

WEDEEN, L. 2008. Peripheral Visions: Publics, Power, and Performance in Yemen. Chicago University Press.

WEEKS, J.L., 2008. Autocratic Audience Costs: Regime Type and Signalling Resolve. *International Organization*, *62*(1), pp. 35–64.

WEEKS, J.L., 2012. Strongmen and Straw Men: Authoritarian Regimes and the Initiation of International Conflict. *American Political Science Review*, *106*(2), pp. 326–347.

WEINBERG, L.B. and EUBANK, W.L., 1998. Terrorism and Democracy: What Recent Events Disclose. *Terrorism and Political Violence*, *10*(1), pp. 108–118.

WEINGAST, B.R., 1997. The Political Foundations of Democracy and the Rule of the Law. *American Political Science Review*, *91*(2), pp. 245–263.

WELCH, C.E., 1970. *Soldier and State in Africa: A Comparative Analysis Of Military Intervention and Political Change*. Northwestern University Press.

WELCH JR, C.E. and SMITH, A.K., 1974. *Military Role and Rule: Perspectives on Civil-Military Relations*. Duxbury Press.

WERTS, H., SCHEEPERS, P., and LUBBERS, M., 2013. Euro-scepticism and Radical Right-Wing Voting in Europe, 2002–2008: Social Cleavages, Socio-Political Attitudes and Contextual Characteristics Determining Voting for the Radical Right. *European Union Politics*, *14*(2), pp. 183–205.

WEYLAND, K., 2017. Autocratic Diffusion and Cooperation: The Impact of Interests vs. Ideology. *Democratization*, 24(7), pp. 1235–1252.

WEYLAND, K., 2001. Clarifying a Contested Concept: Populism in the Study of Latin American Politics. *Comparative Politics*, *34*(1): pp. 1–22.

WEYLAND, K.G., 1998. The Politics of Corruption in Latin America. *Journal of Democracy*, *9*(2), pp. 108–121.

White House, 2011. National Strategy for Counter Terrorism https://obamawhitehouse.archives.gov/sites/default/files/counterterrorism_strategy.pdf. Accessed 23 July 2019.

WHITEHEAD, L., 2009. State Sovereignty and Democracy: An Awkward Coupling. In BURNELL, P. and YOUNGS, R. (eds.), *New Challenges to Democratization*. Routledge, pp. 35–53.

WIGELL, M., 2008. Mapping 'Hybrid Regimes': Regime Types and Concepts in Comparative Politics. *Democratisation*, *15*(2), pp. 230–250.

WIKE, R., SIMMONS, K., STOKES, B., and FETTEROLF, J., 2017. Globally, Broad Support for Representative and Direct Democracy. *Pew Research Center, Washington, DC Google Scholar.*

WIMMER, A., 2018. *Nation Building: Why Some Countries Come Together While Others Fall Apart*. Princeton University Press.

WIMMER, A., 2019. Why Nationalism Works: And Why It Isn't Going Away. *Foreign Affairs, March/April 2019.* https://www.foreignaffairs.com/articles/world/2019-02-12/why-nationalism-works. Accessed 26 July 2019.

WIMMER, A., CEDERMAN, L.E. and MIN, B., 2009. Ethnic Politics and Armed Conflict: A Configurational Analysis of a New Global Data Set. *American Sociological Review*, *74*(2), pp. 316–337.

WINTROBE, R., 2000. *The Political Economy of Dictatorship*. Cambridge University Press.

WINTROBE, R., 1998. Privatisation, the Market for Corporate Control, and Capital Flight from Russia. *World Economy*, 21(5), pp. 603–611.

WITTE, M., 17 Octobe 2014. Kazakh Senate Elections Met International Standards, Say Int'l Observers. *Astana Times* https://astanatimes.com/2014/10/kazakh-senate-elections-met-international-standards-say-intl-observers/ Accessed 27 November 2018.

WOODS, K., LACEY, J. and MURRAY, W., 2006. Saddam's delusions: The view from the Inside. *Foreign Afairs*, 85, p.2.

WORLD BANK. 2018. Combatting Corruption. http://www.worldbank.org/en/topic/governance/brief/anti-corruption. Accessed 7 June 2019.

WRIGHT, J., 2008. Do Authoritarian Institutions Constrain? How Legislatures Affect Economic Growth and Investment. *American Journal of Political Science*, 52(2), pp. 322–343.

WRIGHT, J., 2009. How Foreign Aid Can Foster Democratization in Authoritarian Regimes. *American Journal of Political Science*, 53(3), pp. 552–571.

WRIGHT, N., 10 July 2018. How Artificial Intelligence Will Reshape the Global Order. *Foreign Affairs*. https://www.foreignaffairs.com/articles/world/2018-07-10/how-artificial-intelligence-will-reshape-global-order Accessed 25 February 2019.

WRIGHT, J., DIETRICH, S., and ARIOTTI, M., 2015. *Foreign Aid and Judicial Independence*. Working Paper, pp. 1–38.

WRIGHT, J., FRANTZ, E., and GEDDES, B., 2015. Oil and Autocratic Regime Survival. *British Journal of Political Science*, 45(2), pp. 287–306.

XIAOJUN, Y., 2011. Regime Inclusion and the Resilience of Authoritarianism: The Local People's Political Consultative Conference in Post-Mao Chinese Politics. *The China Journal*, (66), pp. 53–75.

YOM, S.L. and GAUSE III, F.G., 2012. Resilient Royals: How Arab monarchies Hang On. *Journal of Democracy*, 23(4), pp. 74–88.

ZAKARIA, F., 1994. Culture Is Destiny: A Conversation with Lee Kuan Yew. *Foreign Affairs*, 73(2): pp. 109–126.

ZAKARIA, F., 1997. The Rise of Illiberal Democracy. *Foreign Affairs*, 76(6), pp. 22–43.

ZAKARIA, F., 2016. Populism on the March: Why the West is in Trouble. *Foreign Affairs*, 95, p. 9.

ZAKARIA, F., 2011. Why There's No Turning Back in the Middle East. *Time Magazine* 177 (6).

ZHANG, X., FAN, S., ZHANG, L. and HUANG, J., 2004. Local Governance and Public Goods Provision in Rural China. *Journal of Public Economics*, 88(12), pp. 2857–2871.

ZIBLATT, D., 2008. Does Landholding Inequality Block Democratization?: A Test of the 'Bread and Democracy' Thesis and the Case of Prussia. *World Politics*, 60(4), pp. 610–641.

ZUCCO JR, C., 2013. When Payouts Pay Off: Conditional Cash Transfers and Voting Behavior in Brazil 2002–10. *American Journal Of Political Science*, 57(4), pp. 810–822.

Subject Index

Author Index